# The Windows-noob OSD Guides for Configuration Manager 2012 R2

Niall Brady

PUBLISHED BY
Deployment Artist
http://deploymentartist.com

Copyright © 2015 by Deployment Artist
All rights reserved. No part of this book may be reproduced or transmitted in any form or by any means without the prior written permission of the publisher.
ISBN: 978-91-87445-16-3

**Warning and Disclaimer**

Every effort has been made to make this book as complete and as accurate as possible, but no warranty or fitness is implied. The information provided is on an "as is" basis. The authors and the publisher shall have neither liability nor responsibility to any person or entity with respect to any loss or damages arising from the information contained in this book.

**Feedback Information**

We'd like to hear from you! If you have any comments about how we could improve the quality of this book, please don't hesitate to contact us by visiting http://deploymentartist.com, sending an email to feedback@deploymentartist.com, or visiting our Facebook site http://facebook.com/DeploymentArtist.

# Acknowledgments

I'd like to thank my three wonderful boys and my wife Annelie for putting up with the countless hours I've spent writing and researching. I'd also like to thank Johan Arwidmark for encouraging me to write the book and the http://windows-noob.com readers for keeping me on my toes.

## Acknowledgments

# About the Author

**Niall Brady** is an Irishman living in Sweden with three kids and a Swedish wife. He works as a Lead IT Analyst at a global company (Tetra Pak) with a focus on enterprise client management and deployment solutions. He is an active blogger on http://windows-noob.com and http://niallbrady.com.

Niall has been awarded Microsoft Most Valuable Professional (MVP) for more than six years. When he's not working with computers or spending time with his family, he enjoys learning about and attempting to fix his old 1962 Mercedes Benz 180c.

# About the Author

# Contents

Acknowledgments .................................................................................................. iii
About the Author .................................................................................................... v
Contents ................................................................................................................ vii

**Introduction** ........................................................................................................ 1
   Say Hello (Possibly Again) to ViaMonstra Inc. ............................................... 1
   Structure of the Book ...................................................................................... 1
   How to Use This Book .................................................................................... 2
   Sample Files .................................................................................................... 2
   Additional Resources ...................................................................................... 2
   Topics Not Covered ........................................................................................ 2

**Chapter 1** ............................................................................................................ 3

**Tools and Technologies** .................................................................................... 3
   VBScript .......................................................................................................... 3
   JavaScript ....................................................................................................... 4
   PowerShell ...................................................................................................... 4
   Windows Management Instrumentation (WMI) .............................................. 4
   HTML Application (HTA) ................................................................................. 5
   Web Services .................................................................................................. 5
   Hydration ........................................................................................................ 6
   Notepad++ ...................................................................................................... 7
   PowerShell Integrated Scripting Environment (ISE) ....................................... 7
   WBEMTest and WMI Tools ............................................................................ 8

**Chapter 2** .......................................................................................................... 11

**ViaMonstra Inc. and the Proof-of-Concept Environment** ............................ 11
   Step-by-Step Guide Requirements ............................................................... 11
   ViaMonstra Inc. ............................................................................................. 12
      Servers ..................................................................................................... 12
      Clients ...................................................................................................... 12

## Contents

- Internet Access .................................................................................................... 12
- Software ............................................................................................................. 13
- Servers (Detailed Information) ........................................................................... 13
- Clients (Detailed Information) ............................................................................ 14

**Setting Up the ConfigMgr 2012 R2 Infrastructure** ............................................... 15
- Create a New User in the ViaMonstra / Users OU ............................................. 15
- Add a User to the Full Administrator Group Using RBAC .................................. 16
- Add a User to the Local Administrators Group on CM01 ................................... 17
- Install ConfigMgr 2012 R2 CU4 .......................................................................... 18
- Create Software Groups ..................................................................................... 19
- Configure Discovery Methods ............................................................................ 20
- Create a Boundary Group .................................................................................. 27
- Add the Reporting Services Point ...................................................................... 29
- Verify IE Enhanced Security Configuration ........................................................ 31

**Setting Up Software Updates** .............................................................................. 32
- Add a Software Update Point ............................................................................. 32
- Synchronize Updates ......................................................................................... 37
- Review Update Products .................................................................................... 38

**Preparing for OSD** ................................................................................................ 40
- The ConfigMgr 2012 R2 Service Accounts ........................................................ 40
- Set Permissions on the Servers and Workstations OUs .................................... 41
- Create the ConfigMgr 2012 R2 OSD Folder Structure ....................................... 42
- Add the State Migration Point ............................................................................ 43
- Create a New ConfigMgr Client Package .......................................................... 45
- Set Up ConfigMgr 2012 R2 Integration with MDT 2013 ..................................... 47
- Configure the Network Access Account ............................................................ 48
- Configure the Client Settings ............................................................................. 49
- Enable PXE on the CM01 Distribution Point ...................................................... 50

**Creating Boot Images** ........................................................................................... 52
- Create a Custom MDT Integrated x64 Boot Image (WinPE 5.0) ........................ 52

**Adding Operating System Images** ....................................................................... 55
- Extract and Copy the Windows 8.1 Media ......................................................... 56
- Add a Windows 8.1 Operating System Image .................................................... 56

**Creating MDT Toolkit and MDT Settings Packages** ............................................. 57
- Create a MDT Client Task Sequence ................................................................. 58
- Distribute the Packages ...................................................................................... 60

**Creating OSD Collections** .................................................................................... 61
- The All Servers and All Workstations Collections .............................................. 61
- The OSD Collections .......................................................................................... 61

**Forcing Unknown Computers to Prompt for computer name** .............................. 62
- Edit the All Unknown Computers Collection ...................................................... 62
- Verify the Change ............................................................................................... 63

**Adding Applications** .............................................................................................. 66
- Create the Mozilla Firefox Application ................................................................ 67

| | |
|---|---|
| Create the 7Zip Application | 71 |
| Create the Microsoft Office 365 Application | 72 |
| Distribute the Applications | 77 |

# Chapter 3 .................................................................................................................79

# Increasing Log File Size .......................................................................................79
Step-by-Step Guide Requirements ...................................................................79
Description of the Problem ...............................................................................80
    Introducing the smsts.ini File and Associated Options .............................81
Inject smsts.ini into the Boot WIM File via DISM ..............................................82
Inject smsts.ini Using the Extrafiles Method .....................................................90
Making Changes to the Logging Options within Windows ................................93
    Increase Log File Size for a New Computer Scenario ..............................93
    Increase Log File Size for a Refresh Computer Scenario (Replace) ........94
Verifying Log File Size Changes Are in Place ..................................................96
    Verify Log File Size in WinPE ....................................................................96
    Verify Log File Size in Windows ................................................................98

# Chapter 4 ...............................................................................................................101

# Building a Reference Image of Windows 8.1 ....................................................101
Step-by-Step Guide Requirements .................................................................101
Using PowerShell with ConfigMgr ...................................................................102
    Enable PowerShell Integration via the ConfigMgr Console ...................102
    Get Started with ConfigMgr PowerShell Cmdlets ...................................103
    Windows PowerShell ISE ........................................................................105
    Enable PowerShell integration via a PowerShell Script .........................105
A Quick Look at PowerShell Integration .........................................................107
    Create and Distribute a Package Using PowerShell ..............................107
    Create a New Virtual Machine with PowerShell .....................................110
    Import a Computer into ConfigMgr Using PowerShell ............................111
Patching the Image with Windows Updates ...................................................112
    Create a Software Updates Group ..........................................................113
    Decide Which Updates to Keep ..............................................................114
    Deploy the Software Update Group ........................................................117
The Build-and-Capture Process in a Nutshell .................................................120
    Create a Build-and-Capture Task Sequence .........................................121
    Edit the Task Sequence ..........................................................................124
    Distribute the Default x64 Boot Image ....................................................128
    Create a Deployment for the Task Sequence ........................................128
    Start the Task Sequence .........................................................................129
Monitoring the Task Sequence Progress ........................................................130

Contents

    Monitor the Deployment in WinPE ..................................................................130
    Monitor the Deployment in Windows...............................................................131
  Verify the Capture Was Successful .......................................................................134

# Chapter 5 ..........................................................................................................135

# Deploying Windows 8.1 with a Custom Start Screen......................................................135
  Step-by-Step Guide Requirements........................................................................135
  Adding a Captured Reference Image ......................................................................135
    Copy the Image.........................................................................................136
    Add Operating System Image Using PowerShell..................................................136
    Distribute the Operating System Image Using PowerShell......................................137
  Customizing the Start Screen Using the appsfolderlayout Method ..........................137
    Enable the Administrator Account..................................................................138
    Design a Custom Start Screen .......................................................................139
    Export the Start Screen Layout ......................................................................142
    Create and Distribute a Package Using PowerShell.............................................143
  Creating an OSD Task Sequence ..........................................................................143
    Create an OSD Task Sequence Using PowerShell ...............................................143
    Edit the Task Sequence ...............................................................................145
  Deploying the Task Sequence ..............................................................................150
    Deploy a Task sequence using PowerShell.......................................................150
    Target New Windows Updates.......................................................................151
    Deploy a New Computer ..............................................................................151

# Chapter 6 ..........................................................................................................153

# Deploying Windows 8.1 to the Surface Pro 3 ................................................................153
  Step-by-Step Guide Requirements........................................................................153
  About the System Center Configuration Manager Cmdlet Library............................153
    Download the Library .................................................................................154
    Install the Library......................................................................................154
  Downloading Necessary Files ..............................................................................155
    Get the OneNote Update ..............................................................................155
    Download the Latest Surface Pro 3 Drivers.......................................................155
    Extract the drivers .....................................................................................156
    Create an Operating System Hotfixes Package....................................................157
    Create an OOBE Package .............................................................................159
  Creating a Suitable Folder Structure ......................................................................159
    Create the Driver Source Folder Structure ........................................................160
  Importing and Distributing Drivers in ConfigMgr ....................................................160
    Import and Distribute the Drivers Using PowerShell............................................160
    Manually Import the Drivers Using the ConfigMgr Console ..................................161

## Contents

    Manually Distribute the Driver Package ............................................................. 164
  Adding Network Drivers to the x64 Boot Image ........................................................ 166
    Add Network Drivers via PowerShell. ................................................................. 166
    Add Network Drivers via the Boot Image Properties ........................................... 167
    Add Network Drivers via the Drivers Node ......................................................... 170
  Edit the Windows 8.1 Enterprise x64 Task Sequence .............................................. 171
    Add the Apply Driver Package Step .................................................................... 172
    Add the Surface Pro 3 Pen Pairing Support ........................................................ 174
    Disable the Apply Device Drivers Step ............................................................... 177
    Set the OSEnablePrebootInputProtectorsOnSlates Registry Key ....................... 177
    Add the Operating System Hotfixes Steps .......................................................... 179
  Deploying the Surface Pro 3 ....................................................................................... 181

## Chapter 7 ................................................................................................................. 183

## Automatically Syncing Time in WinPE .................................................................. 183
  Step-by-Step Guide Requirements ............................................................................ 183
  The Problem in Detail ................................................................................................. 183
    Fixing the Problem ............................................................................................... 185
  Using net time with a Service Account ...................................................................... 185
    Add a Time Sync Service Account ....................................................................... 186
  Using a Prestart Command ........................................................................................ 187
    Create a Prestart Scripts Folder ........................................................................... 188
    Add a Prestart Command to Your Boot WIM ...................................................... 189
  Verifying the Changes ................................................................................................ 190
    Log Files Associated with the Script ................................................................... 192

## Chapter 8 ................................................................................................................. 193

## Pausing a Task Sequence ..................................................................................... 193
  Step-by-Step Guide Requirements ............................................................................ 193
  Why Pause? ................................................................................................................ 194
    Pausing Effectively ............................................................................................... 194
    Using Selective Pause .......................................................................................... 194
  Method 1: Pausing Using ServiceUI.exe ................................................................... 194
    Create the Pause_TS Package ............................................................................. 195
    Edit a Task Sequence to Add the Pause Functionality ....................................... 196
    Verify the Changes .............................................................................................. 197
  Method 2: Pausing Using cmd .................................................................................... 199
    Edit a Task Sequence to Add the Pause Functionality ....................................... 199
    Verify the Changes .............................................................................................. 200
  Method 3: Pausing Using PowerShell ....................................................................... 201
    Add PowerShell Support to the Boot Image ....................................................... 201

xi

|     |     |
| --- | --- |
| Create the Pause_TS_PowerShell Package | 203 |
| Edit a Task Sequence to Add the Pause Functionality | 205 |
| Verify the Changes | 206 |

# Chapter 9 .................................................................................................209

# Using Devel Mode .....................................................................................209

Step-by-Step Guide Requirements ...............................................................209
Understanding How It All Works ..................................................................210
    Entering Devel Mode ............................................................................210
    Using Listall .........................................................................................212
Preparing for Devel Mode ............................................................................213
    Mount the Boot WIM ............................................................................213
    Copy a Script into the Mounted Boot WIM ...........................................215
    Copy a Script into the Prestart Scripts Folder .....................................216
    Commit the Changes ..........................................................................216
    Add a Prestart Command ....................................................................216
    Create a Local User ............................................................................218
    Share the Hidden Folder and Setting Permissions ..............................219
    Locate a Task Sequence Deployment ID ............................................220
    Populate the Hidden Folder with Files .................................................221
Hiding Task Sequences ...............................................................................222
    Deploy a Task Sequence as Hidden Using the ConfigMgr Console ....222
    Deploy a Task Sequence as Hidden Using PowerShell ......................224
    Modify an Existing Deployment to Make It Hidden ..............................226
Verifying Devel Mode ..................................................................................227
    Incorrectly Entering a Deployment ID .................................................229
    The Devel Mode Log File ....................................................................229

# Chapter 10 ...............................................................................................231

# Implementing MailLog, AssistMe, and ViewLog .....................................231

Step-by-Step Guide Requirements ...............................................................231
Downloading the Required Files ..................................................................232
    Download UltraVNC ............................................................................232
    Download WinRAR .............................................................................232
    Download Blat ....................................................................................232
Preparing Your Environment .......................................................................232
    Install UltraVNC ..................................................................................233
    Install WinRAR ....................................................................................234
    Extract Blat .........................................................................................235
    Create the Folder Structure ................................................................235
    Copy Some Files ................................................................................236
    Edit the MailLog Script ........................................................................237

Contents

    Adding Files to Your Boot Image ..................................................................... 239
        Mount the Boot Image WIM File ................................................................. 239
        Copy the Required Files into the Mounted Boot WIM ................................. 242
        Commit the Changes ................................................................................. 243
        Update the Boot WIM to the Distribution Points .......................................... 244
    Editing the Task Sequence ............................................................................. 244
        Add New Groups ........................................................................................ 244
        Add New Steps .......................................................................................... 248
    Verifying the Changes .................................................................................... 254
        Verify MailLog ............................................................................................ 254
        Verify AssistMe .......................................................................................... 256
        Verify ViewLog .......................................................................................... 259

## Chapter 11 ............................................................................................................. 261

## Checking for Network and Storage Problems in WinPE ..................................... 261
    Step-by-Step Guide Requirements ................................................................. 262
    Preparing Your Environment ........................................................................... 262
        Edit the Script ............................................................................................ 262
        Mount the Boot WIM ................................................................................. 264
        Copy Files into the Mounted Boot Image ................................................... 266
        Edit the Boot Image Registry ..................................................................... 267
        Commit the Changes to the Boot WIM ...................................................... 268
        Update the Boot WIM to the Distribution Points ........................................ 269
    Verifying the Changes .................................................................................... 269
        Verify That the Script Has Run .................................................................. 269
        Verify Network Checks .............................................................................. 270
        Verify Storage Checks ............................................................................... 276
    Fixing Problems Found ................................................................................... 278
        Microsoft Update Catalog .......................................................................... 279
        Obtain Drivers from the Hardware Vendor ................................................ 280
        Use drvload to Inject Drivers ..................................................................... 280
        Add Drivers to the Boot Image ................................................................... 281

## Chapter 12 ............................................................................................................. 283

## Patching an Image Using Offline Servicing ........................................................ 283
    Step-by-Step Guide Requirements ................................................................. 283
    Preparing for Offline Servicing ....................................................................... 284
        Review the Current Update Status ............................................................ 284
        Perform a Sync ......................................................................................... 285
        Select and Download Updates .................................................................. 287
    Servicing an Image ......................................................................................... 289
        Patch the Captured WIM .......................................................................... 289

xiii

Contents

  Monitor the Patching Process ..................................................................292
  Troubleshooting .....................................................................................293
 Verifying the Application of the Updates ....................................................294
  Verify Update Status of the WIM ............................................................294
  Verify Updates Applied on a Virtual Machine .........................................295

## Chapter 13 ....................................................................................................297

## Enforcing BitLocker with MBAM 2.5 ...........................................................297
 Step-by-Step Guide Requirements ............................................................297
 Preparing for MBAM 2.5 ............................................................................298
  Add MBAM Service Accounts ................................................................298
  Configure MBAM Service Accounts .......................................................300
  Add Users to the Three MBAM Helpdesk Groups ..................................302
  Set the Service Principal Name .............................................................303
  Add Additional Roles and Features .......................................................305
  Install the Web Platform Installer ...........................................................306
 Integrating MBAM with ConfigMgr .............................................................307
  Edit the configuration.mof File ...............................................................307
  Import sms_def.mof ...............................................................................308
  Integrate MBAM with ConfigMgr ............................................................310
  Configure MBAM Server ........................................................................311
  Edit the Collection Query .......................................................................313
 Installing the MBAM Server .......................................................................314
  Prepare SQL Server ..............................................................................314
  Install MBAM Server ..............................................................................316
  Configure the Self-Service Portal ...........................................................323
 Configuring MBAM Group Policy ...............................................................326
  Copy Group Policy Templates ................................................................326
  Edit Group Policy ...................................................................................329
 Deploying the MBAM Client Agent .............................................................335
  Create the MBAM Application ................................................................335
  Distribute the MBAM Application ...........................................................337
  Deploy the MBAM Application ...............................................................338
 Verifying MBAM Client Agent Functionality ...............................................339
  Verify the MBAM Client Agent Is Installed .............................................340
  Verify MBAM 2.5 BitLocker Policy ..........................................................340
  The MBAM Client Agent ........................................................................342
  Speed Up MBAM Policy Retrieval and Status Reporting in a Lab (Only) .............344
  Verify That the MBAM Client Agent Is Storing Recovery Information in the MBAM Database ................................................................................345
  Use the Self-Service Portal ....................................................................350
 Enabling BitLocker on Virtual Machines ....................................................352
  Verify BitLocker Encryption Status .........................................................357

## Chapter 14 .........................................................................................................359

## The CM12 UEFI BitLocker HTA ....................................................................359

### Step-by-Step Guide Requirements .............................................................359
### Adding a Web Service ................................................................................359
- Add a Web Service Service Account ...........................................................360
- Prepare Maik Koster's Deployment Webservice Version 7.3....................361
- Add an Application Pool ..............................................................................362
- Install Deployment Webservice ..................................................................363
- Configure Application Settings ...................................................................365
- Add the Web Service User to ConfigMgr ...................................................366
- Test the Web Service ...................................................................................368

### Adding Language Packs ..............................................................................369
- Download the ISO .........................................................................................369
- Create Language Pack Folders ...................................................................369
- Extract the Language Packs .......................................................................370
- Create Language Pack Packages ................................................................372
- Distribute the Language Packs ...................................................................373

### Importing the Task Sequence ....................................................................374
- Import the Task Sequence ...........................................................................374

### Creating Required Packages ......................................................................376
- Create a CM12 UEFI BitLocker HTA Scripts Package .............................376
- Populate the Scep Install Folder .................................................................376
- Create an UEFI BitLocker HTA Package ...................................................377
- Create an Unattend.xml Package ................................................................377
- Distribute the New Packages .....................................................................378

### Adding a SQL Server User ..........................................................................379

### Editing the Task Sequence .........................................................................381
- Fix Package References ..............................................................................382
- Edit Variables in the Task Sequence ..........................................................389
- Add a Step to Copy the USMT Binaries ....................................................390
- Fix a Bug .......................................................................................................391
- Set the Password to Connect to Network Shares .....................................392
- Add the MBAM Client ..................................................................................394

### Editing the CustomSettings.ini File ............................................................395

### Copying a Script to a Share .......................................................................396

### Boot Image Changes ...................................................................................396
- Add MDAC and HTA Support to the Boot Image .....................................397
- Attach the Boot Image to the Task Sequence ...........................................398

### Deploying the Task Sequence ....................................................................399

### Using the Features .....................................................................................399
- About ..............................................................................................................399
- Backup ...........................................................................................................401

Reinstall .................................................................................. 403
New Computer ....................................................................... 403
Tools ..................................................................................... 405
Customizing the HTA ................................................................... 407
Change the Logo ................................................................... 407
Change the CSS .................................................................... 408

## Appendix A ................................................................................................ 411

## Using the Hydration Kit to Build the PoC Environment ........................................ 411

The Base Servers .......................................................................... 411
New York Site Servers (192.168.1.0/24) ................................... 411
The Base Clients ........................................................................... 412
New York Site Clients (192.168.1.0/24) .................................... 412
Internet Access ............................................................................. 412
Setting Up the Hydration Environment ........................................... 412
How Does the Hydration Kit Work? ......................................... 412
Preparing the Downloads Folder ............................................. 413
Preparing the Hydration Environment ..................................... 414
Deploying the New York Site VMs ................................................. 420
Deploy DC01 ............................................................................ 420
Deploy CM01 ........................................................................... 422
Deploy MBAM01 ..................................................................... 423
Deploy PC0001 ........................................................................ 423

## Index ........................................................................................................ 425

## Beyond the Book ...................................................................................... 427

Blog .............................................................................................. 427
Forums ......................................................................................... 427
Twitter .......................................................................................... 427

# Introduction

*The Windows-noob OSD Guides for Configuration Manager 2012 R2* is the ultimate collection of guides for the working IT Pro who wants to customize deployment solutions based on Microsoft Deployment Toolkit (MDT) 2013 and ConfigMgr 2012 R2. Most of the examples and scenarios described in this book are targeted to both deployment solutions, but there are solution-specific parts, as well. Please note that even though I used MDT 2013 and ConfigMgr 2012 R2 and tested all examples against those platforms, many of the examples and guides also work on MDT 2012 Update 1 and ConfigMgr 2012 SP1. Some even work on ConfigMgr 2007 (which you should not still be using, anyway ☺).

Anyway, this is a HOW TO GET IT DONE book, solely focusing on customizing deployment solutions with roots in the real world.

## Say Hello (Possibly Again) to ViaMonstra Inc.

In this book, you customize deployment solutions for the fictive ViaMonstra Inc. organization. ViaMonstra is a midsized company with a single location and 3000 employees. Its site is located in New York.

ViaMonstra has decided to use ConfigMgr 2012 R2 for its main departments, but it also has a development department using the standalone MDT 2013 solution. BTW, the name ViaMonstra comes from *Viam Monstra*, Latin, meaning "Show me the way."

## Structure of the Book

The first chapter explains the tools and technologies I use in the book. The second chapter explains the environment used in the ViaMonstra organization, including what servers and software are used. This chapter also is about finalizing the lab environment, helping you set up your lab environment to match what I'm using in the book, and guiding you through setting up ConfigMgr 2012 R2 for operating system deployment.

Chapter 3 is the first Windows-noob guide chapter. Each of the remaining chapters is a different Windows-noob guide.

Finally, I have the appendix, which include extra material on how to set up the initial proof-of-concept environment, servers and clients, and their roles and configurations.

# Introduction

## How to Use This Book

I have packed this book with step-by-step guides, which mean you can build your solution as you read along.

In numbered steps, I have set all names and paths in bold typeface. I also have used a standard naming convention throughout the book when explaining what to do in each step. The steps normally are something like this:

1. On the **Advanced Properties** page, select the **Confirm** check box, and then click **Next**.

Sample scripts are formatted like the following example, on a grey background.

```
DoNotCreateExtraPartition=YES
MachineObjectOU=ou=Workstations,dc=corp,dc=viamonstra,dc=com
```

Code and commands that you type in the guides are displayed like this:

1. Install **MDT 2013** by running the following command in an elevated **PowerShell prompt** (run as Administrator):

    ```
    & msiexec.exe /i 'C:\Setup\MDT 2013\
    MicrosoftDeploymentToolkit2013_x64.msi' /quiet
    ```

The step-by-step guides in this book assume that you have configured the environment according to the information in Chapter 2, "ViaMonstra Inc. and the Proof-of-Concept Environment," and in Appendix A.

This book is not intended as a reference volume, covering every deployment technology, acronym, or command-line switch known to man, but rather is designed to make sure you learn what you need to know to customize your deployment solution.

## Sample Files

All sample files used in this book can be downloaded from http://deploymentfundamentals.com.

## Additional Resources

In addition to all tips and tricks provided in this book, you can find extra resources like articles and video recordings on my blog, http://windows-noob.com.

## Topics Not Covered

Even though the book examples may work with Windows 10, as well as later versions of ConfigMgr, Windows 10 deployment is not covered in this book, and the examples have not been tested with Windows 10.

# Chapter 1
# Tools and Technologies

In this chapter, you get a crash course in the various tools and technologies that are used in this book.

## VBScript

VBScript (Visual Basic Scripting Edition) is a scripting language that has been installed by default in every release of Microsoft Windows since Windows 98. VBScript is still heavily used in deployment solutions because it's always available on the target operating system and also in the Windows Preinstallation Environment (WinPE). Here is a short VBScript snippet that gets hardware info (model name) from a machine:

```
strComputer = "."
strConn = "winmgmts:{impersonationLevel=impersonate}!\\" & _
    strComputer & "\root\cimv2"
strQuery = "Select * from Win32_Computersystem"

Set objWMI = GetObject(strConn)
Set colItems = objWMI.ExecQuery(strQuery)
For Each Item In colItems
    Wscript.Echo "Model: " & Item.Model
Next
Set objWMI = Nothing
```

## JavaScript

JavaScript (JS) is often used to run client-side scripts inside a web browser. JavaScript does copy many name and naming conventions from Java, but is otherwise not the same language as Java. In deployment solutions, JavaScript is primarily used for frontends (HTAs, or HTML applications). Here is a short JavaScript snippet that sets the window size and position of an HTA page:

```
function Set(){
  var l=(screen.width/2 - 500);
  var t=(screen.height-200);
    self.moveTo(l,t);

    self.resizeTo('900','300');
}
```

## PowerShell

This has to be the coolest technology ever created by Microsoft. PowerShell, or Windows PowerShell, is Microsoft's framework for task automation. It consists of a command-line shell, with an associated scripting language built on top of it, and integrates with .NET Framework, having access to all COM objects and direct access to WMI. PowerShell allows you to perform administrative tasks on both local and remote Windows systems. Since the release of WinPE 4.0, PowerShell can also be added to the boot images used in operating system deployment (OSD).

It's a bit unfair to list samples of what you can do in PowerShell because there are no real limits. Every type of automation task you can imagine can be done in PowerShell, but here are a couple samples:

- Get hardware info (model name) from the machine using PowerShell

    ```
    Get-WmiObject -Class:Win32_ComputerSystem | Select Model
    ```

- Create a device collection in ConfigMgr 2012 R2

    ```
    New-CMDeviceCollection -Name "Install Windows 8.1"
    -LimitingCollectionName "All Systems"
    ```

## Windows Management Instrumentation (WMI)

WMI is a set of extensions to the Windows Driver Model. Windows deployment solutions like MDT 2013 and ConfigMgr 2012 R2 use WMI to get information about the hardware being deployed. ConfigMgr 2012 R2 also uses WMI heavily to store configurations and, for example, to get inventory data. When scripting against ConfigMgr 2012 R2, you can use WMI to read/write configurations, as well. The PowerShell example in the previous section uses WMI to read the hardware information.

# HTML Application (HTA)

HTAs give you the features of HTML together with the advantages of scripting languages. The HTA pages are executed fully trusted so they have access to local computer information (unlike normal webpages). HTAs are commonly used for frontends and other deployment wizards.

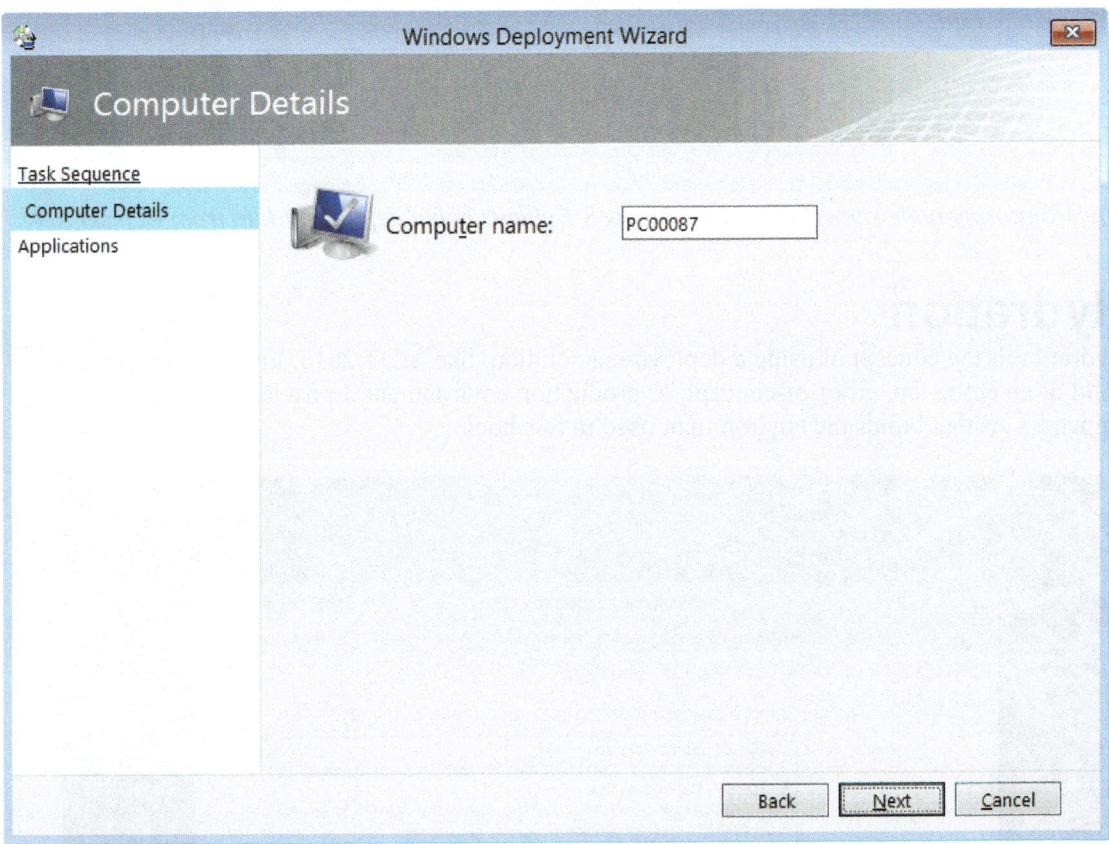

*A sample HTA wizard page (from MDT 2013).*

# Web Services

Web services are used to make it easy for machines to communicate with each other independent of what operating systems they are using. When customizing OSD solutions, web services are mainly used for calling server-side actions. A commonly used scenario is calling a web service that moves a computer from one organizational unit (OU) to another during the deployment process.

Another aspect of web services is reading information, like monitoring information, from the deployment process.

Chapter 1    Tools and Technologies

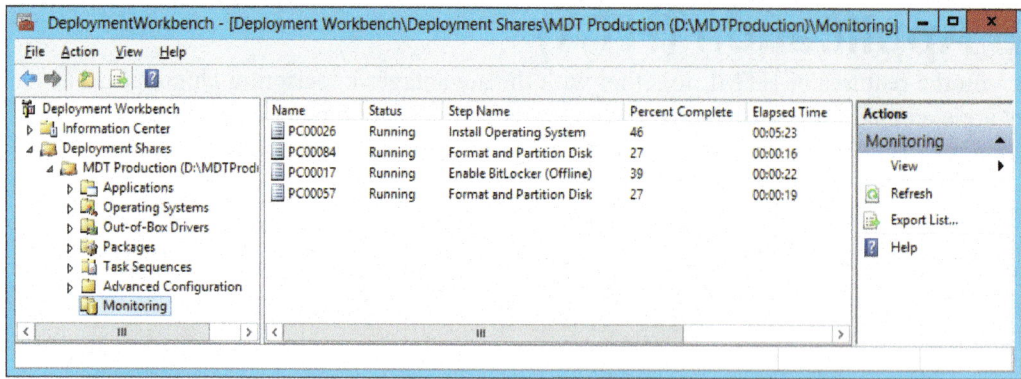

*The Monitoring node showing a few Windows 8.1 clients being deployed (data from web service).*

# Hydration

Hydration is the concept of using a deployment solution, like MDT 2013, to do a fully automated build of an entire lab, proof-of-concept, or production environment. I provide a hydration kit (see Appendix A) that builds the environment used in this book.

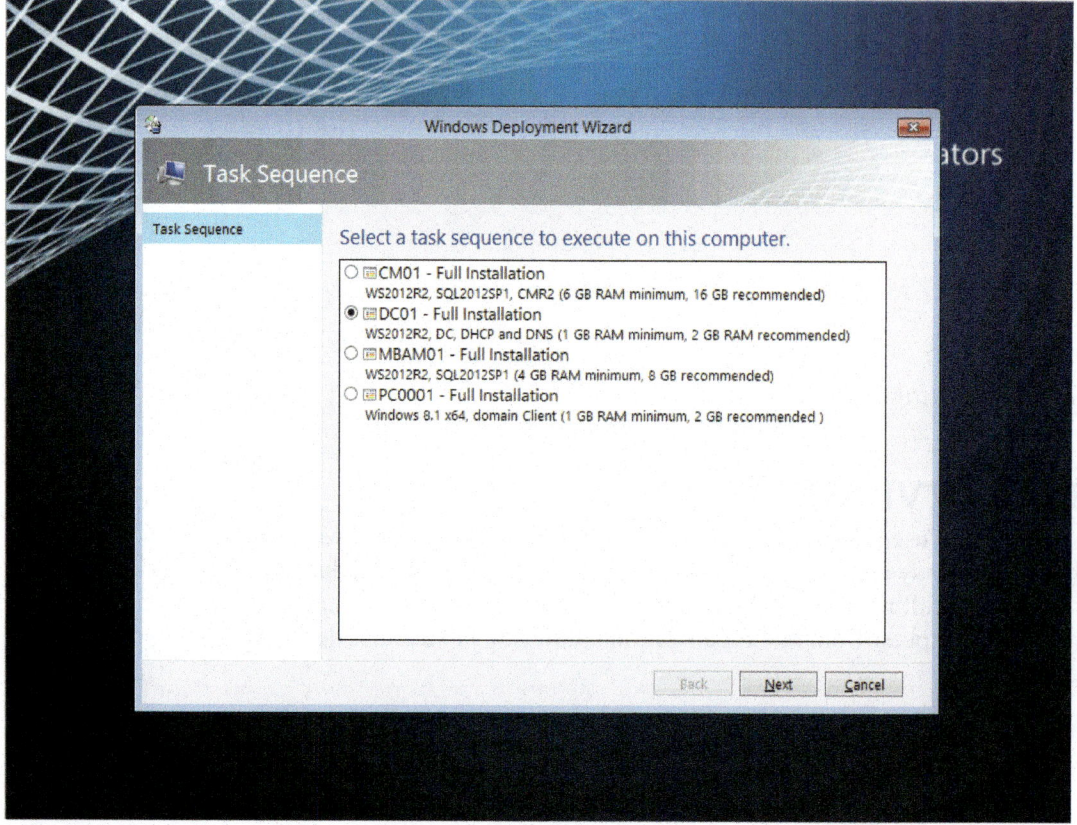

*Creating the virtual machines used in this book. See Appendix A for details.*

# Notepad++

This is a great freeware script editor, perfect for editing VBScripts.

*Notepad++ displaying one of the book sample scripts.*

# PowerShell Integrated Scripting Environment (ISE)

For editing PowerShell scripts, I recommend using the built-in ISE editor available in Windows 7, Windows 8.1, Windows Sever 2012, and Windows Server 2012 R2. It provides you with cmdlets help and Intellisense when writing PowerShell scripts.

Chapter 1   Tools and Technologies

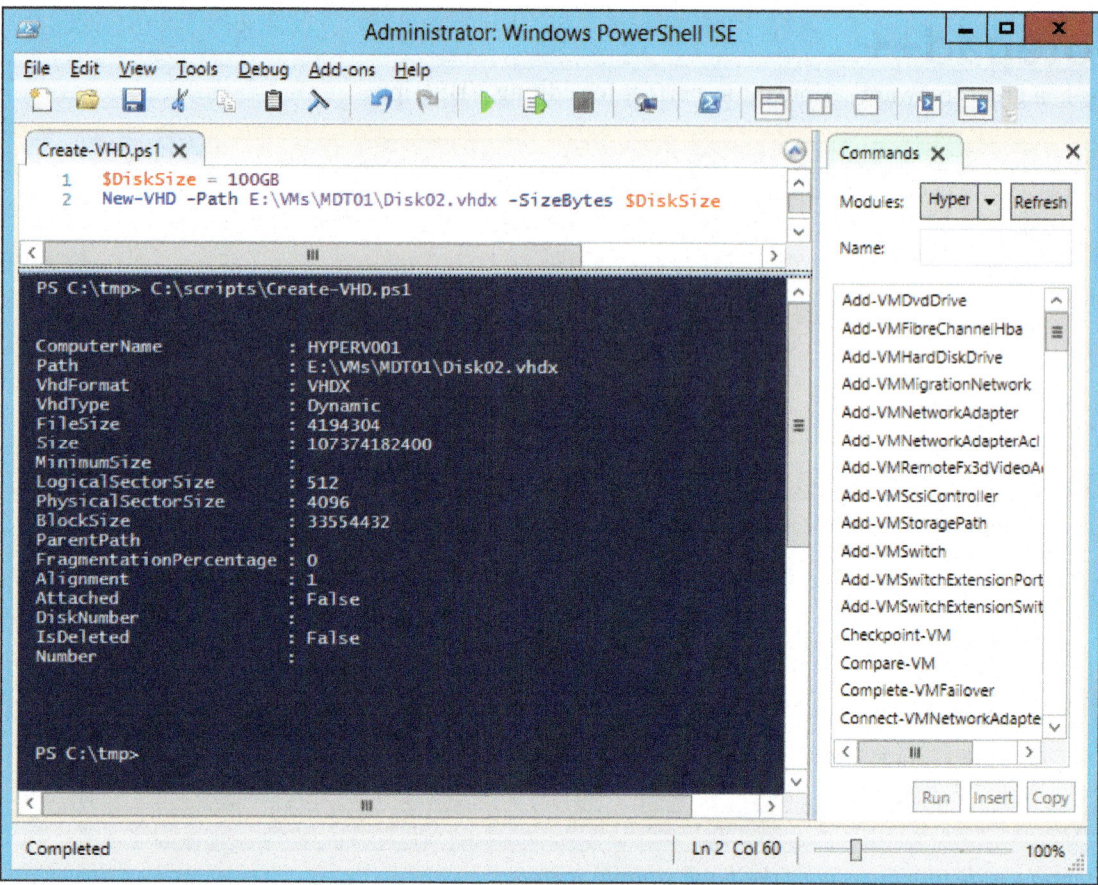

*PowerShell ISE running a script to create a virtual hard disk.*

# WBEMTest and WMI Tools

These are tools for exploring WMI information on a machine. Used to enumerate WMI classes and methods, but also for other things, such as testing WQL queries, WBEMTest is built into Windows and Windows PE. WMI Tools (or WMI Administrative Tools) is a free download from Microsoft that contains the following tools:

- **WMI CIM Studio.** A tool for viewing and editing WMI classes and properties. It can also generate and compile MOF files.

- **WMI Object Browser.** A tool for viewing WMI objects and editing property values.

- **WMI Event Registration Tool.** A tool for creating and configuring permanent event consumers.

- **WMI Event Viewer.** A tool for displaying events for registered consumers.

Chapter 1  Tools and Technologies

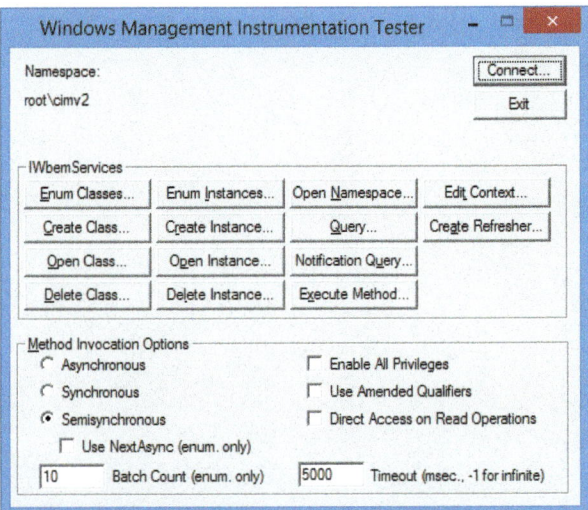

*The WBEMTest tool.*

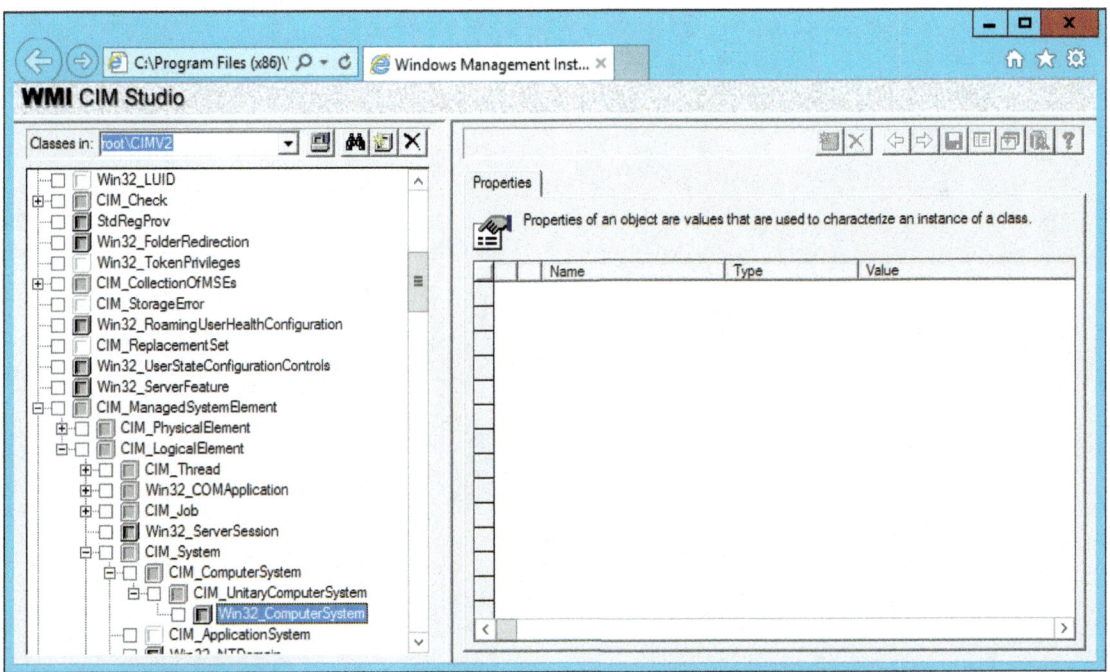

*The WMI CIM Studio tool.*

9

# Chapter 1  Tools and Technologies

Chapter 2

# ViaMonstra Inc. and the Proof-of-Concept Environment

As you remember from the introduction, ViaMonstra Inc. is the fictive company I use throughout this book. In this chapter, I describe the company in more detail, as well as the proof-of-concept environment used in the step-by-step guides.

In this chapter, you also set up a base ConfigMgr 2012 R2 server for software distribution.

## Step-by-Step Guide Requirements

If you want to follow the step-by-step guides in this chapter, you need a lab environment configured as outlined in Appendix A. In this chapter, you use the following virtual machines:

DC01    CM01    PC0002

*The VMs used in this chapter (PC0002 is created in one of the guides).*

You also need to download the following software:

- Microsoft Deployment Toolkit (MDT) 2013 (direct link: http://tinyurl.com/mdt2013download)
- ConfigMgr 2012 R2 CU4 (KB 3026739)
- 7-Zip 9.20 x64
- Mozilla Firefox 36.0.1
- Windows 8.1 Enterprise x64

# ViaMonstra Inc.

ViaMonstra Inc. was invented for the very purpose of having a "real" company for which to build deployment solutions. These deployment solutions come from multiple real-world consulting engagements I have done, consolidating them into a single generic scenario.

ViaMonstra has 3000 employees and a single location in New York.

## Servers

The New York site has the following servers related to software distribution and other supporting infrastructure. All servers are running Windows Server 2012 R2. Detailed configuration of each server is found in the "Servers (Detailed Information)" section in this chapter.

**Friendly Reminder:** Detailed step-by-step guidance on how to deploy the servers used in the book can be found in Appendix A.

- **DC01.** Domain Controller, DNS, and DHCP
- **CM01.** SQL Server 2012 SP1 and ConfigMgr 2012 R2
- **MBAM01.** Microsoft BitLocker Administration and Management 2.5

**Note:** The MBAM01 server is required only if you want to learn about (or use) BitLocker in conjunction with Microsoft BitLocker Administration and Monitoring. The CM12 UEFI BitLocker HTA makes use of the MBAM01 server during computer refresh scenarios.

## Clients

In addition to the servers, you have a Windows 8.1 client that you use in the guides. You also install a few new clients during the various guides.

- **PC0001.** Windows 8.1 Enterprise x64
- **PC0002-PC0013.** New clients that are deployed in the various guides in this book

## Internet Access

Some of the guides in this book require you to have Internet access on the virtual machines. I commonly use a virtual router (running in a VM) to provide Internet access to my lab and test VMs. You can use the Vyatta and VyOS (Vyatta community fork) routers, or a Windows Server 2012 R2 virtual machine with routing configured, as well.

**Note:** For detailed guidance on setting up a virtual router for your lab environment, see this article: http://tinyurl.com/usingvirtualrouter.

## Software

The following list describes the various applications used by ViaMonstra. To be able to follow all the step-by-step guides and configurations in the book, the following software must be downloaded. They can be either trial or full versions.

- 7-Zip 9.20
- Mozilla Firefox 36.0.1
- Windows Assessment and Deployment Toolkit (ADK) 8.1
- ConfigMgr 2012 R2
- ConfigMgr 2012 R2 Toolkit
- Microsoft Deployment Toolkit (MDT) 2013 (http://tinyurl.com/mdt2013download)
- Notepad++ (http://notepad-plus-plus.org/download/v6.2.3.html)
- SQL Server 2012 SP1
- Windows 8.1
- Windows Server 2012 R2

## Servers (Detailed Information)

As mentioned earlier in this chapter, you are using a set of servers in your environment. You use a concept called *hydration* (automated build of entire labs and production environments) when creating the servers.

As mentioned earlier in this chapter, for detailed step-by-step guidance on how to deploy the servers, please review Appendix A, "Using the Hydration Kit to Build the PoC Environment."

To set up a virtual environment with all the servers and clients, you need a host with at least 16 GB of RAM, even though 32 GB RAM is recommended. Either way, make sure you are using SSD drives for your storage. A single 480 GB SSD is enough to run all the scenarios in this book.

**Real World Note:** If using a laptop or desktop when doing the step-by-step guides in this book, please do use a SSD drive for your virtual machines. Using normal spindle-based disks are just too slow for decent lab and test environments. Also, please note that most laptops support at least 16 GB of RAM these days, even if many vendors do not update their specifications with this information.

A detailed description of the servers follows:

- **DC01.** A **Windows Server 2012 R2** machine, fully patched with the latest security updates and configured as Active Directory Domain Controller, DNS Server, and DHCP Server in the **corp.viamonstra.com** domain.
    - Server name: **DC01**
    - IP Address: **192.168.1.200**
    - Roles: **DNS**, **DHCP**, and **Domain Controller**
- **CM01.** A **Windows Server 2012 R2** machine, fully patched with the latest security updates and configured as a member server in the **corp.viamonstra.com** domain. The server has SQL Server 2012 SP1 and ConfigMgr 2012 R2 installed.
    - Server name: **CM01**
    - IP Address: **192.168.1.214**
    - Roles: **WDS** and **IIS**
    - Software: **SQL Server 2012 SP1** and **ConfigMgr 2012 R2**
- **MBAM01.** A **Windows Server 2012 R2** machine, fully patched with the latest security updates and configured as a member server in the **corp.viamonstra.com** domain. The server has SQL Server 2012 SP1 installed.
    - Server name: **MBAM01**
    - IP Address: **192.168.1.243**
    - Roles: **MBAM**
    - Software: **SQL Server 2012 SP1**

## Clients (Detailed Information)

In addition to the servers, you also use a few clients in the step-by-step guides. The required client virtual machines are the following:

- **PC0001.** A **Windows 8.1 Enterprise x64** machine, fully patched with the latest security updates and configured as a member in the **corp.viamonstra.com** domain.
    - Client name: **PC0001**
    - IP Address: **192.168.1.11**
- **PC0002-PC0013.** New clients deployed via the various guides.
    - Client name: **PC0002-PC0013**
    - IP Address: **DHCP**

# Setting Up the ConfigMgr 2012 R2 Infrastructure

In this section, you set up a base ConfigMgr 2012 R2 server for software distribution. In these guides, you use the CM01 virtual machine you configured as part of the hydration kit. The base configuration involves the following:

- Adding a user as Full Administrator in the Configuration Manager (ConfigMgr) console
- Updating to ConfigMgr 2012 R2 CU4
- Configuring Active Directory group membership
- Configuring discovery methods
- Creating a boundary group
- Adding the reporting services point
- Adding the state migration point

## Create a New User in the ViaMonstra / Users OU

To delegate security and roles in ConfigMgr 2012 R2, you can use RBAC (role-based access control). Before doing so, however, you should create a new user matching your name. In these steps, you create a new Active Directory user in the ViaMonstra / Users organizational unit (OU) matching your name:

1. On **DC01**, log in as **VIAMONSTRA\Administrator** using a password of **P@ssw0rd**.
2. Using **Active Directory User and Computers**, in the **ViaMonstra / Users** OU, create a user matching your name, using a password of **P@ssw0rd**, by right-clicking, choosing **New User**, and continuing through the wizard until completion.

Chapter 2  ViaMonstra Inc. and the Proof-of-Concept Environment

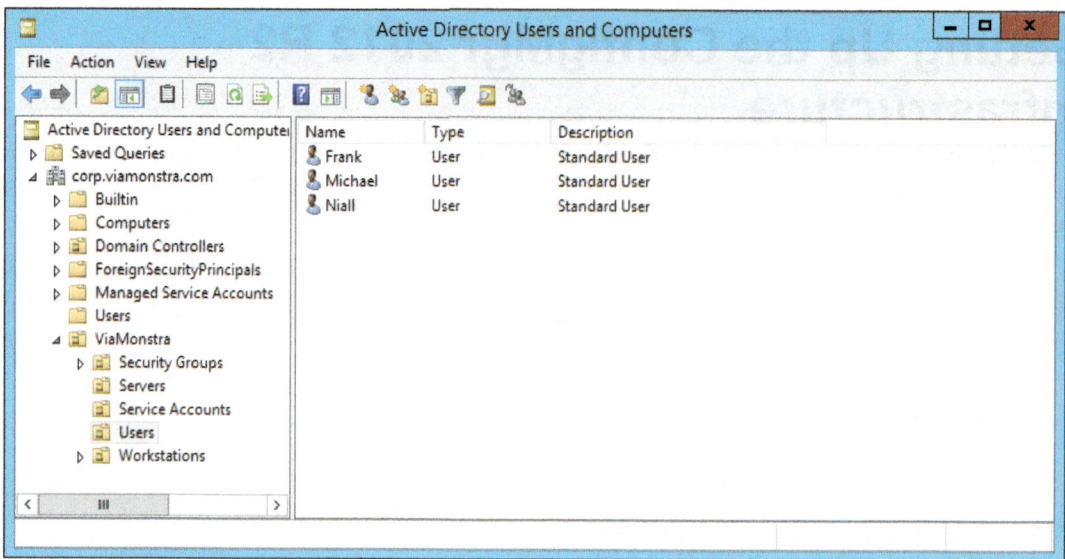

*Configured users in the ViaMonstra / Users OU in Active Directory Users and Computers.*

## Add a User to the Full Administrator Group Using RBAC

ConfigMgr 2012 R2 provides role and security delegation via RBAC. The Full Administrator security group gives access to all objects and abilities within ConfigMgr, so it is wise to grant this roll sparingly. To add a user to the Full Administrator group using RBAC, follow these steps:

1. On **CM01**, log in as **VIAMONSTRA\Administrator** using a password of **P@ssw0rd**.
2. Open the **ConfigMgr console** and browse to the **Administration** workspace.
3. In the **Administration** workspace, select **Security** and expand it.
4. Select **Administrative Users** and click **Add User or Group** on the ribbon.
5. In the **User or Group name** field, do as follows:
    a. Click **Browse** and type in your username (e.g., **VIAMONSTRA\Niall**).
    b. Click **Add** and select **Full Administrator** from the list of available security roles.
6. In the **Assigned Security Scopes and Collections**, select **All instances of the objects that are related to the assigned security roles** as shown in the figure.
7. Click **OK**.

Chapter 2  ViaMonstra Inc. and the Proof-of-Concept Environment

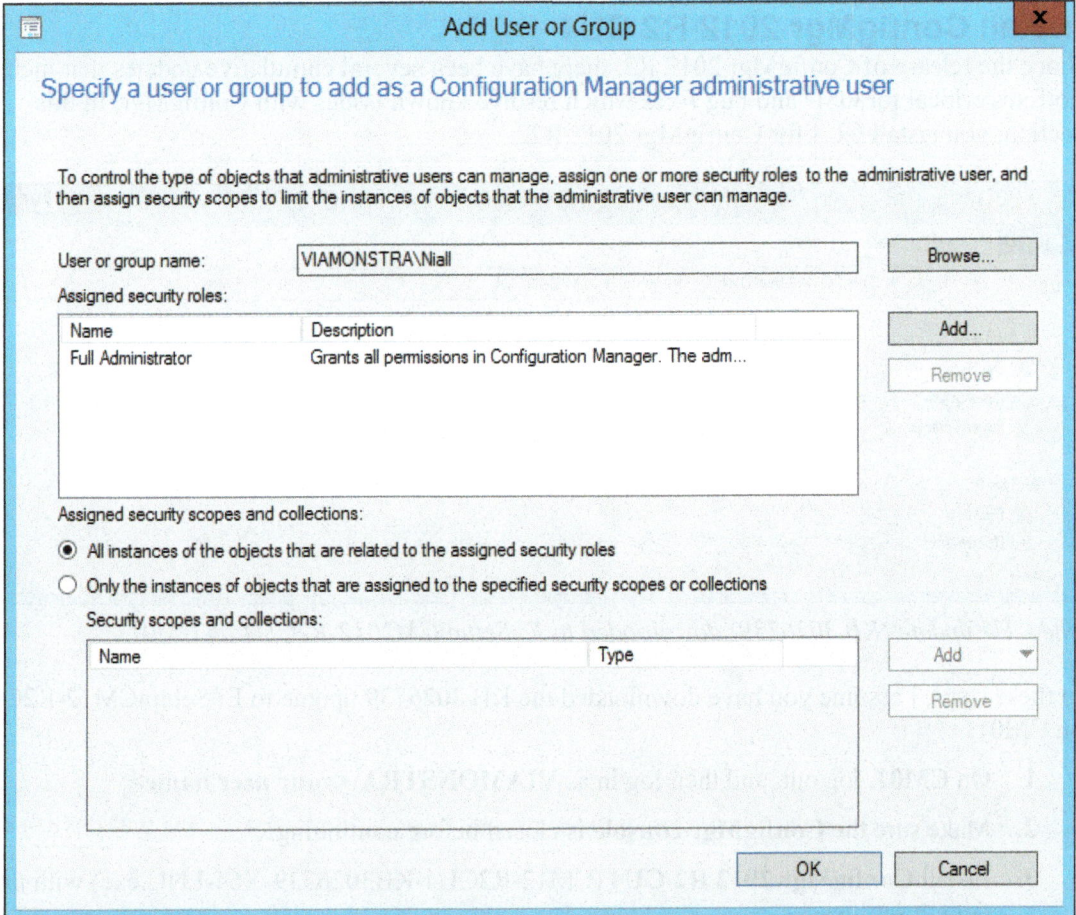

*The Full Administrator role being assigned to all instances of the objects that are related to the assigned security role.*

## Add a User to the Local Administrators Group on CM01

To add a user to the local Administrators group on CM01, follow these steps:

1. On **CM01**, open **Computer Management** and expand the **Local Users and Groups / Groups** node.

2. Double-click the **Administrators** group, click **Add** and type in your username (e.g., **VIAMONSTRA\Niall**).

3. Click **OK** twice.

Chapter 2    ViaMonstra Inc. and the Proof-of-Concept Environment

## Install ConfigMgr 2012 R2 CU4

Since the release of ConfigMgr 2012 R2, there have been several cumulative updates that include hotfixes critical for OSD and bug fixes which resolve known issues with ConfigMgr. In this section, you install CU4 for ConfigMgr 2012 R2.

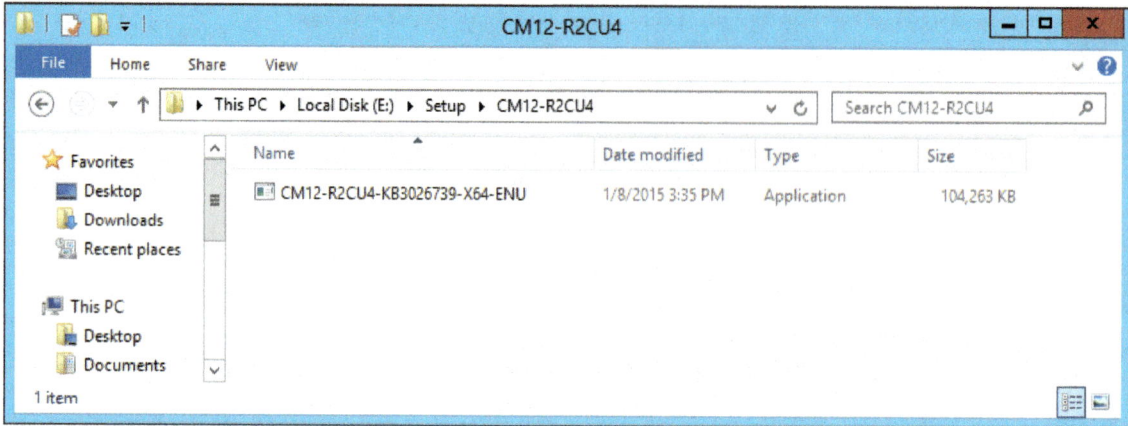

*The CU4 update (KB 3026739) downloaded to E:\Setup\CM2012-R2CU4 on CM01.*

In these steps, I assume you have downloaded the KB 3026739 update to E:\Setup\CM12-R2CU4 on CM01.

1. On **CM01**, log out, and then log in as **VIAMONSTRA\<your user name>**.
2. Make sure the **ConfigMgr console** is closed before continuing.
3. Install **ConfigMgr 2012 R2 CU4** (CM12-R2CU4-KB3026739-X64-ENU.exe) with the default settings.

**Note:** If the setup warns you about an earlier software installation that still has outstanding file rename operations pending, cancel the CU4 setup, restart the server, and then start the CU4 setup again.

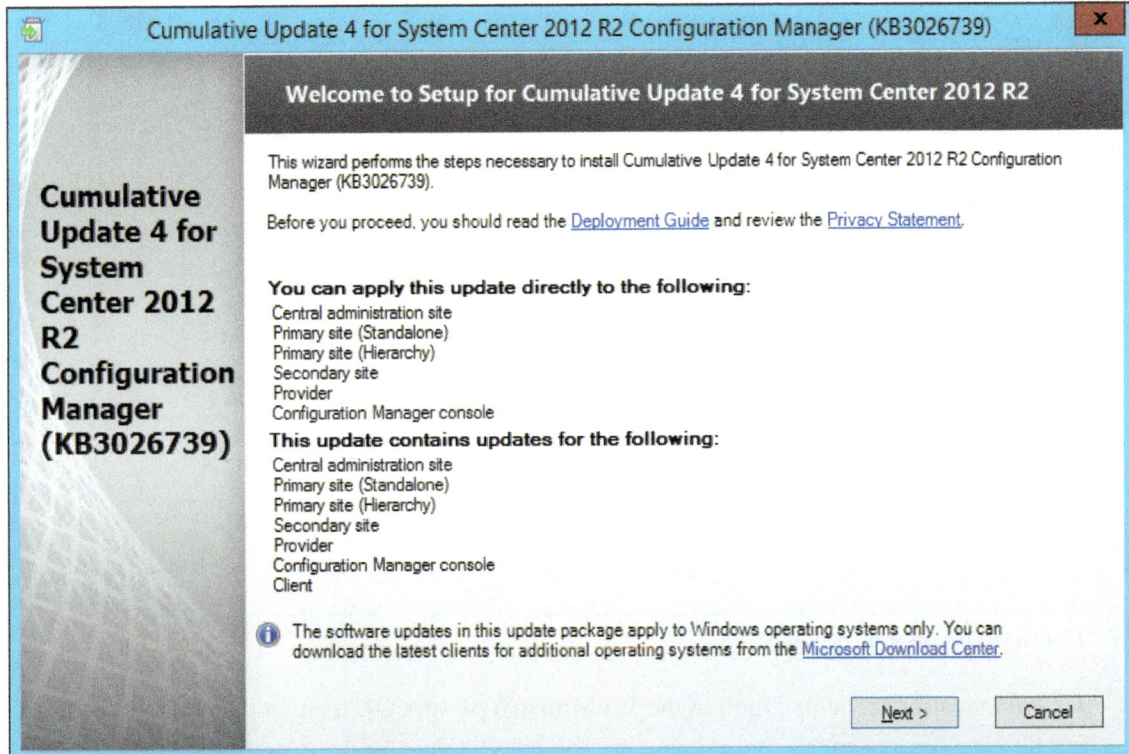

*Running the ConfigMgr 2012 R2 CU4 setup.*

## Create Software Groups

One common way to assign deployments in ConfigMgr 2012 R2 is to use groups in Active Directory. In these steps, you create a few software groups and add test users as members:

1. On **DC01**, log in as **VIAMONSTRA\Administrator** using a password of **P@ssw0rd**.

2. Using **Active Directory User and Computers**, in the **ViaMonstra / Software Groups** OU, create the following global security groups:

    o **7-Zip 9.20 - x64**

    o **Mozilla FireFox - x86**

Chapter 2   ViaMonstra Inc. and the Proof-of-Concept Environment

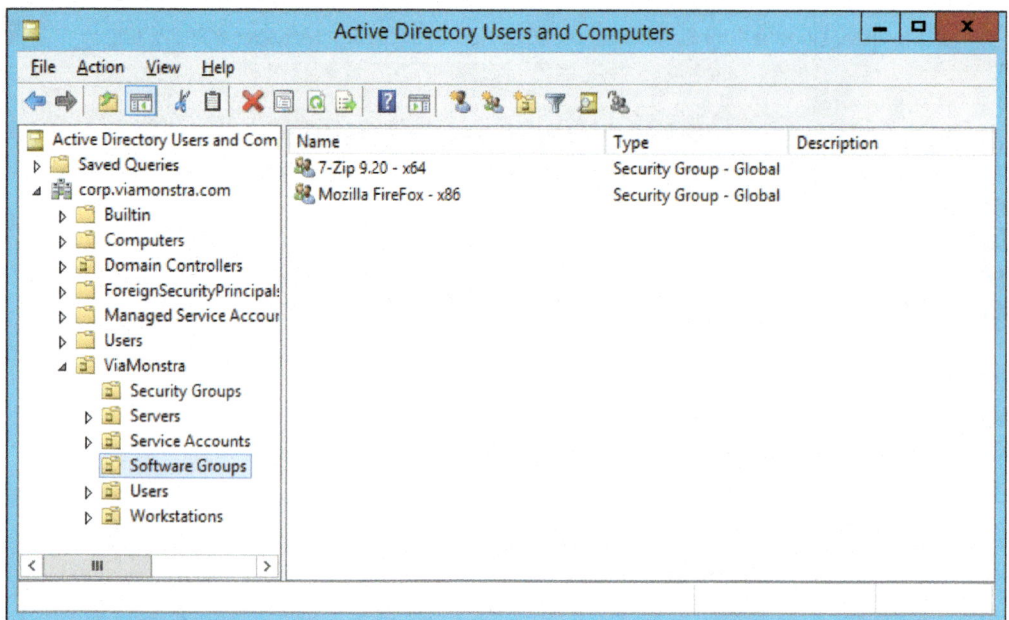

*The software groups created.*

3. Add the user accounts found in the **ViaMonstra / Users** OU as members of the preceding groups.

**Real World Note:** When you create groups that are going to be used for software distribution, they need to contain at least one member for the ConfigMgr group discovery process to find them.

## Configure Discovery Methods

1. On **CM01**, log in as **VIAMONSTRA\<your user name>**, and from the **Start screen**, select the **ConfigMgr console**.

2. In the **Administration** workspace, expand **Hierarchy Configuration / Discovery Methods**.

Chapter 2   ViaMonstra Inc. and the Proof-of-Concept Environment

3. Enable **Active Directory Forest Discovery** and then select the settings to automatically create Active Directory site and IP address range boundaries. When prompted, run the discovery.

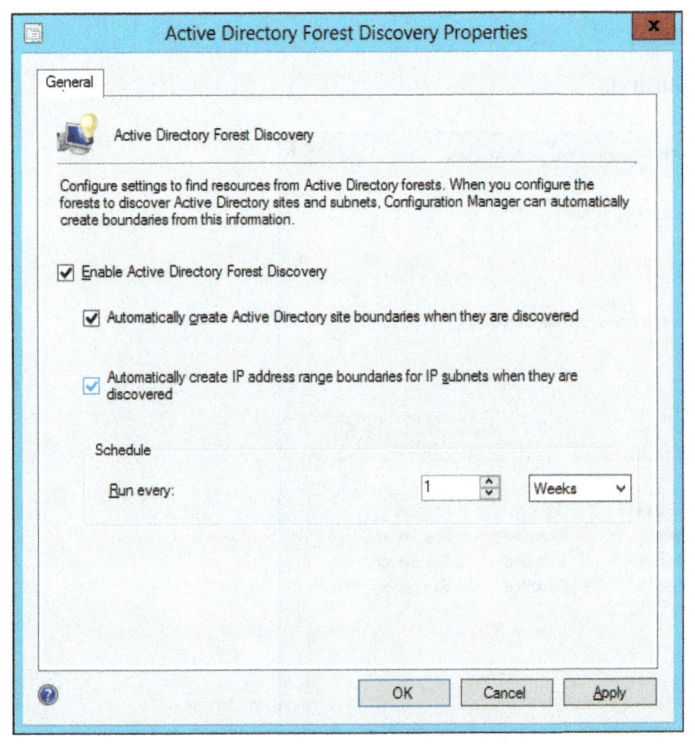

*Configuring Active Directory Forest Discovery.*

4. Using **CMTrace** (located in E:\Program Files\Microsoft Configuration Manager\tools), review the **E:\Program Files\Microsoft Configuration Manager\Logs\ADForestDisc.log** file.

**Real World Note:** In the log, you may see the following error: Discovered subnet 192.168.1.0/24 in AD site NewYork in forest corp.viamonstra.com was not saved in the database. But don't worry, it's a known issue, and the boundary will be created anyway.

5. Still in the **Administration** workspace, select the **Boundaries** node and review the boundaries that were created.

21

6. In the **Discovery Methods** node, enable **Active Directory System Discovery**. Add the following OUs by clicking the * button and clicking **Browse**.
    o Domain Controllers
    o ViaMonstra / Servers
    o ViaMonstra / Workstations

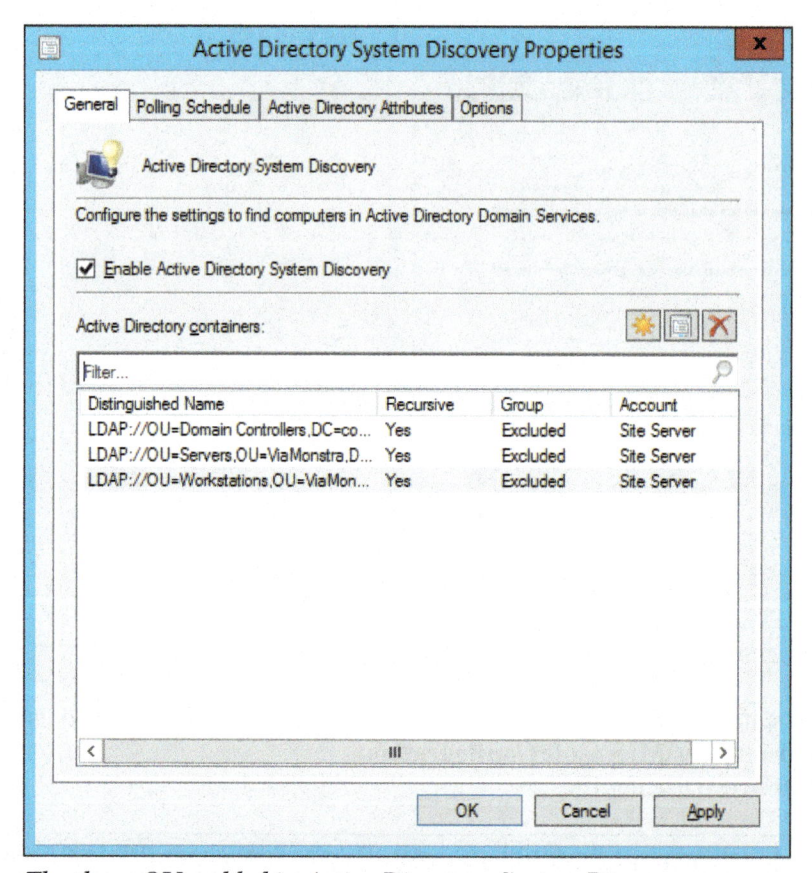

*The three OUs added in Active Directory System Discovery.*

7. Using **CMTrace**, review the **E:\Program Files\Microsoft Configuration Manager\Logs\adsysdis.log** file.

8. In the **Assets and Compliance** workspace, select **Device Collections**. Press **F5** or click the **Refresh** button to refresh the view. You should now see four members in the **All Systems** collection.

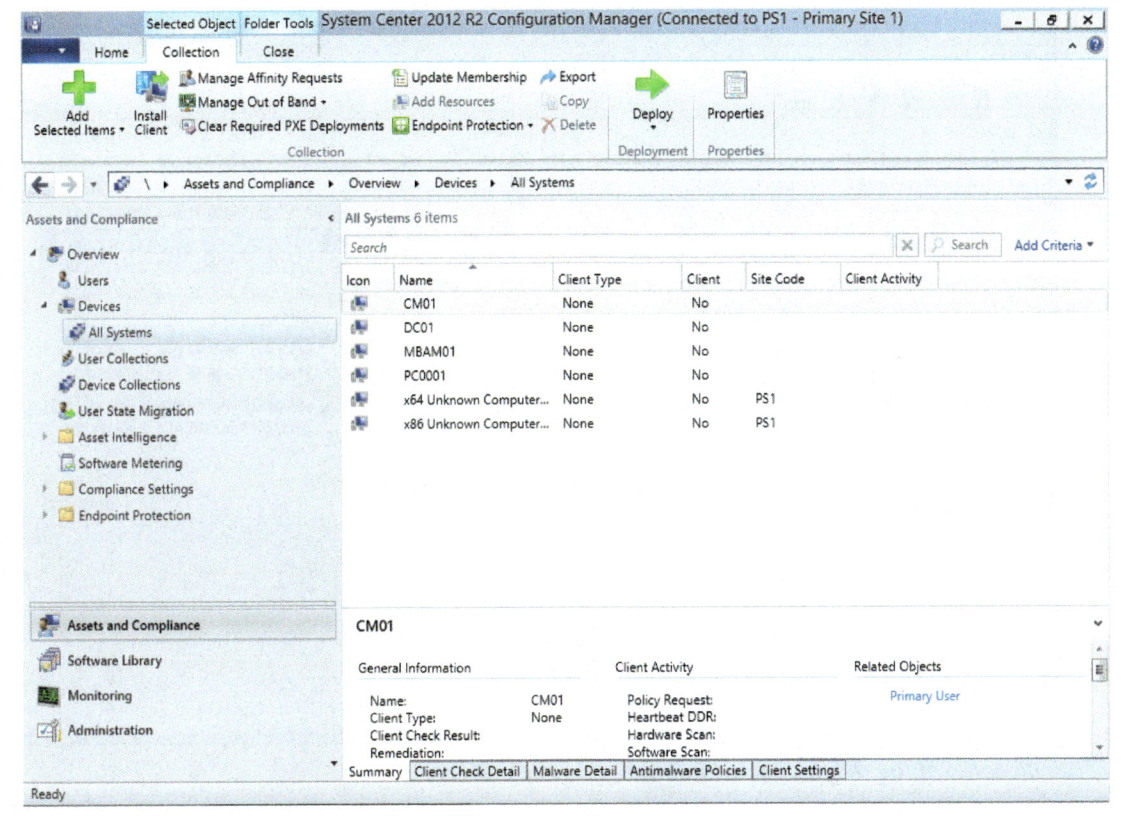

## Chapter 2 ViaMonstra Inc. and the Proof-of-Concept Environment

*Discovered resources listed in the All Systems collection.*

**Note:** It may take a while for the collection to refresh; you can view progress via the colleval.log file. If you want to speed up the process, you can manually update membership on the All Systems collection by right-clicking the collection and selecting Update Membership.

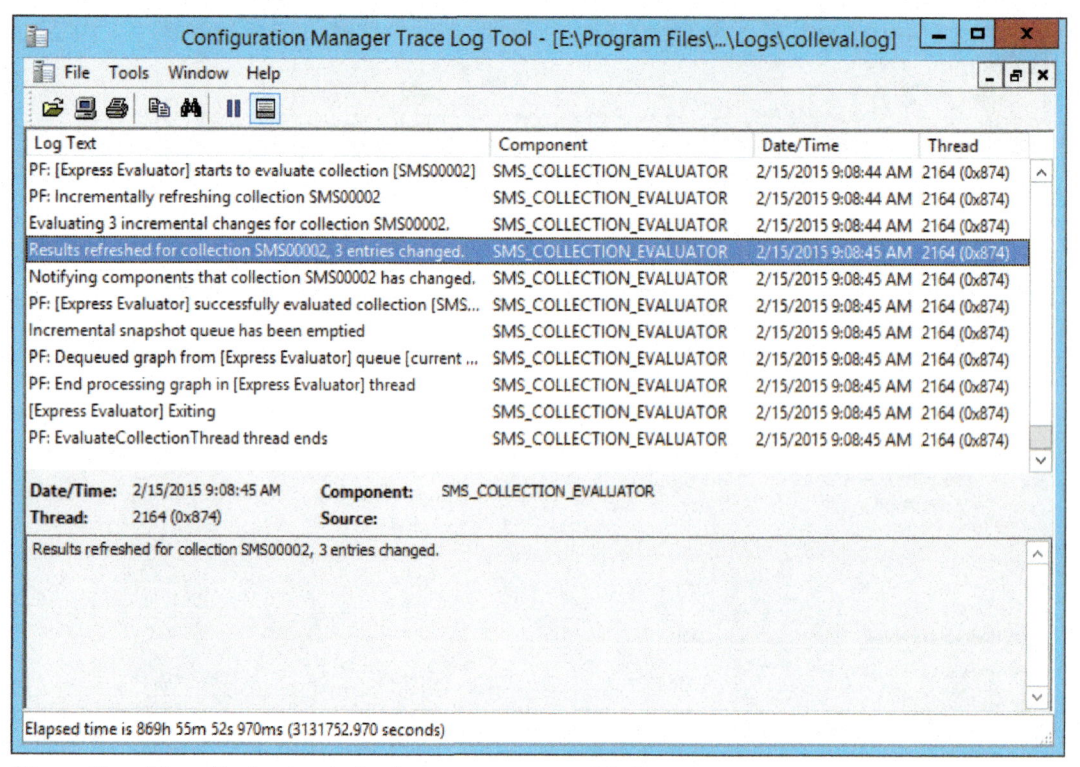

*The colleval.log displaying info about resources added.*

9. In the **Administration** workspace, in the **Discovery Methods** node, enable **Active Directory User Discovery**, add the **ViaMonstra / Users** OU, and run the discovery.

10. Using **CMTrace**, review the **E:\Program Files\Microsoft Configuration Manager\Logs\adusrdis.log** file.

Chapter 2   ViaMonstra Inc. and the Proof-of-Concept Environment

11. In the **Assets and Compliance** workspace, select **Users**. Press **F5** or click the **Refresh** button to refresh the view. You should now see the discovered users.

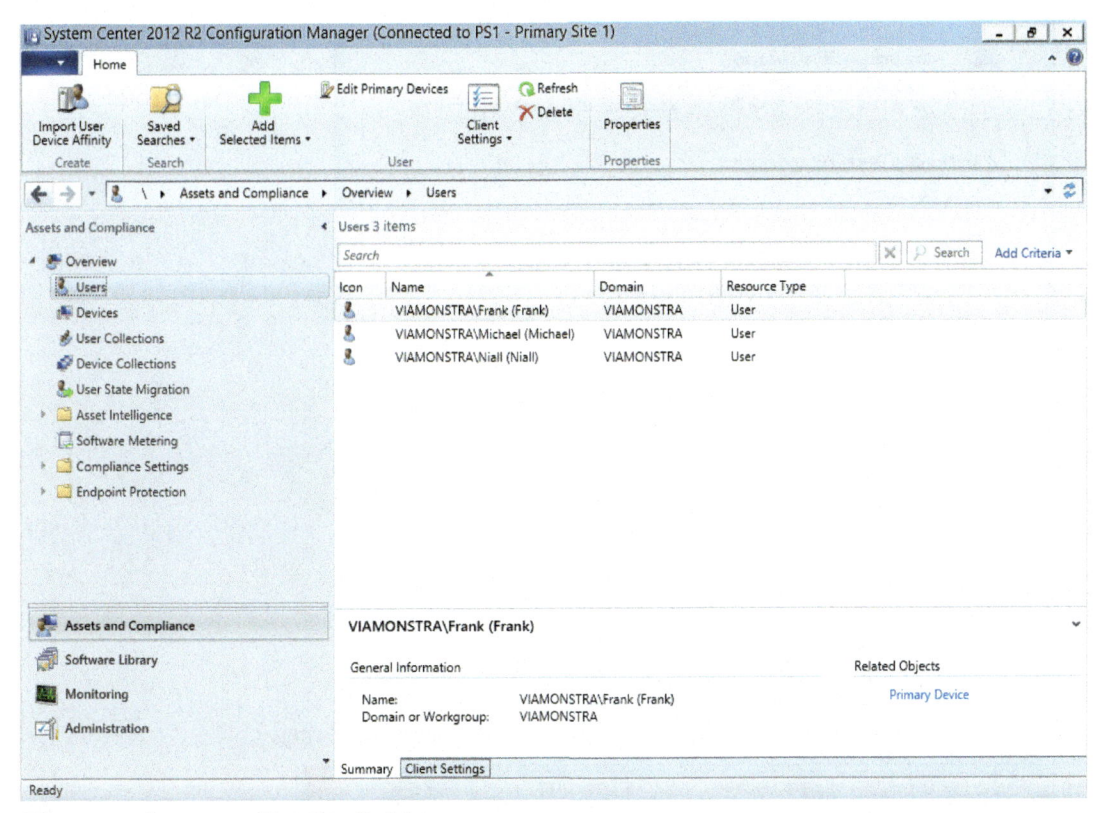

*The users discovered by ConfigMgr.*

12. In the **Discovery Methods** node, enable **Active Directory Group Discovery**, add the **ViaMonstra / Software Groups** OU as the location, name it **Software Groups**, and run the discovery.

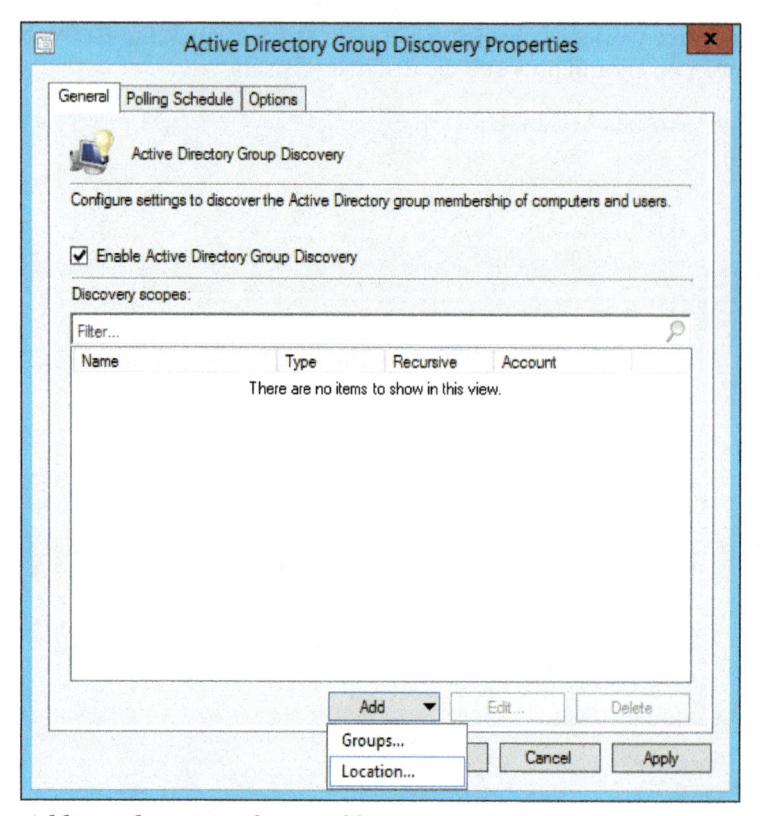

*Adding a location when enabling Active Directory Group Discovery.*

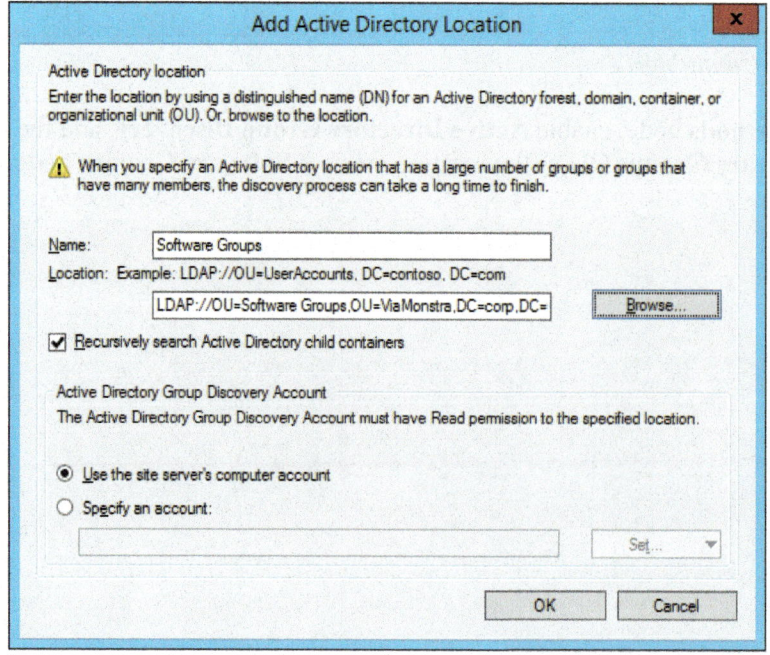

*More details on adding the location for Active Directory Group Discovery.*

13. Using **CMTrace**, review the **E:\Program Files\Microsoft Configuration Manager\Logs\adsgdis.log** file.

14. In the **Assets and Compliance** workspace, select **User Collections**. Press **F5** or click the **Refresh** button to refresh the view. You should now see two members in the **All Users** and **All User Groups** collections, and four members in the **All Users and User Groups** collection.

> **Note:** Again, it may take a while for the collection to refresh, and as for the device collection, you can view progress via the colleval.log file. If you want to speed up the process, you can manually update membership on the collections by right-clicking a collection and selecting Update Membership.

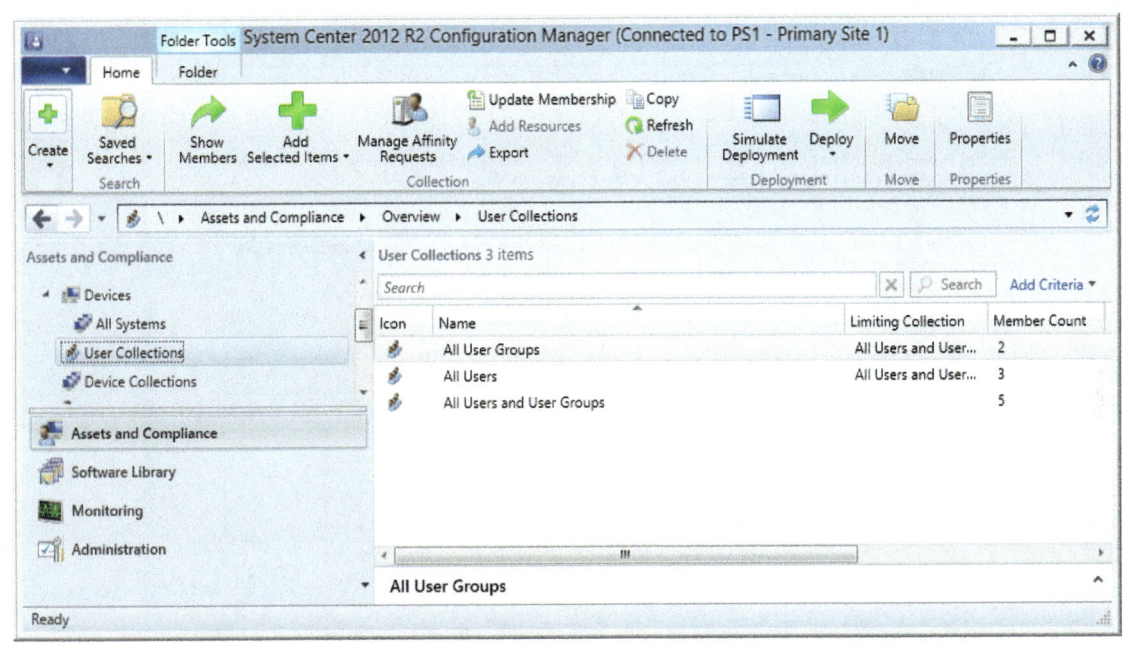

*The User Collections node after the discovery methods have been configured.*

## Create a Boundary Group

To make sure clients can locate content on the distribution point and find the management point, you configure a boundary group.

1. On **CM01**, using the **ConfigMgr console**, in the **Administration** workspace, select **Boundary Groups**.
2. Create a boundary group using the following settings:
    a. In the **General** tab
        - Name: **HQ Assignment**
        - Boundaries: Add the **NewYork** and **192.168.1.1 – 192.168.1.254** boundaries.

b. In the **References** tab

- Site assignment area: Select the **Use the boundary group for site assignment** check box.
- Content location area: Add the **CM01** distribution point.

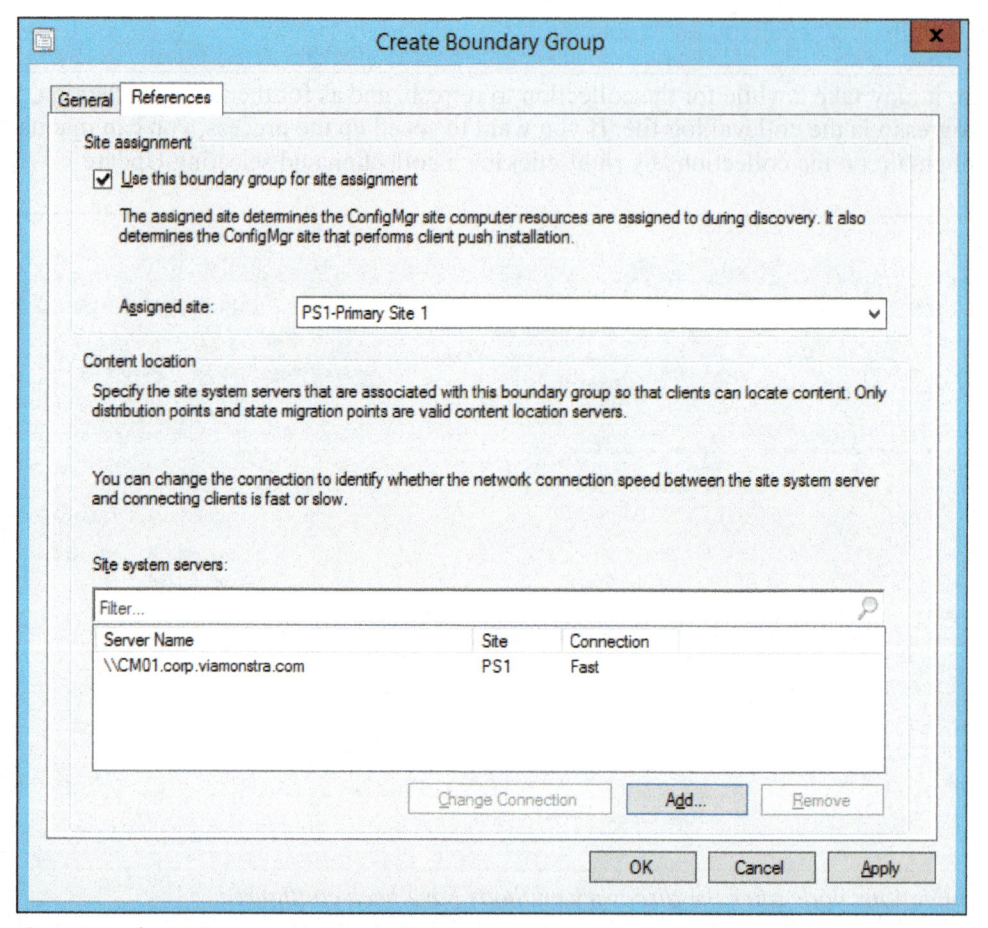

*Creating the HQ Assignment boundary group.*

> **Real World Note:** At this point, I recommend that you verify that your site server is publishing the site information to Active Directory. You can either check the hman.log file on CM01, or review the content in the System Management container using ADSI Edit or Active Directory Users and Computers on DC01.

## Add the Reporting Services Point

Reports in ConfigMgr are very useful for keeping track of deployments, both for applications and task sequences. You also can create custom reports if needed.

1. Using the **ConfigMgr console**, in the **Administration** workspace, expand **Site Configuration** and select **Sites**.
2. On the ribbon, select **Add Site System Roles**, and use the following settings for the **Add Site System Roles Wizard**:
    a. General: **<default>**
    b. Proxy: **<default>**
    c. System Role Selection: **Reporting services point**
    d. Reporting services point: Click **Verify**.
    e. User name: Add a new account
        - User name: **VIAMONSTRA\CM_SR**
        - Password: **P@ss0wrd**
    f. Summary: **<default>**

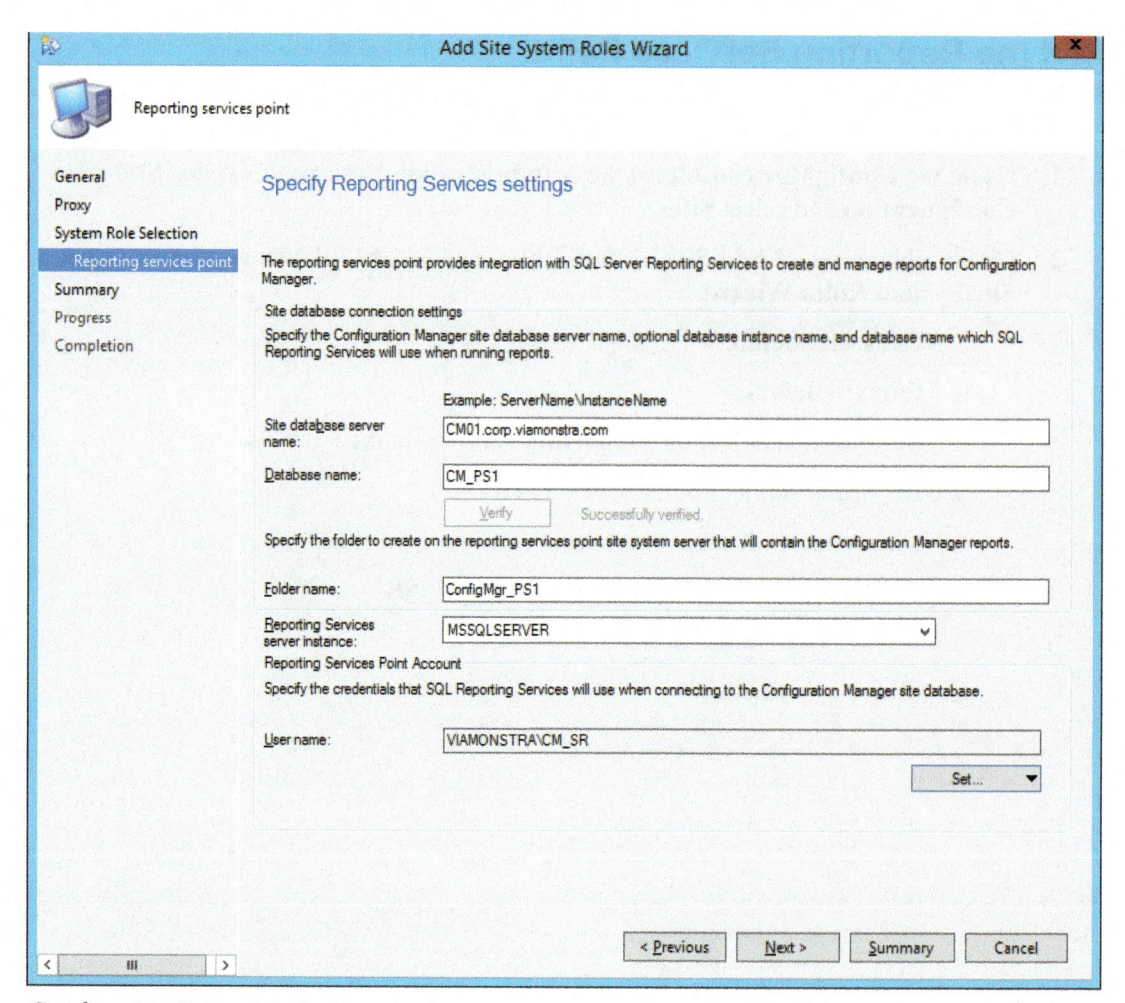

*Configuring Reporting Services settings.*

3. Using **CMTrace**, review the **E:\Program Files\Microsoft Configuration Manager\Logs\srsrpsetup.log** and **E:\Program Files\Microsoft Configuration Manager\Logs\srsrp.log** files.

> **Note:** It will take a short while for the log files to appear. Wait until all reports have been deployed before continuing. You don't need to worry about the red lines in the log; the target folder contains the word error in the name so you see many red lines. Anyway, this is a good time to take a quick break. ☺

Chapter 2    ViaMonstra Inc. and the Proof-of-Concept Environment

4. In the **ConfigMgr console**, in the **Monitoring** workspace, expand the **Reporting / Reports** node, select the **Reports** node, and then review the reports available.

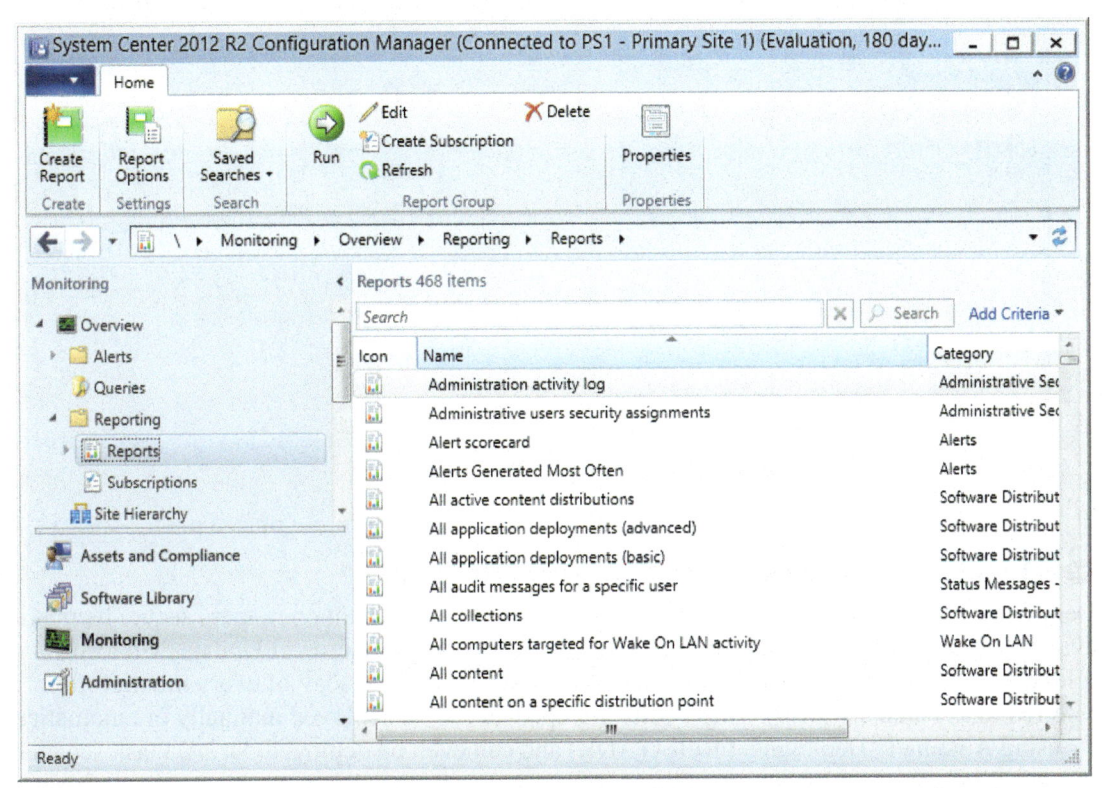

*The Reports node in ConfigMgr 2012 R2 after adding the Reporting services point role.*

## Verify IE Enhanced Security Configuration

Because you probably want to run the reports in a web browser (for better performance), make sure that IE Enhanced Security Configuration is disabled.

1. On **CM01**, using the **Server Manager**, select **Local Server**.
2. In the **PROPERTIES for CM01** pane, make sure the **IE Enhanced Security Configuration** is set to **Off**.

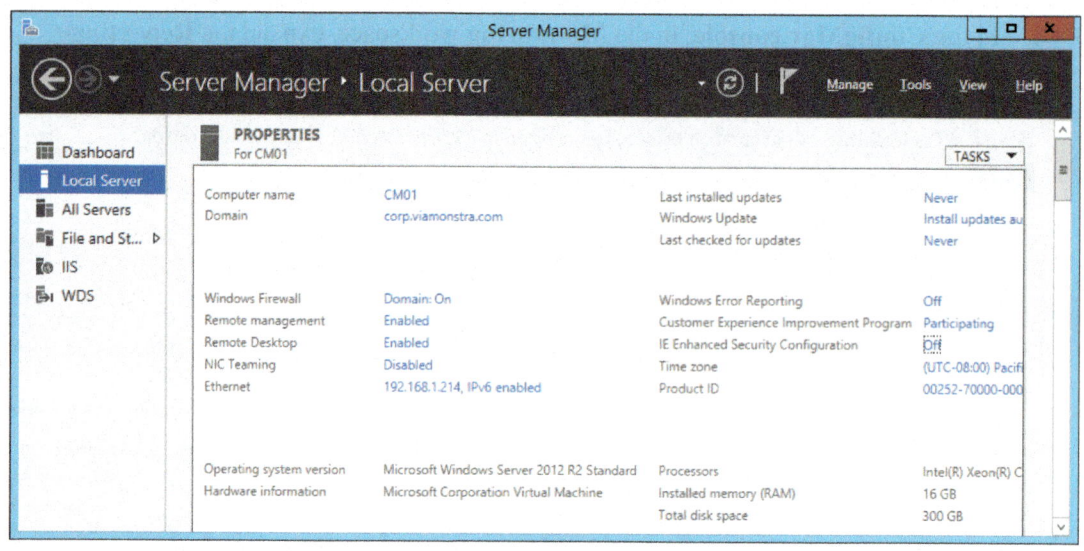

*Making sure IE Enhanced Security Configuration is disabled.*

# Setting Up Software Updates

Deploying software updates in ConfigMgr helps to keep your client computers secure by making available the latest security updates and patches released from Microsoft Update. Microsoft releases Windows updates fairly often, usually on the second Tuesday of every month (often referred to as Patch Tuesday). These software updates can be deployed manually or automatically by using Automatic Deployment Rules (ADR) and can even be deployed during a task sequence.

## Add a Software Update Point

Deploying software updates requires a software update point (SUP) installed and the SUP role itself requires Windows Server Update Services (WSUS). To install the Windows Server WSUS role and then add the ConfigMgr SUP role on CM01 follow this procedure:

> **Note:** Adding a software update point requires that you to have Internet access on the CM01 virtual machine. I commonly use a virtual router (running in a VM) to provide Internet access to my lab and test VMs. You can use the Vyatta and VyOS (Vyatta community fork) routers, or a Windows Server 2012 R2 virtual machine with routing configured.

1. On **CM01**, using the **Server Manager**, select **Add Roles and Features**, and use the following settings for the **Add Roles and Features Wizard**:

    a. Before You Begin: **<default>**

    b. Installation Type: **<default>**

    c. Server Selection: **<default>**

d. Server Roles: **<Windows Server Update Services>**

e. Click **Add Features** when prompted to **Add features that are required for Windows Server Update Services**

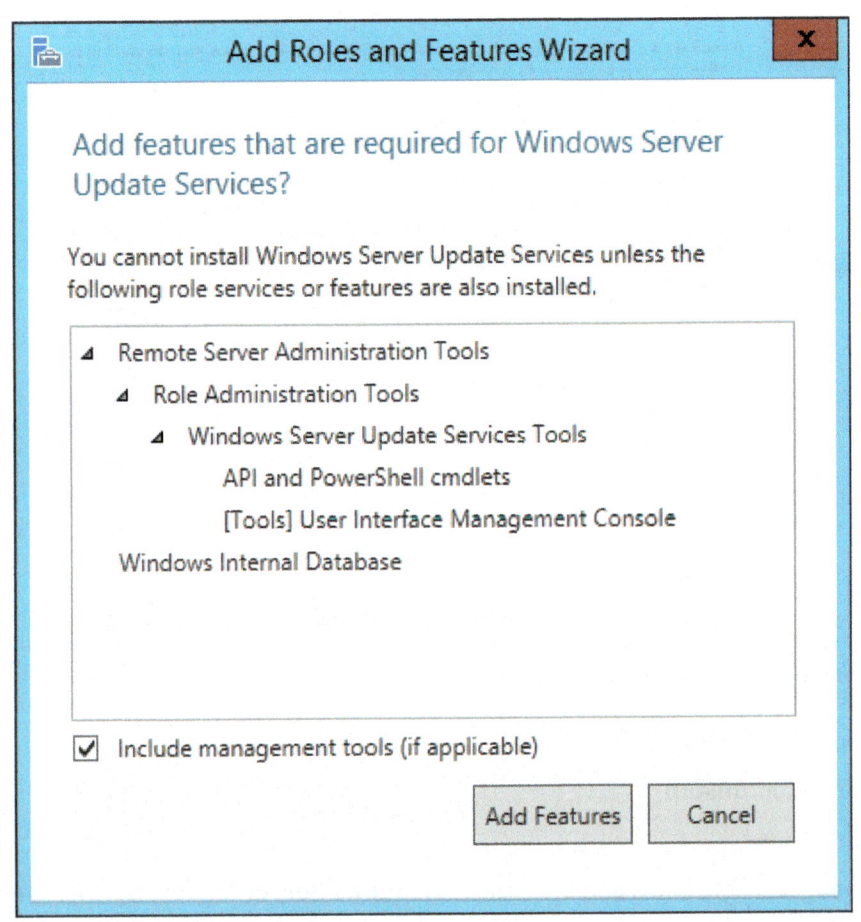

*Adding features required by the WSUS role.*

f. Features: **<default>**

g. WSUS: **<default>**

h. Role Services: Clear the **WID Database** check box, and select the **Database** check box.

i. Content: Specify the following

- **Store Updates in the following location**
- **E:\Sources\WSUS**

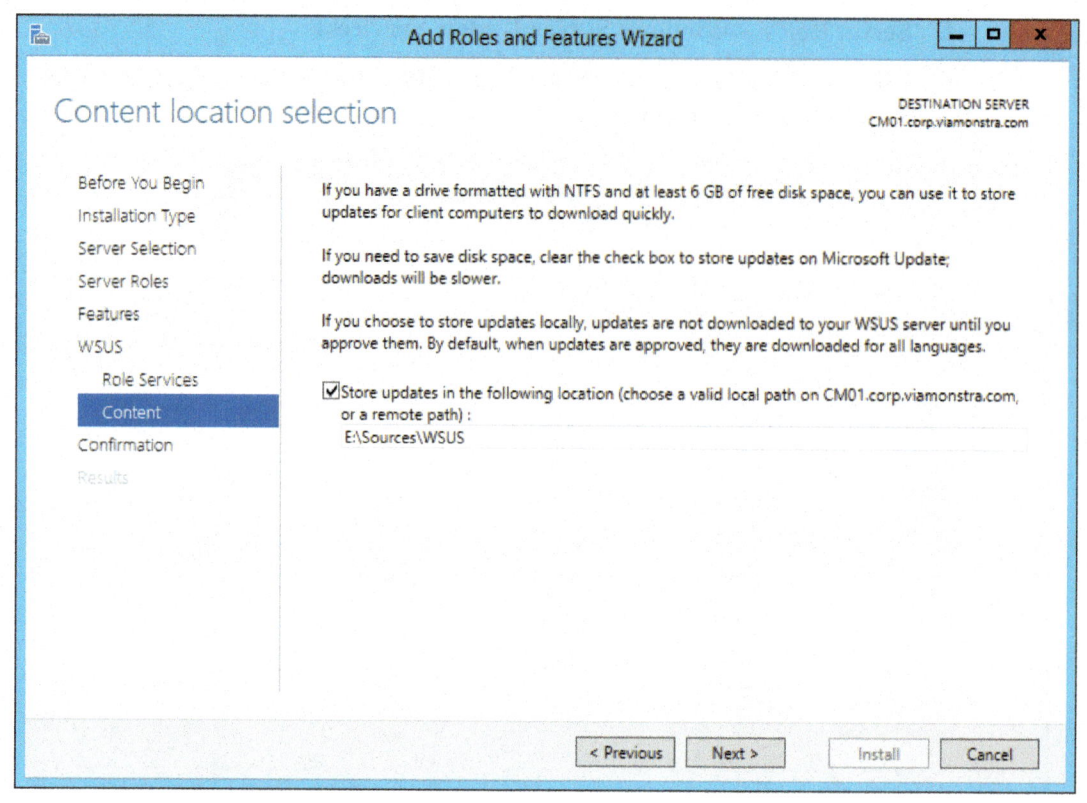

*Store updates in the following location for the WSUS role.*

        j.   DB Instance: **CM01**

        k.   Confirmation: **Install**

        l.   Results: **Close**

2. In **Server Manager**, click **Tools** and then select **Windows Server Update Services** from the options listed.

3. Select **Run** when prompted, let the wizard complete, and then click **Close**.

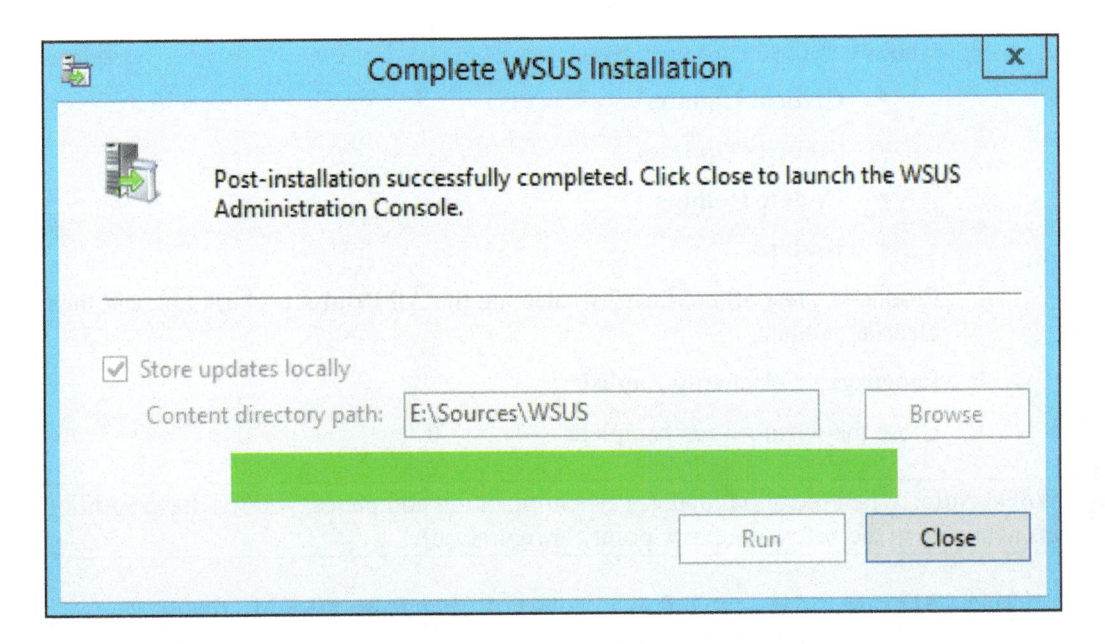

*Final configuration of WSUS is complete.*

4. The **Windows Server Update Services Configuration Wizard** appears. Click **Cancel** and then close the **Windows Server Update Services** UI.
5. Using the **ConfigMgr console**, in the **Administration** workspace, expand **Site Configuration** and select **Sites**.
6. On the ribbon, select **Add Site System Roles**, and use the following settings for the **Add Site System Roles Wizard**:
    a. General: **<default>**
    b. Proxy: **<default>**
    c. System Role Selection: **Software update point**
    d. Software Update Point:
        - WSUS Configuration: **WSUS is configured to use ports 8530 and 8531**
        - Client Connection Type: **Allow intranet-only client connections**
    e. Proxy and Account settings: **<default>**
    f. Synchronization Source: **<default>**
    g. Synchronization Schedule:
        - Enable Synchronization on a schedule **<selected>**
        - Simple Schedule: **7 days**
    h. Supersedence Rules: **<default>**

i. Classifications:
   - **Critical Updates**
   - **Security Updates**
   - **Update Rollups**
   - **Updates**
j. Products: Clear all products by selecting the **All Products** check box and then clearing it again.
k. Languages: Select only **English**
l. Close the wizard when complete.

> **Real World Note:** When the initial updates synchronization completes, you will have additional products available in the software update point configuration.

7. Using **CMTrace**, review the following logs in **E:\Program Files\Microsoft Configuration Manager\Logs\**:
   - SUPSetup.log
   - WCM.log
   - WSUSCtrl.log

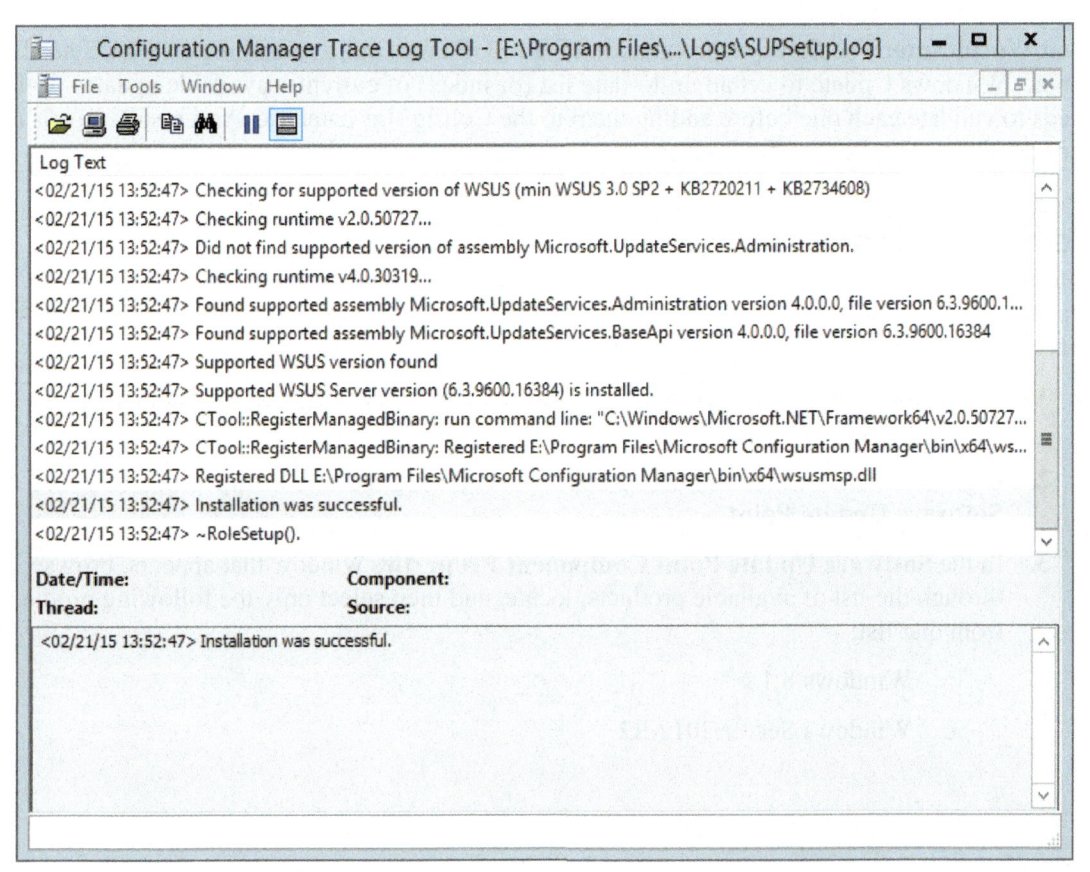

*Successful installation of the SUP role as indicated in the SUPSetup log file.*

## Synchronize Updates

Now that we've enabled the Software Update Point role, it's time to trigger a sync. There are two types of synchronization: Full sync and Delta sync. A Full sync is triggered when run on a schedule as determined by the Sync Schedule tab of the Software Update Point Component Properties, whereas a Delta sync is triggered on demand by selecting Synchronize Software Updates in the ribbon.

Performing a sync is necessary as it updates the index of available products and updates, and this in turn allows you to view new classifications not yet available to ConfigMgr. To synchronize updates, use the following procedure:

1. Using the **ConfigMgr console**, in the **Software Library** workspace, select **Software Updates / All Software Updates**.

2. On the ribbon, click **Synchronize Software Updates** and answer **Yes** when prompted.

3. Using **CMTrace**, review the following log in **E:\Program Files\Microsoft Configuration Manager\Logs\wsyncmgr.log**. Look for a line that states **Sync succeeded. Setting sync alert to canceled state on site PS1.**

> **Real World Note:** The first synchronization of the SUP takes quite some time as WSUS needs to contact Windows Update to get an up-to-date list (or index) of currently available updates. It then needs to validate each one before adding them to the ConfigMgr database. As a result, now is a very good time to take a coffee break.

## Review Update Products

After confirmation of a successful software update sync, it's time to review the updated list of available products and make a new product selection that includes Windows 8.1 and Windows Server 2012 R2. To review and change the update products, do as follows:

1. Using the **ConfigMgr console**, in the **Administration** workspace, expand **Site Configuration** and select **Sites.**

2. Right-click **PS1 – Primary Site 1** and choose **Configure Site Components** followed by **Software Update Point**.

3. In the **Software Update Point Component Properties** window that appears, browse through the list of available products, locate, and then select only the following products from that list:

    o Windows 8.1

    o Windows Server 2012 R2

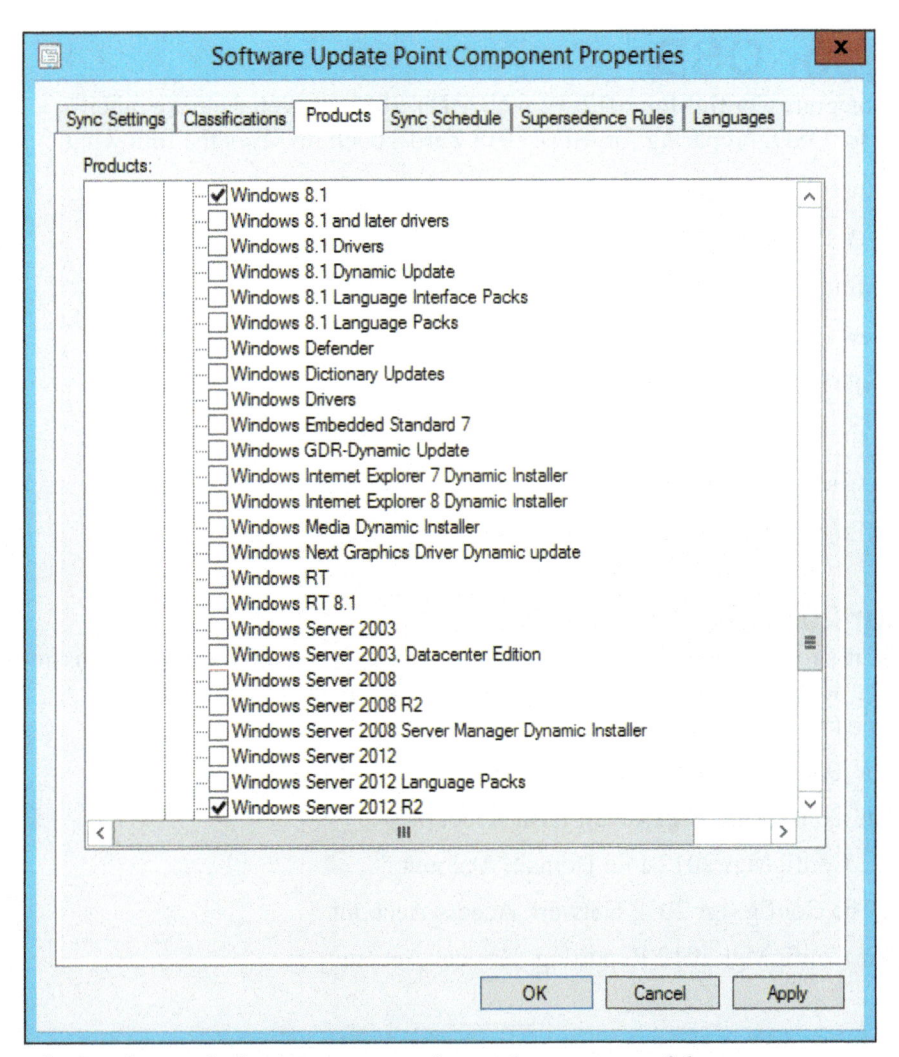

Chapter 2    ViaMonstra Inc. and the Proof-of-Concept Environment

*The Products tab showing new products after a successful sync.*

> **Real World Note**: Many of the newer operating systems such as Windows 8.1 and Windows Server 2012 R2 listed in the preceding figure show up only after a successful sync.

4. After making changes to the **Products** list, click **OK**.
5. Trigger a new sync as explained in the preceding Synchronize Updates section.

# Preparing for OSD

In this section, you integrate ConfigMgr 2012 R2 with MDT 2013, as well as make other preparations needed for OSD. Preparing for MDT 2013 Zero Touch involves the following:

- Reviewing the service accounts
- Configuring Active Directory permissions
- Creating the folder structure
- Creating a new ConfigMgr client package
- Integrating MDT 2013 with ConfigMgr 2012 R2
- Configuring the Network Access account
- Configuring Client Agent settings
- Enabling PXE on the distribution point

## The ConfigMgr 2012 R2 Service Accounts

For security reasons, it's recommended to use a role-based model when configuring permissions for the various service accounts. For the ConfigMgr 2012 R2 setup used in this book, the following service accounts are used:

- **CM_BA.** The ConfigMgr 2012 Build Account
- **CM_CP.** The ConfigMgr 2012 Client Push Account
- **CM_JD.** The ConfigMgr 2012 Join Domain Account
- **CM_NAA.** The ConfigMgr 2012 Network Access Account
- **CM_SR.** The ConfigMgr 2012 Reporting Services Account

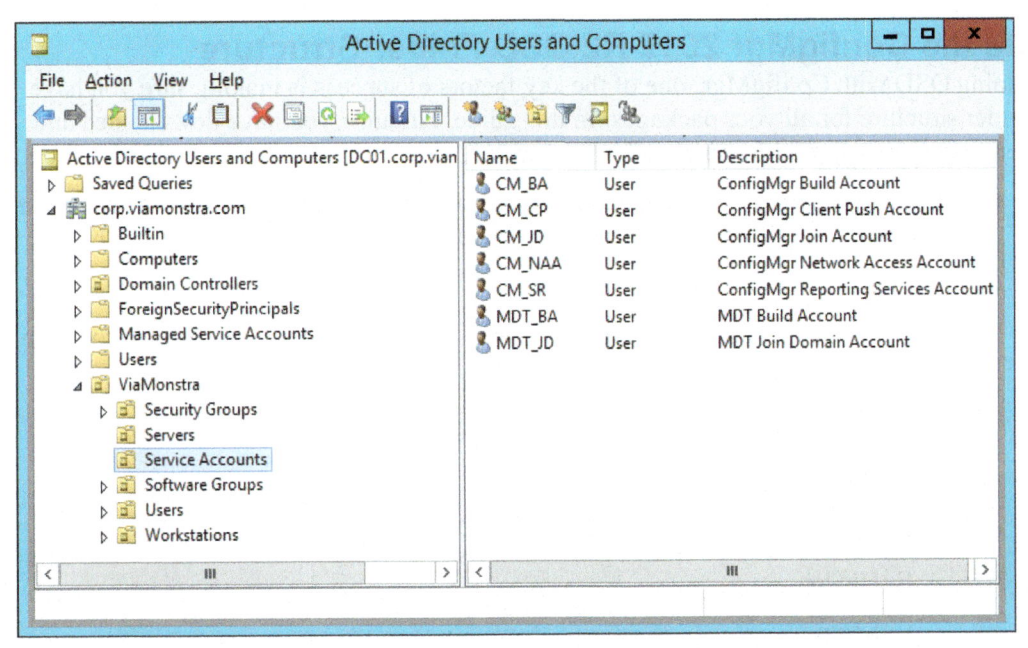

Chapter 2   ViaMonstra Inc. and the Proof-of-Concept Environment

*Active Directory Users and Computers listing the Service Accounts.*

## Set Permissions on the Servers and Workstations OUs

ConfigMgr 2012 deployments need permissions to join machines in Active Directory. In this guide, you grant the join account used for ConfigMgr 2012 R2 (CM_JD) permissions to manage computer accounts in the ViaMonstra / Server and the ViaMonstra / Workstations OUs. In this guide, I assume you have downloaded and extracted the book sample files to C:\Setup on DC01.

1. On **DC01**, in an elevated **PowerShell prompt** (run as Administrator), configure **Execution Policy** in PowerShell by running the following command:

   ```
   Set-ExecutionPolicy -ExecutionPolicy RemoteSigned -Force
   ```

2. On **DC01**, grant permissions for the **CM_JD** account to the **ViaMonstra / Workstations** OU by running the following command:

   ```
   C:\Setup\Scripts\Set-OUPermissions.ps1 -Account CM_JD
   -TargetOU "OU=Workstations,OU=ViaMonstra"
   ```

3. Grant permissions for the **CM_JD** account to the **ViaMonstra / Servers** OU by running the following command:

   ```
   C:\Setup\Scripts\Set-OUPermissions.ps1 -Account CM_JD
   -TargetOU "OU=Servers,OU=ViaMonstra"
   ```

## Create the ConfigMgr 2012 R2 OSD Folder Structure

When doing OSD with ConfigMgr, one of the key factors of success is making sure you have good folder structure for all your packages. In this guide, I assume you have downloaded and extracted the books sample files to E:\Setup on CM01.

1. On **CM01**, review the **E:\Setup\Scripts\Create-ConfigMgrFolders.ps1** script, and if needed modify line 12 to match your user account. The default line 12 is:

    ```
    $CMAdmin = "VIAMONSTRA\Niall"
    ```

2. In an elevated **PowerShell prompt** (run as Administrator), run the following command:

    ```
    E:\Setup\Scripts\Create-ConfigMgrFolders.ps1
    ```

    The preceding script creates the following folder structure:

    E:\Backups

    E:\Captures

    E:\Hidden

    E:\Setup

    E:\Sources

    E:\Sources\OSD

    E:\Sources\OSD\Boot

    E:\Sources\OSD\DriverPackages

    E:\Sources\OSD\Drivers

    E:\Sources\OSD\MDT

    E:\Sources\OSD\OS

    E:\Sources\OSD\OS\Operating System Images

    E:\Sources\OSD\OS\Operating System Installers

    E:\Sources\OSD\Settings

    E:\Sources\Software

    E:\Sources\Software\Microsoft

    E:\Sources\Software\7Zip

    E:\Sources\Software\Mozilla

    E:\USMTStores

    It also shares

    o The E:\Captures folder as Captures$

    o The E:\Sources folder as Sources

- The E:\USMTStores folder as USMTStores$
- The E:\Backups folder as Backups$

## Add the State Migration Point

In computer replace scenarios, the state migration point is used by default to keep track of the backups stored on the server.

1. Using the **ConfigMgr console**, in the **Administration** workspace, expand **Site Configuration** and select **Sites**.
2. On the ribbon, select **Add Site System Roles** and use the following settings for the **Add Site System Roles Wizard**:
    a. General: **<default>**
    b. Proxy: **<default>**
    c. System Role Selection: **State migration point**
    d. Specify state migration point settings: Add a new folder (using the button that looks like an asterisk):
        - Storage Folder: **E:\MigData**
        - Maximum Number of Clients: **500**
        - Minimum Free Space: **20 GB**
        - Deletion policy: **14 days**

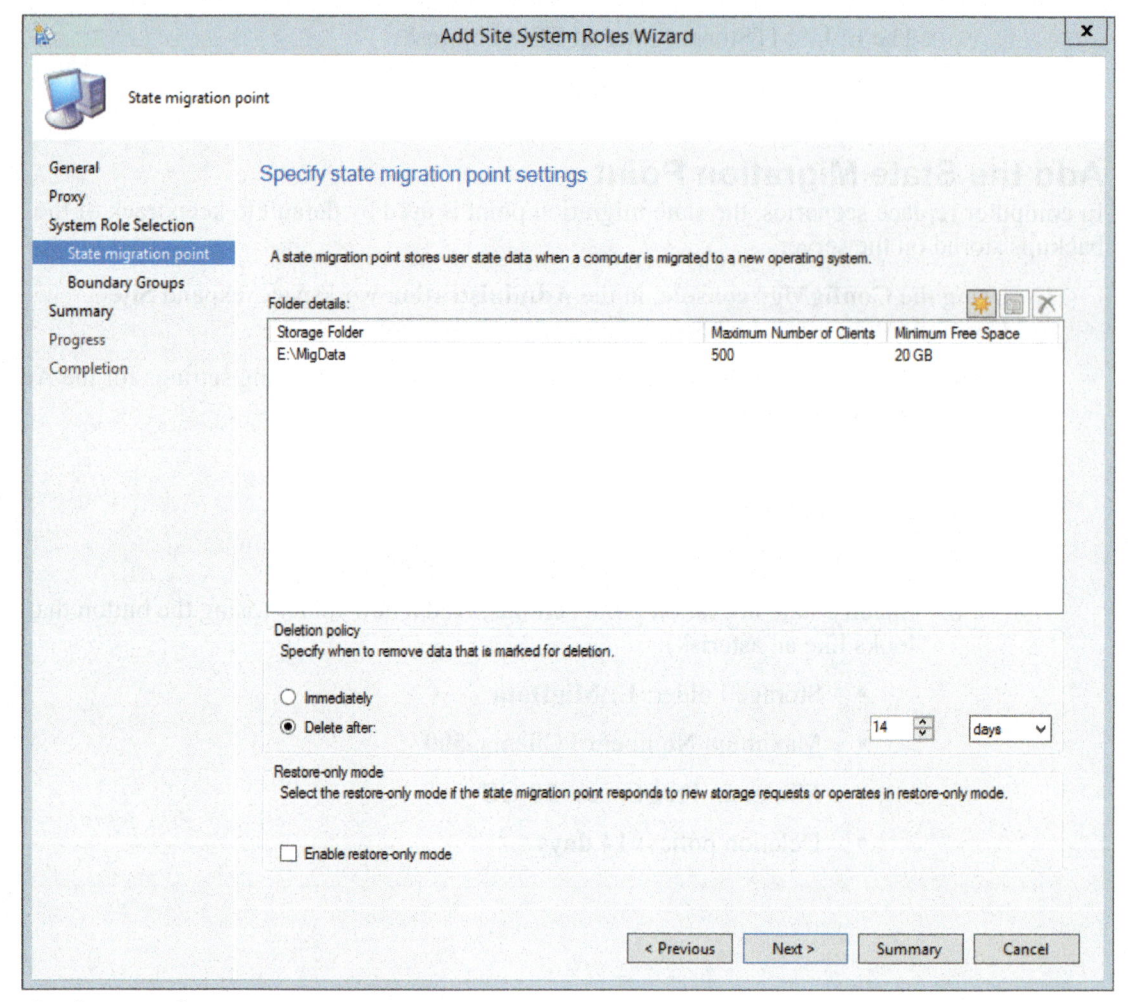

*Configuring the state migration point.*

      e. On the **Boundary Groups** page, make sure the **HQ Assignment** boundary group is added.

3. Using **CMTrace**, in the **E:\Program Files\Microsoft Configuration Manager\Logs** folder, review the following files:

    o **smpmgr.log**

    o **smpMSI.log**

## Create a New ConfigMgr Client Package

Even without the installed update, I recommend that you create a custom ConfigMgr client package for better distribution control. However, because CU4 also has updates for the ConfigMgr 2012 R2 client, it makes even more sense to create a new package. In these steps, you create a new ConfigMgr client package that includes the client update:

1. On **CM01**, in the **E:\Sources** folder, create a subfolder named **ConfigMgr Client with Hotfixes**.

2. Using **File Explorer**, copy the contents of **E:\Program Files\Microsoft Configuration Manager\Client** to the newly created folder (**E:\Sources\ConfigMgr Client with Hotfixes**).

3. In **E:\Sources\ConfigMgr Client with Hotfixes**, create a folder named **Hotfix**.

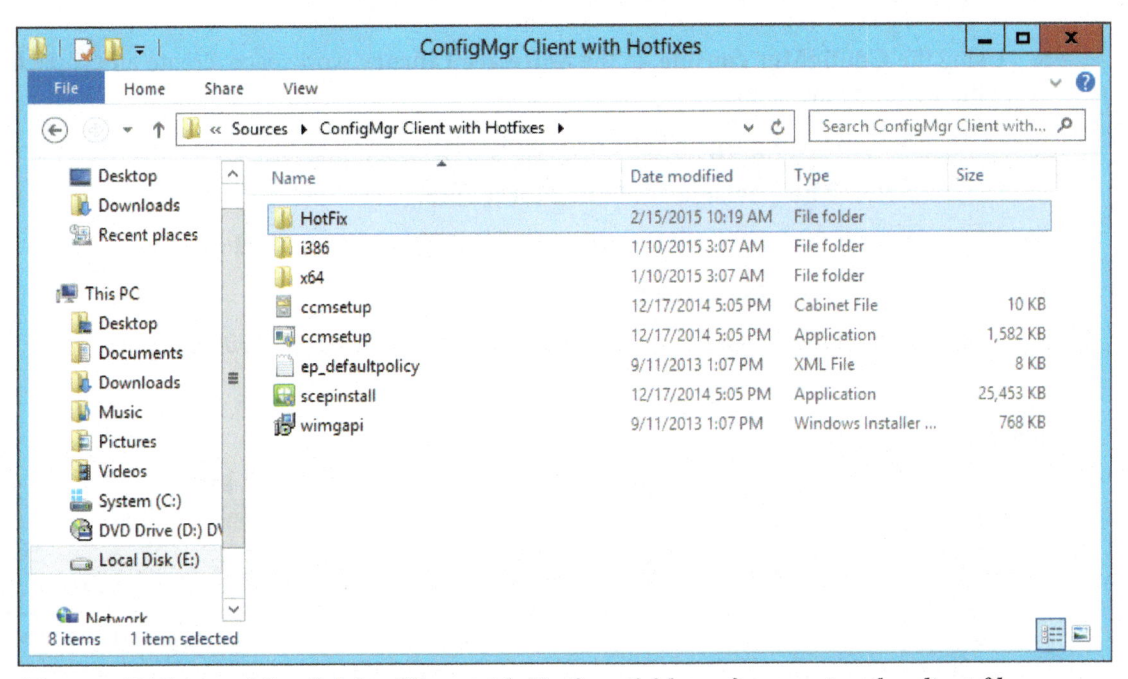

*The new E:\Sources\ConfigMgr Client with Hotfixes folder, after copying the client files.*

4. Using **File Explorer**, navigate to the **E:\Program Files\Microsoft Configuration Manager\hotfix\KB3026739\Client** folder and copy the **i386** and **x64** subfolders to **E:\Sources\ConfigMgr Client with Hotfixes\Hotfix**.

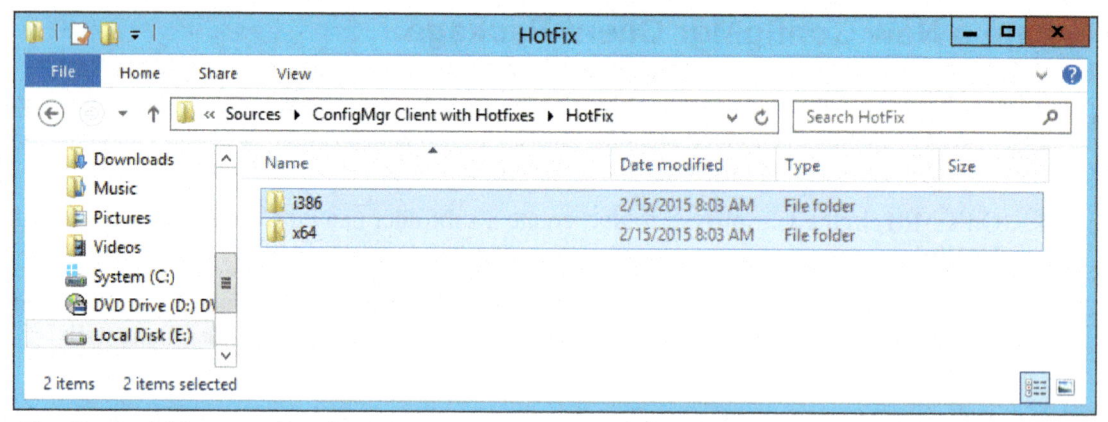

Chapter 2   ViaMonstra Inc. and the Proof-of-Concept Environment

*The Hotfix folder populated with the i386 and x64 subfolders.*

5. Using the **ConfigMgr console**, in the **Software Library** workspace, create a new package with the following settings:

    o   Name: **ConfigMgr Client with Hotfixes**

    o   Select **This package contains source files**.

    o   Source folder: **\\CM01\Sources\ConfigMgr Client with Hotfixes**

    o   Select **Do not create a program**.

6. Make a note of the new package ID. In this environment, it is **PS10000A**.

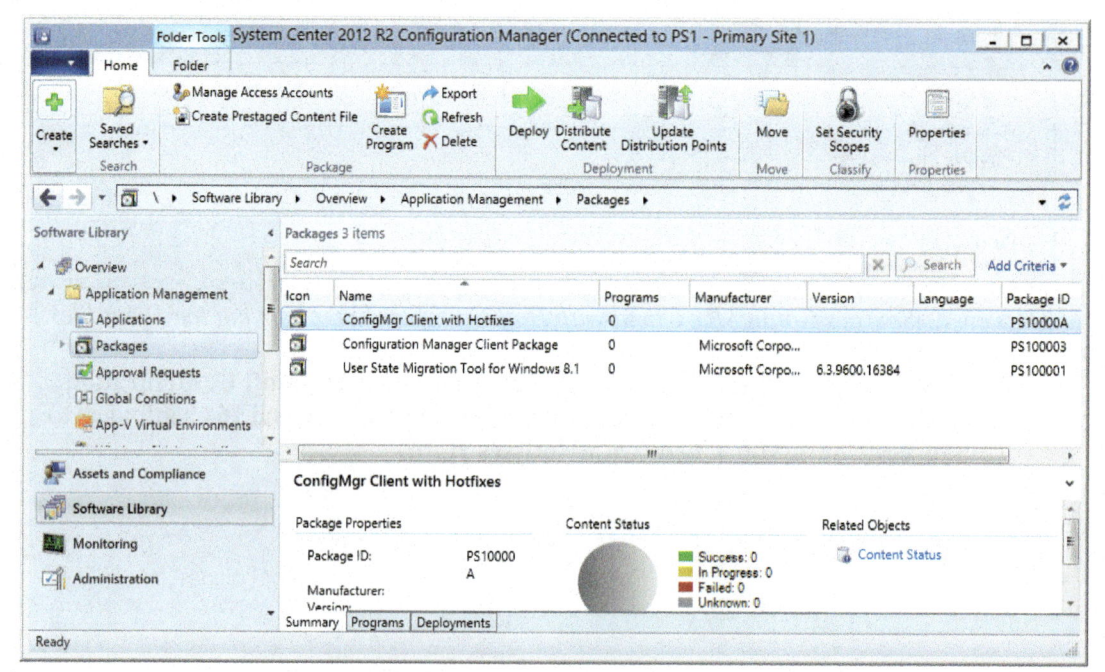

*The new ConfigMgr client package, with its package ID.*

46

7. Distribute the new **ConfigMgr Client with Hotfixes** package to the **CM01** distribution point by right-clicking the **ConfigMgr Client with Hotfixes** package, and selecting **Distribute Content**. Use the following setting for the **Distribute Content Wizard**:

    Content Destination: Add the **CM01** distribution point.

## Set Up ConfigMgr 2012 R2 Integration with MDT 2013

To extend the ConfigMgr console with the new MDT options, you need to run the Configure ConfigMgr Integration wizard that is installed together with MDT 2013. In this guide, I assume that you have downloaded MDT 2013 (http://tinyurl.com/mdt2013download) to the E:\Setup\MDT 2013 folder on CM01.

**Note:** Make sure to use the MDT 2013 version because it matches the Windows ADK and ConfigMgr version used in this environment.

1. On **CM01**, close the **ConfigMgr console** before continuing.
2. Install **MDT 2013** (E:\Setup\MDT 2013\MicrosoftDeploymentToolkit2013_x64.msi) using the default settings.
3. From the **Start screen**, run the **Configure ConfigMgr Integration** application with the following settings:
    - Site Server Name: **CM01.corp.viamonstra.com**
    - Site code: **PS1**

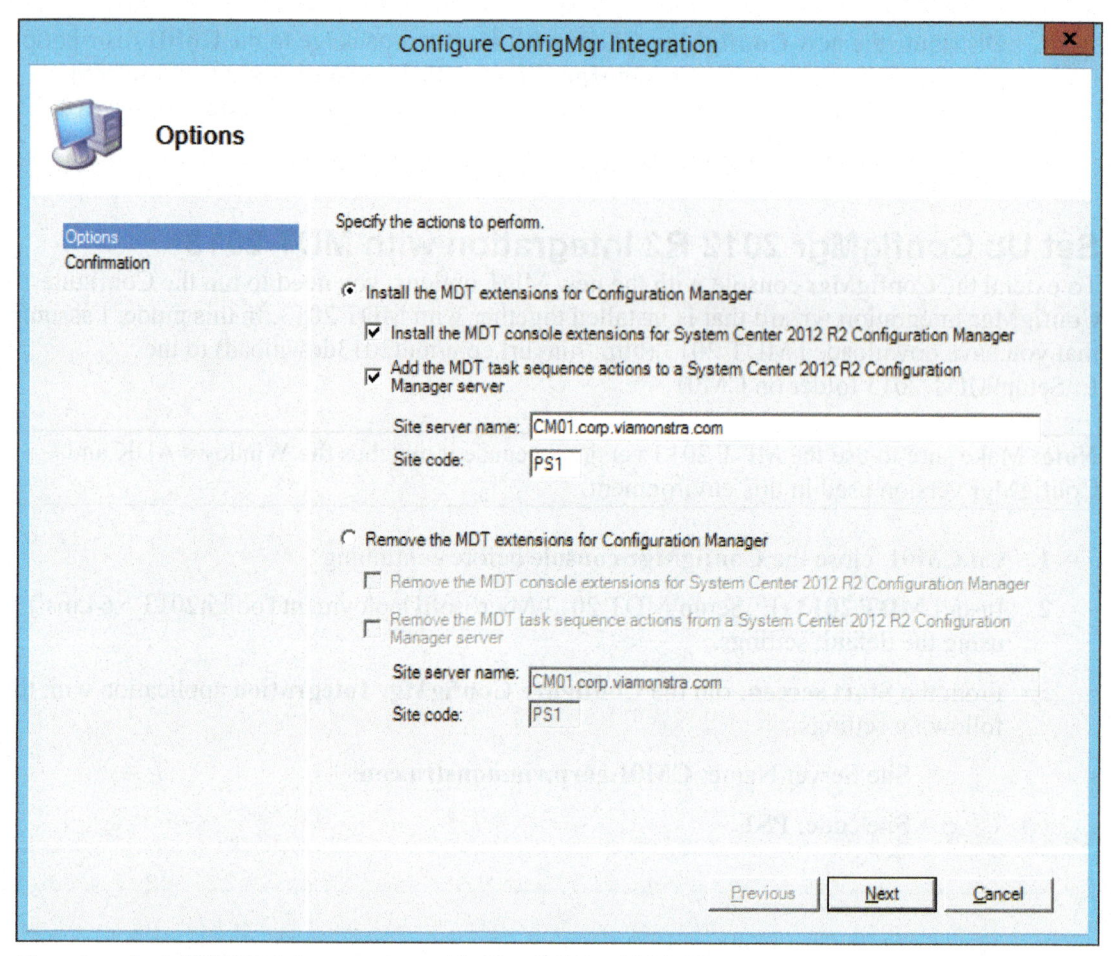

*Running the MDT 2013 integration with ConfigMgr 2012 R2.*

## Configure the Network Access Account

1. On **CM01**, using the **ConfigMgr console**, in the **Administration** workspace, expand **Site Configuration** and select **Sites**.

2. Right-click the **PS1 – Primary Site 1**, and select **Configure Site Components / Software Distribution**.

3. In the **Network Access Account** tab, select the **Specify the account that accesses network locations** option, click the **New** button (which looks like an asterisk), and then select **New Account**.

4. In the **Windows User Account** dialog box, configure the **VIAMONSTRA\CM_NAA** user account as the Network Access account (the password is **P@ssw0rd**). Then use the **Verify** option to verify that the account can connect to **\\DC01\SYSVOL** network share.

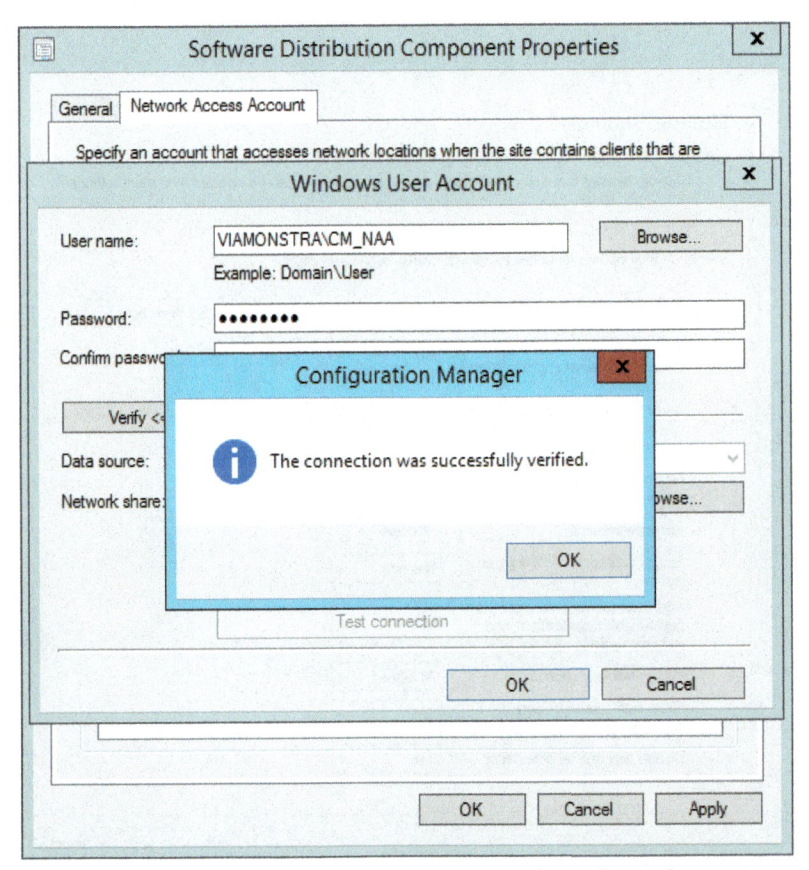

*Configuring the Network Access account and verifying the connection.*

## Configure the Client Settings

In these steps, you configure the organization name in Client Agent settings. This name is visible in the task sequence progress bar when you deploy the Windows 8.1 Enterprise x64 image later in this chapter.

1. On **CM01**, using the **ConfigMgr console**, in the **Administration** workspace, select **Client Settings**.
2. Right-click **Default Client Settings** and select **Properties**.
3. In the **Computer Agent** node, locate the **Organization name displayed in Software center** text box, type in **ViaMonstra**, and click **OK**.

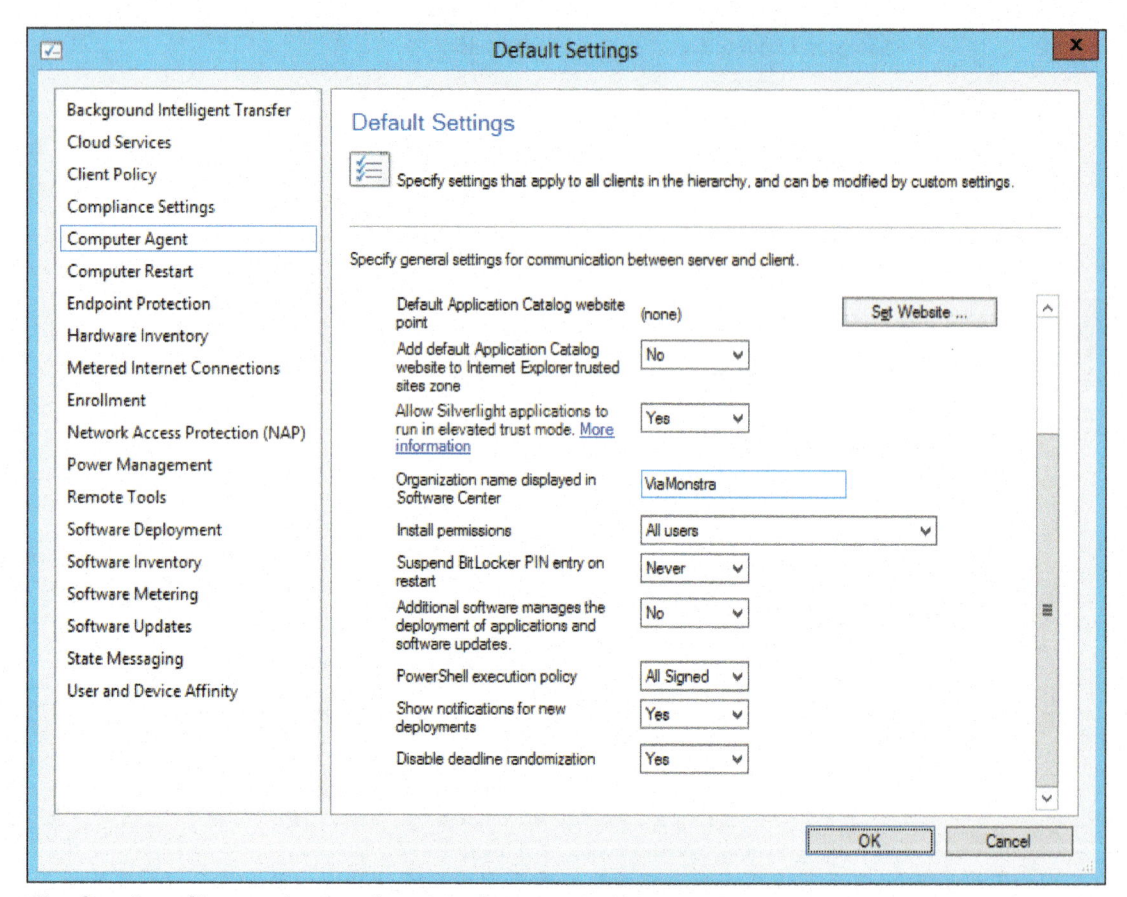

*Configuring client settings and setting the organization name.*

## Enable PXE on the CM01 Distribution Point

In this section, you configure the CM01 for PXE support and also enable unknown computer support. Having PXE enabled is not a requirement for OSD or MDT, but being able to start deployments via PXE is very useful.

1. On **CM01**, using the **ConfigMgr console**, in the **Administration** workspace, select **Distribution Points**.

2. Right-click the **CM01.CORP.VIAMONSTRA.COM** distribution point and select **Properties**.

3. In the **PXE** tab, enable the following settings, and then click **OK**:

    o   Enable PXE support for clients

    o   Allow this distribution point to respond to incoming PXE requests

    o   Enable unknown computer support

- Require a password when computers use PXE
- Password and Confirm password: **P@ssw0rd**

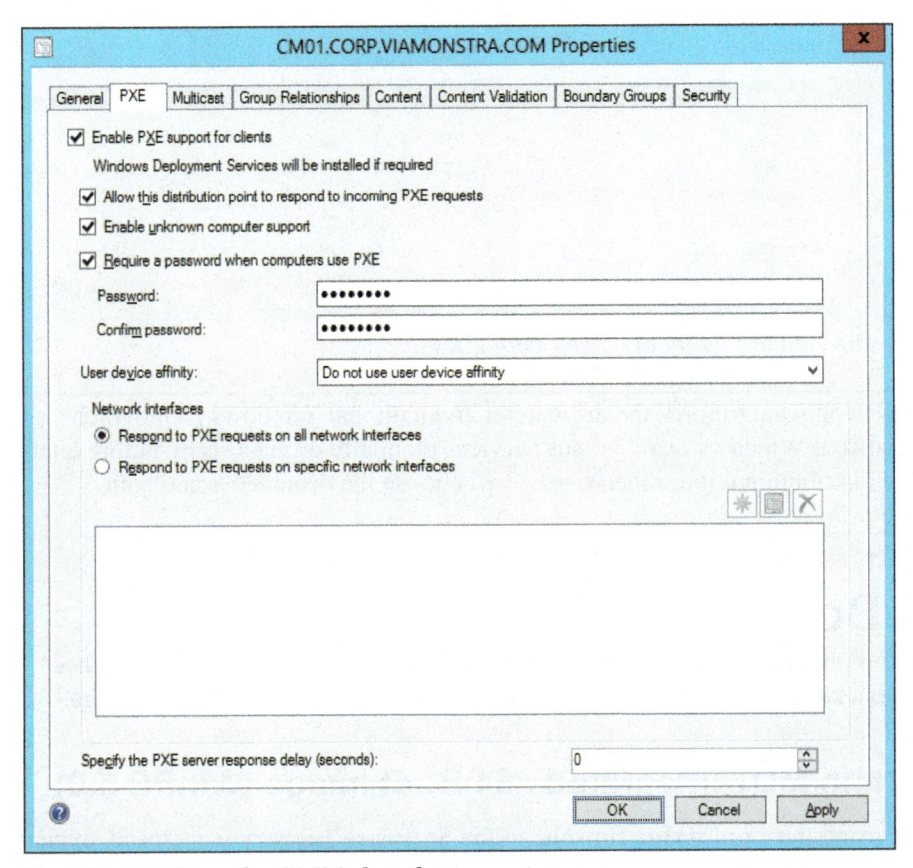

*Enabling PXE on the CM01 distribution point.*

4. Using **CMTrace**, review the **E:\Program Files\Microsoft Configuration Manager\Logs\distmgr.log** file and look for the line **ConfigurePXE**.

5. Using **File Explorer**, verify that you have seven files in the **E:\RemoteInstall\SMSBoot\x86** and **E:\RemoteInstall\SMSBoot\x64** folders.

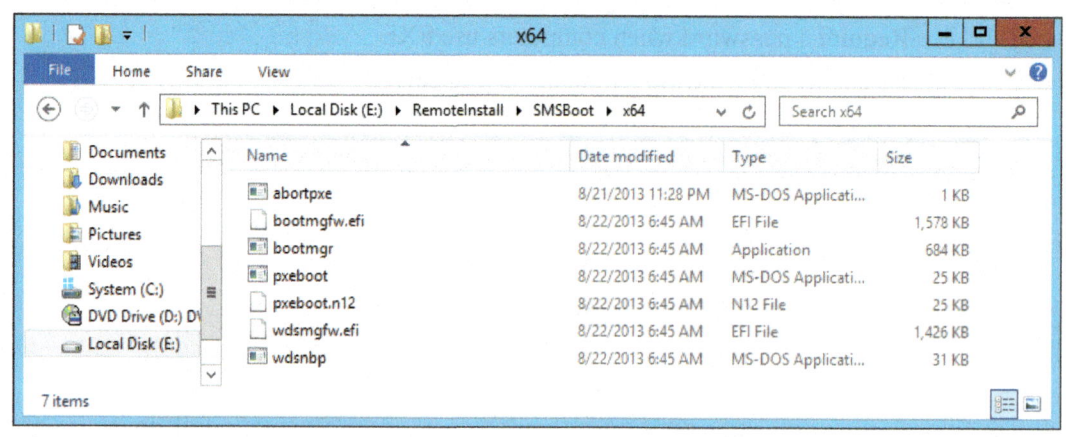

Chapter 2   ViaMonstra Inc. and the Proof-of-Concept Environment

*The netboot files needed to PXE boot an x64 boot image.*

> **Real World Note:** If you want to force the drive letter and path that Windows Deployment Services uses, then install Windows Deployment Services manually or via a script before enabling PXE support on the distribution point; otherwise, it will choose the drive letter and path automatically.

# Creating Boot Images

After the preparations are done, you start creating all the various packages the task sequence needs, and the first package you create is a custom MDT integrated WinPE 5.0 boot image.

## Create a Custom MDT Integrated x64 Boot Image (WinPE 5.0)

1. On **CM01**, using the **ConfigMgr console**, in the **Software Library** workspace, expand **Operating Systems**.

2. Right-click **Boot Images**, select **Create Boot Image using MDT**, and create a new boot image package using the following settings:

    a. On the **Package Source** screen, in the **Package source folder to be created (UNC path):** field, enter the following and click **Next**:

    **\\CM01\Sources\OSD\Boot\WinPE 5.0 x64**

> **Note:** It's a good idea to name the folder based on the WinPE version and architecture of the boot image. The WinPE 5.0 x64 folder will be created by the wizard.

    b. On the **General Settings** screen, for **Name**, enter **WinPE 5.0 x64** and click **Next**.

    c. On the **Options** screen, use the following settings and then click **Next**:

    - Platform: **x64**
    - Scratch Space: **<default>**

Chapter 2 ViaMonstra Inc. and the Proof-of-Concept Environment

**Note:** WinPE 5.0 allocates scratch space dynamically, meaning there is no point in setting a default value. The only time a default value is used is when you have less than 1 GB of RAM in the machine, and if you do, you should not deploy Windows at all to that machine. ☺

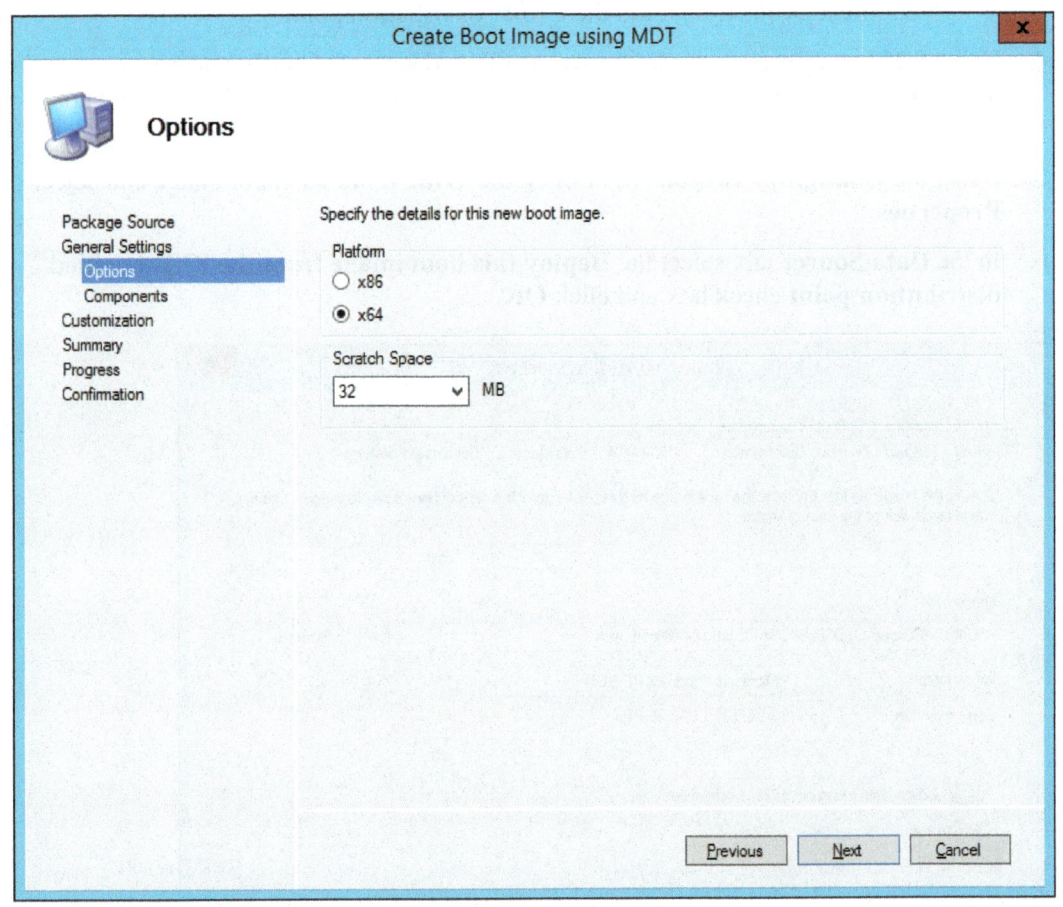

*Selecting the x64 platform.*

    d. On the **Components** screen, keep the defaults and click **Next**.

    e. On the **Customization** screen, select **Enable command support (F8)** and click **Next**.

    f. When you receive confirmation that the process is complete, click **Finish**.

**Real World Note:** The most common reason a boot image creation fails is because of antivirus software. If you have antivirus software running on your ConfigMgr server, make sure to exclude dism.exe from processes that are scanned by the antivirus software, or disable the antivirus software while creating your boot image.

Chapter 2   ViaMonstra Inc. and the Proof-of-Concept Environment

3. Distribute the boot image to the **CM01** distribution point by selecting the **Boot images** node, right-clicking the **WinPE 5.0 x64** boot image, and selecting **Distribute Content**. Use the following setting for the **Distribute Content Wizard**:

    Content Destination: Add the **CM01** distribution point.

4. Using **CMTrace**, review the **E:\Program Files\Microsoft Configuration Manager\Logs\distmgr.log** file. Do not continue until you can see the boot image is distributed. Look for the line with **STATMSG: ID=2301**....

5. Using the **ConfigMgr console**, right-click the **WinPE 5.0 x64** boot image and select **Properties**.

6. In the **Data Source** tab, select the **Deploy this boot image from the PXE-enabled distribution point** check box and click **OK**.

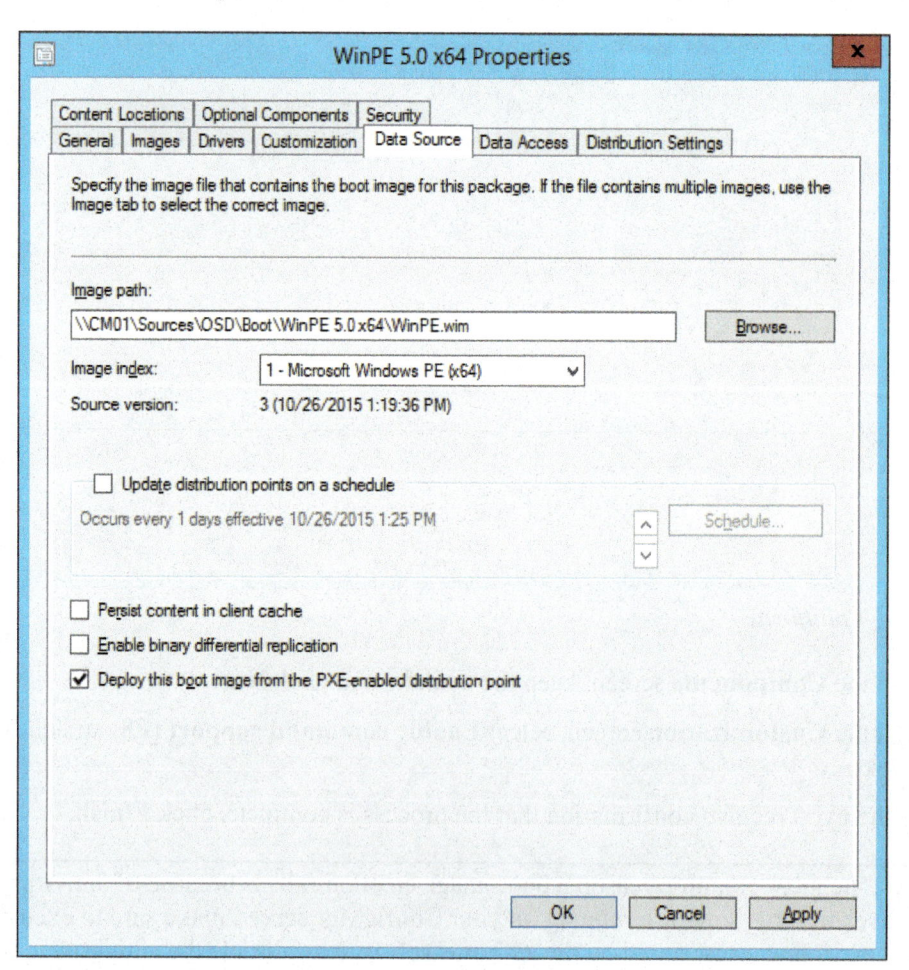

*Enabling the WinPE 5.0 x64 boot image for PXE.*

54

Chapter 2   ViaMonstra Inc. and the Proof-of-Concept Environment

7. Using **CMTrace**, review the **E:\Program Files\Microsoft Configuration Manager\Logs\distmgr.log** file. Look for the line **Expanding <Package ID> to E:\RemoteInstall\SMSImages**.

8. Using **File Explorer**, review the **E:\RemoteInstall\SMSImages** folder. There should be three subfolders containing boot images.

> **Real World Note:** For this environment, you only need an x64 boot image (because you only have an x64 image of Windows 8.1). However, if you want to support both x86 and x64 operating system images (and you are not deploying to 64-bit UEFI hardware), you can instead add an x86 boot image that can deploy both x86 and x64 operating systems.

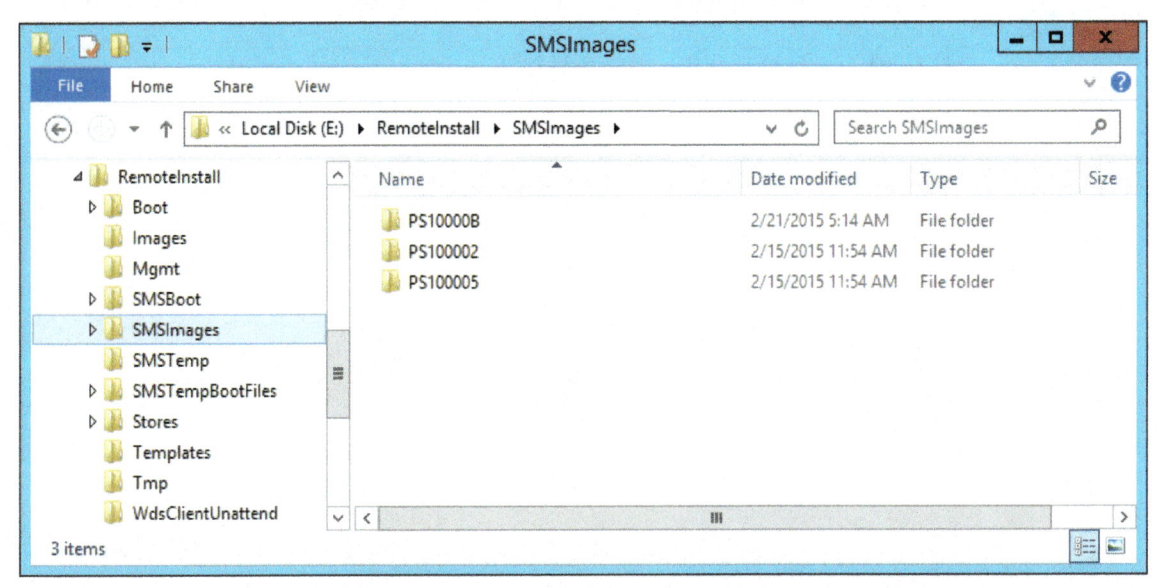

*The E:\RemoteInstall\SMSImages folder after configuring the boot image for PXE.*

# Adding Operating System Images

ConfigMgr 2012 R2 supports two methods for deploying Windows: applying a single WIM file via the operating system image method, or adding a full set of source files using the operating system installer method. The operating system image method is what you should be using because it prevents possible conflicts between Windows PE and Windows setup versions. The operating system installer method is mainly available for backward-compatibility reasons. Using the operating system image method simply provides a more consistent deployment experience.

You can create reference images by different methods, such as using MDT or via ConfigMgr itself using the Build and Capture process. Both methods have their merits and are discussed at length on the Internet. In the following steps, you prepare ConfigMgr for creating a reference image of Windows 8.1.

55

Chapter 2   ViaMonstra Inc. and the Proof-of-Concept Environment

## Extract and Copy the Windows 8.1 Media

To create reference images within ConfigMgr, you need the original media extracted and copied to your source location. Select the previously downloaded Windows 8.1 Enterprise x64 ISO and mount it on the CM01 virtual machine as detailed in the following steps:

1. On the **CM01** virtual machine, mount the **Windows 8.1 Enterprise x64** ISO file.

2. When the ISO is mounted, open **File Explorer** and browse to **D:\**.

3. Select all the files in the folder by pressing **Ctrl + A**.

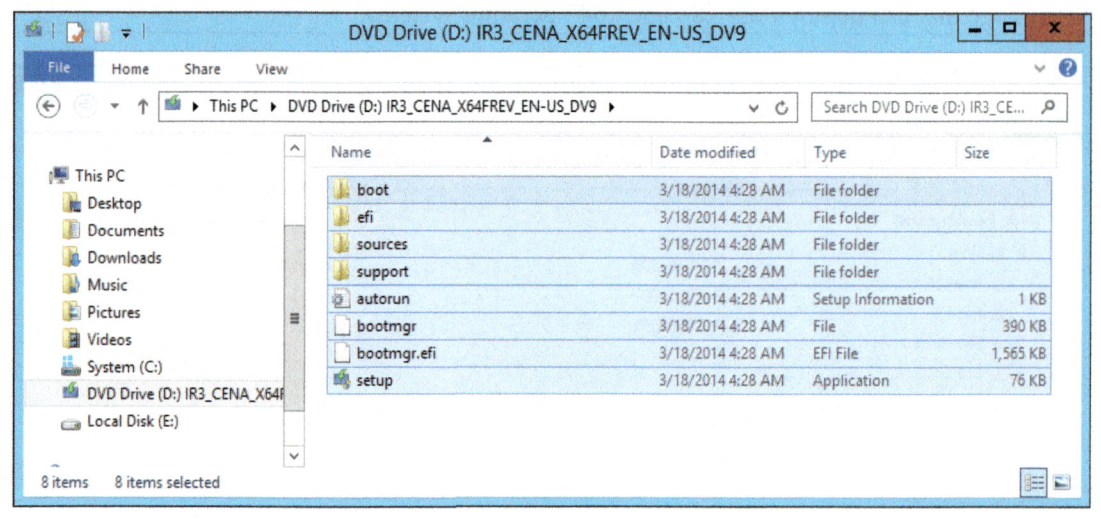

*The Windows 8.1 Enterprise x64 media in File Explorer.*

4. Copy the contents to **E:\Sources\OSD\OS\Operating System Installers\Windows 8.1 Enterprise x64** (you need to create the folder).

## Add a Windows 8.1 Operating System Image

In this example, you add a default image of Windows 8.1 Enterprise x64 image by using the INSTALL.WIM from the Windows 8.1 Enterprise x64 media. You can use this image either to build a new reference image or simply deploy the OS with no customizations to the WIM.

1. Using the **ConfigMgr console**, in the **Software Library** workspace, right-click the **Operating System Image** node and select **Add Operating System Image**.

2. Complete the **Add Operating System Image Wizard** with the following settings. Use default settings for all other options.

    a. Path: **\\CM01\Sources\OSD\OS\Operating System Installers\Windows 8.1 Enterprise x64\Sources\Install.wim**

    b. Name: **Windows 8.1 Enterprise**

    c. Version: **x64**

56

3. Distribute the **Windows 8.1 Enterprise** operating system image to the **CM01** distribution point.

4. In the **Monitoring** workspace, select **Distribution Status**, search for **Windows 8.1 Enterprise**, and review the **content status** for the **Windows 8.1 Enterprise** package. Don't continue until you see the package successfully distributed.

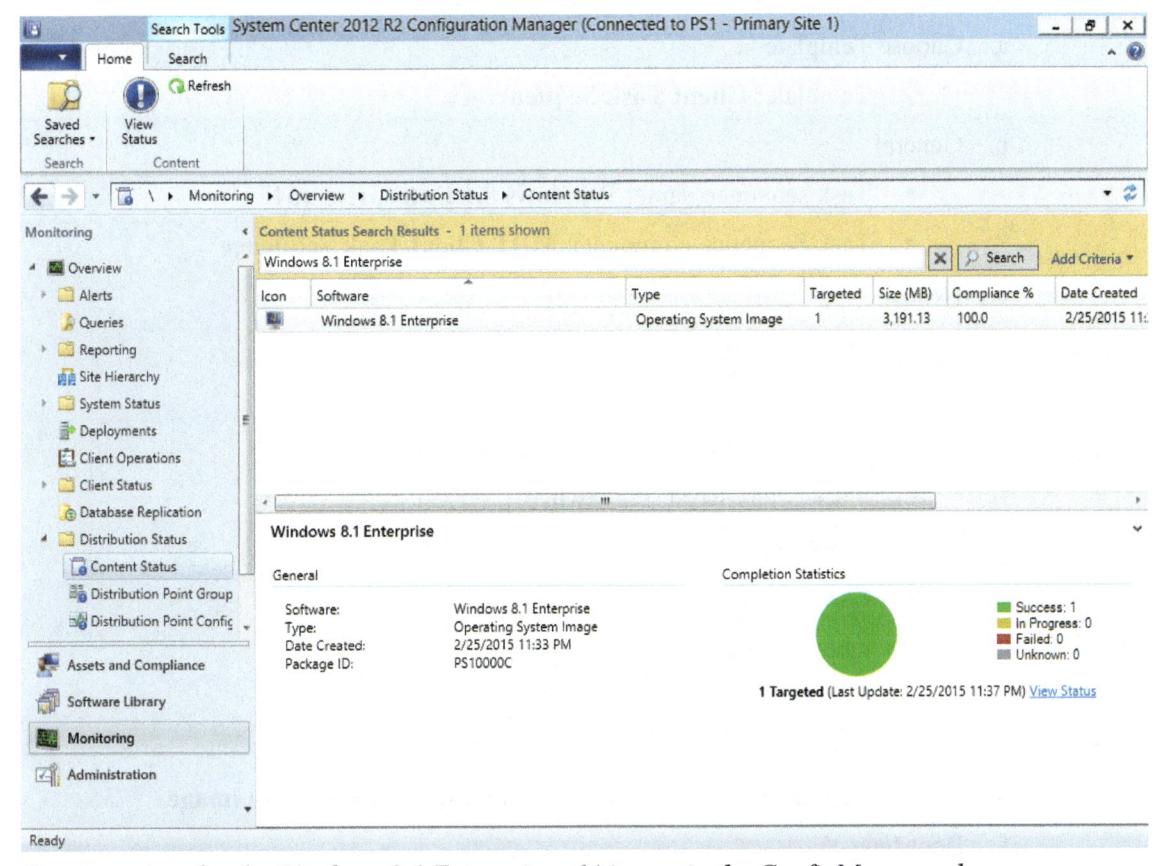

*Content status for the Windows 8.1 Enterprise x64 image in the ConfigMgr console.*

# Creating MDT Toolkit and MDT Settings Packages

The MDT Toolkit and MDT Settings packages are used in MDT-integrated task sequences and, therefore, need to be created. Creating these two packages can be done by simply creating a MDT integrated task sequence as detailed in this section.

## Create a MDT Client Task Sequence

1. On **CM01**, using the **ConfigMgr console**, in the **Software Library** workspace, select **Operating Systems / Task Sequences**.
2. Right-click **Task Sequences**, select **Create MDT Task Sequence**, and then use the following settings for the Create MDT Task Sequence Wizard:

    a. Choose Template

        Template: **Client Task Sequence**

    b. General
    - Task sequence name: **Windows 8.1 Enterprise x64**
    - Task Sequence comments: **MDT Client Task Sequence**

    c. Details

        **Join a Domain**
    - Domain: **corp.viamonstra.com**
    - Account: **VIAMONSTRA\CM_JD**
    - Password: **P@ssw0rd**

    d. Windows Settings
    - User name: **ViaMonstra**
    - Organization name: **ViaMonstra**
    - Product key: **<blank>**

    e. Capture Setting

        **This task sequence will never be used to capture an image**

    f. Boot Image
    - **Specify an existing boot image package**
    - Select the **WinPE 5.0 x64** boot image package.

    g. MDT Package
    - **Create a new Microsoft Deployment Toolkit Files package**
    - Package source folder to be created (UNC path): **\\CM01\Sources\OSD\MDT\MDT 2013**

    h. MDT Details

        Name: **MDT 2013 Toolkit**

    i. OS Image

- **Specify an existing OS Image**
- Select the **Windows 8.1 Enterprise x64** package

j. Deployment Method

**Perform a Zero Touch Installation OS Deployment, with no user interaction**

k. Client Package
- **Specify an existing ConfigMgr client package**
- Select the **ConfigMgr Client with Hotfixes** package.

l. USMT Package
- **Specify an existing USMT package**
- Select the **Microsoft Corporation User State Migration Tool for Windows 8 6.3.9600.16384** package.

m. Settings Package
- **Create a new settings package**
- Package source folder to be created (UNC Path): **\\CM01\Sources\OSD\MDT\MDT 2013 Settings**

n. Settings Details

Name: **MDT 2013 Settings**

o. Sysprep Package

**No Sysprep Package is required**

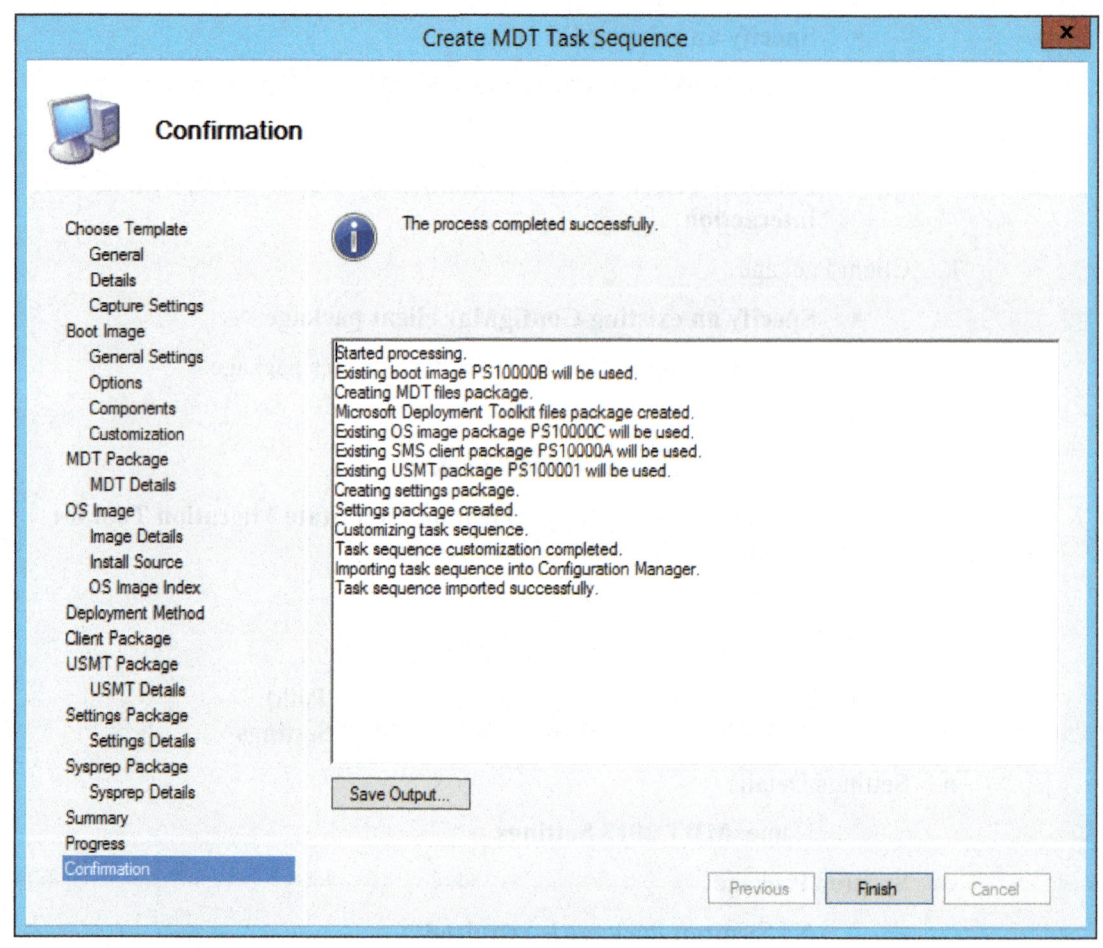

Chapter 2   ViaMonstra Inc. and the Proof-of-Concept Environment

*The Create MDT Task Sequence wizard is complete.*

## Distribute the Packages

In the ConfigMgr console, distribute the default USMT package, and MDT packages created in the preceding process by doing as follows:

1. On **CM01**, using the **ConfigMgr console**, expand the **Software Library** workspace, select **Application Management / Packages**, and then locate and select the **MDT 2013 Toolkit**, **MDT 2013 Settings** and **User State Migration Tool for Windows 8.1** packages.

2. Right-click the selected packages and choose **Distribute content**. Use the following setting for the **Distribute Content Wizard**:

    Content Destination: **CM01.CORP.VIAMONSTRA.COM**

3. Continue through the wizard until completion.

# Creating OSD Collections

To reduce the risk of accidental OSD deployments, it makes sense to limit which computers get those deployments. One way to do that is to separate servers from workstations, which reduces the risk of servers accidently being deployed with an operating system that wasn't intended.

## The All Servers and All Workstations Collections

By building queries to separate servers from workstations, you can create the All Servers and All Workstations collections by assigning the queries to the respective collections.

## The OSD Collections

The OSD Deploy collection will be used primary for targeting OSD task sequences and limited to a collection called *OSD Limiting* so that its members can come only from computers in the All Workstations and All Unknown Computers collections. This removes known servers from the OSD Deploy collection, so even in the worst scenario, if a required deployment is sent to all computers in the OSD Deploy collection, the servers would remain intact and you could rebuild your infrastructure.

As you will be both building and deploying computers using the operating system deployment abilities within ConfigMgr, it makes sense to create specific collections to separate those two tasks. You also want to limit which computers are eligible for task sequence deployments. To set this up, you need to create three collections for that purpose, namely OSD Build, OSD Deploy, and OSD Limiting.

The OSD Build collection will contain a membership query to limit itself to manually imported computers. The OSD Deploy collection will have a membership query to include the OSD Limiting collection, and that collection itself has its membership made up from All Workstations, All Unknown Computers, and manually imported computers. Both the OSD Build and OSD Deploy collections are limited to the OSD Limiting collection which excludes known servers. In total, you create the following five collections:

- All Servers
- All Workstations
- OSD Build
- OSD Deploy
- OSD Limiting

In this guide I assume you have downloaded the book sample files to E:\Setup on CM01.

1. On **CM01**, start **Windows PowerShell ISE** and open the **CreateOSDCollections.ps1** script found in **E:\Setup\Scripts\**.
2. Press **F5** or click the green **Run Script** button to run the script.

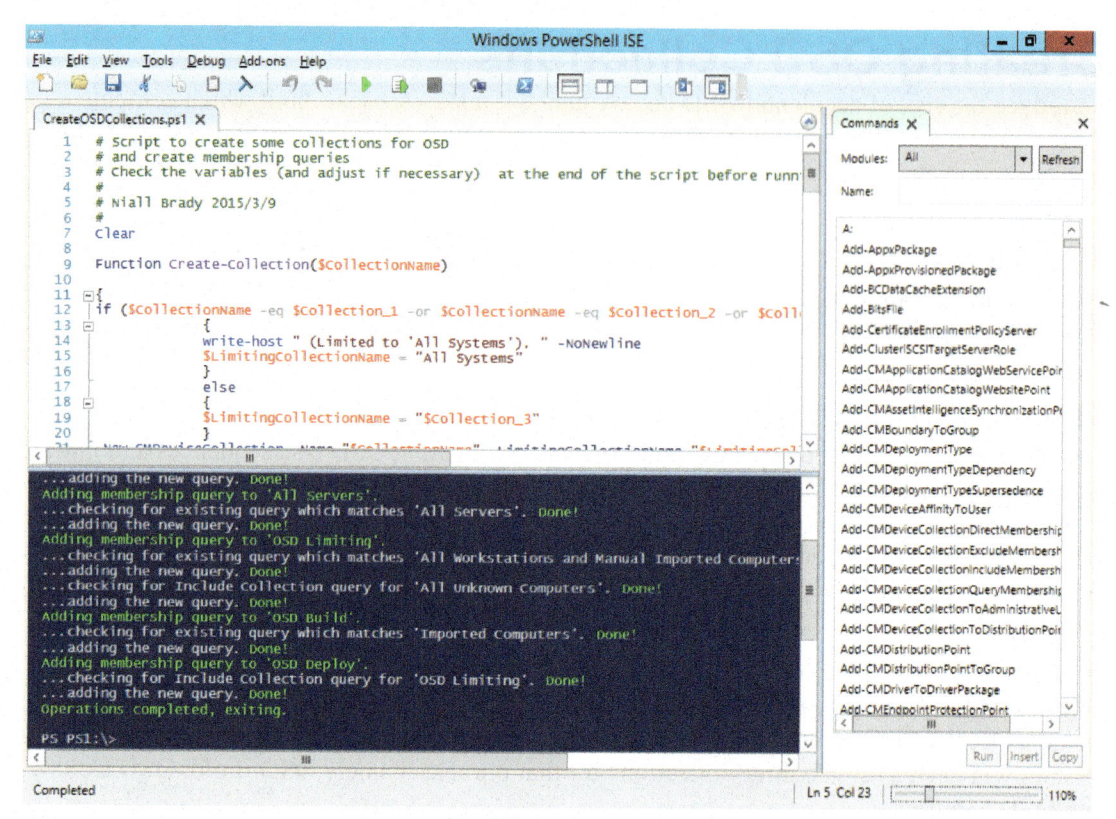

*Creating OSD collections using a PowerShell script in Windows PowerShell ISE.*

3. On **CM01**, using the **ConfigMgr console**, in the **Assets and Compliance** workspace, browse to **Device Collections** and press **F5** to refresh the view. Observe the new OSD collections.

# Forcing Unknown Computers to Prompt for computer name

By default unknown computers (computers that are not yet known to ConfigMgr) get a random MININT computer name, such as MININT-VXADFG3. To force unknown computers to prompt for a computer name during imaging instead of taking the MININT-*random computer name*, complete the guides in this section.

## Edit the All Unknown Computers Collection

1. On **CM01**, using the **ConfigMgr console**, in the **Assets and Compliance** workspace, select **Device Collections**.

2. Right-click the **All Unknown Computers** collection, choose **Properties**, and then select the **Collection Variables** tab.

3. Click the **yellow asterisk** button to add a new collection variable, and use the following settings for the **<New> Variable** wizard:

    o Name: **OSDComputerName**

    o Clear the **Do not display this value in the Configuration Manager console** check box, and click **OK** twice.

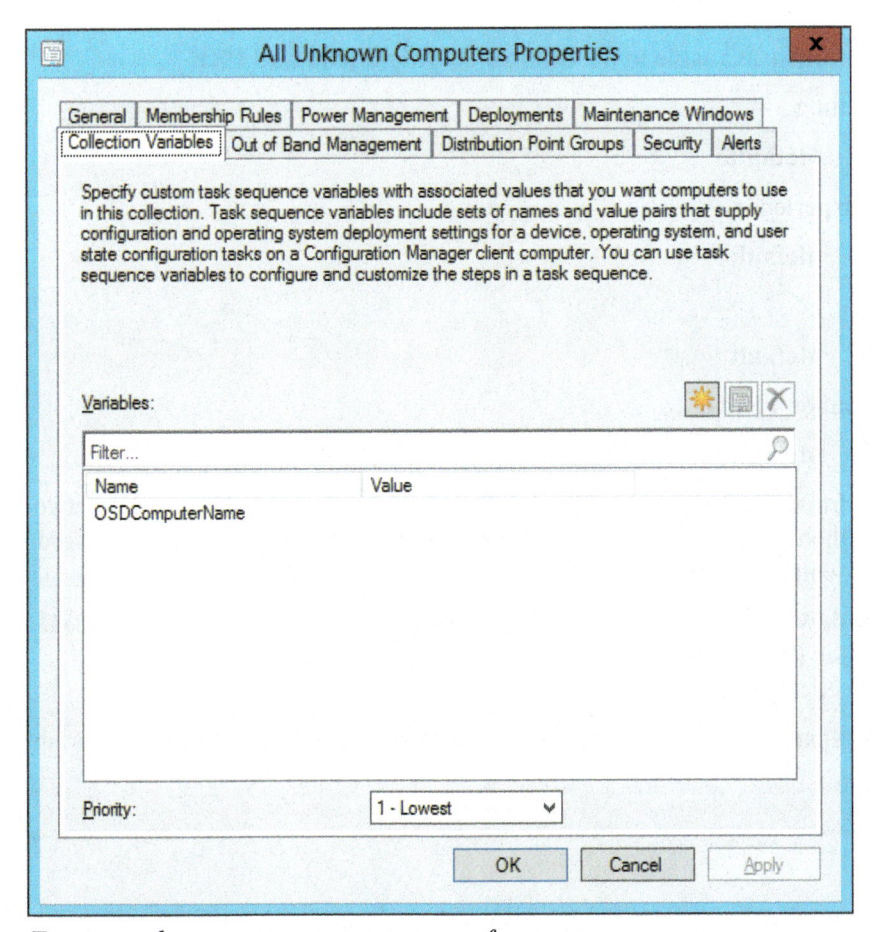

*Forcing unknown computers to prompt for a computer name.*

## Verify the Change

To verify the change, you deploy a task sequence, and PXE boot an unknown computer.

1. On **CM01**, using the **ConfigMgr console**, in the **Software Library** workspace, select **Operating Systems / Task Sequences**, select the **Windows 8.1 Enterprise x64** task sequence, and then select **Deploy**.

2. Use the following settings for the **Deploy Software Wizard**:
    a. General
        Collection: **OSD Deploy**
    b. Deployment Settings
        - Purpose: **Available**
        - Make available to the following: **Only media and PXE**
    c. Scheduling
        **<default>**
    d. User Experience
        **<default>**
    e. Alerts
        **<default>**
    f. Distribution Points
        **<default>**

3. Create a new virtual machine, and verify that the boot order is set to boot to the network then power on the virtual machine. When the **Task Sequence Wizard** PXE password screen appears, enter **P@ssw0rd** and then click **Next**.

4. Select the **Windows 8.1 Enterprise x64** task sequence that you deployed to the **OSD Deploy** collection (which also contains a query for the All Unknown Computers collection) and click **Next**.

5. After clicking **Next**, you are prompted for the **OSDComputerName** collection variable.

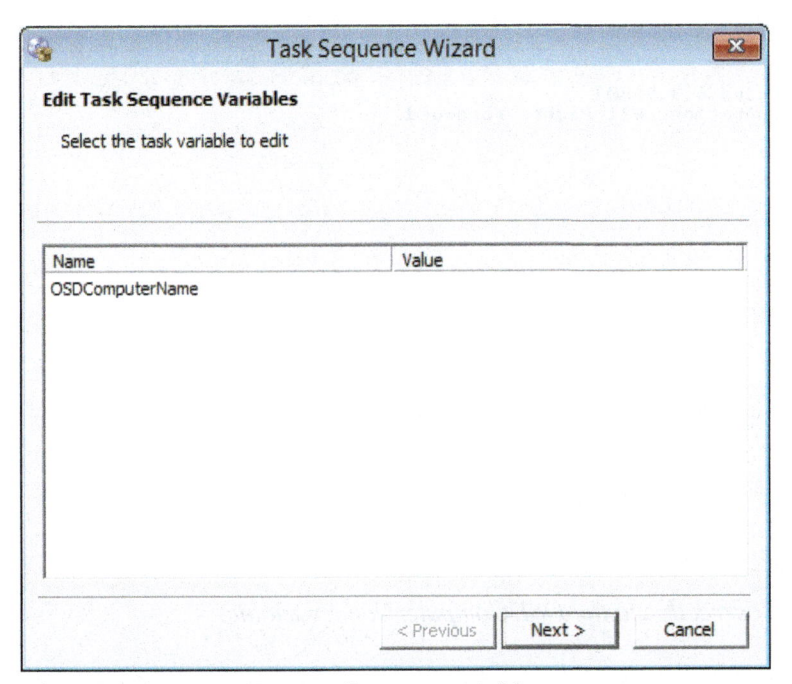

Chapter 2  ViaMonstra Inc. and the Proof-of-Concept Environment

*The OSDComputerName collection variable.*

6. Double-click the **OSDComputerName** variable and enter a name, **PC0002** in this example, for the unknown computer in the Value field. Click **OK** to continue.

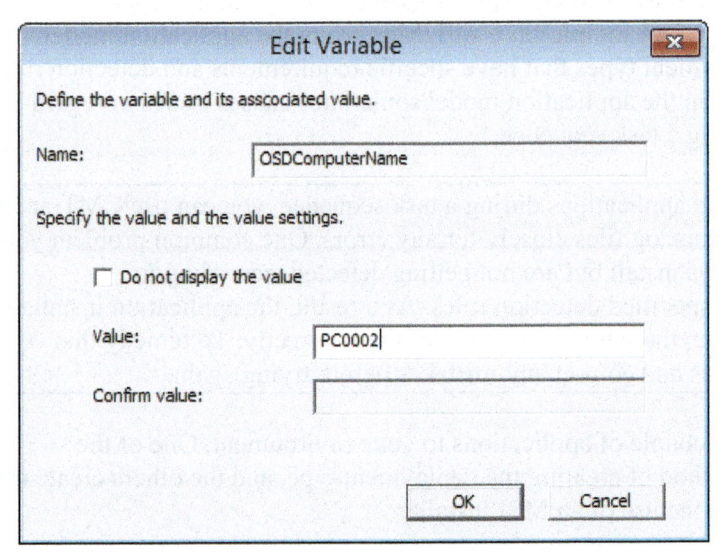

*Enter a suitable name for the unknown computer.*

7. After the operating system deployment is complete, log in to the machine, open a **Command prompt** and type **hostname**. The computer name you entered in the preceding step should be listed.

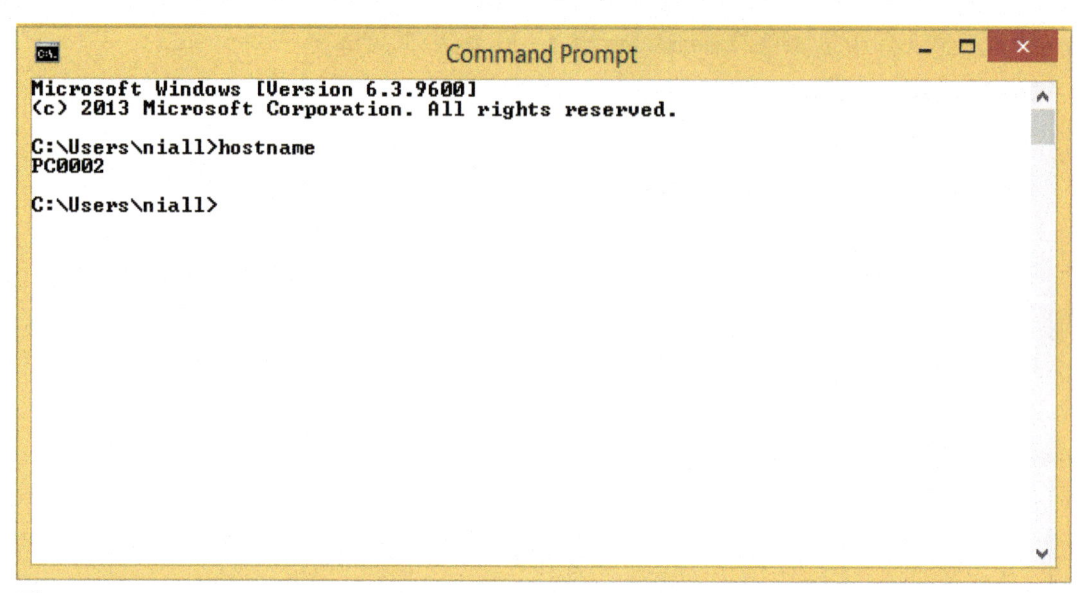

```
Microsoft Windows [Version 6.3.9600]
(c) 2013 Microsoft Corporation. All rights reserved.

C:\Users\niall>hostname
PC0002

C:\Users\niall>
```

*The computer name is set correctly via the OSDComputerName variable.*

## Adding Applications

In any ConfigMgr infrastructure, there is a mix of software that is deployed as packages (legacy) or using the richer, feature-added method of applications. There are pros and cons to using both, particularly when deploying applications in an OSD task sequence. For example, when creating driver applications (Lenovo Hotkey for example) in ConfigMgr, using the application model means you can easily create deployment types that have specific requirements and detection rules; however, the complexity involved in the application model sometimes causes issues in regard to applications getting deployed during a task sequence.

**Real World Note**: When deploying applications during a task sequence, you can use CMTrace to monitor the appenforce.log and smsts.log files closely for any errors. One common problem you may encounter is where applications install but are not getting detected, according to appenforce.log, due to incorrectly specified detection rules. As a result, the application installation is marked as failed in smsts.log even though it may have installed correctly. To remedy this situation, verify your detection rules and correct any mistakes before trying again.

In the following guides, you add a couple of applications to your environment. One of the applications involves a manual method of creating the deployment type, and the others create the deployment type automatically via the use of an MSI installer.

Chapter 2  ViaMonstra Inc. and the Proof-of-Concept Environment

## Create the Mozilla Firefox Application

In this guide, I assume that you have downloaded Mozilla Firefox 36.0.1 (Firefox Setup 36.0.1.exe) to E:\Setup on CM01. Mozilla has all versions on its FTP site: https://ftp.mozilla.org/pub/firefox/releases.

1. On **CM01**, using **File Explorer**, navigate to the **E:\Sources\Software\Mozilla** folder and create the **Mozilla Firefox 36.0 x86** subfolder.

2. Copy the **Mozilla Firefox 36.0** installation file (Firefox Setup 36.0.1.exe) to the following folder:

    **E:\Sources\Software\Mozilla\Mozilla Firefox 36.0 x86**

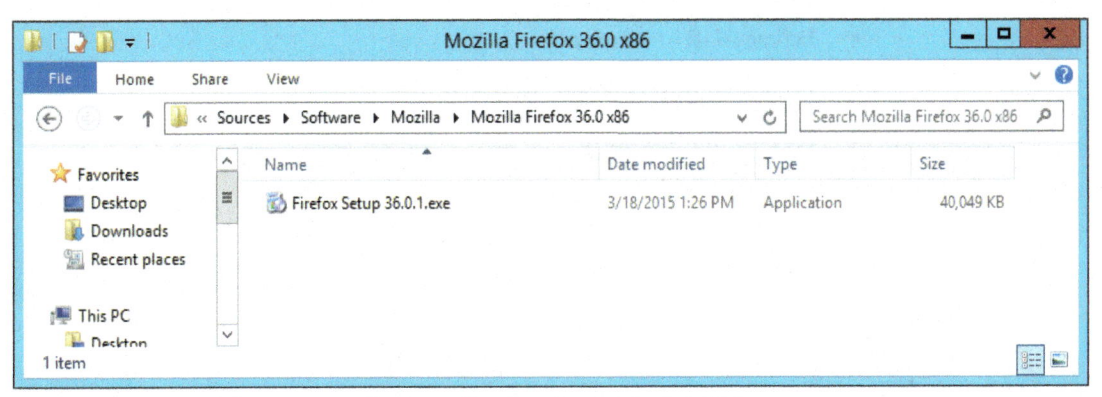

*The E:\Sources\Software\Mozilla\Mozilla Firefox 36.0 x86 folder.*

3. Using the **ConfigMgr console**, in the **Software Library** workspace, right-click **Applications** and select **Create Application**. Use the following settings for the **Create Application Wizard**.

    a. General

        Manually specify the application information

    b. General Information

    - Name: **Firefox**
    - Administrator comments: **<default>**
    - Publisher: **Mozilla**
    - Software version: **36.0.1**
    - Optional reference: **<default>**
    - Administrative categories: **<default>**
    - Date published: **<default>**
    - Select **Allow this application to be installed from the Install Application task sequence without being deployed**

67

- Owners: **<default>**
- Support contacts: **<default>**

   c. Application Catalog
- Selected language: **<default>**
- Localized application name: **<default>**
- User categories: **<default>**
- User documentation: **<default>**
- Link text: **<default>**
- Privacy URL: **<default>**
- Localized description: **<default>**
- Keywords: **<default>**
- Icon: **<default>**
- Display this as a featured app and highlight in the company portal: **<default>**

4. For **Deployment Types**, click **Add**, and for the **Create Deployment Type** wizard, use the following settings:

   a. General

       Type: **Script Installer**

   b. General Information:
- Name: **Mozilla Firefox 36.0.1**
- Administrator comments: **<default>**
- Languages: **<default>**

   c. Content:
- Content location: **\\CM01\Sources\Software\Mozilla\Mozilla Firefox 36.0 x86**
- Persist content in the client cache: **<default>**
- Allow clients to share content with other clients on the same subnet: **<default>**
- Installation program: **"Firefox Setup 36.0.1.exe" -ms**
- Installation start in : **<default>**
- Uninstall program: **"Firefox Setup 36.0.1.exe" /S**

Chapter 2  ViaMonstra Inc. and the Proof-of-Concept Environment

- Uninstall start in: **<default>**
- Run installation and uninstall program as a 32-bit process on 64-bit clients: **<default>**

5. For **Detection Method**, select **Configure rules to detect the presence of this deployment type**, and then select **Add Clause** and use the following settings:

   a. Detection Rule:
      - Setting Type: **Registry**
      - Hive: **HKEY_LOCAL_MACHINE**
      - Key: **SOFTWARE\Wow6432Node\Microsoft\Windows\CurrentVersion\Uninstall\Mozilla Firefox 36.0.1 (x86 en-US)**
      - Value: **DisplayVersion**
      - This registry key is associated with a 64bit application: **<default>**
      - Data Type: **String**
      - This registry setting must exist on the target system to indicate presence of the application

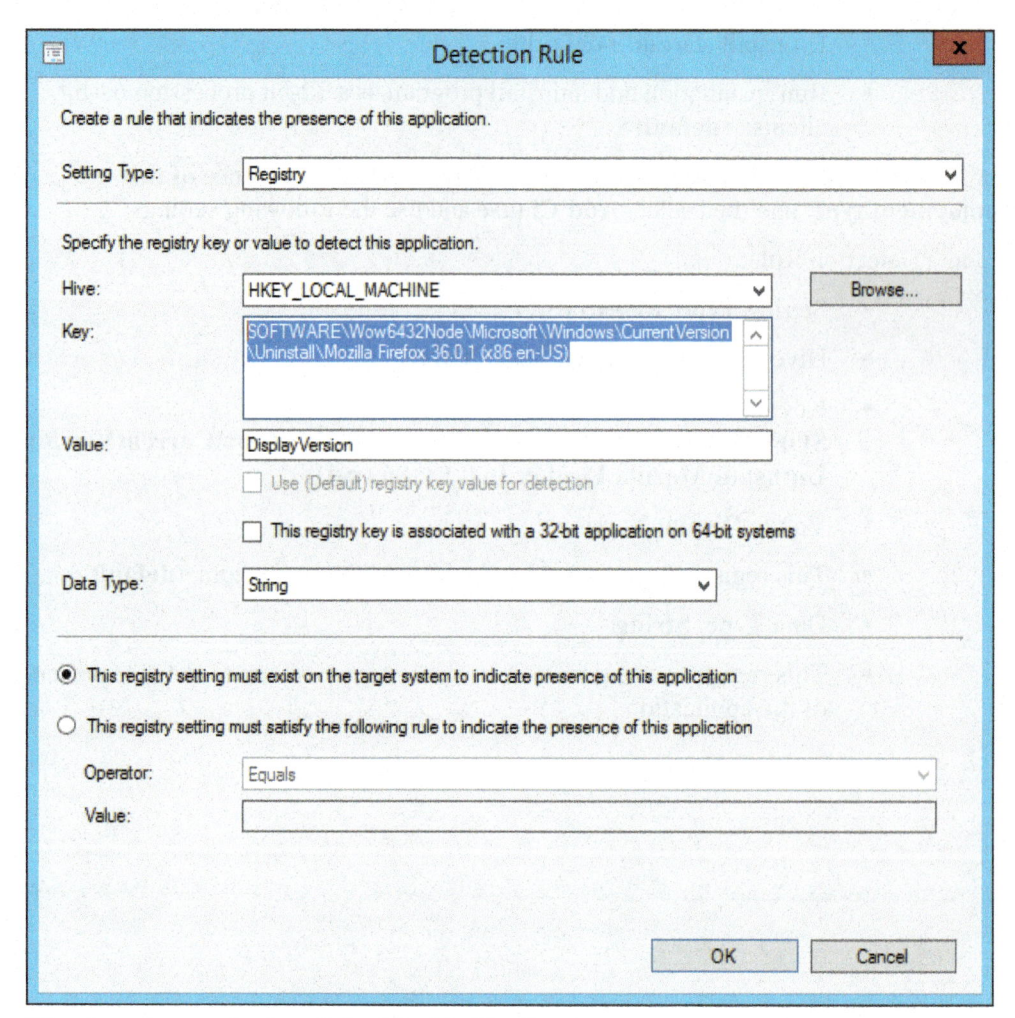

Chapter 2   ViaMonstra Inc. and the Proof-of-Concept Environment

*The detection method used for Mozilla Firefox.*

       b. User Experience
- Installation behavior: **Install for System**
- Logon requirement: **Whether or not a user is logged on**
- Installation program visibility: **Hidden**
- Maximum allowed runtime (minutes): **15**
- Estimated installation time (minutes): **5**

       c. Requirements: **<default>**

       d. Dependencies: **<default>**

       e. Summary: **<default>**

6. After editing the deployment type, continue through the wizard until complete.

## Create the 7Zip Application

In this guide, I assume you have downloaded 7-Zip 9.20 to E:\Setup on CM01. 7-Zip is available on http://7-zip.org.

1. On **CM01**, using **File Explorer**, navigate to the **E:\Sources\Software\7Zip\** folder and create the **7Zip v9.20 x64** subfolder.
2. Copy the **7Zip v9.20 x64** installation file (**7z920-x64.msi**) to the following folder: **E:\Sources\Software\7Zip\7Zip v9.20 x64**.
3. Using the **ConfigMgr console**, right-click **Applications** and select **Create Application**. Use the following settings for the **Create Application Wizard**:
    a. On the **General** screen, select **Automatically detect information about this application from installation files** and then use these settings:
        - Type: **Windows installer (*.msi file)**
        - Location: **\\CM01\Sources\Software\7Zip\7Zip v9.20 x64\7z920-x64.msi**
        - Answer <**Yes**> when prompted that the publisher could not be verified.
    b. General Information
        - Name: **7-Zip 9.20 (x64 edition)**
        - Administrator comments: <**default**>
        - Publisher: <**default**>
        - Software version: <**default**>
        - Optional reference: <**default**>
        - Administrative categories: <**default**>
        - Installation program: <**default**>
        - Run installation and uninstall program as a 32-bit process on 64-bit clients: <**default**>
        - Installation behavior: **Install for system if resource is a device; otherwise install for user.**
    c. Continue through the wizard until complete.
4. Right-click the newly created **7-Zip 9.20 (x64 edition)** application and select **Properties**.
5. Select the **Allow this application to be installed from the Install Application task sequence without being deployed** check box, and click **OK**.

Chapter 2  ViaMonstra Inc. and the Proof-of-Concept Environment

## Create the Microsoft Office 365 Application

In this guide, I assume you have downloaded Office 2013 Deployment Tool for Click-to-Run to E:\Setup on CM01. The tool is available here: http://go.microsoft.com/fwlink/p/?LinkId=282642.

> **Real World Note**: To customize your installation and configuration of Office 365, you use special XML files. These files are used to configure what settings you want in your Office 365 deployment. For details about these XML files and the settings they can contain, see the following page on TechNet: http://technet.microsoft.com/en-us/library/jj219426.aspx.

1. On **CM01**, using **File Explorer**, create a folder **E:\temp**.

2. Copy the **Office Deployment Tool for Click-to-Run** (officedeploymenttool_x86_4747-1000.exe) to **E:\temp**.

3. Double-click the **officedeploymenttool_x86_4747-1000.exe** file and use the following settings for the **Microsoft Office 2013 Click-To-Run Administrator Tool** wizard:

    o **Click here to accept the Microsoft License Terms**.

    o Browse for the **E:\Sources\Software\Microsoft** folder, select **Make New Folder**, create the **Office 365 x86** folder, and click **OK**.

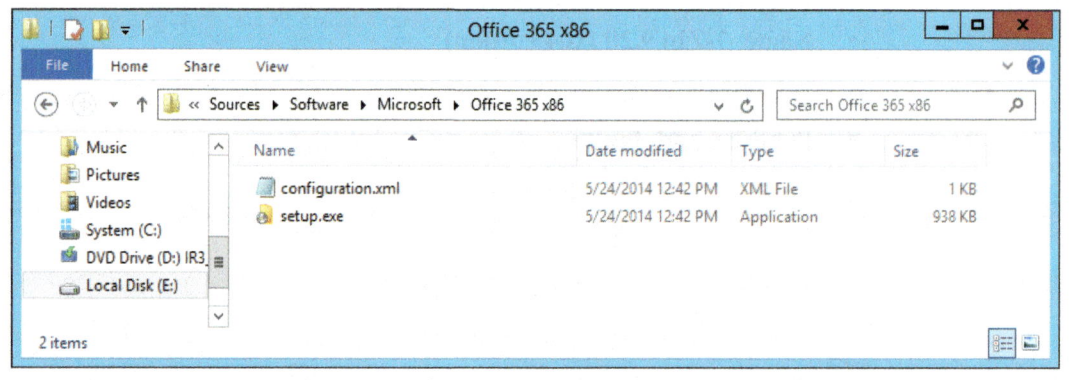

*The downloaded Microsoft Office 2013 Click-To-Run Administrator Tool files.*

4. Copy the three sample XML files found in **E:\Setup\Office 365 sample XMLs** to **E:\Sources\Software\Microsoft\Office 365 x86**.

5. Open an elevated **Command prompt** (run as Administrator) and change directory to **E:\Sources\Software\Microsoft\Office 365 x86**.

6. Use the following command to download the installation files for Office 365. Be aware that this process takes time to download the files, so now is a good time to take a coffee break.

```
setup.exe /download download.xml
```

Chapter 2   ViaMonstra Inc. and the Proof-of-Concept Environment

```
E:\Sources\Software\Microsoft\Office 365 x86>setup.exe /download download.xml
_
```

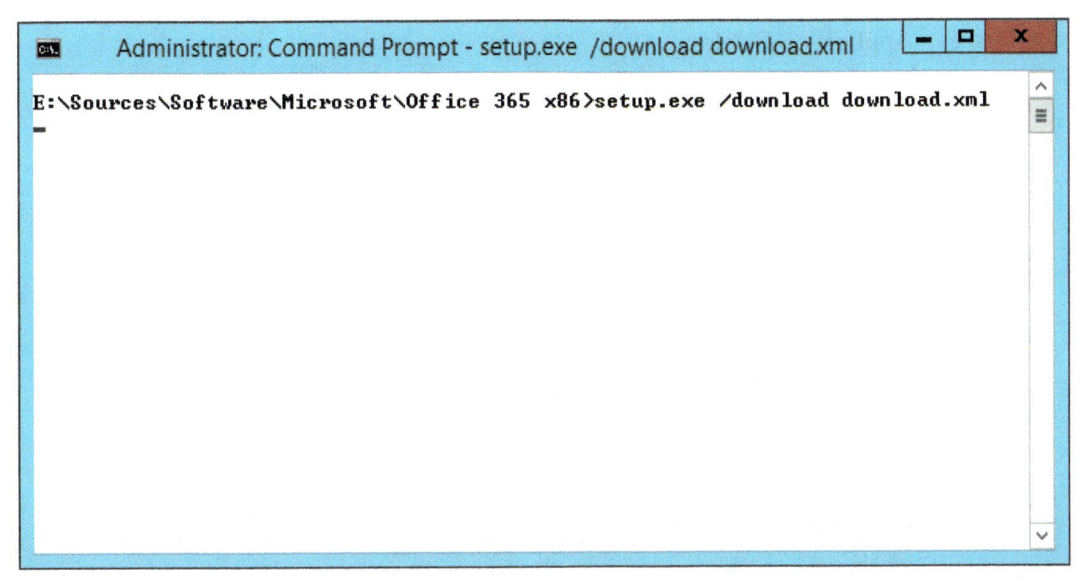

*The tool is downloading the required files. The command prompt underscore stops flashing when complete.*

7. After the files are downloaded, using the **ConfigMgr console**, in the **Software Library** workspace, right-click **Applications** and select **Create Application**. Use the following settings for the **Create Application Wizard**:

   a. General

   Manually specify the application information.

   b. General Information

   - Name: **Office 365**
   - Administrator comments: **<default>**
   - Publisher: **Microsoft**
   - Software version: **15.0.4701.1002**
   - Optional reference: **<default>**
   - Administrative categories: **<default>**
   - Date published: **<default>**
   - Select **Allow this application to be installed from the Install Application task sequence without being deployed**
   - Owners: **<default>**
   - Support contacts: **<default>**

c. Application Catalog

- Selected language: **<default>**
- Localized application name: **<default>**
- User categories: **<default>**
- User documentation: **<default>**
- Link text: **<default>**
- Privacy URL: **<default>**
- Localized description: **<default>**
- Keywords: **<default>**
- Icon: **<default>**
- Display this as a featured app and highlight in the company portal: **<default>**

8. For **Deployment Types**, click **Add**, and for the **Create Deployment Type** wizard, use the following settings:

    a. General

    Type: **Script Installer**

    b. General Information

    - Name: **Microsoft Office 365**
    - Administrator comments: **<default>**
    - Languages: **<default>**

    c. Content

    - Content location: **\\CM01\Sources\Software\Microsoft\Office 365 x86**
    - Persist content in the client cache: **<default>**
    - Allow clients to share content with other clients on the same subnet: **<default>**
    - Installation program: **setup.exe /Configure Install.xml**
    - Installation start in : **<default>**
    - Uninstall program: **setup.exe /Configure Remove.xml**
    - Uninstall start in: **<default>**
    - Run installation and uninstall program as a 32-bit process on 64-bit clients: **<default>**

9. For **Detection Method**, select **Configure rules to detect the presence of this deployment type**, and then select **Add Clause** and use the following settings:

   a. Detection Rule
      - Setting Type: **Registry**
      - Hive: **HKEY_LOCAL_MACHINE**
      - Key: **SOFTWARE\Microsoft\Windows\CurrentVersion\Uninstall\O365ProPlusRetail – en-us**
      - Value: **DisplayName**
      - This registry key is associated with a 32-bit application on 64-bit systems: **<default>**
      - Data Type: **String**
      - This registry setting must satisfy the following rule to indicate the presence of this application:
        - Operator: **Equals**
        - Value: **Microsoft Office 365 ProPlus - en-us**

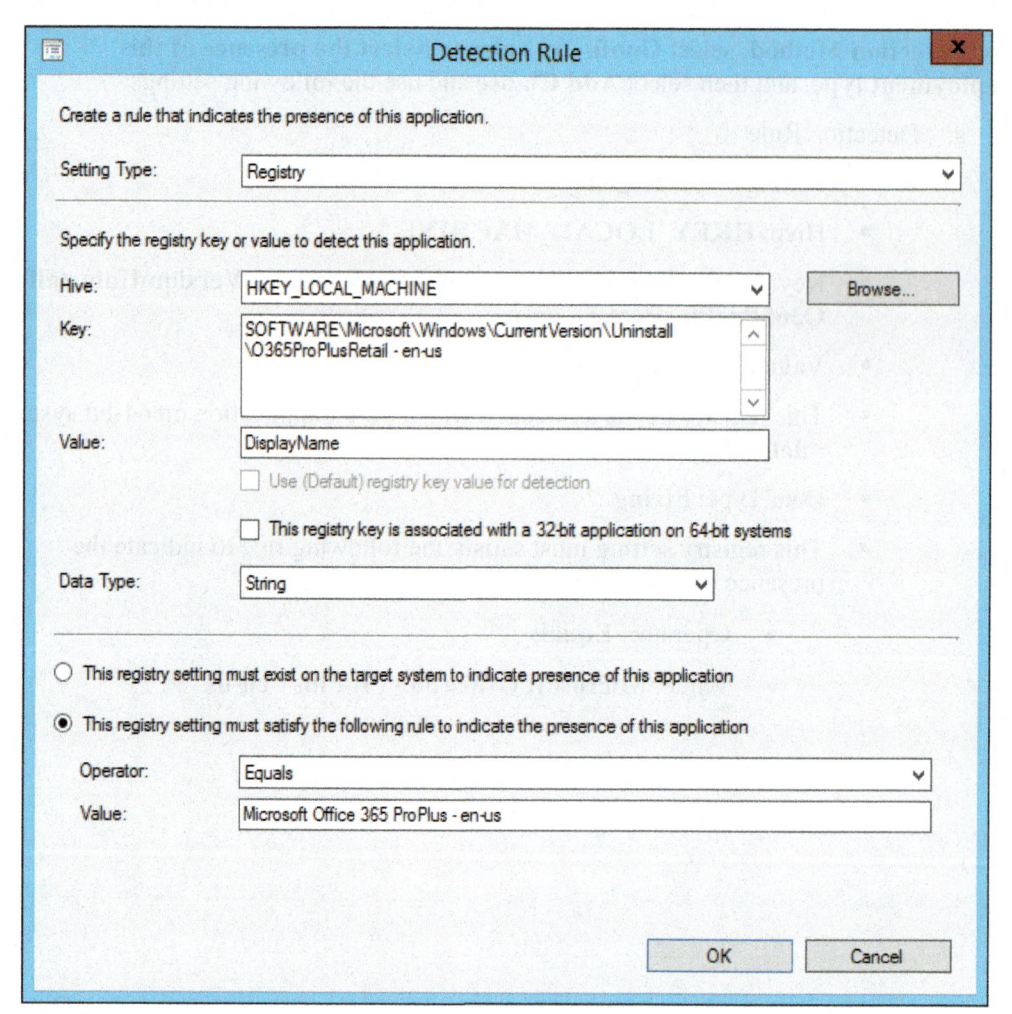

Chapter 2   ViaMonstra Inc. and the Proof-of-Concept Environment

*The detection method used for Microsoft Office 365.*

    b. User Experience

- Installation behavior: **Install for System**
- Logon requirement: **Whether or not a user is logged on**
- Installation program visibility: **Hidden**
- Maximum allowed runtime (minutes): **30**
- Estimated installation time (minutes): 15

    c. Requirements: **<default>**

    d. Dependencies: **<default>**

    e. Summary: **<default>**

**10.** After editing the deployment type, continue through the wizard until complete.

## Distribute the Applications

To be able to install these applications in a task sequence, the content needs to be present on at least one distribution point. To distribute the content for all of the applications at the same time, follow this procedure:

1. On **CM01**, using the **ConfigMgr console**, expand the **Software Library** workspace, select **Application Management / Applications**, and then locate and select all applications created previously.

2. Right-click the applications and choose **Distribute Content**. Use the following setting for the **Distribute Content Wizard**:

    a. Content Destination: **CM01.CORP.VIAMONSTRA.COM**

    b. Continue through the wizard until completion.

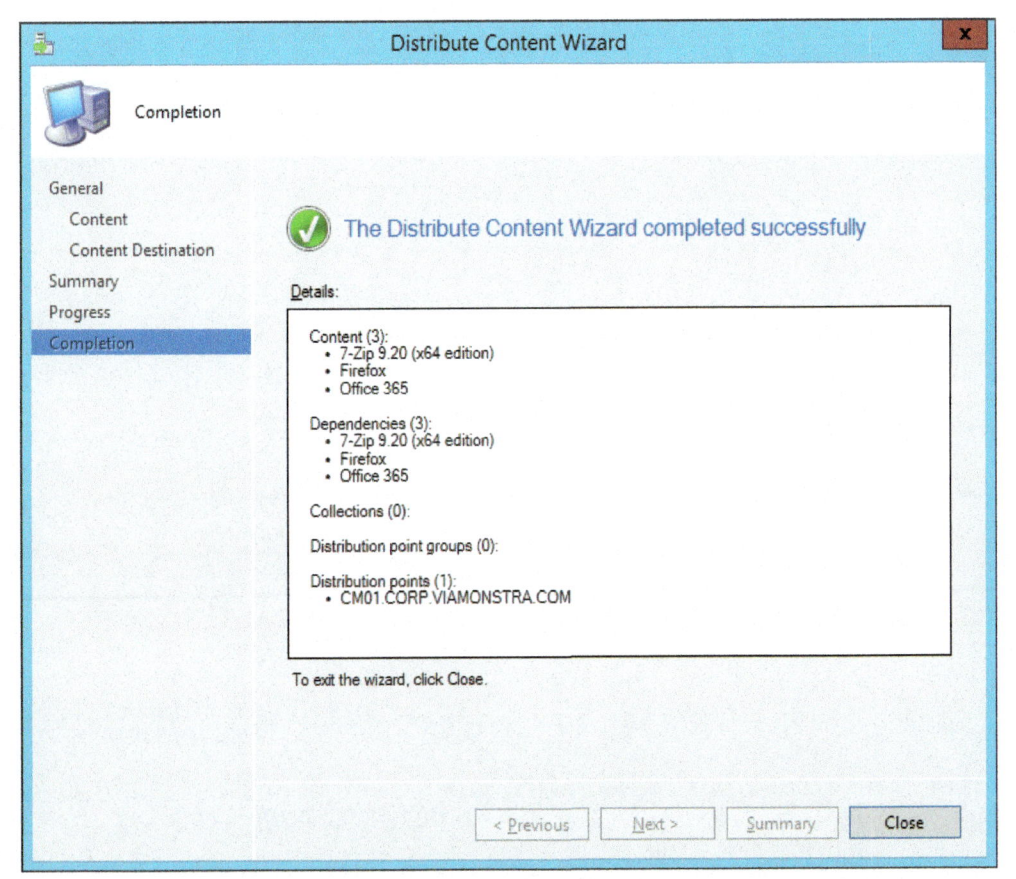

*The applications are distributed to the CM01.CORP.VIAMONSTRA.COM.*

# Chapter 3
# Increasing Log File Size

I've seen a lot of questions on the forums about how you can properly increase the log file size for PXE or boot media-based operating system deployments using System Center 2012 R2 Configuration Manager.

For those of you who work with OSD in ConfigMgr, you should know that when things go wrong the first place to start looking for clues to the problem is in a file called the *smsts.log* file. Opening that log file using a good log parser such as CMTrace (included in the boot images) is also a very good idea as it highlights errors in red and warnings in yellow. In addition, the tool allows you to interpret error codes and more. I recommend you make these changes to your boot images before doing any real OS deployment, particularly if you use any MDT-integrated task sequences as they consume the smsts.log file in minutes.

## Step-by-Step Guide Requirements

If you want to follow the step-by-step guides in this chapter, you need a lab environment configured as outlined in Chapter 2 and Appendix A. In this chapter, you use the following virtual machines:

DC01      CM01      PC0003

*The VMs used in this chapter (PC0003 is a VM created in one of the guides).*

You also need to have downloaded the following software:

> The book sample files (http://deploymentfundamentals.com)

**Note**: This guide assumes that you already have a working PXE environment setup, you've deployed at least one task sequence, and you've also integrated MDT 2013 with ConfigMgr. In addition, this guide assumes that you have enabled F8 command prompt support within your boot WIMs as described in Chapter 2 (Creating Boot Images).

# Description of the Problem

When PXE booting (network boot) or USB boot (bootable media), the default log file size in WinPE is a rather pathetic 1 MB or so, as seen in the following screenshot of the smsts.log file.

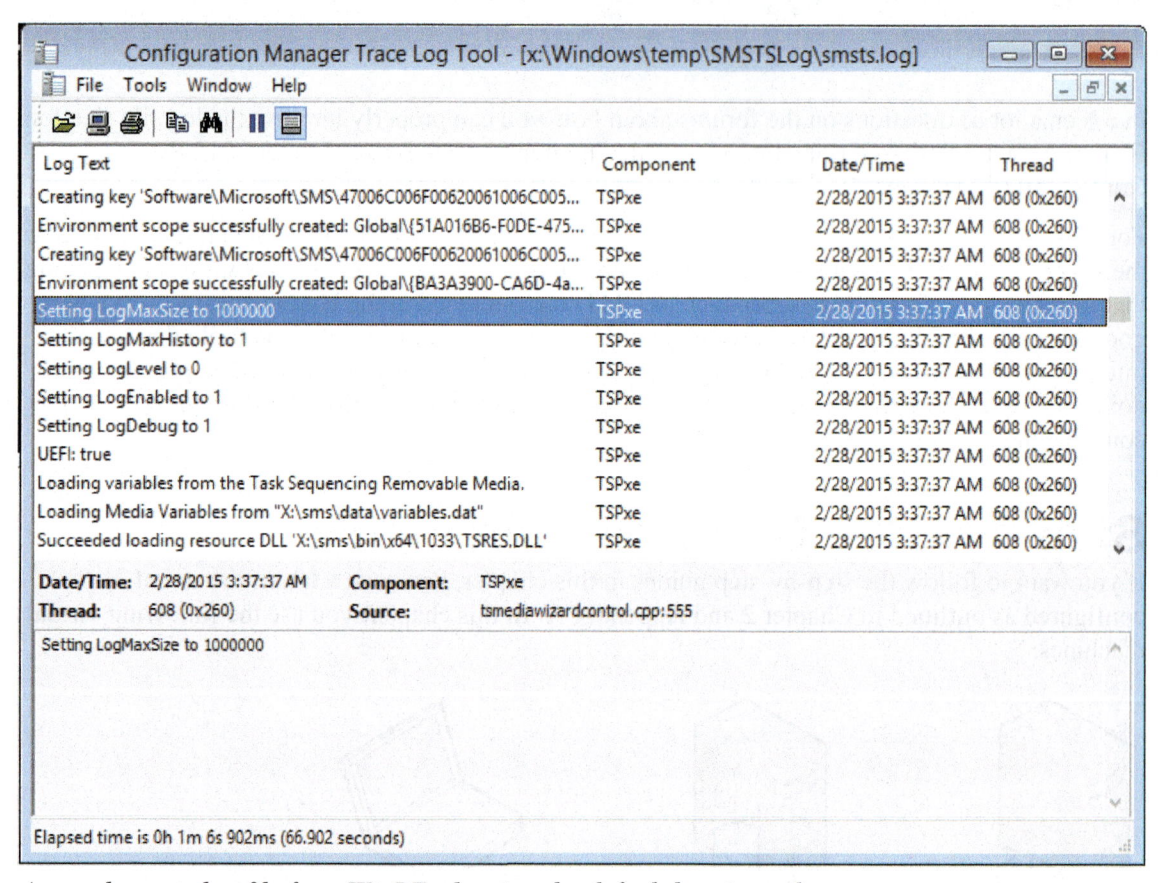

*A sample smsts.log file from WinPE, showing the default logging values.*

As a direct result of this small size, the log file for OSD (smsts.log) will be overwritten for a variety of reasons, including:

- **Large policy to process.** Each task sequence may contain lots of policies to download eating up valuable log file space.
- **MDT-integrated task sequence.** MDT integration means that your log files will overwrite quickly just by downloading the MDT Toolkit package because all the files downloaded in the MDT Toolkit and associated steps are logged to the smsts.log file, quickly filling it.
- **Several packages/applications.** If, for example, you are downloading several files in one or more packages, those files are logged in the smsts.log file, which quickly fills it.

The effect of filling the log file, and therefore the knock effect of rolling over the log file, is as follows: You will most likely miss seeing the real errors you hope to find in the log file as they will have been overwritten due to the log file being so small. In other words, you cannot troubleshoot properly as you've literally lost the important information.

To cut a long story short, if you want to increase the size of your log files during operating system deployment, then a file called *smsts.ini* must be present in the Windows directory of the boot image you are booting from, and it should contain options to specify the new size of log file along with the type of log level you want.

> **Note**: You cannot set the logfile size using a prestart command as that process occurs after the logfile size options are set.

There are two methods used here to increase log file size in WinPE: one is manually injecting the file into your boot images via Deployment Image Servicing and Management (DISM), and the other method relies on the Extrafiles method for MDT-integrated boot images.

## Introducing the smsts.ini File and Associated Options

The smsts.ini file is read by the boot process if it is found in the default location (the Windows directory of your boot WIM). This file is a simple text file containing a few important lines.

To change the smsts.log file size to a maximum of 5 MB, set the log level to the most verbose level, and increase the number of rolled over logs to three while enabling debug logging, use the following options in the smsts.ini file:

```
[Logging]
LOGLEVEL=0
LOGMAXSIZE=5242880
LOGMAXHISTORY=3
DEBUGLOGGING=1
ENABLELOGGING=True
```

The LogLevel=0 line tells the logging engine to log in verbose mode. It can be any value from 0–3 where 0 is the most verbose logging and 3 logs only errors.

The LogMaxSize=5242880 value sets the maximum size that the logfile can grow to before it rolls over. The LogMaxHistory=3 value tells the logging engine how many copies of a file are to be retained after rolling over the original file.

> **Note**: The DebugLogging=1 setting instructs the logging engine to log in Debug mode. This instructs the client to log low-level information that might be useful when troubleshooting problems. As a best practice, avoid using this property in production because excessive logging can occur and affect system performance and disk space consumption.

To get more details about these settings, review the following link on TechNet: https://technet.microsoft.com/en-us/library/gg699356.aspx.

# Inject smsts.ini into the Boot WIM File via DISM

This guide assumes you have not yet added the smsts.ini file to your boot WIM and that you want to add the file to the default x64 boot WIM included with ConfigMgr. Making the change to the source boot WIM file of one architecture (x86 or x64) makes the change for all boot images based on that source boot WIM; however, these changes do not take effect until they have been re-distributed to their distribution points.

> **Real World Note:** If you want to add smsts.ini to other boot images and identify which boot images that a sequence is using, you can simply check the Advanced tab on the task sequence, or start a deployment, and see which boot image that is loaded via PXE.
>
> To identify the boot WIM during PXE boot, look at the example image ID shown in the following screenshot. The image ID is the text in between the words boot and wim. The image ID can then be viewed by selecting the Image ID column in the ConfigMgr console under boot images. By default, it is not selected.

```
Loading files...

IP: 192.168.1.214, File: \SMSImages\PS100005\boot.PS100005.wim
```

*Identifying the boot WIM image ID.*

To add the smsts.ini file to the default x64 boot WIM included with ConfigMgr, follow this procedure:

1. On **CM01**, using **Notepad**, review the **E:\Setup\Scripts\smsts.ini** file. It should match the preceding sample.
2. Using the **ConfigMgr console**, in the **Software Library** workspace, select the **Operating Systems / Boot Images** node.

Chapter 3  Increasing Log File Size

3. Right-click the **Boot image (x64)** boot image and select **Properties**. Then select the **Data Source** tab to identify where the boot image source file (called boot.wim) is located. This is listed in the Image path field.

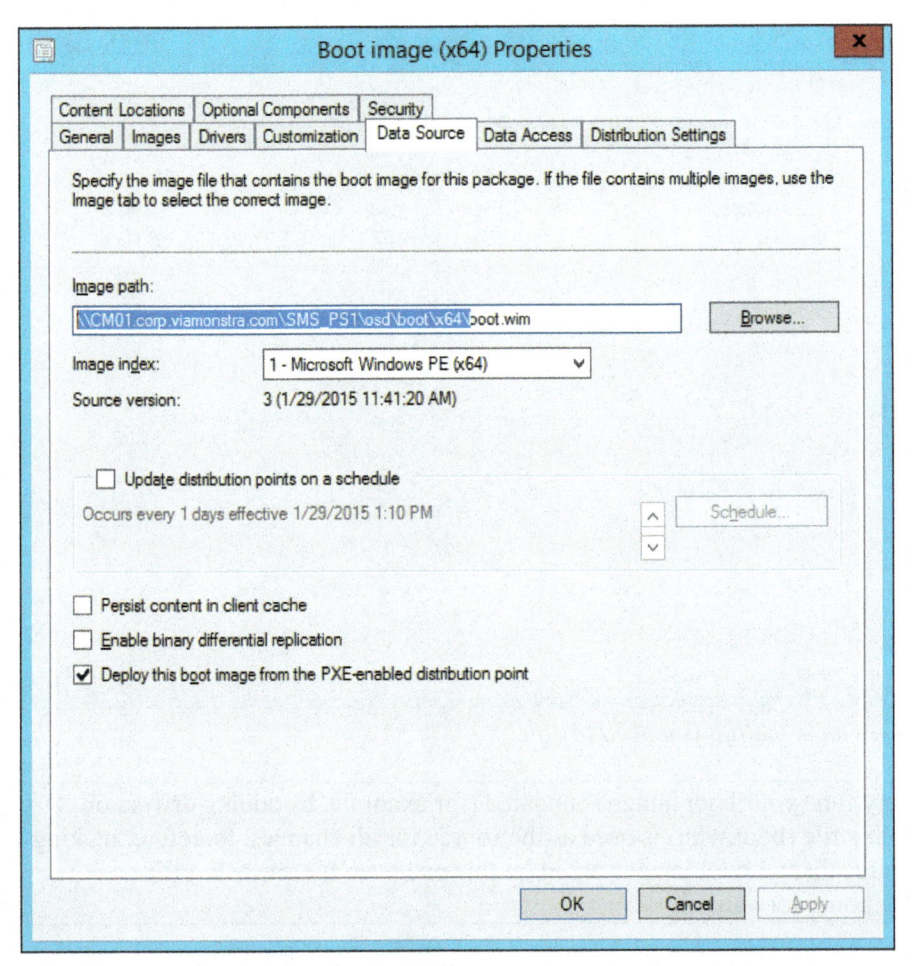

*The boot.wim image path highlighted.*

**Note**: Default boot images created by ConfigMgr are named boot.wim, whereas boot images created using the Create Boot Image using MDT method are named winpe.wim.

83

Chapter 3   Increasing Log File Size

4. Using **File Explorer**, browse to the data source image path listed in the properties. You probably see a few WIM files listed; however, the file in which you are interested is **boot.wim**.

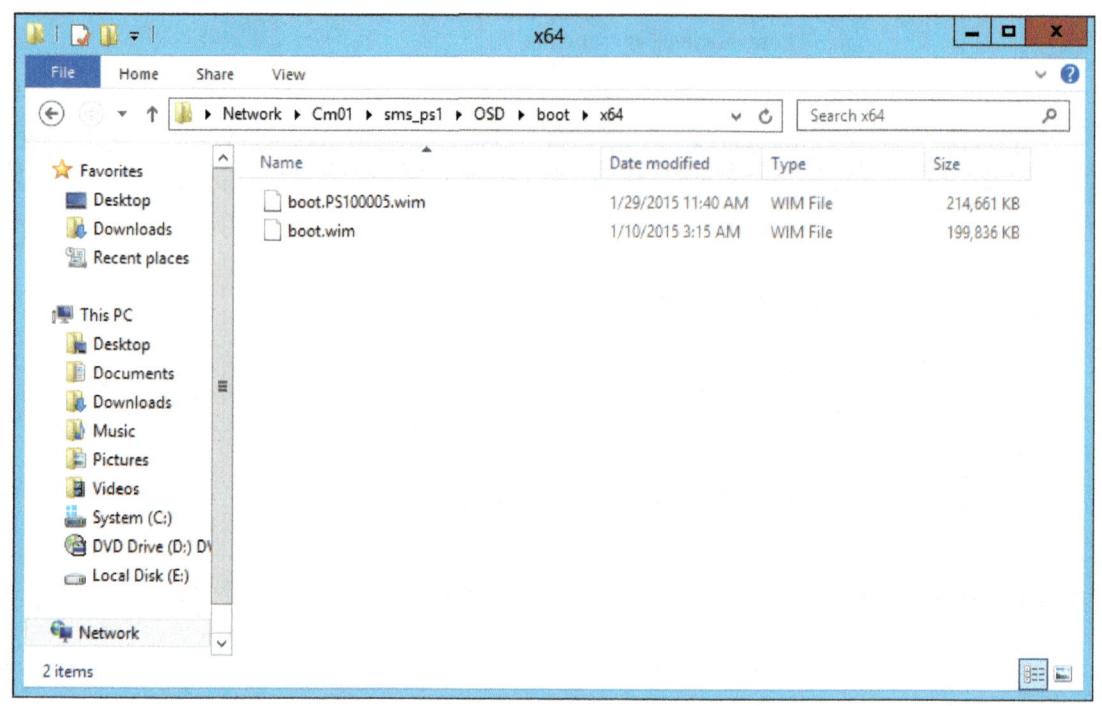

*The file named boot.wim is the file you need to edit.*

> **Real World Note**: Every time your boot image is updated (for example, by adding drivers or optional components), this file (boot.wim) is used as the source for all changes; therefore, making changes to this file ensures that all boot images based on this one have the smsts.log file size changes locked in place going forward.

5. Locate the local copy of the **boot.wim** file shown in the preceding figure. By default, this file is present locally on your ConfigMgr primary server in the following path: **E:\Program Files\Microsoft Configuration Manager\OSD\boot\<Arch>\boot.wim**. (Replace <Arch> with either i386 or x64 depending on the boot WIM architecture you are editing.)

Chapter 3   Increasing Log File Size

6. Make a backup copy of the file before making any changes to it by right-clicking the file and choosing Copy. Rename the copied boot.wim to **boot.wim.bak**. If anything goes wrong with this process, you can always restore the original boot.wim with this backup.

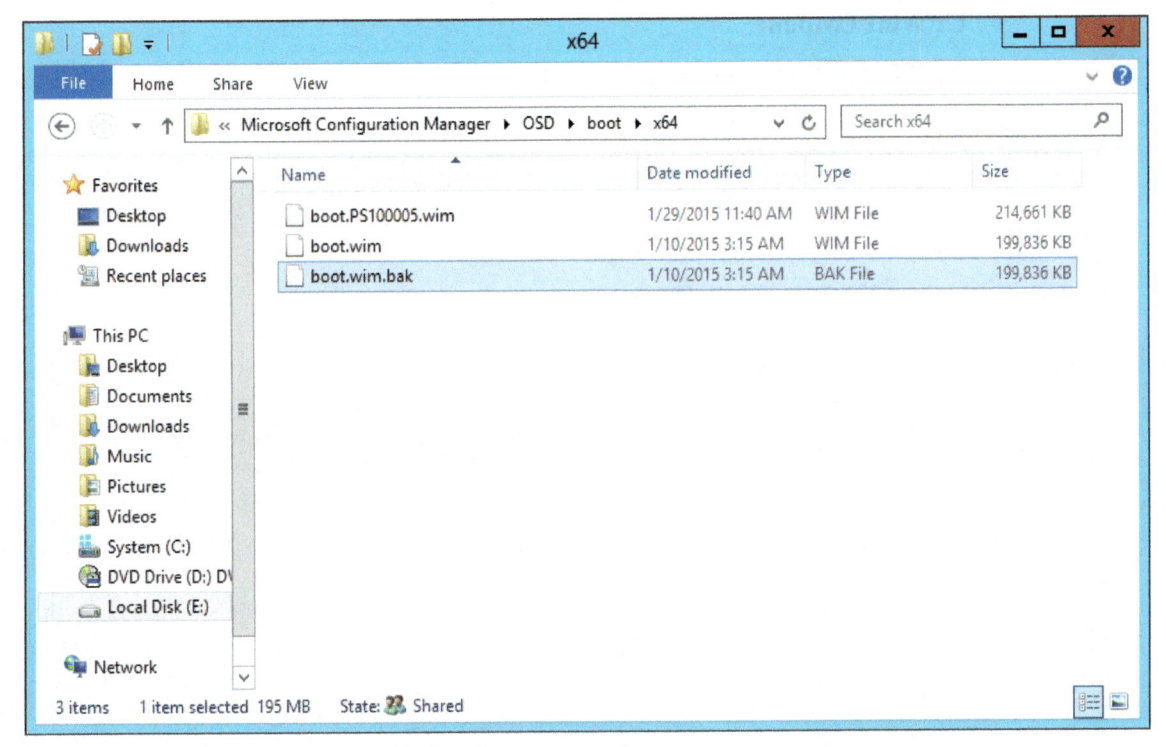

*A backup copy of the boot.wim file has been created.*

85

Chapter 3   Increasing Log File Size

7. To mount the boot WIM, you need some temporary storage for the required files and folders; therefore, create the following folders on **C:\** in an elevated **Command prompt** (run as Administrator):

    o **C:\WinPEMount**
    o **C:\WinPEMount\x86**
    o **C:\WinPEMount\x64**

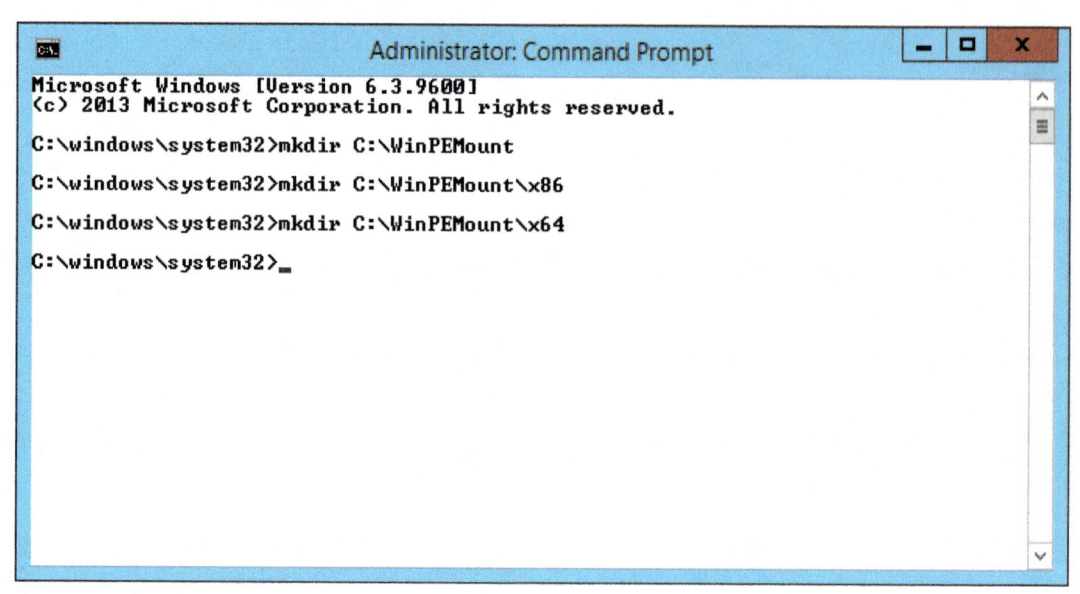

```
Microsoft Windows [Version 6.3.9600]
(c) 2013 Microsoft Corporation. All rights reserved.

C:\windows\system32>mkdir C:\WinPEMount

C:\windows\system32>mkdir C:\WinPEMount\x86

C:\windows\system32>mkdir C:\WinPEMount\x64

C:\windows\system32>
```

*Creating the WinPEMount temporary folders.*

Chapter 3   Increasing Log File Size

8. You modify the boot.wim file in the local path. To inject files, you first need to mount the file with **DISM**. Use the version of DISM that comes with the Windows ADK 8.1, which is 6.3.9600.16384. To start the correct version of DISM, you can locate it in your **Start** menu, right-click the **Deployment Imaging Tools and Environment** command prompt, and then choose **Run as Administrator** as shown in the following figure.

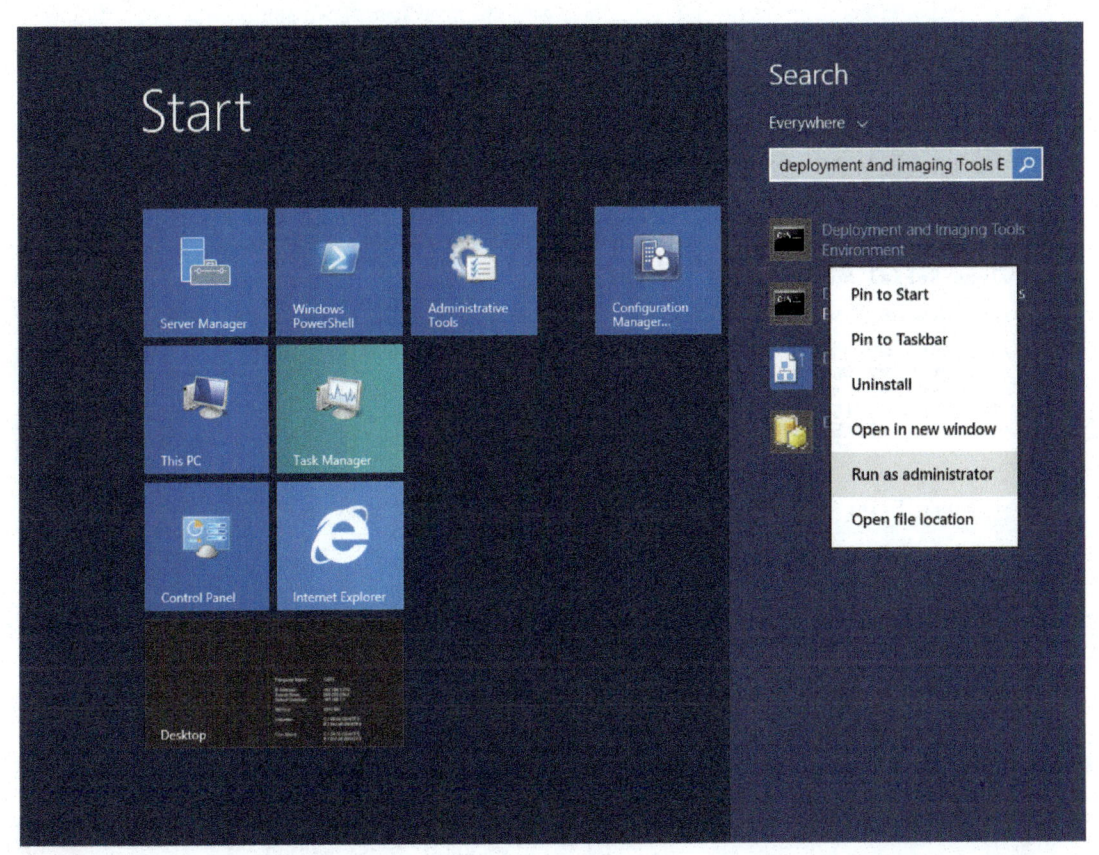

*Running DISM as Administrator.*

87

Chapter 3  Increasing Log File Size

9. Change the drive letter to **E:** and then navigate to the directory containing the local copy of the boot.wim file. That directory is **E:\Program Files\Microsoft Configuration Manager\OSD\boot\x64**. Use the **dir** command to list the contents of the directory to verify that the boot.wim file is present.

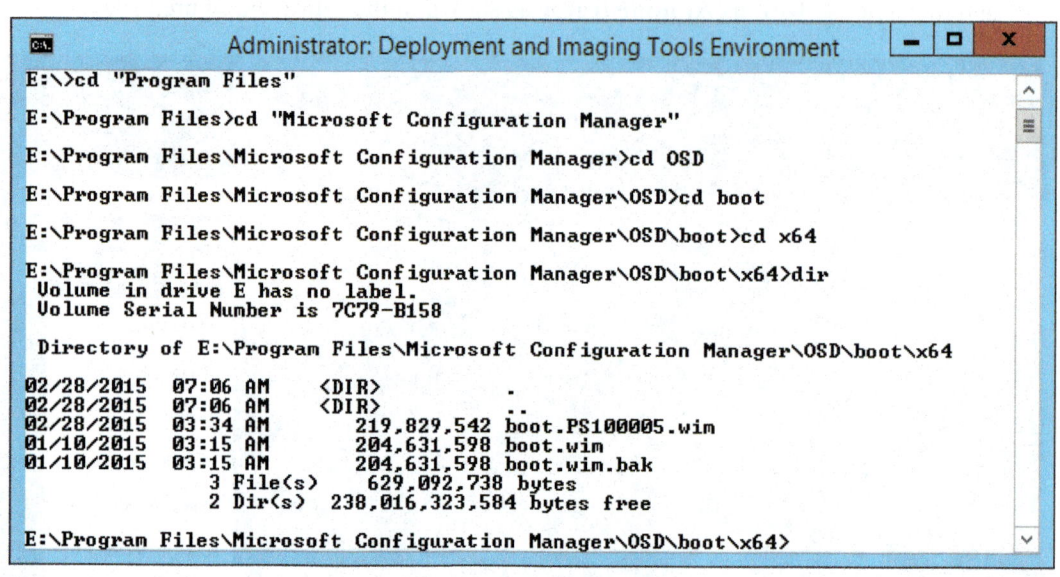

```
E:\>cd "Program Files"

E:\Program Files>cd "Microsoft Configuration Manager"

E:\Program Files\Microsoft Configuration Manager>cd OSD

E:\Program Files\Microsoft Configuration Manager\OSD>cd boot

E:\Program Files\Microsoft Configuration Manager\OSD\boot>cd x64

E:\Program Files\Microsoft Configuration Manager\OSD\boot\x64>dir
 Volume in drive E has no label.
 Volume Serial Number is 7C79-B158

 Directory of E:\Program Files\Microsoft Configuration Manager\OSD\boot\x64

02/28/2015  07:06 AM    <DIR>          .
02/28/2015  07:06 AM    <DIR>          ..
02/28/2015  03:34 AM       219,829,542 boot.PS100005.wim
01/10/2015  03:15 AM       204,631,598 boot.wim
01/10/2015  03:15 AM       204,631,598 boot.wim.bak
               3 File(s)    629,092,738 bytes
               2 Dir(s)  238,016,323,584 bytes free

E:\Program Files\Microsoft Configuration Manager\OSD\boot\x64>
```

*Here you can see your boot.wim file source and the backup copy created previously.*

10. Use the following command to mount your boot WIM file. It should mount the boot WIM successfully as shown in the following screenshot.

    ```
    dism.exe /mount-wim /wimfile:"E:\Program Files\Microsoft
    Configuration Manager\OSD\boot\x64\boot.wim" /index:1
    /mountdir:C:\WinPEMount\x64
    ```

```
E:\Program Files\Microsoft Configuration Manager\OSD\boot\x64>dism.exe /mount-wi
m /wimfile:"E:\Program Files\Microsoft Configuration Manager\OSD\boot\x64\boot.w
im" /index:1 /mountdir:C:\WinPEMount\x64

Deployment Image Servicing and Management tool
Version: 6.3.9600.16384

Mounting image
[==========================100.0%==========================]
The operation completed successfully.

E:\Program Files\Microsoft Configuration Manager\OSD\boot\x64>
```

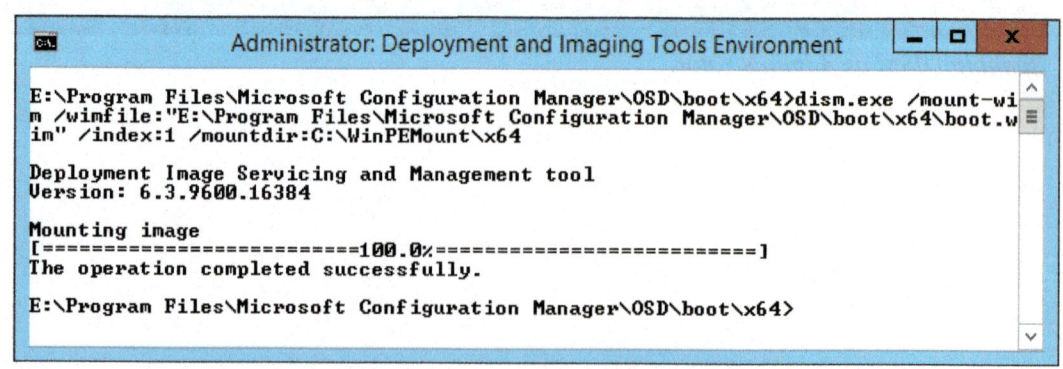

*DISM has successfully mounted the boot wim into the temp folder.*

*Chapter 3  Increasing Log File Size*

11. Copy the **smsts.ini** file created in step 1 to the **Windows** folder in your temporary storage mount directory using the following command:

    ```
    copy E:\Setup\Scripts\smsts.ini C:\WinPEMount\x64\Windows
    ```

12. The smsts.ini file is now in place; however, you need to instruct **DISM** to commit the changes (save those changes) to the **boot.wim** file using the following command and as shown in the screenshot:

    ```
    dism.exe /unmount-wim /mountdir:C:\WinPEMount\x64 /commit
    ```

    ```
    E:\Program Files\Microsoft Configuration Manager\OSD\boot\x64>dism.exe /unmount-wim /mountdir:C:\WinPEMount\x64 /commit

    Deployment Image Servicing and Management tool
    Version: 6.3.9600.16384

    Image File : E:\Program Files\Microsoft Configuration Manager\OSD\boot\x64\boot.wim
    Image Index : 1
    Saving image
    [==========================100.0%==========================]
    Unmounting image
    [==========================100.0%==========================]
    The operation completed successfully.

    E:\Program Files\Microsoft Configuration Manager\OSD\boot\x64>
    ```

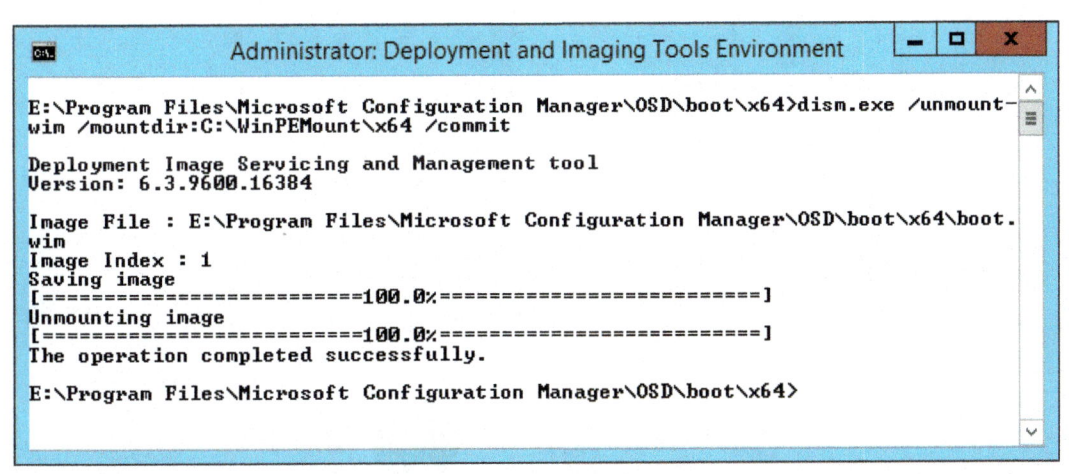

    *DISM has committed the changes to the boot image.*

13. The smsts.ini file has been saved to your source boot.wim, but you need to update it to your distribution points in order to see the new log file size changes in the boot image. In the **ConfigMgr console**, right-click the **Boot Image (x64)** boot image and choose **Update Distribution Points** as shown in the following screenshot. Continue through that wizard until completion.

89

Chapter 3   Increasing Log File Size

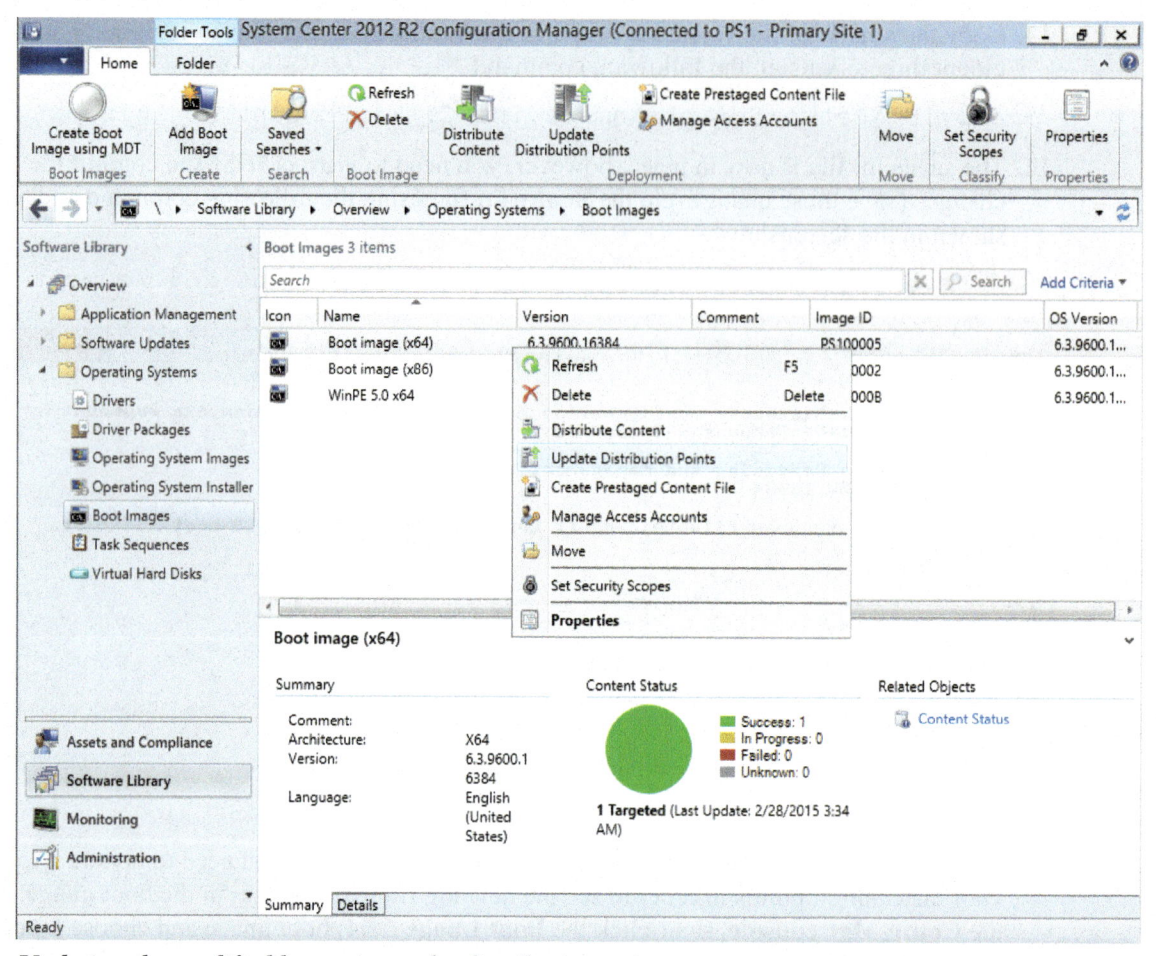

*Updating the modified boot.wim to the distribution points.*

# Inject smsts.ini Using the Extrafiles Method

In this method, you use the Extrafiles method of MDT boot images to inject the smsts.ini file to the correct location.

> **Note**: The Extrafiles method can be used to inject files into MDT boot images during creation of the boot image; therefore, this method is suitable only when creating new MDT boot images. If you already have a boot image and want to extend your log file size, use the DISM method as described in the preceding section. However, adjust your path accordingly for the MDT-created winpe.wim as opposed to boot.wim for ConfigMgr boot images.

Because you want the smsts.ini file copied to the Windows folder in your boot image, you need to create a suitable path in your Extrafiles folder structure. Use the following procedure to create the Extrafiles folder structure:

1. On **CM01**, open a **Command prompt** and browse to **E:\Sources\OSD\MDT**. Create a folder called **Extrafiles** and then create a subfolder within the Extrafiles folder called **Windows**, by running the following command:

    ```
    Mkdir Extrafiles\Windows
    ```

2. Copy the **smsts.ini** file from **C:\Downloads** to the **Extrafiles\Windows** subfolder.

    ```
    copy E:\Setup\Scripts\smsts.ini
    E:\Sources\OSD\MDT\Extrafiles\Windows
    ```

3. On **CM01**, using the **ConfigMgr console**, in the **Software Library** workspace, select **Operating Systems / Boot Images**.

4. Right-click **Boot Images**, select **Create Boot Image using MDT**, and then use the following settings for the wizard:

    a. On the **Package Source** screen, in the **Package source folder to be created (UNC path):** field, enter the following and click **Next**:

    **\\CM01\Sources\OSD\Boot\WinPE 5.0 x86**

    > **Note:** You need to type the preceding path because the final folder (WinPE 5.0 x86) does not yet exist.

    b. On the **General Settings** screen, for **Name**, enter **WinPE 5.0 x86** and click **Next**.

    c. On the **Options** screen, use the following settings and then click **Next**:

    - Platform: **x86**
    - Scratch Space: **<default>**

    d. On the **Components** screen, keep the defaults and click **Next**.

    e. On the **Customization** screen, use the following settings and click **Next**:

    - Add extra files to the new boot image: **Enabled**

        Path: **E:\Sources\OSD\MDT\Extrafiles**

    - Enable command support (F8): **Enabled**

Chapter 3   Increasing Log File Size

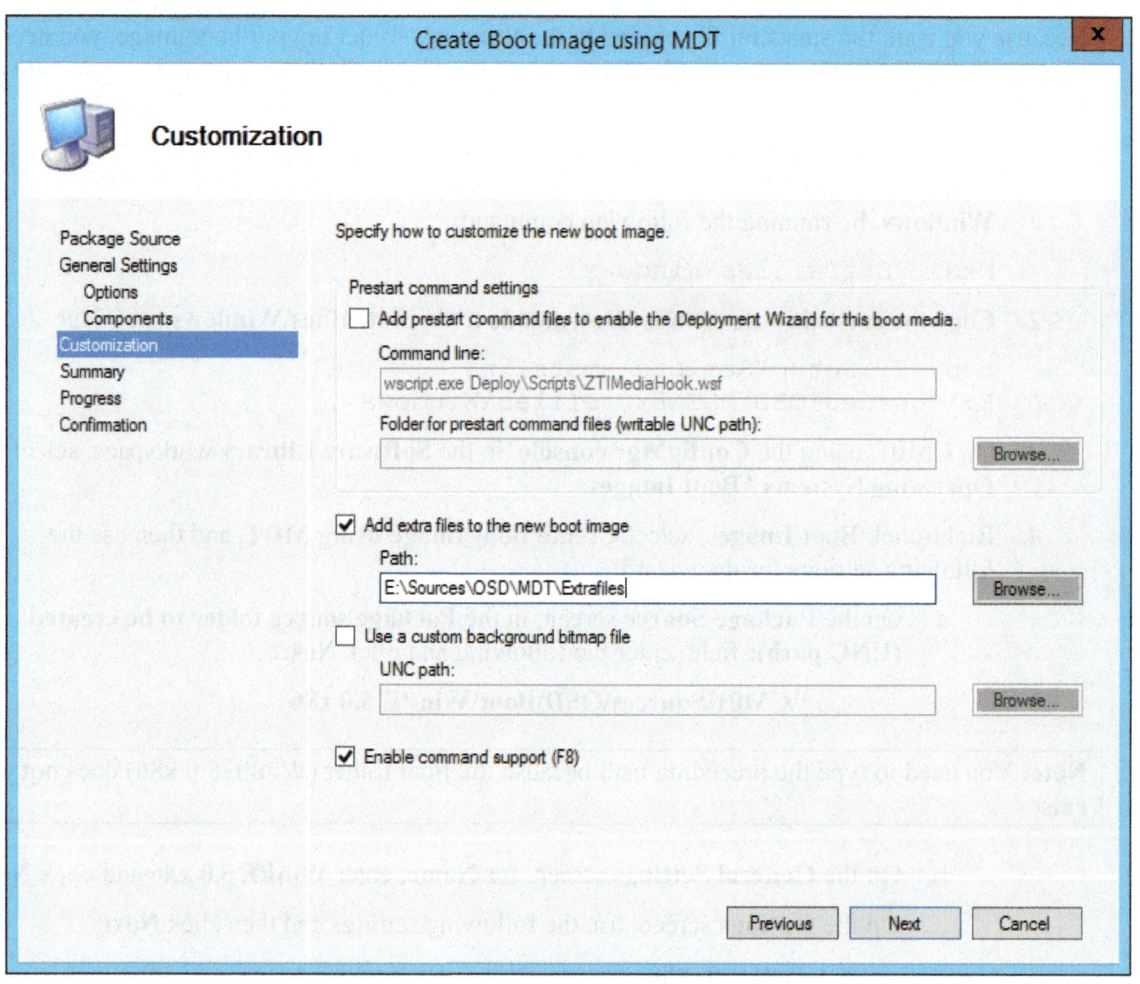

*The Extrafiles folder being added to a new MDT boot image.*

    f.  When you receive confirmation that the process is complete, click **Finish**.

5.  Distribute the boot image to the **CM01** distribution point by selecting the **Boot images** node, right-clicking the **WinPE 5.0 x86** boot image, and selecting **Distribute Content**. Use the following setting for the **Distribute Content Wizard**:

    a.  Content Destination: **Add the CM01 distribution point**.

    b.  Continue through the wizard until completion.

---

**Note**: When you create a new MDT boot image and specify to "Add extra files to the new boot image," that process creates a file called RunCmd.cmd located in the following path: C:\Users\<username>\AppData\Local\Temp\<number>. The RunCmd.cmd file uses xcopy to copy the contents of the specified Extrafiles folder to the root of MDT boot image. You can locate this file after creating the MDT boot image.

---

92

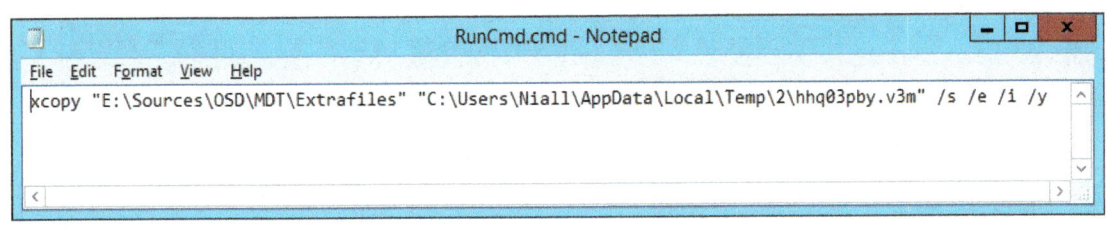

```
RunCmd.cmd - Notepad
File Edit Format View Help
xcopy "E:\Sources\OSD\MDT\Extrafiles" "C:\Users\Niall\AppData\Local\Temp\2\hhq03pby.v3m" /s /e /i /y
```

*The RunCmd.cmd file reveals the xcopy command used during boot image creation.*

# Making Changes to the Logging Options within Windows

The two methods for injecting smsts.ini into boot WIM images make changes that only impact logging during the WinPE Phase of OSD (which is usually where most problems occur). If you also want to increase the log file size within the rest of the task sequence, i.e. during the Windows portion, then the method you use depends on the Windows installation type:

- New computer scenario
- Refresh computer scenario

**Note**: Changing the logging options for either of these scenarios changes the settings for all ConfigMgr client logs, not just the smsts.log.

## Increase Log File Size for a New Computer Scenario

To increase the log file size of all logs within Windows for the new computer scenario, you need to add the following code to your Setup Windows and ConfigMgr step:

```
CCMLOGMAXSIZE=5242880 CCMLOGLEVEL=0 CCMLOGMAXHISTORY=3
```

Those settings instruct the logging engine to create log files with a maximum size of approximately 5 MB during the Windows phase of the task sequence. This also means that all logging from that point onwards will be based on those settings unless otherwise changed. To do this, follow these steps:

1. On **CM01**, using the **ConfigMgr console**, in the **Software Library** workspace, select **Operating Systems / Task Sequences**.

2. Right-click the **Windows 8.1 Enterprise x64** task sequence and choose **Edit**.

3. In the **Post Install** section of the task sequence, locate the **Setup Windows and ConfigMgr** action and type the following into the **Installation Properties** box:

    ```
    CCMLOGMAXSIZE=5242880 CCMLOGLEVEL=0 CCMLOGMAXHISTORY=3
    ```

Chapter 3   Increasing Log File Size

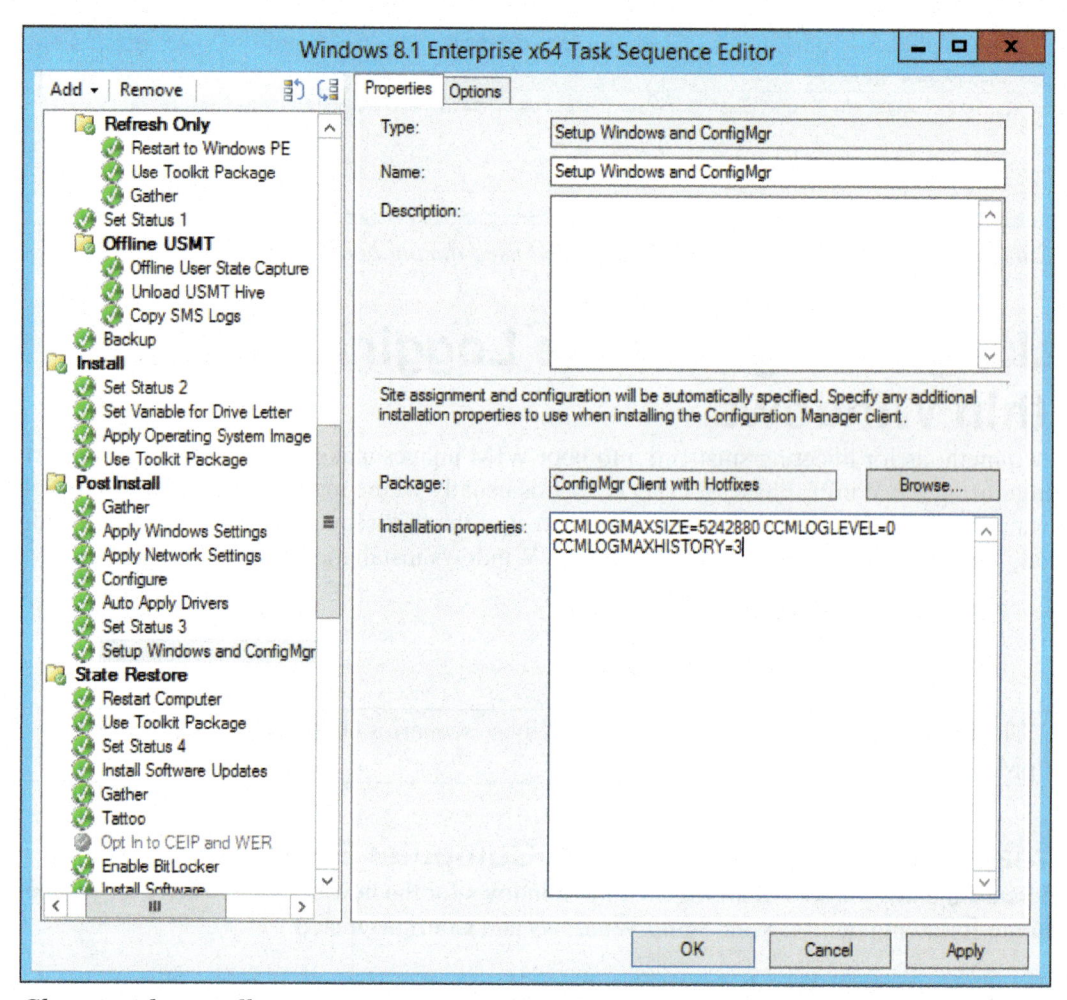

*Changing the installation properties on the Setup Windows and ConfigMgr step.*

4. Click **Apply** to save the changes, and then close the task sequence.

## Increase Log File Size for a Refresh Computer Scenario (Replace)

To change the log file size options in Windows during a refresh computer scenario, follow this procedure, keep in mind that you'll need to make similar edits to any deployed task sequence that you want to change the logging options:

1. On **CM01**, using the **ConfigMgr console**, in the **Software Library** workspace, select **Operating Systems / Task Sequences**.

2. Right-click the **Windows 8.1 Enterprise x64** task sequence and choose **Edit**.

3. Create a new **Run Command Line** action as the first action in the **State Restore** phase by clicking **Add / General / Run Command Line**.

Chapter 3  Increasing Log File Size

4. In the new **Run Command Line** action, set the name to **Change CCM Logging options** and then add the following command line:

```
cmd /c REG.exe ADD
"HKLM\SOFTWARE\Microsoft\CCM\Logging\@GLOBAL" /v LogLevel /t
REG_DWORD /d 0 /f & cmd /c REG.exe ADD
"HKLM\SOFTWARE\Microsoft\CCM\Logging\@GLOBAL" /v
LogMaxHistory /t REG_DWORD /d 3 /f & cmd /c REG.exe ADD
"HKLM\SOFTWARE\Microsoft\CCM\Logging\@GLOBAL" /v LogMaxSize
/t REG_DWORD /d 5242880 /f
```

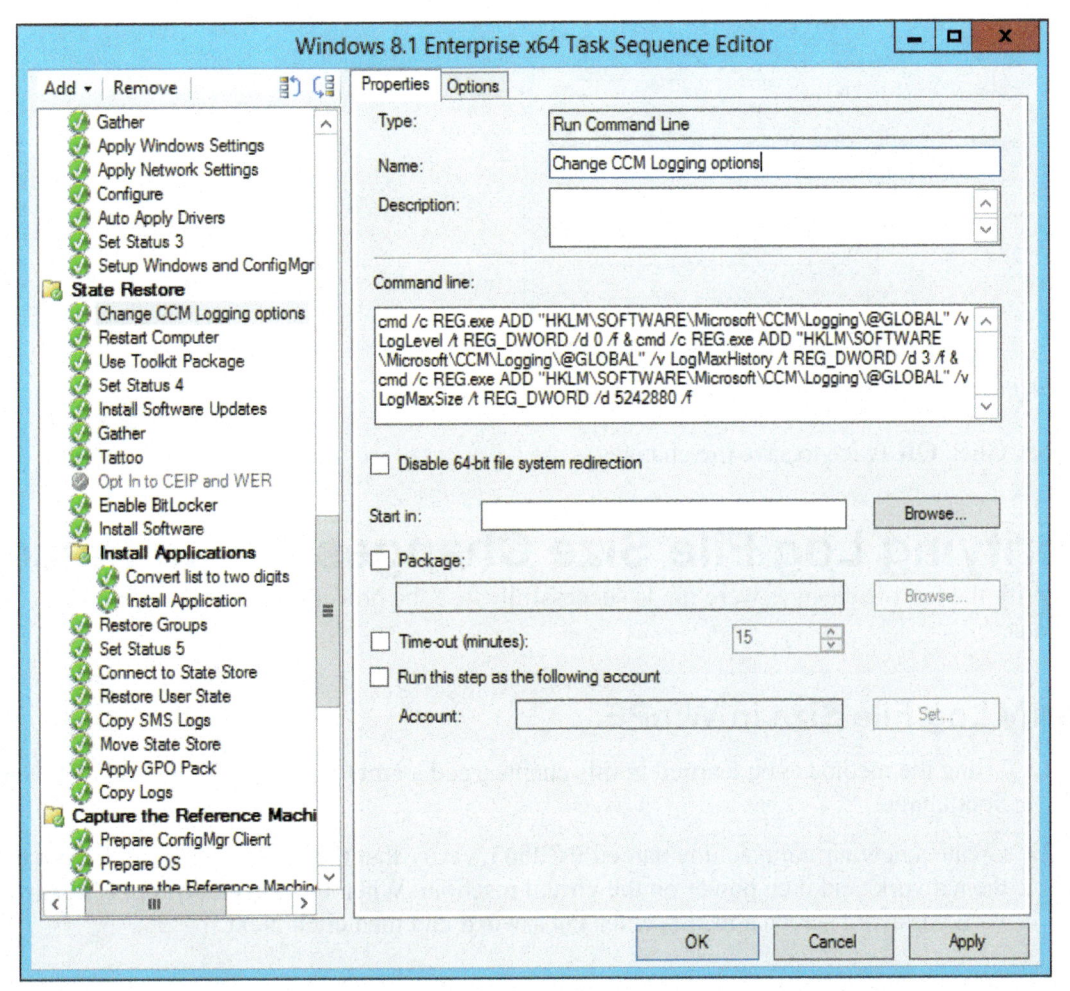

*Changing the CCM logging options via registry keys applied in a Run Command Line action.*

5. Select the **Options** tab, click the **Add Condition** drop-down menu, select **Task Sequence Variable** from the options available, and then use the following settings:
    a. Variable: **DeploymentType**
    b. Condition: **equals**
    c. Value: **Refresh**

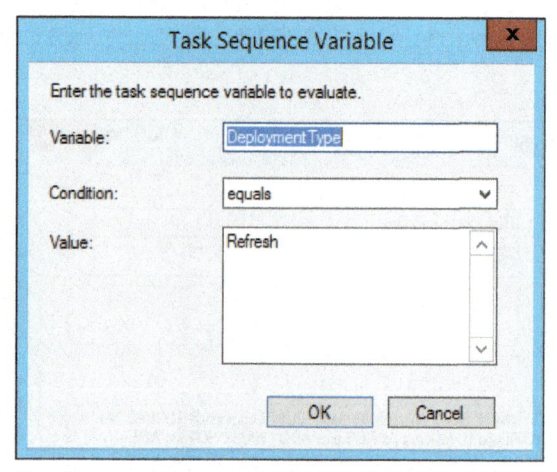

*DeploymentType variable check in Options.*

6. Click **OK** twice to save the changes.

# Verifying Log File Size Changes Are in Place

To verify the log file changes were made successfully, use the procedures in the following sections.

## Verify Log File Size in WinPE

1. Using the methods you learned in this chapter, add a **smts.ini** file to the **WinPE 5.0 x64** boot image.
2. Create a new virtual machine named **PC0003**, verify that the boot order is set to boot to the network, and then power on the virtual machine. When the **Task Sequence Wizard** PXE password screen appears, enter **P@ssw0rd** and then click **Next**.

Chapter 3   Increasing Log File Size

3. When you see the list of available task sequences, press **F8** to bring up the command prompt in your WinPE session. In the command prompt, enter the following to bring up the **smsts.log** file in CMTrace:

```
cmtrace X:\Windows\Temp\SMSTSLOG\smsts.log
```

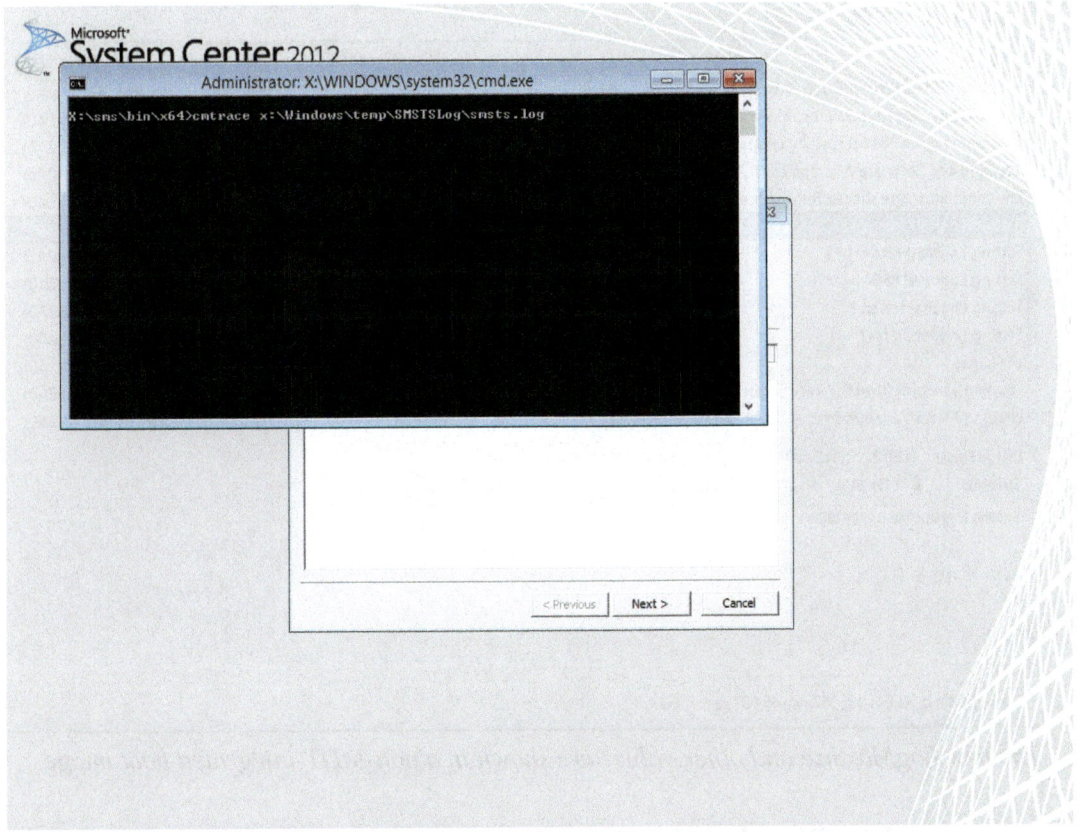

*CMTrace command to bring up the smsts.log file.*

97

4. The smsts.log file appears in CMTrace. Scroll through it to find the new values as shown in the following figure by locating the line that starts with **Setting LogMaxSize**.

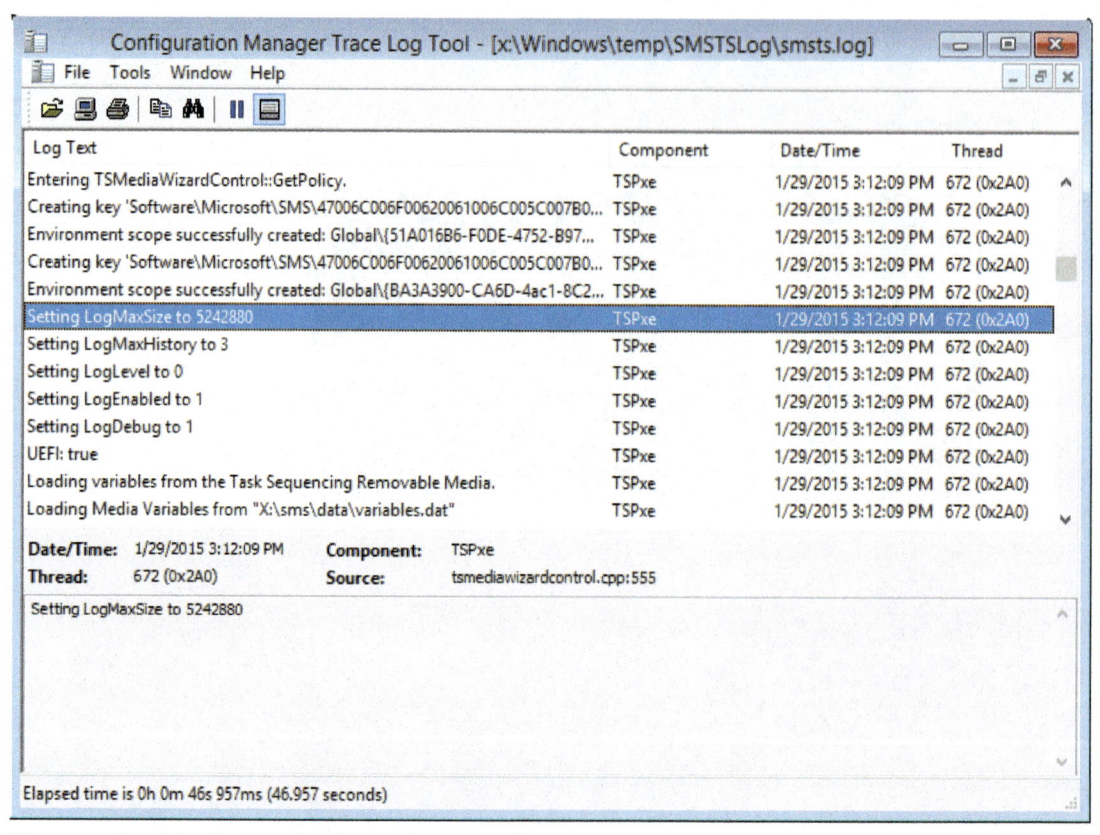

*The new LogMaxSize and other values are shown in a non-MDT-integrated boot image.*

## Verify Log File Size in Windows

If you want to verify the log file size in Windows, you need to complete the deployment of the PC0003 virtual machine.

1. Once again, PXE boot the **PC0003** virtual machine, enter the PXE password **P@ssw0rd** when prompted, and click **Next**. Continue until you see the list of available task sequences.

2. Select the **Windows 8.1 Enterprise x64** task sequence, and allow the OSD process to continue to completion.

3. When the OSD process is complete, log on to the virtual machine as a user with administrative credentials.

Chapter 3   Increasing Log File Size

4. Using **Regedit**, browse to **HKLM\Software\Microsoft\CCM\Logging\@Global** and confirm the **LogMaxSize** and other settings have applied successfully as per the figure.

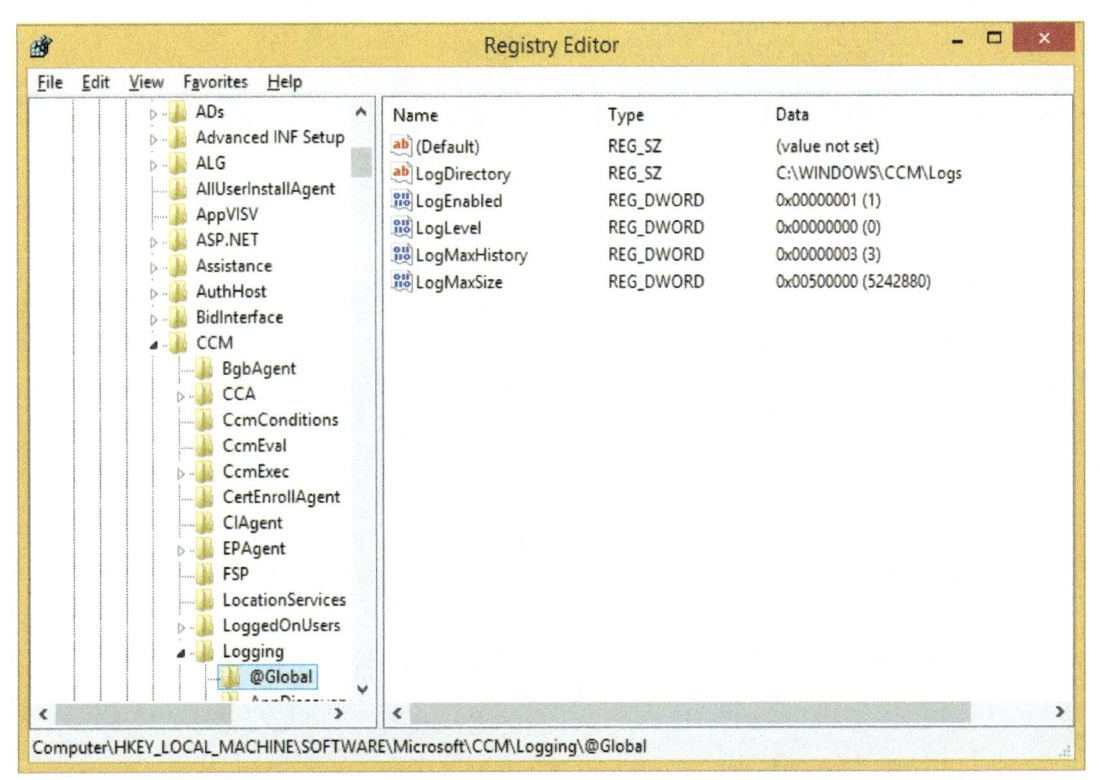

*The LogMaxSize and other settings revealed in the registry of a deployed computer.*

99

Chapter 4

# Building a Reference Image of Windows 8.1

In this chapter, you familiarize yourself with some of the PowerShell capabilities provided in System Center 2012 R2 Configuration Manager. PowerShell gives you the ability to automate many functions and this ability is integrated directly in the ConfigMgr console or can be accessed by importing a ConfigMgr PowerShell module in a script. You will see many PowerShell cmdlets being used in this and other guides in the book, so becoming familiar with PowerShell capabilities is definitely worth your time.

In addition to learning about integrating ConfigMgr with PowerShell, you use native functionality within ConfigMgr to build and capture Windows 8.1 Enterprise x64 with the .NET Framework 3.5 integrated and some key applications like Office 365. There have been many public discussions about which way is the best way to create a reference image, and rather than go into detail about those discussions I'm documenting this method for those of you who want (or have) to capture the reference image using ConfigMgr's built-in functionality.

## Step-by-Step Guide Requirements

If you want to follow the step-by-step guides in this chapter, you need a lab environment configured as outlined in Chapter 2 and Appendix A. In this chapter, you use the following virtual machines:

DC01        CM01        REF001

*The VMs used in this chapter (REF001 is a VM created in one of the guides).*

101

# Using PowerShell with ConfigMgr

Before you can work with ConfigMgr using PowerShell, it needs to be integrated with ConfigMgr. To enable PowerShell integration with ConfigMgr, use either of the following methods:

- PowerShell integration via the ConfigMgr console
- PowerShell integration via a PowerShell script

## Enable PowerShell Integration via the ConfigMgr Console

To enable PowerShell Integration using the built-in ability in the ConfigMgr console, follow this procedure:

1. On **CM01**, using the **ConfigMgr console**, click the white triangle in the blue box to expose the drop-down menu in the top-left corner of the console and select **Connect via Windows PowerShell**.

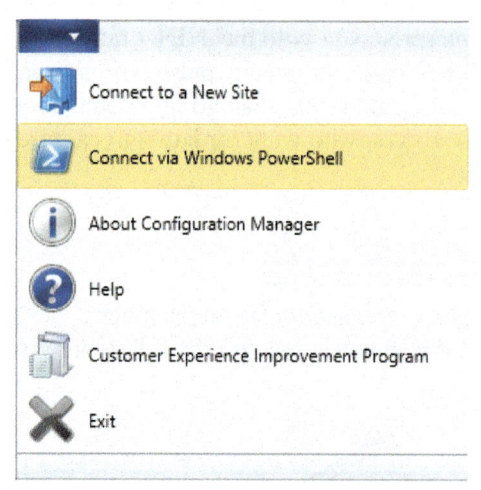

*Connect via Windows PowerShell.*

2. A Windows PowerShell window appears. Select **[A] Always run** when prompted.

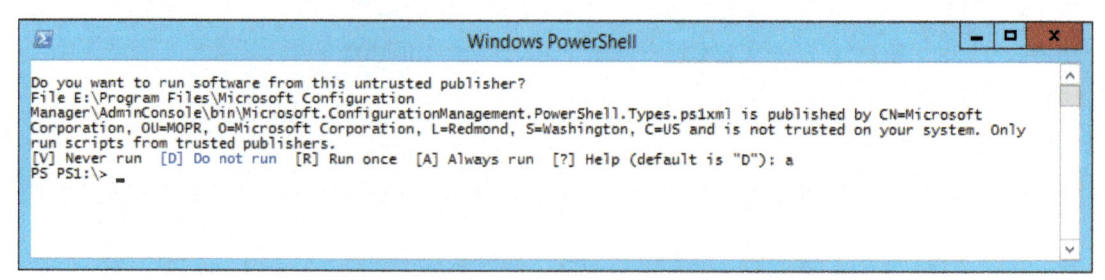

*Windows PowerShell showing the site code of your ConfigMgr site, PS1.*

Chapter 4   Building a Reference Image of Windows 8.1

## Get Started with ConfigMgr PowerShell Cmdlets

Using PowerShell with ConfigMgr does require a basic understanding of how it all works together. In this section, I look at some of the basics so that you get a feeling for the programming language.

- To list the commands available, use the following command:

  `Get-Command -Module ConfigurationManager`

  There are so many commands available that they quickly scroll off screen. You can use the Out-File command described later in this section to output the list of commands into a text file that you can review at your leisure in Notepad.

- To determine how many commands are available, you can use the count ability as follows:

  `(Get-Command -Module ConfigurationManager).count`

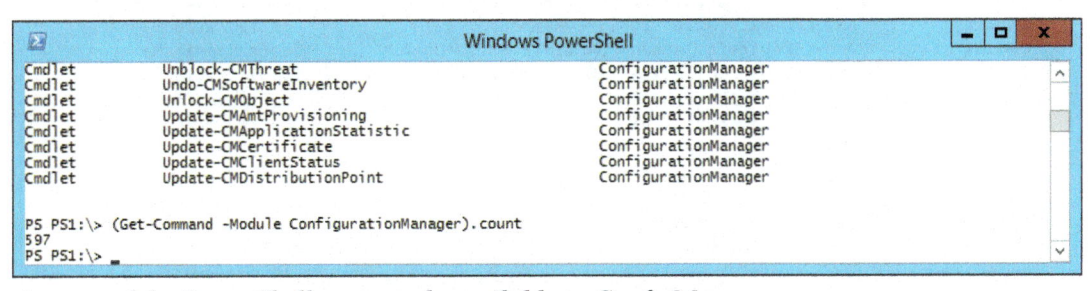

```
Cmdlet    Unblock-CMThreat              ConfigurationManager
Cmdlet    Undo-CMSoftwareInventory      ConfigurationManager
Cmdlet    Unlock-CMObject               ConfigurationManager
Cmdlet    Update-CMAmtProvisioning      ConfigurationManager
Cmdlet    Update-CMApplicationStatistic ConfigurationManager
Cmdlet    Update-CMCertificate          ConfigurationManager
Cmdlet    Update-CMClientStatus         ConfigurationManager
Cmdlet    Update-CMDistributionPoint    ConfigurationManager

PS PS1:\> (Get-Command -Module ConfigurationManager).count
597
PS PS1:\>
```

*A count of the PowerShell commands available to ConfigMgr.*

- To generate a list of these ConfigMgr PowerShell commands in a text file so that you can scroll through them at your leisure or search for a command, use PowerShell's **Out-File** command. You do so as follows:

  a. In the **Windows PowerShell** window, create a folder on **E:** called **E:\Setup\PowerShellCommands** by typing the following:

  `Mkdir E:\Setup\PowerShellCommands`

  b. In the **Windows PowerShell** window, type the following (all on one line):

  `Get-Command -Module ConfigurationManager | Out-File E:\Setup\PowerShellCommands\ConfigMgr_PowerShell_Commands.txt`

103

Chapter 4 Building a Reference Image of Windows 8.1

    c. Using **Notepad**, in the **E:\Setup\PowerShellCommands folder**, open the **ConfigMgr_PowerShell_Commands.txt** file.

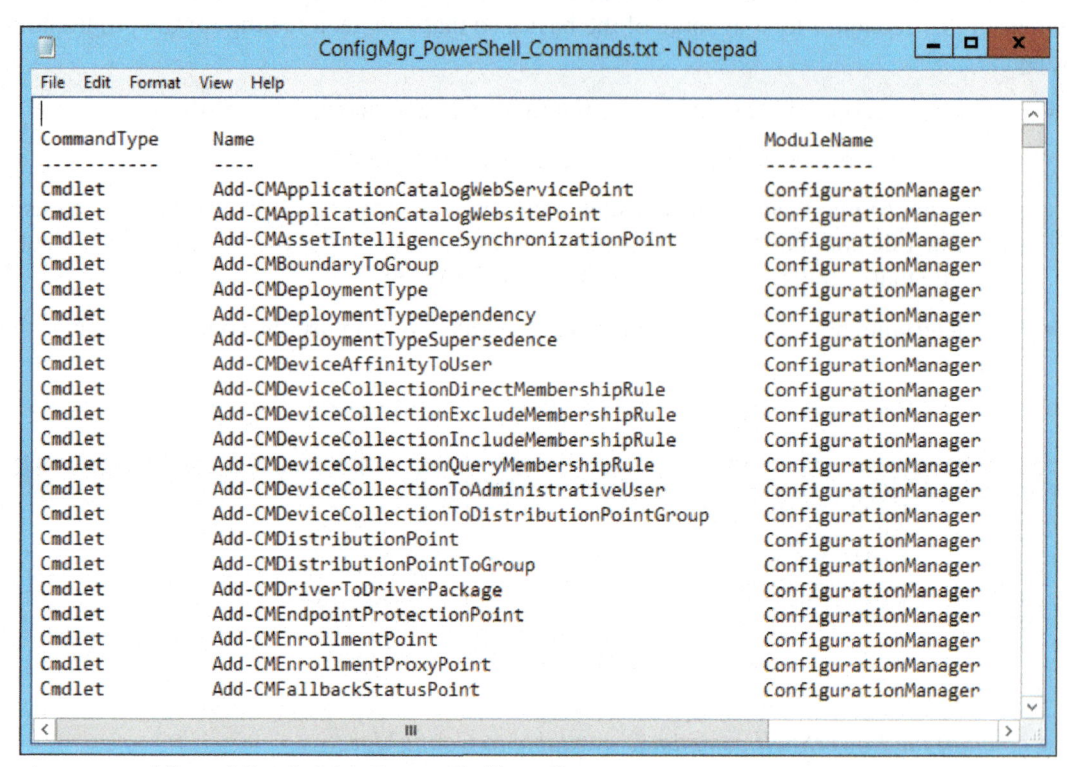

```
ConfigMgr_PowerShell_Commands.txt - Notepad
File  Edit  Format  View  Help

CommandType     Name                                                ModuleName
-----------     ----                                                ----------
Cmdlet          Add-CMApplicationCatalogWebServicePoint              ConfigurationManager
Cmdlet          Add-CMApplicationCatalogWebsitePoint                 ConfigurationManager
Cmdlet          Add-CMAssetIntelligenceSynchronizationPoint          ConfigurationManager
Cmdlet          Add-CMBoundaryToGroup                                ConfigurationManager
Cmdlet          Add-CMDeploymentType                                 ConfigurationManager
Cmdlet          Add-CMDeploymentTypeDependency                       ConfigurationManager
Cmdlet          Add-CMDeploymentTypeSupersedence                     ConfigurationManager
Cmdlet          Add-CMDeviceAffinityToUser                           ConfigurationManager
Cmdlet          Add-CMDeviceCollectionDirectMembershipRule           ConfigurationManager
Cmdlet          Add-CMDeviceCollectionExcludeMembershipRule          ConfigurationManager
Cmdlet          Add-CMDeviceCollectionIncludeMembershipRule          ConfigurationManager
Cmdlet          Add-CMDeviceCollectionQueryMembershipRule            ConfigurationManager
Cmdlet          Add-CMDeviceCollectionToAdministrativeUser           ConfigurationManager
Cmdlet          Add-CMDeviceCollectionToDistributionPointGroup       ConfigurationManager
Cmdlet          Add-CMDistributionPoint                              ConfigurationManager
Cmdlet          Add-CMDistributionPointToGroup                       ConfigurationManager
Cmdlet          Add-CMDriverToDriverPackage                          ConfigurationManager
Cmdlet          Add-CMEndpointProtectionPoint                        ConfigurationManager
Cmdlet          Add-CMEnrollmentPoint                                ConfigurationManager
Cmdlet          Add-CMEnrollmentProxyPoint                           ConfigurationManager
Cmdlet          Add-CMFallbackStatusPoint                            ConfigurationManager
```

*A generated list of ConfigMgr PowerShell cmdlets.*

    d. To get help on any PowerShell cmdlet, try using the **get-help** command. For example, to get help about the ConfigMgr **Update-CMDistributionPoint** cmdlet, do as follows:

```
get-help Update-CMDistributionPoint
```

    e. To search for commands that match a certain name, such as **Get-CM**, you can do as follows:

```
get-command -Name *Get-CM*
```

> **Note**: Microsoft has a page on TechNet dedicated to all the cmdlets included in ConfigMgr. Each cmdlet is listed and clickable. The page's URL: https://technet.microsoft.com/en-us/library/jj821831(v=sc.20).aspx

## Windows PowerShell ISE

You also can integrate PowerShell with ConfigMgr via a script, and the best way by far of doing this is using Windows PowerShell ISE (Integrated Scripting Environment) to create or run your PowerShell scripts. The main advantage it offers is easy access to the cmdlets via drop down menus, and a true scripting environment with color coding and built in help.

To start Windows PowerShell ISE, do as follows:

> Locate the **PowerShell** button in the taskbar. Right-click it and choose **Run ISE as Administrator** as shown in the figure.

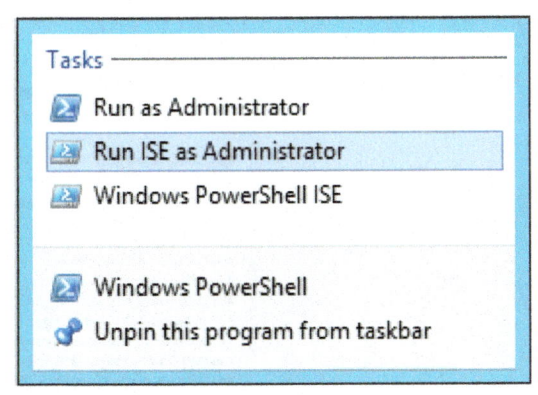

*Run ISE as Administrator.*

## Enable PowerShell integration via a PowerShell Script

Now that you have the PowerShell scripting environment started, you can create or run PowerShell scripts to see the power that PowerShell provides.

1. When **Windows PowerShell ISE** appears, click **File / New** to create a new PowerShell script.

2. Next, you import the **ConfigMgr PowerShell module**. Type in the following line to connect to ConfigMgr via a PowerShell script:

   `Import-Module 'E:\Program Files\Microsoft Configuration Manager\AdminConsole\bin\ConfigurationManager.psd1'`

3. To set the correct location, you need to tell PowerShell what site code to use, as follows:

   `Set-Location PS1:\`

4. Save the script with the following filename **ConnectToConfigMgr.ps1** by clicking **File / Save As** and selecting the following path and file name:

   `E:\Setup\Scripts\ConnectToConfigMgr.ps1.`

5. Run the script by pressing **F5** in Windows PowerShell ISE or clicking the green **Run Script button**.

Chapter 4   Building a Reference Image of Windows 8.1

6. To list the ConfigMgr PowerShell cmdlets in Windows PowerShell ISE, do as follows:

    a. In **Windows PowerShell ISE**, click **Refresh** in the **Commands** pane.

    b. In the **Modules** drop-down list, select **ConfigurationManager** from the available options.

    c. Scroll through the list of available ConfigMgr PowerShell cmdlets as shown in the following figure.

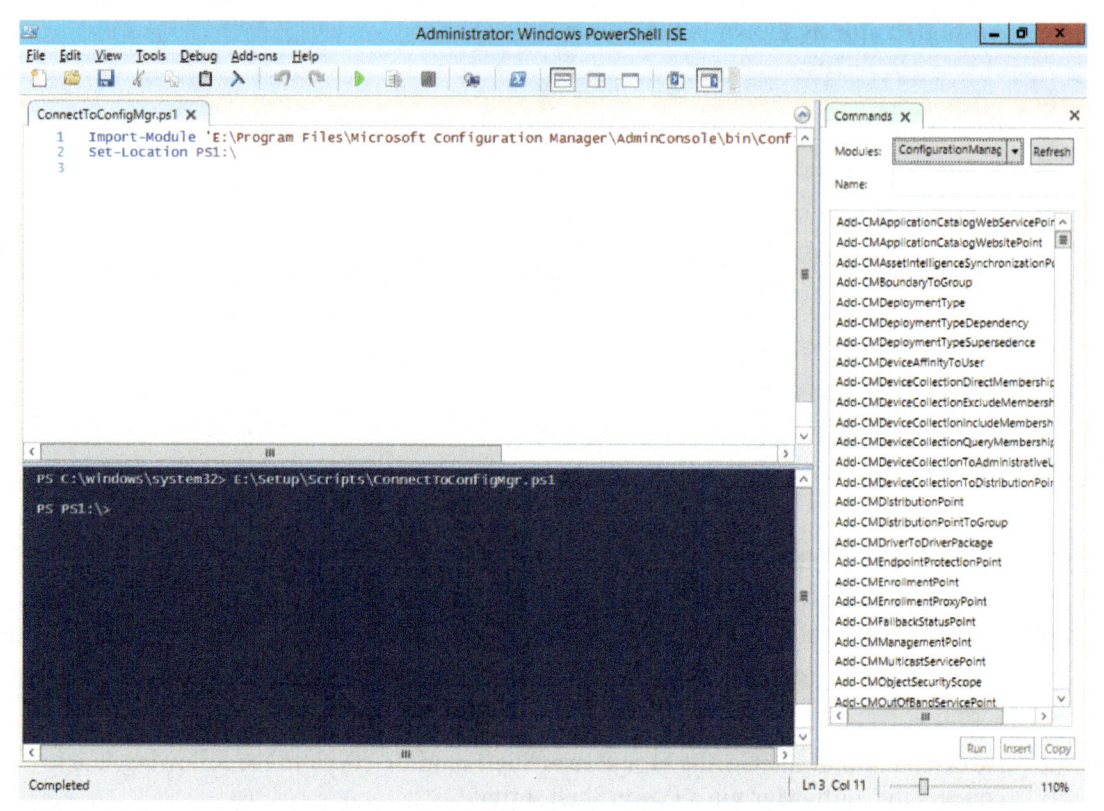

*A list of PowerShell ConfigMgr cmdlets to browse through.*

7. To search for a particular ConfigMgr PowerShell cmdlet, do as follows:

    Enter the cmdlet name or part of the name in the **Name** field of the **Commands** window. For example, enter **Update-CMD**. Notice how the results are displayed as you type.

8. To get more info about a particular ConfigMgr PowerShell cmdlet, do as follows:

    a. Enter the cmdlet name or part of the name in the **Name** field of the **Commands** window. For example, again enter **Update-CMD**.

    b. Click the result that matches your search criteria to display the **Parameters** for that cmdlet.

c. Click the **Help** icon (a white question mark in a blue circle) to get details about that cmdlet.

d. You may be prompted to run the **update-help** cmdlet to update the PowerShell help files directly with the latest version available for download. For more details, see the following TechNet URL: http://go.microsoft.com/fwlink/?LinkId=210614.

Detailed scrollable and searchable help for the chosen cmdlet appears as shown in the figure.

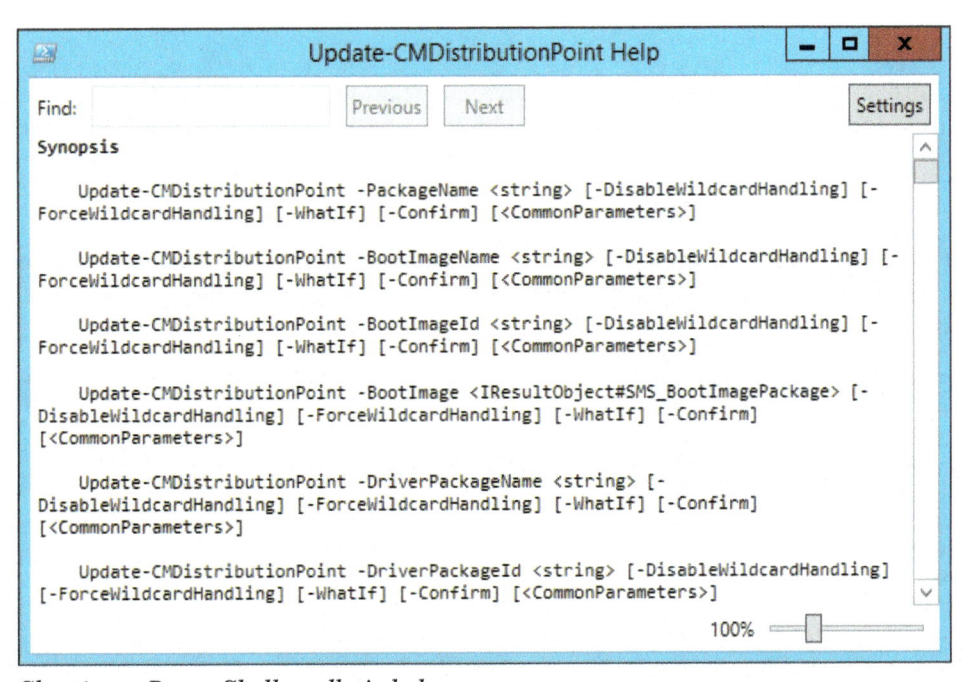

*Showing a PowerShell cmdlet's help.*

# A Quick Look at PowerShell Integration

Using PowerShell integration with ConfigMgr enables the ConfigMgr administrator to do many mundane, repeatable tasks using PowerShell commands bundled together to form scripts and thus saving both time and mouse clicks. In this section, you learn how you can use a couple of ConfigMgr PowerShell cmdlets to do create and distribute a package. There are hundreds of PowerShell cmdlets available for ConfigMgr but covering them all is beyond the scope of this book. The hope here is that once you witness the power of the language, you'll want to do more with it. There are more PowerShell scripts used throughout this book covering a variety of actions.

## Create and Distribute a Package Using PowerShell

In the following example, you create and distribute a ConfigMgr package. This simple script can later be converted to work with variables to make it dynamic. The .NET Framework is an integral part of many applications running on Windows and provides common functionality for those

## Chapter 4  Building a Reference Image of Windows 8.1

applications to run. By default it is not included in Windows 8.1, so you add the .NET 3.5 Windows 8.1 feature to your reference image by creating a package with the source files required for adding roles and features to Windows 8.1.

As the reference image will not be domain joined (it joins a workgroup), you cannot use a Run Command Line action with the Run As User option to specify a domain user. Instead, you create a package and copy the contents of that package locally within your Windows 8.1 reference computer and later install the .NET 3.5 feature using DISM.

To create the Windows 8.1 x64 Features package using PowerShell integration, follow these instructions:

1. On **CM01**, in the **E:\Sources\OSD\OS** folder, create a folder named **Operating System Features**, and then in that folder, create a subfolder named **Windows 8.1 x64 Features**.

2. Browse to the location where you copied the Windows 8.1 source files, which should be **E:\Sources\OSD\OS\Operating System Installers\Windows 8.1 Enterprise x64**.

3. Locate and then select the **sxs** folder within the **Sources** folder. Copy the **sxs** folder (and all its subfolders and files) to the **Windows 8.1 x64 Features** folder that you created previously.

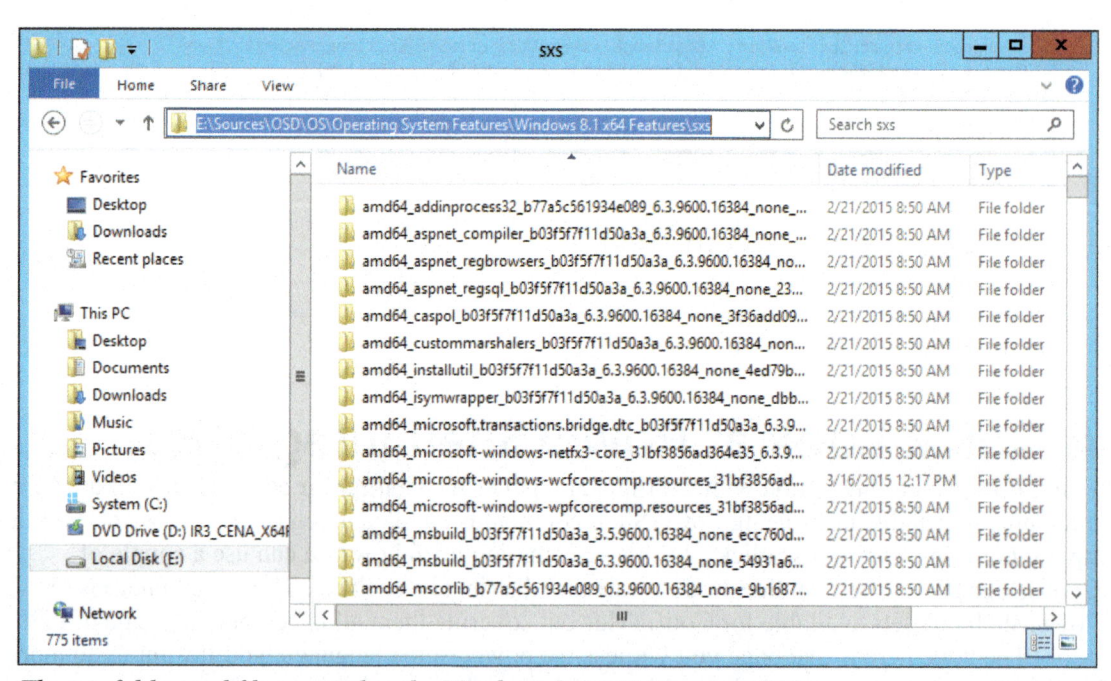

*The sxs folder and files copied to the Windows 8.1 x64 Features folder.*

4. On **CM01**, open **Windows PowerShell ISE** and load the script you created in the preceding section: **E:\Setup\Scripts\ConnectToConfigMgr.ps1**.

Chapter 4   Building a Reference Image of Windows 8.1

5. In **WindowsPowerShell ISE**, create a new line after the **Set-Location PS1:\** line and type in the following command to create the Windows 8.1 x64 Features package:

   ```
   New-CMPackage -Name "Windows 8.1 x64 Features" -Version ""
   -Description "" -Language "" -Manufacturer "" -Path
   "\\CM01.corp.viamonstra.com\Sources\OSD\OS\Operating System
   Features\Windows 8.1 x64 Features"
   ```

6. The package is created using the preceding commands. To distribute it, type the following new line in Windows PowerShell ISE:

   ```
   Start-CMContentDistribution -PackageName "Windows 8.1 x64
   Features" -DistributionPointName "CM01.corp.viamonstra.com"
   ```

7. Run the script in **Windows PowerShell ISE**, by clicking the green **Run Script** button or pressing **F5**.

8. On **CM01**, open up the **ConfigMgr console**, select the **Software Library** workspace, select **Application Management / Packages**, and observe that the **Windows 8.1 x64 Features** package has been created and distributed using PowerShell.

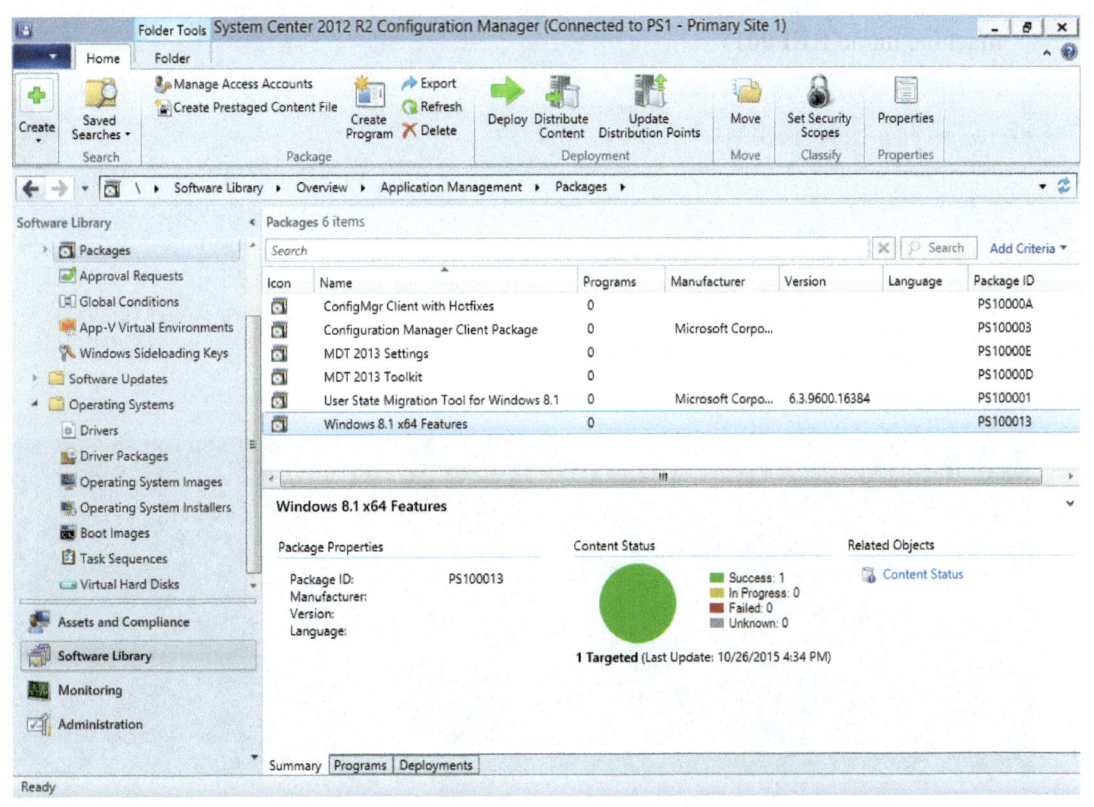

*The Windows 8.1 x64 Features package created and distributed using PowerShell Integration.*

Chapter 4   Building a Reference Image of Windows 8.1

## Create a New Virtual Machine with PowerShell

In this section, you use a script sample to create a new virtual machine (REF001) in Hyper-V. The virtual machine you create is a generation 1 VM, e.g. a BIOS-based VM, which is great for creating reference images because it supports both x86 and x64 builds and also gives you a very generic image. This image can then be deployed to both BIOS-based machines and UEFI-based machines.

> **Note:** If you are using VMWare, just create a virtual machine named REF001 and skip to the next section, "Import a Computer into ConfigMgr Using PowerShell."

1. On **CM01**, browse to the **E:\Setup\Scripts** folder and locate the **Create HyperV VM.ps1** script. Copy the script to your **Hyper-V** host machine.

2. On the **Hyper-V** host machine, open the script in **Windows PowerShell ISE**. Edit the variables within the script as necessary. For example, you may need to change the **$Path** variable to point to the path where you store your Hyper-V virtual machines, or the **$SwitchName** to select the virtual switch you are using.

3. Click the green **Run Script** button or press **F5**. When prompted, enter the new virtual machine name **REF001**.

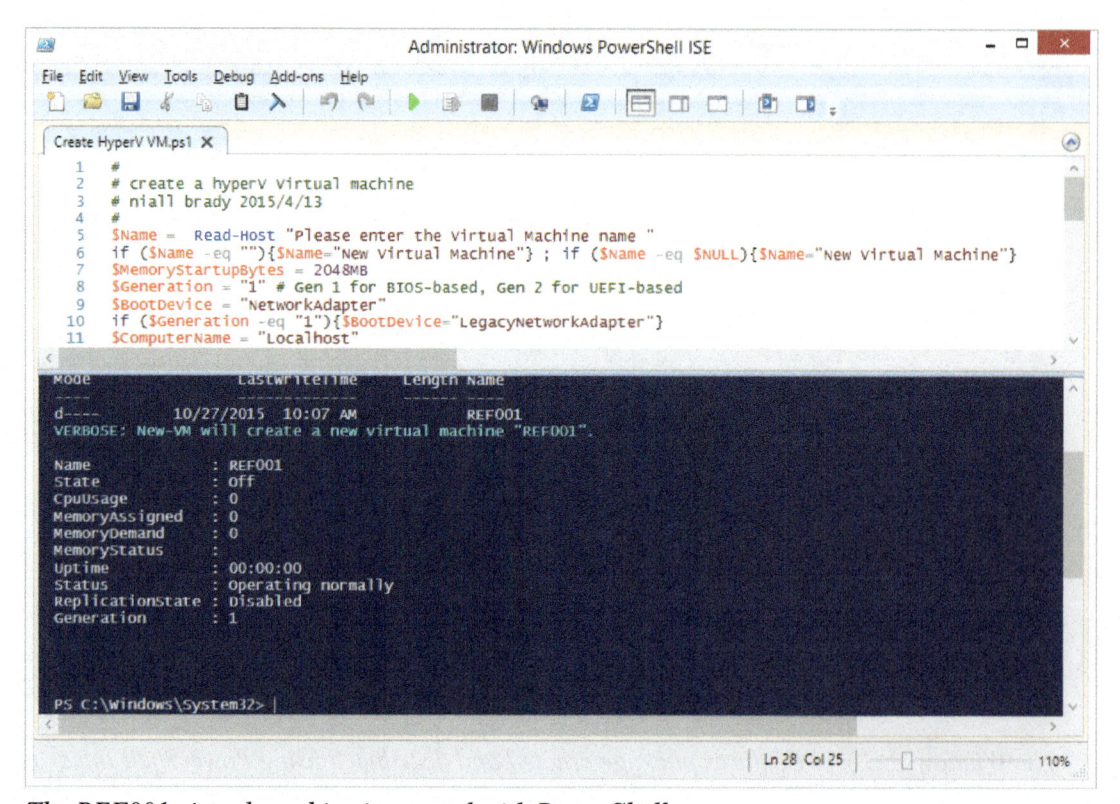

*The REF001 virtual machine is created with PowerShell.*

110

## Import a Computer into ConfigMgr Using PowerShell

After the new virtual machine (REF001) is created in the preceding guide, you import the MAC address and computer name of that virtual machine into ConfigMgr and, as part of that process, add it to the All Systems collection.

1. On **CM01**, browse to the **E:\Setup\Scripts** folder and locate the **Import Computer into ConfigMgr.ps1** script. Open the script in **Windows PowerShell ISE**.

2. Modify the **$MacAddress** variable to match the MAC address of the newly created virtual machine.

> **Note:** Depending on the VM configuration, you may have to start the VM to get a MAC address associated with it. In Hyper-V, you can use the Get-VMNetworkAdapter -VMName REF001 command to retrieve the MAC address.

3. Run the script by clicking the green **Run Script** button or pressing **F5** in Windows PowerShell ISE.

4. After a couple of minutes, on **CM01**, using the **ConfigMgr console**, in the **Assets and Compliance** workspace, select **Device Collections**, and then double-click **All Systems**. The contents of All Systems are presented. Press **F5** to refresh the view, and **REF001** machine should appear.

5. Right-click the collection called **OSD Limiting** and select **Update Membership**. The **REF001** machine should appear there as well.

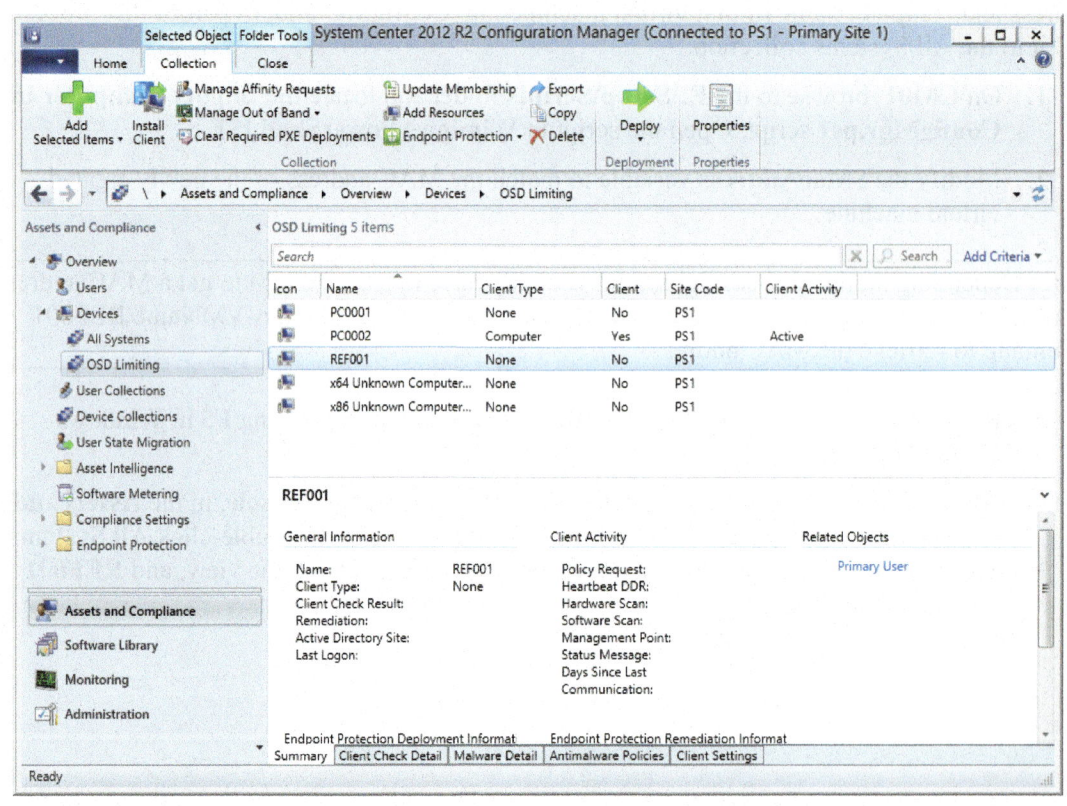

*The imported REF001 machine added to the OSD Limiting collection.*

# Patching the Image with Windows Updates

To keep your Windows 8.1 Enterprise x64 reference image patched with the latest security updates from Microsoft, you first need to decide how often you capture the reference image. If you do it too often, it increases the workload and may even introduce issues with other software or Windows itself due to unanticipated problems with one or more updates. If you wait too long, the operating system eventually becomes vulnerable to attack and, in addition, delivers a bad user experience because the operating system will start downloading updates as soon as the user logs in.

The schedule for reference image creation dictates how often you patch the image, and because of the reasons already mentioned, it's common that people use a cadence of once a quarter to create a reference image.

When you've decided the schedule, you create a software update group containing software updates for the Windows 8.1 operating system and decide which of those updates are suitable to apply; for example, some updates are known to cause a double reboot and that causes task sequences to fail. These types of updates should be removed from the software update group.

> **Real World Note**: Microsoft keeps a list of these troublesome updates at the following address: https://support.microsoft.com/en-us/kb/2894518. You should review the list and take heed of the advice to remove these updates from your OSD task sequences and apply these updates only via the normal software updates process in ConfigMgr.

After deciding which updates to keep, you need to deploy that software update group to the OSD Build collection. This means that during the build and capture process, updates that are included in the software update group are made available for installation in the Install Software Updates action of the task sequence, and this is how you'll patch your reference image.

## Create a Software Updates Group

To prepare a selection of Windows Updates, you need to set certain criteria in order to get the updates you want bundled together in a software update group.

1. On **CM01**, in the **Software Library** workspace, select **Software Updates / All Software Updates**.
2. In the top-right corner of the **All Software Updates** window, select **Add Criteria** and then set the following options from the available choices. When you are done, click the **Search** button.
    - Product: **Windows 8.1**
    - Expired: **No**
    - Superseded: **No**

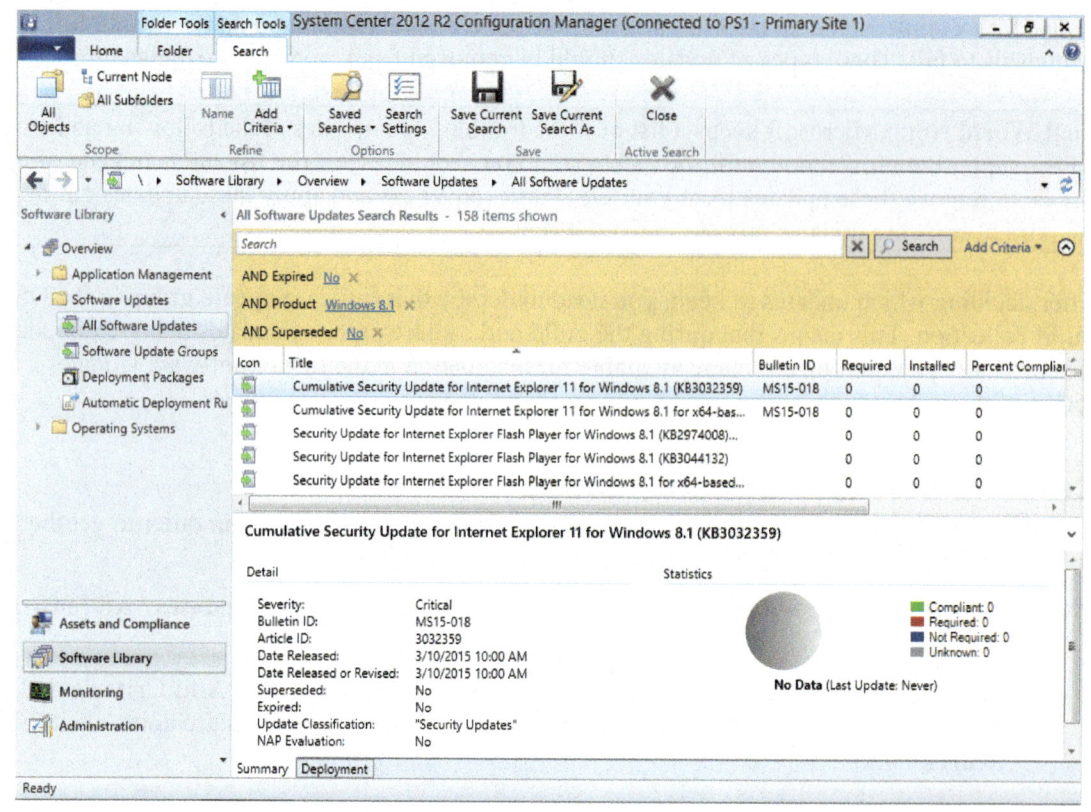

Chapter 4   Building a Reference Image of Windows 8.1

*The Windows 8.1 software updates search criteria.*

3. Select all updates listed by pressing **Ctrl + A**. Then right-click and choose **Create Software Update Group**. Use the following settings in the **Create Software Update Group** window:

    o   Name: **Windows Updates for OSD - W81x64**

    o   Description: **<default>**

## Decide Which Updates to Keep

It's important to remove any updates that can cause a double reboot as those updates will break the task sequence engine. In addition, you may want to remove updates that change core features of the operating system, such as a new Internet Explorer version that might not be compatible with an internal web-based application in your company. To decide which updates to keep, follow this process:

1. On **CM01**, in the **Software Library** workspace, select **Software Update Groups**.

2. Select the **Windows Updates for OSD - W81x64** software update group, right-click, and choose **Show Members**.

3. Using the **Search** field, type the Microsoft Knowledge Base (KB) number of each update from the list of updates mentioned in the preceding section. At the time of writing, the list contains the following updates:

   - **3036493.** MS15-030: Description of the security update for Remote Desktop protocol: March 10, 2015
   - **3039976.** MS15-030: Vulnerability in Remote Desktop protocol could allow denial of service: March 10, 2015
   - **2984976.** RDP 8.0 update for restricted administration on Windows 7 or Windows Server 2008 R2
   - **2981685.** Security updates cannot be installed if BitLocker is not installed on your computer
   - **2966034.** MS14-030: Description of the security update for Remote Desktop Security Release for Windows 8.1 systems that do not have the 2919355 update installed: June 10, 2014
   - **2965788.** MS14-030: Description of the security update for Remote Desktop Security Release for Windows: June 10, 2014
   - **2920189.** Description of the update rollup of revoked noncompliant UEFI modules: May 13, 2014
   - **2871777.** A servicing stack update is available for Windows RT, Windows 8, and Windows Server 2012: September 2013
   - **2871690.** Microsoft security advisory: Update to revoke noncompliant UEFI boot loader modules
   - **2862330.** MS13-081: Description of the security update for USB drivers: October 8, 2013
   - **2771431.** A servicing stack update is available for Windows 8 and Windows Server 2012
   - **2821895.** A servicing stack update is available for Windows RT and Windows 8: June 2013
   - **2545698.** Text in some core fonts appears blurred in Internet Explorer 9 on a computer that is running Windows Vista, Windows Server 2008, Windows 7, or Windows Server 2008 R2
   - **2529073.** Binary files in some USB drivers are not updated after you install Windows 7 SP1 or Windows Server 2008 R2 SP1

4. In the **Windows Updates for OSD - W81x64 results** field, select all updates that were found, right-click, and choose **Edit Membership**.

5. In the **Edit Membership** window that appears, clear the check box for the **Windows Updates for OSD – W81x64** software update group. This action removes those updates from the chosen software update group and means that they will not be deployed during OSD.

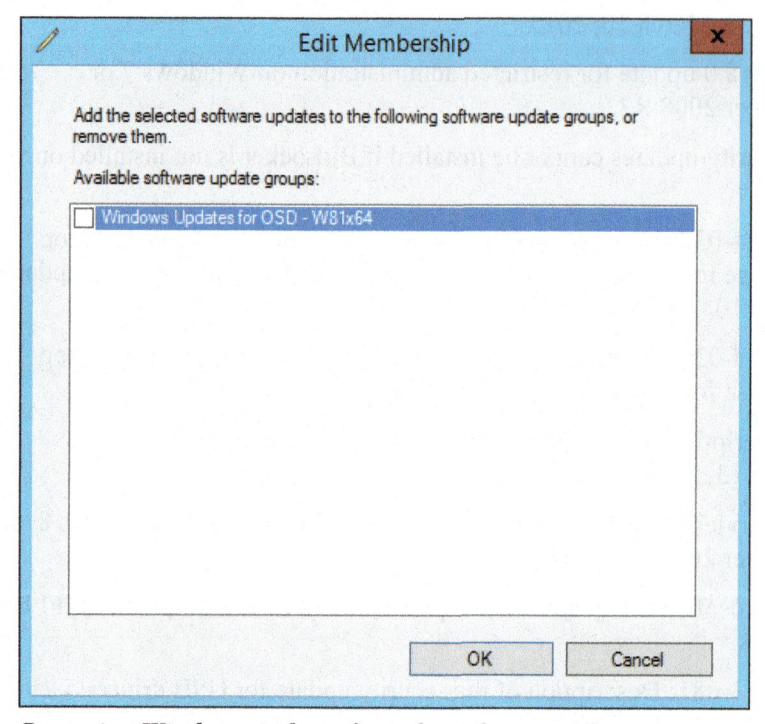

*Removing Windows updates from the software update group.*

6. Repeat the process for any updates you deem necessary to remove. In addition, scroll through the list of updates and decide whether any of them does not meet your company requirements (for example, a new Internet Explorer version).

## Deploy the Software Update Group

After you've decided which updates to keep, it is time to deploy them to the OSD Build collection. This process not only downloads the updates from the Internet, it also places them in a software update package and makes them available for installation to the build and capture process. To deploy the Windows Updates for OSD - W81x64 software update group, follow this process carefully:

1. On **CM01**, using **File Explorer**, create the following folders:
   - **E:\Sources\Updates**
   - **E:\Sources\Updates\Windows Updates for OSD - W81x64**

2. Using the **ConfigMgr console**, in the **Software Library** workspace, select **Software Update Groups**, select the **Windows Updates for OSD - W81x64** software update group, right-click it, and choose **Deploy**.

3. Use the following settings for the **Deploy Software Updates Wizard**:
   a. General
      - Deployment Name: **Windows Updates for OSD - W81x64**
      - Description: **<default>**
      - Select Deployment Template: **<none>**
      - Collection: **OSD Build**
   b. Deployment Settings
      - Type of Deployment: **<default>**
      - Use Wake-on-LAN to wake up clients for required deployments: **<default>**
      - Detail Level: **<default>**
   c. Scheduling
      - Time Based on: **<default>**
      - Software available time: **<default>**
      - Installation deadline: **As Soon as Possible**
   d. User Experience
      - User notifications: **<default>**
      - Deadline behavior
        - Software updates installation: **<Selected>**
        - System restart (if necessary): **<default>**

- Device restart behavior
  - Servers: **<default>**
  - Workstations: **<default>**
- Write filter handling for Windows Embedded devices
  Commit changes at deadline…: **<default>**

e. Alerts
  - Generate an alert when the following conditions are met: **<default>**
  - Disable Operations Manager alerts while…: **<default>**
  - Generate Operation Manager alert when…: **<default>**

f. Download Settings
  - Deployment options: **Download software updates from distribution point and install**
  - Deployment options: **<default>**
  - Allow clients to share content…: **<default>**
  - If software updates are not available on preferred…: **<default>**
  - Allow clients on a metered Internet connection…: **<default>**

g. Deployment Package
  - Name: **Windows Updates for OSD - W81x64**
  - Description: **<default>**
  - Package source: **\\CM01\sources\Updates\Windows Updates for OSD - W81x64**
  - Sending Priority: **<default>**

h. Distribution Points

  Select **Add**, select **Distribution Point** from the drop-down list, and select the **CM01.CORP.VIAMONSTRA.COM** distribution point.

i. Download Location

  Download software updates from the Internet: **<default>**

j. Language Selection

  Specify the languages of the updates: **English**

k. Summary: **<default>**

l. Progress: **<default>**

m. Completion: **<default>**

4. When the deployment completes without errors, verify that the deployment package has distributed to the distribution point before continuing by checking for Stat Msg 2301 for the package ID in distmgr.log as shown in the figure.

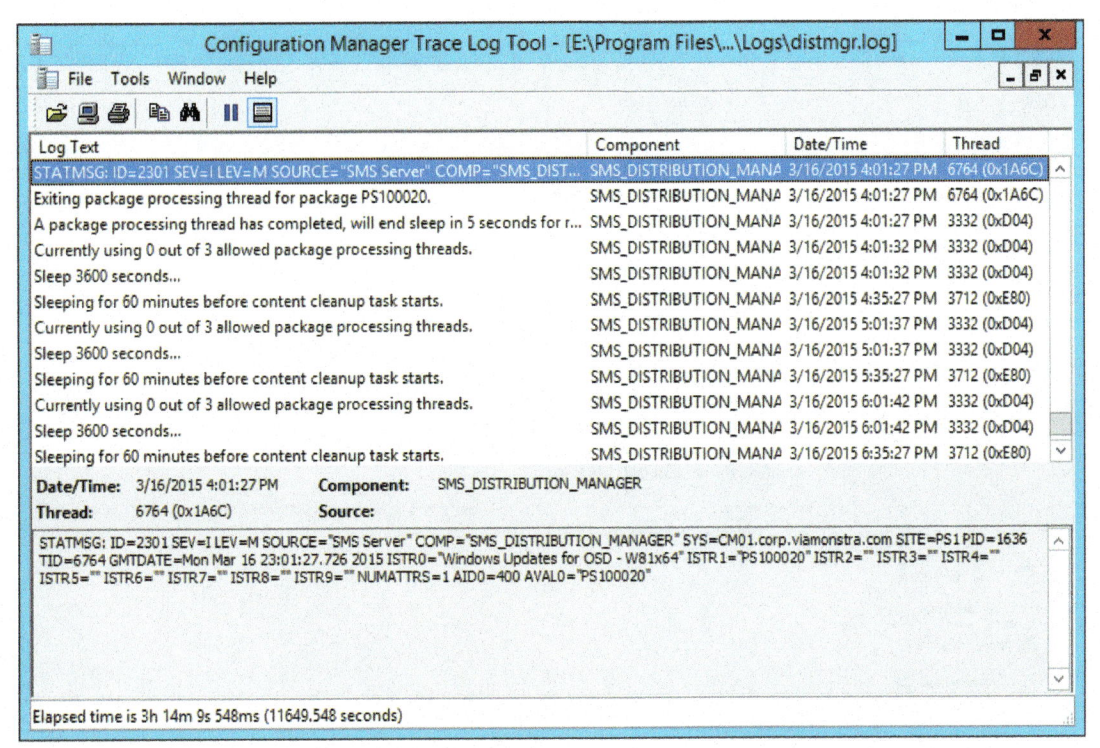

*Look for ID=2301 for the Windows Updates for OSD - W81x64 deployment package*

**Real World Note**: After completing the deployment, the Windows Updates are downloaded to the source specified, and you can view that folder filling up with updates as the wizard progresses to 100 percent. The SMS Provider computer account and the user that is running the wizard to download the software updates must both have Write NTFS permissions on the download location. You should restrict access to that location so that no one can tamper with the software update files.

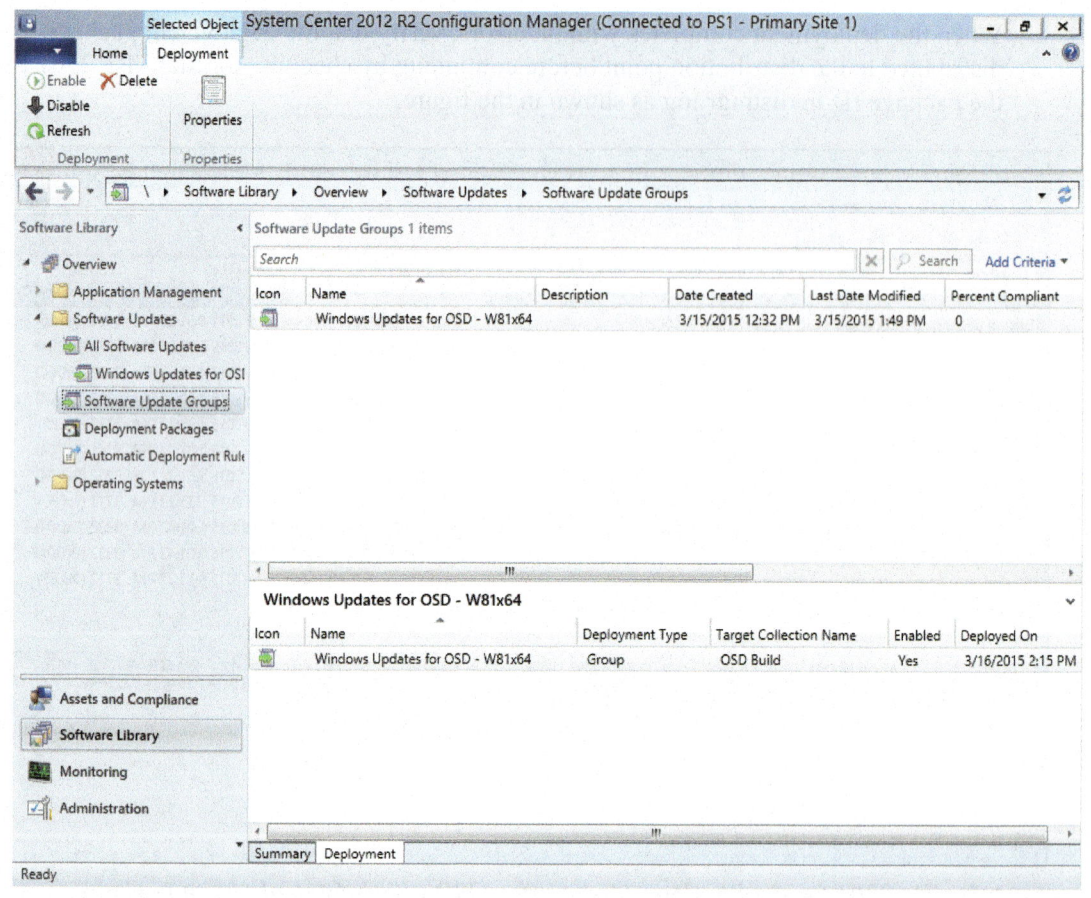

*The Windows Updates for OSD software update group deployed to the OSD Build collection.*

## The Build-and-Capture Process in a Nutshell

The term *build and capture* refers to the process of building an operating system image and then capturing it. The ConfigMgr-created build-and-capture task sequence can be configured to build a reference image and then capture it, all fully automated. The captured image can then be deployed in a separate task sequence.

A build-and-capture task sequence is normally used to create a custom operating system image (WIM file) containing the chosen operating system complete with the latest Windows updates for that OS and occasionally some key applications used in your organization. Those applications would normally be referred to as fat applications as they are usually large in size (for example, Office 365). Having large applications like this baked into the image can cut down on install times later on, but adds to the complexity of updating that software moving forward.

Creating a custom WIM file using a build-and-capture task sequence does allow for greater flexibility and reduced installation time; however, you may have to update this reference image once every quarter or so to include updates for any installed applications and, of course, to keep the image current with the latest Windows Updates.

The image generated by this process can be used in a separate deploy task sequence, and in that task sequence, you can have several custom Apply Driver Package actions to install drivers for various hardware in addition to adding smaller applications and customizations.

## Create a Build-and-Capture Task Sequence

You can create task sequences in ConfigMgr using the wizards built into the console, or via PowerShell cmdlets. To create a build-and-capture task sequence in ConfigMgr using the console, follow this procedure:

1. On **CM01**, using the **ConfigMgr console**, in the **Software Library** workspace, select **Operating Systems / Task Sequences**.
2. Right-click **Task Sequences**, choose **Create Task Sequence**, and use the following settings for the **Create Task Sequence Wizard**:
   a. Create a New Task Sequence
   
      Select a new task sequence to be created: **Build and capture a reference operating system image**
   
   b. Task Sequence Information
      - Name: **Build Windows 8.1 Enterprise x64**
      - Description: **ConfigMgr build and capture task sequence**
      - Boot image: **Boot image (x64) 6.3.9600.16384 en-US**
   
   c. Install Windows
      - Image package: **Windows 8.1 Enterprise x64**
      - Image: **1 – Windows 8.1 Enterprise**
      - Product key: **<leave blank>**
      - Server licensing mode: **<default>**
      - **Enable the account and specify the local administrator password**
         - Password: **P@ssw0rd**
         - Confirm password: **P@ssw0rd**
   
   d. Configure Network
      - Select the domain or workgroup to join: **Join a workgroup**
         
         Workgroup: **workgroup**
      - Specify the account that has permission to join the domain
         
         Account: **<leave blank>**

Chapter 4   Building a Reference Image of Windows 8.1

e. Install ConfigMgr
   - Package: **<default>**
   - Installation Properties: **SMSMP=CM01.corp.viamonstra.com**

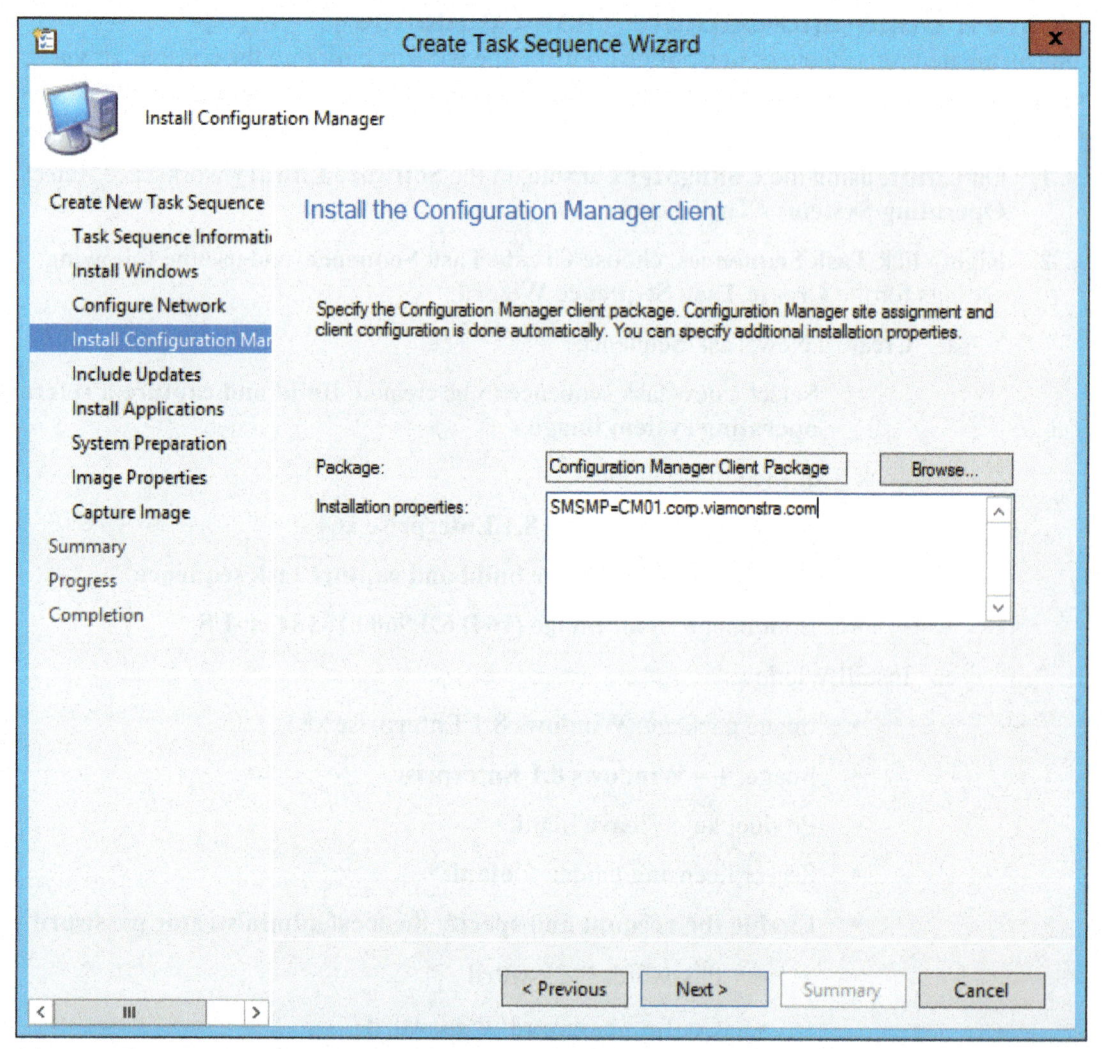

*The installation properties of the ConfigMgr client package.*

f. Include Updates

   **<All software updates>**

g. Install applications

   Select the applications to install with this operating system image: **<default>**

122

Chapter 4   Building a Reference Image of Windows 8.1

    h. System Preparation

        **<default>**

    i. Image Properties

- Created by: **Administrator**
- Version: **<YYMMDD>**
- Description: **Windows 8.1 Enterprise x64 with Windows Updates**

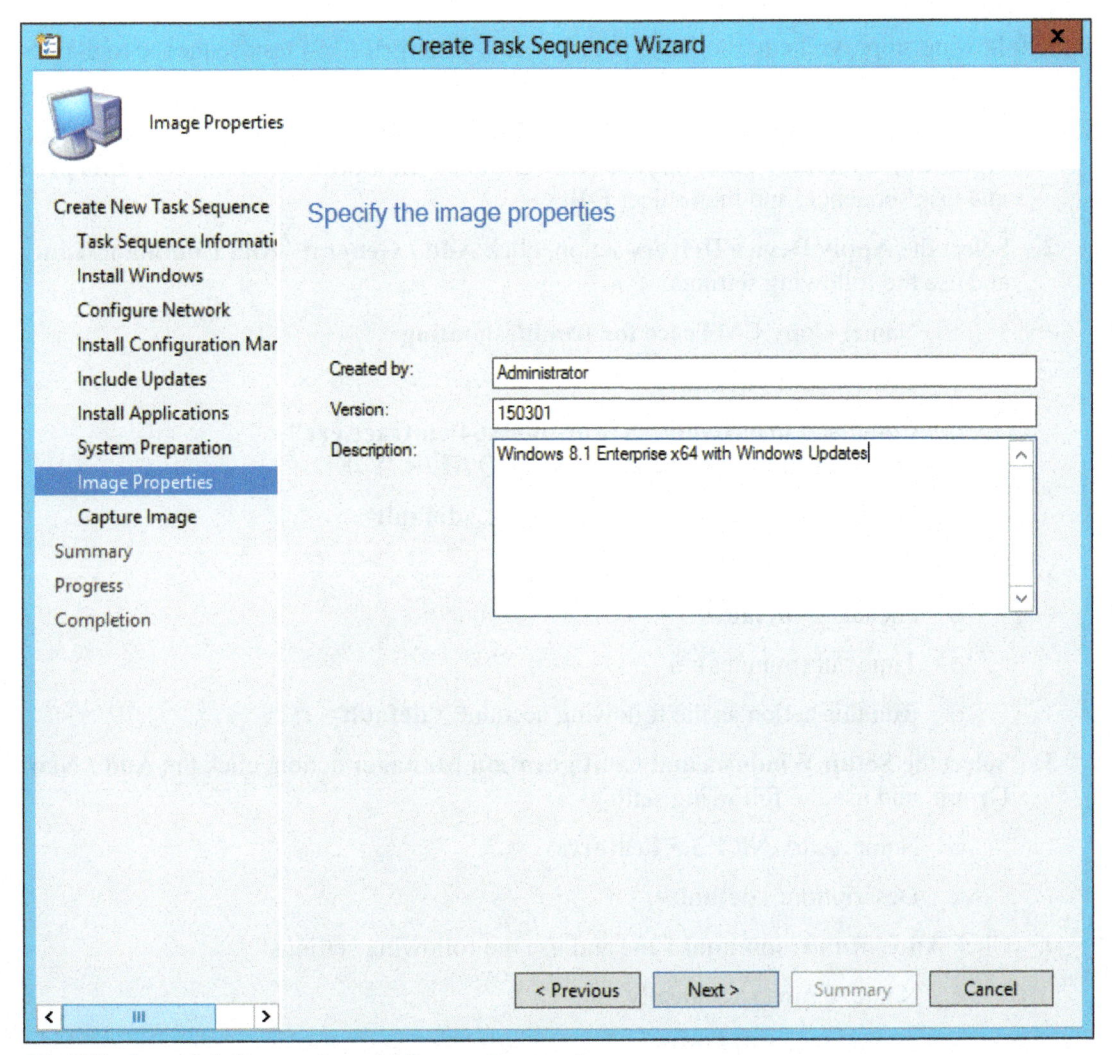

*The Windows 8.1 Enterprise x64 Image Properties.*

j. Capture Image

- Path: **\\CM01\Captures$\W81_150301.wim**
- Account:
  - UserName: **VIAMONSTRA\CM_BA**
  - Password: **P@ssw0rd**

## Edit the Task Sequence

In the following steps, you edit the Build Windows 8.1 Enterprise x64 task sequence to the OSD Build collection:

1. On **CM01**, using the **ConfigMgr console**, in the **Software Library** workspace, select **Operating Systems / Task Sequences**, right-click the **Build Windows 8.1 Enterprise x64** task sequence, and then select **Edit**.

2. Select the **Apply Device Drivers** action, click **Add / General / Run Command Line**, and use the following settings:
   - Name: **Copy CMTrace for troubleshooting**
   - Description: **<default>**
   - Command line: **xcopy "X:\sms\bin\x64\cmtrace.exe" "C:\Windows\System32" /E /C /I /Q /H /R /Y /S**
   - Disable 64-bit file system redirection: **<default>**
   - Start in: **<default>**
   - Package: **<default>**
   - Time out (minutes): **5**
   - Run this action as the following account: **<default>**

3. Select the **Setup Windows and Configuration Manager** action, click the **Add / New Group**, and use the following settings:
   - Name: **Add .NET 3.5 Features**
   - Description: **<default>**

4. Click **Add / Run Command Line** and use the following settings:
   - Name: **Copy SXS locally**
   - Description: **<default>**
   - Command line:
     **xcopy ".\*.*" "C:\Windows\Temp\" /D /E /C /I /Q /H /R /Y /S**
   - Disable 64-bit file system redirection: **<default>**

Chapter 4   Building a Reference Image of Windows 8.1

- Start in: **<default>**
- Package: **Windows 8.1 x64 Features**
- Time out (minutes): **5**
- Run this step as the following account: **<default>**

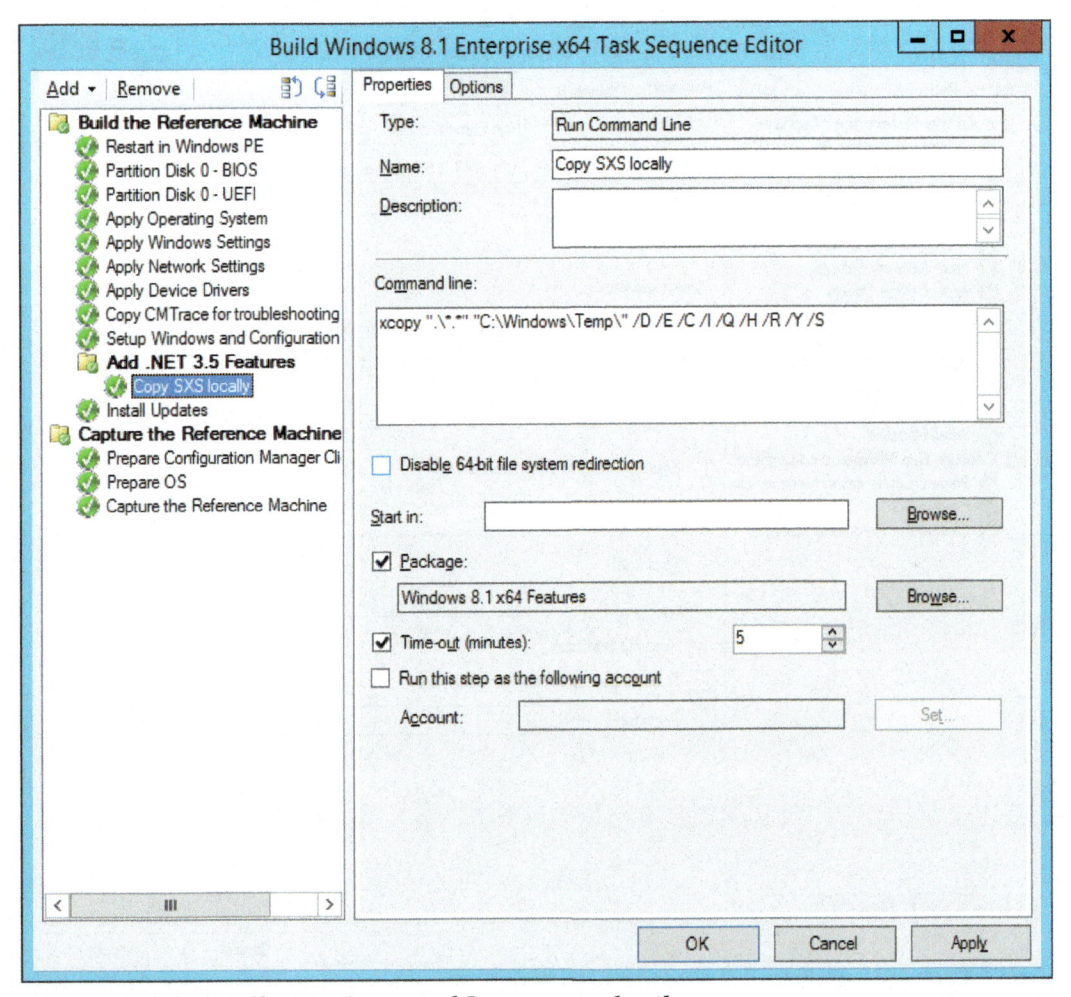

*The xcopy SXS locally Run Command Line step in detail*

5. Click **Add / Run Command Line** and use the following settings:

    - Name: **Add .NET 3.5 Features using dism**
    - Description: **<default>**
    - Command line: **dism.exe /Online /Enable-Feature /FeatureName:NetFx3 /all /limitaccess /source:C:\Windows\Temp\SXS**
    - Disable 64-bit file system redirection: **<default>**

125

Chapter 4   Building a Reference Image of Windows 8.1

- o   Start in: **<default>**
- o   Package: **<default>**
- o   Time out (minutes): **5**
- o   Run this step as the following account: **<default>**

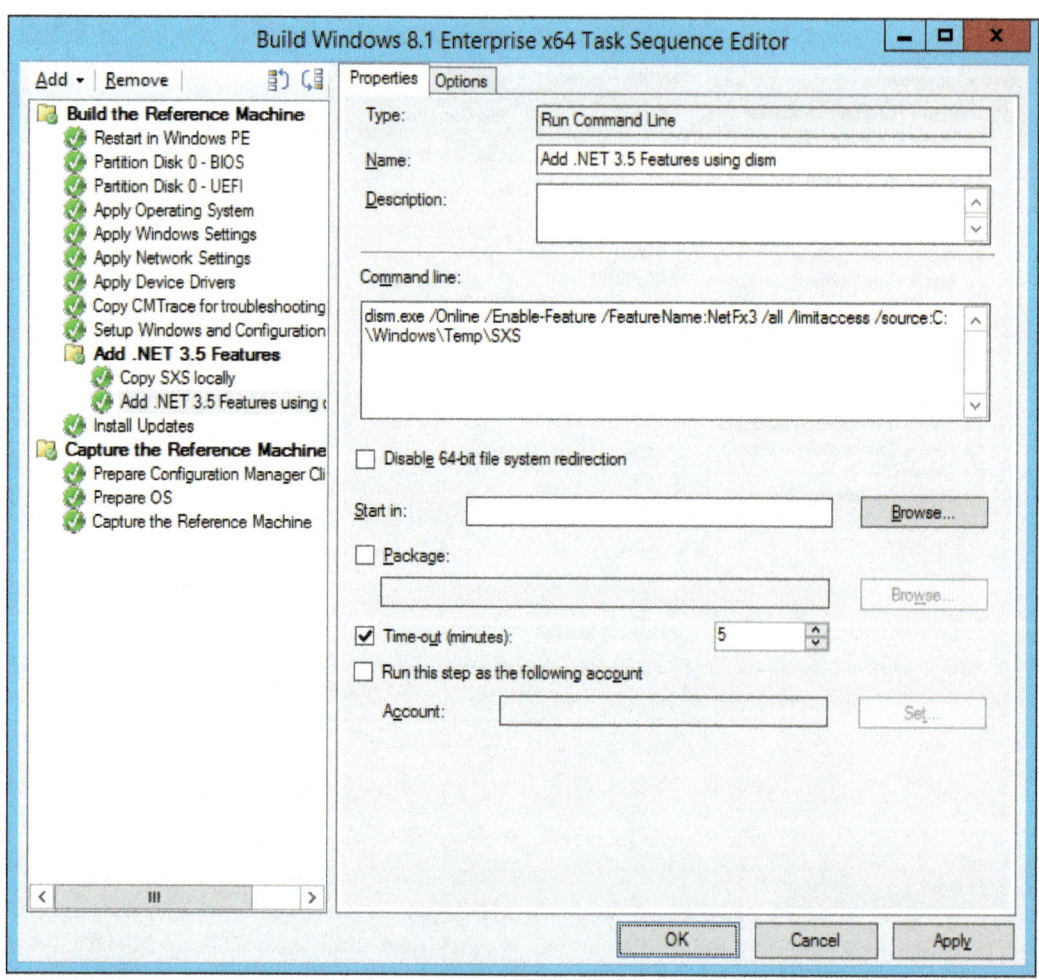

*Adding the .NET 3.5 features using DISM.*

6.  Select the **Install Updates** step, click the **Add / General / Install Application**.

7.  In the **Install Application** window, click the **yellow asterisk** button to add an application and use the following settings:

    - o   Name: **Install Applications**

Chapter 4   Building a Reference Image of Windows 8.1

- o   Install the following applications:
    - **7-Zip 9.20 (x64 edition)**
    - **Firefox**
    - **Office 365**
- o   Select **If an application fails, continue installing other applications in the list**
8. Click **OK**.

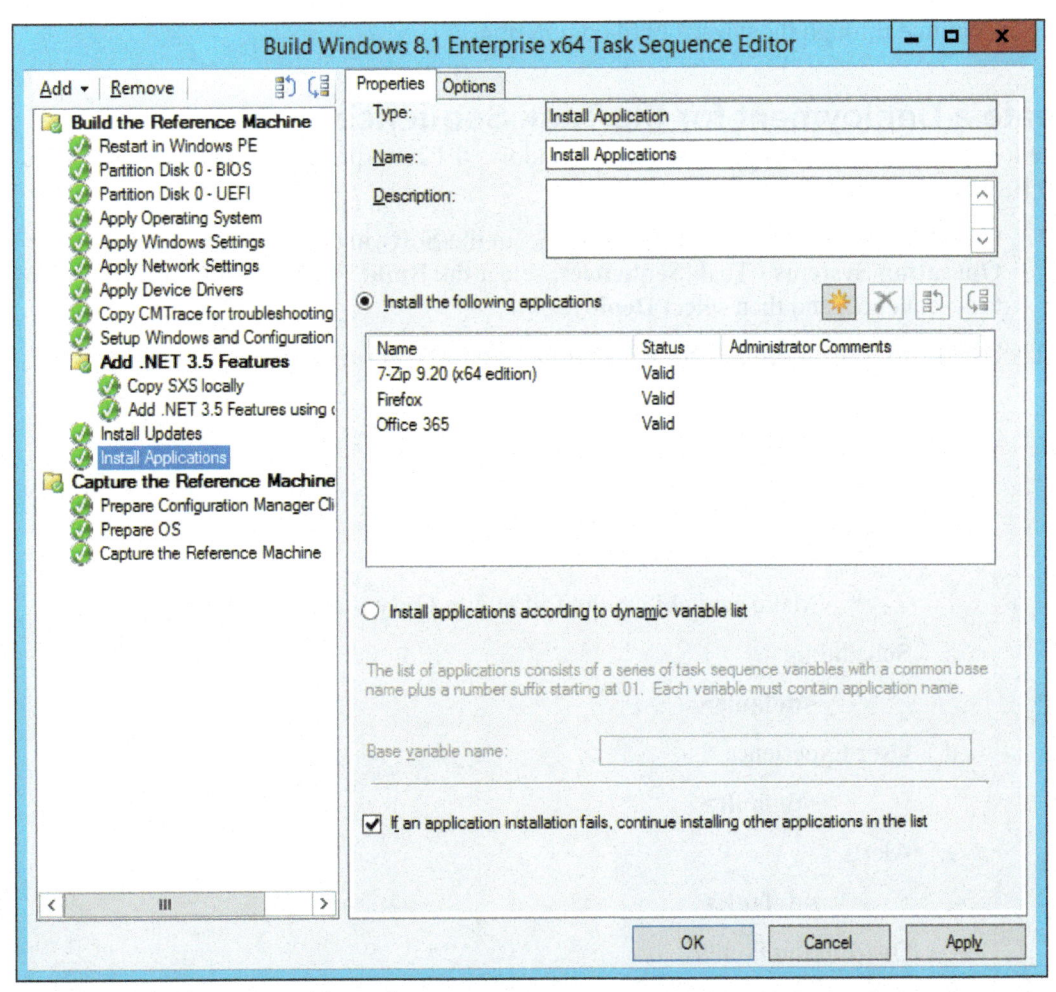

*Installing applications in the task sequence.*

## Distribute the Default x64 Boot Image

In the ConfigMgr console, distribute the default x64 boot image by doing as follows:

1. On **CM01**, using the **ConfigMgr console**, expand the **Software Library** workspace and select **Operating Systems / Boot Images**.

2. Right-click the **Boot image (x64)** boot image and choose **Distribute content**. Use the following setting for the **Distribute Content Wizard**:

    Content Destination: **CM01.CORP.VIAMONSTRA.COM**

3. Continue through the wizard until completion.

## Create a Deployment for the Task Sequence

In the following steps, you deploy the Build Windows 8.1 Enterprise x64 task sequence to the OSD Build collection:

1. On **CM01**, using the **ConfigMgr console**, in the **Software Library** workspace, select **Operating Systems / Task Sequences**, select the **Build Windows 8.1 Enterprise x64** task sequence, and then select **Deploy**.

2. Use the following settings for the **Deploy Software Wizard**:

    a. General

        Collection: **OSD Build**

    b. Deployment Settings

    - Purpose: **Available**
    - Make available to the following: **Only media and PXE**

    c. Scheduling

        **<default>**

    d. User Experience

        **<default>**

    e. Alerts

        **<default>**

    f. Distribution Points

        **<default>**

## Start the Task Sequence

The preceding steps get everything in place for the actual build-and-capture process. Now all that's needed to start the ball rolling is to PXE-boot the client computer REF001. To start that process, follow these instructions:

1. Power on **REF001** and when prompted, press **F12** for network boot service.
2. When the **Task Sequence Wizard** PXE password screen appears, enter **P@ssw0rd** and click **Next**.
3. In the **Select a task sequence to run** list of task sequences, select **Build Windows 8.1 x64 Enterprise**, and click **Next**.

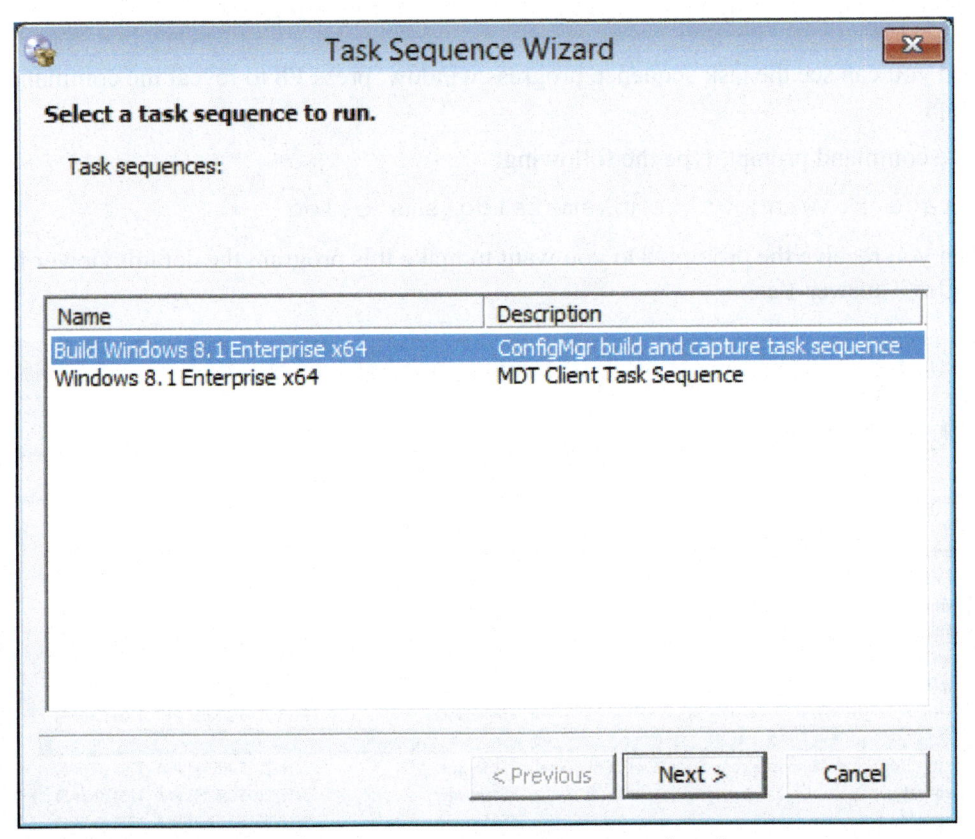

*The Build Windows 8.1 Enterprise x64 task sequence is listed.*

Once started, the task sequence formats the hard disk and begins to process its individual steps sequentially.

# Monitoring the Task Sequence Progress

As you are creating a reference image, it's a good idea to monitor the deployment by reviewing the deployment logs using CMTrace throughout the lifetime of the task sequence, especially after it has rebooted into Windows. To monitor the progress of the build-and-capture deployment, use the procedures in the following sections.

## Monitor the Deployment in WinPE

To monitor the process during the WinPE phase, do as follows:

> **Note**: This assumes that you enabled command support in the boot image used.

1. When you can see the task sequence progress window, press **F8** to reveal the command prompt.

2. At the command prompt, type the following:
   ```
   Cmtrace x:\windows\temp\smstslog\smsts.log
   ```

3. When you receive the prompt "Do you want to make this program the default viewer for log files," answer **Yes**.

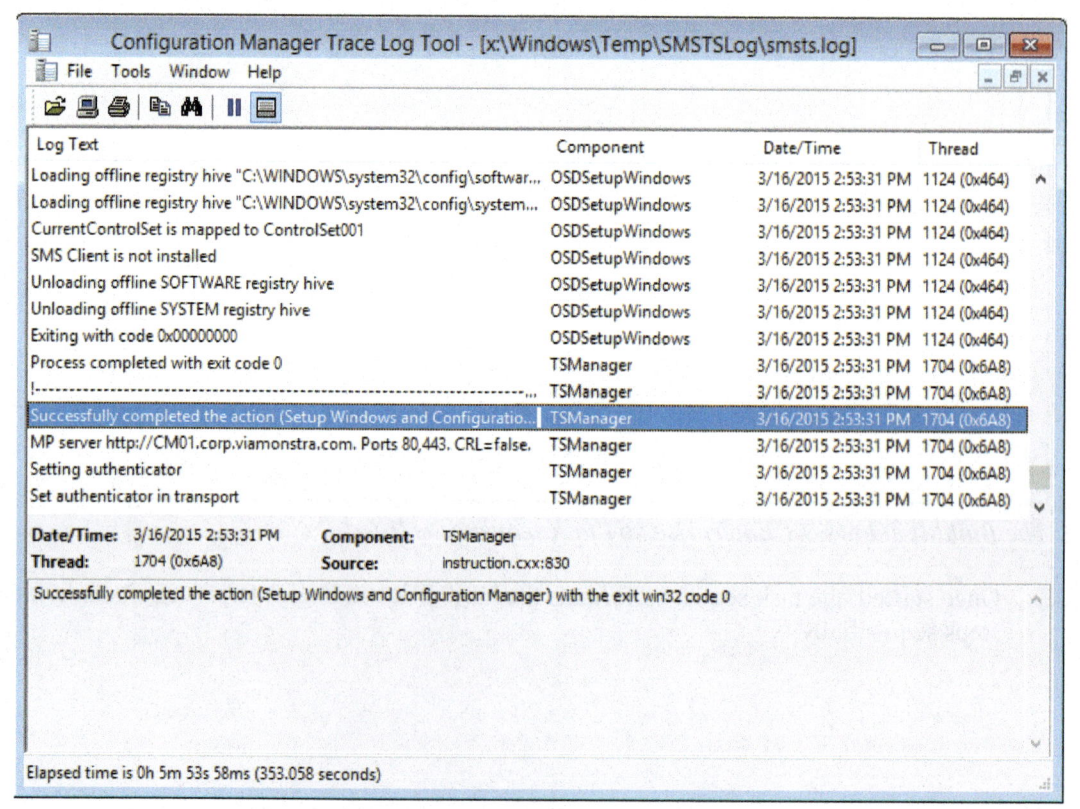

*Monitoring the smsts.log file in WinPE.*

4. When finished looking through the log, close CMTrace by clicking **File / Exit**.

5. At the command prompt, type **Exit** and press **Enter** to allow the task sequence to continue.

## Monitor the Deployment in Windows

To monitor the process during the Windows phase that occurs after the Setup Windows and ConfigMgr step reboots the computer, you need to be aware that the smsts.log file can be in a couple of locations based on whether the ConfigMgr client is installed and running:

- Before the ConfigMgr client is installed, you can locate the smsts.log file in C:\_SMSTaskSequence\Logs.

- After the ConfigMgr client is installed (and running), you can find the smsts.log file in C:\Windows\CCM\Logs\SMSTSLOG.

You can monitor the deployment with CMTrace as it happens while in Windows as follows:

1. When you can see the task sequence progress window, press **F8** to reveal the command prompt.

## Chapter 4   Building a Reference Image of Windows 8.1

2. At the command prompt, type one of the following commands depending on whether the client is installed:

    o   Client not installed:

    `cmtrace C:\_SMSTaskSequence\Logs\smsts.log`

    o   Client installed and running:

    `cmtrace C:\Windows\CCM\Logs\SMSTSLOG\smsts.log`

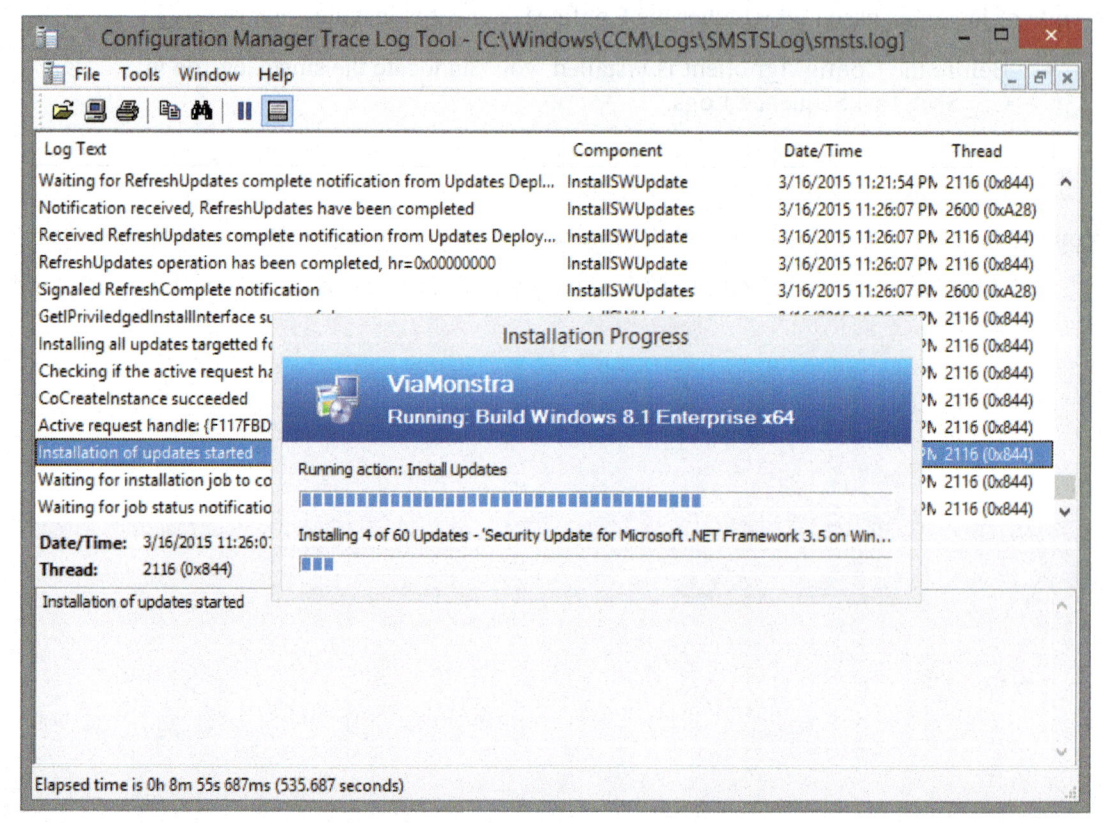

*Monitoring the smsts.log via CMTrace in Windows.*

Chapter 4  Building a Reference Image of Windows 8.1

3. In addition to the smsts.log file, you should review the following logs to keep track of the deployments progress:

    o   In **C:\Windows**, review the following file to view information about update installation and retrieval: **WindowsUpdate.log**.

    o   To review information about how the applications are installed, review the following log file in **C:\Windows\CCM\Logs\**: **Appenforce.log**.

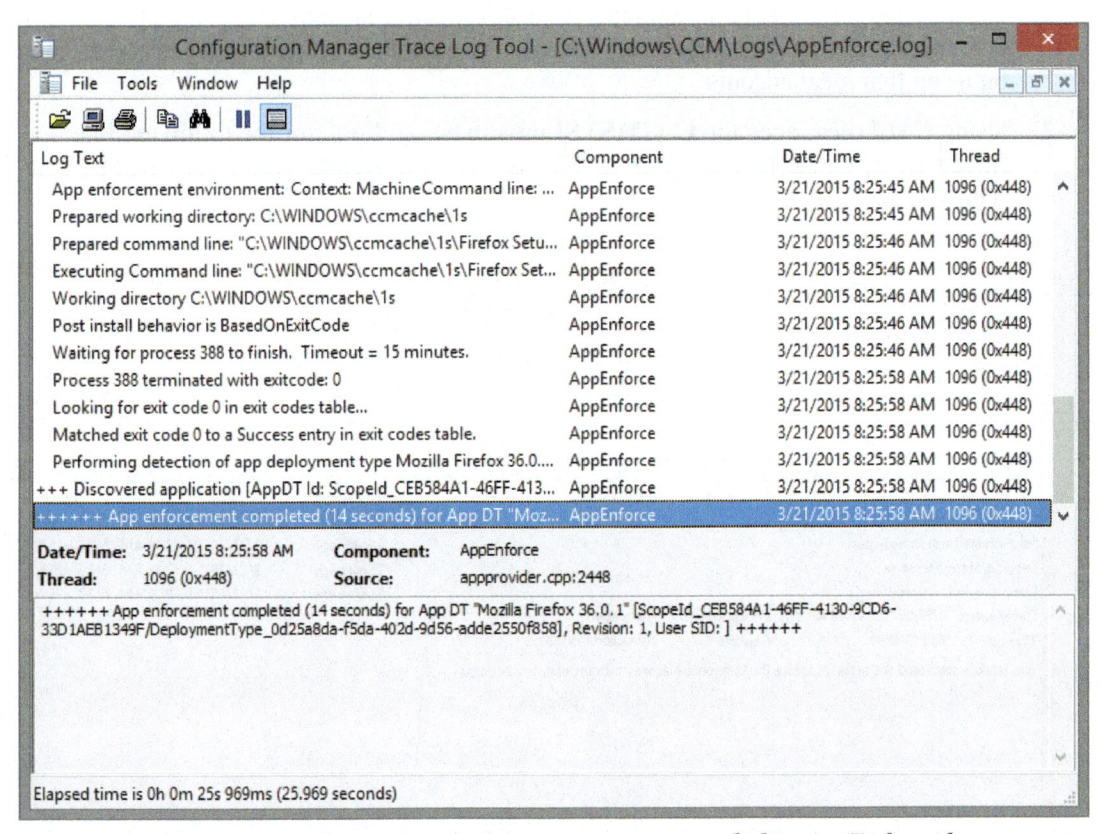

*The detection of the Mozilla Firefox deployment type as revealed in AppEnforce.log.*

133

# Verify the Capture Was Successful

To verify that the capture is complete, you once again turn to the smsts.log file for verification. To do so, proceed as follows:

> **Note:** You also can verify that the WIM file was created in the E:\Captures folder on CM01.

1. On **REF001**, after the build-and-capture task sequence is complete, complete the out-of-box experience (OOBE) phase and select to create a local account in the process. Then log on using that local account.

2. Using **CMTrace**, open the **C:\SMSTSLog\smsts.log**. Look for the following line: **Successfully completed the action (Capture the Reference Machine) with the exit win32 code 0**.

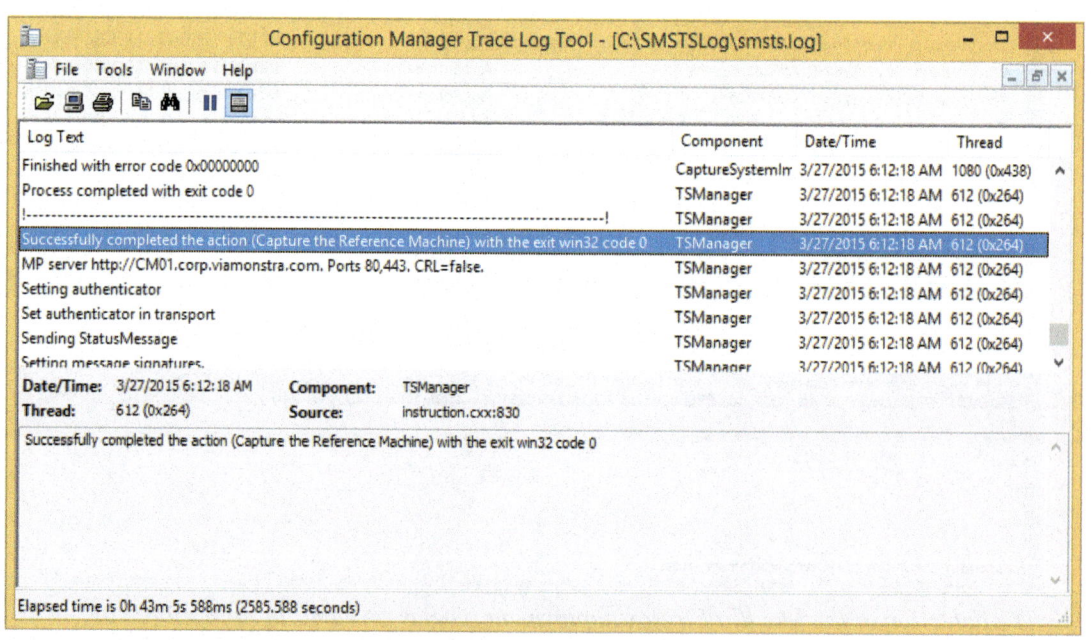

*The capture was successful according to the smsts.log file.*

# Chapter 5
# Deploying Windows 8.1 with a Custom Start Screen

In this chapter, you learn to customize the Windows 8.1 Start screen during deployment and deploy the Windows 8.1 reference image captured with ConfigMgr in the preceding chapter. That image not only contains the base operating system, but it also contains all applicable Windows updates available for Windows 8.1 up to the date when it was captured. In addition, you installed some core applications such as Office 365 for your organization.

You use that captured image to save time when deploying new computers with Windows 8.1 as the end result is quicker deployments (less time waiting for applications to install and less time waiting for Windows updates to install). In addition, you have a predictable, automated, professional, enterprise-ready experience for your end users. They will have a clean Start screen with only the approved applications and icons that you want appearing on the Start screen for your organization.

## Step-by-Step Guide Requirements
If you want to follow the step-by-step guides in this chapter, you need a lab environment configured as outlined in Chapter 2 and Appendix A. In this chapter, you use the following virtual machines:

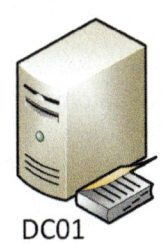

DC01   CM01   REF001   PC0004

*The VMs used in this chapter (PC0004 is a VM created in one of the guides).*

## Adding a Captured Reference Image
In the preceding chapter, you used ConfigMgr to build and capture a reference image of Windows 8.1 Enterprise x64. Now you add that image to ConfigMgr to make it available for use in an OSD task sequence. You add the captured image using a ConfigMgr PowerShell cmdlet called New-CMOperatingSystemImage.

## Copy the Image

Before you can use that cmdlet, though, you want to copy the captured reference image to your ConfigMgr OSD Operating System Images folder. To copy the captured image, follow this process:

1. On **CM01**, open **File Explorer** and browse to **E:\Captures**. The previously captured reference image (example: **W81_150301.wim**) should be there. Select the file and press **Ctrl + C** to copy it.

2. Using **File Explorer**, browse to **E:\Sources\OSD\OS\Operating System Images** and create the **Windows 8.1 Enterprise x64** subfolder.

3. In the **E:\Sources\OSD\OS\Operating System Images\Windows 8.1 Enterprise x64** folder press **Ctrl + V** to paste the captured image.

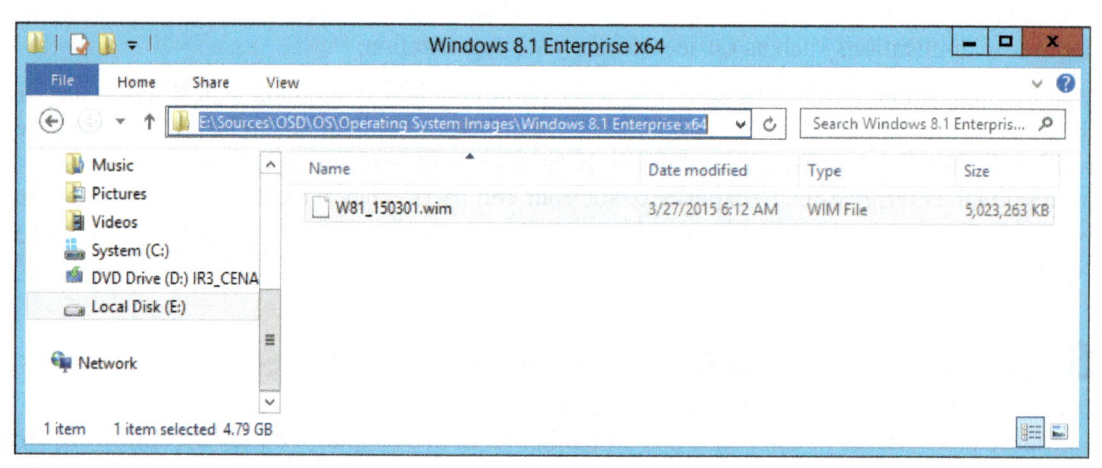

*The previously captured image is copied to its new destination.*

## Add Operating System Image Using PowerShell

As you learned in Chapter 4, there are hundreds of PowerShell cmdlets that help you to automate everyday tasks in ConfigMgr, and the Add Operating System Image step has a corresponding cmdlet for that called *New-CMOperatingSystemImage*.

1. On **CM01**, start an elevated **PowerShell prompt** (run as Administrator).

2. Connect to the **ConfigMgr PowerShell drive** by running the following command:

    `E:\Setup\Scripts\ConnectToConfigMgr.ps1`

3. Add the previously captured operating system image to ConfigMgr using PowerShell by running the following command:

    ```
    New-CMOperatingSystemImage
    -Name "Windows 8.1 Enterprise - 150301" -Path
    "\\CM01\Sources\OSD\OS\Operating System Images\Windows 8.1
    Enterprise x64\W81_150301.wim" -Version "x64"
    ```

## Distribute the Operating System Image Using PowerShell

To distribute the operating system image to the CM01 distribution point using PowerShell, do the following:

1. On **CM01**, start an elevated **PowerShell prompt** (run as Administrator).

2. Connect to the **ConfigMgr PowerShell drive** by running the following command:

   ```
   E:\Setup\Scripts\ConnectToConfigMgr.ps1
   ```

3. Add the previously captured operating system image to ConfigMgr using PowerShell by running the following command:

   ```
   Start-CMContentDistribution -OperatingSystemImageName
   "Windows 8.1 Enterprise - 150301" -DistributionPointName
   "CM01.corp.viamonstra.com"
   ```

> **Note**: The preceding two PowerShell commands have been merged together along with variables to make a script for doing both tasks. To view the script, refer to the script called "Create and distribute an operating system image.ps1" in E:\Setup\Scripts. This script uses variables so that you can customize it to easily add different operating system images with various versions and architectures.

# Customizing the Start Screen Using the *appsfolderlayout* Method

There are a few methods for customizing Start screens (such as Export-Layout documented on TechNet at https://technet.microsoft.com/en-us/%5Clibrary/dn283401%28v=wps.630%29.aspx). I recommend that you use whichever works best for your organization. The method covered in this section is referred to as the *appsfolderlayout* method as it involves copying a file with that name that applies the change to the every user profile when that profile is created for the first time during user logon. It also allows users to change their Start screen icon placement as they see fit.

To customize the Start screen, you of course need a Start screen to start with (oh, the irony). As you have previously used PC0002 to build and capture a reference image, that virtual machine should now be in a state ready to be used for this guide. Before making any changes to the virtual machine, take a snapshot of it (checkpoint) so that you can return to this point in time later if needed (for example if you want to change the Start screen layout).

> **Real World Note**: It's worthwhile taking some time thinking about the design and layout of the Start screen that is right for your organization, as it will be the Start screen that all users get by default. Providing them with too many tiles may be confusing; however, the converse is also true. If you remove too much stuff, they might not be able to find the application they are looking for.

It makes sense to customize the Start screen layout to suit the functionality of your organization, keeping it clean and simple also means that your users can find the apps they need to do their job effectively, faster. To customize the Start screen using the appsfolderlayout.bin file, follow the process outlined in this section.

## Enable the Administrator Account

1. On **REF001**, unless you already completed the out-of-box experience (OOBE) screens to set up a new user profile in the preceding chapter, please do that now.

2. Open an elevated **Command prompt** (run as Administrator) and type the following:

   ```
   net user administrator /active:yes
   ```

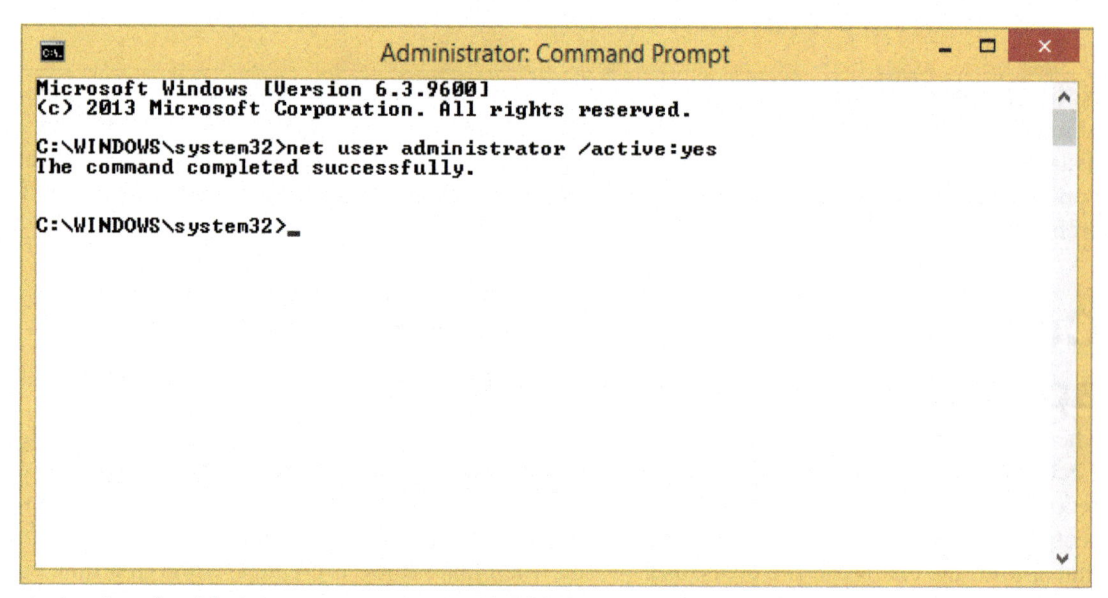

*Activating the Administrator account on PC0002.*

3. Sign out as the current user.

Chapter 5   Deploying Windows 8.1 with a Custom Start Screen

## Design a Custom Start Screen

1. On **REF001**, log in as **Administrator**. Review the default **Start screen** before any customization has taken place.

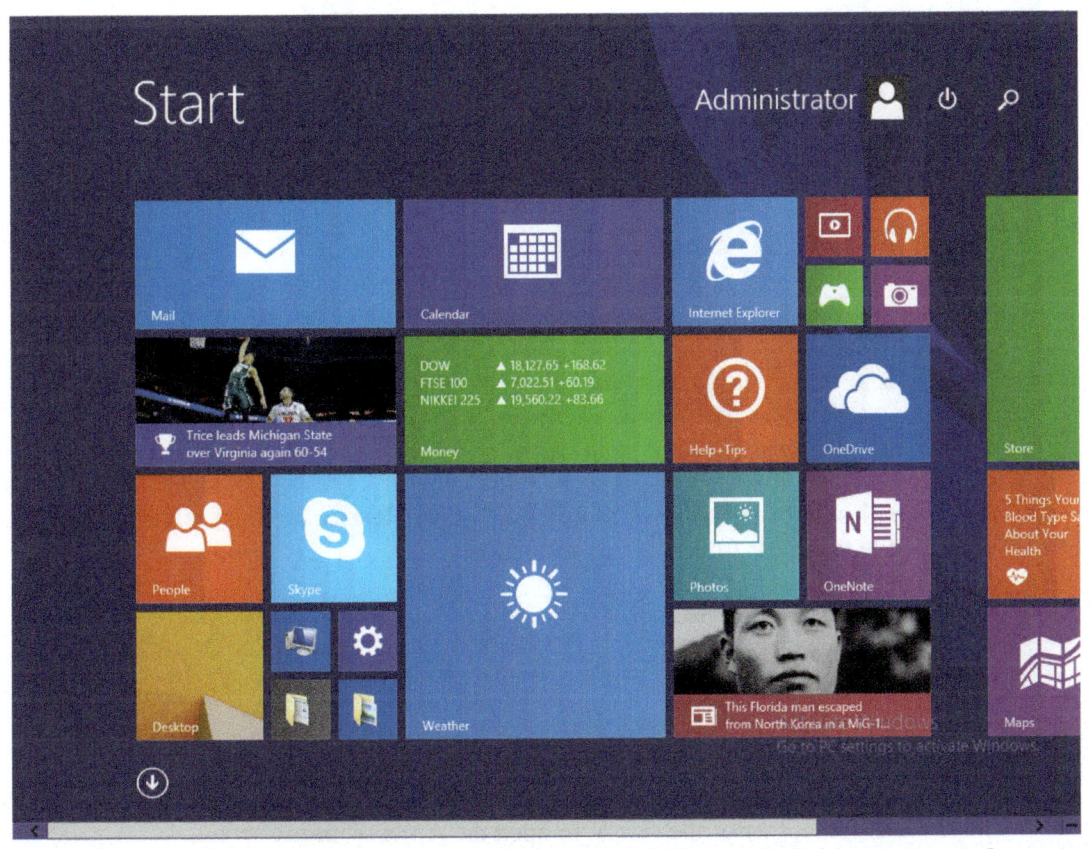

*The Start screen before any customization has occurred. Overcrowded comes to mind.*

2. Using your own preferences, remove any tiles that you don't want to appear in your captured image by right-clicking that tile and choosing **Unpin from Start**. You can select more than one tile by pressing and holding the **Ctrl** key as click additional tiles.

139

Chapter 5  Deploying Windows 8.1 with a Custom Start Screen

*Removing a tile by choosing Unpin from Start.*

3. To **resize** tiles, right-click one or more tiles, choose **Resize**, and then select the size you want the tile to appear from the following choices:

    Small

    Medium

    Wide

    Large

4. To add your enterprise apps to the customized **Start screen**, click the white down arrow in the lower left corner of the screen to open the **Apps by name** screen.

5. Using search or by scrolling through the list of apps, find **Mozilla Firefox** and **7Zip File Manager**. Hold down the **Ctrl** key and select both apps, and then right-click and select choose **Pin to Start**.

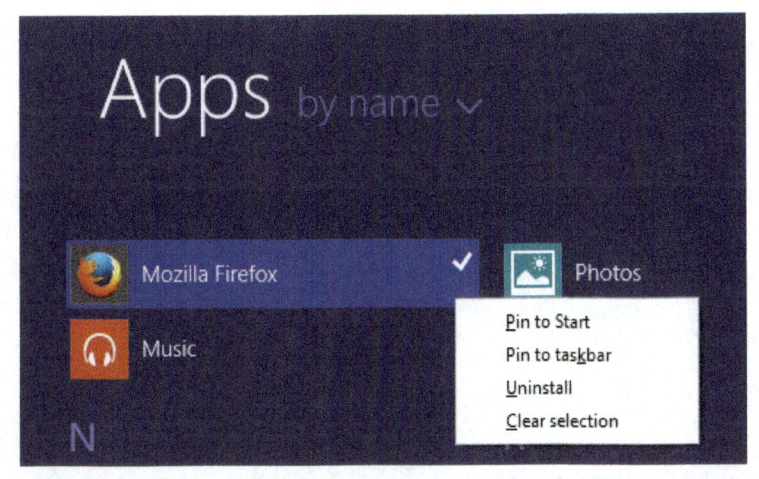

Chapter 5   Deploying Windows 8.1 with a Custom Start Screen

*Using Pin to Start to pin one or more apps to the Start screen.*

6. After you have your chosen tiles in place on the Start screen, you can click a tile and then drag it from one position on the Start screen to another. Repeat this process with the pinned tiles until you are happy with the overall layout.

7. When you are happy with the layout of tiles on the Start screen, create name groups by right-clicking above any group of tiles, selecting **Name groups**, and entering a name for each group, for example, **Office 365**.

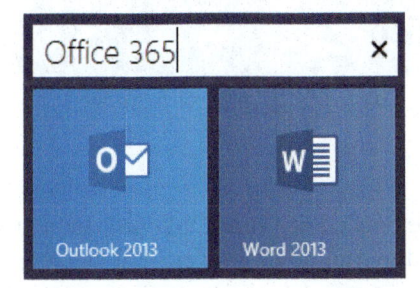

*Adding a custom name group.*

   After you have carefully added, removed, resized, pinned, and arranged your tiles and then created name groups, the finished Start screen is ready.

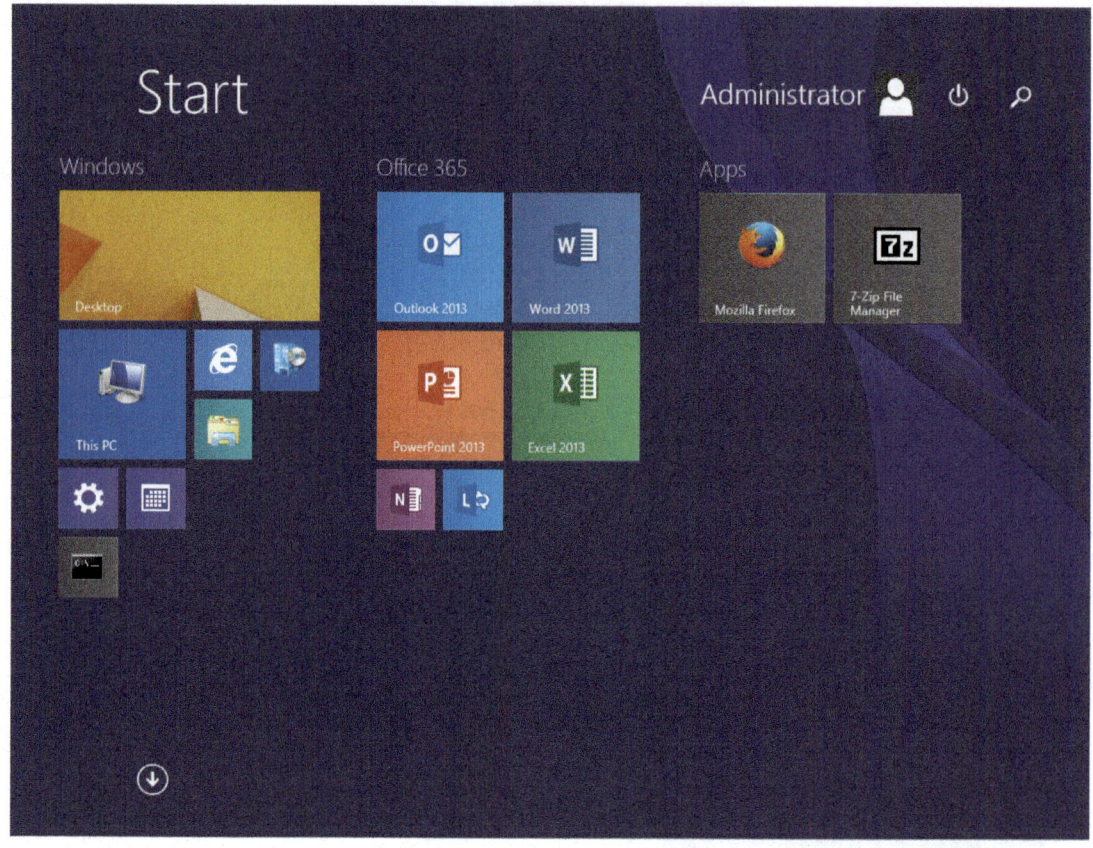

Chapter 5   Deploying Windows 8.1 with a Custom Start Screen

*The finished customized Start screen with custom name groups, clean and purposeful.*

## Export the Start Screen Layout

After customizing the Start screen, you need to create the file needed for your OSD task sequence, and that file is called *appsfolderlayout.bin*. The file is created by running a PowerShell cmdlet named Export-StartLayout.

> **Real World Note:** The appsfolderlayout.bin file can also be created by running the sysprep process on the machine, and then copy the file from the C:\Users\Administrator\Appdata\Local\Microsoft\Windows folder. But it's much easier to just use PowerShell.

1. On **REF001**, as **Administrator**, open an elevated PowerShell prompt (run as Administrator).

2. Export the Start screen layout by running the following command:

   ```
   Export-StartLayout -As Bin
   -Path C:\Windows\Temp\appsFolderLayout.bin
   ```

3. Copy the **C:\Windows\Temp\appsFolderLayout.bin** to **E:\Setup** on **CM01**.

142

## Create and Distribute a Package Using PowerShell

Now that you have the customized Start screen captured in a file, you need to create a package. To create a package, you could use the ConfigMgr console and use the Create Package wizard, or save time and use the Create and Distribute a Package.ps1 PowerShell script in Windows PowerShell ISE.

To create and then distribute the Windows 8.1 x64 Start Screen package, do as follows:

1. On **CM01**, using **File Explorer**, browse to **E:\Sources\OSD\OS** and create the following folder structure:

    **Operating System Start Screens\Windows 8.1 x64 Start Screen**

2. Copy the **E:\Setup\appsfolderlayout.bin** file to **E:\Sources\OSD\OS\Operating System Start Screens\Windows 8.1 x64 Start Screen**

3. Start an elevated **Windows PowerShell ISE** (run as Administrator), and open the **E:\Setup\Scripts\Create and Distribute a Package.ps1** PowerShell script.

4. Locate and then edit the **$PackageSource** and **$PackageName** variables in the script:

    ```
    $PackageSource = "\\CM01.corp.viamonstra.com\Sources\OSD\OS\
    Operating System Start Screens\Windows 8.1 x64 Start Screen"
    ```

    ```
    $PackageName = "Windows 8.1 x64 Start Screen"
    ```

5. Run the script by clicking the green **Run Script** button, or by pressing **F5** in **Windows PowerShell ISE**.

# Creating an OSD Task Sequence

Now it's time to create an OSD task sequence. This task sequence is used to deploy your previously captured image. An OSD task sequence can be as flexible, simple, or complex as you require. I recommend that you start simple, get the deployment working, and then add additional functionality as needed one step at a time, with plenty of testing in between changes.

Task sequences can be created in the console via the available wizards or created using PowerShell. In the preceding chapter, you saw how to create a task sequence using the wizard available in the console. In this chapter, you create a task sequence using a ConfigMgr PowerShell cmdlet.

## Create an OSD Task Sequence Using PowerShell

The PowerShell cmdlet for creating a task sequence is called *New-CMTaskSequence*, and it accepts many options, including the type of task sequence (listed below). There are currently four types of task sequence:

- InstallOperatingSystemImageOption
- BuildOperatingSystemImageOption

Chapter 5   Deploying Windows 8.1 with a Custom Start Screen

- InstallOperatingSystemImageVhdOption
- CustomOption

As you are going to create an OSD task sequence, you use the first option. To create an OSD task sequence using PowerShell, you can experiment with the New-CMTaskSequence cmdlet yourself or save time and use the provided script called *Create a deploy task sequence.ps1* in E:\Setup\Scripts.

The script is written to make all the choices for you. You can customize it later to change settings as appropriate. To create the OSD task sequence, run the PowerShell script by doing as follows:

1. On **CM01**, start an elevated **Windows PowerShell ISE** (run as Administrator), and open the **E:\Setup\Scripts\Create a deploy task sequence.ps1** PowerShell script.

2. Review and if necessary edit the variables in the script. For example, **$CMDrive** may need to be changed to point to the drive letter where ConfigMgr is installed in your environment.

3. Run the script by pressing **F5** or clicking the green **Run Script** button.

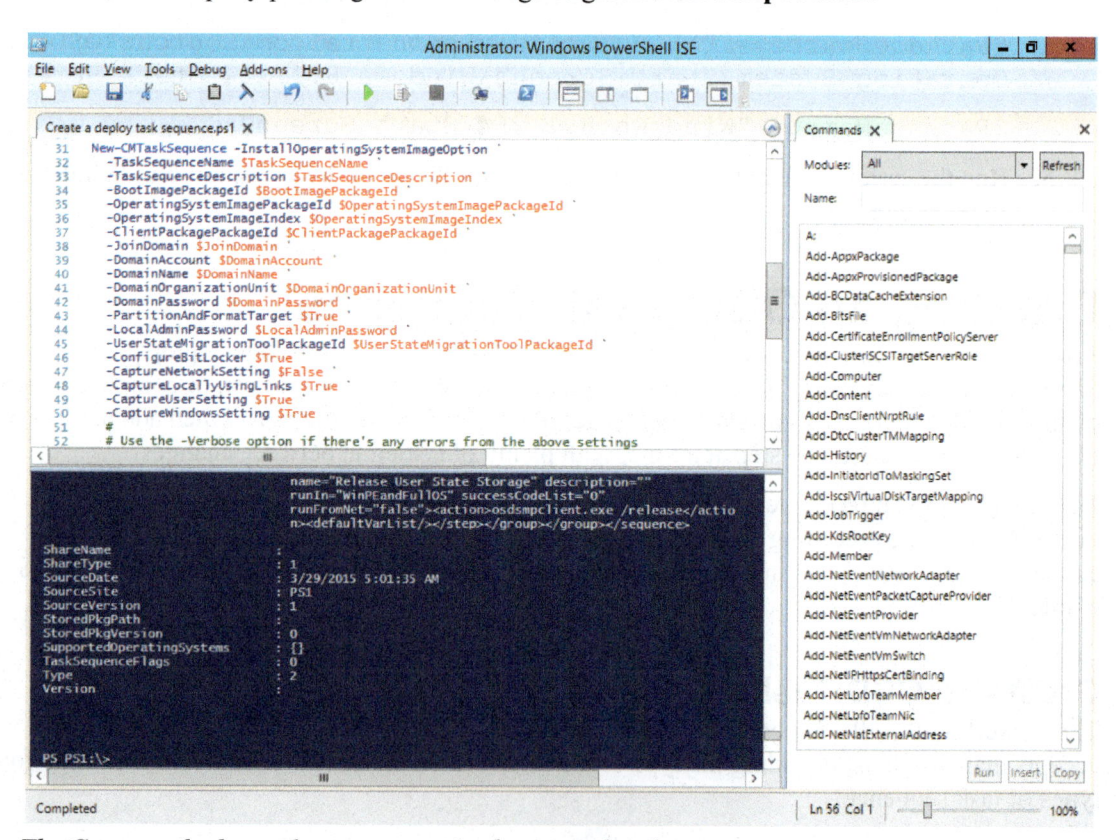

*The Create a deploy task sequence script has completed.*

144

Chapter 5 Deploying Windows 8.1 with a Custom Start Screen

> **Real World Note**: When making any changes to PowerShell scripts, you are likely to see errors in red text when something unexpected occurs. To enable you to get more details about why that is happening, most PowerShell cmdlets allow the use of the -Verbose switch. If your PowerShell script fails after making a change, then add the -Verbose switch, run the script again, and see what additional information it reveals.

## Edit the Task Sequence

Now that you have an OSD task sequence, it is time to fine tune it and add some additional steps. These steps apply the custom Start screen settings and change the way the Enable BitLocker step functions in regard to Hyper-V virtual machines. To edit the task sequence, do as follows:

1. On **CM01**, expand **Operating Systems** and select **Task Sequences**. Refresh the view in the console, and you should see the newly created **Windows 8.1 Enterprise x64 - 150301** task sequence. Right-click the task sequence and choose **Edit** from the available options.

2. When the Task Sequence Editor appears, select the **Partition Disk 0 - Bios** step and double-click the **Windows (Primary)** partition to bring up its properties. Under **Advanced Options**, enter **OSDISK** for the **Variable** option, and click **OK**.

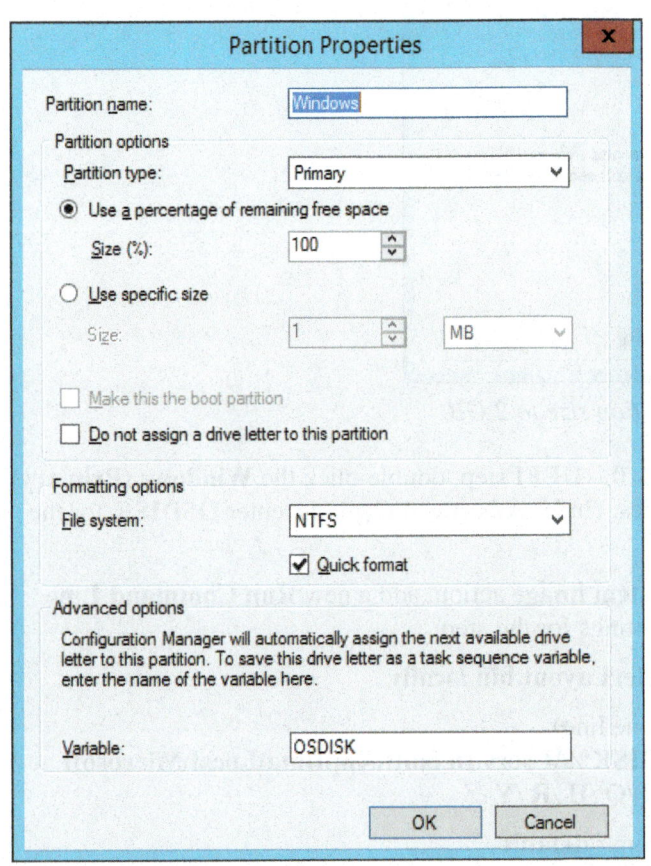

*Setting the Windows partition to a variable called OSDISK.*

145

Chapter 5    Deploying Windows 8.1 with a Custom Start Screen

3. Select the **Partition Disk 0 – UEFI** step, and double-click the **Windows (Recovery)** partition to bring up its properties. Under **Partition Options**, for the **Use specific size** option, enter **2048**, and click **OK**.

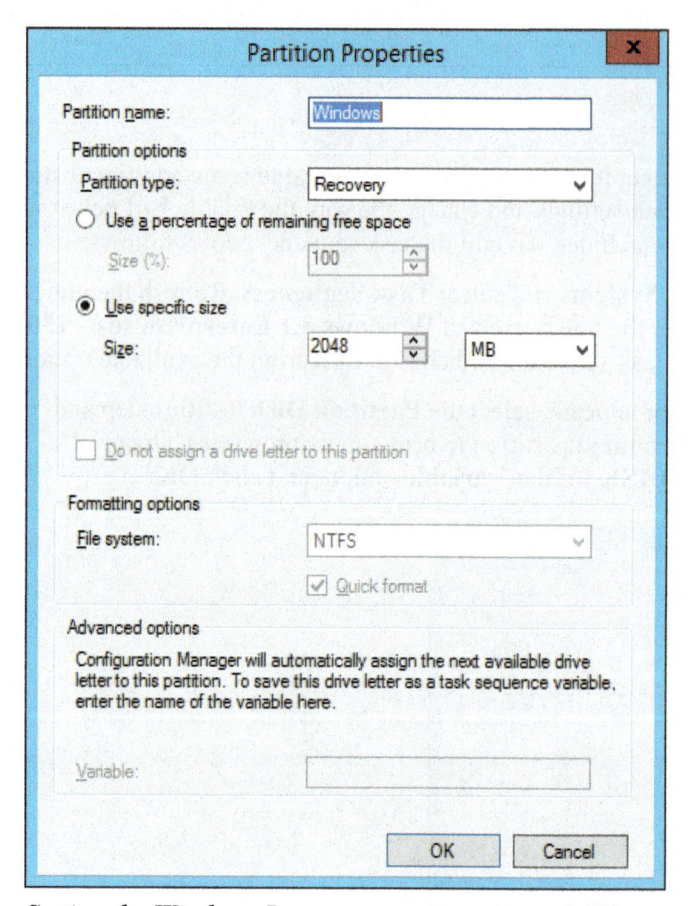

*Setting the Windows Recovery partition size to 2 GB.*

4. While still in the **Partition Disk 0 – UEFI** step, double-click the **Windows (Primary)** partition to bring up its properties. Under **Advanced Options**, enter **OSDISK** for the **Variable** option, and click **OK**.

5. After the **Apply Operating System image** action, add a new **Run Command Line** action, and use the following settings for the step:

    o Name: **Copy AppsFolderLayout.bin locally**

    o Command line (all on one line):
    **xcopy ".\*.*" "%OSDISK%\Users\Default\AppData\Local\Microsoft\Windows" /D /E /C /I /Q /H /R /Y /S**

    o Disable 64 bit redirection: **<default>**

    o Package: **Windows 8.1 x64 Start Screen**

Chapter 5   Deploying Windows 8.1 with a Custom Start Screen

- o Time-out (minutes): **3**
- o Run this step as the following account: **<default>**

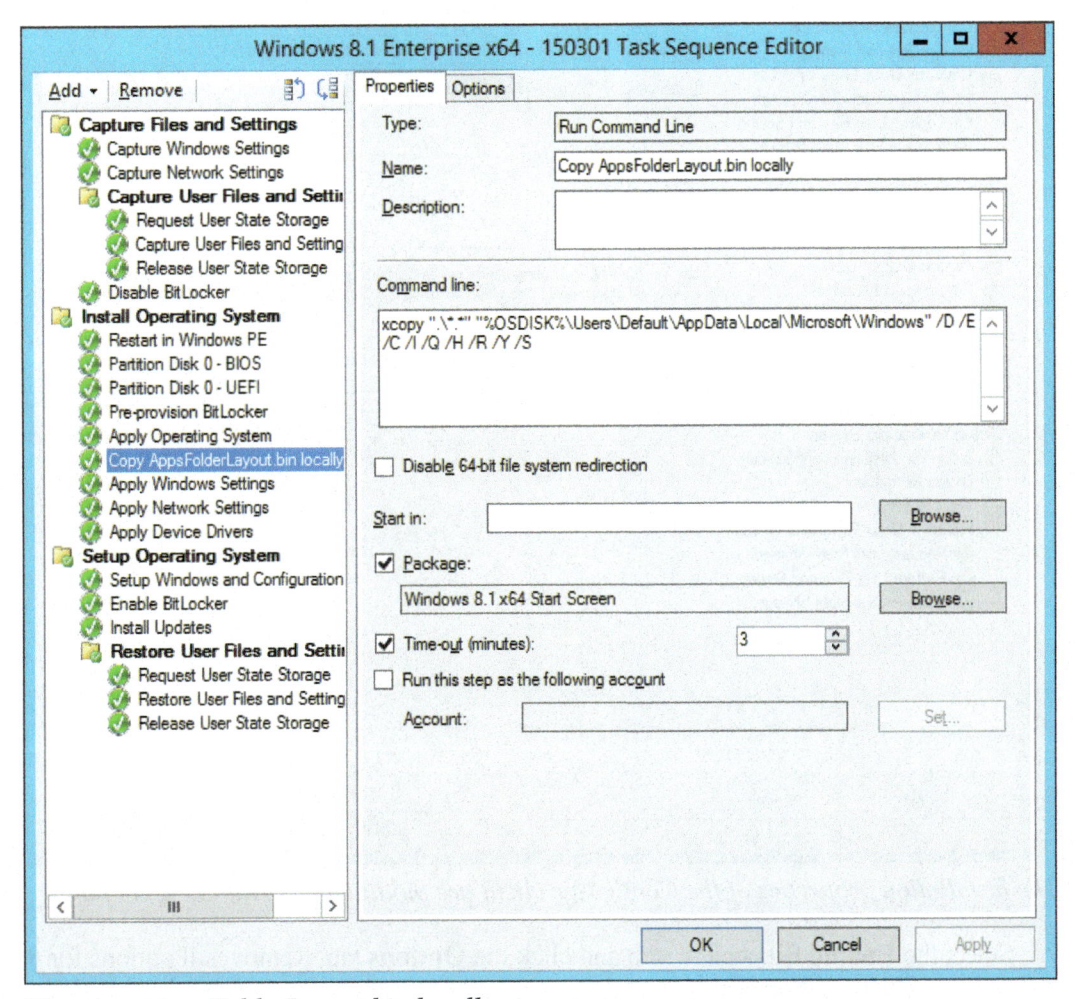

*The xcopy AppsFolderLayout.bin locally step.*

6. Next, you add the **CU4** patch and **CCM Logging** properties. Select the **Setup Windows and Configuration Manager** step and in the **Installation properties**, type in the following where <PS1000A> is the Package ID of your **ConfigMgr Client with Hotfixes** package:
Patch="C:\_SMSTaskSequence\OSD\PS10000A\Hotfix\x64\configmgr2012ac-r2-kb3026739-x64.msp" CCMLOGMAXSIZE=5242880 CCMLOGLEVEL=0 CCMLOGMAXHISTORY=3

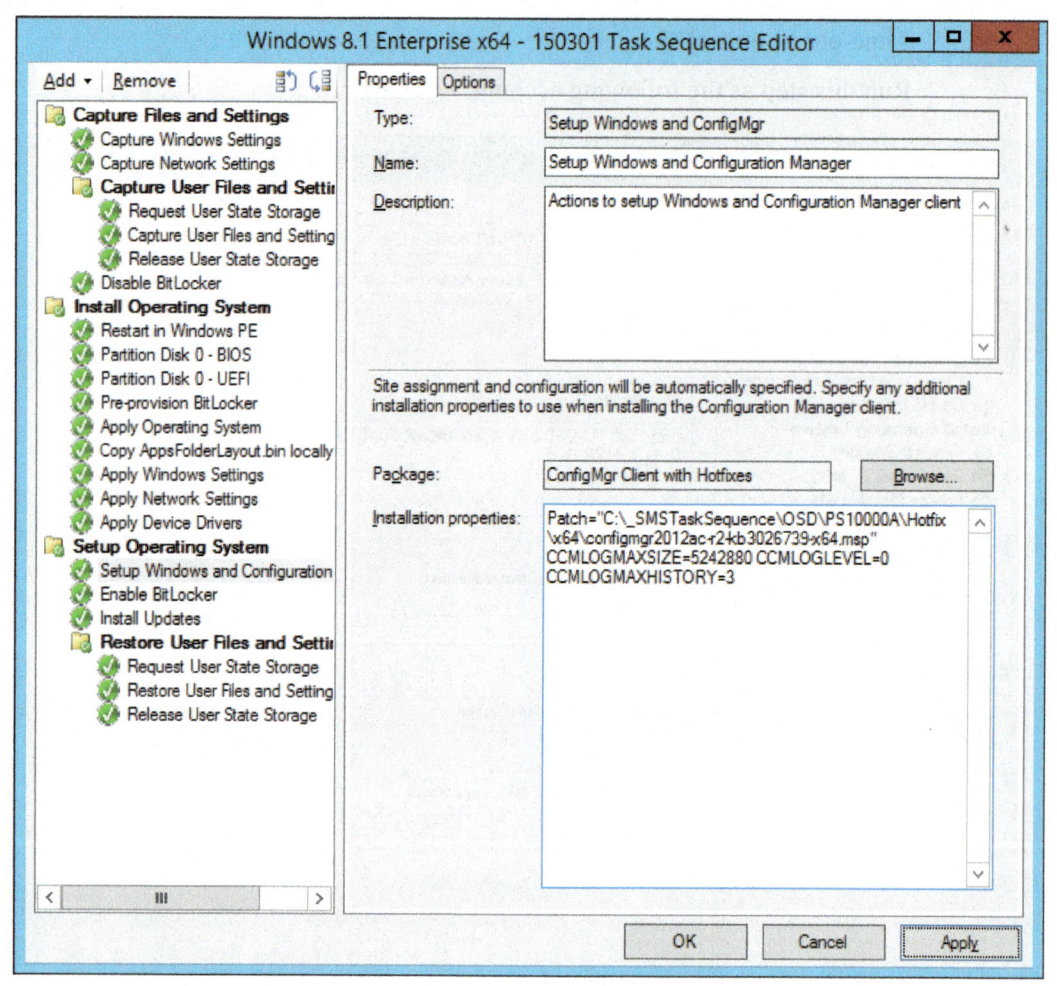

*The installation properties of the ConfigMgr client are modified to install the CU4 patch.*

7. Select the **Enable BitLocker** step and click the **Options** tab. Remove all options for the step by selecting **Remove All**.

8. Add options by selecting the **Add Condition** drop-down menu, selecting **If statement**, and then selecting **All conditions** in the **If Statement Properties** window. Click the **Add Condition** drop-down menu again, select **Task Sequence Variable** from the options, and enter the following when the **Task Sequence Variable** window appears:

    o   Variable: **_SMSTSWTG**

    o   Condition: **not equals**

    o   Value: **True**

Chapter 5   Deploying Windows 8.1 with a Custom Start Screen

9. Click the **Add Condition** drop-down menu again, select **Query WMI** from the options, and enter the following when the **WMI Query Properties** appears:

    o   WMI Namespace: **root\cimv2**

    o   WQL Query: **select * from Win32_ComputerSystem where Model <> "Virtual Machine"**

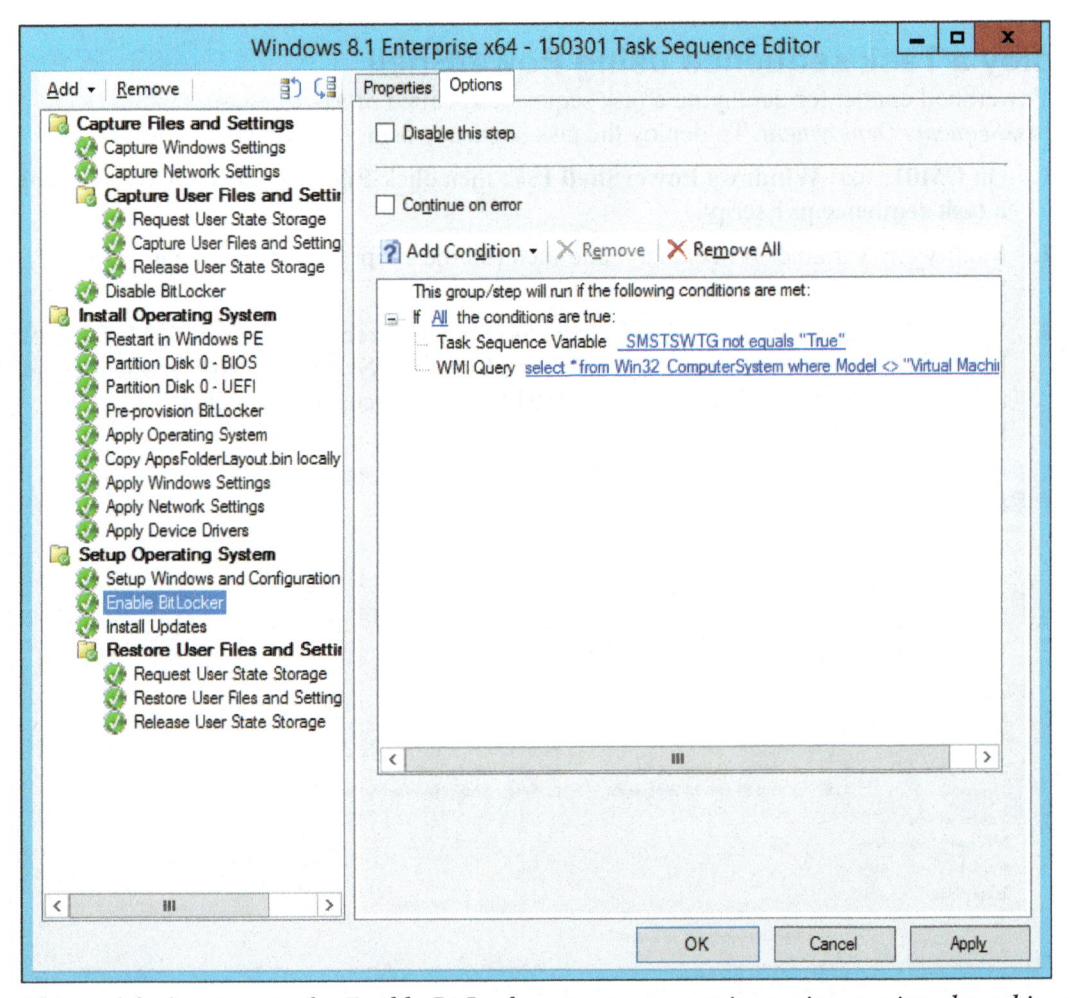

*The modified options in the Enable BitLocker step to prevent it running on virtual machines.*

10. Save all the changes and close the **Task Sequence Editor** by clicking **OK**.

Chapter 5   Deploying Windows 8.1 with a Custom Start Screen

# Deploying the Task Sequence

After you edit the task sequence, it is ready to be deployed. To deploy the task sequence, you can simply right-click the task sequence and choose Deploy from the options available and continue through the wizard, targeting the task sequence to the OSD_Deploy collection. Alternatively, you can increase your use of PowerShell and deploy via another built-in cmdlet.

## Deploy a Task sequence using PowerShell

The PowerShell cmdlet for deploying a task sequence is called *Start-CMTaskSequenceDeployment*. To deploy the task sequence using PowerShell, do as follows:

1. On **CM01**, start **Windows PowerShell ISE**; then click **File / Open** and open the **Deploy a task sequence.ps1** script.
2. Modify any variables if necessary, and then run the script by clicking the green **Run Script** button or by pressing **F5**.
3. Verify that the task sequence deployment is created correctly in the ConfigMgr console. In the **Software Library** workspace, select **Operating Systems / Task Sequences**, select the **Windows 8.1 Enterprise x64 - 150301** task sequence, and then click the **Deployments** tab.

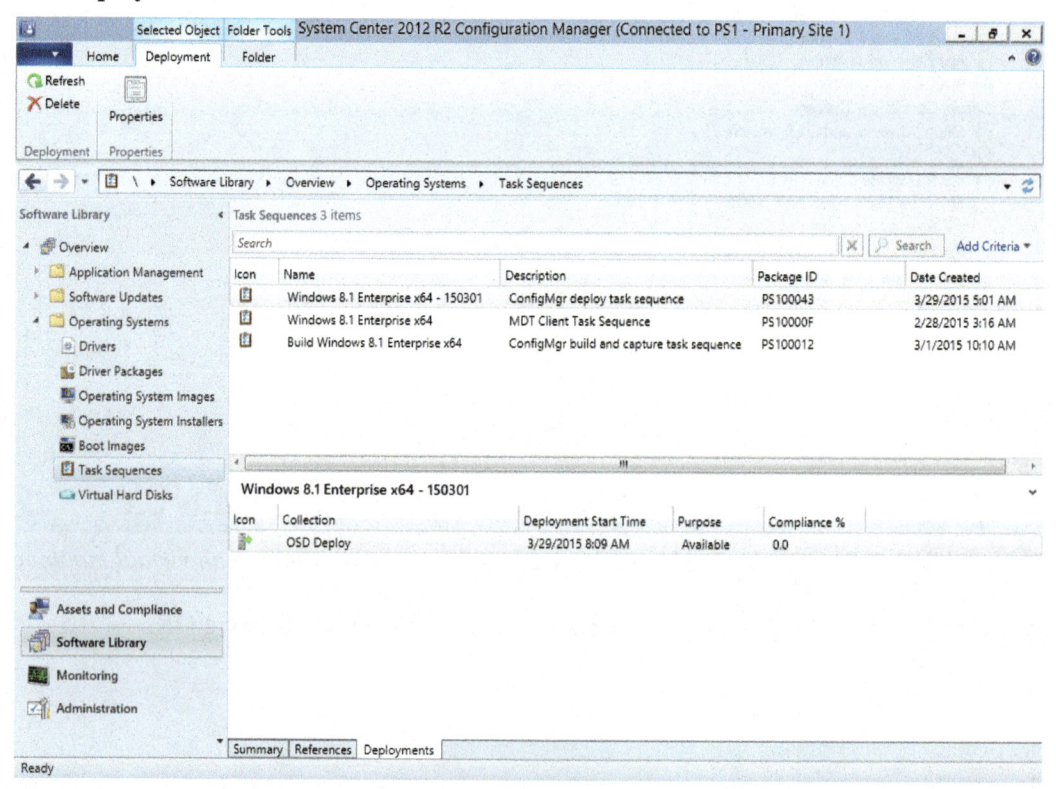

*The Windows 8.1 Enterprise x64 - 150301 task sequence is deployed using PowerShell to the OSD Deploy collection.*

## Target New Windows Updates

This is an optional but recommended step. In production, you obviously want to keep your computers up to date with the latest patches as they become available. If you want those Windows updates to be included as part of the OSD task sequence process, then you need to select applicable Windows updates and target them to the OSD Deploy collection.

## Deploy a New Computer

Now everything is ready to start deploying computers with your custom image with apps like Office 365, .NET 3.5 integrated, and a custom Start screen. Follow the process below to image it with the Windows 8.1 Enterprise x64 - 150301 task sequence:

1. Create a virtual machine named **PC0004**.
2. Power on **PC0004** and when prompted press **Enter** (or F12) for network boot service.
3. When the **Task Sequence Wizard** PXE password screen appears, enter **P@ssw0rd** and click **Next** to continue.
4. Select **Windows 8.1 Enterprise x64 - 150301** in the **Select a task sequence to run** list of task sequences and click **Next**.
5. Assign the **PC0004** computer name, and then click **Next**.

## Chapter 5   Deploying Windows 8.1 with a Custom Start Screen

6. Let the task sequence complete operations and when done, log in using the credentials of a domain user. Verify that the Start screen shows the customizations carried out earlier in this chapter.

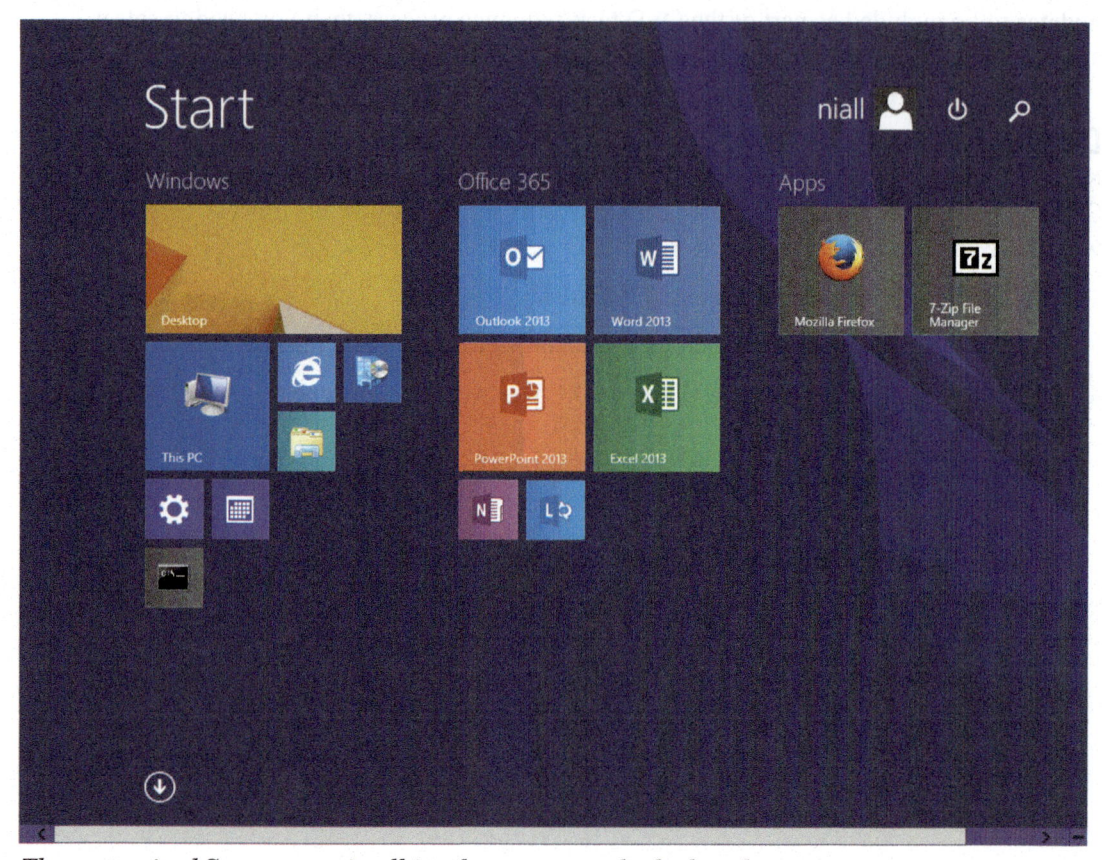

*The customized Start screen in all its glory on a newly deployed computer.*

# Chapter 6
# Deploying Windows 8.1 to the Surface Pro 3

In this chapter, you learn how to install Windows 8.1 x64 Enterprise on Microsoft Surface Pro 3 devices. The Surface Pro 3 is a true 64-bit UEFI device with custom hardware such as the Bluetooth pen and as a result poses some challenges for correct deployment.

## Step-by-Step Guide Requirements
If you want to follow the step-by-step guides in this chapter, you need a lab environment configured as outlined in Chapter 2 and Appendix A. In this chapter, you use the following virtual machines, or if you have access to a Surface Pro 3, use that instead of PC0005:

DC01    CM01    PC0005

*The VMs used in this chapter (PC0005 is a virtual machine that you create if you don't have a real Surface Pro 3 you can use).*

You also need to have downloaded the following software:

KB 2968599

## About the System Center Configuration Manager Cmdlet Library
There are a few issues with some of the PowerShell cmdlets in the CU4 release used in this guide. For example, the New-CMDriverPackage cmdlet doesn't work. This problem is fixed with the release of System Center Configuration Manager Cmdlet Library.

This library is the new method of delivering new, changed, or fixed PowerShell cmdlets for ConfigMgr, and it even checks for newer versions and alerts you.

## Download the Library

To download the library visit this link: https://microsoft.com/en-us/download/details.aspx?id=46681 and download the ConfigMgr2012PowerShellCmdlets.msi. There is also a ConfigurationManagerCmdletLibraryReleaseNotes.docx file containing release notes and information about the new cmdlets and what has changed. I recommend reading it.

## Install the Library

In this guide I assume you have downloaded the System Center Configuration Manager Cmdlet Library to E:\Setup on CM01. To install the library, follow these steps:

1. On **CM01**, close any open sessions of **Windows PowerShell ISE** and close any **ConfigMgr consoles**. As a user with Administrator privileges, double-click the **ConfigMgr2012PowerShellCmdlets.msi**.

2. When the **System Center Configuration Manager Cmdlet Library Setup Wizard** appears, click **Next**. When you get the information about the self-update checking feature, read through it and click **Next**. Accept the EULA and click **Next**, answer **Yes** to the UAC prompt, and finally click **Finish** to close the wizard.

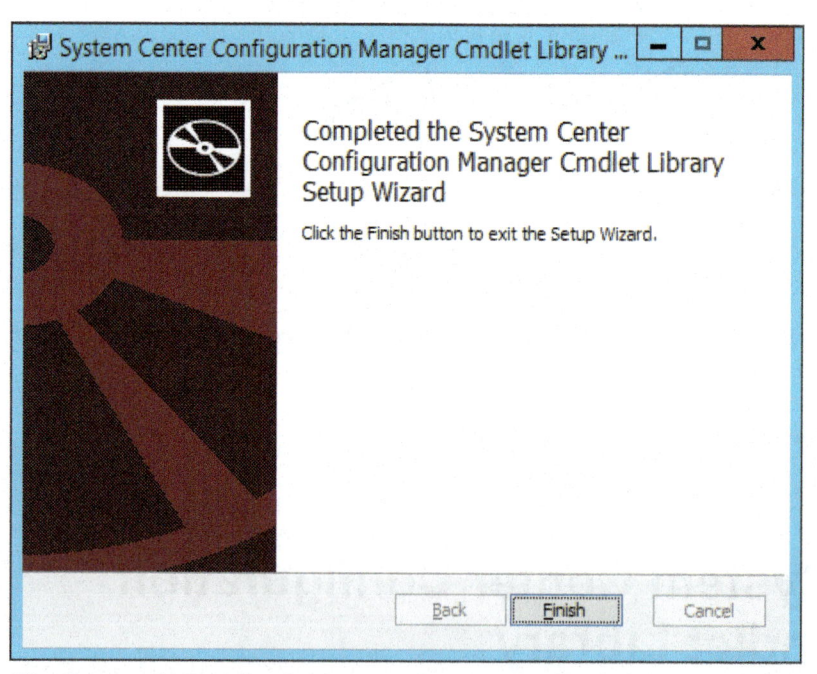

*The System Center Configuration Manager Cmdlet Library is installed.*

# Downloading Necessary Files

To properly support the Surface Pro 3, you need to download not only drivers but some updates too. The Windows updates fix problems with pen interaction with OneNote among other things.

## Get the OneNote Update

If you deploy a custom image to Surface Pro 3 the Pen button does not bring up modern OneNote. To resolve that problem, KB2968599 needs to be installed during deployment.

1. On **CM01**, using **Internet Explorer**, navigate to http://download.windowsupdate.com/d/msdownload/update/software/crup/2014/06/windows8.1-kb2968599-x64_de4ca043bf6ba84330fd96cb374e801071c4b8aa.msu

2. Download the file to **E:\Setup**.

There are more updates included in the Surface Pro 3 drivers in the next section.

## Download the Latest Surface Pro 3 Drivers

Microsoft releases new drivers for the Surface Pro family of devices on a fairly regular basis. Those updated drivers are released to fix issues identified in the field, so before creating the task sequence, check the Microsoft website for the latest drivers. You can download drivers for all Microsoft Surface devices including the Surface Pro 3 from the following URL http://microsoft.com/en-us/download/details.aspx?id=38826.

1. On **CM01**, using **Internet Explorer**, navigate to http://microsoft.com/en-us/download/details.aspx?id=38826

2. Download all ZIP files that match **Surface Pro 3** to **E:\Setup**.

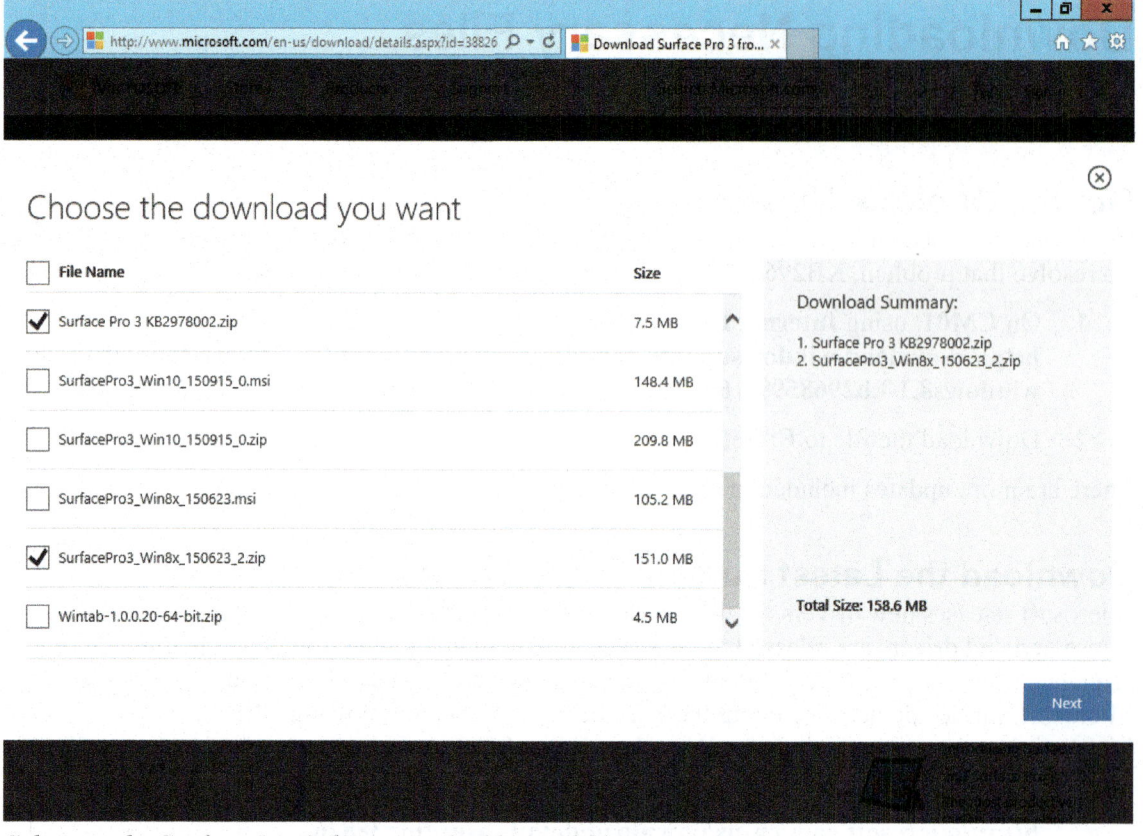

*Selecting the Surface Pro 3 drivers and additional files to download.*

## Extract the drivers

After you have download the drivers, unzip those that are zipped to a folder such as E:\Setup\Surface Pro 3. That folder does not exist, so you need to create it.

1. On **CM01**, using **File Explorer**, create the **E:\Setup\Surface Pro 3** folder.
2. Extracted the downloaded Surface Pro 3 ZIP files to the **E:\Setup\Surface Pro 3** folder.

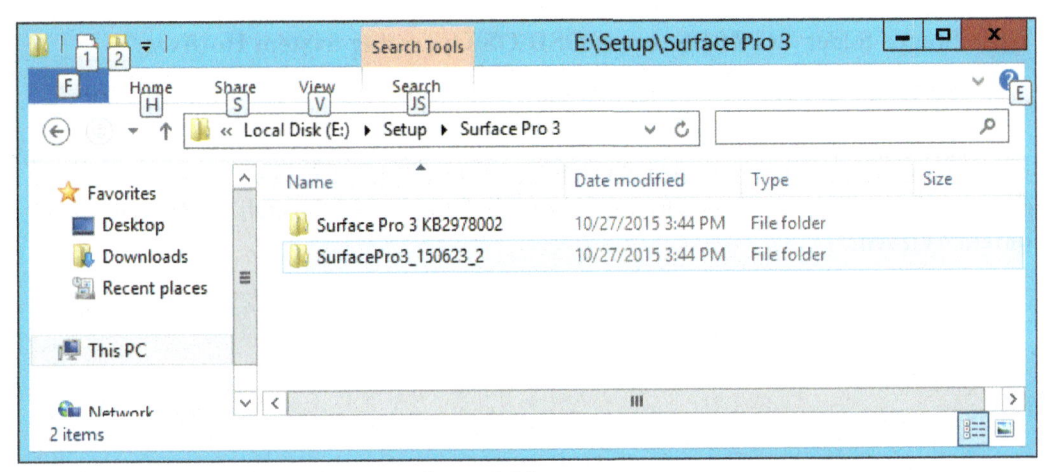

Chapter 6   Deploying Windows 8.1 to the Surface Pro 3

*The Surface Pro 3 drivers extracted to a folder.*

## Create an Operating System Hotfixes Package
This package contains updates needed to support the Surface Pro 3. To create the Operating System Hotfixes package, follow these steps:

1. On **CM01**, using **File Explorer**, create the following directory: **E:\Sources\OSD\OS\Operating System Hotfixes**.

2. Uncompress **Surface Click Note POC.EXE** by running it. The uncompressed file is Windows8.1-KB2978002-x64.msu. Copy that file with any other previously downloaded hotfixes for the Surface Pro 3 to **E:\Sources\OSD\OS\Operating System Hotfixes**.

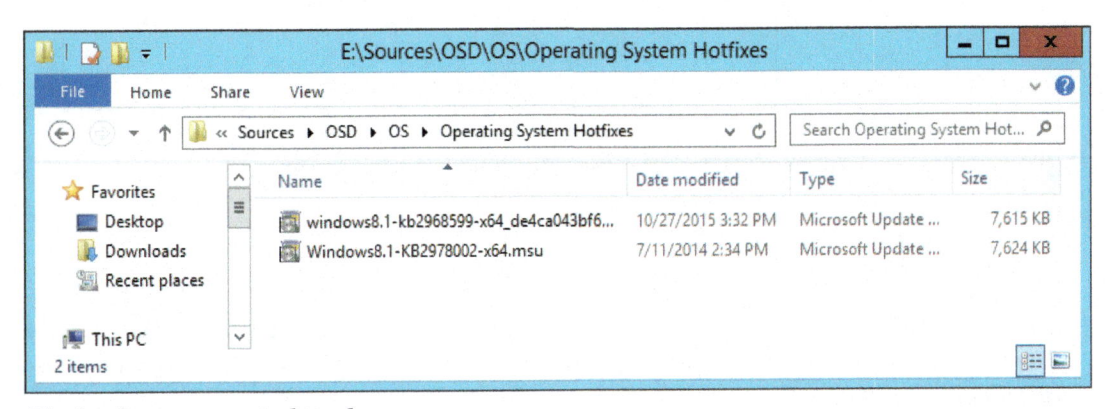

*The hotfixes are copied in place.*

3. On **CM01**, using the **ConfigMgr console**, in the **Software Library** workspace, select **Application Management / Packages**. Right-click and choose **Create Package**. Use the following settings for the **Create Package and Program** wizard:

    a. Name: **Operating System Hotfixes**

    b. Description: **Hotfixes needed for the Surface Pro 3 deployment**

157

c. Source folder: **\\CM01\Sources\OSD\OS\Operating System Hotfixes**

d. Select **Do not create a program** and continue through the rest of the wizard (accepting the default settings) until completion.

4. Distribute the package to the **CM01.CORP.VIAMONSTRA.COM** distribution point by right-clicking it, choosing **Distribute Content**, and continuing through the **Distribute Content Wizard**.

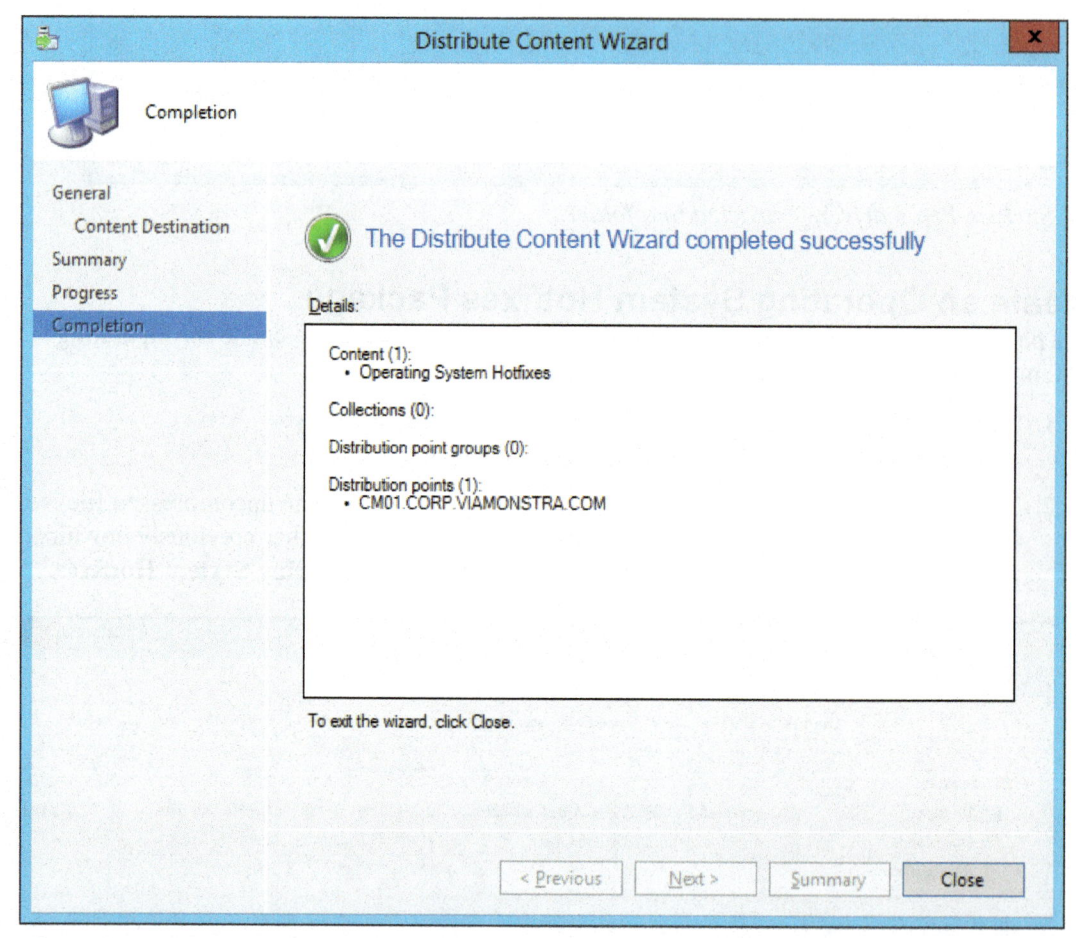

*The Operating System Hotfixes package is distributed to the CM01.VIAMONSTRA.COM distribution point.*

## Create an OOBE Package

This OOBE package is used for providing the ability to pair your Surface Pen during the out-of-box experience (OOBE) portion of Windows. To create the OOBE package, follow these steps:

1. On **CM01**, create the **E:\Sources\Software\Microsoft\Surface Pro 3 OOBE** folder.

2. From an existing OEM installation of Surface Pro 3, copy the following files to **E:\Sources\Software\Microsoft\Surface Pro 3 OOBE** folder on **CM01**.

    - C:\Windows\system32\oobe\info\default\1033\oobe.xml
    - C:\Windows\system32\oobe\info\default\1033\PenPairing_en-US.png
    - C:\Windows\system32\oobe\info\default\1033\PenError_en-US.png
    - C:\Windows\system32\oobe\info\default\1033\PenSuccess_en-US.png

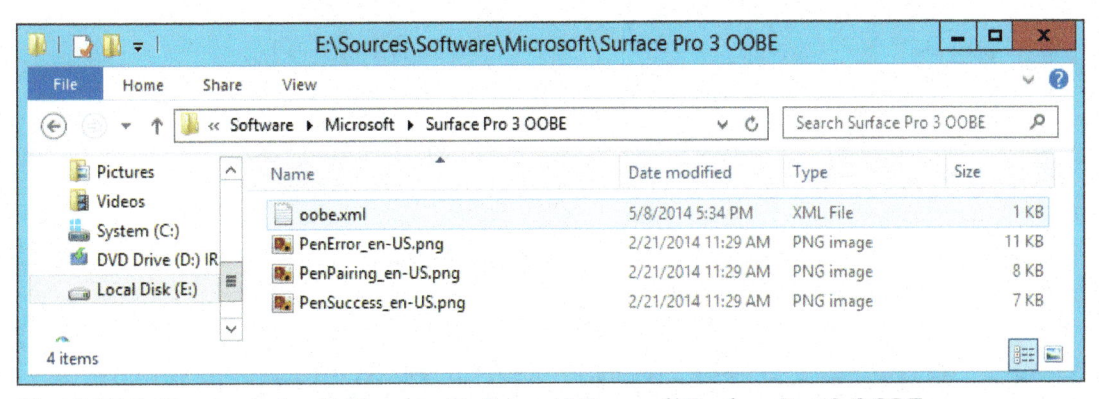

*The OOBE files copied to E:\Sources\Software\Microsoft\Surface Pro 3 OOBE.*

3. On **CM01**, using the **ConfigMgr console**, in the **Software Library** workspace, select **Application Management / Packages**. Right-click and choose **Create Package**. Use the following settings for the **Create Package and Program** wizard:

    - Name: **Surface Pro 3 Pen Support**
    - Source folder: **\\CM01\Sources\Software\Microsoft\Surface Pro 3 OOBE**
    - Select **Do not create a program**.

4. Continue through the wizard until completion. Finally, distribute the package to the **CM01.CORP.VIAMONSTRA.COM** distribution point.

# Creating a Suitable Folder Structure

After downloading and extracting the drivers, the next thing to do is to create a logical driver source and destination folder structure so that it is easy to navigate through those drivers and see which drivers are used in your environment. You could, for example, separate your drivers into Operating System (Windows 8.1 x64), Make (Microsoft), and finally Model (Surface Pro 3). By following this approach you can easily see which drivers are in use in your organization.

## Create the Driver Source Folder Structure

To create the driver source folder structure for the Surface Pro 3, follow these steps:

1. On **CM01**, using **File Explorer**, browse to **E:\Sources\OSD\Drivers** and create the following folder structure:

    **Windows 8.1 x64\Microsoft\Surface Pro 3**

2. Using **File Explorer**, copy the extracted drivers from **E:\Setup\Surface Pro 3\SurfacePro3_150623_2** to **E:\Sources\OSD\Drivers\Windows 8.1 x64\Microsoft\Surface Pro 3**.

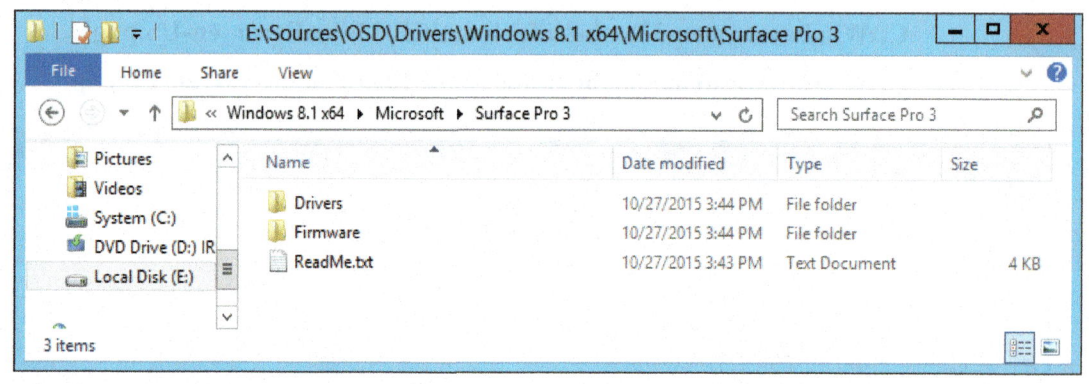

*The drivers are copied to their destination.*

# Importing and Distributing Drivers in ConfigMgr

Now that you have downloaded the drivers and copied them to an appropriately named driver source location, it's time to import the drivers into ConfigMgr. You can do this in two ways: manually, using the ConfigMgr console, or automatically, using PowerShell. Let's start with the PowerShell method.

## Import and Distribute the Drivers Using PowerShell

This method uses a PowerShell script containing ConfigMgr PowerShell cmdlets to automate the processes described in the preceding sections. All you have to do is run the script. After the script is complete, it will have imported all of the drivers into ConfigMgr and then distributed the driver package to the distribution point. In addition, the script updates the driver package to the distribution points. To import the Surface Pro 3 drivers into ConfigMgr using PowerShell, follow these steps:

> **Note:** If you want to import and distribute the drivers manually, skip this step.

Chapter 6   Deploying Windows 8.1 to the Surface Pro 3

1. On **CM01**, using the **Windows PowerShell ISE** as Administrator, load the script called **Import Drivers and Create a driver package.ps1** found in **E:\Setup\Scripts**.

2. To run the script, press **F5** or click the green **Run Script** button in **Windows PowerShell ISE**.

## Manually Import the Drivers Using the ConfigMgr Console

To manually import the drivers using the ConfigMgr console, follow this process:

1. On **CM01**, using the **ConfigMgr console**, expand **Software Library** and select **Operating Systems / Drivers**.

2. In the **Drivers** node, right-click and choose **Import Driver**. Use the following settings for the **Import New Driver Wizard**:

    a. On the **Locate Driver** screen, select **Import all drivers in the following network path (UNC)** and use the following settings:

    - Source folder: **\\CM01\Sources\OSD\Drivers\Windows 8.1 x64\Microsoft\Surface Pro 3**
    - Specify the option for duplicate drivers: **<default>**

    b. On the **Driver Details** screen, use the following settings:

    - The following drivers will be imported: **Select All**
    - Enable these drivers and allow computers to install them: **<default>**

    c. For the **Assign this driver to one or more categories for filtering** option, click **Categories**.

    d. Click **Create** and when the **Create Administrative Category** window appears, enter **Windows 8.1 x64 - Microsoft Surface Pro 3** in the **Specify the name of the new administrative category** field.

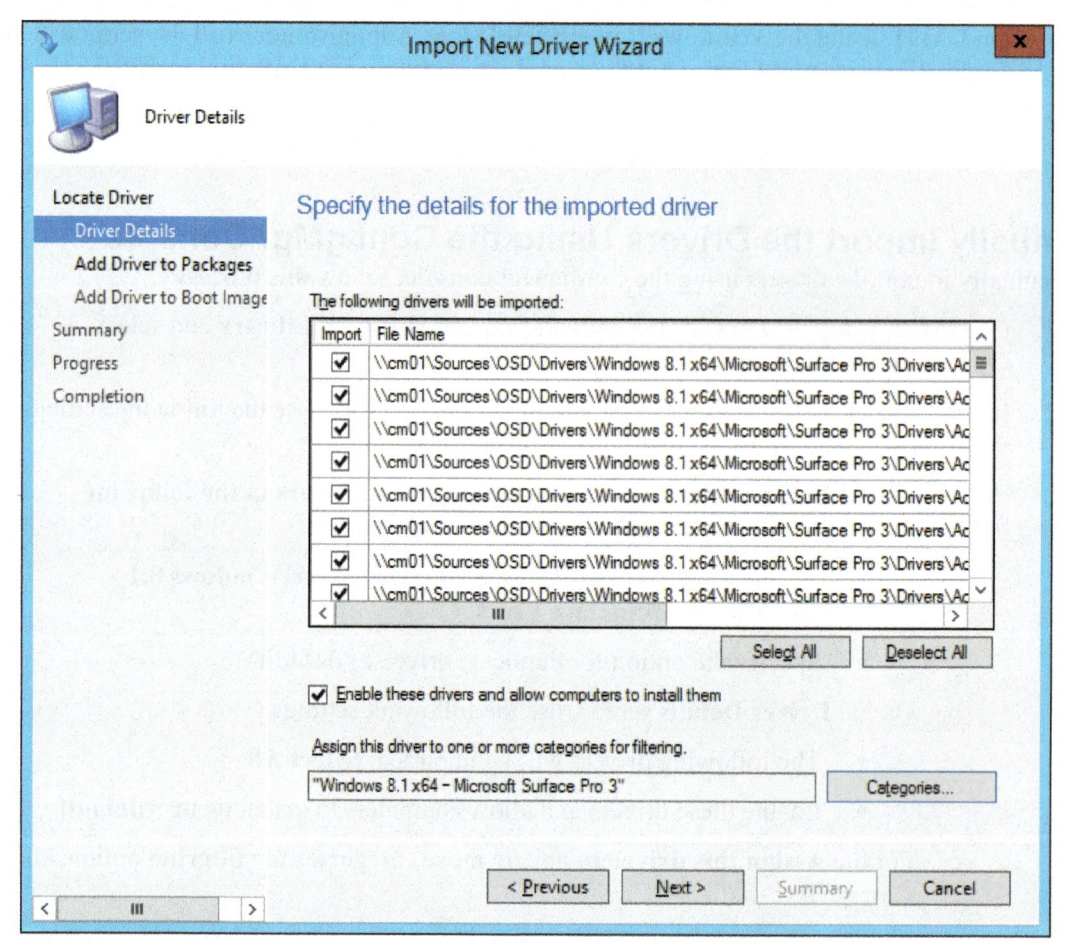

Chapter 6   Deploying Windows 8.1 to the Surface Pro 3

*Assigning categories to drivers that are being imported.*

- e. On the **Add Drivers to Packages** screen, clear the **Update distribution points when finished** check box, and then select **New Package** and use the following settings.
    - Name: **Windows 8.1 x64 - Microsoft Surface Pro 3**
    - Comment:
    - Path: **\\CM01\Sources\OSD\Drivers\Windows 8.1 x64\Microsoft\Surface Pro 3**

162

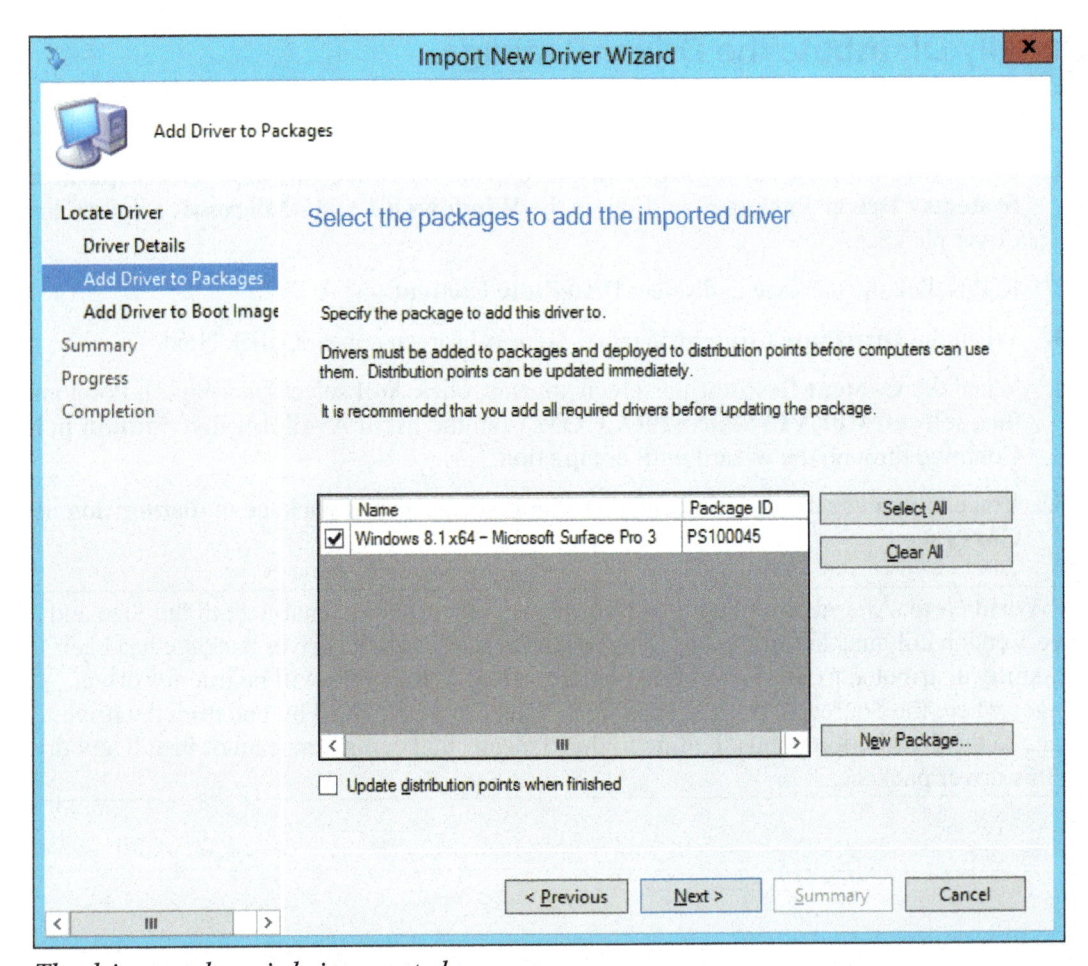

*The driver package is being created.*

    f. On the **Add Driver to Boot Image** screen, make sure nothing is selected because you add drivers to the boot image in a separate step. Then continue through the **Import New Driver Wizard** until completion.

**Real World Note**: If you want to monitor the driver imports in real time, use CMTrace and open SMSProv.log and DriverCatalog.log located in E:\Program Files\Microsoft Configuration Manager\Logs. The SMSProv.log file lists any issues you may have with permissions or file access and is very useful for troubleshooting. The DriverCatalog.log file reveals other issues, such as duplicate drivers.

## Manually Distribute the Driver Package

In order for computers to install drivers, they need those drivers located on a distribution point. To manually distribute the Windows 8.1 x64 - Microsoft Surface Pro 3 driver package, do as follows:

1. On **CM01**, using the **ConfigMgr console**, expand **Software Library**, select **Operating Systems / Driver Packages**, and select the **Windows 8.1 x64 - Microsoft Surface Pro 3** driver package.

2. Right-click the package and select **Distribute Content**.

3. When the **Distribute Content Wizard General** screen appears, click **Next**.

4. When the **Content Destination** screen appears, click **Add** select Distribution Point and then select **CM01.VIAMONSTRA.COM** from the list of **Available distribution points**. Continue through the wizard until completion.

5. You can monitor the updating and distribution of the driver package in **distmgr.log** using **CMTrace**.

**Real World Note**: After distributing the driver package, you should enable both the Size and Source Version columns in the console. Notice that even though the driver package has been successfully distributed to the distribution point, its size is 0KB. This will be true for driver packages where the Source Version is equal to 1. This can be resolved by updating the driver package to the distribution points. Failure to do so means that computers cannot install any drivers from this driver package.

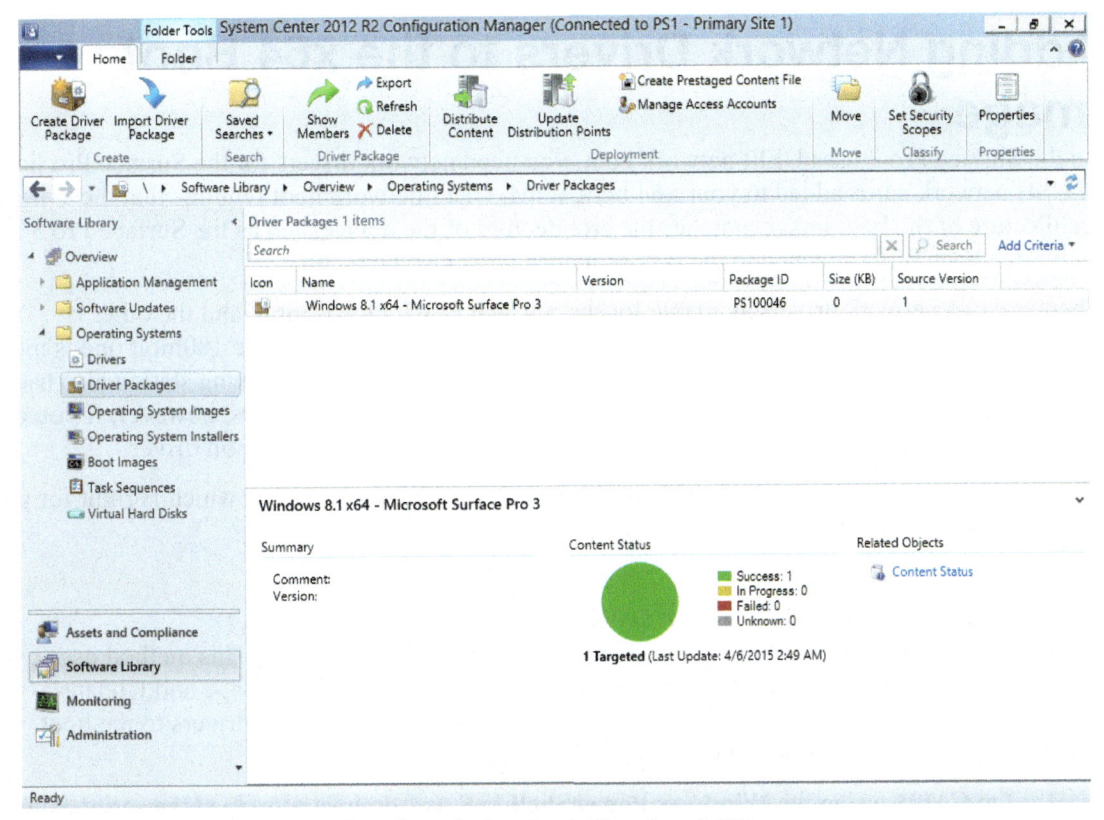

Chapter 6   Deploying Windows 8.1 to the Surface Pro 3

*After the driver package is distributed, the size is listed as 0 KB.*

6. To resolve the 0 KB size problem, right-click the **Windows 8.1 x64 - Microsoft Surface Pro 3** driver package and select **Update Distribution Points**. When prompted whether you are sure you want to update, click **OK**.

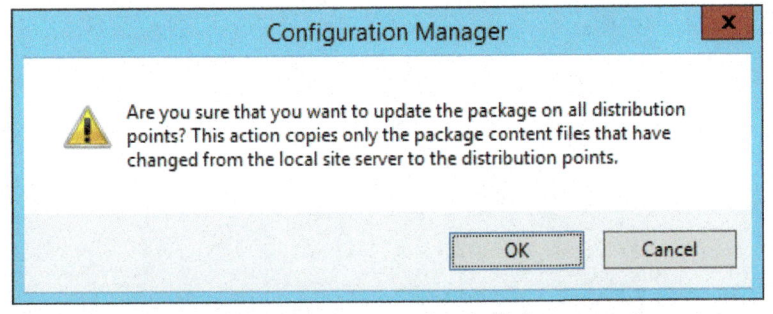

*Click OK to update the package to the distribution points.*

7. Wait a few minutes to allow the content to distribute.
8. Refresh the console by selecting the driver package and pressing **F5**. Confirm that the driver package has a **Source Version** of **2** and that the driver package size equals the actual driver package size in kilobytes.

# Adding Network Drivers to the x64 Boot Image

As the Surface Pro 3 uses UEFI network boot, you need network drivers for the Surface Pro line of USB network cards added to your x64 boot WIM. UEFI network boot requires that the architecture of the boot image matches the architecture of the device, and as the Surface Pro 3 is 64 bit, the boot WIM attached to the task sequence must also be 64 bit.

There are two network drivers available for the Surface Pro 3. One is mbit, and the other is gigabit. You can identify which adapter is which via the model number. The 100mbit one is model 1552, whereas the gigabit one is called model 1663. The Surface Pro 3 docking station also uses the same gigabit driver. In the examples that follow, you import both drivers; however, if you only have the gigabit model in your organization, you don't need to import the mbit driver.

There are a variety of ways to add drivers to your boot image, and deciding which is right for you is up to you. Here are three alternative options.

### Add Network Drivers via PowerShell.

This method works well for those of you who like to automate everything. This method uses two of ConfigMgr's built-in PowerShell cmdlets, namely Set-CMDriverBootImage and Update-CMDistributionPoint. All you have to do is run the script. To add network drivers to the boot WIM using PowerShell, follow these steps:

1. On **CM01**, using the **Windows PowerShell ISE** as Administrator, load the script called **Add Drivers to boot image.ps1** found in **E:\Setup\Scripts**.

2. To run the script press **F5** or click the green **Run Script** button in **Windows PowerShell ISE**. After the script is complete, it will have imported the network drivers and updated the boot WIM image to the distribution point.

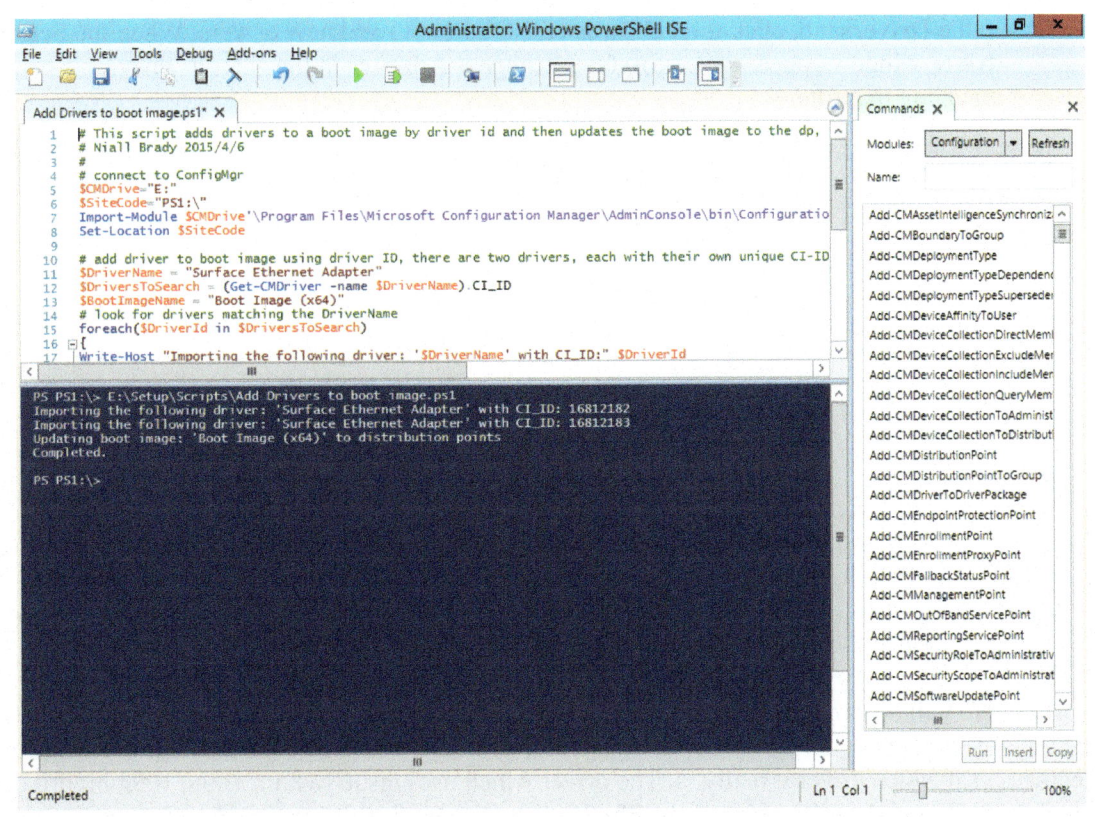

*Adding network drivers via PowerShell.*

## Add Network Drivers via the Boot Image Properties

This method is easy but limited to selecting one driver at a time. So, for that reason, it is suitable only when adding one or two network drivers to a boot image. To add the Surface Pro 3 network drivers to your x64 boot WIM via the boot image properties, follow this process:

1. On **CM01**, using the **ConfigMgr console**, expand **Software Library**, select **Operating System / Boot Images**, and then select the **Boot Image (x64)**.

2. Right-click and choose **Properties**. When the **Boot image (x64) Properties** window appears, select the **Drivers** tab.

3. In the **Drivers** tab, click the **yellow asterisk** button to add new drivers. When the **Select a driver** window appears, type **Surface Ethernet Adapter** in the filter to search for results matching that filter.

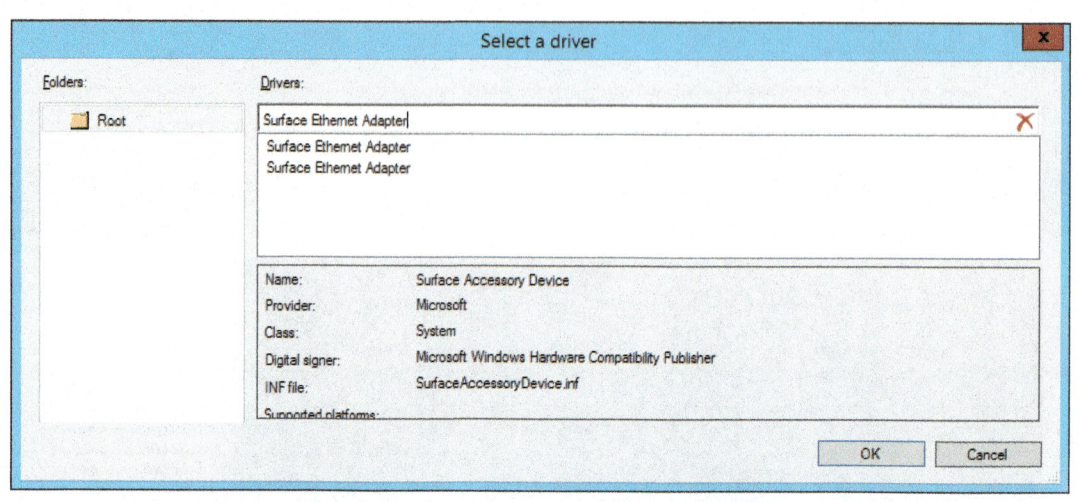

*Selecting a driver by using the filter to search for suitable drivers.*

> **Note**: There will be two Surface Ethernet Adapters drivers listed, one is the 100mbit driver, and the other is the gigabit driver. To differentiate between the drivers, select one and the INF file details reveal which driver it really is. The driver which uses msu64w8.inf is the 100mbit driver (model 1552), and the other driver (msu30x64w8.inf) is for gigabit (model 1663).

4. Select one of the drivers listed and click **OK**. You cannot select more than one driver using this method. If you want to add the other driver, then repeat the preceding process to do so.

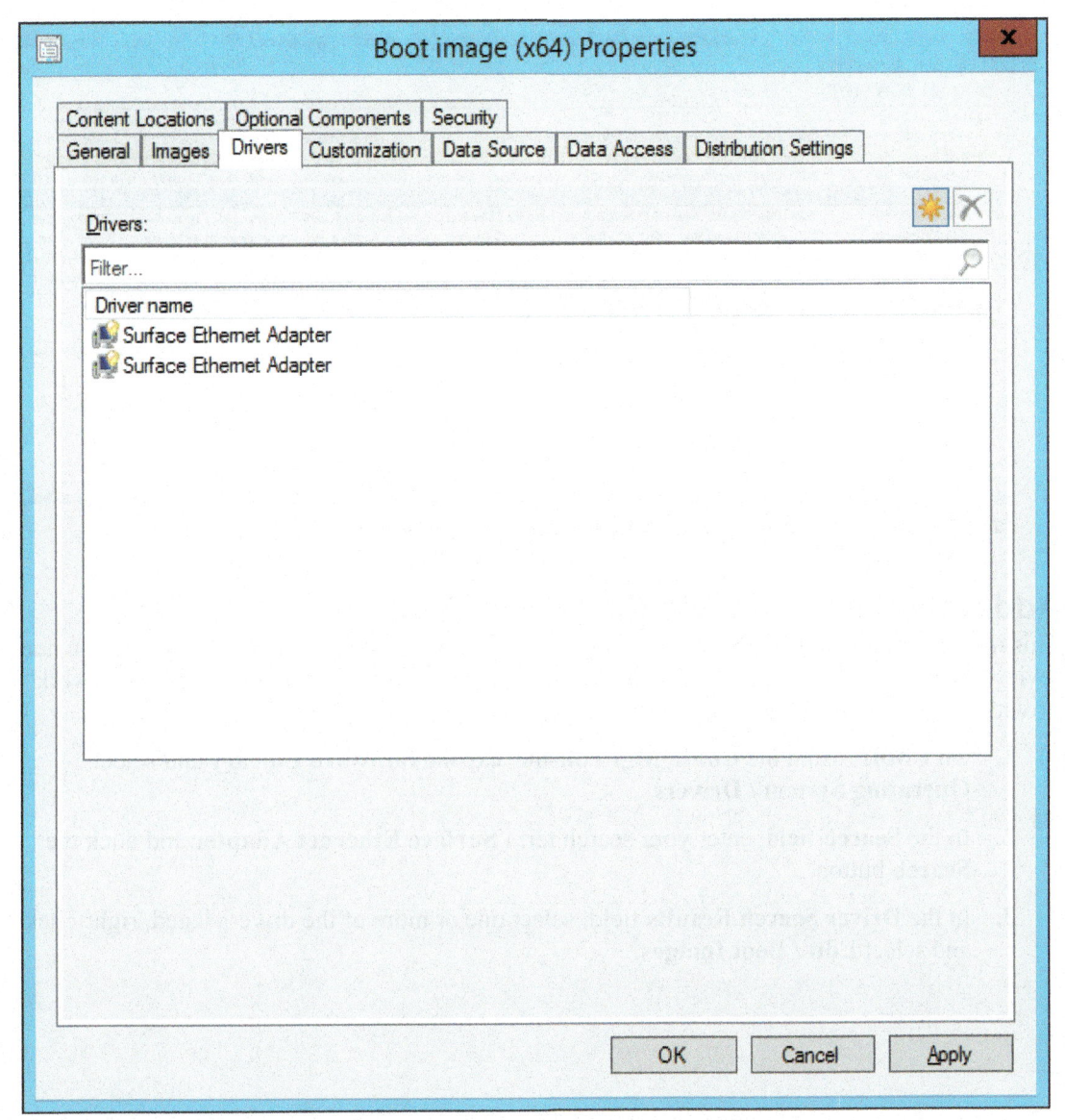

Chapter 6   Deploying Windows 8.1 to the Surface Pro 3

*Both the Surface Pro 3 mbit and gigabit network drivers are added to the boot WIM.*

5. To complete the process, click **Apply**. You are prompted as to whether you want to update the boot image to your distribution points. Click **Yes**. After clicking Yes, you see the **Update Distribution Points Wizard** appear. Click **Next** to view the progress of the driver injection. Click **Close** when the wizard is complete.

**Note**: Drivers are added or removed from boot images using DISM (Deployment Image Servicing and Management). If anything goes wrong with the driver injection process, you can review that process in CMTrace by opening dism.log located in C:\Windows\Logs\Dism.

169

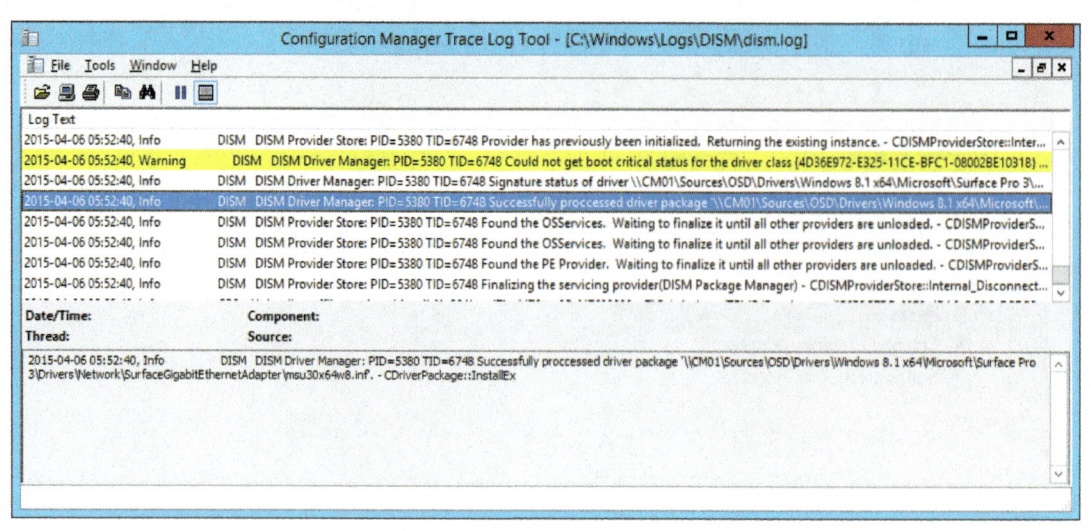

*Monitoring driver injection into boot images using dism.log.*

## Add Network Drivers via the Drivers Node

This method works well if you are adding or removing more than one driver; however you need to review the log files (such as dism.log or smsprov.log) to verify all went well. To add network drivers to the boot WIM using this process, follow these steps:

1. On **CM01**, using the **ConfigMgr console**, expand **Software Library** and select **Operating System / Drivers**.

2. In the **Search** field, enter your search term **Surface Ethernet Adapter** and click the **Search** button.

3. In the **Driver Search Results** field, select one or more of the drivers listed, right-click, and select **Edit / Boot Images**.

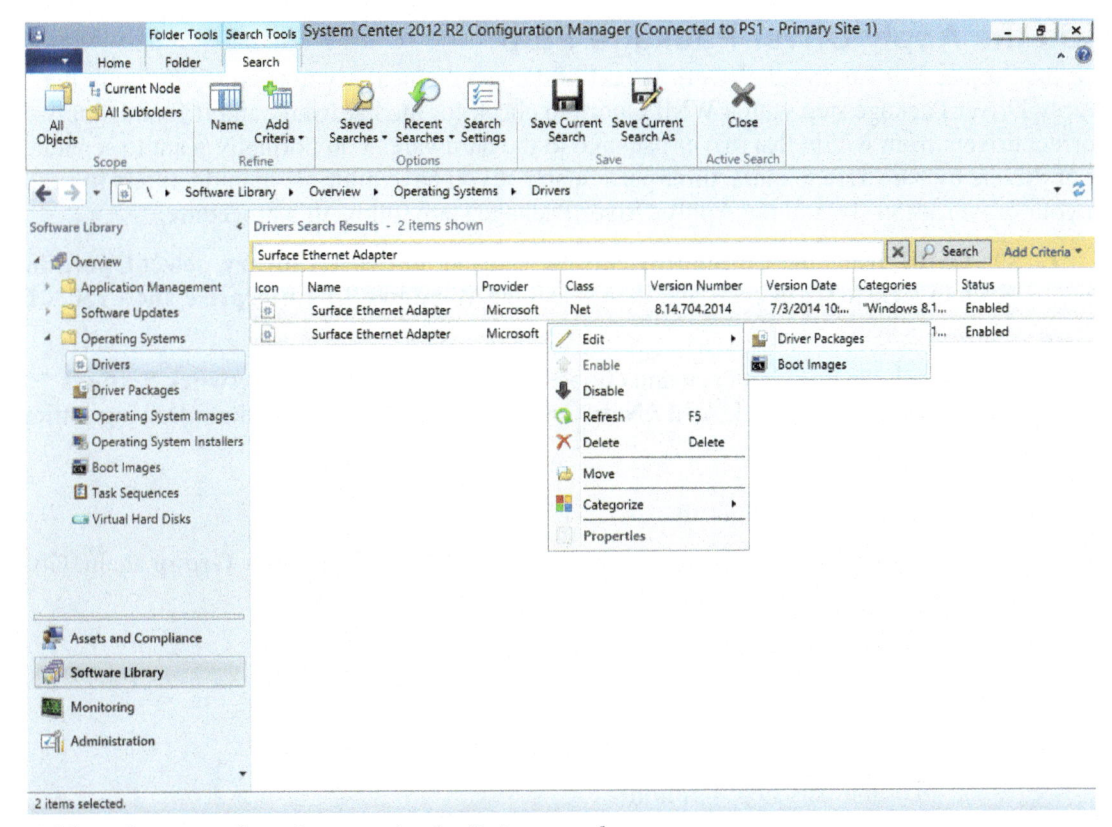

*Adding drivers to boot images via the Drivers node.*

4. When the **Add or Remove Drivers to Boot Images** wizard appears, select the **Boot Image (x64)** boot image and click **OK**. Note that this window closes when the process is complete without any notification of success or error.

# Edit the Windows 8.1 Enterprise x64 Task Sequence

In Chapter 5, you created a Windows 8.1 Enterprise x64 - 150301 task sequence containing your reference image with a custom Start screen, Windows updates, and apps for your organization. That task sequence already contains the correct boot image needed to deploy the Surface Pro 3, namely Boot Image (x64). As you have already added the network drivers to the boot WIM, all that is remaining is to add some new steps to the task sequence.

In this section, you make edits to that task sequence to properly support deployments of the Surface Pro 3.

## Add the Apply Driver Package Step

For the Surface Pro 3 to install drivers as part of the task sequence, you need to configure the Apply Driver Package step with a WMI Query to check for the hardware, and if found, apply the correct drivers from within that driver package to the hardware. You normally want to separate your drivers by hardware manufacturer particularly if you have multiple manufacturers to support in your organization. To add the Apply Driver Package step, follow this procedure:

1. On **CM01**, using the **ConfigMgr console**, expand **Software Library**, select **Operating System / Task Sequences**, and then select the **Windows 8.1 Enterprise x64 - 150301** task sequence.

2. Right-click the task sequence and choose **Edit**; locate the **Apply Network Settings** action, select it, and click **Add / New Group**. Give the new group the following settings:
   - Name: **Drivers**
   - Description: **<default>**

3. Now you create a subgroup within the first group. Click **Add / New Group** again. Give the new group the following settings:
   - Name: **Microsoft**
   - Description: **<default>**

4. Use the following settings for the **Microsoft** group's **Options** tab:
   a. Disable this step: **<default>**
   b. Continue on error: **<default>**
   c. Click the **Add Condition** drop-down menu, select **Query WMI** from the options available, and then use the following settings for the **WMI Query Properties**:
      - WMI Namespace: **<default>**
      - WQL Query: **Select \* from Win32_ComputerSystem WHERE Manufacturer like "Microsoft%"**

5. Next, choose **Add / Drivers**, and select the **Apply Driver Package** option. Use the following settings for the **Apply Driver Package** step's **Properties** tab:
   - Name: **Windows 8.1 x64 - Microsoft Surface Pro 3**
   - Driver Package: **Windows 8.1 x64 - Microsoft Surface Pro 3**
   - Select the mass storage driver…: **<default>**
   - Do unattend installation of unsigned drivers…: **<default>**

Chapter 6   Deploying Windows 8.1 to the Surface Pro 3

6. Use the following settings for the **Apply Driver Package** step's **Options** tab:
   - Disable this step: **<default>**
   - Continue on error: **<default>**
7. While still in the **Options** tab, click the **Add Condition** drop-down menu, select **Query WMI** from the options available, and then use the following settings for the **WMI Query Properties**:
   - WMI Namespace: **<default>**
   - WQL Query: **SELECT * FROM Win32_ComputerSystem WHERE Model Like "%Surface Pro 3%"**
8. Test the query by clicking **Test Query**. It should contain valid syntax as shown here.

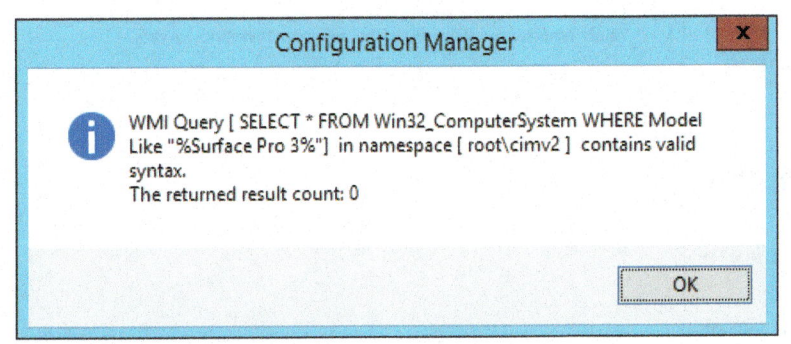

*Testing the Microsoft Surface Pro 3 WMI Query.*

9. Click **OK** to save the changes to the step.

*The Surface Pro 3 driver package is added to the task sequence.*

## Add the Surface Pro 3 Pen Pairing Support

If you want to prompt your users with an OOBE to pair the Surface Pro 3 pen, then you must add the following steps to the task sequence, and they must occur before the Setup Windows and Configuration Manger step. To add pen pairing support, follow this procedure:

1. On **CM01**, using the **ConfigMgr console**, expand **Software Library**, select **Operating System / Task Sequences**. Right-click the **Windows 8.1 Enterprise x64 - 150301** task sequence and select **Edit**.

2. Select the **Apply Driver Package** step named **Windows 8.1 x64 - Microsoft Surface Pro 3** and click **Add / General / Run Command Line**. Use the following options for the **Run Command Line** step:
    - Name: **Surface Pro 3 Pen Support**
    - Description: **<default>**
    - Command line: **xcopy ".\*.*" "C:\Windows\System32\oobe\info\default\1033" /D /E /C /I /Q /H /R /Y /S**
    - Disable 64-bit file system redirection: **<default>**
    - Start in: **<default>**
    - Package: **Surface Pro 3 Pen Support**
    - Time-out (minutes): **3**
    - Run this step as the following account: **<default>**
3. As you want this step to run only on Surface Pro 3s, you want to make the step check the type of hardware it's running on. To do that, click the **Options** tab, click the **Add Condition** drop-down menu, and select **Query WMI** from the options available. Then use the following settings for the **WMI Query Properties**:
    - WMI Namespace: **<default>**
    - WQL Query: **SELECT * FROM Win32_ComputerSystem WHERE Model Like "%Surface Pro 3%"**

## Chapter 6   Deploying Windows 8.1 to the Surface Pro 3

4. Test the query by clicking **Test Query**. It should contain valid syntax. Click **OK** to close the Test Query window and then click **OK** to save your changes.

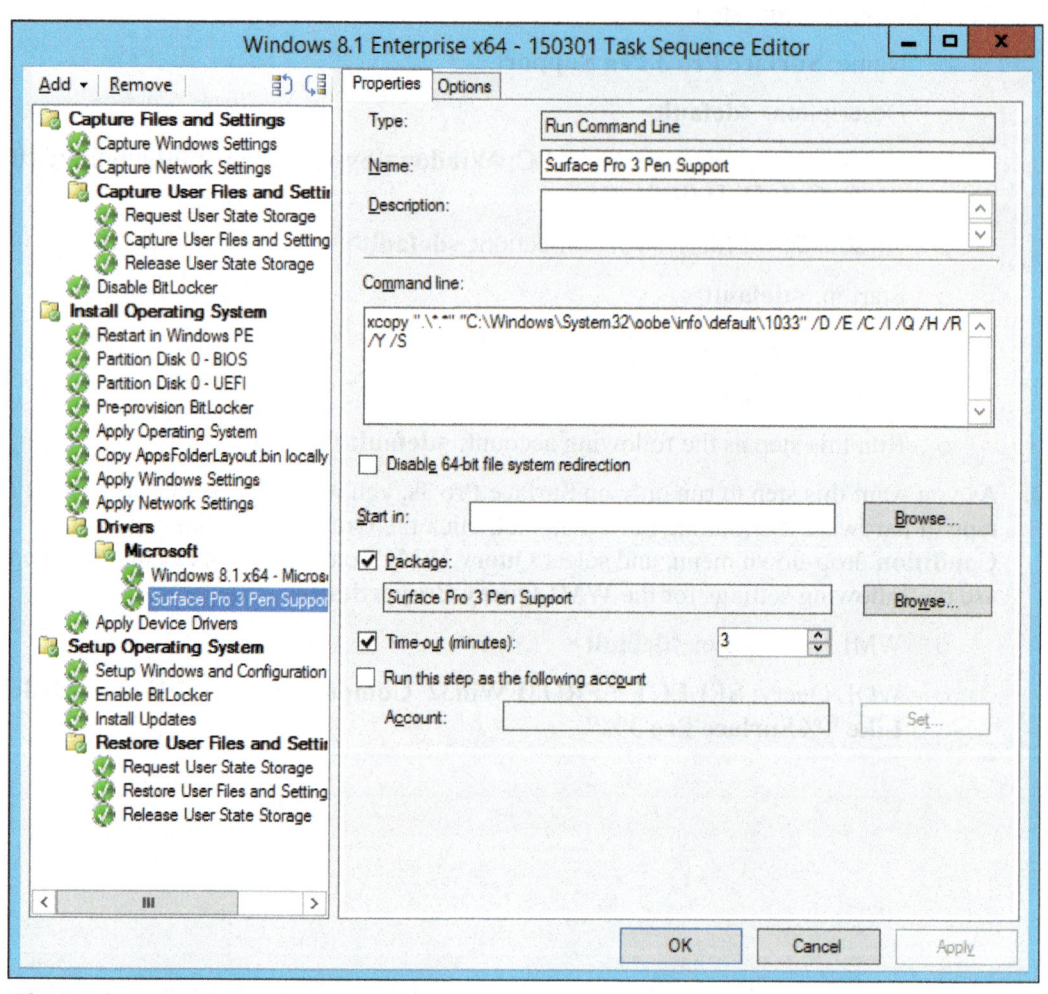

*The Surface Pro 3 Pen Support step.*

**Real World Note**: The changes in the preceding steps require that a user is actually physically present to do the Bluetooth pen pairing when the step runs; otherwise, it times out and the user will have to click Next anyway with no pairing having been completed. As a result, you should test this and decide whether it is something you want in your deployments or whether you want to pair the pen in Windows manually. To see how the OOBE pairing process works, please watch this video: https://youtu.be/8eAsMPV5v84.

## Disable the Apply Device Drivers Step

As you want to have complete control over what hardware gets which driver, it makes sense to disable the Apply Device Drivers step. To disable the step, do as follows:

1. On **CM01**, using the **ConfigMgr console**, expand **Software Library**, select **Operating System / Task Sequences**. Right-click the **Windows 8.1 Enterprise x64 - 150301** task sequence and select **Edit**.

2. Select the **Apply Device Drivers** step and click the **Options** tab. Select the **Disable this step** check box and click **OK**.

## Set the OSEnablePrebootInputProtectorsOnSlates Registry Key

The Surface Pro 3 is a tablet/hybrid device that can have a keyboard attached (or not). As a result, it's treated differently than a standard laptop or desktop when it comes to BitLocker (because a keyboard may or may not be attached, and it might be needed for TPM/Pin authentication).

If you deploy Windows 8.1 to the Surface Pro 3 and use the Enable BitLocker step, when the deployment is complete the device may end up not being BitLockered. To resolve this problem, simply add a registry key after the Setup Windows and Configuration Manager step and before the Enable BitLocker step to set the registry key.

To set the OSEnablePrebootInputProtectorsOnSlates registry key, do as follows:

1. On **CM01** using the **ConfigMgr console**, expand **Software Library**, select **Operating System / Task Sequences**. Right-click the **Windows 8.1 Enterprise x64 - 150301** task sequence and select **Edit**.

2. Select the **Setup Windows and Configuration Manager** action and click **Add / General / Run Command Line**.

3. Use the following settings for the **Run Command Line** step's **Properties** tab:

    - Name: **Set OSEnablePrebootInputProtectorsOnSlates reg key**
    - Description: **<default>**
    - Command line (you can copy and paste from E:\Setup\Scripts\Set the OSEnablePrebootInputProtectorsOnSlates Registry Key.txt): **powershell.exe -command "New-Item -Path HKLM:\SOFTWARE\Policies\Microsoft -Name FVE; Set-ItemProperty -Path HKLM:\SOFTWARE\Policies\Microsoft\FVE -Name OSEnablePrebootInputProtectorsOnSlates -Value 1 -Type DWord -Force"**
    - Disable 64-bit file system redirection: **<default>**
    - Start in: **<default>**
    - Package: **<default>**
    - Time-out (minutes): **3**
    - Run this step as the following account: **<default>**

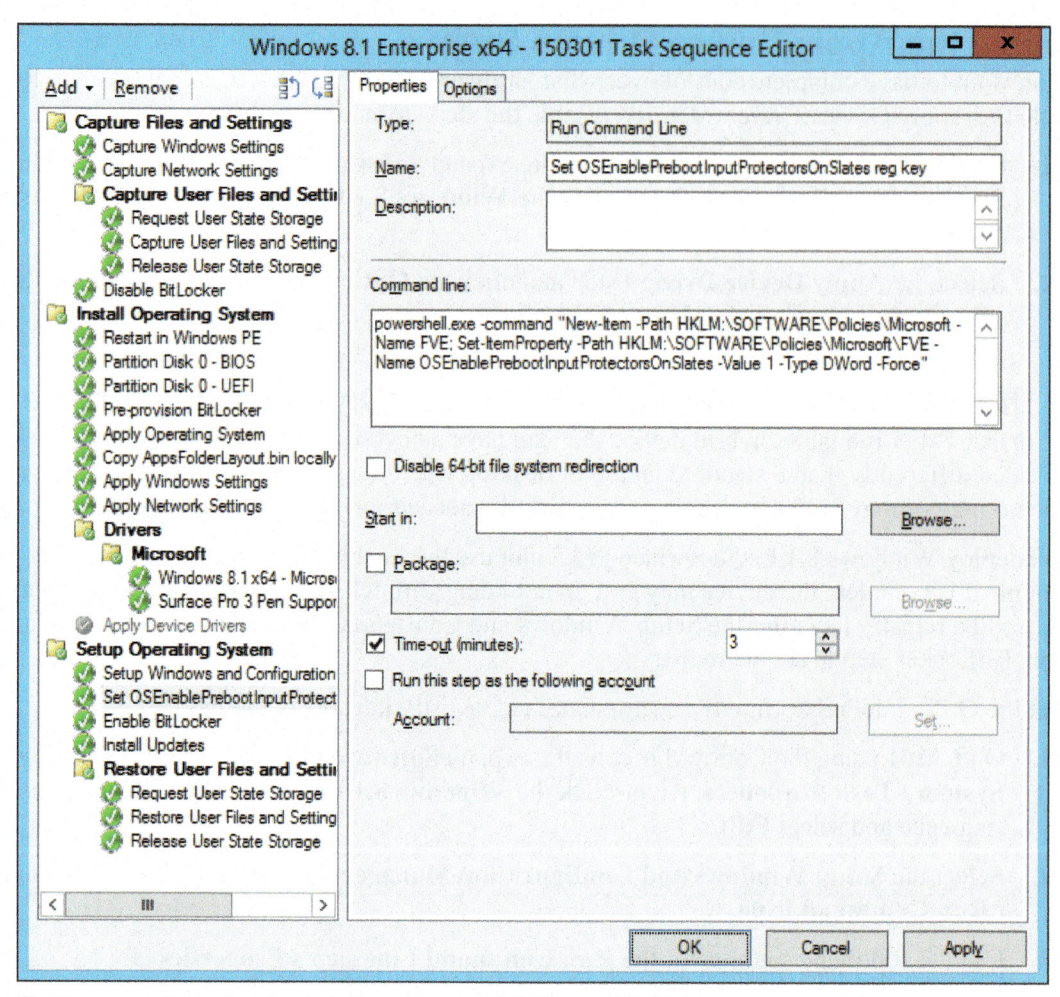

*Setting a registry key in a task sequence with PowerShell.*

4. Use the following settings for the **Run Command Line** step's **Options** tab:

    a. Disable this step: **<default>**

    b. Continue on error: **<default>**

    c. Click the **Add Condition** drop-down menu, select **Query WMI** from the options available, and then use the following settings for the **WMI Query Properties**:

        - WMI Namespace: **<default>**
        - WQL Query: **SELECT * FROM Win32_ComputerSystem WHERE Model Like "%Surface Pro 3%"**

5. Test the query by clicking **Test Query**. It should contain valid syntax.

## Add the Operating System Hotfixes Steps

To add the Operating System Hotfixes steps to your task sequence, do as follows:

1. On **CM01**, using the **ConfigMgr console**, expand **Software Library**, select **Operating System / Task Sequences**. Right-click the **Windows 8.1 Enterprise x64 - 150301** task sequence and select **Edit**.

2. Locate the **OSEnablePrebootInputProtectorsOnSlates** action and click **Add / New Group**. Give the new group the following settings:
   - Name: **Add Office updates for Pen Support**
   - Description: **For Surface Pro 3**

3. Use the following settings for the **Add Office updates for Pen Support** action's **Options** tab:
   a. Disable this step: **<default>**
   b. Continue on error: **<default>**
   c. Click the **Add Condition** drop-down menu, select **Query WMI** from the options available, and then use the following settings for the **WMI Query Properties**:
      - WMI Namespace: **<default>**
      - WQL Query: **SELECT * FROM Win32_ComputerSystem WHERE Model Like "%Surface Pro 3%"**

4. Test the query by clicking **Test Query**. It should contain valid syntax.

5. Click **Add / General / Run Command Line**. Use the following settings for the **Run Command Line** step:
   - Name: **Copy updates to C:\Windows\Temp folder**
   - Description: **<default>**
   - Command line: **xcopy ".\*.*" "C:\Windows\Temp\" /D /E /C /I /Q /H /R /Y /S**
   - Disable 64-bit file system redirection: **<default>**
   - Start in: **<default>**
   - Package: **Operating System Hotfixes**
   - Time-out (minutes): **3**
   - Run this step as the following account: **<default>**

6. Click **Add / General / Run Command Line**. Use the following settings for the **Run Command Line** step:
   - Name: **Install KB2978002**
   - Description: **<default>**

- Command line: **wusa.exe C:\Windows\Temp\Windows8.1-KB2978002-x64.msu /quiet /norestart**
- Disable 64-bit file system redirection: **&lt;default&gt;**
- Start in: **&lt;default&gt;**
- Package: **Operating System Hotfixes**
- Time-out (minutes): **15**
- Run this step as the following account: **&lt;default&gt;**

7. Click **Add / General / Run Command Line**. Use the following settings for the **Run Command Line** step:
   - Name: **Install KB2968599**
   - Description: **&lt;default&gt;**
   - Command line: **wusa.exe C:\Windows\Temp\windows8.1-kb2968599-x64_de4ca043bf6ba84330fd96cb374e801071c4b8aa.msu /quiet /norestart**
   - Disable 64-bit file system redirection: **&lt;default&gt;**
   - Start in: **&lt;default&gt;**
   - Package: **Operating System Hotfixes**
   - Time-out (minutes): **15**
   - Run this step as the following account: **&lt;default&gt;**

8. The preceding hotfixes require a reboot. To avoid that on first login, add a **Restart Computer** step. To add that step, click **Add / General / Restart Computer**. Use the following settings for the **Restart Computer** step:
   - Specify what to run after the restart: **The currently installed default operating system.**
   - Message display time-out (seconds): **5**

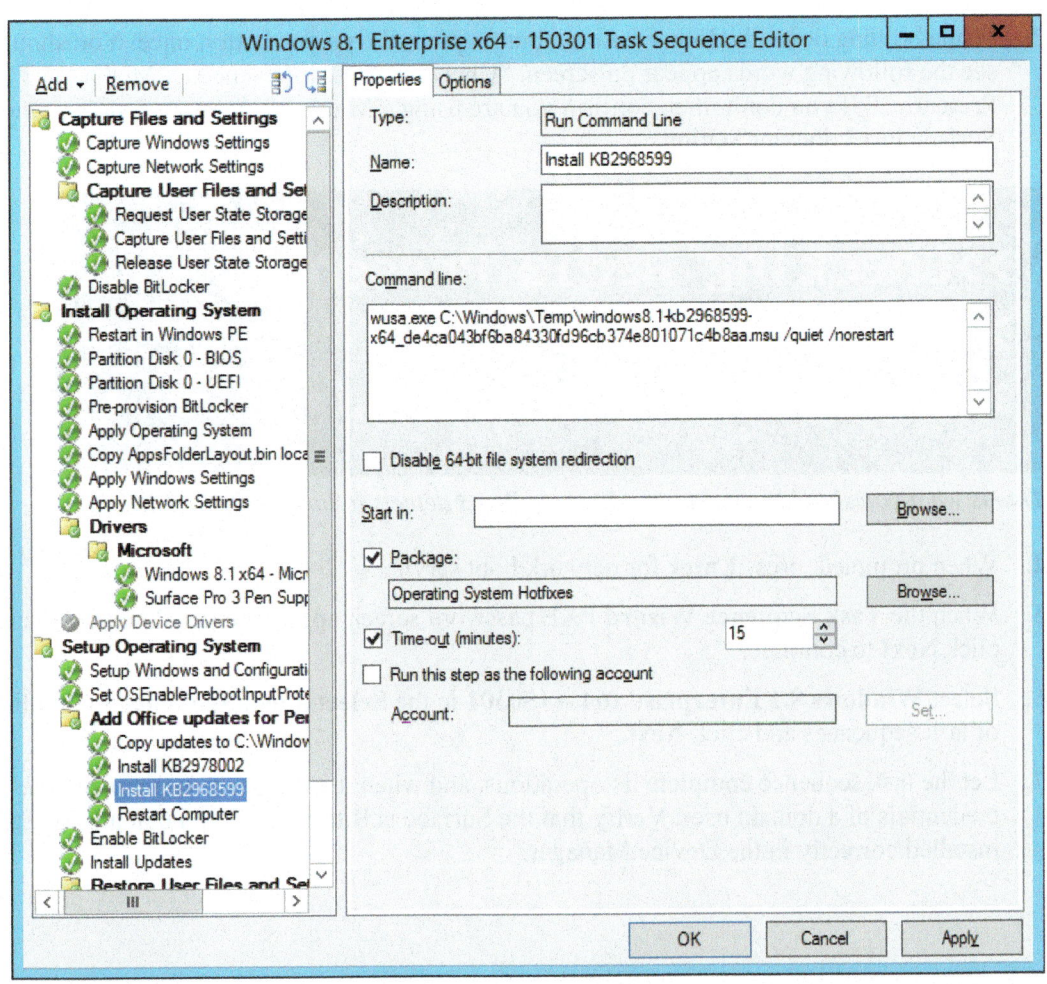

Chapter 6   Deploying Windows 8.1 to the Surface Pro 3

*The Add Office updates for Pen Support group showing the Install KB2968599 step.*

# Deploying the Surface Pro 3

Now everything is in place to start deploying Surface Pro 3. Follow this process to deploy a Surface Pro 3 with the task sequence called Windows 8.1 Enterprise x64 – 15030:

> **Note:** If you don't have a Surface Pro 3 machine, you can create a virtual machine named PC0005 to test at least part of the task sequence.

1. Make sure to properly shut down your Surface Pro 3; otherwise, it will not UEFI network boot properly. To shut it down properly in **Windows**, choose **Shutdown** and let it shut down.
2. Connect either a Microsoft USB network dongle (mbit or gigabit) to the Surface Pro 3 or dock the Surface in its docking station and ensure that it is connected to your network.

Chapter 6   Deploying Windows 8.1 to the Surface Pro 3

3. While holding down the **lower volume** button press the **power** button once. You should see the following words appear on screen: "Checking Media Presence…, Media Present…." If you don't, then confirm you are using a Microsoft network dongle or the Surface Pro 3 docking station.

```
>>Checking Media Presence......
>>Media Present......
>>Start PXE over IPv4.
```

*This is what you should see when the Surface Pro 3 detects a Surface Pro 3 NIC.*

4. When prompted, press **Enter** for network boot service.
5. When the **Task Sequence Wizard** PXE password screen appears, enter **P@ssw0rd** and click **Next** to continue.
6. Select **Windows 8.1 Enterprise x64 – 150301** in the **Select a task sequence to run** list of task sequences and click **Next**.
7. Let the task sequence complete its operations, and when it is finished, log in using the credentials of a domain user. Verify that the Surface is BitLockered and that all drivers are installed correctly in the Device Manager.

# Chapter 7
# Automatically Syncing Time in WinPE

I've seen this problem occur occasionally with laptops and tablets, and I've read reports of it happening on the Surface Pro 3. What seems to happen is that when the battery is left without power for extended periods of time, the computer forgets the real date/time and reverts to the manufacturing date/time or some other preprogrammed date/time.

When you later try to PXE boot those devices, it causes policy retrieval problems from ConfigMgr's management point that result in a "Failed to Run Task Sequence" error in the task sequence wizard.

## Step-by-Step Guide Requirements
If you want to follow the step-by-step guides in this chapter, you need a lab environment configured as outlined in Chapter 2 and Appendix A. In this chapter, you use the following virtual machines:

DC01    CM01    PC0006

*The VMs used in this chapter (PC0006 is a VM created in one of the guides).*

## The Problem in Detail
Failure to retrieve policy means you cannot run any task sequences and the failure in turn produces an error just before running any required (mandatory) task sequences or displaying a list of one or more available (optional) task sequences.

## Chapter 7   Automatically Syncing Time in WinPE

The error produced occurs immediately after the PXE password is entered, if one is set. The error message displayed to the end user is shown in the following figure.

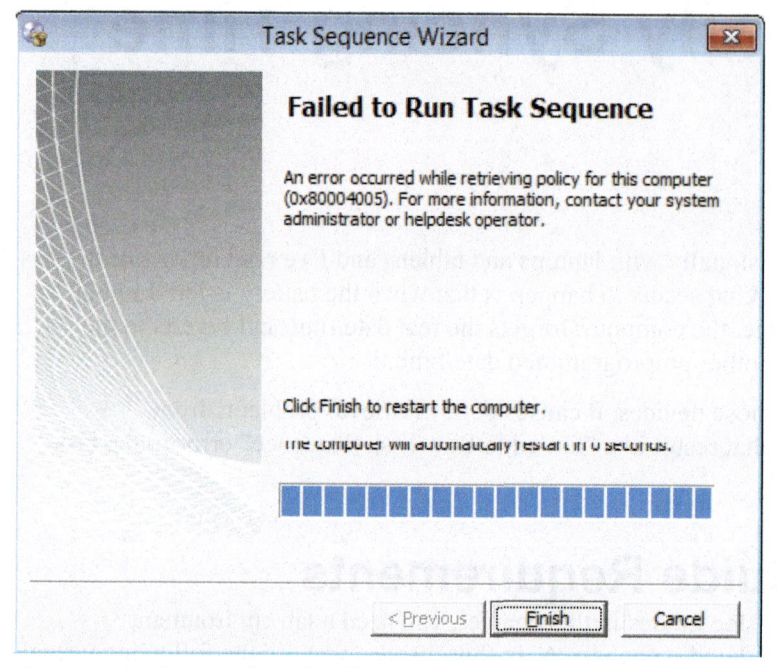

*An error is shown when the date is wrong in the BIOS and you attempt to PXE boot.*

The actual errors can be viewed using the CMTrace tool and are highlighted in red text in the smsts.log file shown in the next figure. The smsts.log file is found at the following location: x:\windows\temp\smstslog\smsts.log.

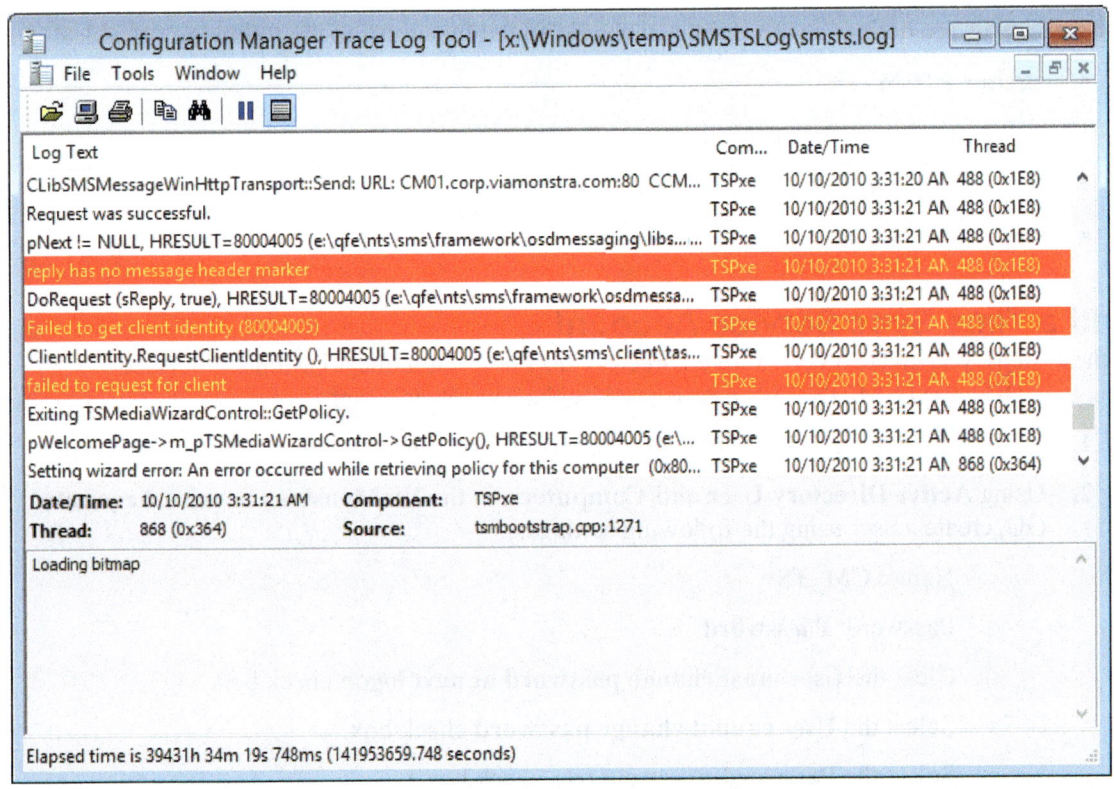

*The smsts.log file reveals more details including the incorrect date in the Date/Time column.*

## Fixing the Problem

Fixing this problem is easy enough: simply set the correct date in the BIOS, reboot the client computer, and PXE boot again. This time it should not get the error and should receive the policy correctly.

Although that is an easy fix, it does require manual steps and also requires a reboot; therefore, you might want to create a solution that runs automatically every time you boot a computer, particularly if you are imaging a lot of computers and especially tablets.

To automate the sync process for all of your computers that PXE boot or use standalone or bootable media, complete the steps in the following sections.

# Using net time with a Service Account

To get the correct time, use a script that uses the built-in Windows *net time* command to sync the time with a known server. This method requires domain logon credentials. As a result, you need to create a user account to be used in the script.

The credentials are defined in the script and can be edited by adjusting the following variables:

- strUser = "CM_TS"
- strPassword = "P@ssw0rd"
- strDomain = "ViaMonstra"
- strServer = "DC01"

## Add a Time Sync Service Account

In these steps, you create a new Active Directory user account in the ViaMonstra/Service Accounts OU called CM_TS. This user is used by the TimeSync script.

1. On **DC01**, log in as **VIAMONSTRA\Administrator** using a password of **P@ssw0rd**.
2. Using **Active Directory User and Computers**, in the **ViaMonstra / Service Accounts** OU, create a user using the following settings:
    - Name: **CM_TS**
    - Password: **P@ssw0rd**
    - Clear the **User must change password at next logon** check box.
    - Select the **User cannot change password** check box.
    - Select the **Password never expires** check box.
    - Description: **TimeSync Service Account**

Chapter 7    Automatically Syncing Time in WinPE

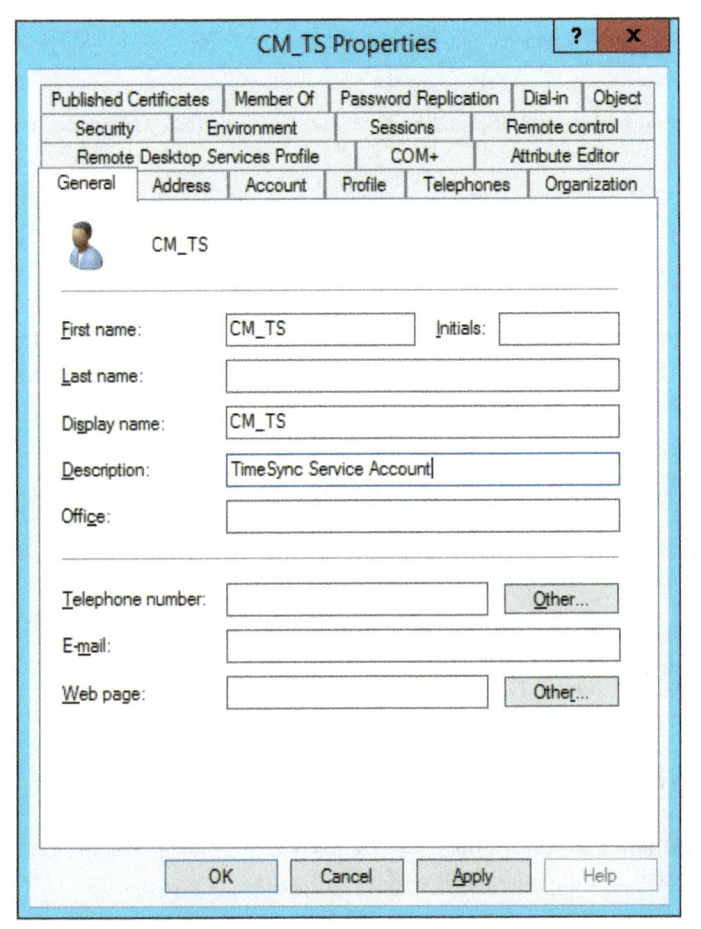

*The CM_TS Service Account properties in Active Directory.*

# Using a Prestart Command

The fix to this problem involves using a feature in the ConfigMgr boot image properties called a *prestart* command to run a script in Windows PE to sync time using net time with a server you specify in your domain.

A prestart command is a script or executable that runs before any task sequence is selected and can interact with the user in Windows PE. It's a useful way of fixing things dynamically before the task sequence engine starts. Any prestart command entered in the Command line field on the boot image's Customization tab will end up in a text file in the root of the boot image (X:\) called TSConfig.ini.

## Chapter 7 Automatically Syncing Time in WinPE

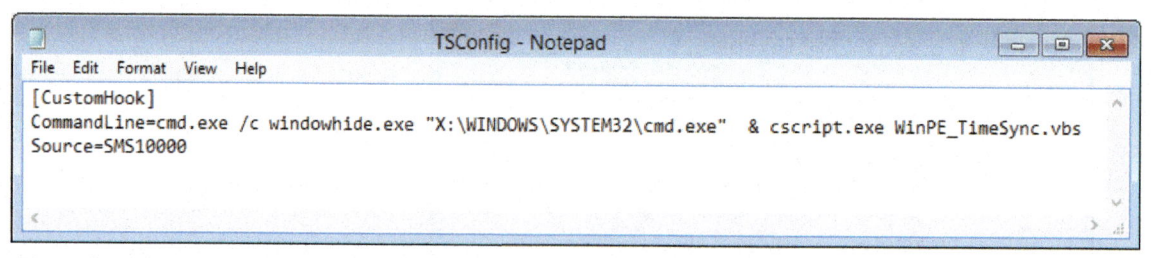

```
[CustomHook]
CommandLine=cmd.exe /c windowhide.exe "X:\WINDOWS\SYSTEM32\cmd.exe" & cscript.exe WinPE_TimeSync.vbs
Source=SMS10000
```

*TSconfig.ini revealing a prestart command (CustomHook) and the SMS package source.*

This text file also contains the name of the SMS package used to store the prestart scripts, namely SMS10000. This package is basically the contents of the prestart scripts folder you create in the next section and is located in the boot image at X:\sms\PKG\SMS10000.

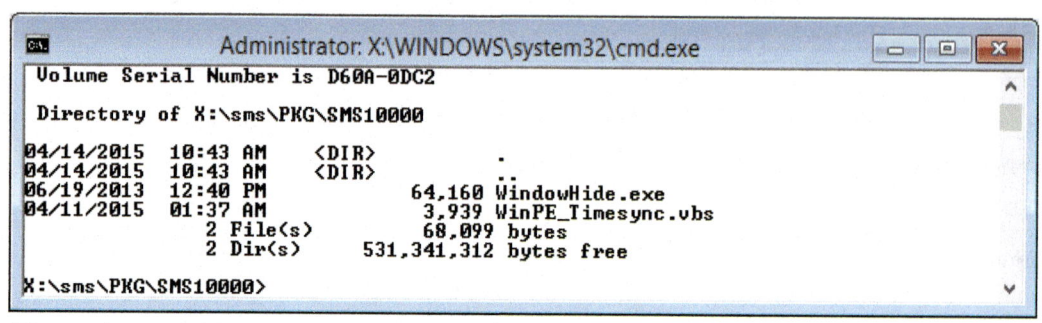

```
Volume Serial Number is D60A-0DC2

 Directory of X:\sms\PKG\SMS10000

04/14/2015  10:43 AM    <DIR>          .
04/14/2015  10:43 AM    <DIR>          ..
06/19/2013  12:40 PM            64,160 WindowHide.exe
04/11/2015  01:37 AM             3,939 WinPE_Timesync.vbs
               2 File(s)         68,099 bytes
               2 Dir(s)     531,341,312 bytes free

X:\sms\PKG\SMS10000>
```

*The sms\PKG folder containing the prestart scripts.*

For more information on prestart commands and how they can be used with media, see this TechNet article: https://technet.microsoft.com/en-us/library/jj651034.aspx.

## Create a Prestart Scripts Folder

As you will be using one or more prestart scripts throughout this book, it makes sense to store those scripts where the ConfigMgr console can access them when updating boot images. You can actually run multiple prestart scripts via the prestart command line as long as you know how to do it.

The trick to using more than one prestart in a boot image is to launch them via a command prompt or via another script. The following sample prestart command launches a command prompt, which in turn runs two prestart scripts in the order specified.

```
cmd.exe /c cscript.exe prestart1.vbs & cscript.exe prestart2.vbs
```

## Chapter 7  Automatically Syncing Time in WinPE

To create a folder called Prestart Scripts that will store the prestart scripts used in this book, follow these steps.

1. On **CM01**, using an elevated **Command prompt** (run as Administrator), browse to **E:\Sources\OSD\Boot** and create the following folder: **Prestart Scripts**.

```
E:\Sources\OSD\Boot>mkdir "Prestart Scripts"
E:\Sources\OSD\Boot>_
```

*A place to store prestart scripts used in boot images.*

2. Using **File Explorer**, copy the script called **WinPE_TimeSync.vbs** in **E:\Setup\Scripts** on **CM01** to **E:\Sources\OSD\Boot\Prestart Scripts**.

3. Using **File Explorer**, copy a file called **windowhide.exe** in **E:\Sources\OSD\MDT\MDT 2013\Tools\<arch>** on **CM01** to **E:\Sources\OSD\Boot\Prestart Scripts**, where <arch> corresponds to the boot media architecture (either x86 or x64). In this guide, you use the **x64** version.

## Add a Prestart Command to Your Boot WIM

Adding a prestart command to a boot image affects only that boot image. As a result, you should add the prestart command only to a boot image attached to your task sequence(s) in use. In this step, you add the prestart command to the Boot Image (x64).

The prestart does a couple of things, first it launches a command prompt and then swiftly hides it using a tool called windowhide.exe. Next, it runs the actual prestart script before exiting. To add the prestart command to the boot image, follow these steps:

1. On **CM01**, using the **ConfigMgr console**, expand **Software Library**, select **Operating System / Boot Images**, and then select the **Boot Image (x64)** boot image.

2. Right-click the **Boot Image (x64)** boot image and choose **Properties**, click the **Customization** tab, select the **Enable Prestart Command** and **Include files for the prestart command** check boxes, and then use the following settings:

    o  Command line: **cmd.exe /c windowhide.exe "X:\WINDOWS\SYSTEM32\cmd.exe" & cscript.exe WinPE_TimeSync.vbs**

    o  Source directory: **\\CM01\Sources\OSD\Boot\Prestart Scripts**

    o  Select **Enable command support (testing only)**

189

3. Click **OK** and answer **Yes** when prompted to update the distribution points now; continue through that wizard until completion and click **Close**.

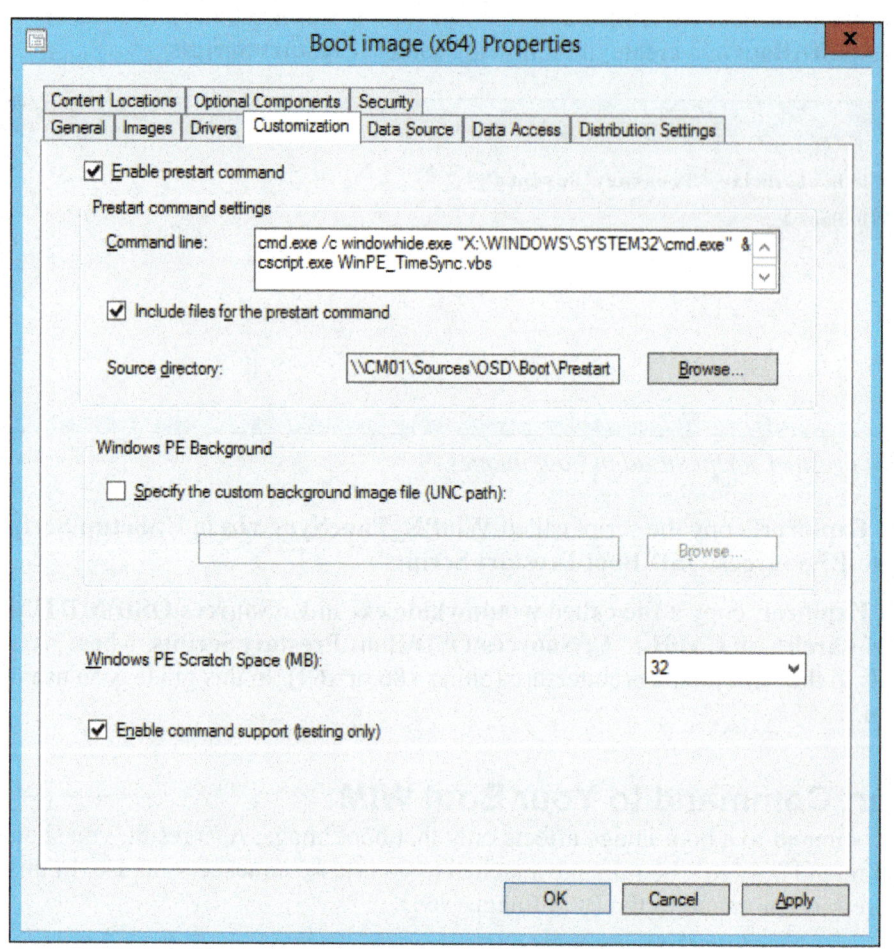

*The WinPE_Timesync prestart command has been added to Boot Image (x64).*

# Verifying the Changes

Everything is in place to test and verify the prestart changes to your boot image. To verify that the prestart command and associated script do what they are supposed to do, follow this procedure:

1. Create a virtual machine named **PC0006**, and verify that the boot order is set to boot to network, as explained in Chapter 5, and then power the virtual machine on. When the **Task Sequence Wizard** PXE password screen appears, press **F8**.

2. Using the **date** command change the date to something before today, such as **10/10/10**.

Chapter 7   Automatically Syncing Time in WinPE

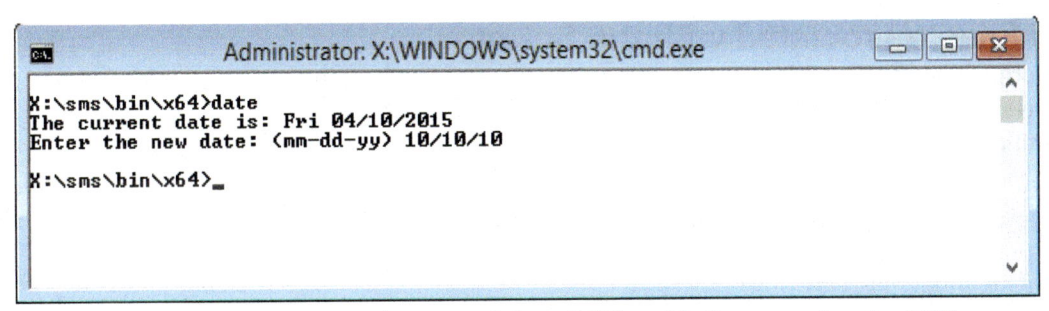

```
X:\sms\bin\x64>date
The current date is: Fri 04/10/2015
Enter the new date: (mm-dd-yy) 10/10/10

X:\sms\bin\x64>_
```

*Changing the date to a date in the past while in PXE and before entering the PXE password.*

3. Next, enter the PXE password (**P@ssw0rd**) and press **Enter**. After a couple of moments, the **Windows 8.1 x64 – 1501** task sequence is listed in the list of task sequences. This is an indication of success as the policy was retrieved successfully from the management point even though the date of the computer was set to October 10, 2010, five years or so in the past.

4. To further verify the change, using **CMTrace**, open **x:\windows\temp\smstslog\smsts.log**. Notice the date before and after the script is run. This date correction occurs before the management point is contacted for retrieval of the policy.

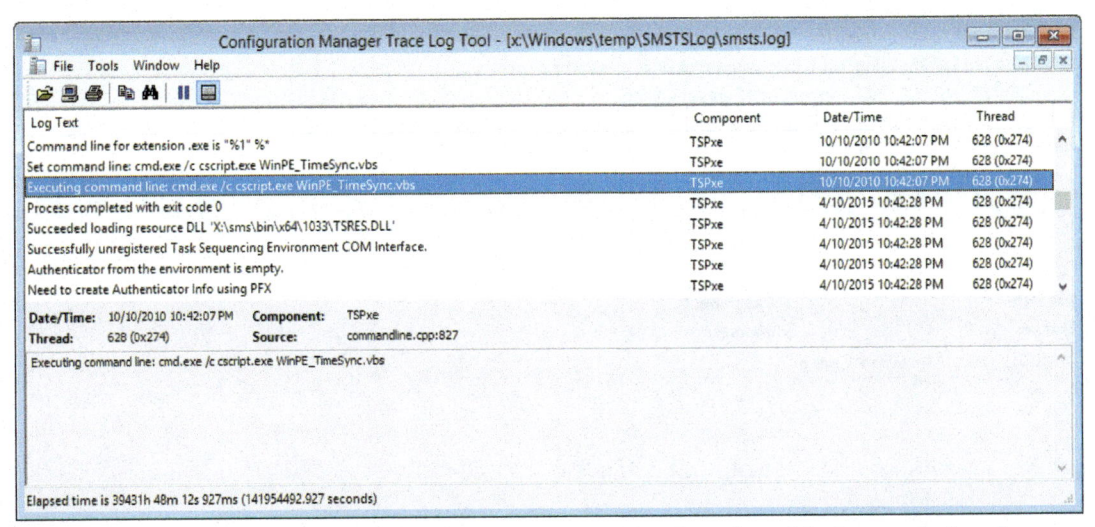

*CMTrace reveals the prestart script running. Notice the dates listed before and after the event.*

## Log Files Associated with the Script

The script generates the following three log files. These log files can help you troubleshoot scenarios in which the script isn't working as expected, for example when you've entered credentials in the script incorrectly.

- WinPE_TimeSync.log
- WinPE_Net_Use.log
- WinPE_Net_Time.log

These three log files should be present in X:\Windows\Temp\SMSTSLOG after the script has run and can be opened in Notepad or CMTrace for viewing. The figure shows the WinPE_TimeSync.log file after successfully syncing time with the domain controller. The date change is clearly visible in the log.

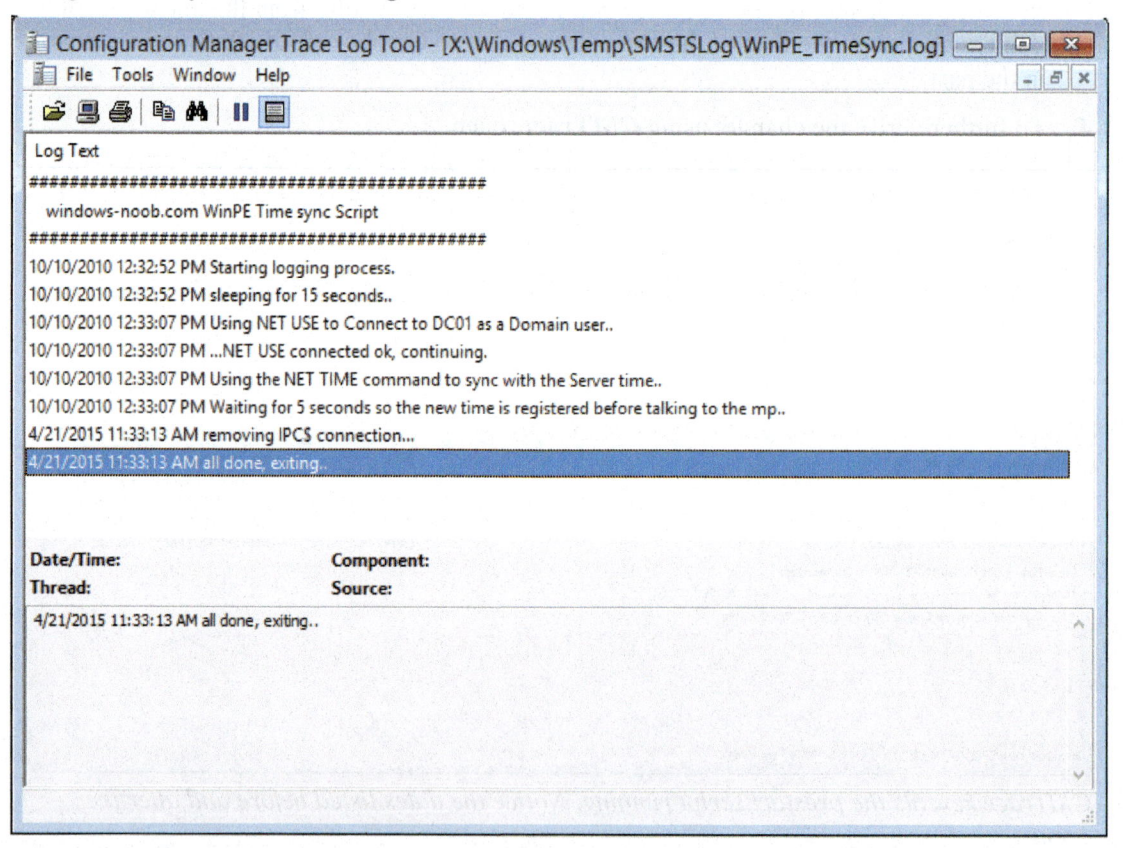

*The X:\WinPE_TimeSync.log file in CMTrace showing successful completion.*

**Real World Note**: If you have issues getting the script to work in your environment, and the preceding logs don't reveal the problem to you, locate any lines in the script that start with 'wscript.echo strCommand and remove the single quote (') in front of them. This will echo the command line on-screen (to the command prompt window) so that you can view it easily to help recognize typos or other problems.

# Chapter 8
# Pausing a Task Sequence

Sometimes things don't go as planned. You are deploying an operating system to a computer and the task sequence fails. You can use normal troubleshooting methods such as these:

- Press F8 and review the smsts.log in CMTrace
- Review a report or query the status of the task sequence progress
- Review other operating system deployment related logs
- Review application or package content status

Or you can pause your task sequence during normal task sequence operations using one of the methods described in this chapter.

## Step-by-Step Guide Requirements
If you want to follow the step-by-step guides in this chapter, you need a lab environment configured as outlined in Chapter 2 and Appendix A. In this chapter, you use the following virtual machines:

DC01        CM01        PC0007

*The VMs used in this chapter (PC0007 is a VM created in one of the guides).*

You also need to have downloaded the following software:

The book sample files (http://deploymentfundamentals.com)

> **Note**: This guide assumes that you have already got a working PXE environment setup, that you've deployed at least one task sequence, and that you've also integrated MDT 2013 with ConfigMgr. In addition, this guide assumes that you have enabled F8 command prompt support within your boot WIMs as described in Chapter 2.

# Why Pause?

Pausing your task sequence gives you the power to perform additional diagnosis during a deployment. It also enables you to monitor a step "live" while it's happening, for example, checking how and when variables are being set rather than reviewing the logs after the event.

When you start using the pause functionality in your task sequences, you'll wonder how you ever managed without it. There are a variety of different ways to pause a task sequence, some require a bit of work, such as those covered as Methods 1 and 3 in this chapter; whereas others, such as Method 2, are very simple but also lack the finesse or clarity of the other methods.

## Pausing Effectively

I recommend that you place a pause step both before and after the step or group that you want to monitor. The reason behind this is that it allows you to get prepared for the troubleshooting actions and then monitor the results. In addition, having two pauses means you can gather variable values both before and after the step (or group) is complete to validate the results.

To get details of how you can dump task sequence variables, see the following post on TechNet: http://blogs.technet.com/b/mniehaus/archive/2010/04/26/dumping-task-sequence-variables.aspx.

When adding the Pause Task Sequence step, it's a good idea to surround the step with highly visible # marks so that you can quickly locate the pause steps in a complex task sequence. When you are using the pause functionality, you can either completely delete the steps or simply disable them.

## Using Selective Pause

You can take this one step further and only pause based on a criteria set; for example, you can selectively pause if the computer in question has a variable set such as Pause_TS=True. This can be set on the computer object in the ConfigMgr console and checked via the Options tab on the pause task sequence step itself.

The advantage of using selective pause is that it allows you to troubleshoot new steps in a production environment without other users seeing the pause.

# Method 1: Pausing Using ServiceUI.exe

This method makes use of the functionality provided by a file called ServiceUI.exe from the Microsoft Deployment Toolkit. This file allows you to pop up messages and run interactive actions with users while in the SYSTEM context in Windows PE or Windows.

You do not need to use MDT or have MDT integrated with ConfigMgr in order to use this method. However, you do need to prepare a package containing both the script used in this guide and ServiceUI.exe from MDT so that you can easily add a pause to your task sequences.

## Create the Pause_TS Package

You need two files. The first is the script called pause_ts.vbs, which is located in E:\Setup\Scripts, and the second is ServiceUI.exe from MDT. This second file is located by default in C:\ProgramFiles\Microsoft Deployment Toolkit\Templates\Distribution\Tools\<arch> where <arch> matches the architecture (x86 or x64) of your boot image.

> **Note**: The boot image attached to your task sequence decides which version of ServiceUI.exe you need to use, so if you are using a 64-bit boot image, you must use the X64 version of ServiceUI.exe; otherwise, you get a subsystem missing error when you try to run it.

To create the Pause_TS package, follow these steps:

1. On **CM01**, using a **Command prompt**, create the following directory: **E:\Sources\Software\ViaMonstra\Pause_TS**.

2. Using **File Explorer**, copy **Pause_TS.vbs** from **E:\Setup\Scripts** and **ServiceUI.exe** from **E:\Sources\OSD\MDT\MDT 2013\Tools\x64** to **E:\Sources\Software\ViaMonstra\Pause_TS**.

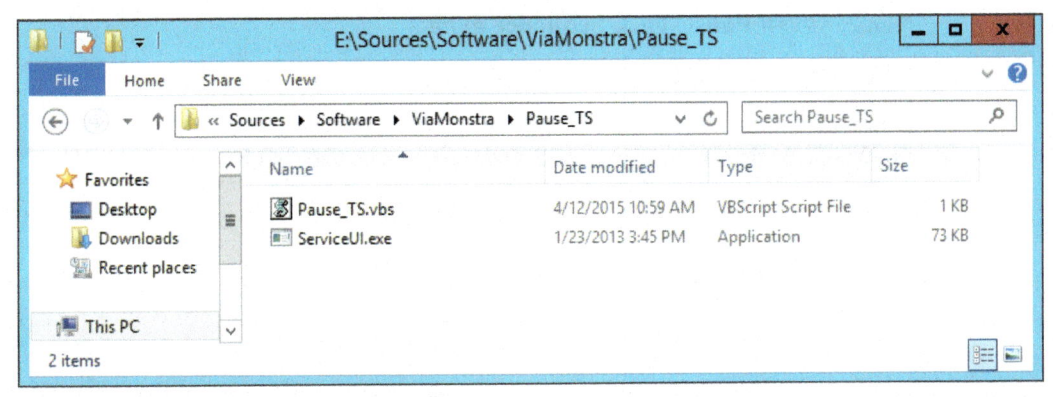

*The files used in the Pause_TS package.*

3. On **CM01**, using the **ConfigMgr console**, in the **Software Library** workspace, select **Application Management / Packages**. Right-click and choose **Create Package**. Use the following settings for the **Create Package and Program** wizard:

    o Name: **Pause_TS**

    o Source folder: **\\CM01\Sources\Software\ViaMonstra\Pause_TS**

    o Select **Do not create a program**.

4. Continue through the wizard until completion. Finally, distribute the package to the **CM01.CORP.VIAMONSTRA.COM** distribution point by right-clicking the package and completing the **Distribute Content Wizard**.

## Edit a Task Sequence to Add the Pause Functionality

Now that you've created the Pause_TS package, it's time to add the pause functionality to a task sequence.

It is worth pointing out that this pause functionality method only works when the computer can access the package on the distribution point. So if you feel that there are occasions during which you may not be able to access a distribution point for whatever reason, you could inject the files into your boot image using DISM instead, or use one of the other methods of pausing a task sequence as detailed in this chapter.

To add the pause functionality to the task sequence, follow these steps:

1. On **CM01**, using the **ConfigMgr console**, expand **Software Library**, select **Operating System / Task Sequences**, and then select the **Windows 8.1 Enterprise x64 - 150301** task sequence.

2. Right-click the task sequence and choose **Edit**; locate the **Apply Operating System** step and click it; next choose **Add / General / Run Command Line**.

3. Use the following settings for the **Run Command Line** step:
   - Name: ##### **Pause Task Sequence** #####
   - Description: **<default>**
   - Command line: **serviceUI.exe -process:TSProgressUI.exe %SYSTEMROOT%\System32\wscript.exe pause_ts.vbs**
   - Disable 64-bit file system redirection: **<default>**
   - Start in: **<default>**
   - Package: **Pause_TS**
   - Time-out (minutes): **<default>**
   - Run this step as the following account: **<default>**

4. Select the ##### **Pause Task Sequence** ##### line, right-click it, and choose **Copy**; then directly after the **Copy AppsFolderLayout.bin locally** line, right-click, and choose **Paste**.

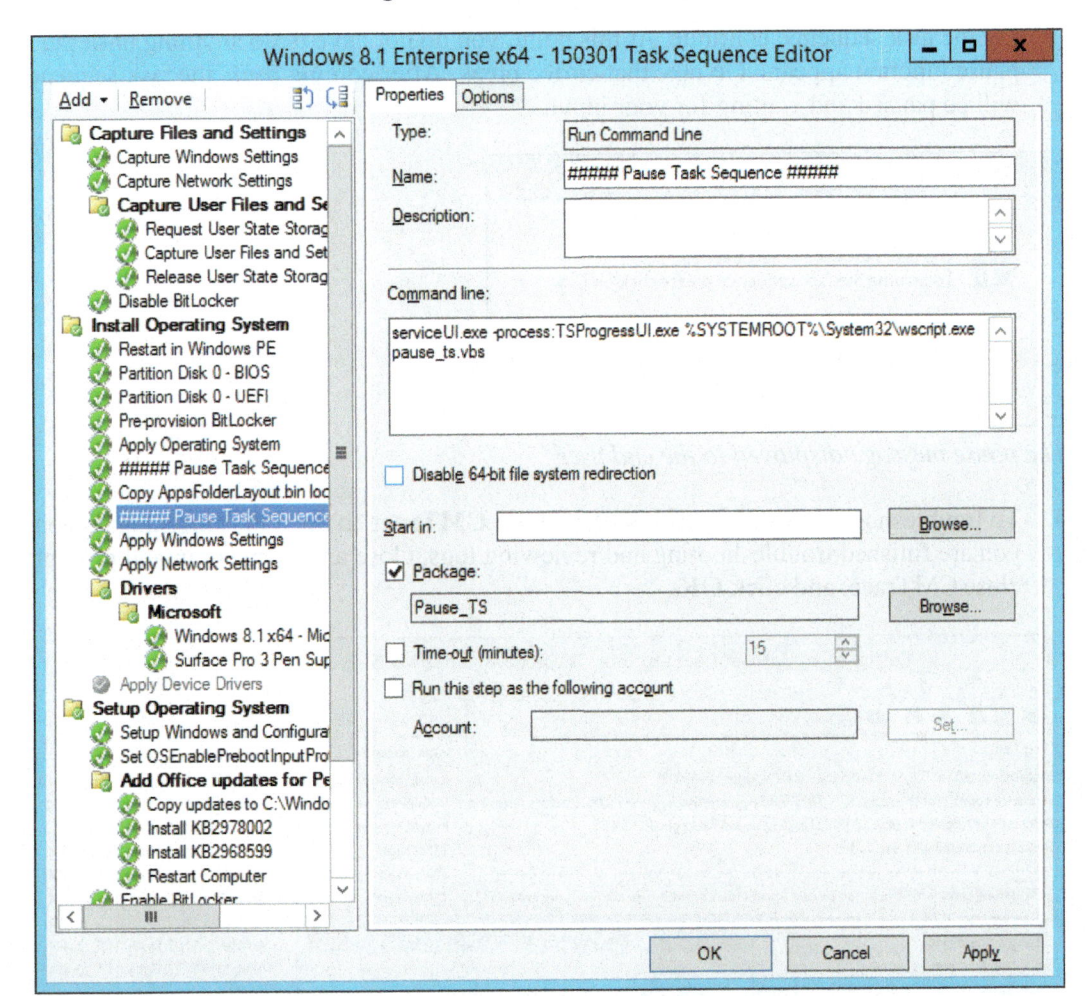

5. Click **OK** to save the changes and close the Task Sequence.

*Pausing a task sequence step with the ServiceUI method.*

## Verify the Changes

You've added your pause steps to your task sequence and now you want to view them in action. To view the pause functionality using the ServiceUI method, do as follows:

1. Create a virtual machine named **PC0007**, and verify that the boot order is set to boot to network as explained in Chapter 5 and then power the virtual machine on. When the **Task Sequence Wizard** PXE password screen appears, enter **P@ssw0rd** and click **Next**.

2. Select the **Windows 8.1 Enterprise x64 - 150301** task sequence and click **Next**.

## Chapter 8   Pausing a Task Sequence

3. Assign the **PC0007** computer name, and click **Next**.

   Let the task sequence continue. At this point, you do not have to do anything until the pause function appears. Go take that coffee break. After coming back, the task sequence will be paused and waiting for your input.

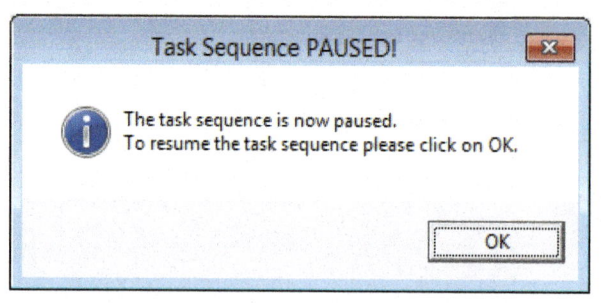

   *The pause message displayed to the end user.*

4. To troubleshoot at this point, press **F8** and use **CMTrace** to open the **smsts.log**. When you are finished troubleshooting and reviewing logs, close any open command prompts, close CMTrace, and click **OK**.

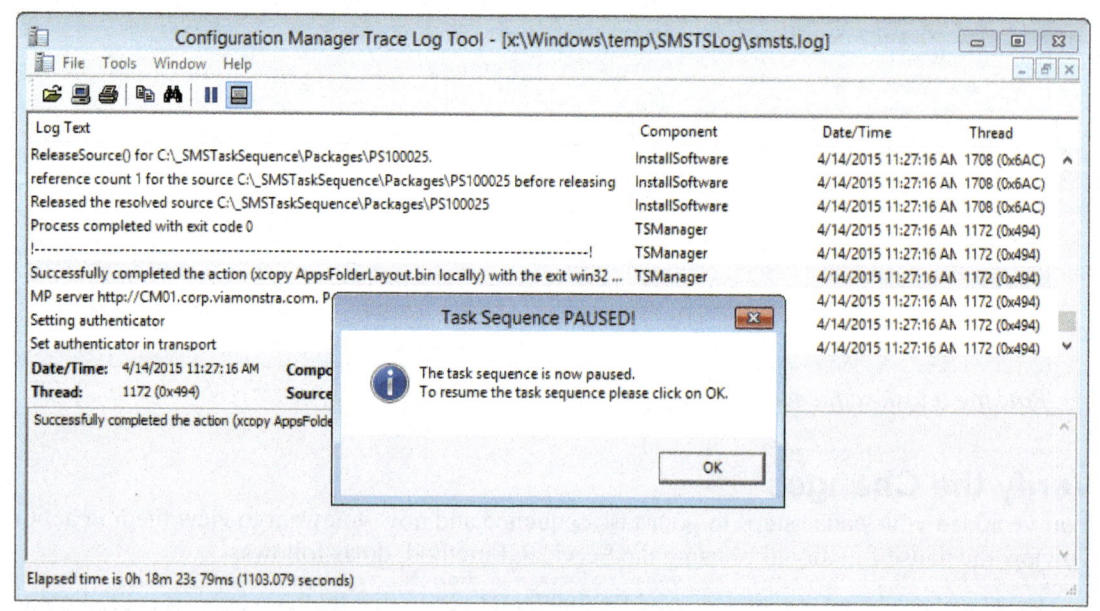

   *After the step has run, another pause is issued to allow you to verify the step ran successfully.*

198

Chapter 8  Pausing a Task Sequence

# Method 2: Pausing Using cmd

This method makes use of the cmd command, and its advantage is that no package needs to be created or downloaded. That also means it is simple to implement for a quick pause in a task sequence.

The downside of this method is that it may not be immediately clear to the end user what has occurred other than a command prompt window popping up, and the user is not informed to close the command prompt in order to continue.

## Edit a Task Sequence to Add the Pause Functionality

For this method, I assume you have not added the pause steps from the preceding method. The method pauses the task sequence by opening a command prompt. To add a pause to your task sequence using the cmd command, do as follows:

1. On **CM01**, using the **ConfigMgr console**, expand **Software Library**, select **Operating System / Task Sequences**, and then select the **Windows 8.1 Enterprise x64 - 150301** task sequence.

2. Right-click the task sequence and choose **Edit**; locate the **Apply Operating System** step and click it; next choose **Add / General / Run Command Line**.

3. Use the following settings for the **Run Command Line** step:
   - Name: ##### **Pause Task Sequence** #####
   - Description: **<default>**
   - Command line: **cmd /c start "cmd" /wait cmd**
   - Disable 64-bit file system redirection: **<default>**
   - Start in: **<default>**
   - Package**: <default>**
   - Time-out (minutes): **<default>**
   - Run this step as the following account: **<default>**

4. Select the ##### **Pause Task Sequence** ##### line, right-click it, and choose **Copy**; then directly after the **xcopy AppsFolderLayout.bin locally** line, right-click, and choose **Paste**.

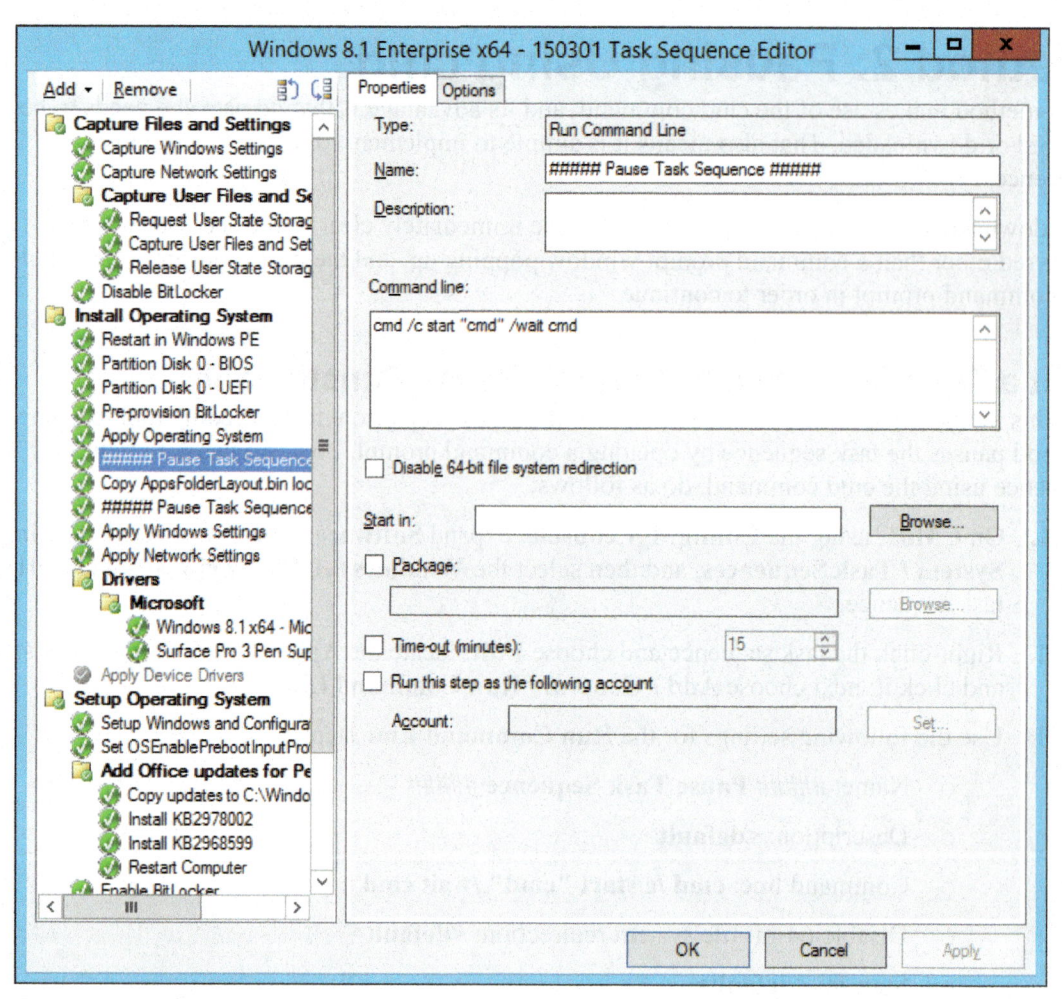

*Pausing a task sequence using the cmd command.*

## Verify the Changes

To view the pause functionality using the cmd method, do as follows:

1. Create a virtual machine named **PC0007**, and verify that the boot order is set to boot to network as explained in Chapter 5 and then power the virtual machine on. When the **Task Sequence Wizard** PXE password screen appears, enter **P@ssw0rd** and click **Next**.

2. Select the **Windows 8.1 Enterprise x64 – 150301** task sequence and click **Next**.

3. Assign the **PC0007** computer name, and click **Next**.

   Let the task sequence continue. When you see the task sequence Installation Progress window state "Running action: ##### Pause Task Sequence #####", a command prompt opens and you can begin your troubleshooting.

Chapter 8  Pausing a Task Sequence

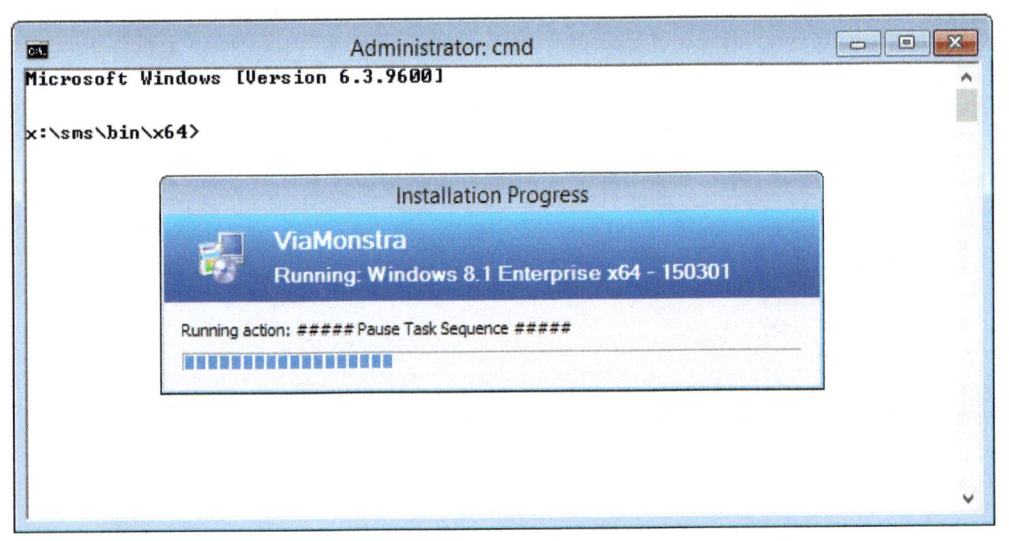

*Pausing the task sequence using a command prompt. Simple yet effective.*

4. After troubleshooting is complete, simply close the command prompt and the task sequence will continue.

# Method 3: Pausing Using PowerShell

This method makes use of PowerShell to pause the task sequence whether you are in Windows PE or Windows. However, using PowerShell in Windows PE requires that PowerShell support is added to your boot image via the Optional Components tab in the boot image. PowerShell purists will probably want to use this method, and having PowerShell support added to your boot image images is useful indeed.

## Add PowerShell Support to the Boot Image

To add PowerShell support to your boot image, do as follows:

1. On **CM01**, using the **ConfigMgr console**, expand **Software Library**, select **Operating Systems / Boot Images**, and then select the **Boot image (x64)** boot image.

2. Right-click the file and choose **Properties**. Select the **Optional Components** tab.

3. In the **Components** section, click the **yellow asterisk** button and select **Windows PowerShell (WinPE-PowerShell)** from the list of available components.

4. When you are prompted to add the optional **Microsoft .NET (WinPE-NetFx)** component, click **OK**.

# Chapter 8  Pausing a Task Sequence

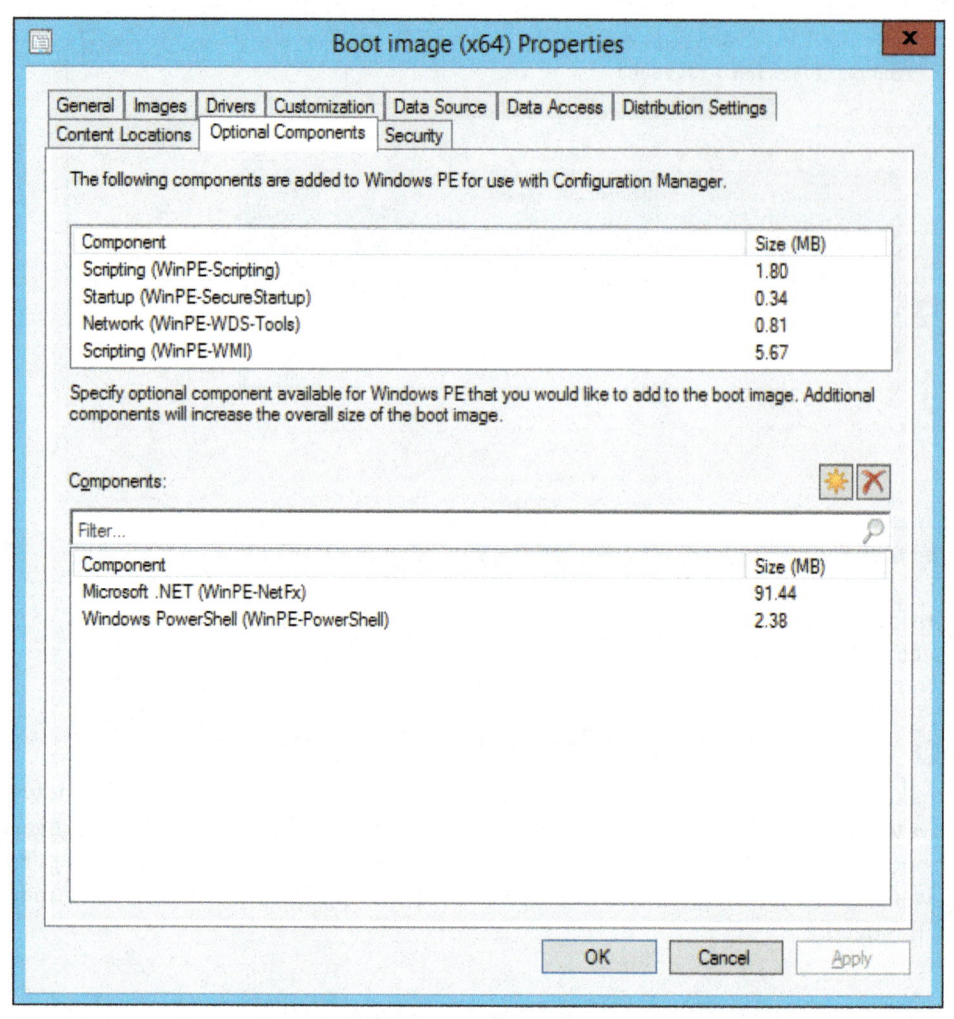

*The Windows PowerShell (WinPE-PowerShell) optional components.*

5. Click **OK** again and select **Apply**. When you are prompted to update the boot image to its distribution points, select **Yes** and continue through the **Update Distribution Points Wizard** until completion.

Chapter 8   Pausing a Task Sequence

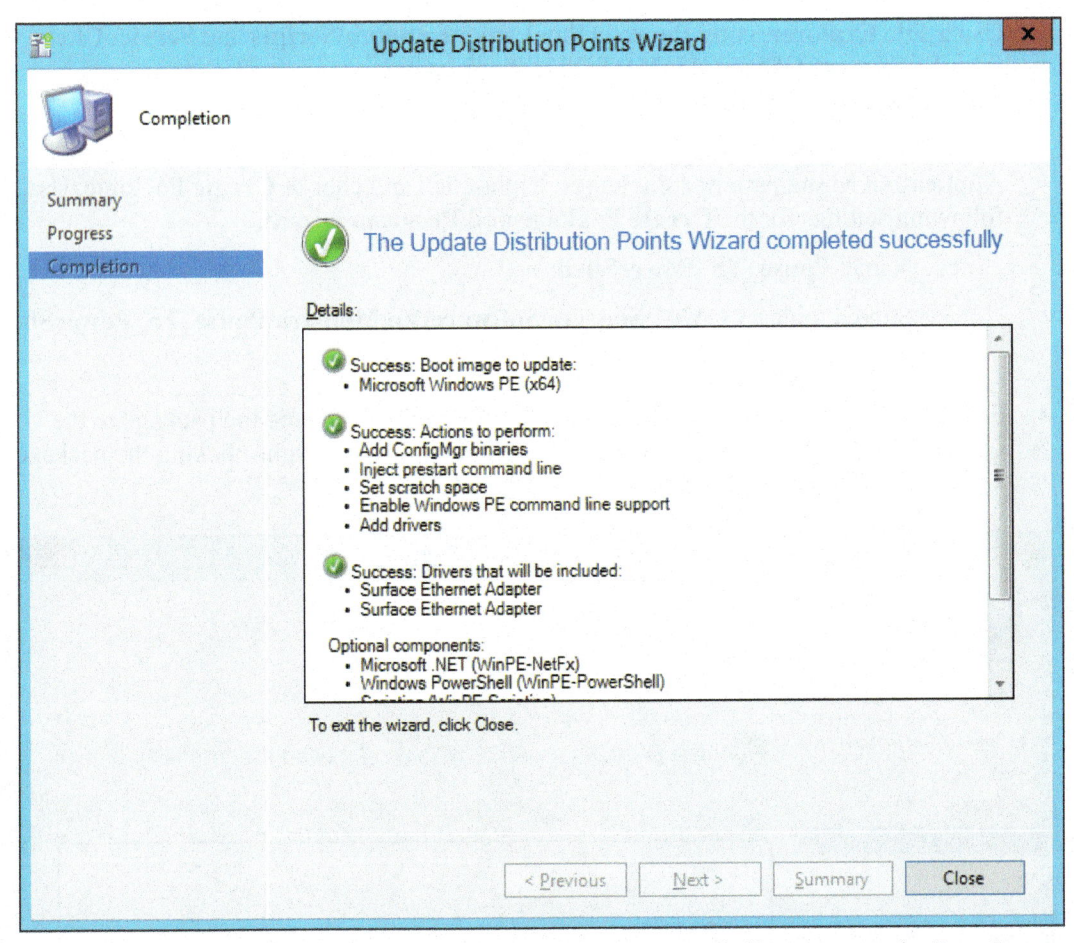

*The Update Distribution Points Wizard after adding PowerShell support to the Boot Image (x64)*

## Create the Pause_TS_PowerShell Package
You need two files. The first is the script called pause_ts.ps1, which is located in E:\Setup\Scripts, and the second is ServiceUI.exe from MDT. This second file is located by default in C:\ProgramFiles\Microsoft Deployment Toolkit\Templates\Distribution\Tools\<arch> where <arch> matches the architecture (x86 or x64) of your boot image.

> **Note**: The boot image attached to your task sequence decides which version of ServiceUI.exe you need to use. So if you are using a 64-bit boot image, you must use the X64 version of ServiceUI.exe; otherwise, you get a subsystem missing error when you try to run it.

To create the Pause_TS_PowerShell package, follow these steps:

1. On **CM01**, using a **Command prompt**, create the following directory:
   **E:\Sources\Software\ViaMonstra\Pause_TS_PowerShell**.

Chapter 8   Pausing a Task Sequence

2. Using **File Explorer**, copy **Pause_TS.ps1** from **E:\Setup\Scripts** and **ServiceUI.exe** from **E:\Sources\OSD\MDT\MDT 2013\Tools\x64** to **E:\Sources\Software\ViaMonstra\ Pause_TS_PowerShell**.

3. On **CM01**, using the **ConfigMgr console**, in the **Software Library** workspace, select **Application Management / Packages**. Right-click and choose **Create Package**. Use the following settings for the **Create Package and Program** wizard:
   o Name: **Pause_TS_PowerShell**
   o Source folder: **\\CM01\Sources\Software\ViaMonstra\Pause_TS_PowerShell**
   o Select **Do not create a program**.

4. Continue through the wizard until completion. Finally, distribute the package to the **CM01.CORP.VIAMONSTRA.COM** distribution point by right-clicking the package and completing the **Distribute Content Wizard**.

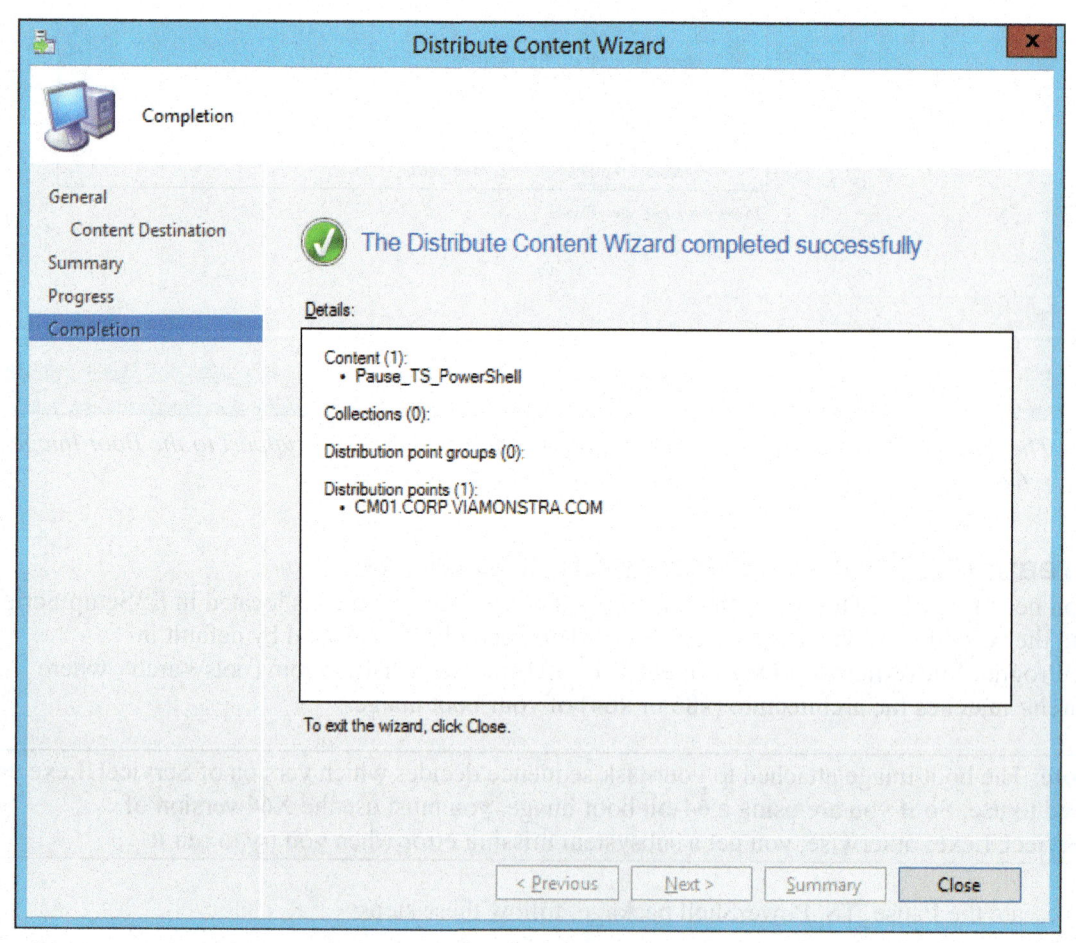

*The Pause_TS_PowerShell package is created and distributed.*

204

Chapter 8 Pausing a Task Sequence

## Edit a Task Sequence to Add the Pause Functionality

For this method, I assume you have not added the pause steps from the preceding methods. The Pause_TS.ps1 PowerShell script hides the UI window of the task sequence before sending the pause pop-up message. Next, it waits for the user to click OK before resuming the task sequence. To edit the task sequence and add these steps, do as follows:-

1. On **CM01**, using the **ConfigMgr console**, expand **Software Library**, select **Operating System / Task Sequences**, and then select the **Windows 8.1 Enterprise x64 - 150301** task sequence.

2. Right-click the task sequence and choose **Edit**; locate the **Apply Operating System** step and click it; and choose **Add / General / Run Command Line**.

3. Use the following settings for the **Run Command Line** step:
   - Name: **##### Pause Task Sequence #####**
   - Description: **<default>**
   - Command line: **serviceUI.exe -process:TSProgressUI.exe %SYSTEMROOT%\System32\WindowsPowerShell\v1.0\powershell.exe -NoProfile -WindowStyle Hidden -ExecutionPolicy Bypass -File pause_ts.ps1**
   - Disable 64-bit file system redirection: **<default>**
   - Start in: **<default>**
   - Package: **Pause_TS_PowerShell**
   - Time-out (minutes): **<default>**
   - Run this step as the following account: **<default>**

4. Select the **##### Pause Task Sequence #####** line, right-click it, and choose **Copy**; then directly after the **xcopy AppsFolderLayout.bin locally** line, right-click and choose **Paste**.

205

Chapter 8   Pausing a Task Sequence

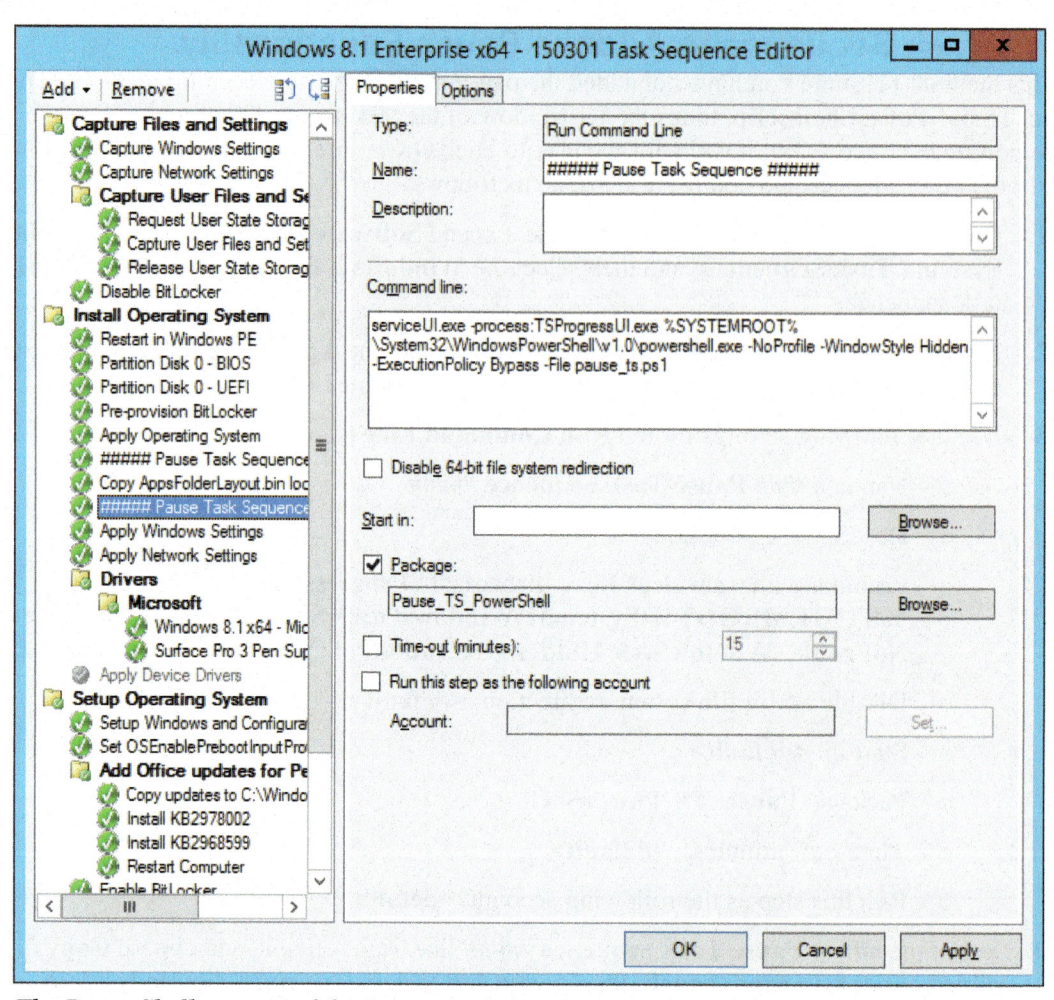

*The PowerShell version of the Pause Task Sequence step.*

## Verify the Changes

You've added your pause steps to your task sequence and now you want to view them in action. To view the pause functionality using the ServiceUI method, do as follows:

1. Create a virtual machine named **PC0007**, and verify that the boot order is set to boot to network as explained in Chapter 5 and then power the virtual machine on. When the **Task Sequence Wizard** PXE password screen appears, enter **P@ssw0rd** and click **Next**.

2. Select the **Windows 8.1 Enterprise x64 - 150301** task sequence and click **Next**.

3. Assign the **PC0007** computer name, and click **Next**.

Chapter 8 Pausing a Task Sequence

4. Let the task sequence continue. At this point you do not have to do anything until the task sequence pauses itself. After the task sequence has run the pause task sequence step, the task sequence pauses and waits for your input.

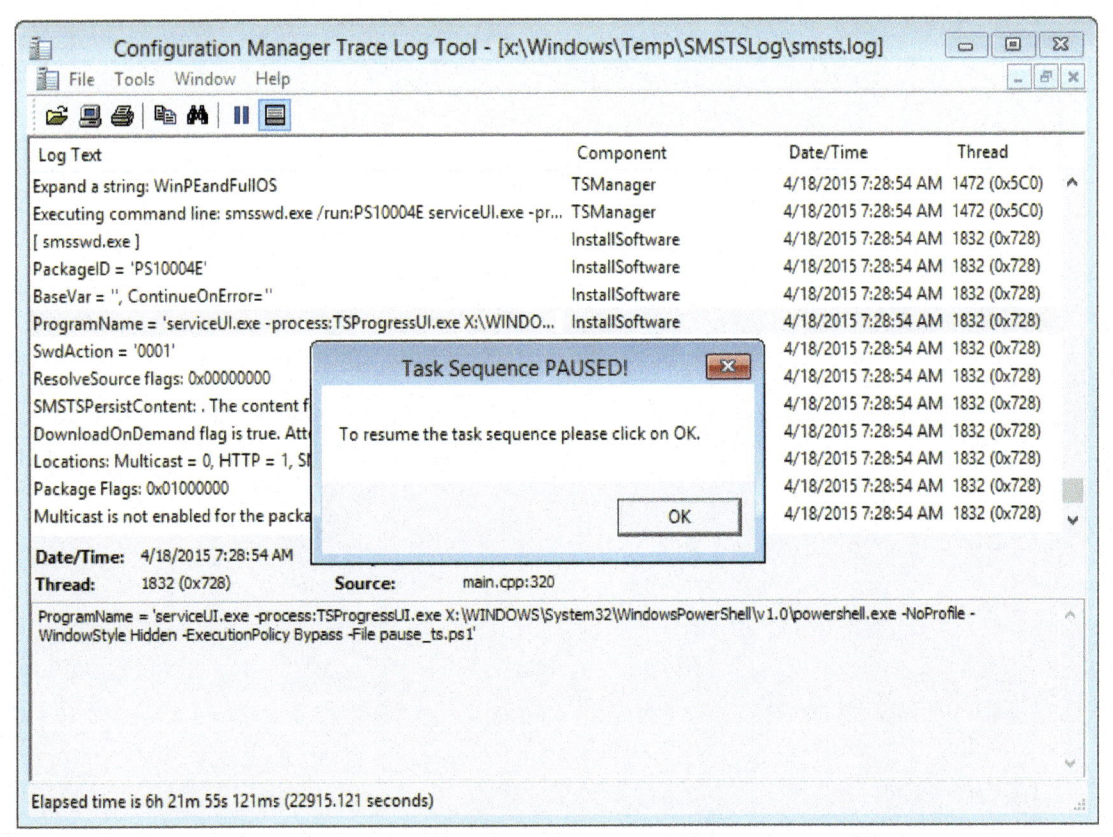

*The task sequence is paused using PowerShell, and troubleshooting can begin.*

# Chapter 9
# Using Devel Mode

In most organizations, task sequences are developed for new operating systems or for special scenarios such as verifying driver support for new hardware. These task sequences are usually not targeted to all computers because they are still being developed. Some task sequences are created to support legacy operating systems, or server-only installs.

ConfigMgr administrators usually deal with this by creating special collections for deploying these task sequences and then importing computers into those collections so that only those computers see the task sequence targeted to the collection. Having the ability to do this without creating new collections or importing computer objects is useful and dare I say it, fun. This method is called *devel mode*. When you start using devel (developer) mode, you'll wonder how you managed without it!

## Step-by-Step Guide Requirements

If you want to follow the step-by-step guides in this chapter, you need a lab environment configured as outlined in Chapter 2 and Appendix A. In this chapter, you use the following virtual machines:

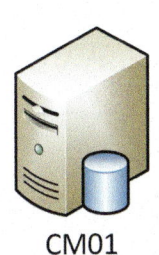

DC01    CM01    PC0008

*The VMs used in this chapter (PC0008 is a VM created in one of the guides).*

You also need to have downloaded the following software:

> The book sample files (http://deploymentfundamentals.com)

**Note**: This guide assumes that you have already got a working PXE environment setup, you've deployed at least one task sequence, and you've enabled F8 command prompt support within your boot WIMs as described in Chapter 2.

# Understanding How It All Works

The magic behind devel mode is made possible by using the following capabilities within ConfigMgr or on the ConfigMgr server directly in conjunction with some scripts:

- The SMSTSPrefferredAdvertID variable
- Hidden deployments
- Prestart commands
- cmd support in boot images
- A hidden share containing some files.

The prestart command used for devel mode pops up a prompt only if a file called hidden.txt is present in the root of X: when a client is booting from PXE or booting from media. The hidden.txt file is placed there by using a script called devel.vbs but only after being invoked by a user.

## Entering Devel Mode

The devel.vbs script is invoked prior to entering the PXE password and running a prestart, when a user presses F8 to bring up a command prompt and then enters the word devel.

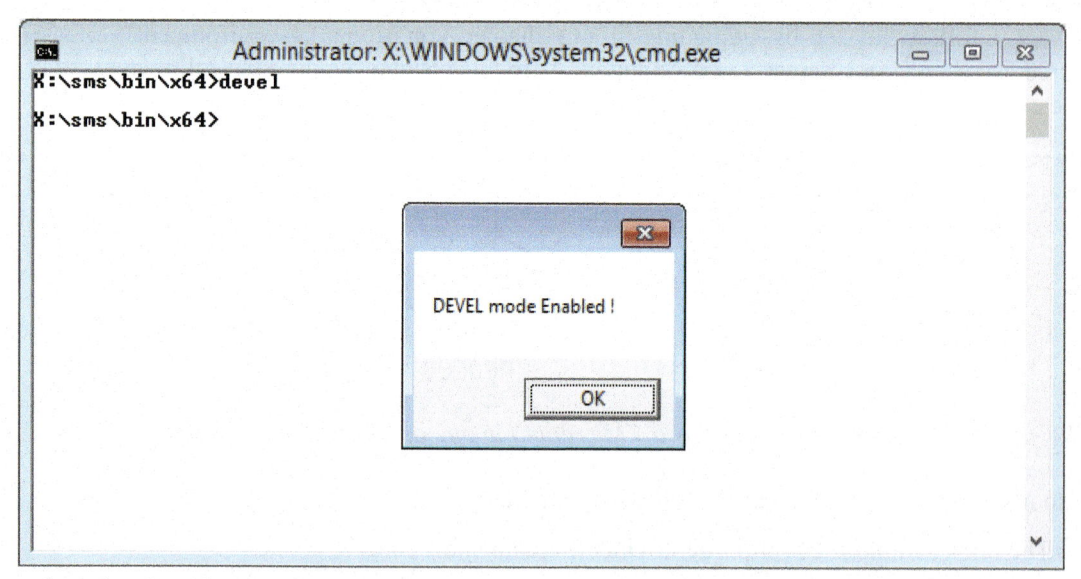

*When devel mode is enabled, clicking OK closes the command prompt window.*

After OK is clicked, the command prompt closes automatically, and the user can continue the PXE process as normal and enter a PXE password. After the user correctly enters the PXE password and clicks Next, the prestart script verifies whether the hidden.txt file is present and, if it is, connects to an UNC share on a server specified in the devel_mode.vbs prestart script. From there, it checks for a file called DeploymentIDs.txt.

Chapter 9   Using Devel Mode

If that file is found, the script displays the contents of the file in a prompt to the end user. The contents of that file (and the AllDeploymentIDs.txt file) are added manually by the ConfigMgr administrator (that's you). Those two text files are placed in the hidden$ share on your ConfigMgr server. Of course, you could make it more dynamic and use PowerShell and task scheduler to auto-populate the files; however, that's beyond the scope of this guide.

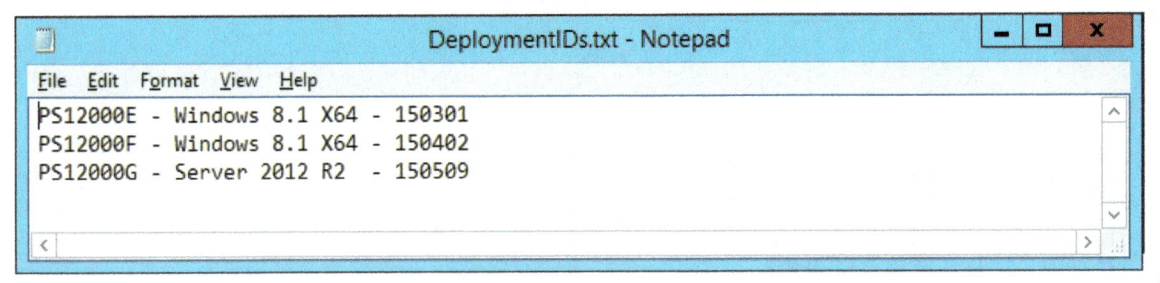

![DeploymentIDs.txt - Notepad showing:
PS12000E - Windows 8.1 X64 - 150301
PS12000F - Windows 8.1 X64 - 150402
PS12000G - Server 2012 R2  - 150509]

*The contents of the sample DeploymentIDs.txt file—edit it to suit your environment.*

The end user can now enter their choice of hidden task sequence by inputting the deployment ID in the box provided, and the script sets the SMSTSPreferredAdvertID variable.

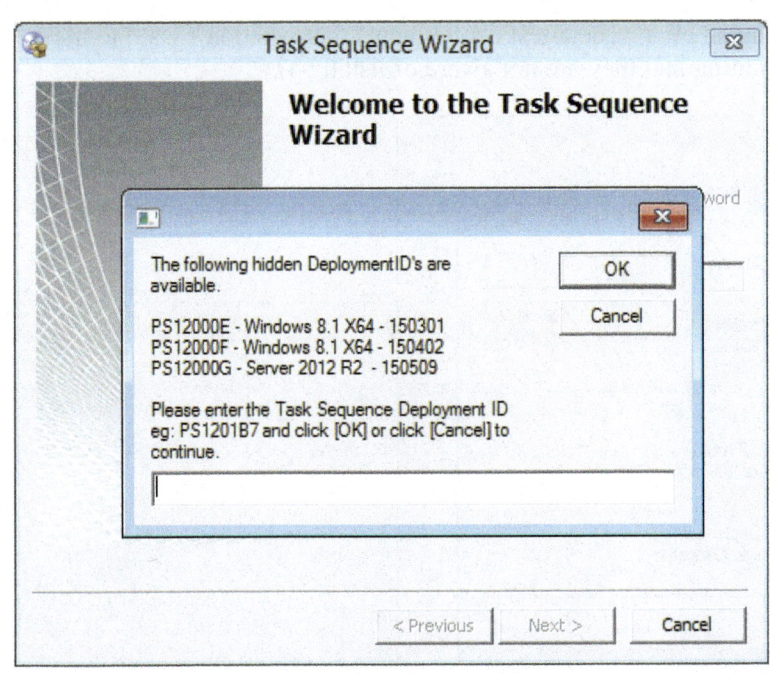

![Task Sequence Wizard dialog showing the prompt: "The following hidden DeploymentID's are available. PS12000E - Windows 8.1 X64 - 150301, PS12000F - Windows 8.1 X64 - 150402, PS12000G - Server 2012 R2 - 150509. Please enter the Task Sequence Deployment ID eg: PS1201B7 and click [OK] or click [Cancel] to continue."]

*Enter a deployment ID from the list provided in the input box and click OK.*

**Note**: Failing to enter a deployment ID correctly or clicking Cancel in the popup message displays the normal list of optional task sequences (those that are not hidden) available to that computer.

Chapter 9   Using Devel Mode

## Using Listall

In addition to being able to enter a deployment Id, the user can type the word "listall" in the input box and then click OK. This displays any additional deployment IDs listed in a file called AllDeploymentIDs.txt located in the hidden folder. These deployment IDS are hidden from the original popup.

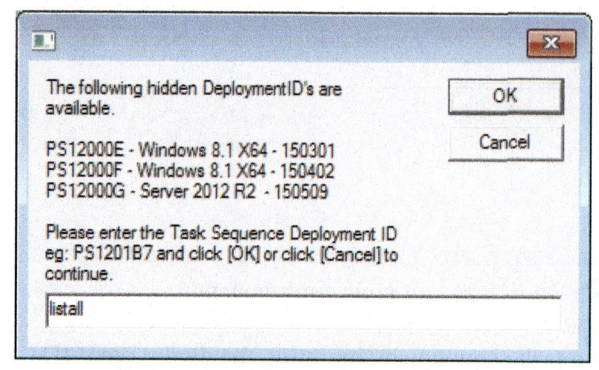

*Using listall in devel mode.*

This scenario could be useful for some of your beta/test deployments that you don't want to make available to your technicians (assuming that they are not aware of listall ;-)).

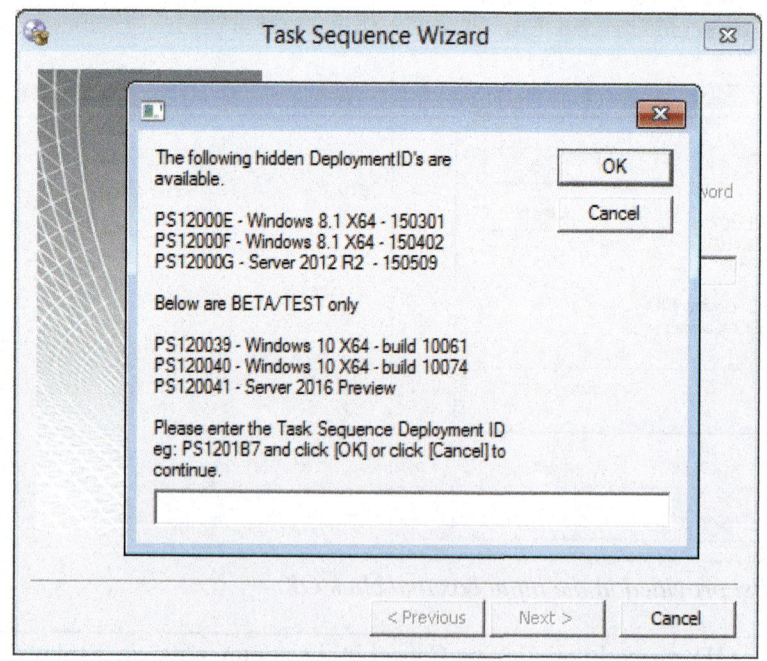

*This is what happens after entering listall.*

212

# Preparing for Devel Mode

To prepare your environment for devel mode, you need to modify a boot image attached to your production task sequences, and after you have completed those modifications, the boot image must be distributed to your distribution points.

To use the new functionality, you also must deploy any development or test task sequences differently that you normally deploy a production task sequence. That process is explained in the section in this chapter called "Hiding Task Sequences."

To prepare the environment for devel mode in ViaMonstra, follow the steps in this section.

## Mount the Boot WIM

1. On **CM01**, using the **ConfigMgr console**, expand **Software Library**, select **Operating System / Boot Images**, and then select the **Boot Image (x64)** boot image.
2. Right-click the boot image and select **Properties**. The **Data Source** tab reveals where this boot image is located.

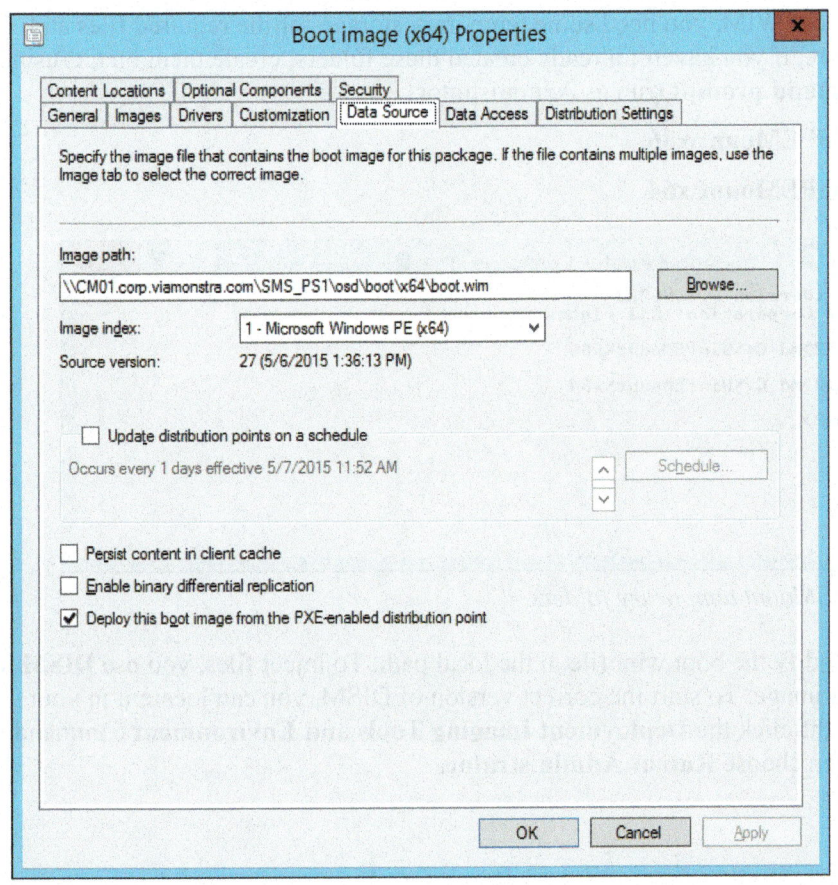

*The data source of the boot WIM.*

3. Using **File Explorer**, browse to the data source image path listed in the properties of the boot WIM you intend to edit. You probably see a few WIM files listed; however, the file in which you are interested is **boot.wim**.

> **Real World Note**: Every time your boot image is updated (for example, by adding drivers or optional components), this file (boot.wim) is used as the source for all changes; therefore, making changes to this file ensures that all boot images based on this one have the smsts.log file size changes locked in place going forward.

4. Locate the local copy of the boot.wim file shown in the preceding figure. By default, this file is present locally on your ConfigMgr primary server in the following path: **E:\Program Files\Microsoft Configuration Manager\OSD\boot\<Arch>\boot.wim**. (Replace <Arch> with either i386 or x64 depending on the boot WIM architecture you are editing.)

5. Make a backup copy of the file before making any changes to it by right-clicking it and choosing **Copy**. Rename the copied boot.wim to **boot.wim.bak**. If anything goes wrong with this process, you can always restore the original boot.wim with this backup.

6. To mount the boot WIM, you need some temporary storage for the required files and folders; therefore, if you haven't already created these folders, create them on **C:\** using an elevated **Command prompt** (run as Administrator):

    o **C:\WinPEMount\x86**

    o **C:\WinPEMount\x64**

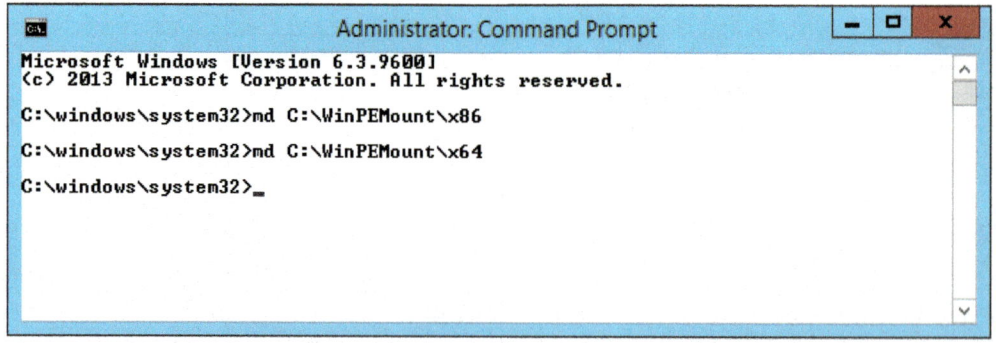

```
Microsoft Windows [Version 6.3.9600]
(c) 2013 Microsoft Corporation. All rights reserved.

C:\windows\system32>md C:\WinPEMount\x86

C:\windows\system32>md C:\WinPEMount\x64

C:\windows\system32>_
```

*Creating the WinPEMount temporary folders.*

7. You need to modify the boot.wim file in the local path. To inject files, you use **DISM** to mount the boot image. To start the correct version of DISM, you can locate it in your **Start** menu, right-click the **Deployment Imaging Tools and Environment** command prompt, and then choose **Run as Administrator**.

8. Change the drive letter to **E:** and then navigate to the directory containing the local copy of the boot.wim file. That directory is **E:\Program Files\Microsoft Configuration Manager\OSD\boot\x64**. Use **DIR** to list the contents of the directory to verify that the boot.wim file is present.

9. Use the following command to mount your boot WIM file. It should mount the boot WIM successfully as shown in the corresponding figure.

```
dism.exe /mount-wim /wimfile:"E:\Program Files\Microsoft
Configuration Manager\OSD\boot\x64\boot.wim" /index:1
/mountdir:C:\WinPEMount\x64
```

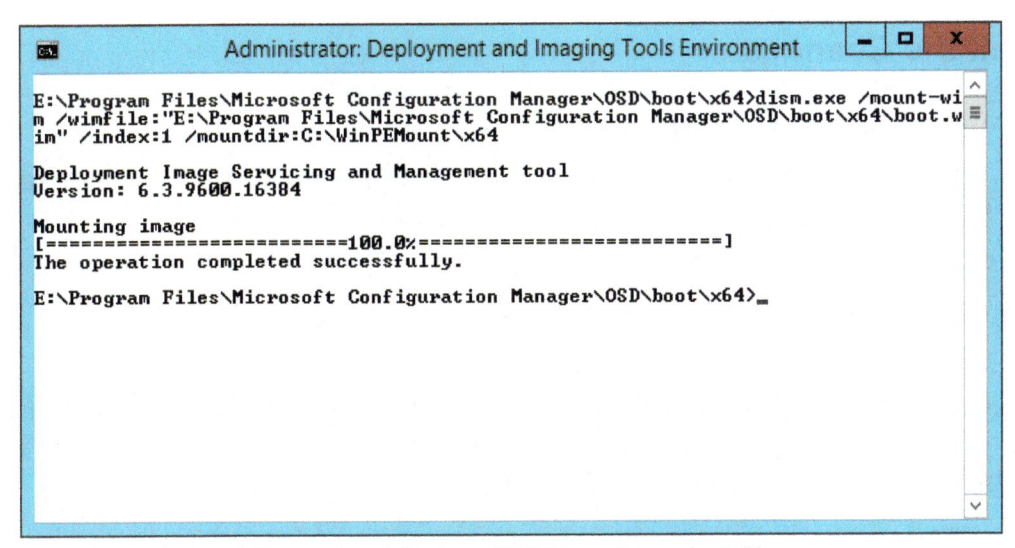

*DISM has successfully mounted the boot WIM into the temp folder.*

## Copy a Script into the Mounted Boot WIM

Now that you've mounted the boot WIM, you need to add some scripts. The scripts needed for this guide are located in E:\Setup\Scripts\Devel Mode. To copy devel.vbs to the mounted WIM file path, follow this step:

1. On **CM01**, switch to the previously opened **Command prompt** (Deployment Imaging Tools and Environment).

2. Copy the **devel.vbs** file in **E:\Setup\Scripts\Devel Mode** to **C:\WinPEMount\X64\Windows\System32** by using the following command:

```
xcopy "E:\Setup\Scripts\devel.vbs" /y /q
C:\WinPEMount\X64\Windows\System32\
```

## Copy a Script into the Prestart Scripts Folder
To copy the prestart script to the correct destination, follow this step:

1. On **CM01**, switch to the previously opened **Command prompt** (Deployment Imaging Tools and Environment).

2. Copy the **devel_mode.vbs** file in **E:\Setup\Scripts\Devel Mode** to **E:\Sources\OSD\Boot\Prestart Scripts** by using the following command:
   ```
   xcopy "E:\Setup\Scripts\devel_mode.vbs" /y /q
   "E:\Sources\OSD\Boot\Prestart Scripts"
   ```

## Commit the Changes
After copying the script to the boot.wim, you need to save those changes. To do so, you use the /commit switch. To commit the changes, do as follows:

1. On **CM01**, switch to the previously opened **Command prompt** (Deployment Imaging Tools and Environment).

2. Commit the changes to the **boot.wim** file by running the following command:
   ```
   dism.exe /unmount-wim /mountdir:C:\WinPEMount\x64 /commit
   ```

> **Real World Note**: Sometimes even your best efforts at boot image mounting may fail. For example, you may have one or more files open when trying to commit the changes resulting in a mount error. If you think you've made any mistake and want to abort the changes made, then you can use the /discard switch to discard the changes like so:
>
> ```
> dism.exe /unmount-wim /mountdir:C:\WinPEMount\x64 /commit
> ```

## Add a Prestart Command
Now that you have edited the boot image, it is time to add a (or modify an existing) prestart command. This prestart command runs a script that checks for a hidden text file in the root of X: that allows you to run task sequences that are normally invisible (hidden). To modify the boot image and add the necessary prestart command, do as follows:

1. On **CM01**, using the **ConfigMgr console**, expand **Software Library**, select **Operating System / Boot Images**, and then select the **Boot Image (x64)** boot image.

2. Right-click and choose **Properties**; click the **Customization** tab, select the **Enable Prestart Command** option, and then use the following settings if no prestart command is already present:
   - Command line: **cmd.exe /c cscript.exe devel_mode.vbs**
   - Source directory: **\\CM01\Sources\OSD\Boot\Prestart Scripts**

Chapter 9  Using Devel Mode

3. Click **Apply** and answer **Yes** when prompted to update the distribution points now; then continue through the wizard until completion and click **Close**.

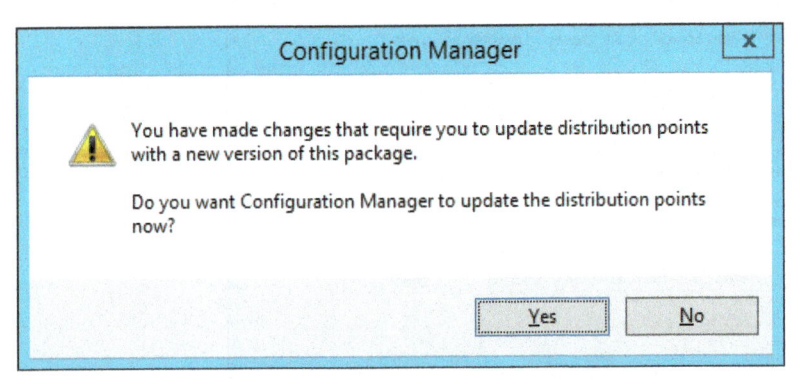

*Applying the change triggers a distribution of the boot image.*

> **Note**: If a prestart command was already in use (for example, if you have already added the WinPE TimeSync prestart command explained in Chapter 7), then you must append this new prestart by adding a "& cscript.exe <prestart.cmd>" where prestart.cmd is the name of script you want to run as a prestart. In addition, the entire prestart command line must be prefixed with cmd.exe /c as shown in the following figure.

217

Chapter 9  Using Devel Mode

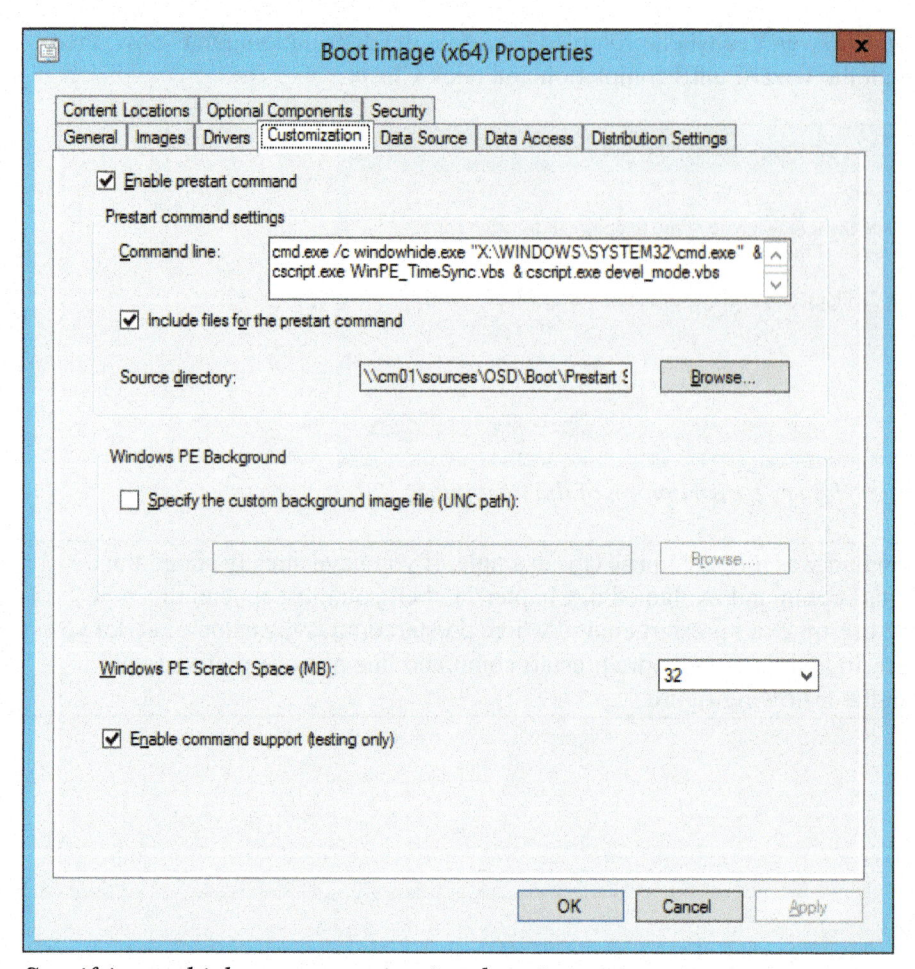

*Specifying multiple prestart scripts in a boot image.*

## Create a Local User

In order to read the list of deployment IDs, the boot image prestart script connects to a UNC share called hidden$ using a local user called CM_HL on a server of your choice. You can edit the script to point to a different server/share if you wish. In this guide, you create a local user on the CM01 server. To create the CM_HL local user, follow these steps:

1. On **CM01**, start **Computer Management** and browse to **Local Users and Groups**; then select **Users**. Right-click **Users** and select **New User**. Use the following settings for the **New User** wizard:

    a. User name: **CM_HL**

    b. Full name: **CM_HL**

    c. Description: **HiddenList Local User**

    d. Password: **P@ssw0rd**

Chapter 9   Using Devel Mode

    e. Confirm password: **P@ssw0rd**
    f. Clear the **User must change password at next logon** check box.
    g. Select the **User cannot change password** check box.
    h. Select the **Password next expires** check box.
    i. Clear the **Account is disabled** check box.

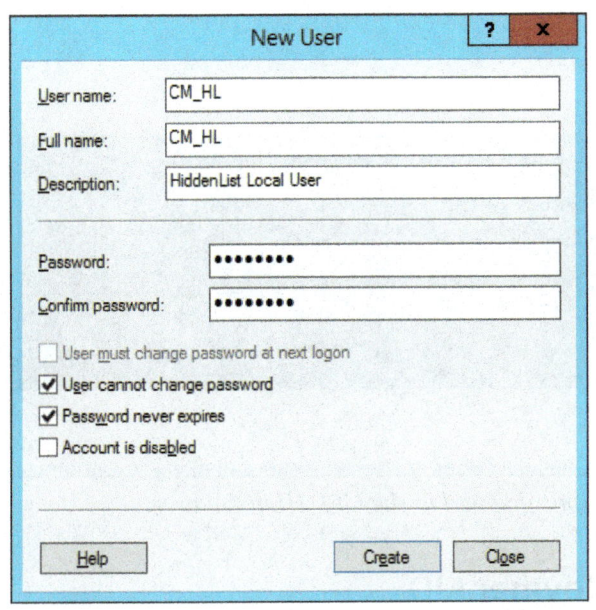

*The New User wizard settings for the CM_HL local user.*

2. In the **New User** wizard, after entering the settings, click **Create** and then click **Close**.

## Share the Hidden Folder and Setting Permissions

To grant the CM_HL local user permissions to read the text files from the hidden$ share, use the following process:

1. On **CM01**, start **Windows PowerShell ISE** as **Administrator** and locate the following script **Share hidden folder.ps1** in **E:\Setup\Scripts**.
2. Run the script by pressing **F5** or clicking the green **Run Script** button in **Windows PowerShell ISE**.

219

Chapter 9   Using Devel Mode

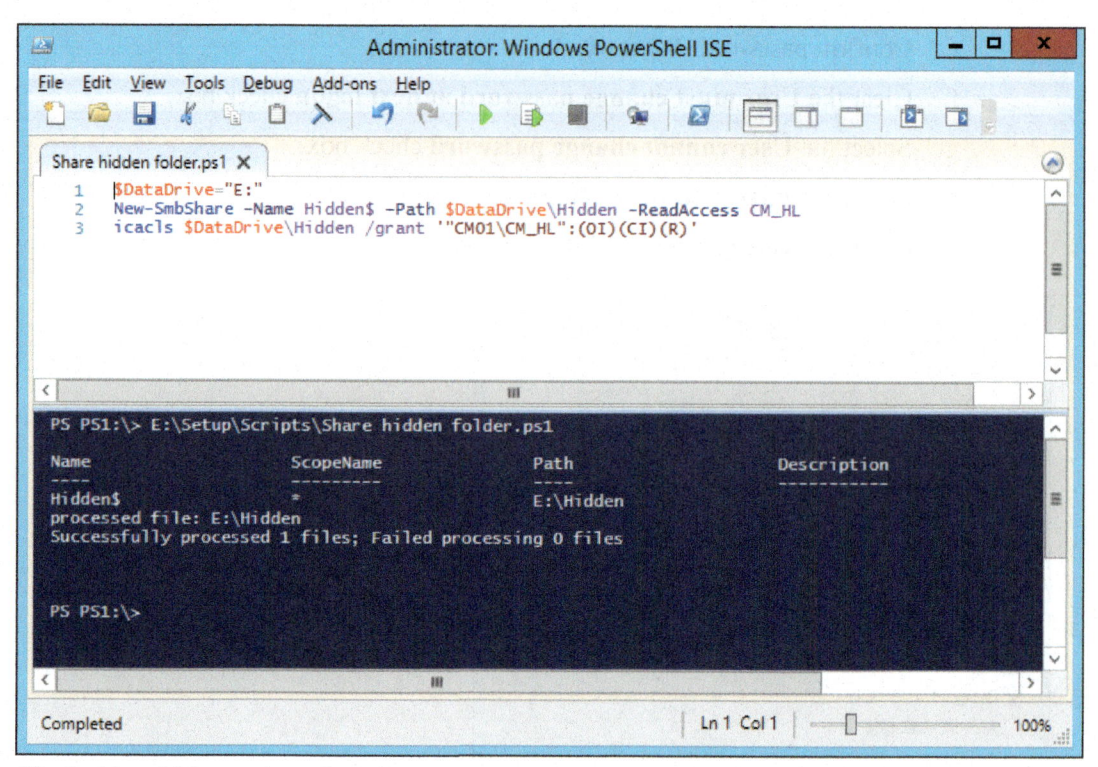

*The hidden folder is shared and permissions granted to the CM_HL local user.*

## Locate a Task Sequence Deployment ID

When a task sequence is deployed, that deployment has its own unique deployment ID. The deployment ID values can be viewed by enabling a column view when viewing a task sequence Deployments tab in the ConfigMgr console.

> **Note**: The Deployment ID column view is not enabled by default in the ConfigMgr console.

To add the Deployment ID column view, do as follows:

1. On **CM01**, in the **Software Library**, select **Operating Systems / Task Sequences**, and then select a task sequence with deployments.

2. Click the **Deployments** tab and right-click anywhere in the columns that appear for the selected task sequence. In the list of available columns that appears, select **Deployment ID**.

Chapter 9  Using Devel Mode

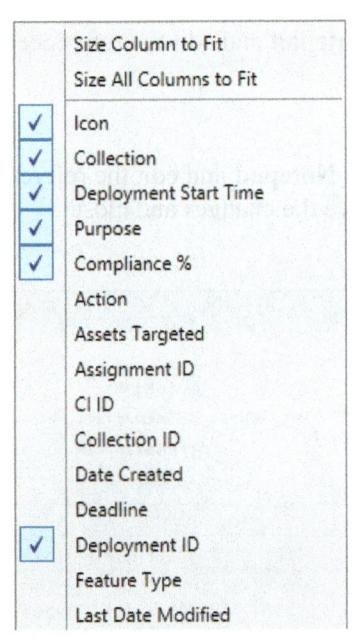

*The Deployment ID column is now enabled.*

After you enable the Deployment ID column, you can see the deployment ID of each deployment listed in the Deployment ID column view as shown here. Deployment IDs always begin with the three-character site code for the site you are connected to, such as PS1.

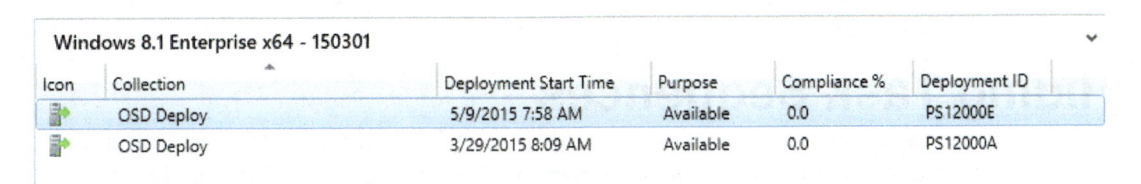

*The deployment IDs are listed in the Deployment ID column on the right.*

## Populate the Hidden Folder with Files

In order for the prestart to display deployment IDs, you need two simple text files in the hidden folder. These text files contain deployment IDs of hidden task sequences and the corresponding task sequence names.

You do not need to enter all your hidden task sequences here. You only need to enter the deployment IDs that you wish to make available via devel mode. In other words, if you want to keep a task sequence totally private, then do not add its deployment ID to the files. To populate the folder with the files needed for devel mode, do as follows:

1. On **CM01**, locate the sample files in **E:\Setup\Devel Mode**, and using **File Explorer**, copy them to **E:\Hidden**.

2. In the **Hidden** folder, open **DeploymentIDs.txt** using **Notepad** and edit the references within to match your chosen hidden task sequences.

3. Save the changes and close **Notepad**.

4. In the **Hidden** folder, open **AllDeploymentIDs.txt** using **Notepad** and edit the references within to match your beta/test hidden task sequences. Save the changes and close **Notepad**.

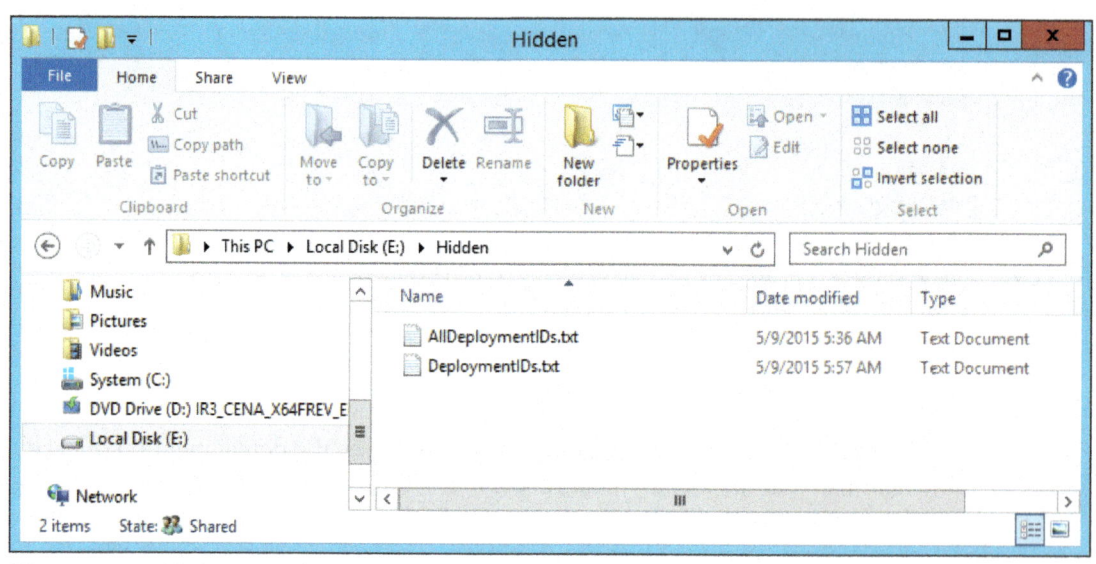

*The two text files are in place.*

# Hiding Task Sequences

Devel mode works because of a new feature added to ConfigMgr in SP1. The new feature is the ability to make task sequences available as hidden to PXE and media. You can deploy task sequences as hidden either manually using the console, or automatically using PowerShell. You can even change which task sequences are made available by modifying the deployment settings after it has been deployed.

## Deploy a Task Sequence as Hidden Using the ConfigMgr Console

This method works by using task sequences that have been deployed using a special deployment setting purpose called Only media and PXE (hidden). To deploy a task sequence as hidden, follow this process:

1. On **CM01**, using the **ConfigMgr console**, in the **Software Library** workspace, select **Operating Systems / Task Sequences**, select the **Windows 8.1 Enterprise x64 - 150301** task sequence, and then select **Deploy**.

2. Use the following settings for the **Deploy Software Wizard**:
    a. General

    Collection: **OSD Deploy**

    b. Deployment Settings
        - Purpose: **Available**
        - Make available to the following: **Only media and PXE (hidden)**

    c. Scheduling

    **<default>**

    d. User Experience

    **<default>**

    e. Alerts

    **<default>**

    f. Distribution Points

    **<default>**

Chapter 9   Using Devel Mode

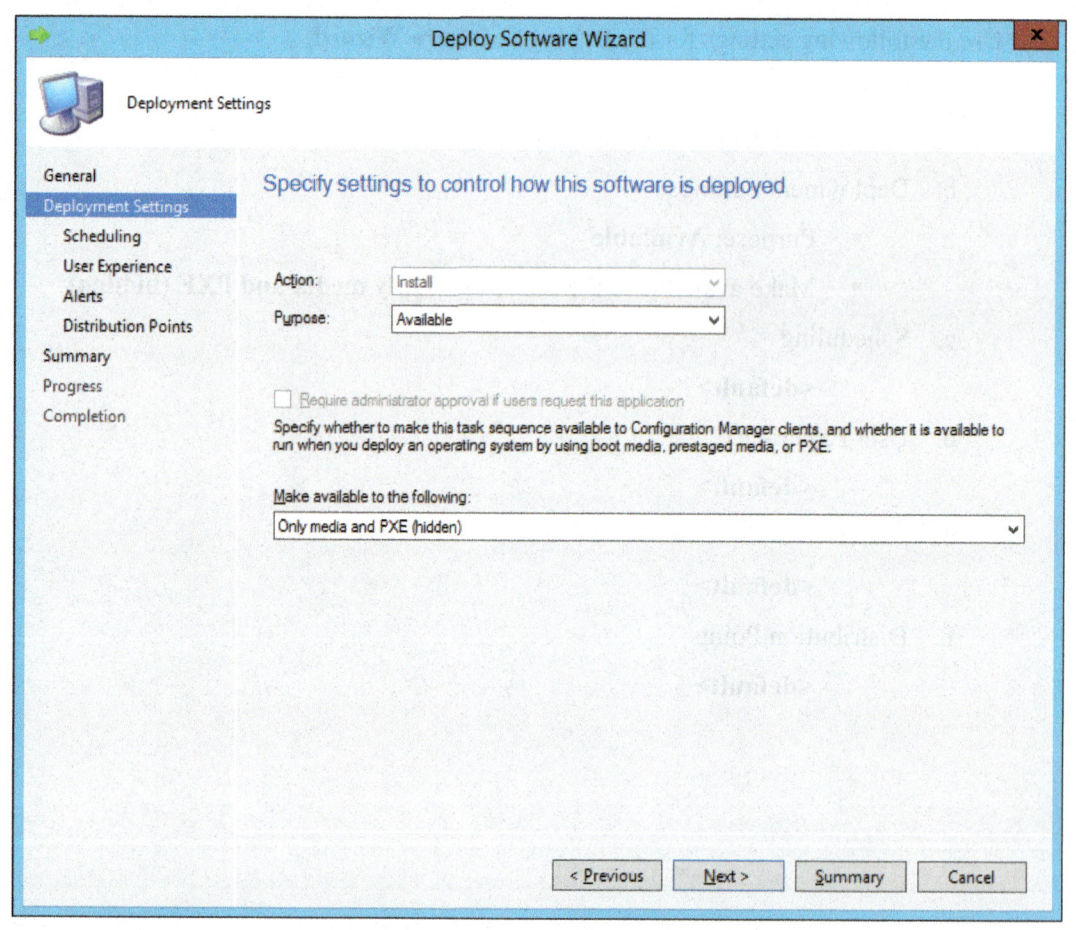

*Deploying a task sequence as hidden using the ConfigMgr console.*

## Deploy a Task Sequence as Hidden Using PowerShell

To deploy a task sequence as hidden using PowerShell, use the ConfigMgr cmdlet called Start-CMTaskSequenceDeployment and specify that the MakeAvailableToType value is set to MediaAndPxeHidden.

There are four possible values for MakeAvailableToType:

- Clients
- ClientsMediaAndPxe
- MediaAndPxe
- MediaAndPxeHidden

**Note**: For more details on the Start-CMTaskSequenceDeployment cmdlet, see the following TechNet URL: https://technet.microsoft.com/en-us/library/jj870935%28v=sc.20%29.aspx.

Chapter 9   Using Devel Mode

To deploy a task sequence as hidden using PowerShell, follow this process:

1. On **CM01**, start **Windows PowerShell ISE**, click **File / Open**, and open the **Deploy a task sequence as hidden.ps1** script.

2. Modify any variables if necessary and then run the script by clicking the green **Run Script** button or by pressing **F5**.

3. Verify that the task sequence deployment is created correctly in the ConfigMgr console by selecting the **Software Library**, choosing **Operating Systems / Task Sequences**, selecting the **Windows 8.1 Enterprise x64 - 150301** task sequence, and clicking the **Deployments** tab. There should be two deployments, one of which is set with the following deployment settings and made available only to media and PXE (hidden).

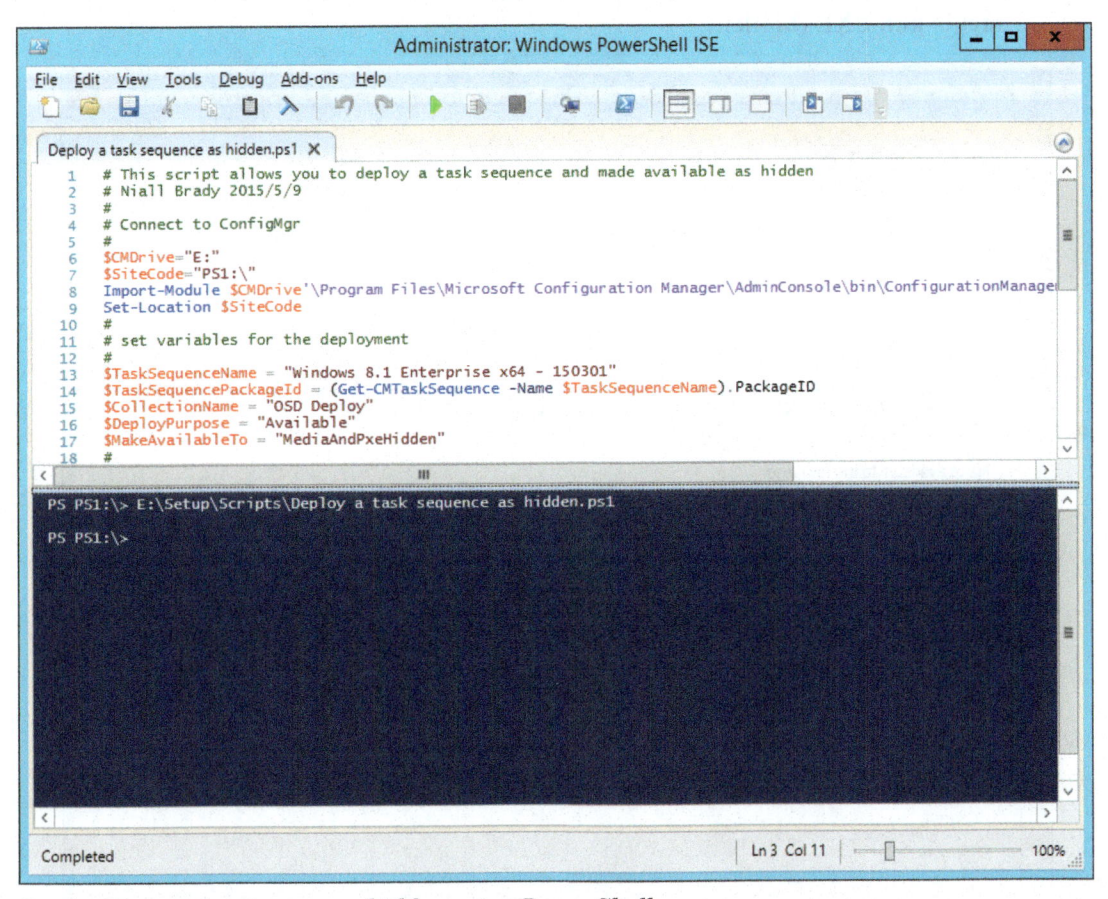

*Deploying a task sequence as hidden using PowerShell.*

225

## Modify an Existing Deployment to Make It Hidden

You can change what a task sequence is made available to by using the drop-down menu in the Deployment Settings tab of the task sequence deployment properties. To change what a task sequence is made available to, follow this process:

1. On **CM01**, using the **ConfigMgr console**, in the **Software Library** workspace, select **Operating Systems / Task Sequences**, select the **Windows 8.1 Enterprise x64 - 150301** task sequence, and then click the **Deployments** tab.

2. Select a previous deployment that was not made available as hidden, right-click it, select **Properties**, and click the **Deployment Settings** tab.

3. Using the drop-down list available for **Make available to the following**, select **Only media and PXE (hidden)**.

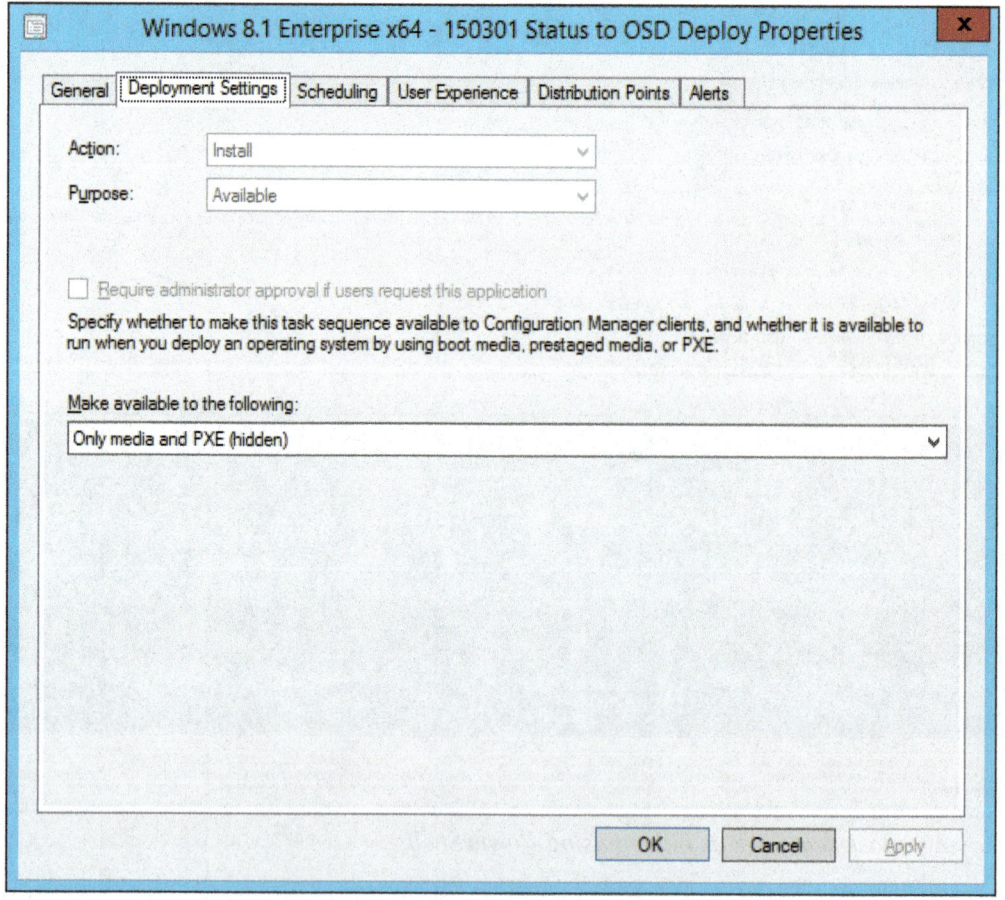

*Modifying the deployment settings of a task sequence deployment.*

Chapter 9　Using Devel Mode

# Verifying Devel Mode

To verify that devel mode is working correctly, use the following process:

1. Create a virtual machine named **PC0008**, and verify that the boot order is set to boot to network as explained in Chapter 5 and then power the virtual machine on.

2. Before entering the PXE password, press **F8** to bring up the command prompt. Type **devel** and press **Enter**. The DEVEL mode Enabled! popup should appear.

3. Before clicking OK in the popup, manually check that the **x:\hidden.txt** file is present using this command:

   ```
   dir x:\
   ```

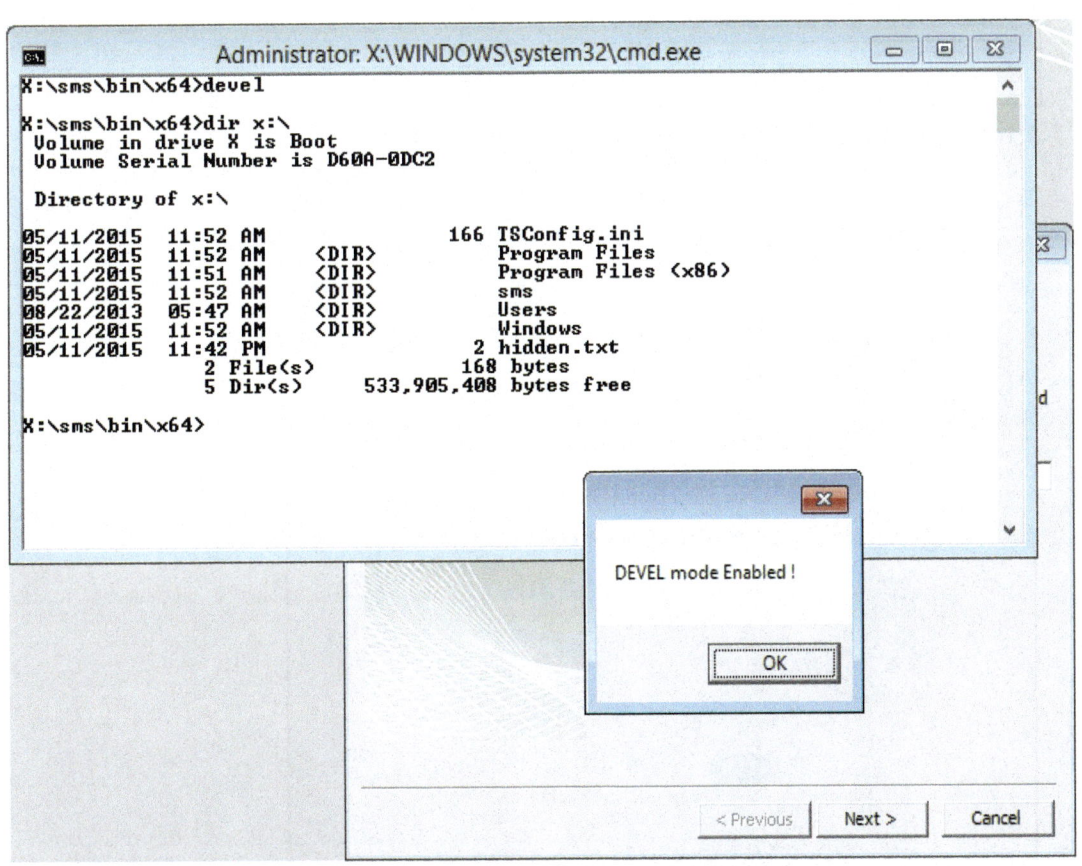

*The hidden.txt file is present in the root of X: after entering devel mode.*

4. Click **OK** on the **DEVEL mode Enabled!** message. The command prompt automatically disappears.

5. Enter the PXE password (**P@ssw0rd**), and click **Next**.

227

Chapter 9   Using Devel Mode

6. After a few moments, the prestart command should pop up an input box requesting that you enter a deployment ID. Enter a deployment ID corresponding to a previously deployed task sequence that is made available to Only Media and PXE (hidden). The deployment ID can be lowercase, uppercase, or a mixture of both, as long as it is valid.

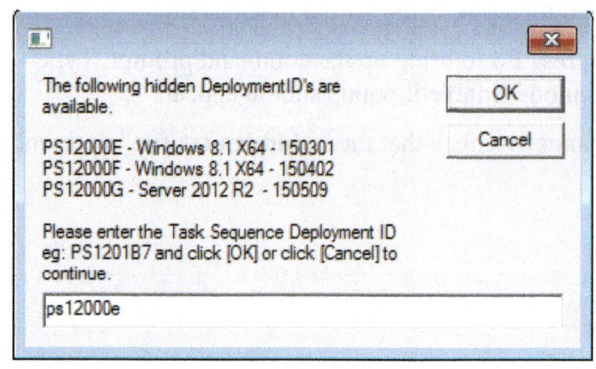

*A valid deployment ID must be entered in the input box.*

7. After entering the deployment ID, click **OK**. The prestart script checks whether this deployment ID exists and, if it does, processes it as a required task sequence.

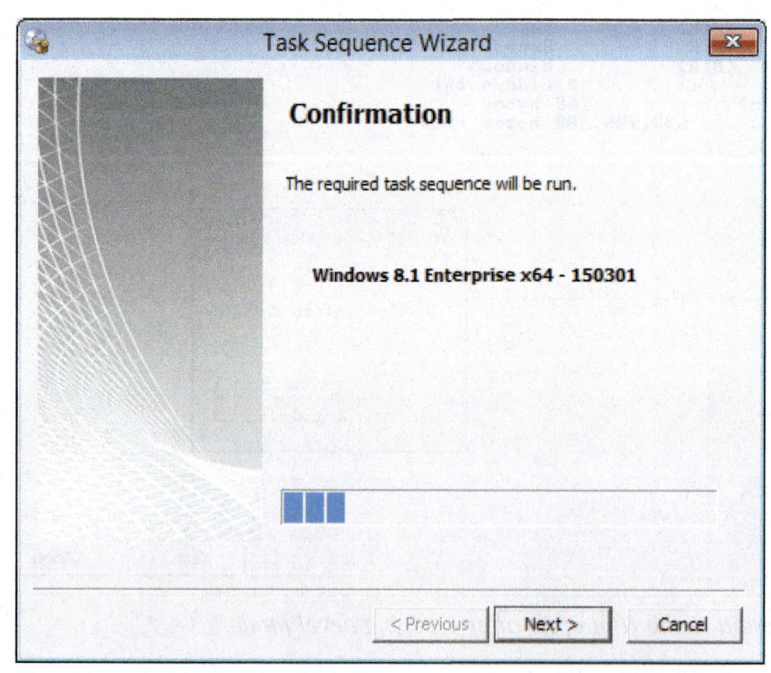

*The deployment ID is accepted, and a confirmation is displayed.*

8. Click **Next** to continue. The Task Sequence Wizard continues as normal.

## Incorrectly Entering a Deployment ID

The prestart attempts to set the SMSTSPreferredAdvertID variable to whatever text is entered by the user in the input box. However, if that text is not valid, or if the deployment ID does not exist, the prestart falls back to displaying any valid available task sequences deployed to that computer in the list of available task sequences.

In the event that an incorrect or invalid deployment ID is entered in the devel mode input box, the following error message is logged in the smsts.log file: "Provided preferred deployment <deploymentID> is not found among the available deployments" where <deploymentID> is the deployment ID entered in the input box.

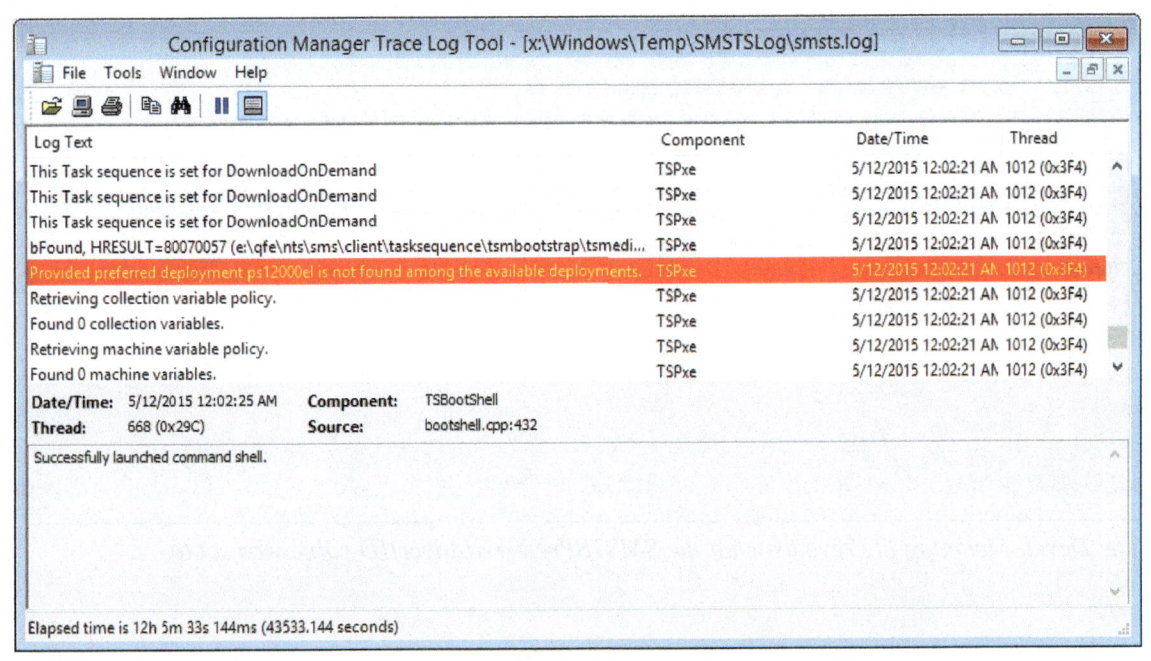

*An error is logged in the smsts.log file if a deployment ID is incorrectly entered.*

## The Devel Mode Log File

The devel_mode.vbs prestart script writes to a log file called devel_mode.log located in X:\Windows\Temp\SMSTSLOG. The log file is created when the prestart script runs (not when you type devel in the command prompt). Use CMTrace to review the log file for troubleshooting any issues with the tool itself.

## Chapter 9  Using Devel Mode

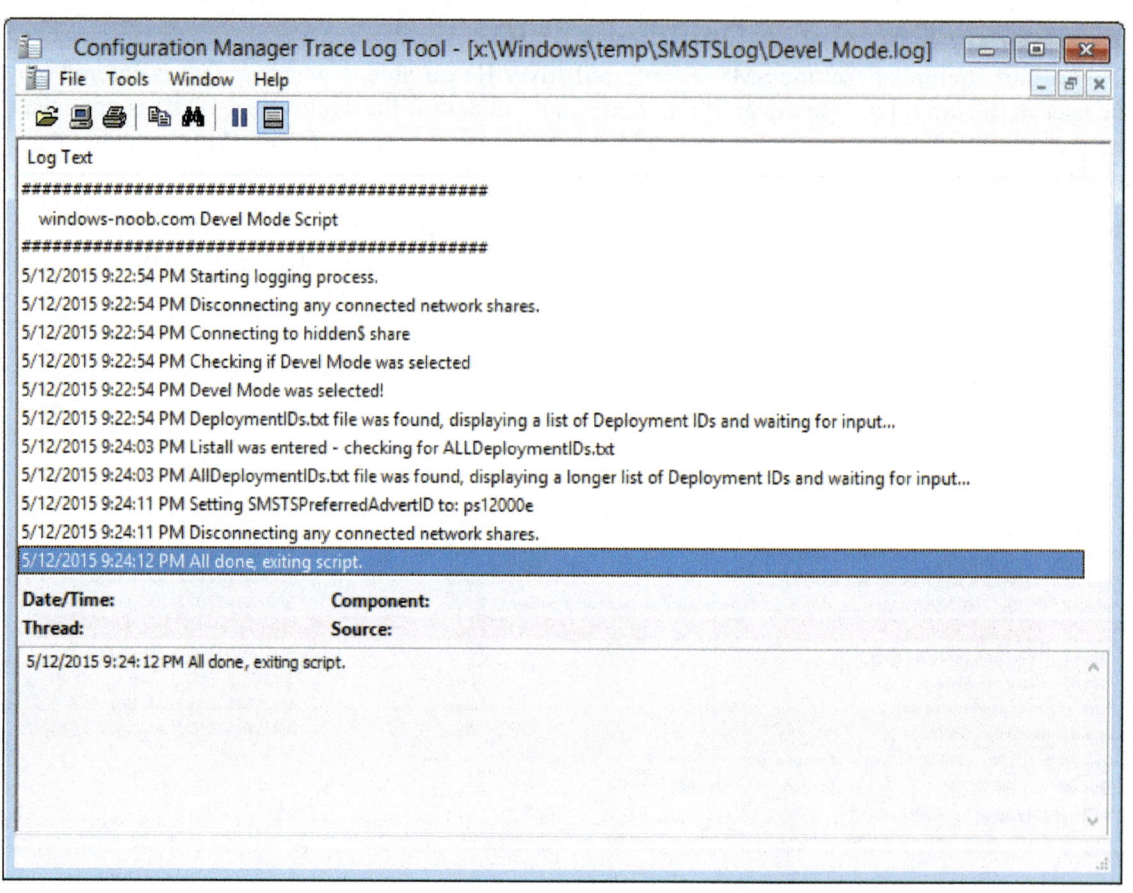

![Configuration Manager Trace Log Tool screenshot showing Devel_Mode.log contents]

```
windows-noob.com Devel Mode Script
##############################################
5/12/2015 9:22:54 PM Starting logging process.
5/12/2015 9:22:54 PM Disconnecting any connected network shares.
5/12/2015 9:22:54 PM Connecting to hidden$ share
5/12/2015 9:22:54 PM Checking if Devel Mode was selected
5/12/2015 9:22:54 PM Devel Mode was selected!
5/12/2015 9:22:54 PM DeploymentIDs.txt file was found, displaying a list of Deployment IDs and waiting for input...
5/12/2015 9:24:03 PM Listall was entered - checking for ALLDeploymentIDs.txt
5/12/2015 9:24:03 PM AllDeploymentIDs.txt file was found, displaying a longer list of Deployment IDs and waiting for input...
5/12/2015 9:24:11 PM Setting SMSTSPreferredAdvertID to: ps12000e
5/12/2015 9:24:11 PM Disconnecting any connected network shares.
5/12/2015 9:24:12 PM All done, exiting script.
```

*The Devel_Mode.log file reveals what the SMSTSPreferredAdvertID value was set to.*

# Chapter 10
# Implementing MailLog, AssistMe, and ViewLog

Any ConfigMgr administrator who deals with operating system deployments experiences occasional failures for various reasons. Those reasons can be varied and may include issues such as network congestion, packages or applications not being present on a distribution point, hash failures, or other problems.

When a task sequence fails, it is good practice to have capabilities to troubleshoot further built in to your deployment. There are capabilities from Microsoft, such as the Diagnostics and Recovery Toolkit (DaRT), but that requires additional licensing (MDOP).

MailLog, AssistMe, and ViewLog comprise a cool alternative to DaRT. These scripts offer new capabilities that are beneficial to any onsite support technician. These capabilities are summarized here:

- **MailLog.** Gathers deployment information and compresses and then mails the SMSTS logs to an email address specified
- **AssistMe.** Lists the IP address, disables the firewall, and enables UltraVNC so that a technician can remotely control the computer to troubleshoot further by entering a password
- **ViewLog.** Opens the smsts.log file with CMTrace.exe whether in Windows PE or Windows

## Step-by-Step Guide Requirements
If you want to follow the step-by-step guides in this chapter, you need a lab environment configured as outlined in Chapter 2 and Appendix A. In this chapter, you use the following virtual machines:

DC01  CM01  PC0009  PC0010  PC0011

*The VMs used in this chapter (PC0009 – PC0011 are VMs created in the guides).*

You also need to have downloaded the software listed in the Download the Required Files section.

> **Note**: This guide assumes that you have already got a working PXE environment setup, deployed at least one task sequence, and enabled F8 command prompt support within your boot WIMs as described in Chapter 2.

## Downloading the Required Files

In order to complete this guide, you need some third-party files to support the scripts. These files are free/shareware applications. As this guide uses the 64-bit boot image and 64-bit operating system, you should download the 64-bit version of these files. If you plan on using an x86 boot WIM and x86 operating system, download the matching architecture of the files listed in this section.

### Download UltraVNC

UltraVNC is used to do the remote sessions. You can download the latest version of UltraVNC from the following location, noting that you need to accept the agreement in order to download the MSI: http://uvnc.com/downloads/ultravnc.html. I'm using UltraVnc_1205_X64.msi for this guide.

### Download WinRAR

RAR is used to compress the log files prior to emailing. To obtain WinRAR use the following URL and select the x64 English version: http://rarlabs.com/. The version of WinRAR used in this guide is the 64-bit architecture named winrar-x64-521.exe located at http://rarlabs.com/rar/winrar-x64-521.exe.

### Download Blat

Blat is a Windows (32- and 64-bit) command-line utility that sends email using SMTP. The version of Blat used in this guide is the 64-bit architecture named blat324_64.full.zip located at http://sourceforge.net/projects/blat/files/Blat%20Full%20Version/64%20bit%20versions/blat324_64.full.zip/download.

## Preparing Your Environment

To prepare for MailLog, AssistMe, and ViewLog, you need files grouped together in a specific order. These files contain everything you need to add the additional functionality to troubleshoot task sequences. To do that, however, you need to install both UltraVNC and WinRAR on CM01. In addition, you extract Blat.

After doing those tasks, you copy the respective files to specific folders before editing the MailLog.vbs script to point to your mail server.

Chapter 10  Implementing MailLog, AssistMe, and ViewLog

## Install UltraVNC

In order to support deployments both in Windows PE and in Windows, you use UltraVNC Viewer to connect to remote desktops in case something goes wrong. In this guide I assume you downloaded UltraVNC to E:\Setup\MailLog Software\UVNC on CM01.

1. On **CM01**, open an elevated **Command prompt** (run as Administrator) and browse to **E:\Setup\MailLog Software\UVNC**.

2. Install **UltraVNC** using **msiexec** by entering the following command:

   ```
   msiexec /i UltraVnc_1205_X64.msi /q /l C:\Windows\Temp\uvnc.log
   ```

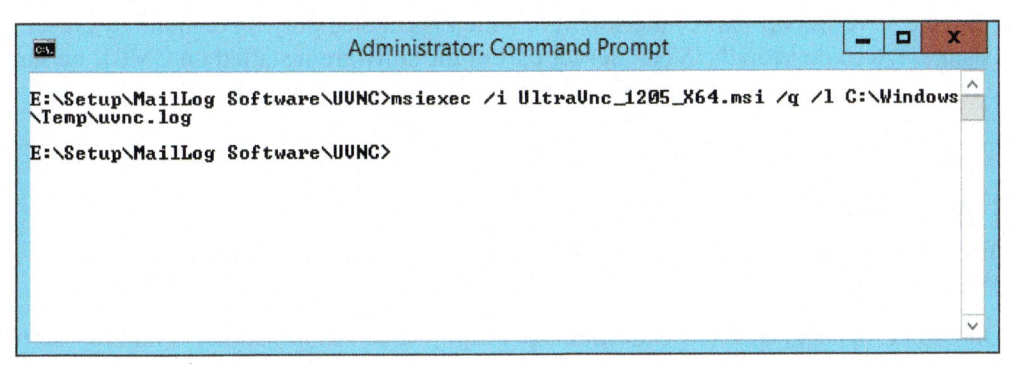

*UltraVNC is installed via msiexec.*

3. Verify the installation was successful by opening the **uvnc.log** in **CMTrace** and looking for a line containing **Installation completed successfully**. The file is located in **C:\Windows\Temp**.

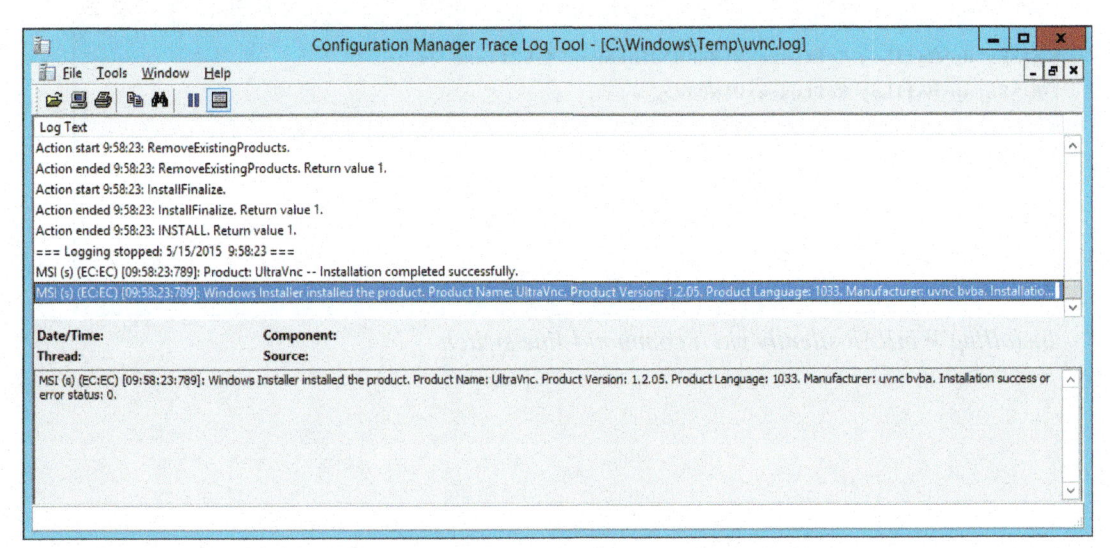

*To verify successful installation, look for a line that reads "Installation completed successfully."*

4. Installation of the MSI also installs the VNC Server software. To stop the VNC Server service and then disable it, use the following commands in an elevated **Command prompt** (run as Administrator):

   ```
   sc stop "uvnc_service"
   sc config "uvnc_service" start=disabled
   ```

> **Real World Note**: Although the UltraVNC software is free under the GNU License, it is prudent for security reasons to use only the VNC Viewer part of this software and install it on a client operating system instead of on a server operating system. You only need the VNC Viewer component of this software to connect to remote systems being deployed. Those systems, however, use the VNC Server part of the software which is enabled only on demand by a user typing assistme. If you do keep the VNC Server part of the software installed on CM01, be sure to configure it to make it as secure as possible via the settings provided or stop and disable the service as shown in the preceding step.

## Install WinRAR

In this guide I assume you have downloaded WinRAR x64 (64 bit) 5.21 to E:\Setup\MailLog software\WinRAR on CM01.

1. On **CM01**, open an elevated **Command prompt** (run as Administrator) and browse to **E:\Setup\MailLog Software\WinRAR**.

2. Run the following command to install **WinRAR** silently:

   ```
   winrar-x64-521.exe /s
   ```

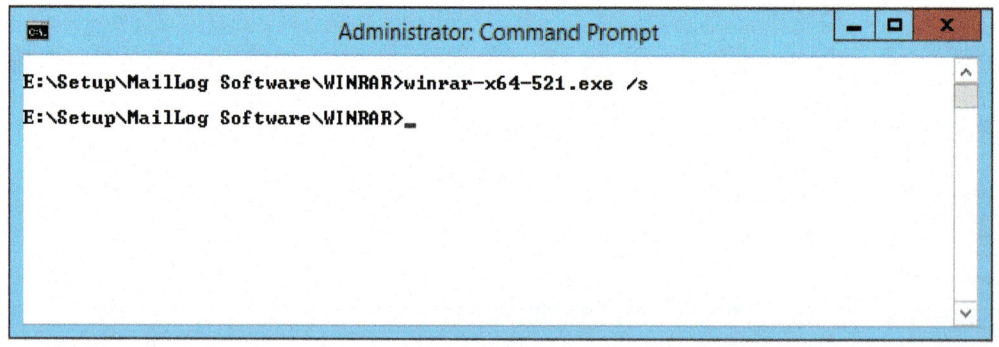

*Installing WinRAR silently via a command-line switch.*

Chapter 10  Implementing MailLog, AssistMe, and ViewLog

## Extract Blat

In this guide I assume you have downloaded Blat v3.2.4 to E:\Setup\MailLog Software\Blat on CM01.

1. On **CM01**, open **File Explorer** and browse to **E:\Setup\MailLog Software\Blat**.
2. Right-click **blat324_64.full.zip** and choose **Extract to blat324_64.full** (using WinRAR).

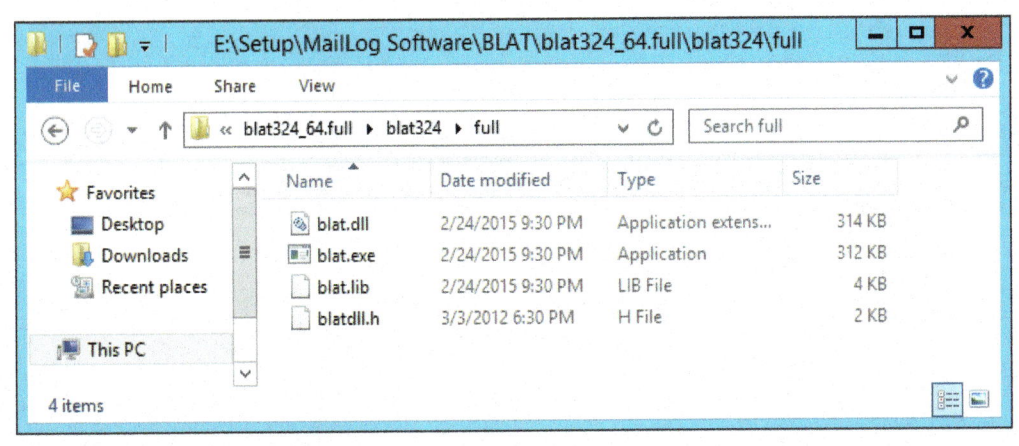

*The extracted Blat software.*

## Create the Folder Structure

Create the folder structure by following this process:

1. On **CM01**, using a **Command prompt**, browse to **E:\Sources\Software\ViaMonstra** and create the following folders using these commands:

   ```
   mkdir MailLog\VNC

   mkdir MailLog\Mailer
   ```

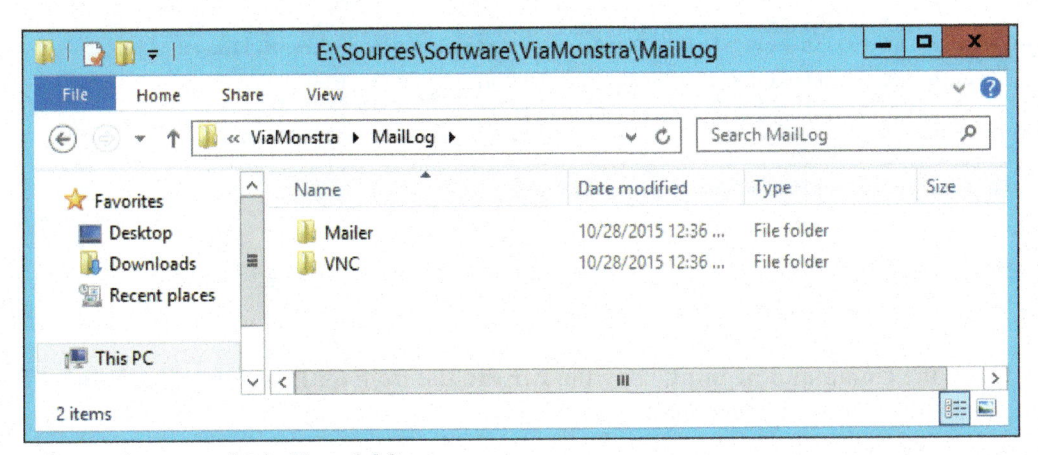

*The newly created MailLog folders.*

235

Chapter 10 Implementing MailLog, AssistMe, and ViewLog

## Copy Some Files

To populate the folders with the necessary files, do as follows:

1. On **CM01**, using an elevated **Command prompt** (run as Administrator), browse to **E:\Sources\Software\ViaMonstra\MailLog** and then issue the following command to copy the three required scripts:

   ```
   copy E:\Setup\Scripts\assistme.cmd . & copy
   E:\Setup\Scripts\viewlog.cmd . & copy
   E:\Setup\Scripts\maillog.vbs .
   ```

*Copying the scripts to the MailLog package folder.*

2. Using the **Command prompt**, change to the **Mailer** folder and issue the following command to xcopy the **Blat** files you need to the **Mailer** folder:

   ```
   xcopy "E:\Setup\MailLog
   software\BLAT\blat324_64.full\blat324\full"
   "E:\Sources\Software\ViaMonstra\MailLog\Mailer" /E /Y /R /H
   ```

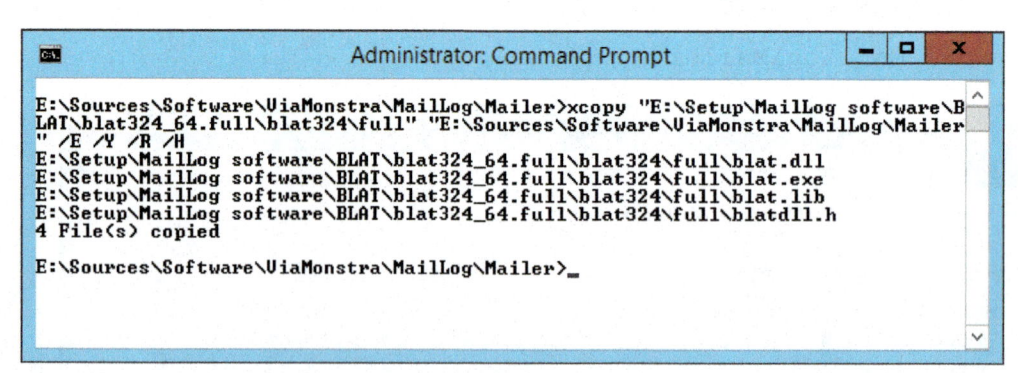

*The Blat files are copied to their destination.*

3. Using the **Command prompt**, copy the **rar.exe** file from **C:\Program Files\WinRAR** by issuing the following command:

   ```
   copy "C:\Program Files\WinRAR\rar.exe"
   "E:\Sources\Software\ViaMonstra\MailLog\Mailer"
   ```

4. Using the **Command prompt**, change to the **E:\Sources\Software\ViaMonstra\ MailLog\VNC** folder and issue the following command to xcopy the **UltraVNC** files you need to the **VNC** folder:

   ```
   xcopy "C:\Program Files\uvnc bvba\UltraVnc"
   "E:\Sources\Software\ViaMonstra\MailLog\VNC" /D /E /C /I /Q
   /H /R /Y /S
   ```

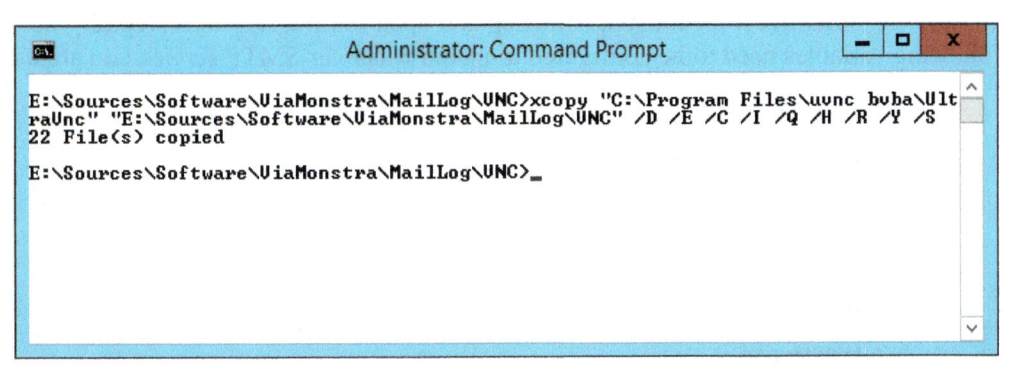

   ```
   Administrator: Command Prompt
   E:\Sources\Software\ViaMonstra\MailLog\UNC>xcopy "C:\Program Files\uvnc bvba\Ult
   raUnc" "E:\Sources\Software\ViaMonstra\MailLog\UNC" /D /E /C /I /Q /H /R /Y /S
   22 File(s) copied

   E:\Sources\Software\ViaMonstra\MailLog\UNC>_
   ```

   *The VNC files are copied to the VNC folder.*

5. Using the **Command prompt**, in the **E:\Sources\Software\ViaMonstra\MailLog\VNC** folder, copy the **UltraVNC.ini** and **vnc.reg** files by issuing the following command:

   ```
   copy "E:\Setup\MailLog software\UVNC\UltraVNC.ini" . & copy
   "E:\Setup\MailLog software\UVNC\vnc.reg" .
   ```

> **Real World Note**: You can configure the UltraVNC settings yourself by running uvnc_settings.exe from within the E:\Sources\Software\ViaMonstra\MailLog\VNC folder and setting the password used to connect to the remote machine (and any other settings you feel like configuring). The password configured in the supplied UltraVNC.ini file is P@ssw0rd.

6. Using the **Command prompt**, change to the **E:\Sources\Software\ViaMonstra\MailLog** folder and copy **findstr.exe** by doing as follows:

   ```
   copy "C:\Windows\System32\findstr.exe"
   "E:\Sources\Software\ViaMonstra\MailLog"
   ```

> **Note**: The file (findstr.exe) is not present in Windows PE, but the assistme.cmd script requires it for correctly displaying the IP address of the remote computer.

## Edit the MailLog Script

The maillog.vbs script needs to be configured with settings so that it knows where to send email; therefore, you have to define certain settings within the script before you add the script to the boot image and task sequence.

> **Note**: The values in the sample maillog.vbs script in E:\Setup\Scripts are for reference purposes only and must be changed to match the mail server in your environment; otherwise, the ability to mail log files will not work.

To edit the script and add your mail server settings, do as follows:

1. On **CM01**, using an elevated **Command prompt** (run as Administrator), browse to **E:\Sources\Software\ViaMonstra\MailLog** and open **maillog.vbs** in **Notepad**. The following variables need to be configured to match whatever SMTP service you are using:
    - **MailServer**
    - **MailPort**
    - **MailTo**
    - **MailFrom**
    - **MailUser**
    - **MailPassword**

> **Real World Note**: It's a good idea to use an email address that is shared so that one or more members of a helpdesk team have access to and can read the email messages sent to that address.

2. In the **maillog.vbs** script, there is an **EmailLogs** function which has some lines that output the commands used to send the email (for debugging purposes). If you want to obscure the username and password used to send email from the MailLog.log file, then locate two lines in that function which state **LogText "About to run " & strCMD** and place an apostrophe (') in front of them so that they are not executed.

*Removing sensitive details from being logged by the maillog.vbs script.*

3. When you are finished editing the **maillog.vbs** script, save the file and close Notepad.

> **Real World Note**: Most organizations will probably block port 25 for SMTP on the firewall. In my lab, I used an SMTP service from https://sendgrid.com and configured maillog.vbs to use port 2525. This service offers up to 400 email messages per day for free, and I can definitely recommend it for lab purposes.

# Adding Files to Your Boot Image

To gain access to the features that MailLog provides, you need to copy the files and folders prepared in the preceding section to your boot image. To do that, follow the process in this section.

## Mount the Boot Image WIM File

1. On **CM01**, using the **ConfigMgr console**, expand **Software Library**, select **Operating System / Boot Images**, and then select the **Boot Image (x64)** boot image.
2. Right-click the file and select **Properties**. The **Data Source** tab reveals where this boot image is located.

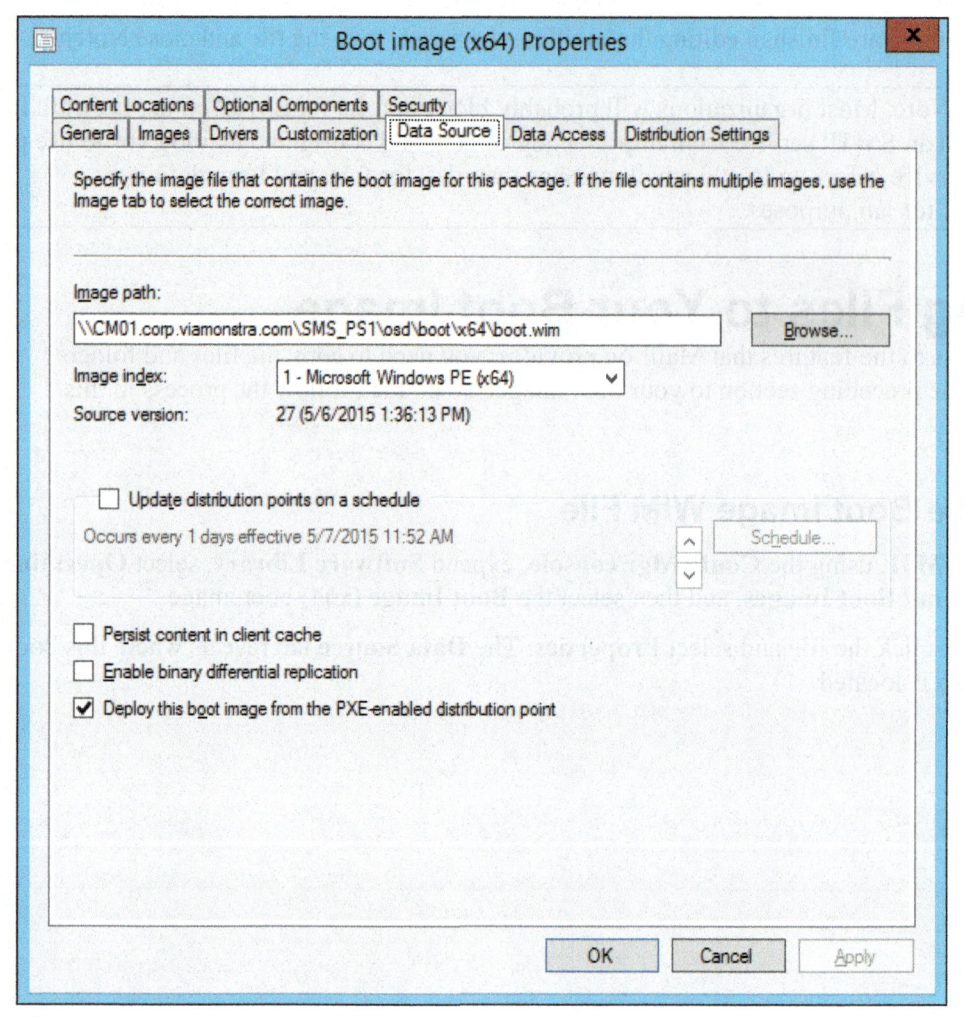

Chapter 10   Implementing MailLog, AssistMe, and ViewLog

*The data source of the boot WIM.*

3.  Using **File Explorer**, browse to the data source image path listed in the properties of the boot WIM you intend to edit. You probably see a few WIM files listed; however, the file in which you are interested is **boot.wim**.

4.  Locate the **local copy** of the boot.wim file shown in the preceding figure. By default, this file is present locally on your ConfigMgr primary server in the following path: **E:\Program Files\Microsoft Configuration Manager\OSD\boot\<Arch>\boot.wim** (replace <Arch> with either i386 or x64 depending on the boot WIM architecture you are editing).

5.  Make a backup copy of the file before making any changes to it by right-clicking it and choosing **Copy**. Rename the copied boot.wim to **boot.wim.bak**. If anything goes wrong with this process, you can always restore the original boot.wim with this backup.

240

6. To mount the boot WIM, you need some temporary storage for the required files and folders; therefore, if you haven't already created these folders, create them on **C:\** using an elevated **Command prompt** (run as Administrator):

    o **C:\WinPEMount\x86**

    o **C:\WinPEMount\x64**

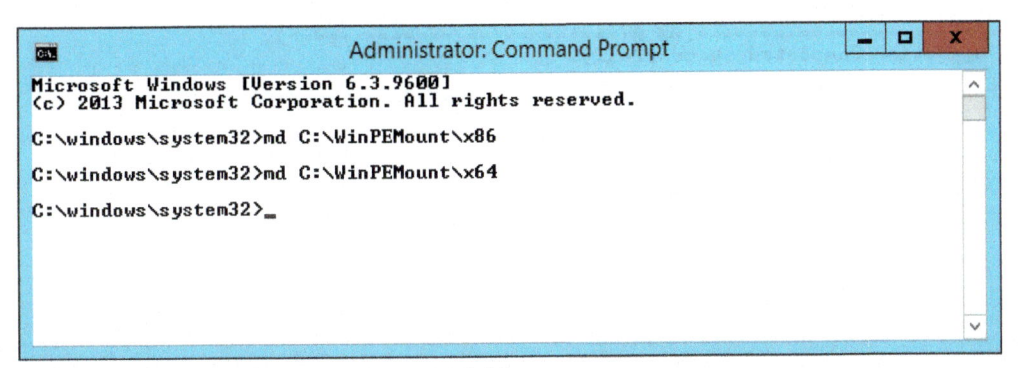

```
Microsoft Windows [Version 6.3.9600]
(c) 2013 Microsoft Corporation. All rights reserved.

C:\windows\system32>md C:\WinPEMount\x86

C:\windows\system32>md C:\WinPEMount\x64

C:\windows\system32>_
```

*Creating the WinPEMount temporary folders.*

7. You need to modify the boot.wim file in the local path. To inject files, you use DISM to mount the boot image. To start the correct version of **DISM**, you can locate it in your **Start** menu, right-click the **Deployment Imaging Tools and Environment** command prompt, and then choose **Run as Administrator**.

8. Change the drive letter to **E:** and then navigate to the directory containing the local copy of the boot.wim file. That directory is **E:\Program Files\Microsoft Configuration Manager\OSD\boot\x64**. Use **DIR** to list the contents of the directory to verify that the boot.wim file is present.

9. Use the following command to mount your boot WIM file. It should mount the boot WIM successfully as shown in the corresponding figure.

```
dism.exe /mount-wim /wimfile:"E:\Program Files\Microsoft
Configuration Manager\OSD\boot\x64\boot.wim" /index:1
/mountdir:C:\WinPEMount\x64
```

Chapter 10  Implementing MailLog, AssistMe, and ViewLog

```
E:\Program Files\Microsoft Configuration Manager\OSD\boot\x64>dism.exe /mount-wi
m /wimfile:"E:\Program Files\Microsoft Configuration Manager\OSD\boot\x64\boot.w
im" /index:1 /mountdir:C:\WinPEMount\x64

Deployment Image Servicing and Management tool
Version: 6.3.9600.16384

Mounting image
[============================100.0%==========================]
The operation completed successfully.

E:\Program Files\Microsoft Configuration Manager\OSD\boot\x64>
```

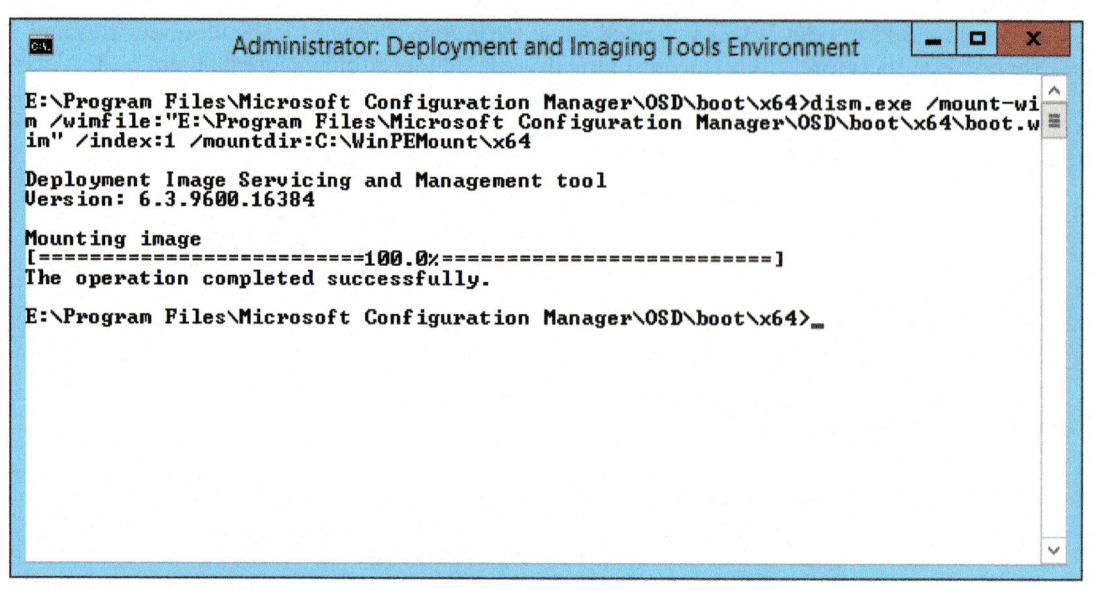

*DISM has successfully mounted the boot WIM into the temp folder.*

## Copy the Required Files into the Mounted Boot WIM

Now that you've mounted the boot WIM, you need to copy all the files and folders prepared in the preceding section. Those files are located in E:\Sources\Software\ViaMonstra\MailLog. To copy all those files to the mounted WIM file path, follow this step:

1. On **CM01**, switch to the previously opened **Command prompt**.

2. Copy all the files in **E:\Sources\Software\ViaMonstra\MailLog** to **C:\WinPEMount\X64\Windows\System32** by using the following command:

   ```
   xcopy "E:\Sources\Software\ViaMonstra\MailLog"
   "C:\WinPEMount\X64\Windows\System32" /D /E /C /I /Q /H /R /Y
   /S
   ```

# Chapter 10  Implementing MailLog, AssistMe, and ViewLog

```
Administrator: Deployment and Imaging Tools Environment
Image Index : 1
Saving image
[========================100.0%==========================]
Unmounting image
[========================100.0%==========================]
The operation completed successfully.

C:\Program Files (x86)\Windows Kits\8.1\Assessment and Deployment Kit\Deployment
 Tools>dism.exe /mount-wim /wimfile:"E:\Program Files\Microsoft Configuration Ma
nager\OSD\boot\x64\boot.wim" /index:1 /mountdir:C:\WinPEMount\x64

Deployment Image Servicing and Management tool
Version: 6.3.9600.16384

Mounting image
[========================100.0%==========================]
The operation completed successfully.

C:\Program Files (x86)\Windows Kits\8.1\Assessment and Deployment Kit\Deployment
 Tools>xcopy "E:\Sources\Software\ViaMonstra\MailLog" "C:\WinPEMount\X64\Windows
\System32" /D /E /C /I /Q /H /R /Y /S
33 File(s) copied

C:\Program Files (x86)\Windows Kits\8.1\Assessment and Deployment Kit\Deployment
 Tools>_
```

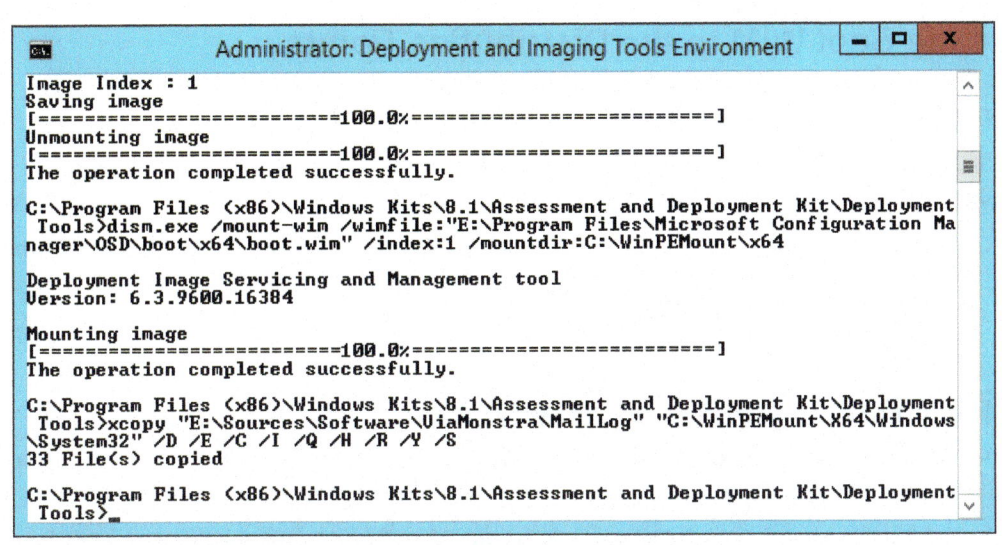

*The required files are copied into the mounted boot WIM.*

## Commit the Changes

After copying the script to the boot.wim file, you need to save those changes. To do so, you use the /commit switch. To commit the changes, do as follows.

1. On **CM01**, switch to the previously opened **Command prompt**.

2. Save the changes by running the following command:

   ```
   dism.exe /unmount-wim /mountdir:C:\WinPEMount\x64 /commit
   ```

```
Administrator: Deployment and Imaging Tools Environment
E:\Program Files\Microsoft Configuration Manager\OSD\boot\x64>dism.exe /unmount-
wim /mountdir:C:\WinPEMount\x64 /commit

Deployment Image Servicing and Management tool
Version: 6.3.9600.16384

Image File : E:\Program Files\Microsoft Configuration Manager\OSD\boot\x64\boot.
wim
Image Index : 1
Saving image
[========================100.0%==========================]
Unmounting image
[========================100.0%==========================]
The operation completed successfully.

E:\Program Files\Microsoft Configuration Manager\OSD\boot\x64>_
```

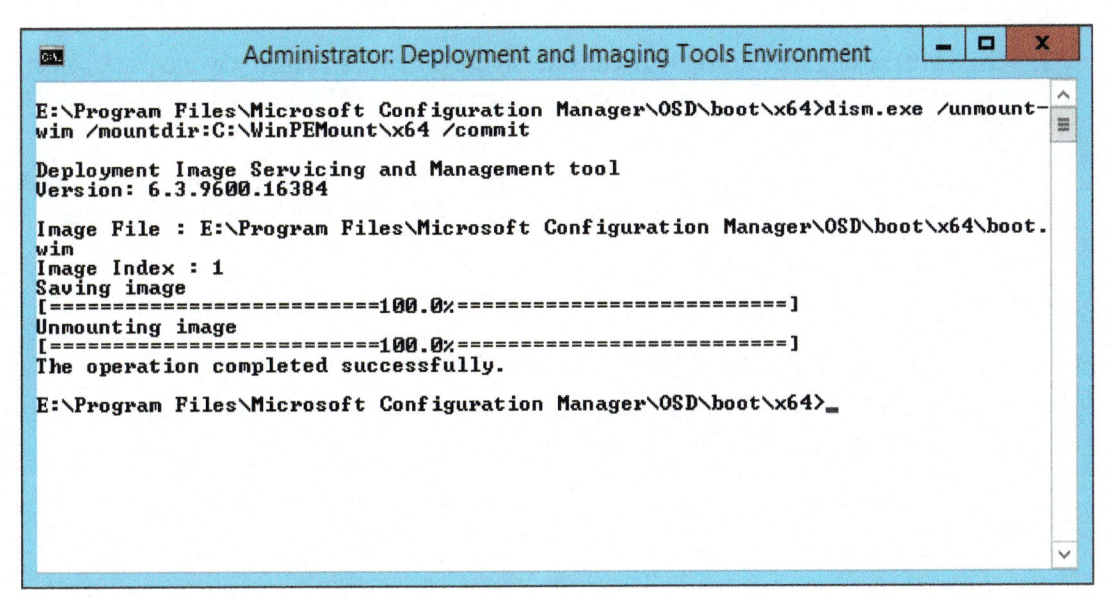

*Committing (saving) the changes to the boot.wim file.*

## Update the Boot WIM to the Distribution Points

Now that the boot image has the required files added, you must update it to your distribution points for the new capabilities to be useable. To do this, follow this process:

1. On **CM01**, using the **ConfigMgr console**, select **Software Library**, and then select **Operating Systems / Boot Images**.

2. Right-click the **Boot Image (x64)** boot image and choose **Update Distribution Points**. Click **Next** and continue through the **Update Distribution Points Wizard** until completion.

# Editing the Task Sequence

To add the MailLog, ViewLog, and AssistMe functionality within a task sequence, you must add additional groups and steps to any task sequence that will use the new functionality.

To force the task sequence to failover to a special group if any step in the task sequence fails, you can use a task sequence variable called _SMSTSLastActionSucceeded. If that variable is equal to false, then the previous step failed. This works well for catching errors, but sometimes you need to exercise caution. For example, when any step in the Restore User Files and Settings group fails, you don't necessarily want that group to failover to a MailLog scenario if there were no files previously captured.

## Add New Groups

You want the task sequence engine to failover to MailLog automatically in the event of a task sequence failure. To do this, you need to create two new groups in the task sequence. Follow this process:

1. On **CM01**, using the **ConfigMgr console**, in the **Software Library** workspace, select **Operating System / Task Sequences** and then select the **Windows 8.1 Enterprise x64 - 150301** task sequence.

2. Right-click the task sequence and choose **Edit**; locate the first step of the task sequence and select it; click **Add / New Group**. Use the following settings for the new group:

    a. Name: **Execute Task Sequence**

    b. Description: **<default>**

    c. Click the **Options** tab and select the **Continue on Error** check box.

3. Using the **Move Up** button, position **Execute Task Sequence** as the first group in the task sequence as it appears in the next figure.

Chapter 10   Implementing MailLog, AssistMe, and ViewLog

4. Select the **Capture Files and Settings** group, and using the **Move Up** button, move the group up one step so that it becomes a child of the **Execute Task Sequence** group. A child group appears below and slightly to the right of its parent group. Repeat this process for each major group heading (but not the groups within those groups) as shown in the figure.

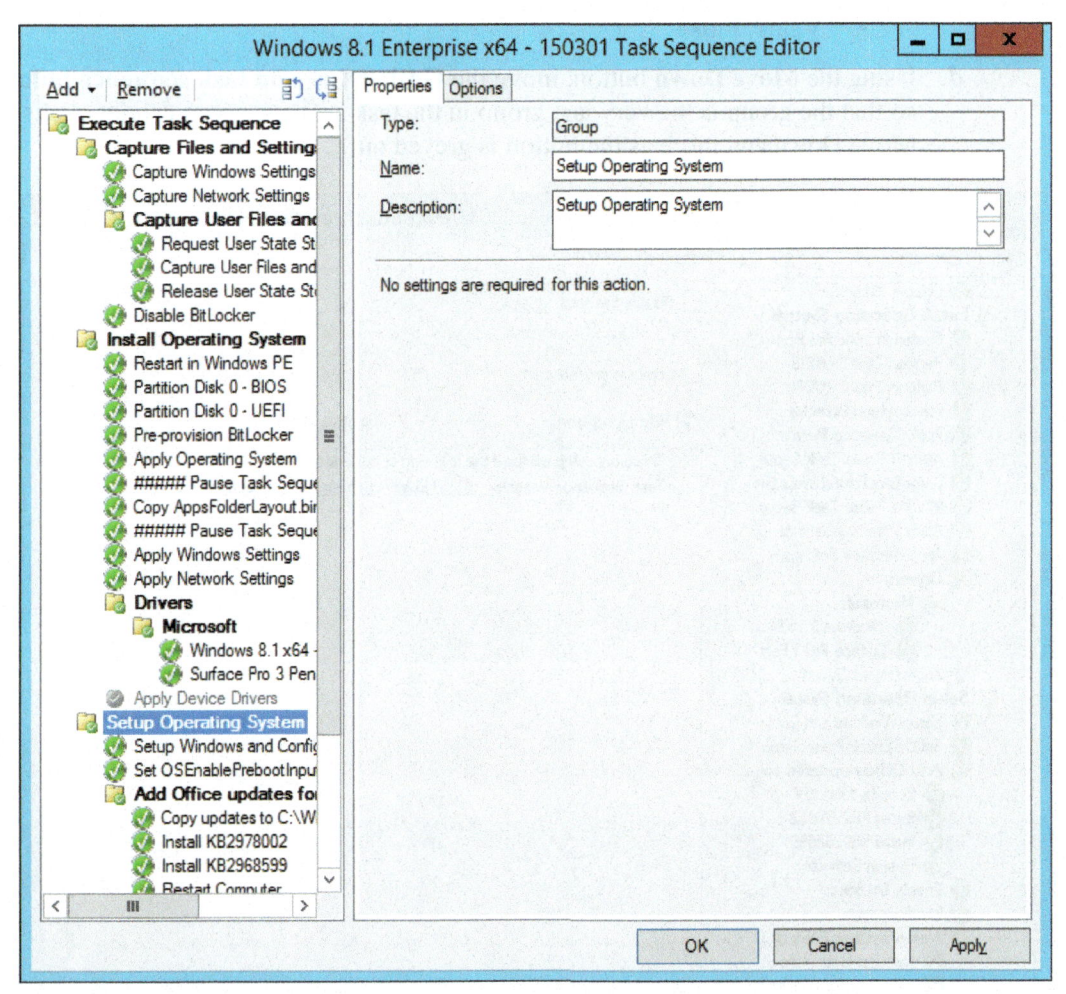

*Organizing groups under the Execute Task Sequence group.*

5. Next, locate the last step of the task sequence and select it. Click the **Add / New Group** again and use the following settings for the new group:

    a. Name: **Gather Logs on task sequence failure**

    b. Description: **<default>**

245

Chapter 10   Implementing MailLog, AssistMe, and ViewLog

c. Click the **Options** tab and select the **Add Condition** drop-down menu. Select **Task Sequence Variable** from the list of options and fill in the following values:

- Variable: **_SMSTSLastActionSucceeded**
- Condition: **equals**
- Value: **False**

d. Using the **Move Down** button, move the **Gather Logs on task sequence failure** so that the group is the very last group in the task sequence (you cannot click Move Down any more as the button is greyed out).

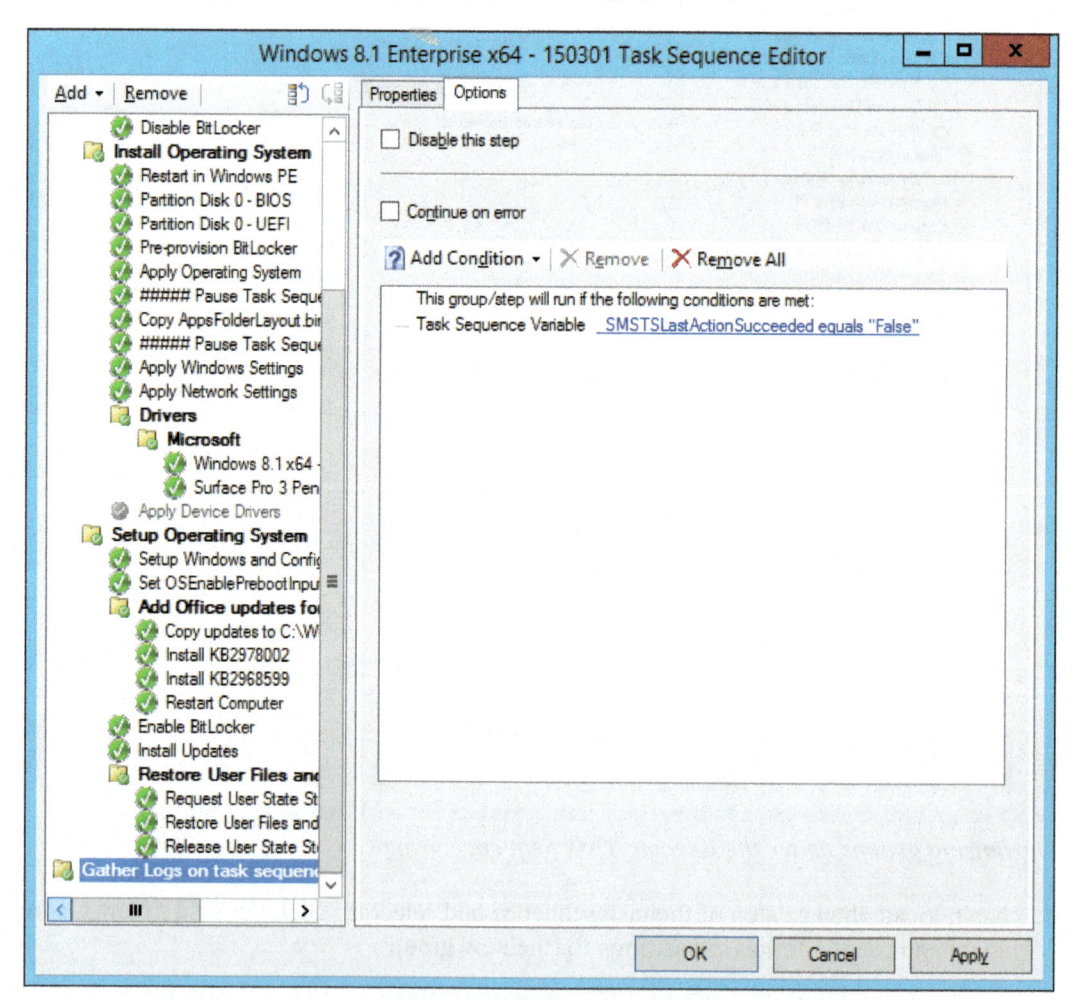

*The Gather Logs on task sequence failure group is created.*

6. Finally, locate the first step of the task sequence and select it. Click the **Add / New Group** and use the following settings for the new group:

   a. Name: **Task Sequence completed successfully**

   b. Description: **<default>**

   c. Click the **Options** tab and select the **Add Condition** drop-down menu. Select **If Statement** and then **All Conditions**.

   d. Click **If All conditions are true** and select the **Add Condition** drop-down menu. Select **Task Sequence Variable** from the list of options and fill in the following values:

      - Variable: **_SMSTSLastActionSucceeded**
      - Condition: **equals**
      - Value: **True**

   e. Click **If All conditions are true** and select the **Add Condition** drop-down menu. Select **Task Sequence Variable** from the list of options and fill in the following values:

      - Variable: **TS_Failed**
      - Condition: **not equals**
      - Value: **True**

   f. Using the **Move Down** button, move the **Task Sequence completed successfully** so that the group is the very last group in the task sequence (you cannot click Move Down any more as the button is greyed out).

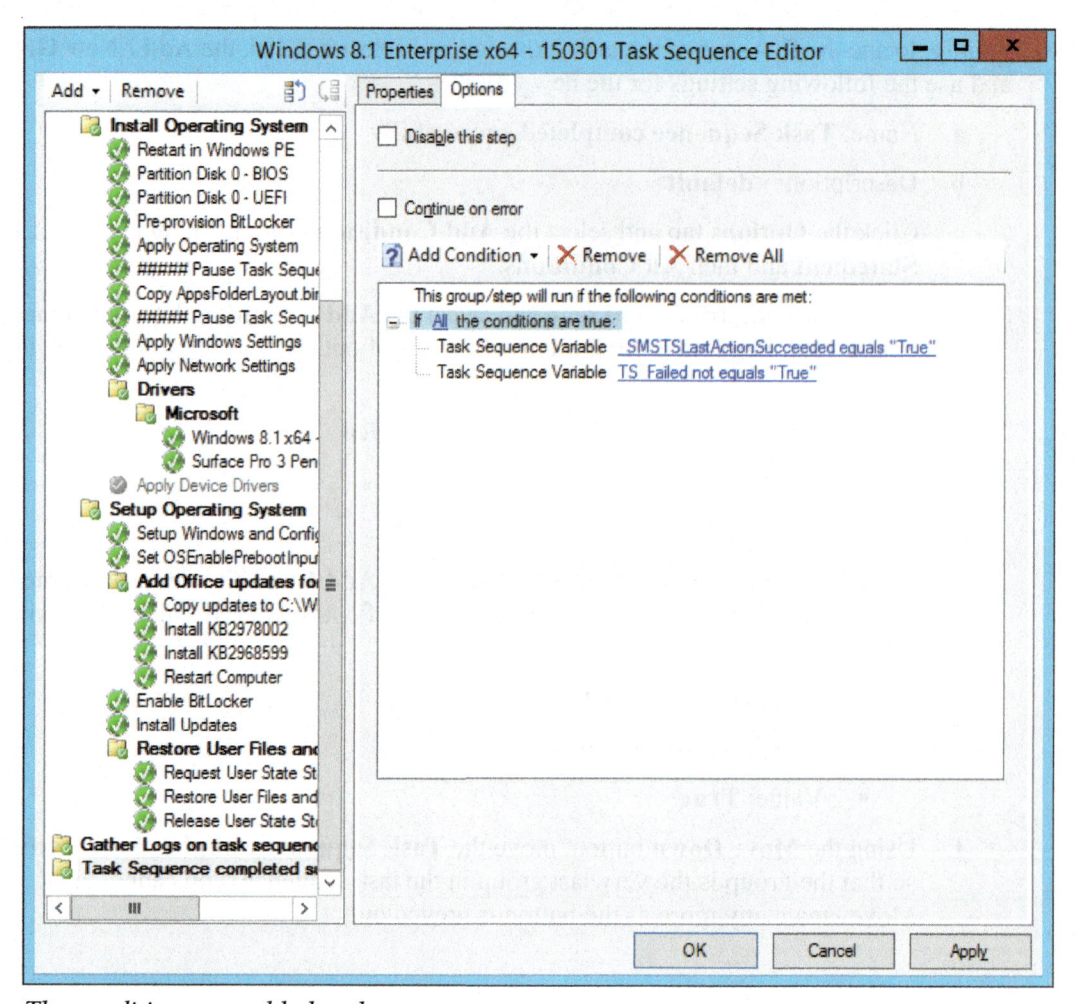

Chapter 10   Implementing MailLog, AssistMe, and ViewLog

*The conditions are added to the group.*

7. Save the changes by clicking **OK**.

## Add New Steps

Next you need to add some additional steps to the task sequence. One step resets _SMSTSLastActionSucceeded in case any step in the Restore User Files and Settings group fails. Another step copies the required files to the hard disk so that they can be used within the Windows phase of OSD, and a further step invokes MailLog after a task sequence failure. The final step removes the MailLog files after a successful OSD.

To add the new steps, follow this process:

1. On **CM01**, using the **ConfigMgr console**, expand **Software Library**, select **Operating System / Task Sequences**, and then select the **Windows 8.1 Enterprise x64 - 150301** task sequence.

248

Chapter 10   Implementing MailLog, AssistMe, and ViewLog

2. Right-click the task sequence and choose **Edit**; locate the **Apply Operating System** step and click it; next choose **Add / General / Run Command Line**.

3. Use the following settings for the **Run Command Line** step:

    a. Name: **Copy MailLog files for the Windows phase**

    b. Description: **<default>**

    c. Command line (you can also copy and paste from E:\Setup\Scripts\Copy MailLog files for the Windows phase.txt) :
    **cmd.exe /c xcopy "X:\Windows\System32\VNC" "%OSDISK%\Windows\System32\VNC" /D /E /C /I /Q /H /R /Y /S & xcopy "X:\Windows\System32\mailer" "%OSDISK%\Windows\System32\mailer" /D /E /C /I /Q /H /R /Y /S & copy "X:\Windows\System32\maillog.vbs" "%OSDISK%\Windows\System32\" & copy "X:\Windows\System32\assistme.cmd" "%OSDISK%\Windows\System32\" & copy "X:\Windows\System32\viewlog.cmd" "%OSDISK%\Windows\System32\"**

    d. Disable 64-bit file system redirection: **<default>**

    e. Start in: **<default>**

    f. Package: **<default>**

    g. Time-out (minutes): **5**

    h. Run this step as the following account: **<default>**

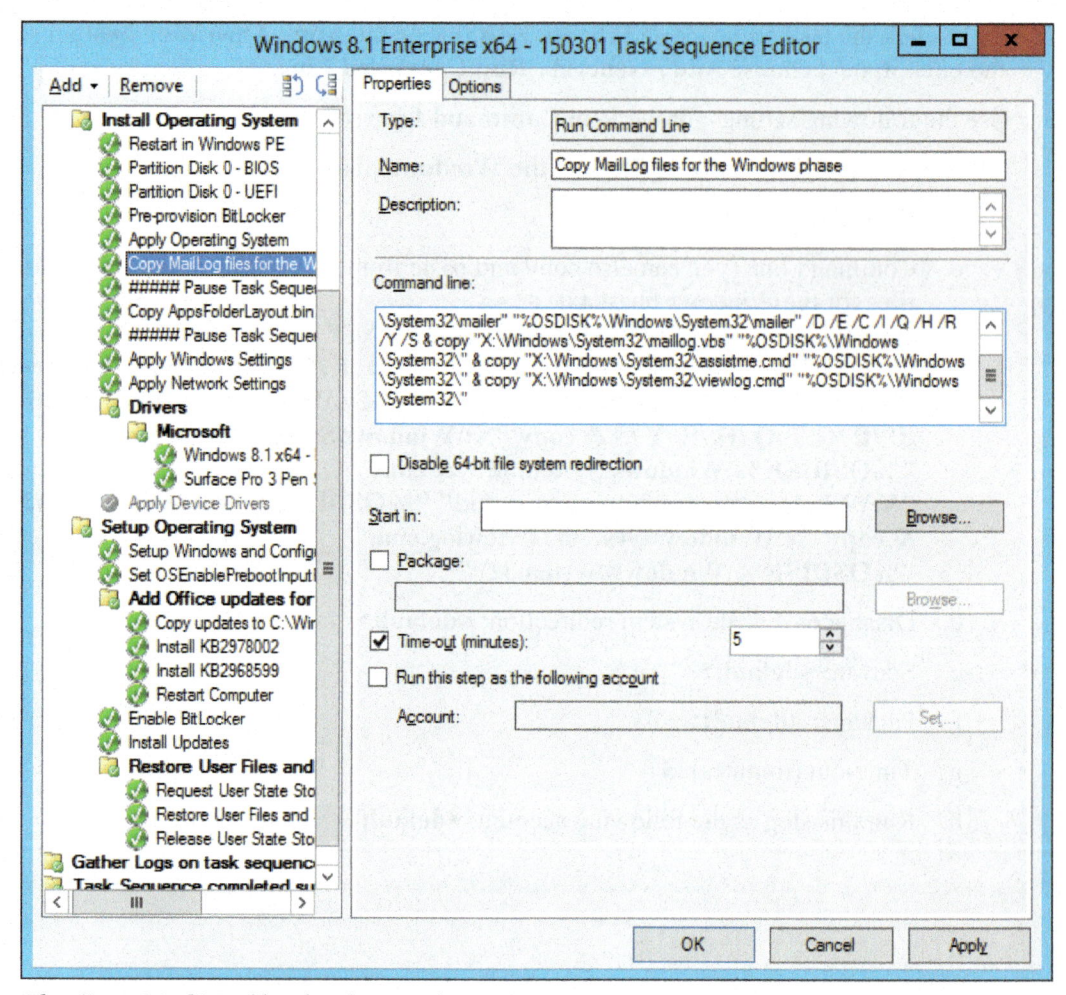

*The Copy MailLog files for the Windows phase step.*

4. Next, locate the **Restore User Files and Settings** group, and add a step directly after the last one in the group. Choose **Add / General / Set Task Sequence Variable**.

5. Use the following settings for the **Set Task Sequence Variable** step:

    a. Name: **Set Dummy_Var**

    b. Description: **<default>**

    c. Task Sequence Variable: **Dummy_Var**

    d. Value: **True**

6. Use the **Move Down** button to move the **Set Dummy_Var** step beneath the group as shown in the figure. This way if any step in the **Restore User Files and Settings** group fails (such as when there is no user data to restore), it will run the dummy step prior to checking for a failed condition. This avoids unnecessarily failing a task sequence.

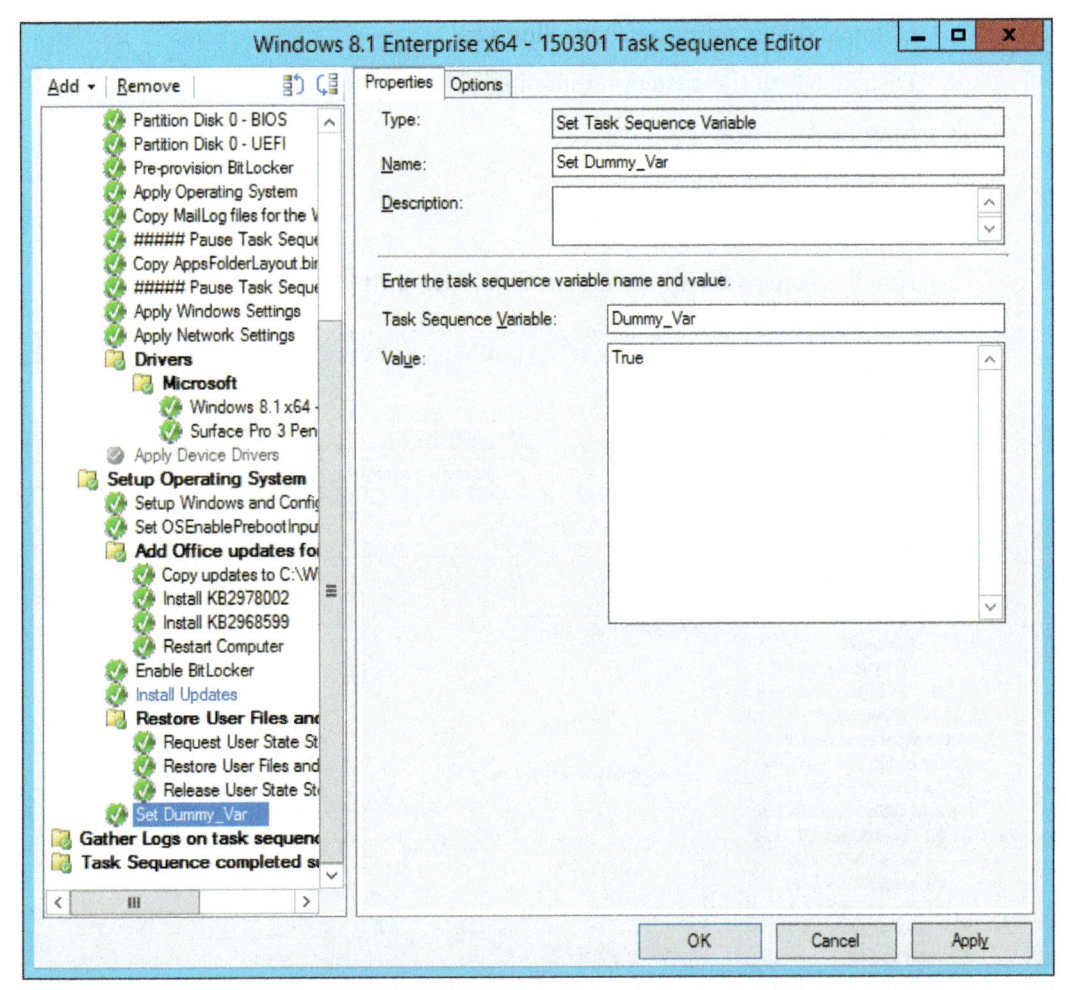

Chapter 10 Implementing MailLog, AssistMe, and ViewLog

*Setting a dummy variable to force _SMSTSLastActionSucceeded behavior to True.*

7. Next, locate the **Gather Logs on task sequence failure** group, select it, choose **Add / General / Set Task Sequence Variable**, and use the following settings for the **Set Task Sequence Variable** step:

    a. Name: **Set TS_Failed**

    b. Description: **<default>**

    c. Task Sequence Variable: **TS_Failed**

    d. Value: **True**

8. Next, choose **Add / General / Run Command Line**. Use the following settings for the **Run Command Line** step:

    a. Name: **Invoke MailLog on failure**

    b. Description: **<default>**

251

Chapter 10 Implementing MailLog, AssistMe, and ViewLog

    c. Command line: **cmd.exe /c maillog.vbs**

    d. Disable 64-bit file system redirection: **<default>**

    e. Start in: **<default>**

    f. Package: **<default>**

    g. Time-out (minutes): **<default>**

    h. Run this step as the following account: **<default>**

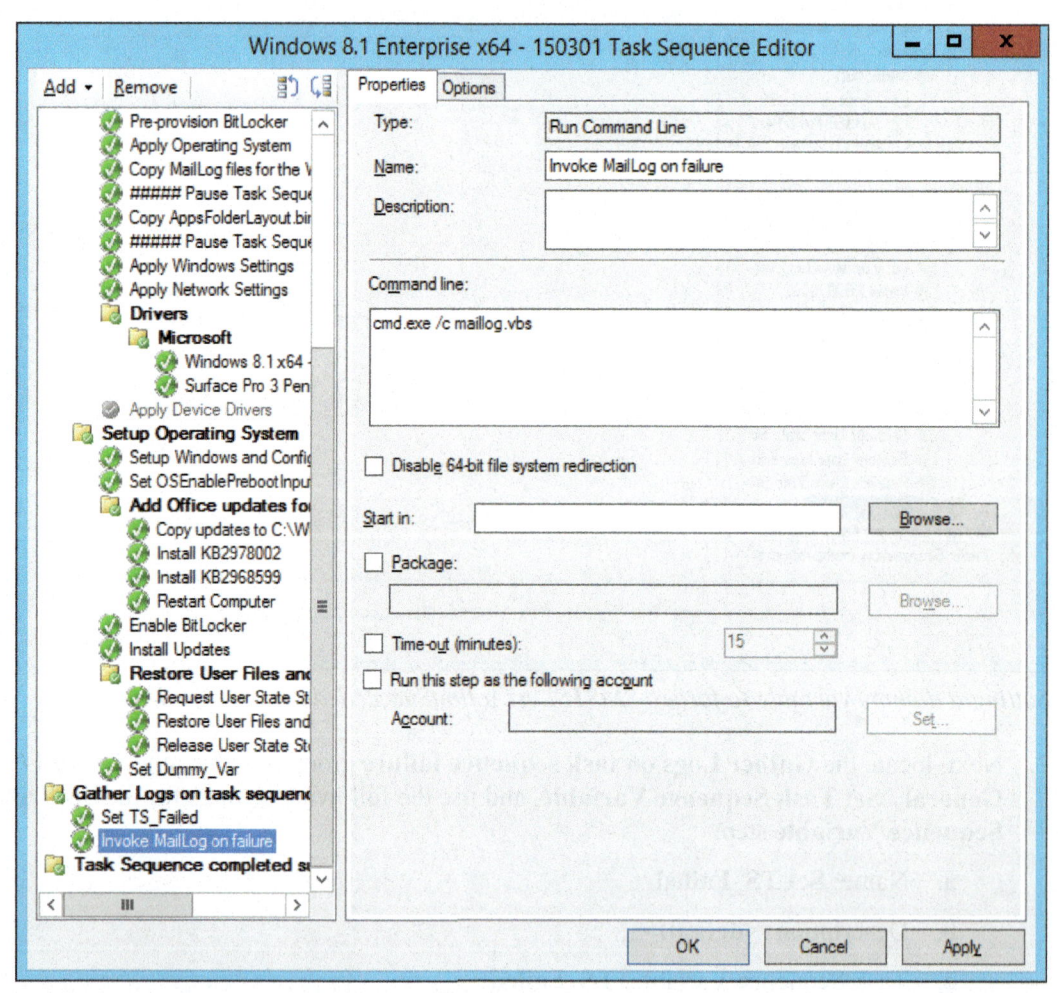

*The Invoke MailLog on failure step is added.*

9. Select the **Task Sequence completed successfully** group, choose **Add / General / Run Command Line**, and use the following settings for the **Run Command Line** step:

    a. Name: **Cleanup AssistMe, ViewLog and MailLog files**

    b. Description: **<default>**

Chapter 10   Implementing MailLog, AssistMe, and ViewLog

    c. Command line (you can copy and paste from the E:\Setup\Scripts\Cleanup AssistMe, ViewLog and MailLog files.txt file):
**cmd.exe /c echo Y | rd /s C:\Windows\System32\Mailer & echo Y | rd /s C:\Windows\System32\vnc & del C:\Windows\System32\assistme.cmd & del C:\Windows\System32\viewlog.cmd & del C:\Windows\System32\maillog.vbs**

    d. Disable 64-bit file system redirection: **<default>**

    e. Start in: **<default>**

    f. Package: **<default>**

    g. Time-out (minutes): **5**

    h. Run this step as the following account: **<default>**

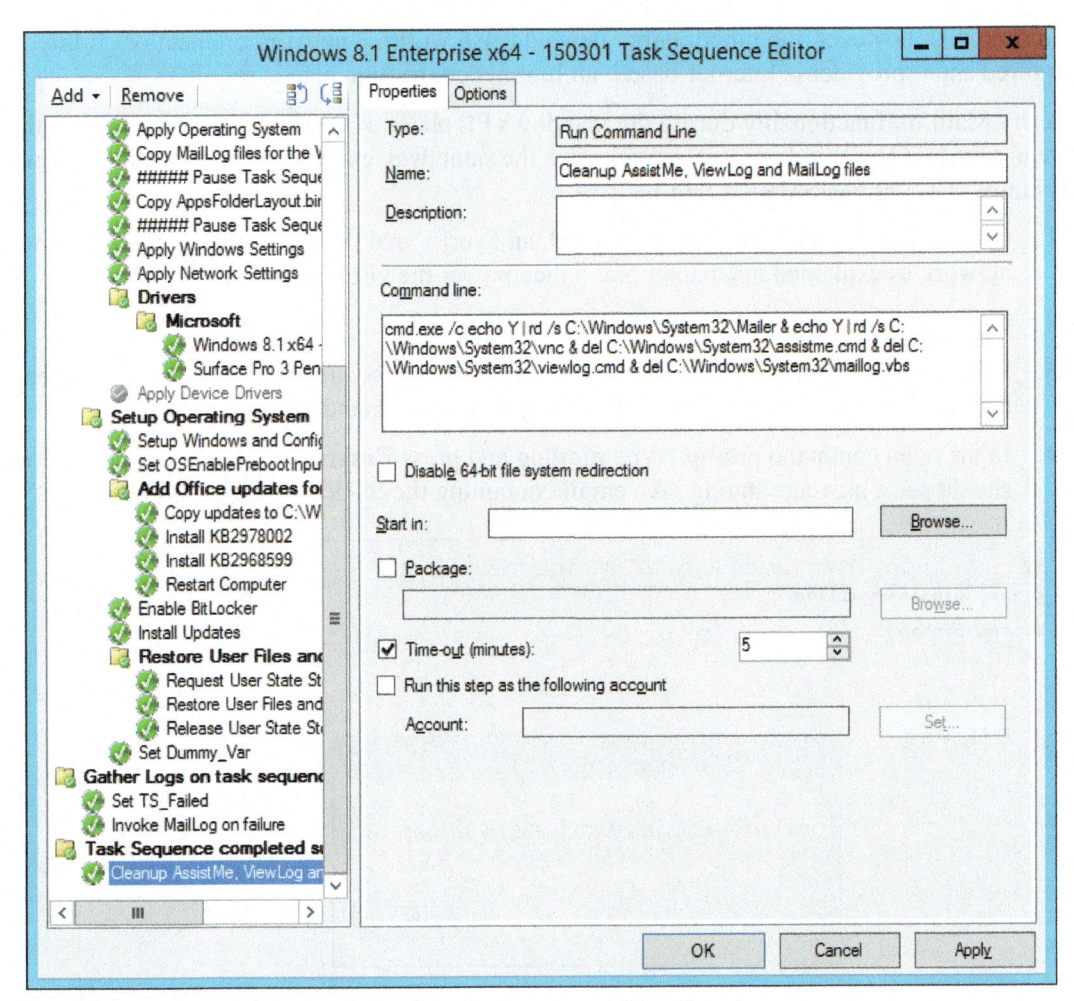

*Cleaning up after a successful task sequence is completed.*

**10.** Save the changes by clicking **OK**.

253

## Verifying the Changes

Now that you've prepared your environment for the new capabilities, it's time to verify that everything is working as expected.

### Verify MailLog

MailLog is designed to give you a quick overview of key information when a deployment goes wrong. It provides you with the computer name, the make/model, whether it is UEFI or legacy, and at what stage of an OSD it is in, all of which you can see by quickly glancing at the email. In addition, it contain a compressed attachment containing one or more log files. Those log files can be useful when additional troubleshooting is necessary.

MailLog has the ability to email logs whether it is running in the Windows PE or the Windows portion of OSD; however, the functionality depends on a working network connection. If the configured email provider is Internet-based, an Internet connection also is required.

To verify MailLog functionality during the Windows PE phase of OSD, perform the steps in the following guide. (The Windows phase works just the same way except that it stores the logs in C:\Windows\CCM\Logs\SMSTSLOG.)

1. Create a virtual machine named **PC0009**, and verify that the boot order is set to boot to network as explained in Chapter 5 and then power the virtual machine on.
2. Enter the PXE password **P@ssw0rd**, and click **Next**.
3. Select the **Windows 8.1 Enterprise x64 - 150301** task sequence and click **Next**. After the task sequence has started, press **F8** to bring up the command prompt.
4. In the open command prompt, type **maillog** and press **Enter**. After some moments, you should see a message stating "An email containing the SMSTS logfiles has been sent."

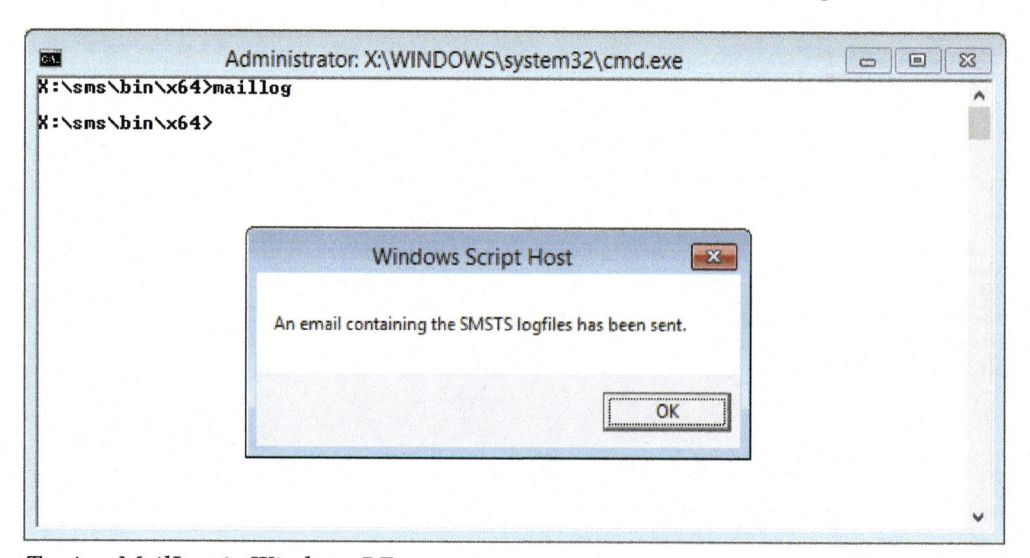

*Testing MailLog in Windows PE.*

Chapter 10   Implementing MailLog, AssistMe, and ViewLog

5. To review the log created by MailLog, using **CMTrace**, open the following log file **x:\Windows\Temp\SMSTSLog\MailLog.log**.

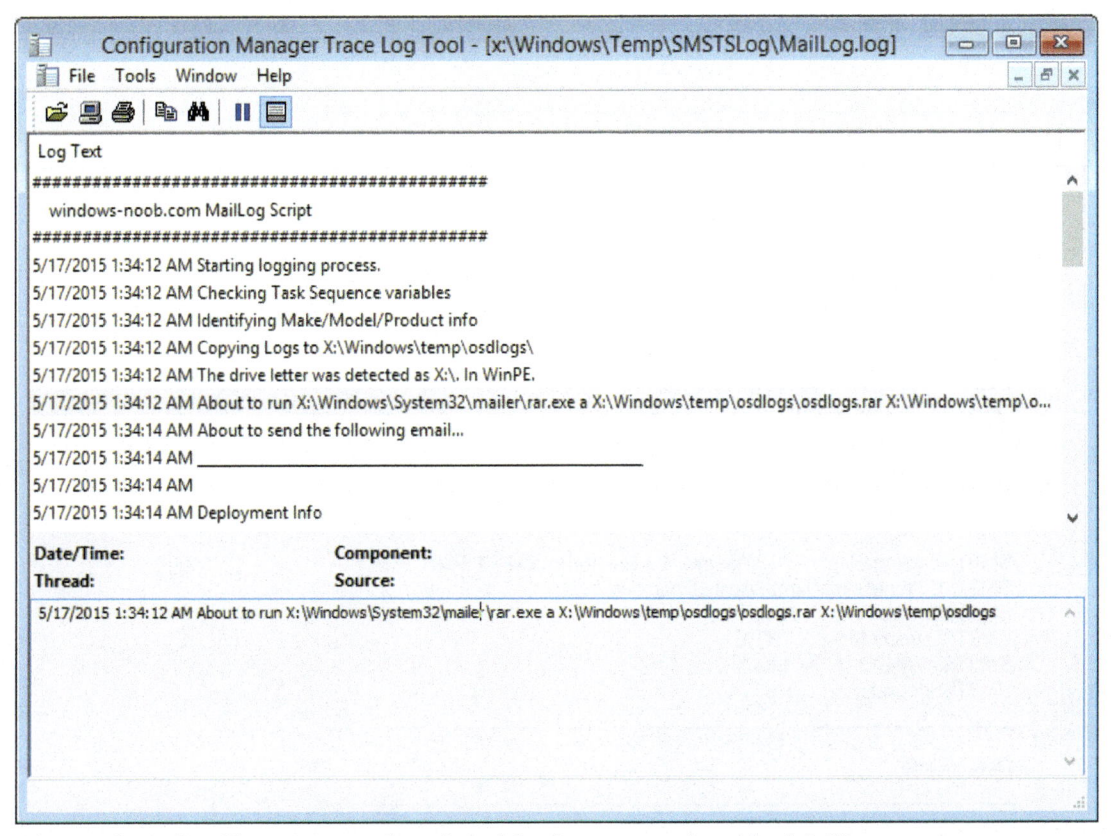

*The MailLog.log file contains a lot of useful information about the MailLog process.*

6. After the email message is sent, verify that it has arrived in the inbox of the configured MailTo address. Check the attachment that is included in the email, which should contain log files in a compressed format (osdlogs.rar).

**Note:** If the email message does not arrive in the configured inbox due to network or other problems, it is worth noting that a local copy of the email is saved on the client in the MailLog.log file. This local copy of the email is saved irrespective of whether the contents can be emailed to the configured MailTo address.

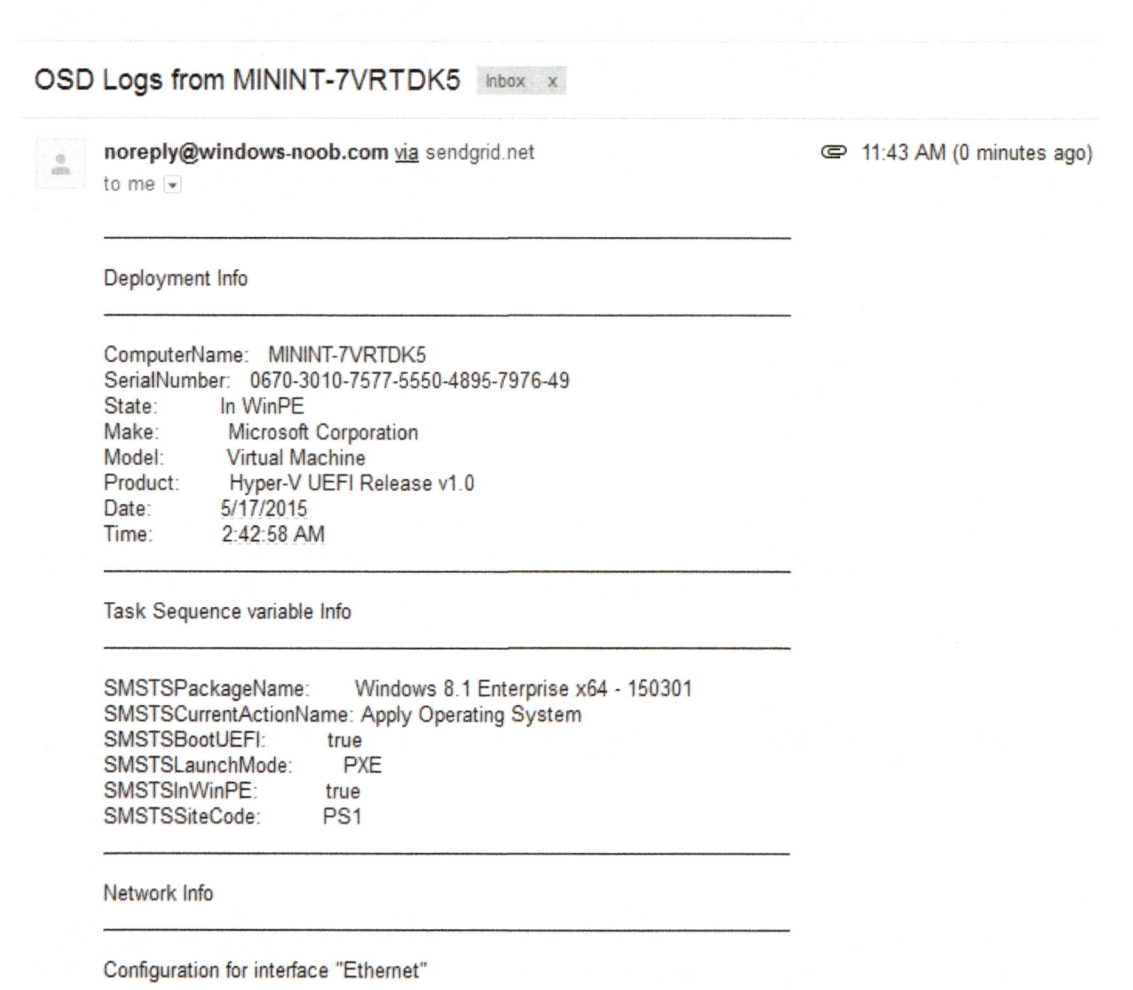

```
OSD Logs from MININT-7VRTDK5  Inbox  x

noreply@windows-noob.com via sendgrid.net          11:43 AM (0 minutes ago)
to me

─────────────────────────────────────────────────
Deployment Info
─────────────────────────────────────────────────

ComputerName:   MININT-7VRTDK5
SerialNumber:   0670-3010-7577-5550-4895-7976-49
State:          In WinPE
Make:           Microsoft Corporation
Model:          Virtual Machine
Product:        Hyper-V UEFI Release v1.0
Date:           5/17/2015
Time:           2:42:58 AM

─────────────────────────────────────────────────
Task Sequence variable Info
─────────────────────────────────────────────────

SMSTSPackageName:       Windows 8.1 Enterprise x64 - 150301
SMSTSCurrentActionName: Apply Operating System
SMSTSBootUEFI:          true
SMSTSLaunchMode:        PXE
SMSTSInWinPE:           true
SMSTSSiteCode:          PS1

─────────────────────────────────────────────────
Network Info
─────────────────────────────────────────────────

Configuration for interface "Ethernet"
```

*The OSD Logs email and associated attachment has arrived in the inbox.*

> **Real World Note**: The OSD Logs email contains information that should aid with troubleshooting a failed deployment. For example, the email reveals what state the computer was in when the email was sent (in WinPE or in Windows). You can even configure which task sequence variables are revealed in the email by changing the maillog script to suit your needs. Be aware that the task sequence variable info is populated only after a task sequence has been selected and run.

## Verify AssistMe

AssistMe also can be used in both the Windows PE and Windows portions of an operating system deployment. AssistMe can be instigated by a user calling the helpdesk and asking for help. The helpdesk operator can then instruct the user how to allow a remote connection by running AssistMe.

Chapter 10 Implementing MailLog, AssistMe, and ViewLog

AssistMe usually requires two users, one with a problem and another to support that user (for example, a helpdesk user). To verify AssistMe during the Windows PE phase of OSD, do as follows:

1. Create a virtual machine named **PC0010**, and verify that the boot order is set to boot to network as explained in Chapter 5 and then power the virtual machine on.

2. Enter the PXE password **P@ssw0rd**, and click **Next**.

3. Select the **Windows 8.1 Enterprise x64 - 150301** task sequence and click **Next**. After the task sequence has started, press **F8** to bring up the command prompt.

4. The user with the problem can type **AssistMe** in the command prompt and then press **Enter**. After some moments, a message listing the IP address and some other information about the deployment appears. The IP address should be provided to the helpdesk user supporting the session.

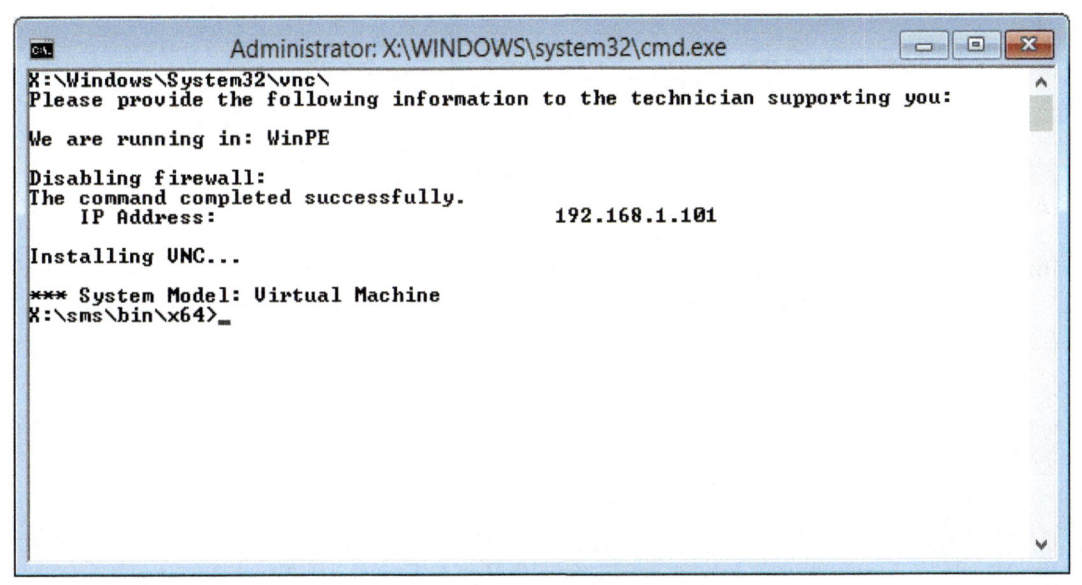

*AssistMe has been entered in a command prompt by the user during OSD.*

5. On **CM01**, the helpdesk user can now remotely connect to the IP address provided by the user with the problem by using VNC Viewer. Start **VNC Viewer** and enter the **IP address** provided.

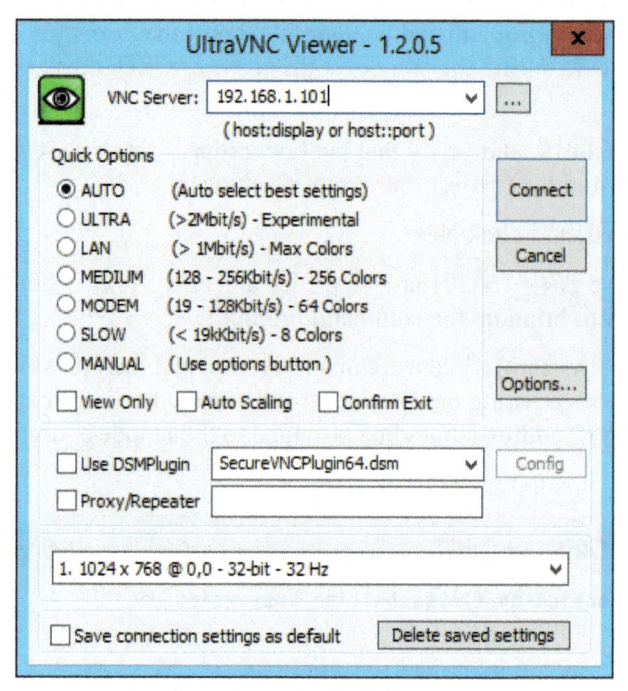

Chapter 10   Implementing MailLog, AssistMe, and ViewLog

*Entering the IP address in VNC Viewer.*

6. After entering the IP address, click **Connect**. You are prompted for a password by a VNC Authentication window. Enter the configured password **P@ssw0rd** and click **Log On** to continue.

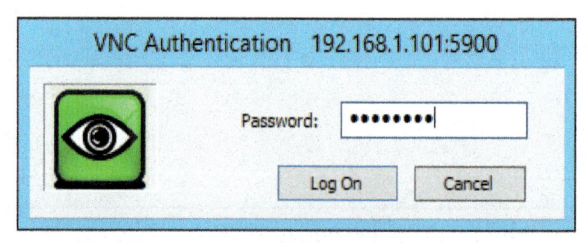

*The VNC Viewer Password prompt.*

After entering the password correctly, the VNC session appear in the service mode window of VNC Viewer on CM01. This session gives the helpdesk user full control of the connected computer to allow them to troubleshoot as they wish.

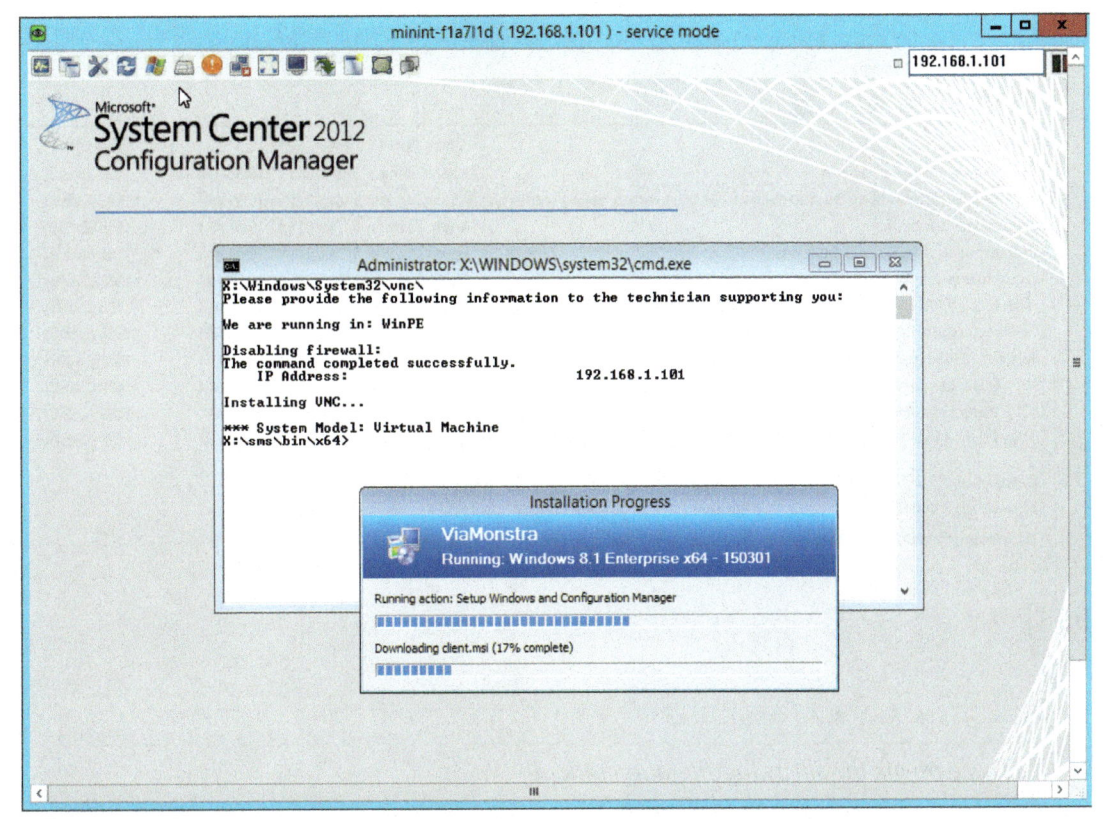

Chapter 10   Implementing MailLog, AssistMe, and ViewLog

*A VNC session while OSD is in progress.*

7. After the troubleshooting session is complete, close that session by optionally closing any open log files and close the open command prompt window before clicking the red (Close) X in the top-right corner of the VNC Viewer service mode window.

## Verify ViewLog

ViewLog opens the appropriate smsts.log file in CMTrace to save you having to find the file whether you are in Windows PE or Windows (with or without the CCM agent installed). To verify ViewLog functionality during the Windows PE phase of OSD do as follows:

1. Create a virtual machine named **PC0011**, and verify that the boot order is set to boot to network as explained in Chapter 5 and then power the virtual machine on.

2. Enter the PXE password **P@ssw0rd**, and click **Next**.

3. Select the **Windows 8.1 Enterprise x64 - 150301** task sequence and click **Next**. After the task sequence has started, press **F8** to bring up the command prompt.

4. In the open command prompt, type **viewlog** and press **Enter**. After some moments, CMTrace appears and loads the smsts.log file without prompting.

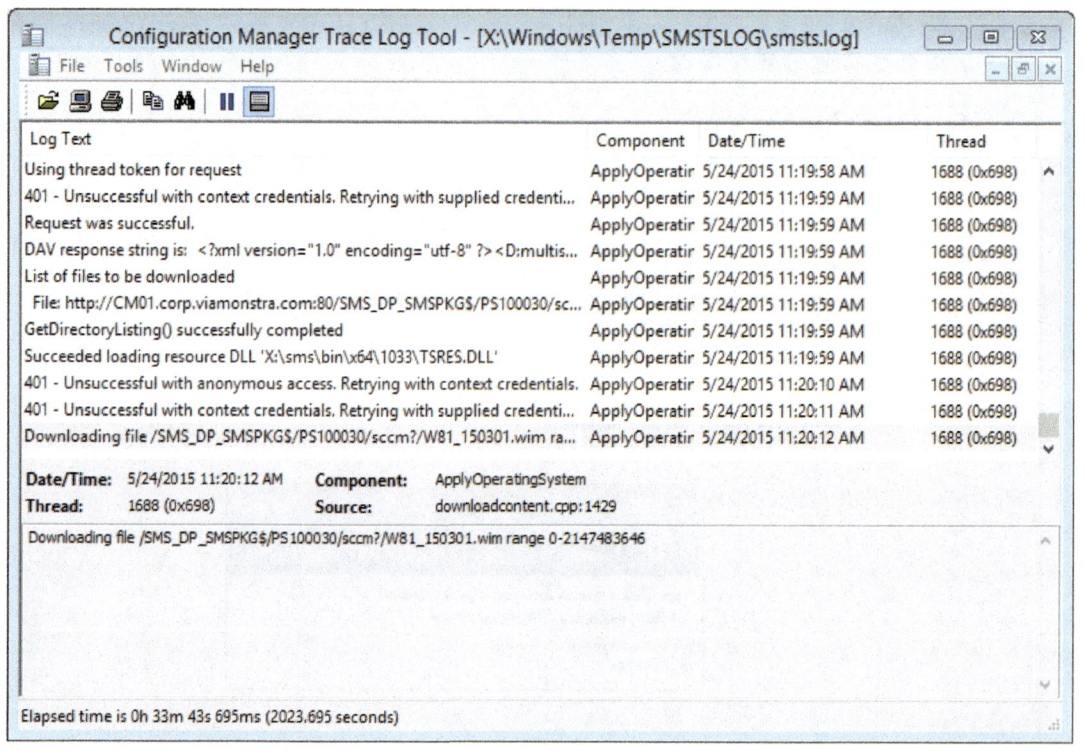

Chapter 10   Implementing MailLog, AssistMe, and ViewLog

*CMTrace opens the smsts.log file automatically.*

5. After reviewing the **smsts.log** file in **CMTrace**, you can close CMTrace.

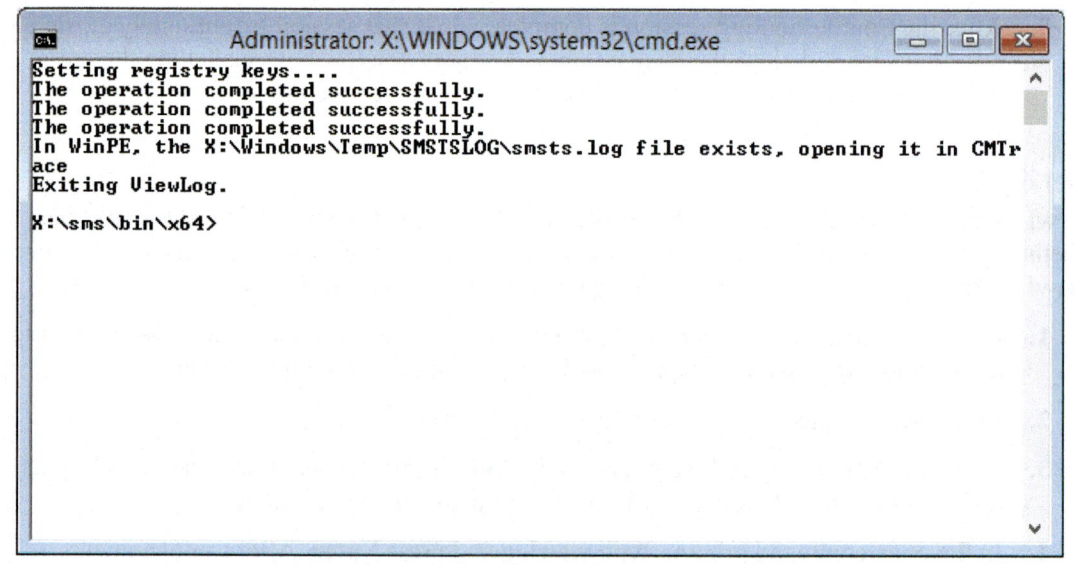

*The command prompt after running ViewLog and after CMTrace is closed.*

260

# Chapter 11
# Checking for Network and Storage Problems in WinPE

I'm sure you've come across this problem before. Someone in your organization purchases new hardware. It is connected to the network to install the corporate image, but it fails after attempting to PXE boot. Usually the failure is attributed to missing network or storage drivers in the boot image attached to the task sequence. Either way, the problem usually ends up at your desk.

> **Real World Note**: Identifying a problem with missing network or storage drivers is not always straightforward. You can use a tool called wbemtest to connect to WMI on a computer that has an issue with a missing network or missing storage driver and then attempt to identify the hardware using queries. This troubleshooting capability is explained in the following blog post: http://niallbrady.com/2011/08/31/missing-nic-driver-in-winpe-boot-image-no-problem/.

You can implement the solution provided in this chapter to make the troubleshooting process easier and receive clear information about what the actual problem is when an attempted PXE boot fails. However, adding the capability to detect when there are issues with network connectivity or storage requires certain changes to the default booting process in WinPE.

Those changes trigger a script which checks for network and storage capability. The checks must occur before the task sequence engine kicks off. This is done via a registry hack in the boot image, which in turn launches the detection script before either starting the normal task sequence environment or presenting troubleshooting information to the end user.

After a failure is observed and the message is given to the end user, you still have to resolve the issue by adding appropriate drivers to the boot image and updating that boot image to the distribution points. However, having this technology in place should make the overall process easier.

Chapter 11 Checking for Network and Storage Problems in WinPE

# Step-by-Step Guide Requirements

If you want to follow the step-by-step guides in this chapter, you need a lab environment configured as outlined in Chapter 2 and Appendix A. In this chapter, you use the following virtual machines:

DC01　　　　CM01　　　　PC0012

*The VMs used in this chapter (PC0012 is a VM created in one of the guides).*

In order to complete this guide, you need the following two files:

- WindowHide.exe
- CheckForNetwork.vbs

The WindowHide.exe file is located in the Tools\<arch> folder of MDT, where <arch> matches the architecture of the boot image you plan to use. If, for example, you are editing a 64-bit boot image, it is in E:\Sources\OSD\MDT\MDT 2013\Tools\x64. The CheckForNetwork.vbs script itself is located in E:\Setup\Scripts.

> **Note**: This guide assumes that you have already got a working PXE environment setup, deployed at least one task sequence, and enabled F8 command prompt support within your boot WIMs as described in Chapter 2.

# Preparing Your Environment

Preparing your boot image with the needed files requires editing the script to verify that the array of servers listed matches servers in your environment that are pingable. Next, the boot image must be mounted and, in addition, the boot image registry is modified to run your script. To perform those actions, follow the steps in this section.

## Edit the Script

To make changes to the array of servers defined in the script, do as follows:

1. On **CM01**, using a **Command prompt**, ping one or more server **IP addresses** in turn to verify that they are pingable. Each server IP address that you can ping successfully will be used in the script. Make note of the server IP addresses that you intend to use.

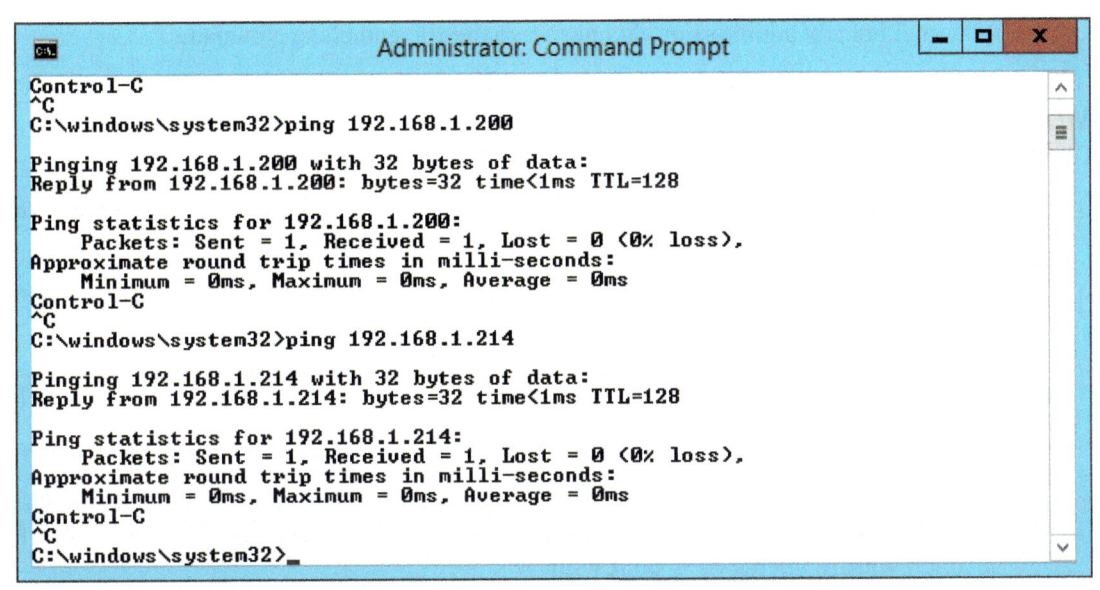

Chapter 11   Checking for Network and Storage Problems in WinPE

```
Administrator: Command Prompt                     _ □ x
Control-C
^C
C:\windows\system32>ping 192.168.1.200

Pinging 192.168.1.200 with 32 bytes of data:
Reply from 192.168.1.200: bytes=32 time<1ms TTL=128

Ping statistics for 192.168.1.200:
    Packets: Sent = 1, Received = 1, Lost = 0 (0% loss),
Approximate round trip times in milli-seconds:
    Minimum = 0ms, Maximum = 0ms, Average = 0ms
Control-C
^C
C:\windows\system32>ping 192.168.1.214

Pinging 192.168.1.214 with 32 bytes of data:
Reply from 192.168.1.214: bytes=32 time<1ms TTL=128

Ping statistics for 192.168.1.214:
    Packets: Sent = 1, Received = 1, Lost = 0 (0% loss),
Approximate round trip times in milli-seconds:
    Minimum = 0ms, Maximum = 0ms, Average = 0ms
Control-C
^C
C:\windows\system32>_
```

*Pinging server IP addresses manually to verify that they respond to pings.*

2. On **CM01**, using **Notepad**, open **E:\Setup\Scripts\CheckForNetwork.vbs**. Scroll down to the **ServersToPing** line and verify that the addresses entered in the array match servers that you can ping in your environment. Remove any servers that are not pingable.

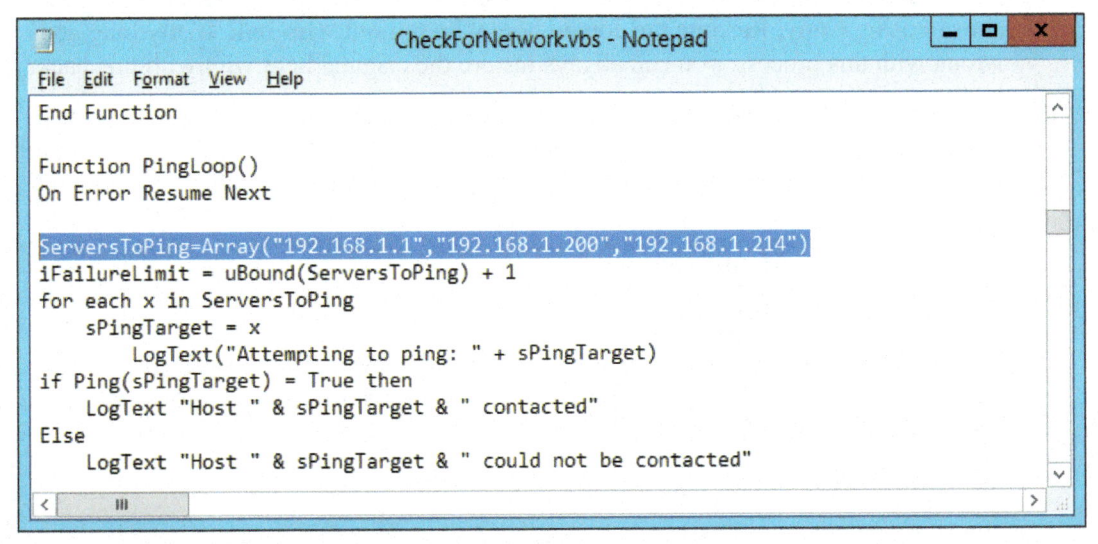

```
CheckForNetwork.vbs - Notepad                     _ □ x
File  Edit  Format  View  Help

End Function

Function PingLoop()
On Error Resume Next

ServersToPing=Array("192.168.1.1","192.168.1.200","192.168.1.214")
iFailureLimit = uBound(ServersToPing) + 1
for each x in ServersToPing
    sPingTarget = x
        LogText("Attempting to ping: " + sPingTarget)
if Ping(sPingTarget) = True then
    LogText "Host " & sPingTarget & " contacted"
Else
    LogText "Host " & sPingTarget & " could not be contacted"
```

*The IP addresses added here should be pingable.*

**Note**: Be very careful with any edits to this script as this script runs before the task sequence engine. A missing quotation mark in the ServersToPing array or any mistake made while editing the script is enough to cause it to fail. That failure forces the boot image to reboot without any visible error, making troubleshooting even harder. Test your changes in a virtual machine thoroughly before implementing in production.

263

3. After making any additions or changes, save the file and close Notepad.

## Mount the Boot WIM

To mount the boot WIM in order to inject the script, do as follows:

1. On **CM01**, using the **ConfigMgr console**, expand **Software Library**, select **Operating System / Boot Images**, and then select the **Boot Image (x64)** boot image.

2. Right-click the file and select **Properties**. The **Data Source** tab reveals where this boot image is located and its file name.

> **Note**: If the boot image is an MDT-created boot image, it is called winpe.wim. If it is created by ConfigMgr, it is called boot.wim.

3. Using **File Explorer**, browse to the data source image path listed in the properties of the boot WIM you intend to edit. You probably see a few WIM files listed; however, the file in which you are interested is **boot.wim**.

4. Locate the local copy of the boot.wim file. By default, this file is present locally on your ConfigMgr primary server in the following path **E:\Program Files\Microsoft Configuration Manager\OSD\boot\<Arch>\boot.wim**. (Replace <Arch> with either i386 or x64 depending on the boot WIM architecture you are editing.)

5. Make a backup copy of the file before making any changes to it by right-clicking the file and choosing **Copy**. Rename the copied boot.wim to **boot.wim.bak**. If anything goes wrong with this process, you can always restore the original boot.wim with this backup.

6. To mount the boot WIM, you need some temporary storage for the required files and folders; therefore, if you haven't already created these folders, create the following folder structure on **C:\** using an elevated **Command prompt** (run as Administrator) and the **mkdir** command:
   - **C:\WinPEMount\x86**
   - **C:\WinPEMount\x64**

7. To start **DISM** correctly, locate it in your **Start** menu by searching for **Deployment Imaging Tools and Environment**, right-clicking the **Command prompt**, and then choosing **Run as Administrator**.

Chapter 11   Checking for Network and Storage Problems in WinPE

*Running DISM as administrator.*

8. In the **DISM** command prompt, change the drive letter to **E:** and then navigate to the directory containing the local copy of the boot.wim file that you need to mount. That directory is **E:\Program Files\Microsoft Configuration Manager\OSD\boot\<arch>** where **<arch>** is the architecture (x64 or x86) of your boot image. Use **dir** to list the contents of the directory and to verify that the boot.wim file is present.

9. Use the following command to mount your boot.wim file where <arch> is the architecture of your boot image. It should mount the boot.wim successfully as shown in the corresponding figure.

```
dism.exe /mount-wim /wimfile:"E:\Program Files\Microsoft
Configuration Manager\OSD\boot\<arch>\boot.wim" /index:1
/mountdir:C:\WinPEMount\<arch>
```

```
Administrator: Deployment and Imaging Tools Environment

E:\Program Files\Microsoft Configuration Manager\OSD\boot\x64>dism.exe /mount-wim /wimfile:"E:\Program Files\Microsoft Configuration Manager\OSD\boot\x64\boot.wim" /index:1 /mountdir:C:\WinPEMount\x64

Deployment Image Servicing and Management tool
Version: 6.3.9600.16384

Mounting image
[==========================100.0%==========================]
The operation completed successfully.

E:\Program Files\Microsoft Configuration Manager\OSD\boot\x64>_
```

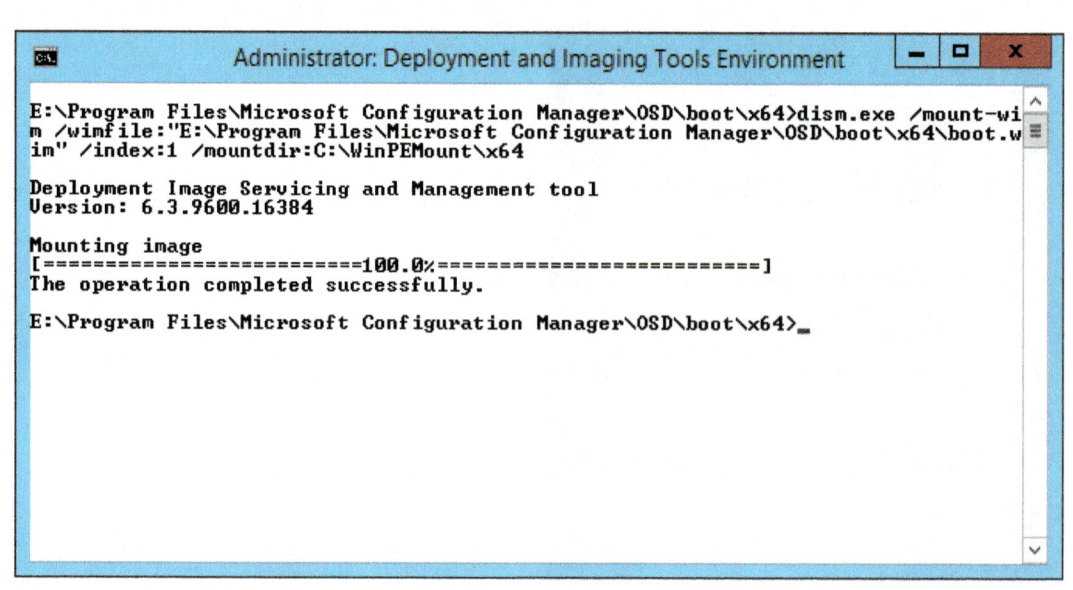

*Mounting the x64 boot image with DISM.*

## Copy Files into the Mounted Boot Image

To copy the two required files to the correct location, follow these steps:

1. On **CM01**, using the **DISM** command prompt, issue the following command to copy the script to its destination folder. Replace <arch> with the architecture of the boot image you are editing, in this case that is **x64**.

   ```
   copy E:\Setup\Scripts\CheckForNetwork.vbs
   C:\WinPEMount\<arch>\Windows\System32
   ```

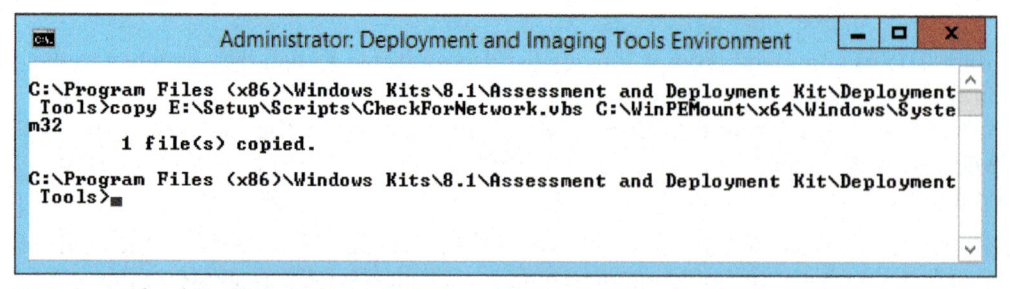

```
Administrator: Deployment and Imaging Tools Environment

C:\Program Files (x86)\Windows Kits\8.1\Assessment and Deployment Kit\Deployment Tools>copy E:\Setup\Scripts\CheckForNetwork.vbs C:\WinPEMount\x64\Windows\System32
        1 file(s) copied.

C:\Program Files (x86)\Windows Kits\8.1\Assessment and Deployment Kit\Deployment Tools>_
```

*Copying CheckForNetwork.vbs to the correct location.*

2. Next, copy **WindowHide.exe** from the MDT **Tools** folder to its destination by using the following command, where <arch> is the architecture of the boot image you are editing:

   ```
   copy "E:\Sources\OSD\MDT\MDT 2013\Tools\<arch>\
   WindowHide.exe" C:\WinPEMount\<arch>\Windows\System32
   ```

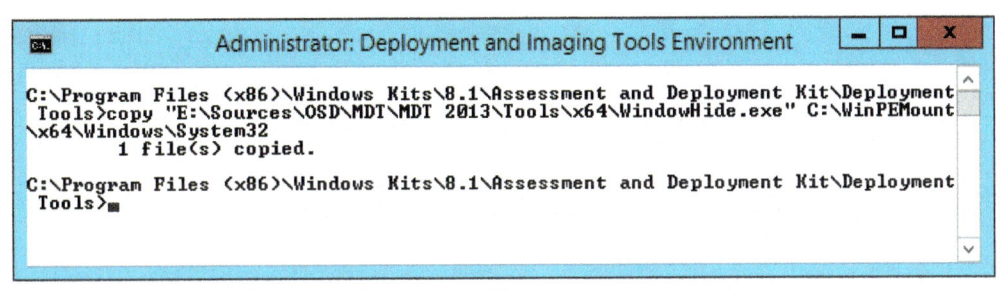

# Chapter 11 Checking for Network and Storage Problems in WinPE

*Copying WindowHide.exe to the mounted boot image.*

## Edit the Boot Image Registry

You need to use reg.exe to mount the system hive of the mounted boot WIM. This is necessary to force your script to run instead of the normal sequence of events when booting up. To mount the SYSTEM hive of the registry of the boot image and make appropriate changes, follow these steps:

1. On **CM01**, using the **DISM** command prompt, issue the following command where <arch> matches the architecture of your boot image:

   ```
   REG.EXE load HKEY_LOCAL_MACHINE\Mount\
   "C:\WinPEMount\<arch>\Windows\System32\Config\SYSTEM"
   ```

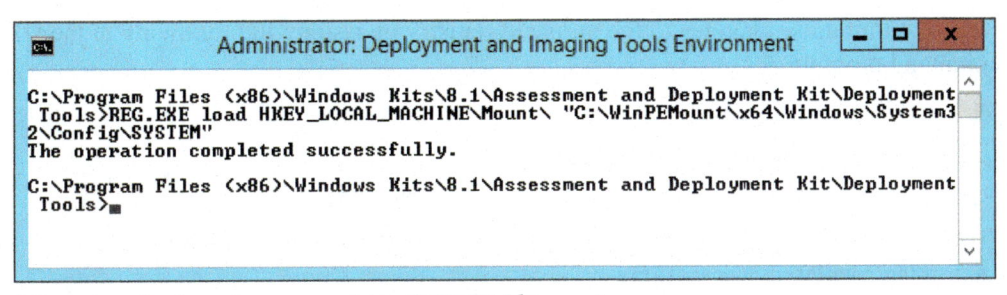

*Mounting the boot image registry SYSTEM hive using reg.exe.*

2. Next, using the **DISM** command prompt, issue the following command to change the current value (winpeshl.exe) for **CmdLine** in the mounted registry hive to run our script instead:

   ```
   reg add "HKEY_LOCAL_MACHINE\Mount\Setup" /v CmdLine /t
   REG_SZ /d "cscript.exe CheckForNetwork.vbs" /f
   ```

267

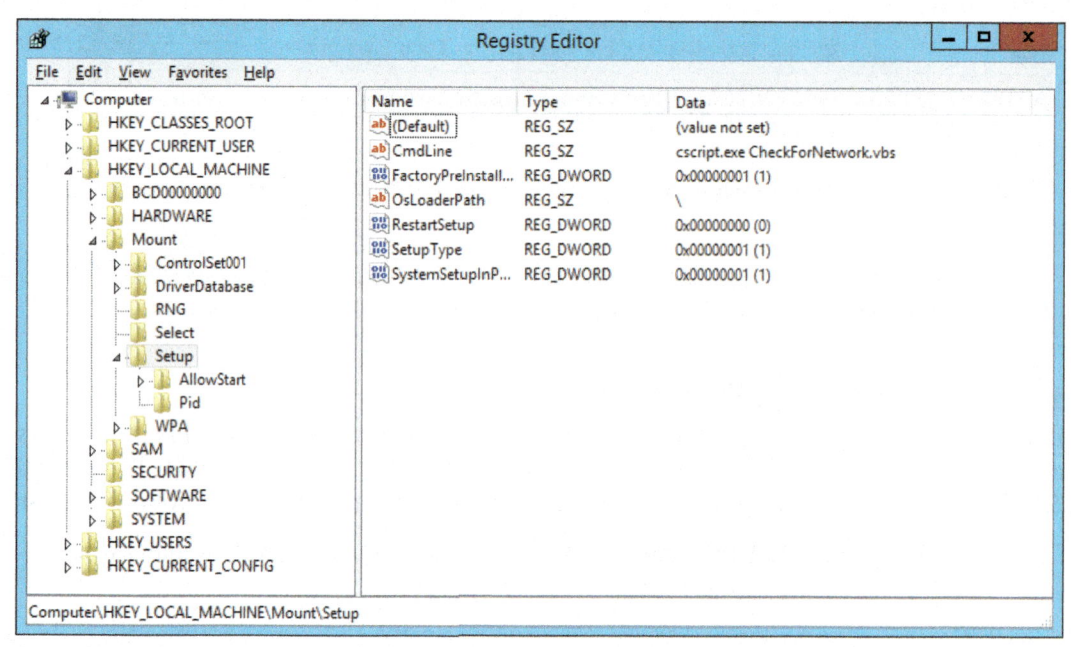

Chapter 11 Checking for Network and Storage Problems in WinPE

*Using regedit to view the mounted registry and to see the injected change.*

3. Next, commit those changes to the mounted registry by issuing the following in the **DISM** command prompt:

   ```
   REG.EXE unload HKEY_LOCAL_MACHINE\Mount
   ```

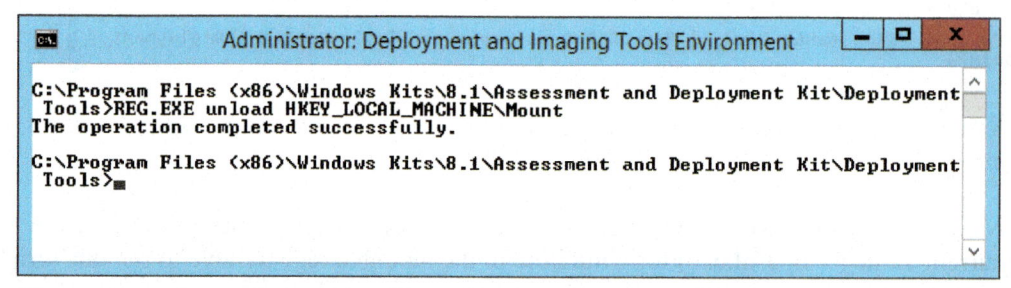

*The registry change is committed by unloading the mounted hive.*

## Commit the Changes to the Boot WIM

Now that you've made the required changes, you need to commit them to the boot.wim file. To commit (or write) the changes, do as follows:

1. On **CM01**, verify that you do not have any files open, and verify that you do not have **File Explorer** browsing in the mounted folder. This is important because you cannot commit the changes if any file is open.

2. Using the **DISM** command prompt, issue the following command:

   ```
   dism /unmount-wim /mountdir:c:\WinpeMount\X64 /commit
   ```

268

```
C:\Program Files (x86)\Windows Kits\8.1\Assessment and Deployment Kit\Deployment
 Tools>dism /unmount-wim /mountdir:c:\WinpeMount\X64 /commit

Deployment Image Servicing and Management tool
Version: 6.3.9600.16384

Image File : E:\Program Files\Microsoft Configuration Manager\OSD\boot\x64\boot.
wim
Image Index : 1
Saving image
[==========================100.0%==========================]
Unmounting image
[==========================100.0%==========================]
The operation completed successfully.

C:\Program Files (x86)\Windows Kits\8.1\Assessment and Deployment Kit\Deployment
 Tools>
```

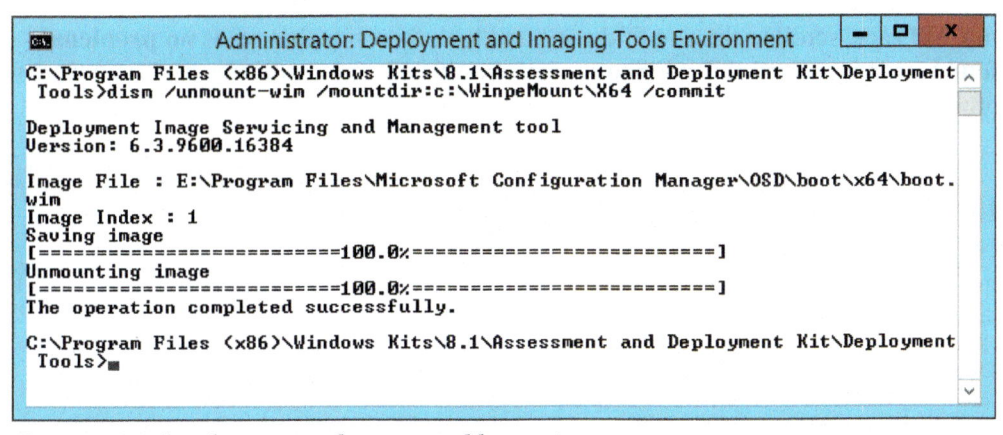

*Committing the changes to the mounted boot.wim.*

## Update the Boot WIM to the Distribution Points

For all computers in your organization to utilize the changes, you need to update the boot image to the distribution points. To do this, follow this process:

1. On **CM01**, using the **ConfigMgr console**, select **Software Library** and then select **Operating Systems / Boot Images**.

2. Right-click the **Boot Image (x64)** boot image and choose **Update Distribution Points**. Click **Next** and continue through the **Update Distribution Points Wizard** until completion.

# Verifying the Changes

Now that you've prepared your environment with the capability to test for network and storage issues in WinPE, it's time to verify that everything is working as expected. Normally, when there is no issue with the network or storage drivers in your boot image, you don't see anything out of the ordinary. The only way you know the script has run is by reviewing the log it creates.

However, in the event that the script detects a problem with network connectivity or storage, it informs the user and gives useful information to assist with solving the problem.

## Verify That the Script Has Run

To verify that the **CheckForNetwork** script has run, do as follows:

1. Create a virtual machine named **PC0012**, and verify that the boot order is set to boot to network as explained in Chapter 5 and then power the virtual machine on.

2. Before entering any password at the PXE password prompt, press **F8** to bring up a command prompt.

3. In the open command prompt, navigate to **X:\Windows\Temp\SMSTSLOG** and open **CheckForNetwork.log** using **CMTrace**.

4. In **CMTrace**, scroll to the end of the log and look for a line that reads **no problems found, starting normal Task Sequence env**. This message indicates that there were no problems identified with either network or storage.

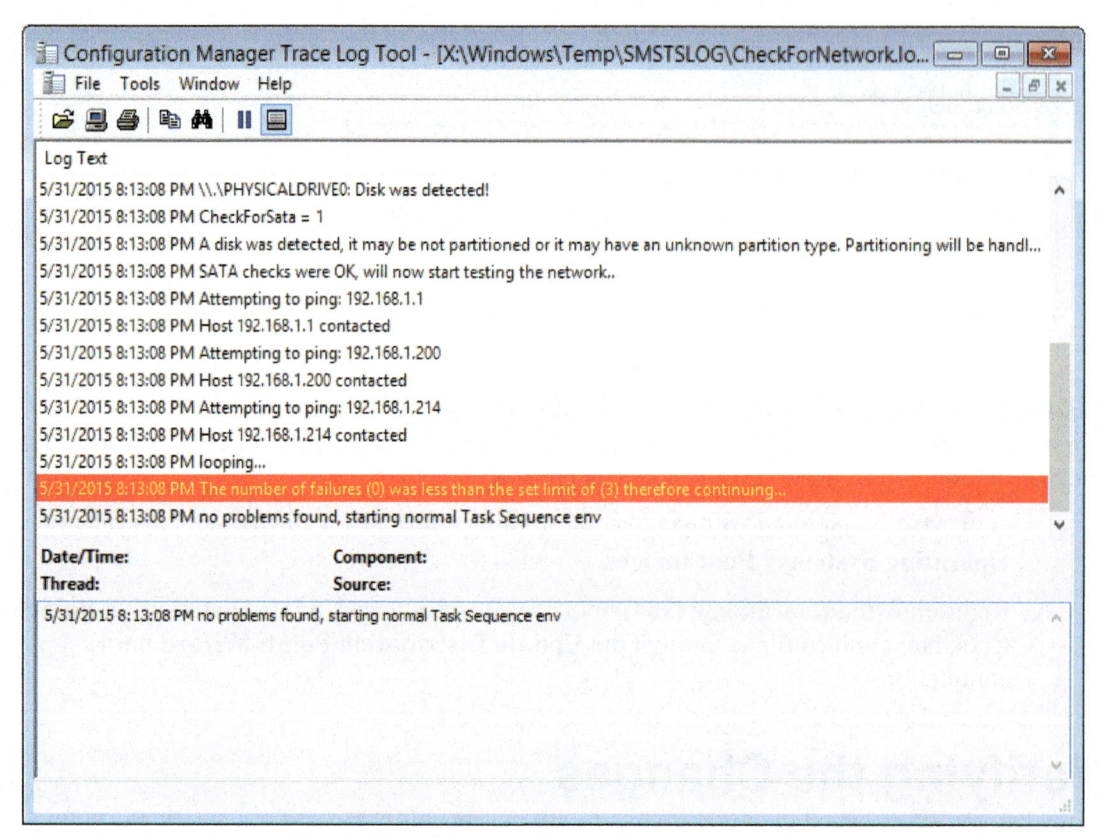

*Verifying the functionality via the CheckForNetwork log file.*

5. Turn off the **PC0012** virtual machine.

## Verify Network Checks

To verify what happens when the script cannot ping any of the servers in the previously defined array, you can simulate a network failure by removing a virtual machine's network card connection and by booting that virtual machine using removable media.

This media should contain the boot image you edited earlier in this chapter. To perform the simulation, do as follows:

1. On **CM01**, using the **ConfigMgr console**, in the **Software Library** workspace, select **Operating Systems / Task Sequences** and select the **Windows 8.1 Enterprise x64 - 150301** task sequence.

Chapter 11  Checking for Network and Storage Problems in WinPE

2. On the ribbon, click **Create Task Sequence Media** and use the following settings for the **Create Task Sequence Media Wizard**:

   a. Select Media Type: **Bootable media**

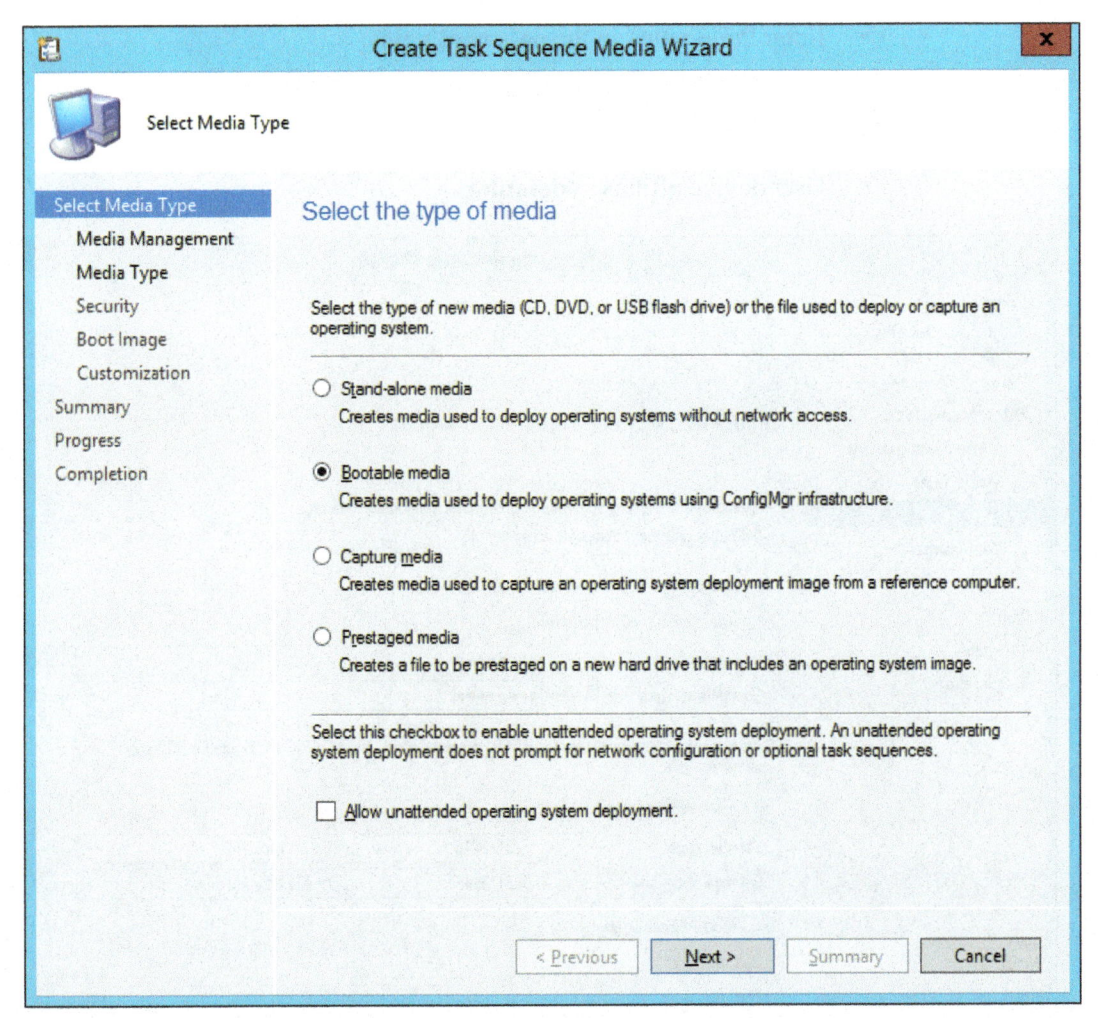

*Selecting bootable media in the Create Task Sequence Media Wizard.*

   b. Media Management: **Dynamic media**
   c. Media Type:
      - Select **CD/DVD Set**.
      - Media file: **E:\Setup\CheckForNetwork.iso**

271

Chapter 11   Checking for Network and Storage Problems in WinPE

d. Security:
- Select **Enable unknown computer support**.
- Select **Protect media with a password**.
- Enter **P@ssw0rd** in the password fields.
- Create a self-signed media certificate...: **<default>**
- Import PKI certificate: **<default>**
- User device affinity: **<default>**

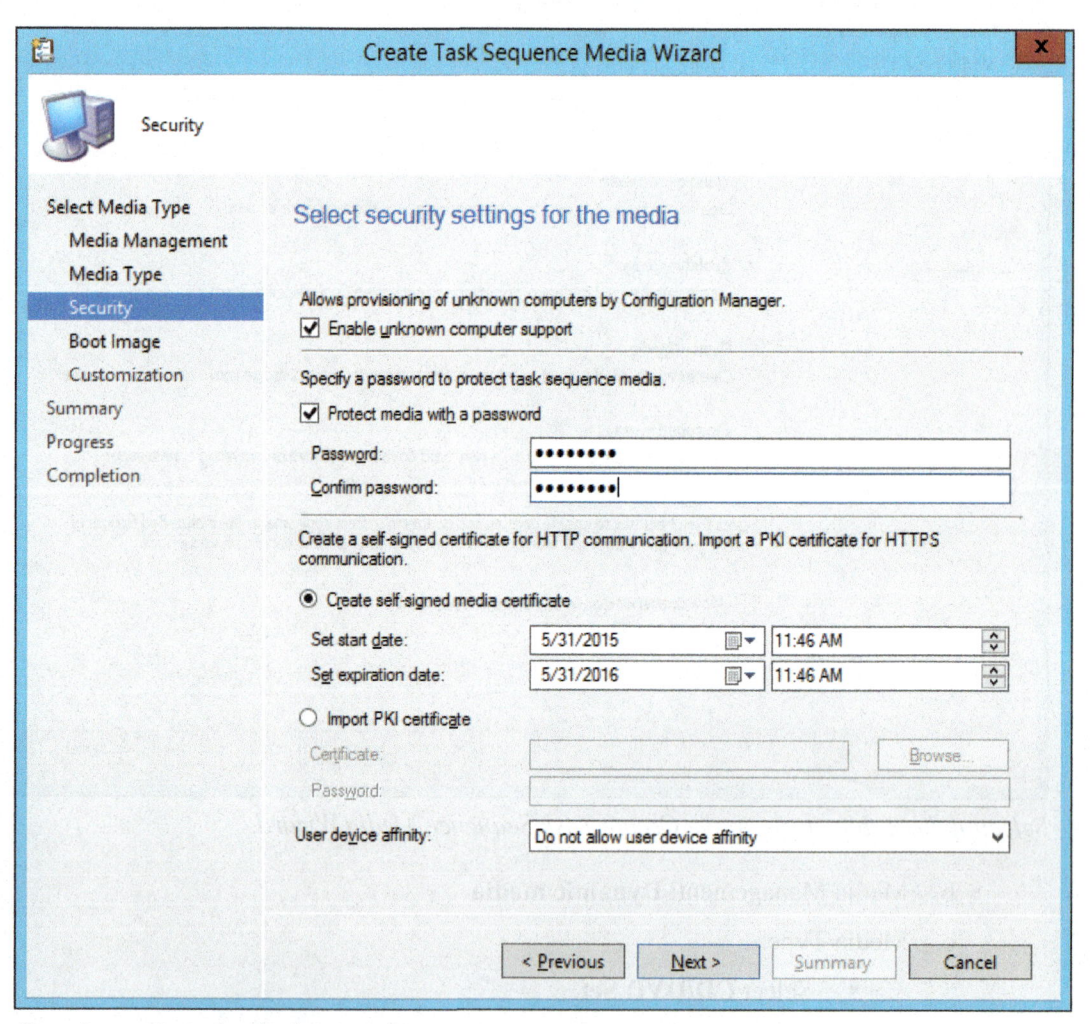

*Security settings for the boot media.*

e. Boot Image:

- Boot image: **Boot Image (x64)**
- Distribution point: **CM01.CORP.VIAMONSTRA.COM**
- Associated management points: **CM01.corp.viamonstra.com**

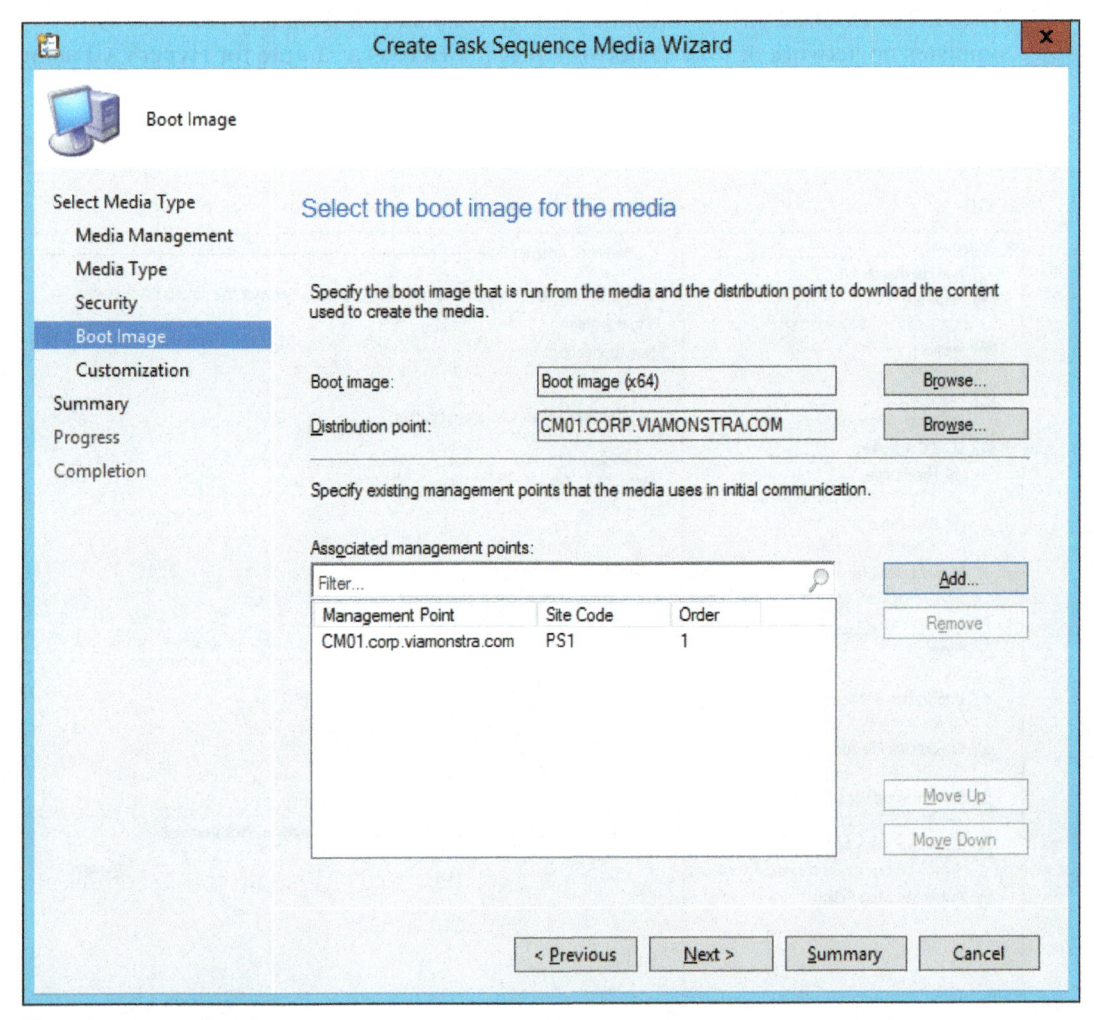

*Boot image settings.*

f. Customization:

- Variables: **<default>**
- Enable prestart command: **<default>**

3. On **CM01**, using **File Explorer**, copy the **CheckForNetwork.iso** file from **E:\Setup** to **C:\ISO** on the Hyper-V host (you may need to create this folder).

Chapter 11   Checking for Network and Storage Problems in WinPE

> **Note:** If using VMware, copy or upload the CheckForNetwork.iso to a location where you can mount it on your virtual machines.

4. Edit the **PC0012** virtual machine, and configure it to boot from the **CheckForNetwork.iso** file.

5. Also, in the **PC0012** virtual machine setting, disconnect it from any network. This simulates no network or lack of network drivers. Here is a sample for HyperV (if using VMware there are similar settings).

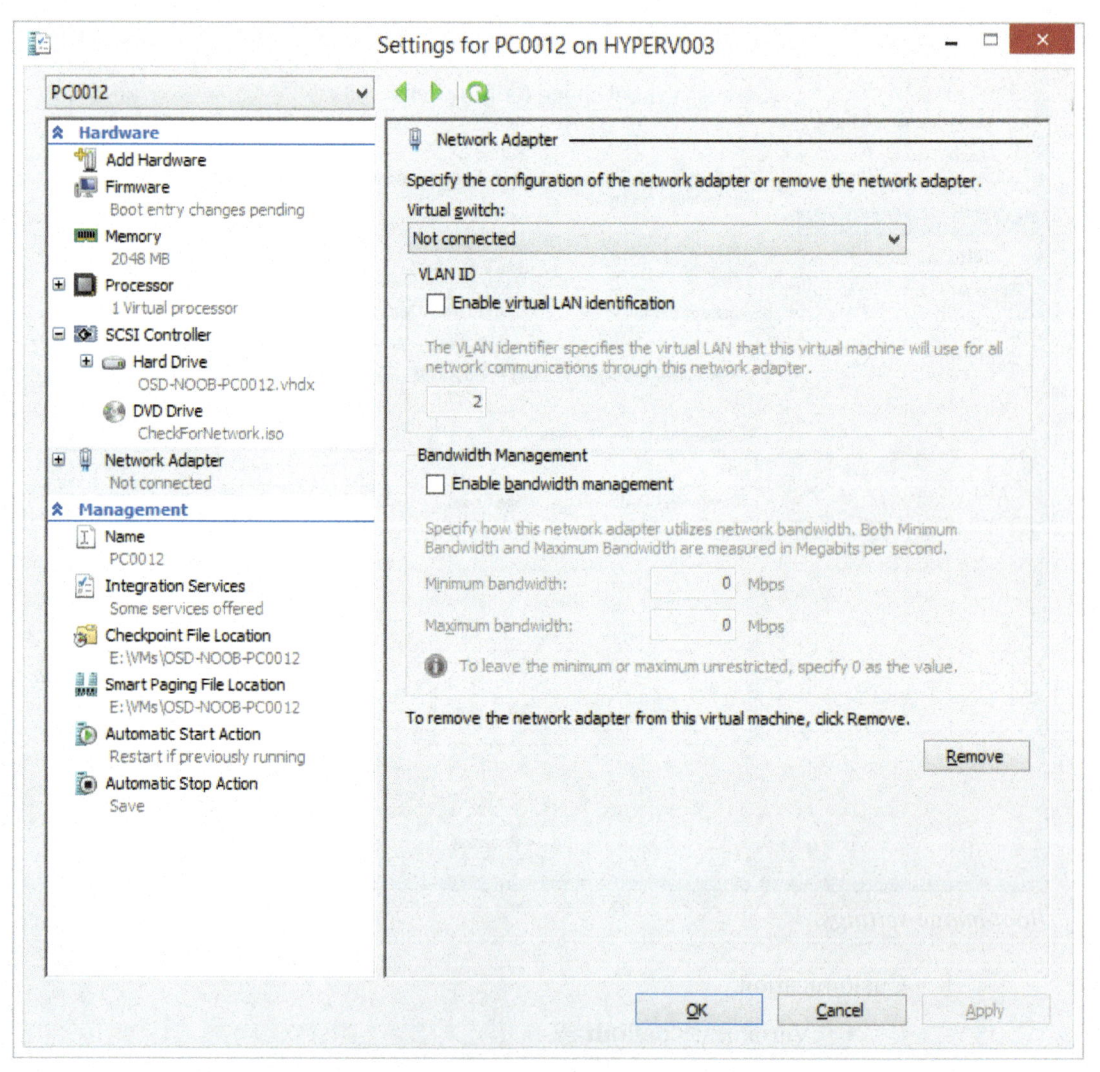

*Disconnecting the network adapter from the network.*

6. Power on the **PC0012** virtual machine and press a key to boot from the ISO file when you see this message: "Press any key to boot from CD or DVD…."

Chapter 11   Checking for Network and Storage Problems in WinPE

The virtual machine boots from the media, and as expected, the network checks fail. The failure triggers the warning "Cannot connect the network message," which has three choices for the user:

- o **Yes**: Press this to retry (if a network cable is missing, for example).
- o **No**: To exit and reboot.
- o **Cancel**: To troubleshoot further with a command prompt.

In addition to the choices, it lists possible reasons for the failure and gives details about the hardware that was detected, such as the make and model, and perhaps most importantly, it lists the PNP Device ID of any network cards identified by the script.

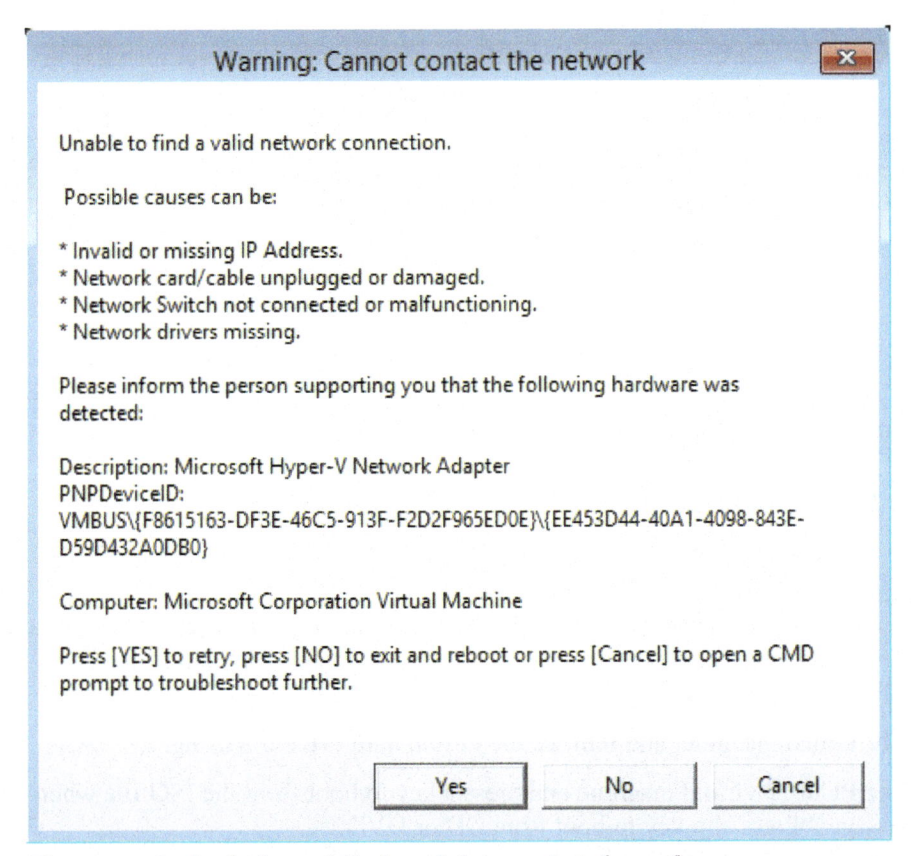

```
Warning: Cannot contact the network

Unable to find a valid network connection.

 Possible causes can be:

* Invalid or missing IP Address.
* Network card/cable unplugged or damaged.
* Network Switch not connected or malfunctioning.
* Network drivers missing.

Please inform the person supporting you that the following hardware was
detected:

Description: Microsoft Hyper-V Network Adapter
PNPDeviceID:
VMBUS\{F8615163-DF3E-46C5-913F-F2D2F965ED0E}\{EE453D44-40A1-4098-843E-
D59D432A0DB0}

Computer: Microsoft Corporation Virtual Machine

Press [YES] to retry, press [NO] to exit and reboot or press [Cancel] to open a CMD
prompt to troubleshoot further.

            [ Yes ]    [ No ]    [ Cancel ]
```

*The network checks have failed, and the user is informed.*

7. To review the **CheckForNetwork.log** after a network failure is detected, click **Cancel**. At the command prompt, open the **CheckForNetwork.log** with **CMTrace** by using the following command where **<arch>** matches the architecture of the boot WIM:

```
X:\SMS\BIN\<arch>\cmtrace.exe
X:\Windows\Temp\SMSTSLOG\CheckForNetwork.log
```

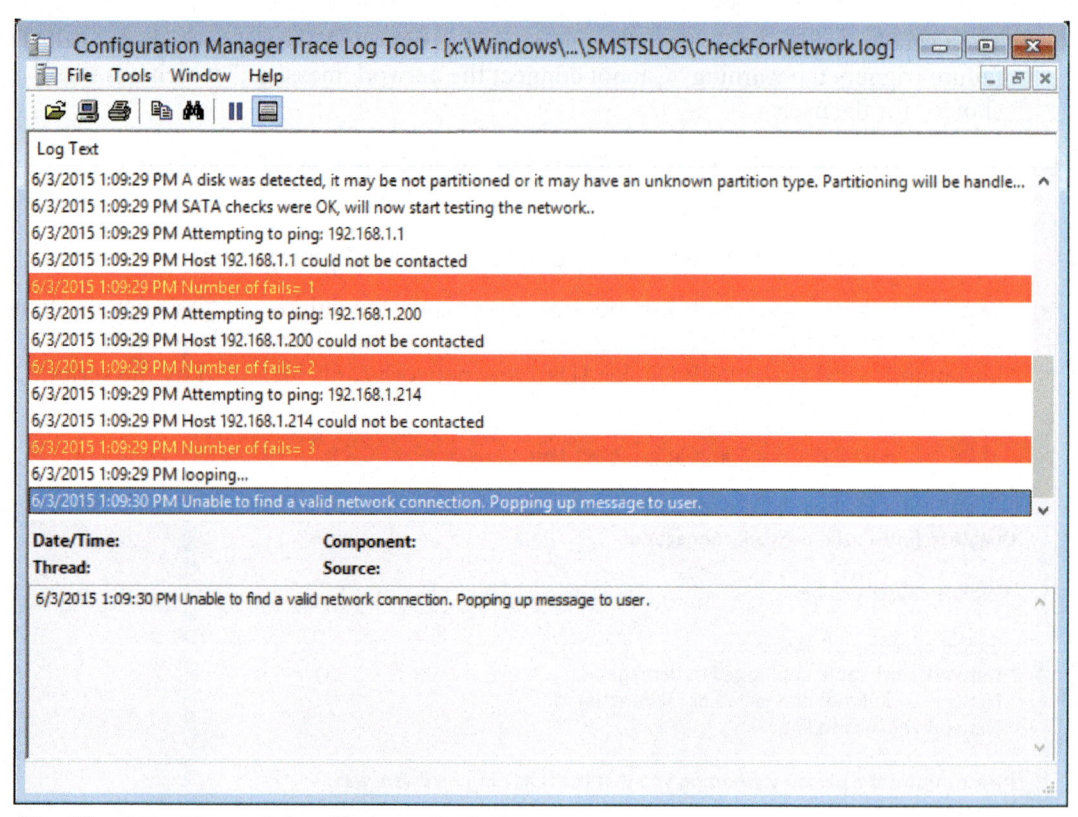

*The CheckForNetwork.log file logs the failure.*

8. Turn of the **PC0012** virtual machine.

## Verify Storage Checks

To verify what happens when the script cannot detect adequate storage, once again you simulate this by using the virtual machine created previously. To perform the steps necessary for this simulation, do as follows:

1. Edit **PC0012** virtual machine, and remove the virtual hard drive it's using.

2. Power on the **PC0012** virtual machine and press a key to boot from the ISO file when you see this message: "Press any key to boot from CD or DVD…."

After booting up, the Warning: Unable to continue message appears informing the user that no valid storage device was found. In addition, the PNP Device ID of the detected storage controllers are listed, as well as the make and model of the device that was booted.

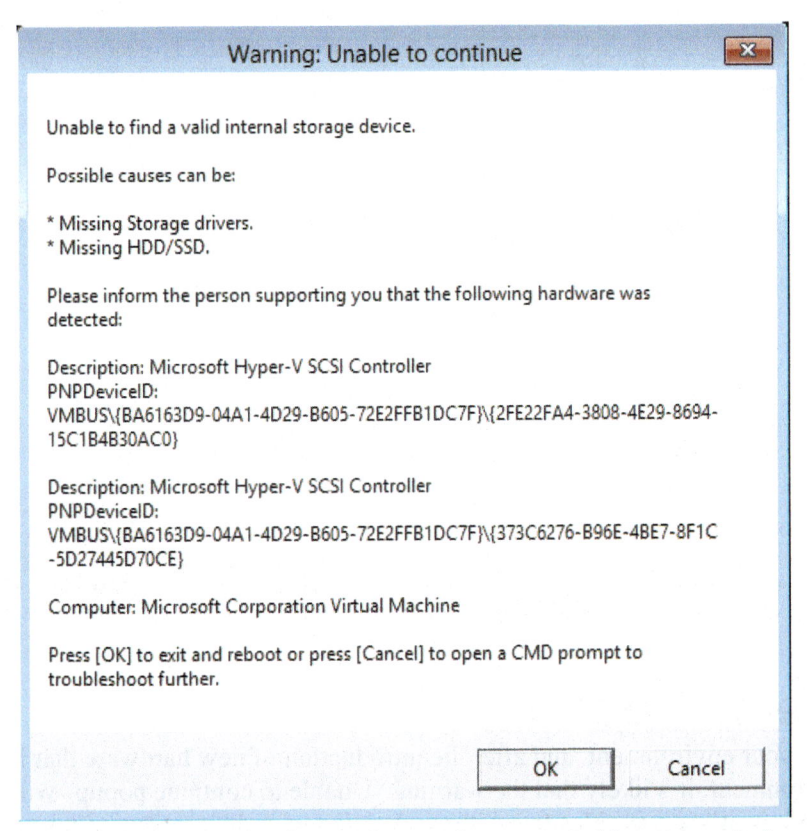

## Chapter 11  Checking for Network and Storage Problems in WinPE

**Warning: Unable to continue**

Unable to find a valid internal storage device.

Possible causes can be:

* Missing Storage drivers.
* Missing HDD/SSD.

Please inform the person supporting you that the following hardware was detected:

Description: Microsoft Hyper-V SCSI Controller
PNPDeviceID:
VMBUS\{BA6163D9-04A1-4D29-B605-72E2FFB1DC7F}\{2FE22FA4-3808-4E29-8694-15C1B4B30AC0}

Description: Microsoft Hyper-V SCSI Controller
PNPDeviceID:
VMBUS\{BA6163D9-04A1-4D29-B605-72E2FFB1DC7F}\{373C6276-B96E-4BE7-8F1C-5D27445D70CE}

Computer: Microsoft Corporation Virtual Machine

Press [OK] to exit and reboot or press [Cancel] to open a CMD prompt to troubleshoot further.

[OK]  [Cancel]

*The warning message that is shown when no suitable storage is found.*

The user has the choice of clicking OK to exit and reboot, or clicking Cancel to open a command prompt for further troubleshooting. After the command prompt opens, another message appears. You can click OK to close it when troubleshooting is complete.

277

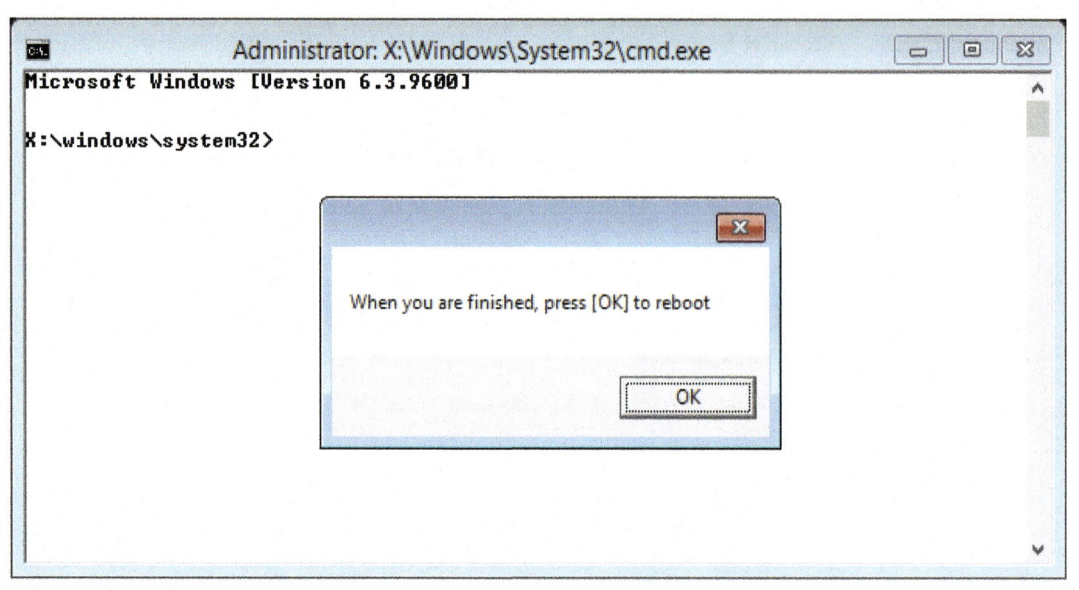

*After troubleshooting is complete, press OK to reboot the computer.*

## Fixing Problems Found

After implementing this in your environment, and after the introduction of new hardware that isn't yet supported in your environment, it's likely that the warning "Unable to continue popup" will be seen sooner or later. When it is, it's a good idea to ask the technician with the problem to take a photo or screenshot of the popup to assist you with getting the right drivers for your boot WIM.

> **Real World Note**: Using MailLog or AssistMe would be great in this type of scenario, except that both of those tools depend on a working Ethernet connection, and that may be exactly what is missing when things go wrong. For that reason, this version of the tool does not attempt to provide support via either of those options.

The important thing is that you get the PNP Device ID of the network or storage hardware and the make and model of the hardware on which the problem occurred. When you have this information, you can attempt to fix the problem.

The PNP Device ID is broken up into a few components listed here:

> Vendor > Device > Subsystem

The vendor is the hardware vendor of the device in question (e.g. Intel) and not necessarily the hardware vendor of the computer (e.g. Dell). The device itself is the network or storage card, and the subsystem is a version of that card.

## Microsoft Update Catalog

In the event of missing network or storage drivers, the popup message should reveal the PNP Device ID of the identified hardware. This information should be enough to help you locate the missing drivers on Microsoft's Update Catalog website (which contains Microsoft WHQL supported drivers).

To search for drivers on the Microsoft Update Catalog website using the PNP Device ID listed in the popup, do as follows:

1. Using **Internet Explorer**, browse to the following URL: **http://catalog.update.microsoft.com/v7/site/Home.aspx**.

2. In the **Search** box provided, enter the PNP Device ID using the following format: PCI\VEN_<XXXX>&DEV_<YYYY>, where <XXXX> is a four-character vendor ID and <YYYY> is a four-character device ID. For example: **PCI\VEN_8086&DEV_1507**.

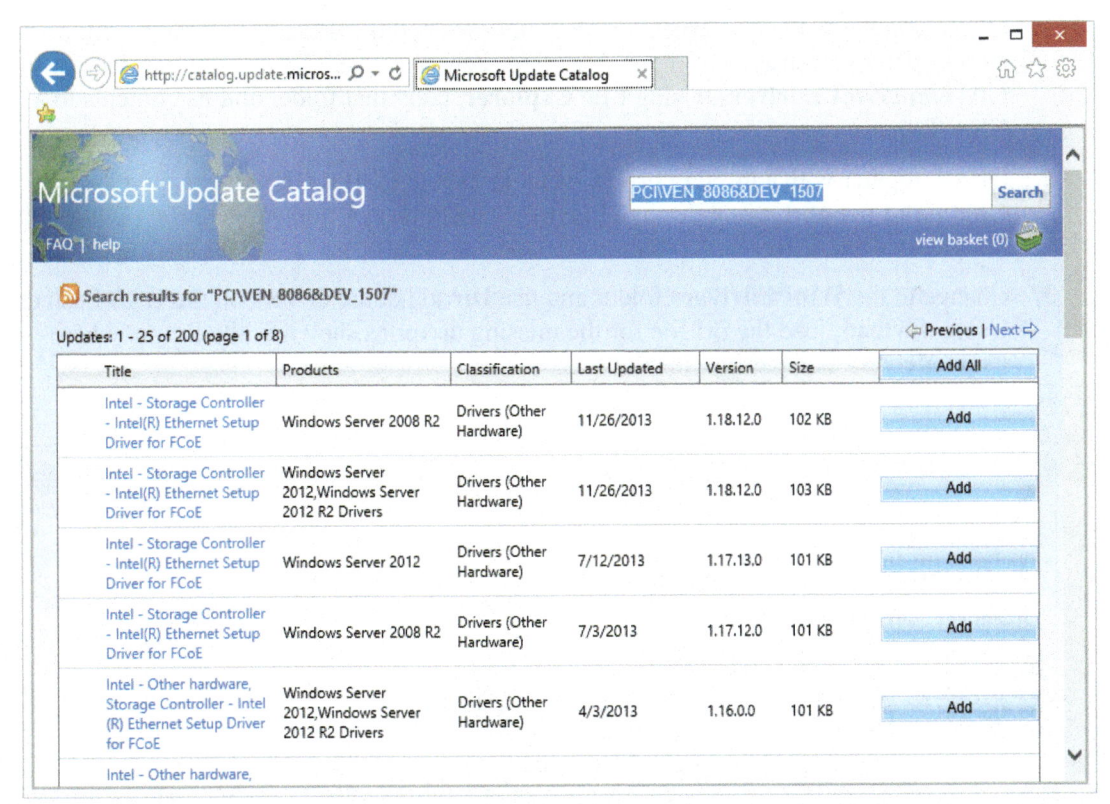

*Searching for supported drivers on Microsoft's Update Catalog website.*

Assuming the search results provided some hits, you can further refine the drivers listed based on what product (operating system) they support. In fact, you should try to find drivers for Windows 8.1 to properly support WinPE 5 as used in ConfigMgr. You also can sort based on when the drivers were last updated or by the version of the driver. Clicking Add in the right pane adds the driver to your basket, and you can choose to download any selected drivers for testing.

## Obtain Drivers from the Hardware Vendor

In the event that you cannot locate drivers on Microsoft's Update Catalog website, the next logical place to search is the hardware vendor itself. By hardware vendor, I mean the vendor of the failing item, whether that is a network card or storage card and not necessarily the vendor of the device (laptop, tablet, or desktop).

For example, if it is an Intel network card that was identified (e.g. VEN_8086), then you can search http://support.intel.com for drivers for the network card in question. However, instead searching for the PNP Device ID, use the description of the card as was detailed in the popup.

## Use drvload to Inject Drivers

After you've downloaded the driver required, you can use a failed Windows PE session to test the drivers. To do this, perform the following:

1. On a computer with an Internet connection, download the drivers for the network or storage device as described in the preceding sections and extract them to a folder such as **C:\Temp\WinPEdrivers**. Using **File Explorer**, copy that folder and its contents to a USB flash drive.

2. On a computer with a missing driver issue, insert the **USB flash drive**. Using the **Command prompt**, cycle through the drive letters from **C:** onwards until you locate the USB flash drive letter.

3. Change to the **WinPEdrivers** folder and use **Dir** to list the drivers on the USB flash drive. Using **drvload**, load the **inf** file for the missing driver as shown in the figure, where **<somedriver>** is the driver inf file:

   ```
   Drvload <somedriver>.inf
   ```

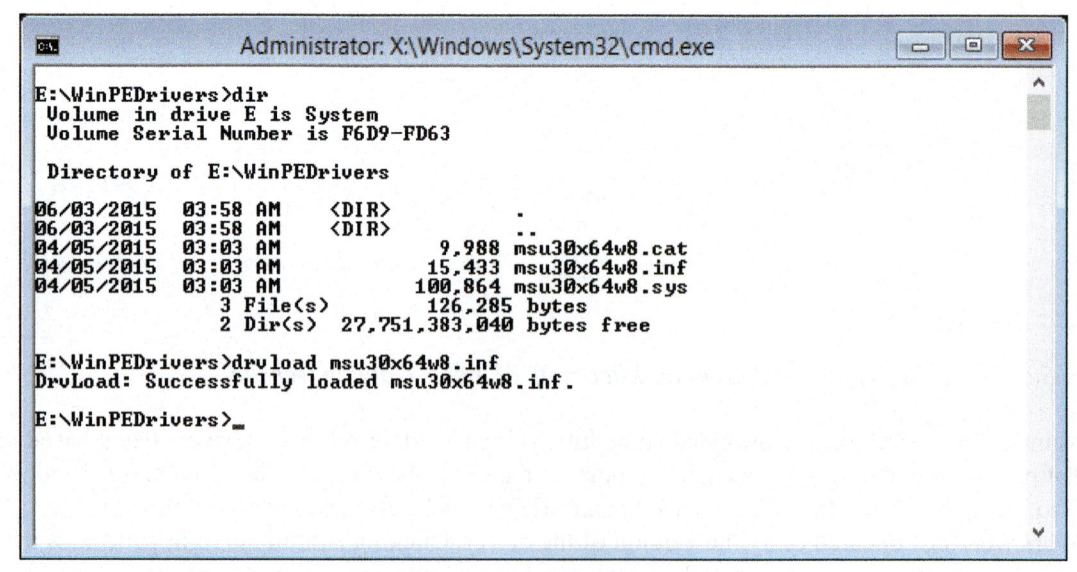

```
E:\WinPEDrivers>dir
 Volume in drive E is System
 Volume Serial Number is F6D9-FD63

 Directory of E:\WinPEDrivers

06/03/2015  03:58 AM    <DIR>          .
06/03/2015  03:58 AM    <DIR>          ..
04/05/2015  03:03 AM             9,988 msu30x64w8.cat
04/05/2015  03:03 AM            15,433 msu30x64w8.inf
04/05/2015  03:03 AM           100,864 msu30x64w8.sys
               3 File(s)        126,285 bytes
               2 Dir(s)  27,751,383,040 bytes free

E:\WinPEDrivers>drvload msu30x64w8.inf
DrvLoad: Successfully loaded msu30x64w8.inf.

E:\WinPEDrivers>_
```

*Loading a missing driver in WinPE using drvload.*

After loading the selected driver, verify whether it worked based on the functionality of the driver. For example, if it was a network driver, run wpeinit to start the network, do ipconfig and see if you get a valid IP address. If it was a storage driver, verify if you can browse (or see) the hard disk drive after loading the driver.

## Add Drivers to the Boot Image

After you have identified the missing driver, the next step is to add that driver to the boot image. This process is described in Chapter 6.

# Chapter 12
# Patching an Image Using Offline Servicing

Keeping images up to date when it comes to security is a difficult task in any enterprise. Some organizations patch the images quarterly, others monthly, and some patch the image during the imaging process itself, or just after the user's first logon.

Leaving the patching to just after logon means an unwelcome surprise for the end user. For example, imagine a scenario in which a user gets their new Windows 8.1 computer, log on, and before long are told 151 updates are to be installed. You can just imagine the inconvenience that brings to the user's day.

This is where offline servicing comes into play. You can use this feature in ConfigMgr to offline service (patch) the image with available updates on a schedule as you see fit (once a month, for example), leaving your end users with a much better experience. You can even patch the image on a schedule, or do it manually. The choice is yours.

As the patching takes place offline, there is little or no "hit" on the image. You also can use offline servicing to patch your WIM file before going through the build-and-capture process to avoid issues with software updates breaking the task sequence. Offline servicing uses DISM to inject the patches, and it works with CBS (Component-Based Servicing). CBS allows components and features from different elements of Windows, such as Windows Media Player, to be packaged as small modules. By using CBS, it's possible to patch many different parts of the operating system.

## Step-by-Step Guide Requirements
If you want to follow the step-by-step guides in this chapter, you need a lab environment configured as outlined in Chapter 2 and Appendix A. In this chapter, you use the following virtual machines:

DC01　　　CM01　　　PC0013

*The VMs used in this chapter (PC0013 is a VM created in one of the guides).*

# Preparing for Offline Servicing

Before you can begin any patching, you need to be sure that you follow a plan. To ensure a smooth process, follow the steps in this section.

## Review the Current Update Status

You should review the current update status of the image you intend to work on. This gives you a visual clue as to the patched state of the image. Images that have not yet been through this process appear unpatched even if they've had patches injected during the reference image creation process; however, any of those updates detected as installed in the image are flagged as installed after the offline servicing process is complete.

> **Note**: The update status of a WIM file that has not had any offline servicing actions performed on it shows no items. On WIM files that have had offline servicing performed, the update status shows the date of the servicing only for updates that have been injected into the WIM image via the offline servicing option, whereas any updates detected as installed by another method (for example, during reference image creation) during the offline servicing process are listed but without a date.

To review the update status, do as follows:

1. On **CM01**, using the **ConfigMgr console**, in the **Software Library** workspace, select **Operating Systems / Operating System Images** and then click the previously captured WIM file called **Windows 8.1 Enterprise - 150301**.

2. At the bottom of the console, there are four tabs. Click **Update Status**. It lists nothing in the image currently as no updates have been applied via offline servicing.

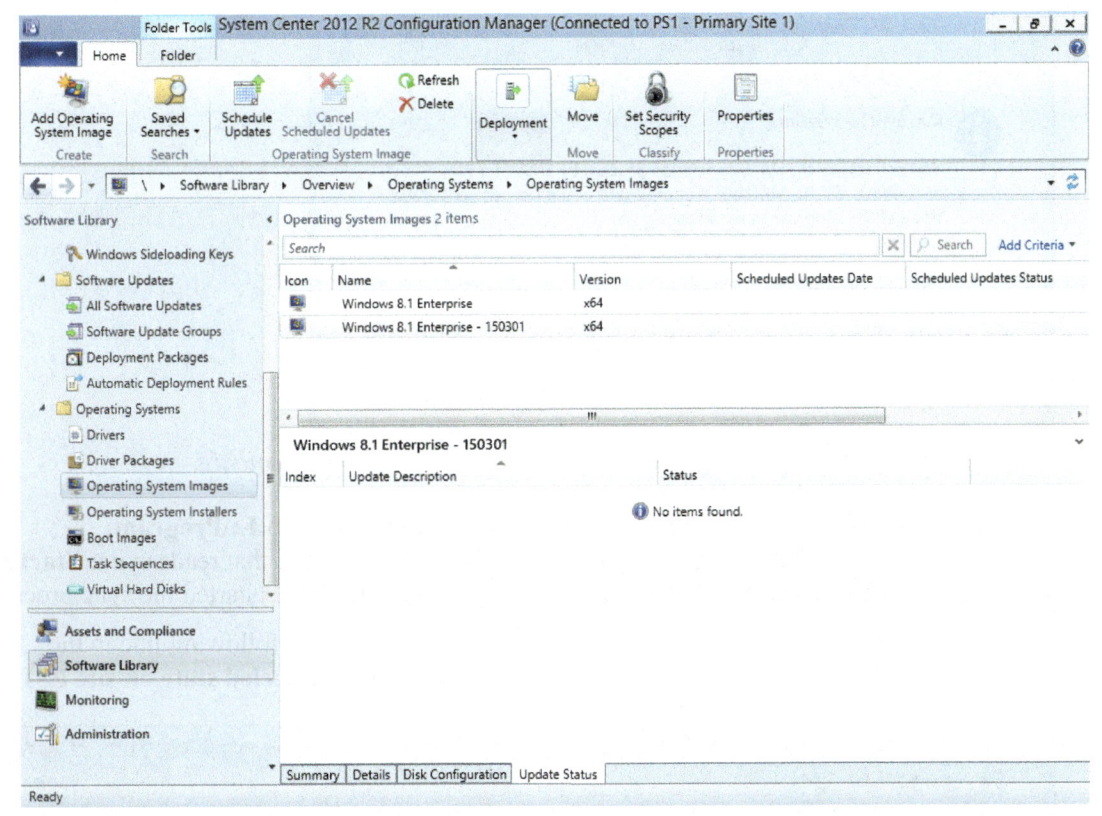

Chapter 12   Patching an Image Using Offline Servicing

*The Update Status tab of the selected image before offline servicing has been initiated.*

## Perform a Sync

Before starting the offline servicing activity, it's a good idea to make sure that the updates used are current and relevant. Doing that involves synchronizing the software update point with Microsoft Windows Update.

> **Note**: There are two types of sync, Full or Delta. A Full sync is performed on schedule as defined in the Software Update Point Sync Schedule, whereas a Delta sync occurs when you manually initiate a sync in the console via Synchronize Software Updates. If a sync fails for any reason, it is retried every 60 minutes. A Delta sync is forced to a Full sync if any change has been made to the categories (for example, adding an additional product, or adding or removing a classification).

To perform a sync, follow the process described here:

1. On **CM01**, using the **ConfigMgr console**, in the **Software Library** workspace, select **Software Updates / All Software Updates** and then click **Synchronize Software Updates** on the ribbon.

2. A popup appears asking whether you are sure that you want to initiate a site-wide synchronization of software updates. Answer **Yes**.

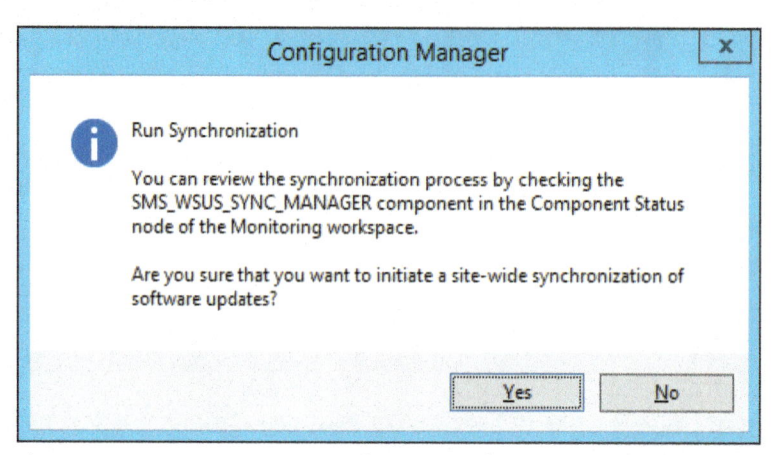

Chapter 12   Patching an Image Using Offline Servicing

*Are you sure you want to synchronize software updates? Of course you are.*

3. Using **CMTrace**, open a log file called **wsyncmgr.log** located in **E:\Program Files\Microsoft Configuration Manager\Logs**. Look for a line that reads **sync: Starting WSUS synchronization**. This should correspond to the time you started the sync process.

4. When the sync is complete, you can verify it by looking for the following line in the **wsyncmgr.log** file: **Sync succeeded. Setting sync alert to canceled state on site PS1**.

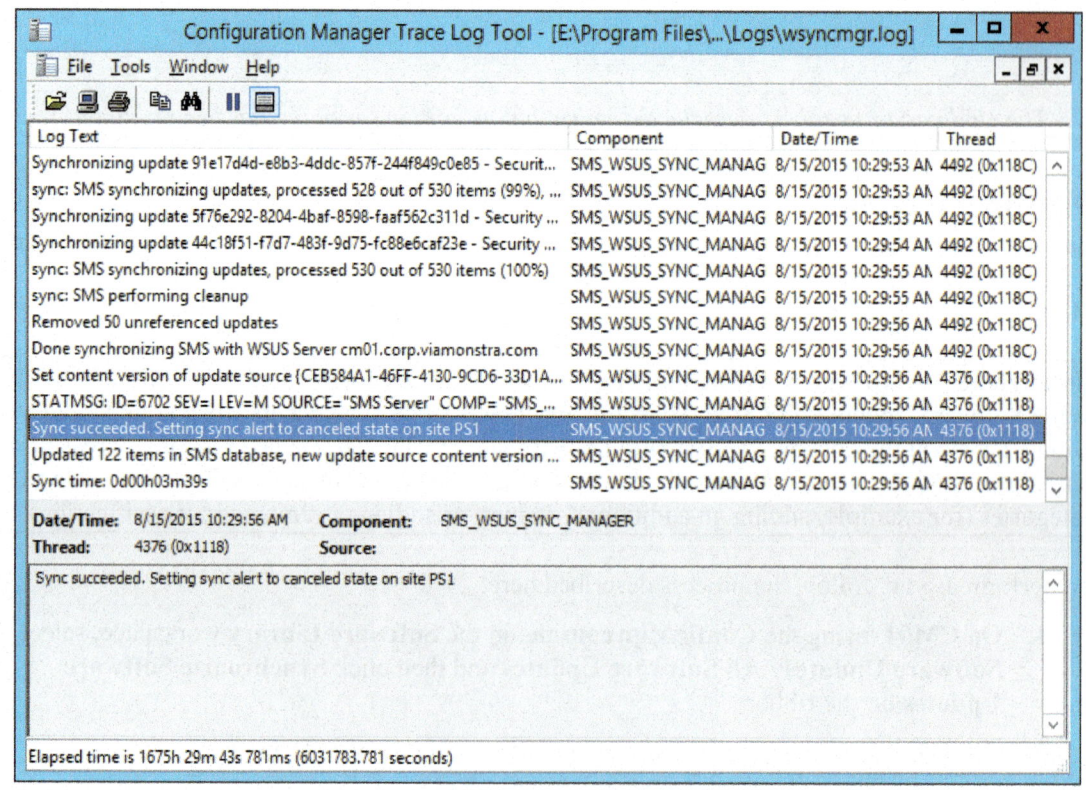

*Verifying sync status using CMTrace and the wsyncmgr.log file.*

286

## Select and Download Updates

After performing a successful sync, it's time to sort your Windows updates. To sort them, use the following steps.

1. On **CM01**, using the **ConfigMgr console**, in the **Software Library** workspace, select **Software Updates / All Software Updates** to see the list of available updates in the right pane.

2. Click **Add Criteria** (top right) and select the following search criteria:
   - Expired: **<no>**
   - Superseded: **<no>**
   - Product: **<Windows 8.1>**

3. Click **Search** to produce a list of suitable updates. Select the first update listed, scroll to the bottom of the list, and while holding down the **Shift** key, select the last update listed (you can also press Ctrl +A to select all updates).

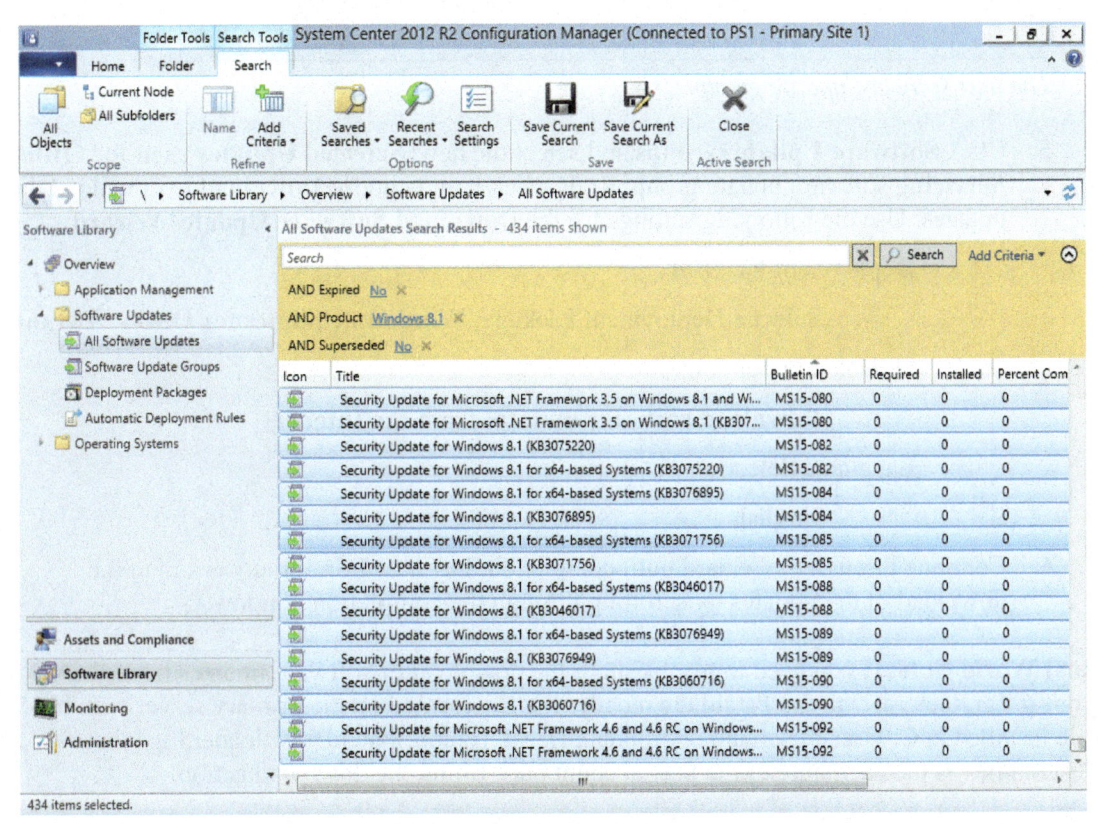

*Selecting Windows 8.1 software updates for use with offline servicing.*

Chapter 12  Patching an Image Using Offline Servicing

4. Right-click the selected updates and choose **Create Software Update Group**. Use the following settings for the **Create Software Update Group** window and then click **Create**:

    o Name: **Updates used for Offline Servicing**

    o Description:

    > OS: Windows 8.1
    >
    > Created: <todays date in YYMMDD format>

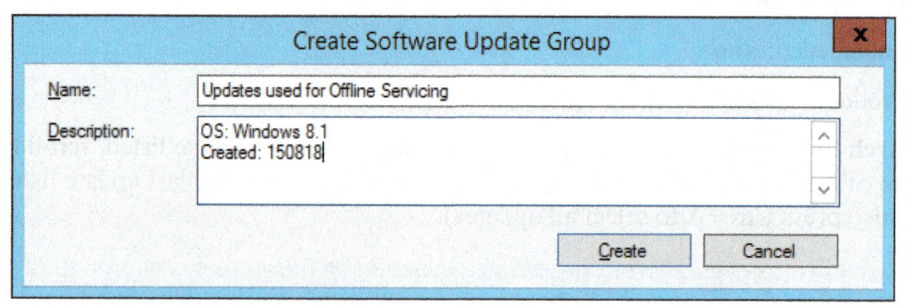

*The new software update group.*

5. Click **Software Update Groups** and select the newly created **Updates used for Offline Servicing** software update group. Right-click it and choose **Download** to download the updates. Use the following settings for the **Download Software Updates Wizard**:

    a. Deployment Package

    > Select a Deployment Package: **Windows Updates for OSD - W81x64**

    b. Download Location

    > **Download software updates from the Internet**

    c. Language Selection

    > **English**

6. Continue through the wizard until completion. Pay attention for any errors in the download of the updates by scrolling through the completion window.

**Real World Note**: If you need to troubleshoot the download of software updates from WSUS into ConfigMgr, then refer to the PatchDownloader.log file located on the primary server with the SUP role installed in C:\User\<username>\Appdata\Local\Temp\2\PatchDownloader.log where <username> is the username of the user account performing the download action.

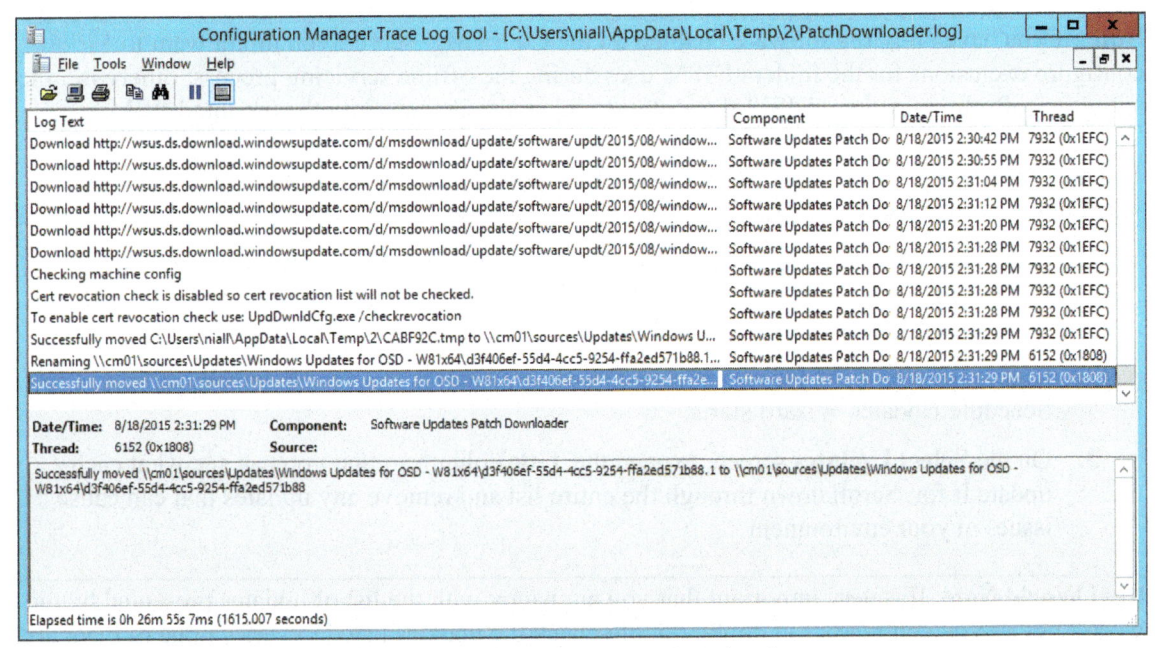

Chapter 12  Patching an Image Using Offline Servicing

*The PatchDownloader.log is useful for troubleshooting download issues.*

# Servicing an Image

When you have completed the preparations for offline servicing and confirmed that suitable updates are downloaded, you can commence the offline servicing process. To do offline servicing on a previously captured WIM image, follow the processes in this section.

## Patch the Captured WIM

Injecting updates into the WIM images offline is disk intensive so you should not perform this operation except when the server is "at rest," for example on a weekend. You should allow for plenty of free space on the drive where ConfigMgr is installed as the WIM image is duplicated (a backup copy created) during this process. The backup copy renamed with a .bak extension.

> **Real World Note**: If you need to change the drive letter used by offline servicing, then refer to this TechNet blog post:
> http://blogs.technet.com/b/configmgrteam/archive/2013/07/15/customizing-offline-servicing-of-operating-system-images.aspx.

When using offline servicing, you can run the process "as soon as possible" or on a defined schedule. Running it on a schedule can be useful if you cannot be present at the time the server is in a state suitable for carrying out the patching process.

Chapter 12   Patching an Image Using Offline Servicing

> **Note**: If you have antivirus software enabled on the ConfigMgr server, you might want to configure exclusions for the folders DISM uses during the offline servicing process; otherwise, the antivirus software may deny DISM the ability to inject the changes into the mounted WIM.

To patch the previously captured Windows 8.1 Enterprise - 150301 image without defining a schedule, use the following steps:

1. On **CM01**, using the **ConfigMgr console**, in the **Software Library** workspace, select **Operating Systems / Operating System Images** and then select the previously captured **Windows 8.1 Enterprise - 150301** image.

2. Right-click the WIM file and choose **Schedule Updates** from the available choices. The Schedule Updates Wizard starts.

3. On the **Select Updates** screen, expand the **Title** column so that you can see what each update if for. Scroll down through the entire list and remove any updates that can cause issues in your environment

> **Real World Note**: It is very important that you are happy with the list of updates presented by the wizard before you continue. If in doubt, double-check the updates listed to verify none of them are known to cause issues with any software in your environment. In the event that you patch the image and one or more updates causes an issue, you can revert to the backup copy of the WIM and start the process again without the suspect patches. It is not currently possible within the wizard to remove updates from an already serviced WIM. To remove updates from an already serviced WIM, you have to mount the image using DISM and uninstall the affected update before committing the changes.

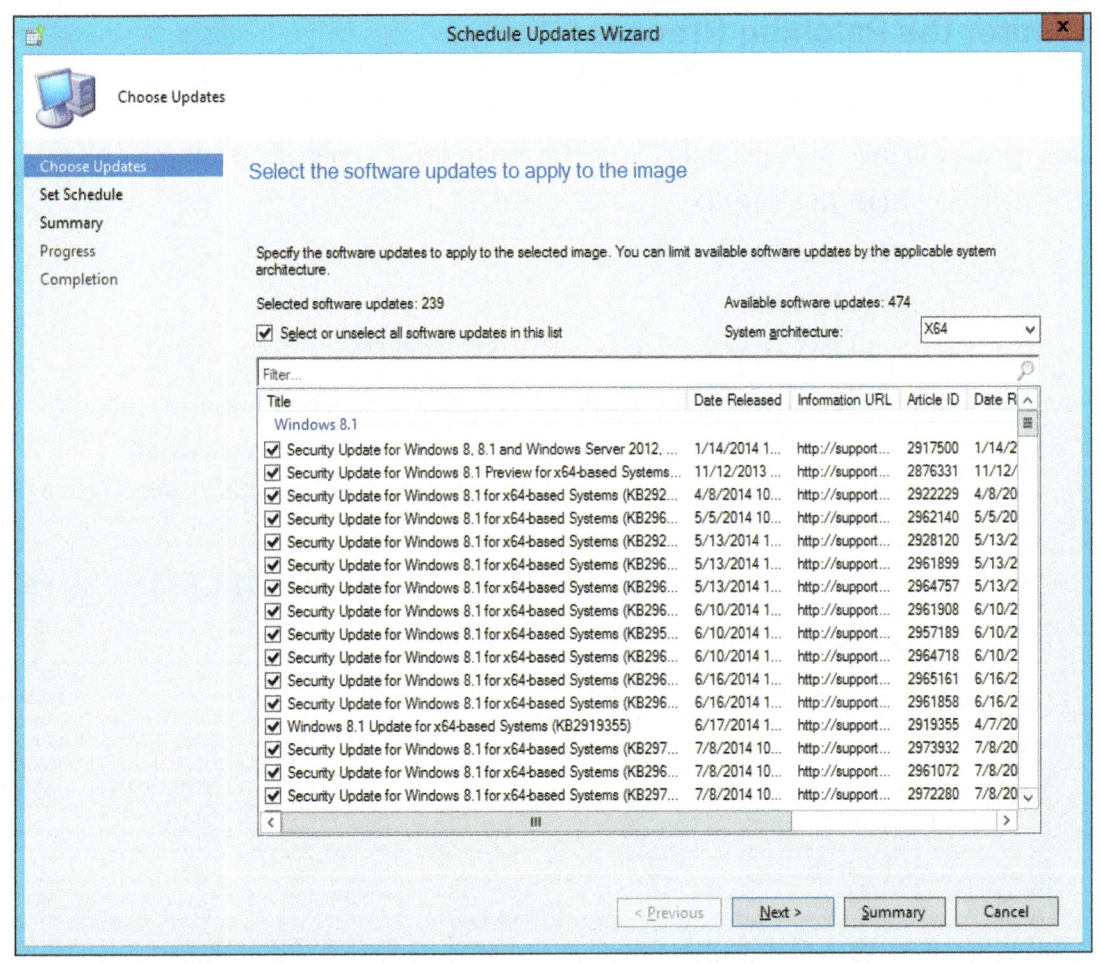

Chapter 12   Patching an Image Using Offline Servicing

*Selecting suitable updates from those made available to offline servicing.*

4. On the **Set Schedule** screen, choose **As soon as possible**. In addition, confirm that **Continue on error** and **Update distribution points with image** are selected.

5. Continue through the rest of the wizard until completion. Click **Close** when done.

> **Note**: When you select the option to continue on error if any errors occur during the application of one or more patches, the process still continues to attempt to install the remaining patches. In production, avoid selecting to update distribution points with the patched image after offline servicing as you are putting yourself at risk of pushing out an image that has not been tested yet. In a lab, it's okay to do this as you can test the patched WIM at your leisure, but in production, clear the Update distribution points with image check box and manually distribute that image to a distribution point for testing even if it means adding a new operating system image. The original WIM file is in the same data source location but with a .bak file extension. In worst-case scenarios, you can always restore the file by renaming it to .wim.

291

Chapter 12   Patching an Image Using Offline Servicing

## Monitor the Patching Process

The OfflineServicingMgr.log file logs each attempt to install the selected updates, and after some time, it checks all available updates to see whether they are applicable to the image.

Each update will have an Applicability State that can be listed as any of the following:

- NOT_REQUIRED
- INSTALLED
- APPLICABLE
- APPLICABILITY_CHECK_NOT_SUPPORTED

To monitor the patching process by reviewing the OffLineServicingMgr.log, do as follows:

1. On **CM01**, using the **File Explorer**, browse to **E:\Program Files\Microsoft Configuration Manager\Logs** and double-click **OfflineServicingMgr.log**. The log file opens in **CMTrace**.

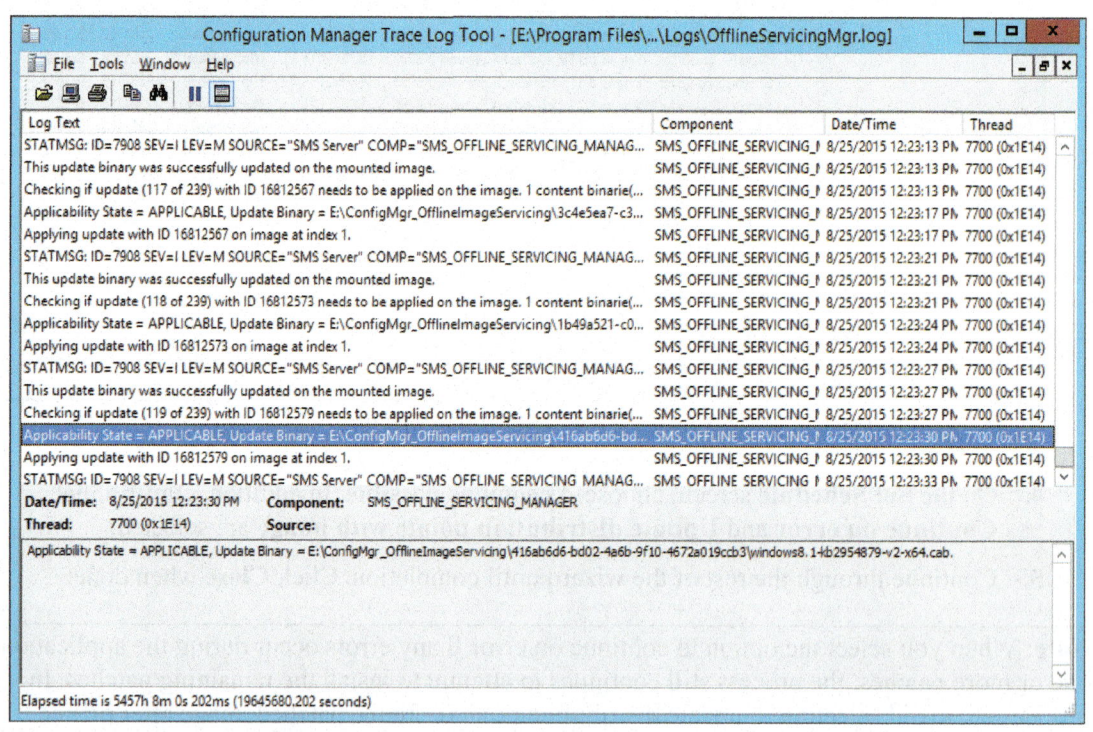

*The OfflineServicingMgr.log reveals how the patching process is going.*

2. To find out how many updates are applied, look for a line that reads **Total number of updates that have been successfully applied on the mounted image is <number>** where **<number>** is the number of updates applied.

Chapter 12  Patching an Image Using Offline Servicing

3. When done with the servicing, the log file exposes the copying of the current WIM to a backup file. Look for **Create backup copy for image <ImageID>** where **<ImageID>** is the image ID of the WIM file.

4. In addition, it logs the distribution of the WIM file. Look for a line that reads **Successfully requested image <ImageID> to be updated from its source** where **<ImageID>** is the image ID of the WIM file.

5. To verify that the process is complete, look for the following line: **Schedule processing succeeded**.

## Troubleshooting

In the event of problems with the offline servicing process, pay close attention to the logs DISM creates in %WINDIR%Windows\Logs\DISM on the ConfigMgr server that is doing the offline servicing. For example, the log dism_sccmAMD64.log contains information pertaining to injecting individual updates and can highlight access permission problems or other issues.

If a failure occurs in offline servicing, look at the DISM.log file (and associated DISM logs) first for specific errors. If the DISM.log file doesn't contain any errors, review the Sessions.xml log file second, and then the CBS.log file.

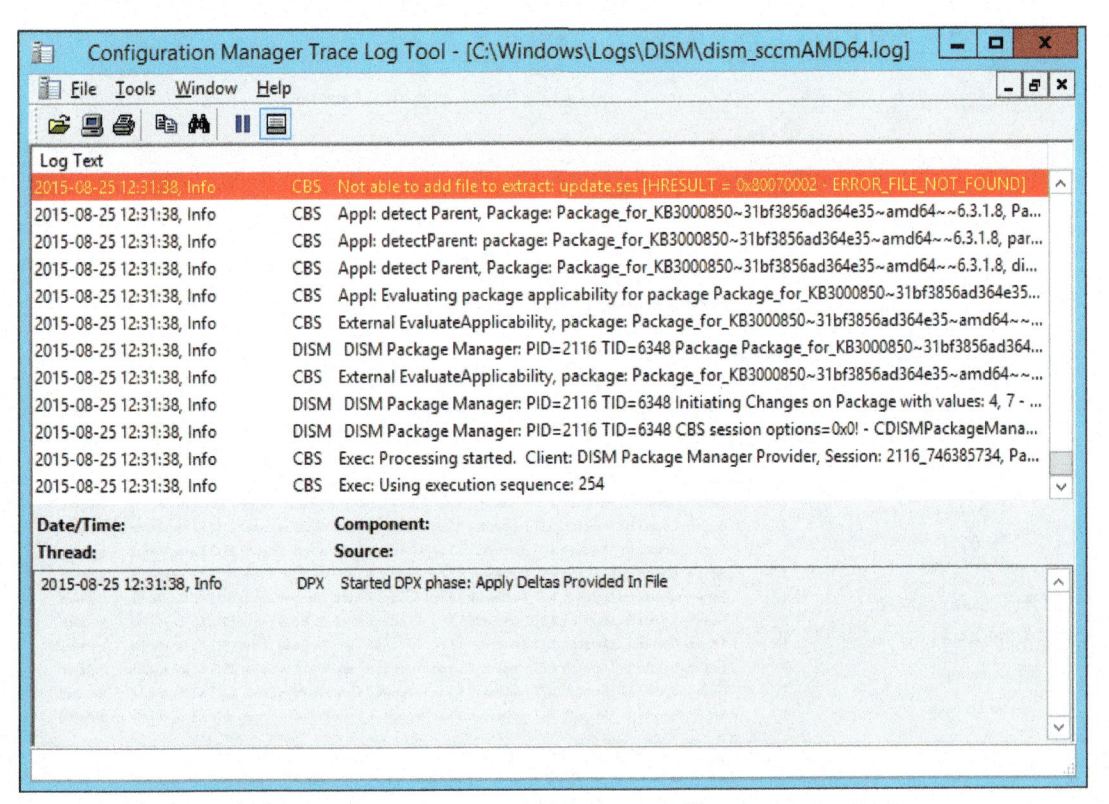

*Another log file worth looking at when troubleshooting offline servicing.*

293

# Verifying the Application of the Updates

To verify that updates are indeed applied, you can review the update status of the WIM file, or simply deploy a new computer and check the updates installed in Control Panel. These processes are described in this section.

## Verify Update Status of the WIM

To check what the update status of the patched WIM is, do as follows:

1. On **CM01**, using the **ConfigMgr console**, in the **Software Library** workspace, select **Operating Systems / Operating System Images** and click the previously captured WIM file called **Windows 8.1 Enterprise - 150301**.

2. At the bottom of the console, there are four tabs. Click **Update Status**. It lists all the updates successfully applied to the image, including those it detected as installed during the offline servicing process.

3. The Scheduled Update Status column should read **Successful** for a successful offline servicing session. You may have to refresh the console view to see this status.

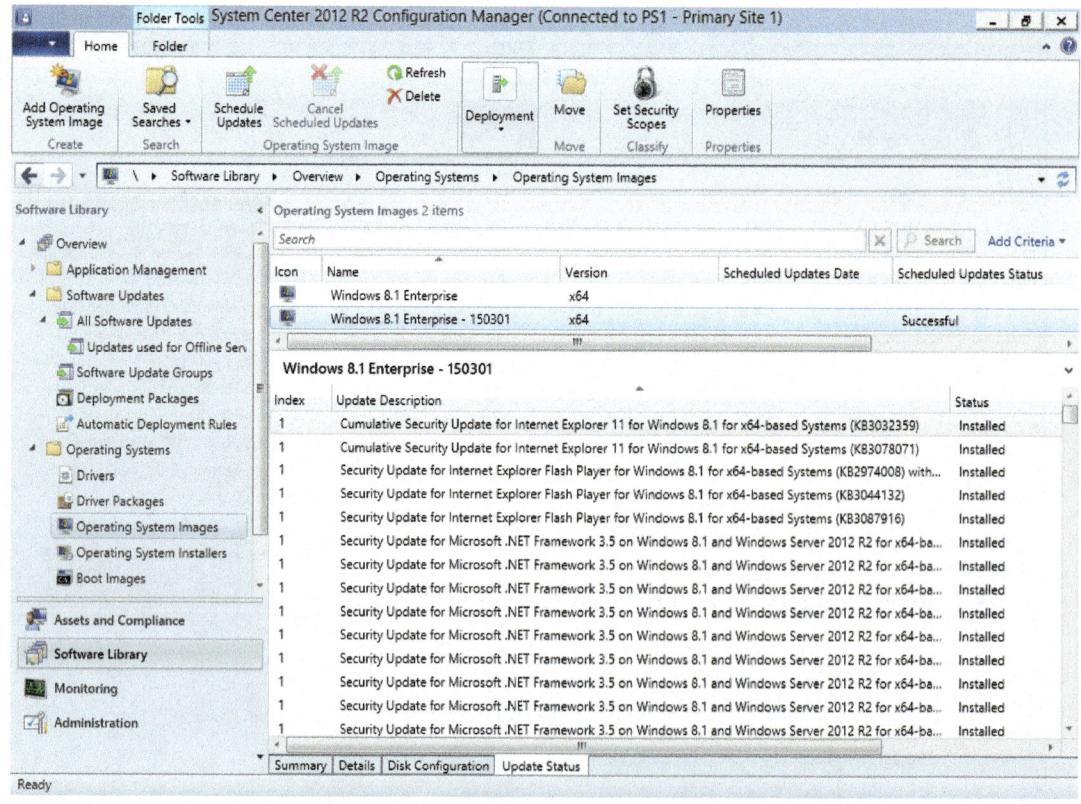

*The long list of updates installed in the WIM image using offline servicing.*

Chapter 12   Patching an Image Using Offline Servicing

## Verify Updates Applied on a Virtual Machine

To verify that the offline servicing process has worked, you need to PXE boot a virtual machine and reimage it with the patched and recently distributed WIM.

> **Note**: The installed date (displayed in Control Panel) of some patches applied via the offline servicing process will vary. Some will match the date of the offline servicing scheduled operation, whereas some will match the date when you PXE-booted the machine to lay down the patched image. This is okay. It just means that some updates needed to finish the installation on first boot.

To verify the patches installed, do as follows:

1. Create a virtual machine named **PC0013**, and verify that the boot order is set to boot to network as explained in Chapter 5 and then power the virtual machine on.
2. Enter the PXE password **P@ssw0rd**, and click **Next**.
3. Select the **Windows 8.1 Enterprise x64 - 150301** task sequence and click **Next**.
4. Let the task sequence continue until completion. When complete, log on as an administrative user and open **Control Panel**. Then select **System and Security**, and under the **Windows Update** heading, click **View Update History**. Finally, click **Installed Updates** to get a list of installed updates.

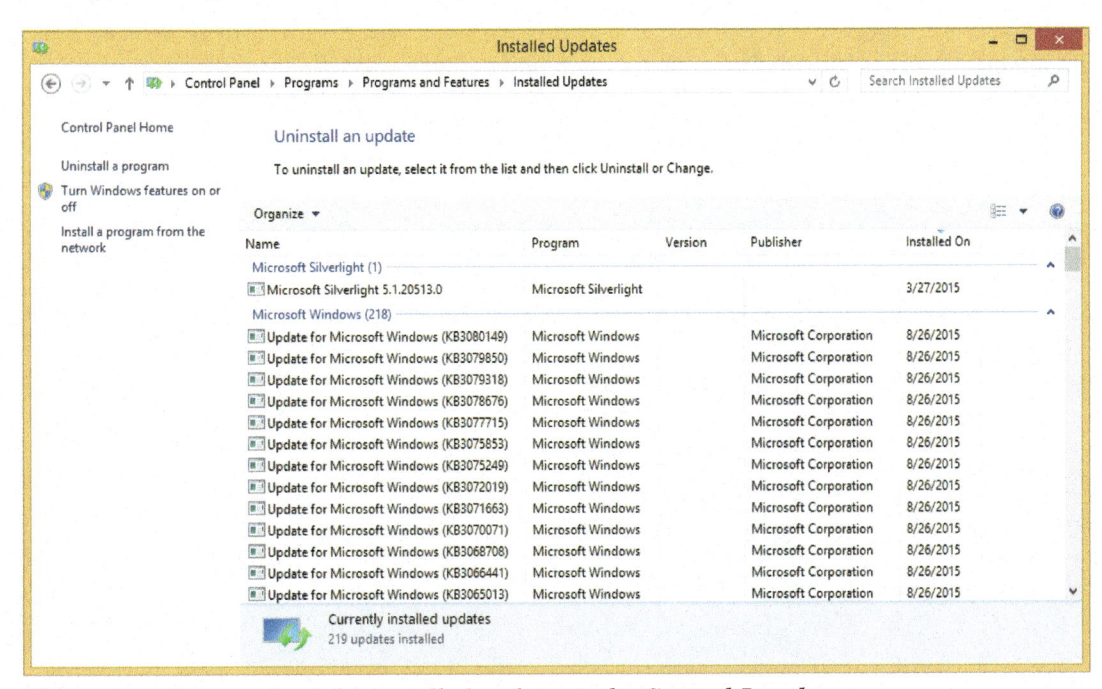

*The easiest place to check for installed updates is the Control Panel.*

295

## Chapter 12  Patching an Image Using Offline Servicing

Double-check the preceding list with the list shown in Update Status in the console. They should match. Any updates that didn't apply may have been incompatible. To get further details about individual update applications, you can refer to the setupact.log file in C:\Windows\Panther.

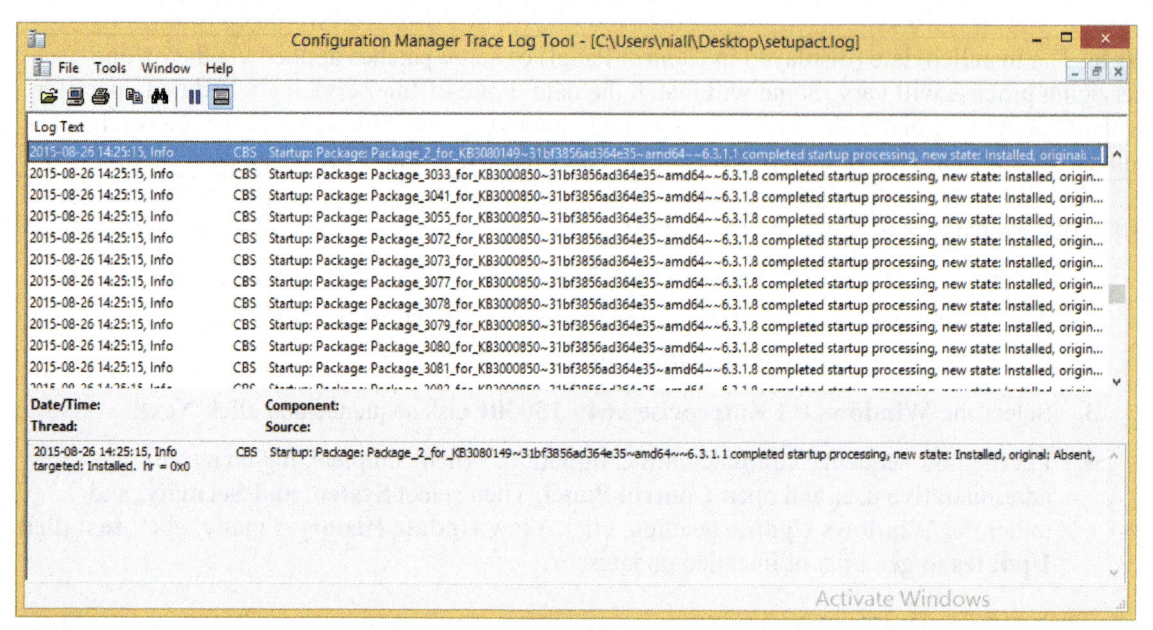

*The setupact.log is useful for finding out why an update didn't install.*

# Chapter 13
# Enforcing BitLocker with MBAM 2.5

Microsoft BitLocker and Monitoring (MBAM) enables administrators to automate the process of encrypting volumes on client computers across the enterprise. In addition, it comes with many features that make managing BitLocker easier, such as providing helpdesk and self-service functionality.

The CM12 UEFI BitLocker HTA (see the detailed setup guide in Chapter 14) also depends on a working MBAM backend infrastructure to allow the task sequence to make a connection to the MBAM server to unlock BitLockered drives while still in Windows PE. This means that you need to implement this in your organization before attempting to use the features that the HTA provides.

## Step-by-Step Guide Requirements
If you want to follow the step-by-step guides in this chapter, you need a lab environment configured as outlined in Chapter 2 and Appendix A. In this chapter, you use the following virtual machines:

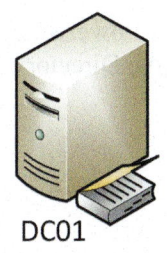

DC01    MBAM01    CM01    PC0001

*The VMs used in this chapter.*

You also need to have downloaded the following software:

    MBAM 2.5 (part of Microsoft Desktop Optimization Pack 2014 R2)

# Preparing for MBAM 2.5

MBAM is a part of the Microsoft Desktop Optimization Pack (MDOP) 2014 R2. MDOP is part of the Microsoft Software Assurance program. For more information about the Microsoft Software Assurance program and how to acquire the MDOP, see
http://go.microsoft.com/fwlink/?LinkId=322049.

> **Note**: To get an overview of the features MBAM provides, please see https://technet.microsoft.com/en-us/library/dn656930.aspx. Implementing MBAM 2.5 in production is no easy task; therefore, be sure to read through all the steps listed in the MBAM 2.5 Planning Checklist as detailed at https://technet.microsoft.com/en-us/library/dn645385.aspx.

To install and configure MBAM for this guide, you need to make configuration changes and apply settings on multiple servers (DC01, MBAM01, and CM01) as illustrated in this chapter.

## Add MBAM Service Accounts

In these steps, you create a few new MBAM service accounts and groups in Active Directory. These users and groups facilitate management of MBAM.

> **Note**: For an overview of planning for the different user and group accounts in MBAM 2.5, please see the following TechNet article: https://technet.microsoft.com/en-us/library/dn645328.aspx.

1. On **DC01**, using the **Windows PowerShell ISE** as Administrator, load the script called **Create MBAM Users Usergroups and OU in AD.ps1**, which is found on the **CM01** server in **C:\Setup\Scripts**.

2. To run the script, press **F5** or click the green **Run Script** button in **Windows PowerShell ISE**. After the script is complete, it will have added users and groups to Active Directory.

Chapter 13   Enforcing BitLocker with MBAM 2.5

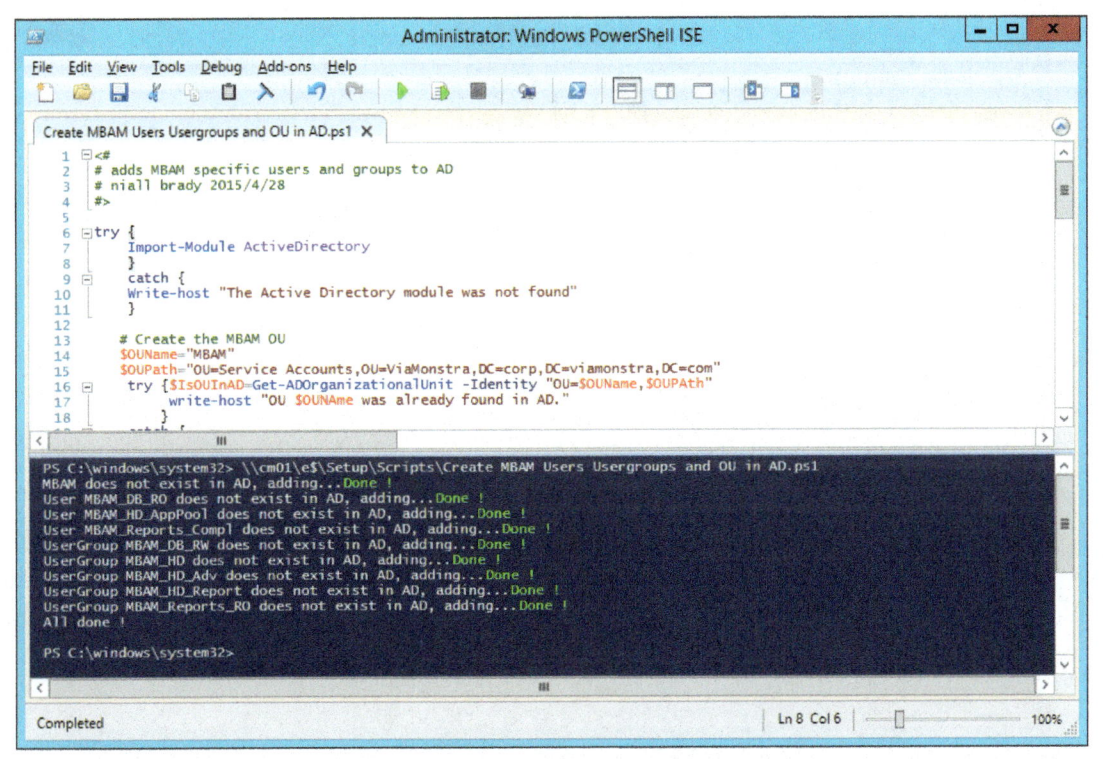

*Creating service accounts in Active Directory for MBAM 2.5 using PowerShell.*

3. On **DC01**, using **Active Directory Users and Computers**, browse to the **ViaMonstra / Service Accounts** OU and select the newly created **MBAM** OU. Observe the created users and groups.

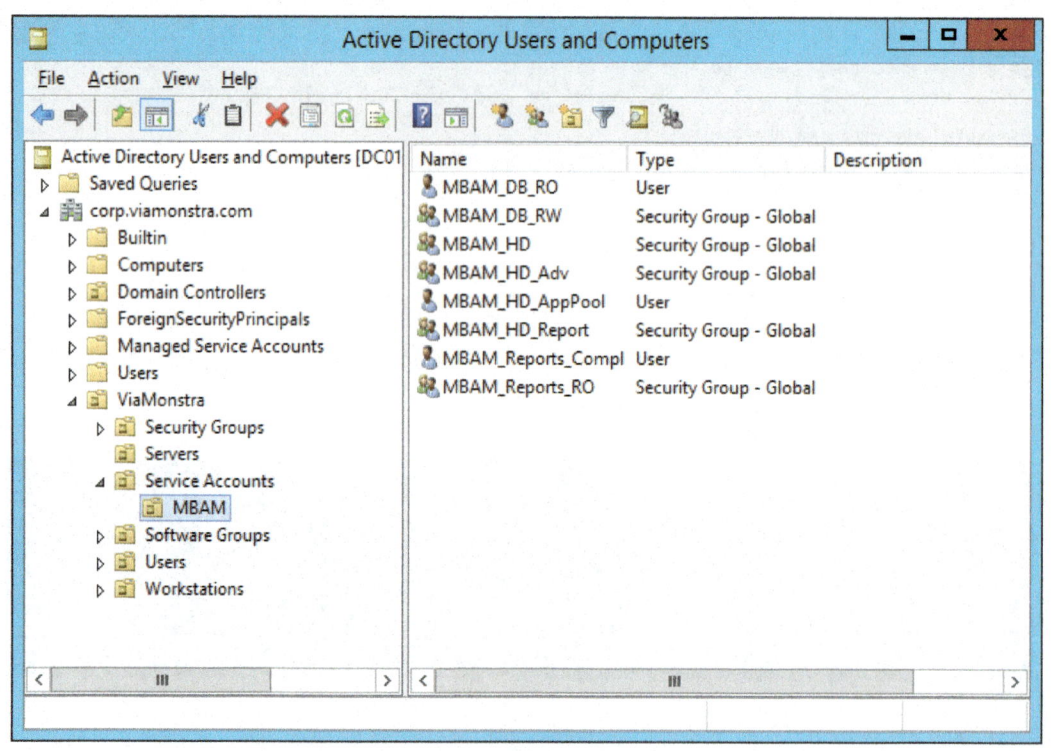

*The newly created MBAM OU with users and groups.*

## Configure MBAM Service Accounts

Next, you add the MBAM_Reports_Compl user to the MBAM_DB_RW security group by doing as follows:

1. On **DC01**, using **Active Directory Users and Computers**, browse to the **ViaMonstra / Service Accounts / MBAM** OU and double-click the **MBAM_DB_RW** security group.

2. Click the **Members** tab and select **Add**. Add the following user: **MBAM_Reports_Compl**.

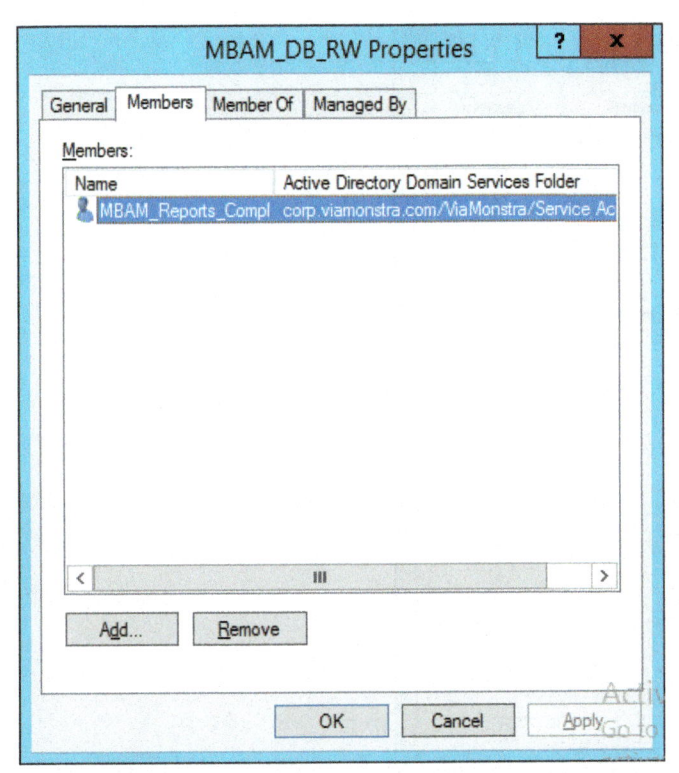

*The MBAM_Reports_Compl user is added to the MBAM_DB_RW group.*

Next, set the password expiration option to never expire by doing as follows for both the MBAM_Reports_Compl user and the MBAM_HD_AppPool user accounts:

1. On **DC01**, using **Active Directory Users and Computers**, browse to the **ViaMonstra\Service Accounts\MBAM OU** and double-click the **MBAM_Reports_Compl** user.
2. Select the **Account** tab and select the **Password never expires** check box. Click **Apply**.

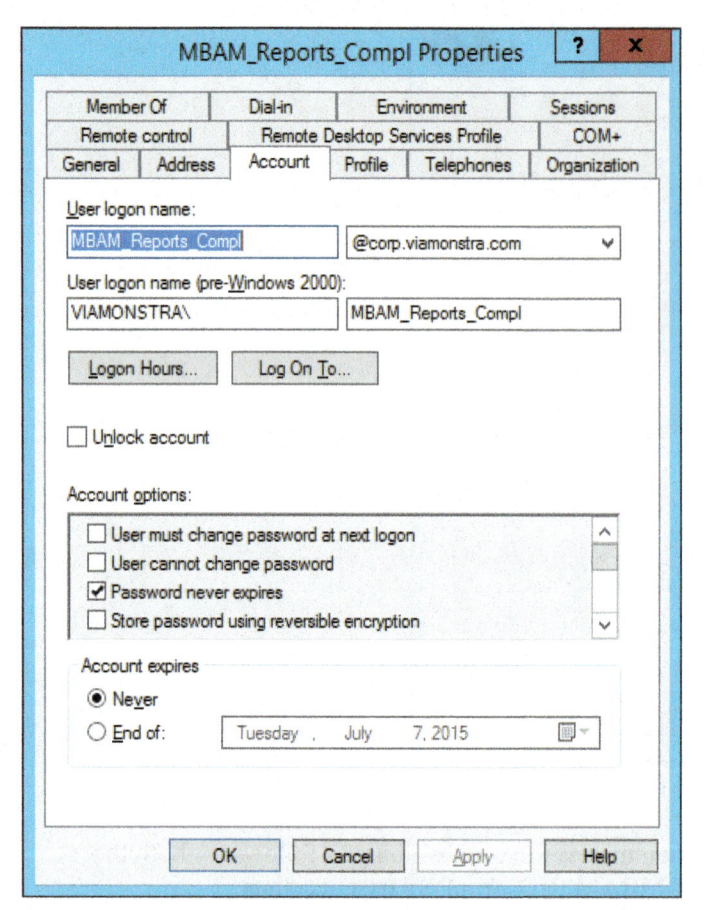

*Setting a password to never expire.*

3. Repeat steps 1 and 2 for the **MBAM_HD_AppPool** user.

## Add Users to the Three MBAM Helpdesk Groups

MBAM comes with three helpdesk groups to categorize permissions available to helpdesk users. One group is for general helpdesk users (MBAM_HD), one is for advanced helpdesk users (MBAM_HD_ADV), and the remaining group (MBAM_HD_Report) is for users who can run reports. Consequently, if you are in all three groups, then you have full helpdesk functionality.

It's up to you to decide who in your organization ends up in those user groups. In this section, you add one user to all three security groups, giving that user full access to all functionality of the helpdesk:

1. On **DC01**, using **Active Directory Users and Computers**, browse to the **ViaMonstra / Service Accounts / MBAM** OU and double-click the **MBAM_HD** security group.

2. Click the **Members** tab and select **Add**. Add the user matching your **<username>**.

Chapter 13 Enforcing BitLocker with MBAM 2.5

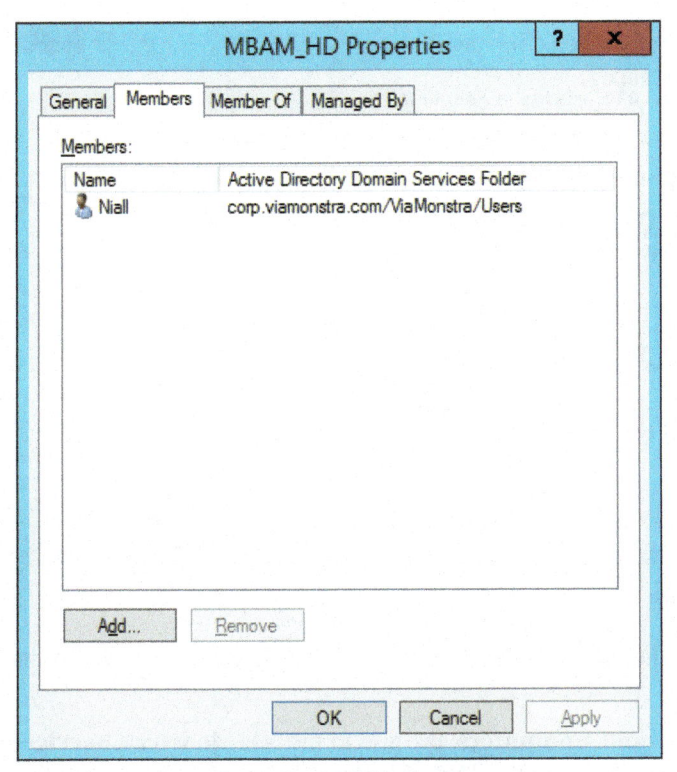

*Adding a user to the MBAM Helpdesk user group.*

3. Repeat the above process for the **MBAM_HD_ADV** and **MBAM_HD_Report** security groups.

## Set the Service Principal Name

Next, you need to set the Service Principal Name (SPN) for the user who will be used by the application pool for the MBAM web application. To do this, follow these steps:

1. On **DC01**, using an elevated **Command prompt** (run as Administrator), issue the following command to set the SPN for the **MBAM_HD_AppPool** user:

   ```
   Setspn -S HTTP/MBAM01.CORP.VIAMONSTRA.COM
   VIAMONSTRA\MBAM_HD_AppPool
   ```

2. To verify that it's set, using an elevated **Command prompt** (run as Administrator), issue the following command:

   ```
   Setspn -L VIAMONSTRA\MBAM_HD_AppPool
   ```

303

### Chapter 13   Enforcing BitLocker with MBAM 2.5

```
Microsoft Windows [Version 6.3.9600]
(c) 2013 Microsoft Corporation. All rights reserved.

C:\windows\system32>Setspn -S HTTP/MBAM01.CORP.VIAMONSTRA.COM VIAMONSTRA\MBAM_HD
_AppPool
Checking domain DC=corp,DC=viamonstra,DC=com

Registering ServicePrincipalNames for CN=MBAM_HD_AppPool,OU=MBAM,OU=Service Acco
unts,OU=ViaMonstra,DC=corp,DC=viamonstra,DC=com
        HTTP/MBAM01.CORP.VIAMONSTRA.COM
Updated object

C:\windows\system32>Setspn -L VIAMONSTRA\MBAM_HD_AppPool
Registered ServicePrincipalNames for CN=MBAM_HD_AppPool,OU=MBAM,OU=Service Accou
nts,OU=ViaMonstra,DC=corp,DC=viamonstra,DC=com:
        HTTP/MBAM01.CORP.VIAMONSTRA.COM

C:\windows\system32>
```

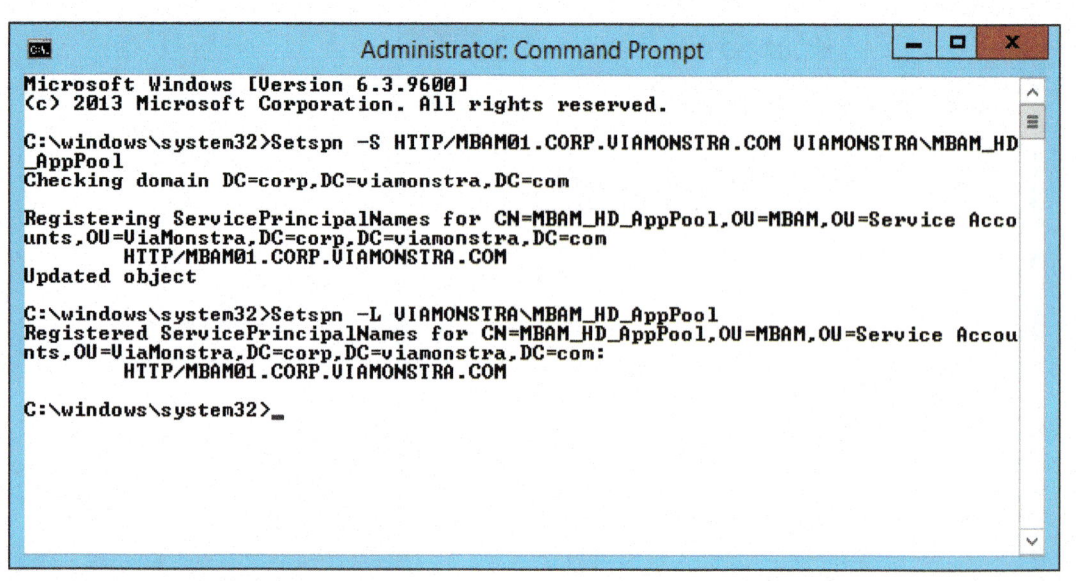

*Setting and then verifying the SPN.*

3. After registering the SPN for the account, an additional tab (**Delegation**) appears in that user's properties.

4. Using **Active Directory Users and Computers**, browse to the **ViaMonstra / Service Accounts / MBAM** OU and double-click the **MBAM_HD_AppPool** user.

5. In the new **Delegation** tab, select the **Trust this user for delegation to any service (Kerberos only)** option and then click **OK**.

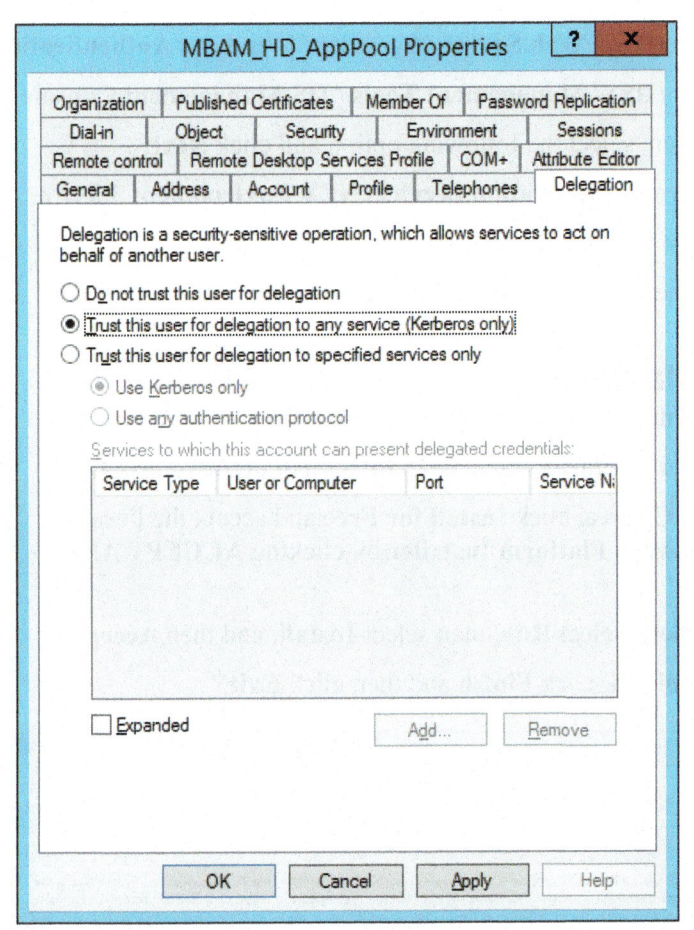

*The Delegation tab with appropriate setting for the selected MBAM user.*

## Add Additional Roles and Features

In these steps, you add features required by MBAM on the MBAM01 server:

1. On **MBAM01**, log in as **VIAMONSTRA\Administrator**, and using **Server Manager**, select **Add Roles and Features**.

2. In the **Add Roles or Features Wizard**, click **Next** and use the following settings:

    a. On the **Installation Type** screen, select **Role-based or feature-based installation** and click **Next**.

    b. On the **Server Selection** screen, click **Select a server from the server pool**, use **MBAM01.corp.viamonstra.com** as the specified server, and click **Next**.

    c. At the **Server Roles** screen, select **Web Server (IIS)**; then select the following options and click **Next**:

        - **Web Server (IIS) / Web Server / Common HTTP Features / Static Content**

- **Web Server (IIS) / Web Server / Security / Windows Authentication**
- **Web Server (IIS) / Management Tools / IIS Management Console**

d. At the **Features** screen, select the following option and click **Next**:

**Windows Process Activation Service\.NET Environment 3.5**

e. On the **Confirmation** screen, click **Install** to install the features.

f. When complete, at the **Results** screen, click **Close**.

## Install the Web Platform Installer

You install ASP .NET MVC 4 from http://asp.net/mvc/mvc4. Follow these steps:

1. On **MBAM01**, using **Internet Explorer**, navigate to **http://asp.net/mvc/mvc4**.

2. In the **Install ASP.NET MVC4** area, click **Install for Free** and accept the license agreement for the **Microsoft Web Platform Installer** by clicking **ACCEPT AND INSTALL**.

3. When the download is complete, select **Run**, then select **Install**, and then **Accept**.

4. When the installation is completed, click **Finish** and then click **Exit**.

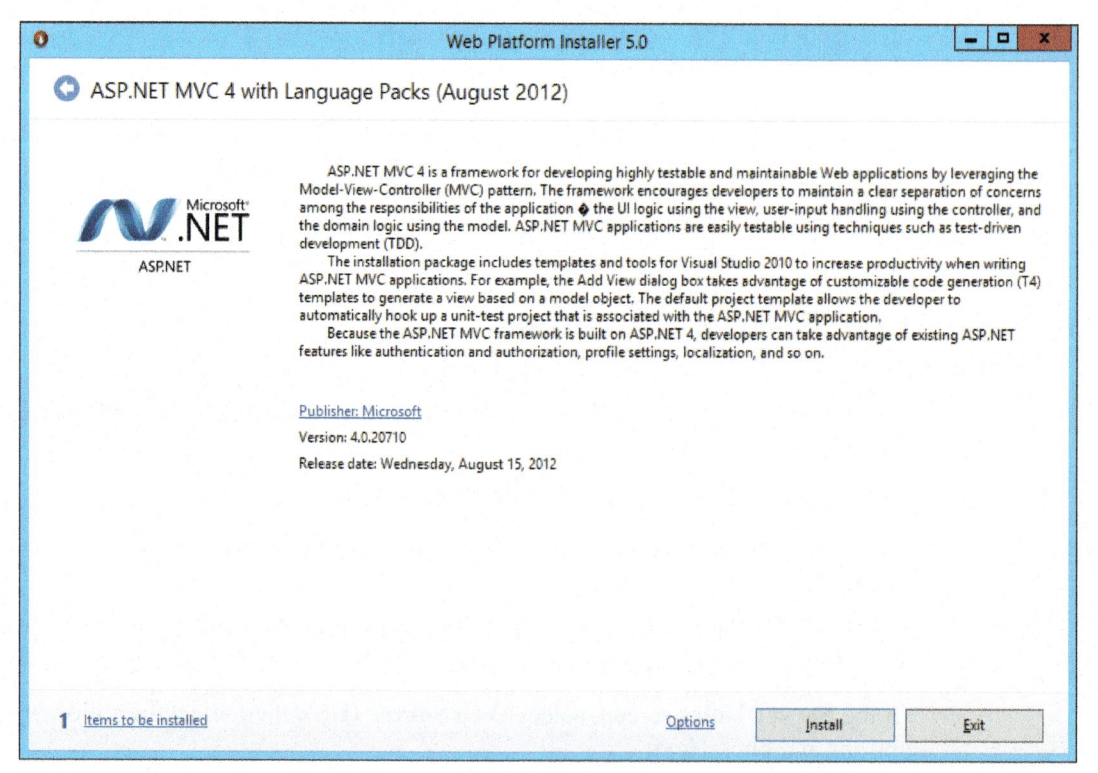

*The Web Platform Installer 5.0.*

# Integrating MBAM with ConfigMgr

Integrating MBAM with ConfigMgr provides reporting ability and target collections for MBAM computers in addition to Compliance Settings for BitLocker. Follow the steps below to integrate MBAM with ConfigMgr.

## Edit the configuration.mof File

To enable client computers to report BitLocker compliance details through MBAM ConfigMgr reports, you need to edit the configuration.mof file. To do this, do as follows:

1. On **CM01**, using an elevated **Command prompt** (run as Administrator), browse to **E:\Program Files\Microsoft Configuration Manager\inboxes\clifiles.src\hinv** and issue the following command to open the **configuration.mof** file using **Notepad**:

   ```
   Notepad configuration.mof
   ```

2. On **CM01**, using another elevated **Command prompt** (run as Administrator), browse to **E:\Setup\MBAM** and, using the following command, open the **mbam_changes_for_configuration.mof** file in **Notepad**:

   ```
   Notepad mbam_changes_for_configuration.mof
   ```

3. Using **Notepad**, select everything in the **mbam_changes_for_configuration.mof** file by pressing **Ctrl + A**. Then copy everything by pressing **Ctrl + C**.

4. Using **Notepad**, scroll to the end of the **configuration.mof** file and press **Ctrl + V** to paste the mbam_changes_for_configuration.mof changes into the configuration.mof file.

5. Save the changes by pressing **Ctrl + S**.

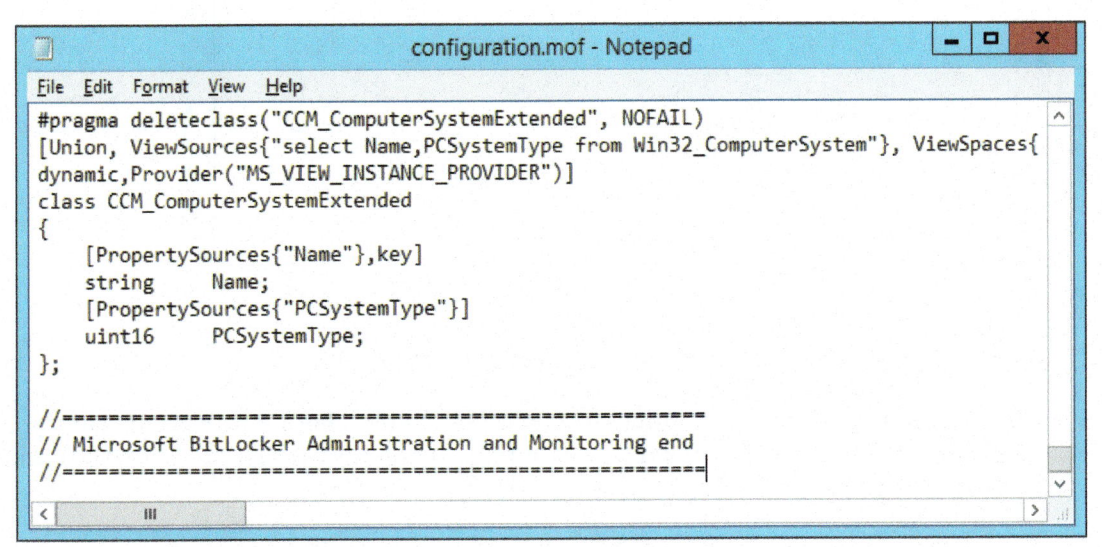

*Applying the contents of mbam_changes_for_configuration.mof to the end of the configuration.mof file.*

## Import sms_def.mof

To support your clients properly, you also need to import the sms_def.mof file into ConfigMgr. To do this, do as follows:

1. On **CM01**, using the **ConfigMgr console**, select the **Administration** workplace, select **Client Settings**, and then right-click **Default Client Settings** and select **Properties**.

2. Select **Hardware Inventory** from the options in the left pane, and then click **Set Classes**. Click the **Import** button, browse to **E:\Setup\MBAM**, select the **sms_def.mof** file, and click **Open**.

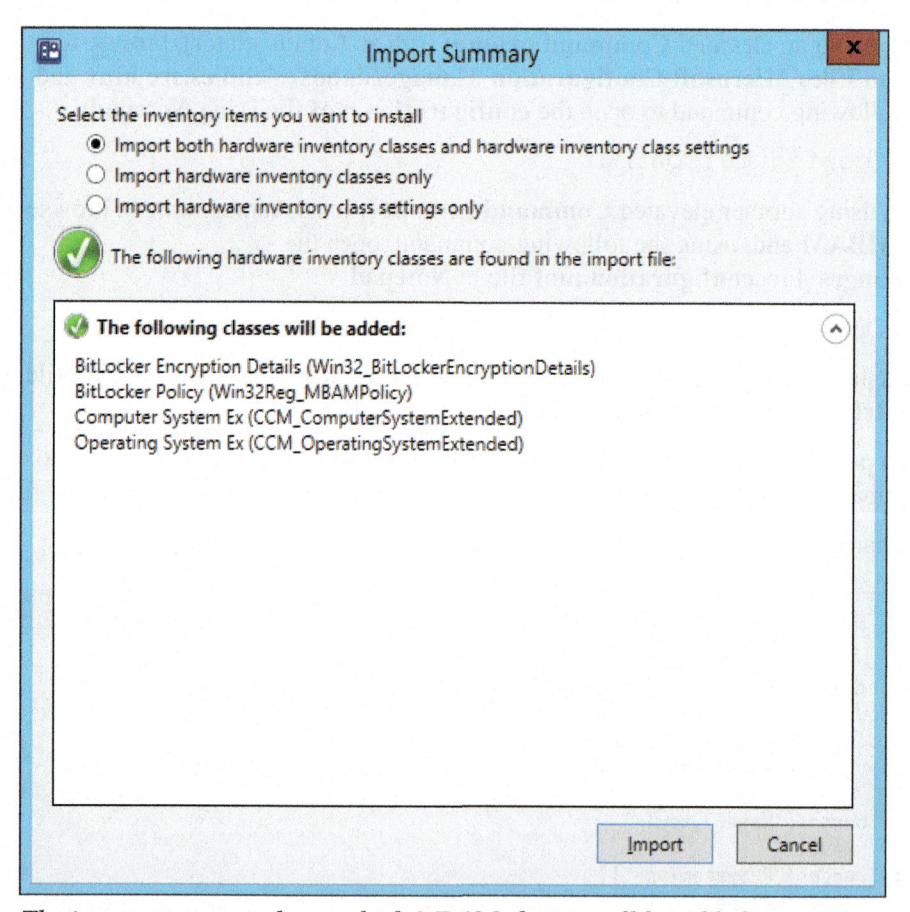

*The import summary shows which MBAM classes will be added.*

3. In the **Import Summary** window, ensure that the **Import both hardware inventory classes and hardware inventory class settings** option is selected (it's the default), and then click **Import**.

4. In the **Hardware Inventory Classes** window, scroll down to the **TPM (Win32_Tpm)** class, expand it, and select all the check boxes within that class. Click **OK** when done.

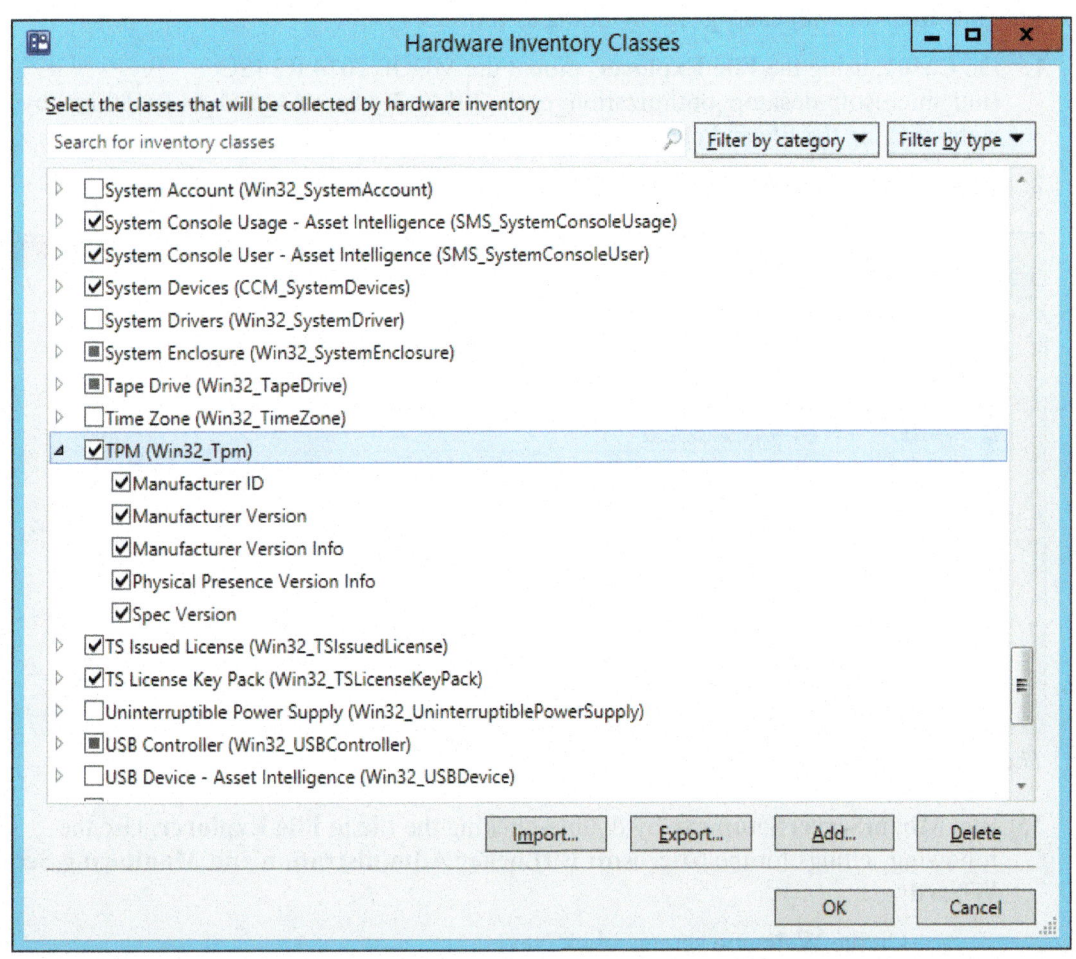

*The TPM(Win32_Tpm) class.*

5. In the **Default Client Settings** window, click **OK** to close.

## Integrate MBAM with ConfigMgr

In this guide I assume you have downloaded MDOP 2014 R2 ISO to E:\Setup on CM01. Next, you integrate MBAM with ConfigMgr by doing as follows:

1. On **CM01**, using the **File Explorer**, mount the MDOP 2014 R2 ISO (mu_microsoft_desktop_optimization_pack_2014_r2_x86_x64_dvd_6110480.iso) by right-clicking the file and choosing **Mount** (or double-click the file).

2. Browse to the **<drive>\MBAM\MBAM 2.5\Installers\x64** folder.

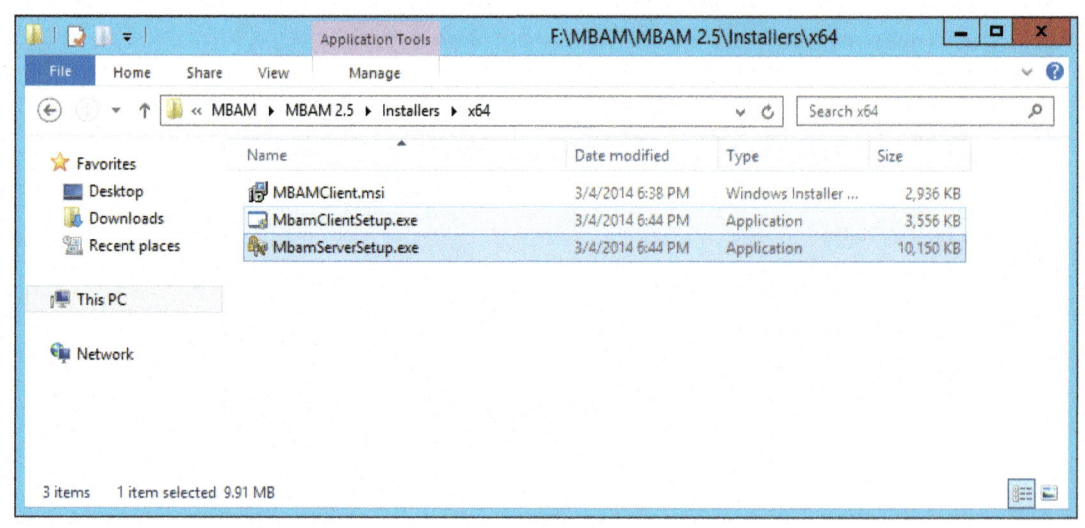

*The MBAM 2.5 Installers folder.*

3. Run **MbamServerSetup.exe** by double-clicking the file in **File Explorer**. Use the following settings for the **Microsoft BitLocker Administration and Monitoring Setup Wizard**:

    a. On the **Welcome** screen, click **Next**.

    b. On the **End-User License Agreement** screen, accept the agreement by selecting the **I accept the terms in the License Agreement** check box and clicking **Next**.

    c. On the **Microsoft Update** screen, select **Do not use Microsoft Update** and click **Next**.

    d. On the **Customer Experience Improvement Program** screen, select **Do not join the program at this time** and click **Next**.

    e. On the **Begin the Installation** screen, click **Install** and accept the UAC prompt.

    f. After the **Microsoft BitLocker Administration and Monitoring Setup Wizard** is completed, click **Finish**.

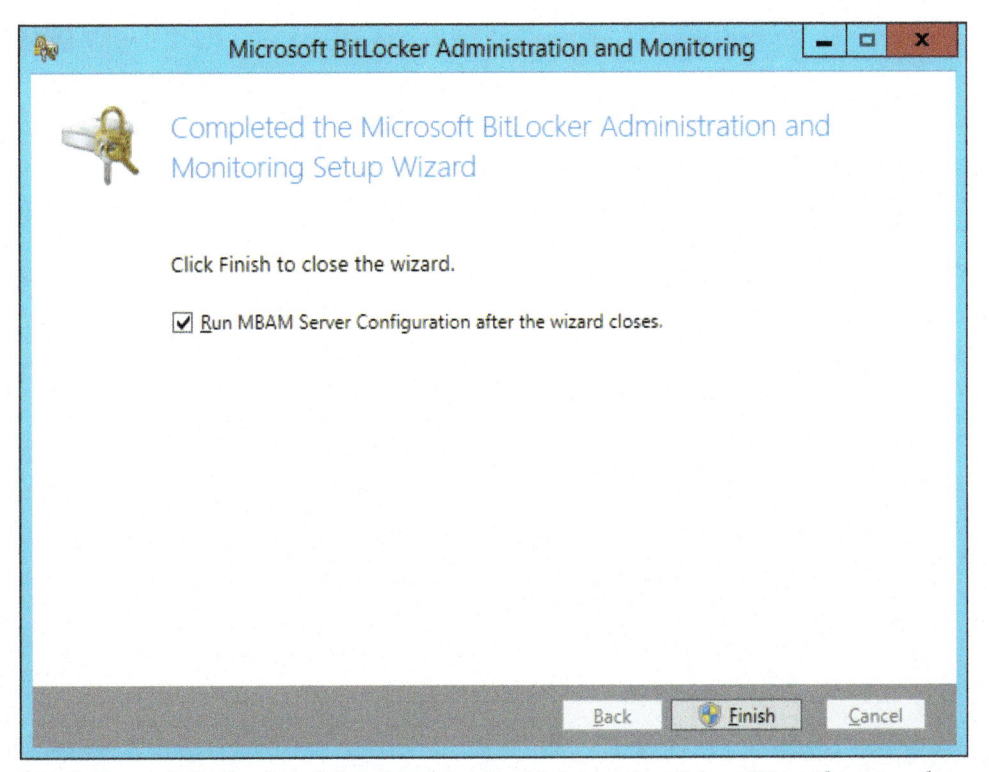

*The Microsoft BitLocker Administration and Monitoring Setup Wizard is complete.*

## Configure MBAM Server

After the preceding wizard has completed, the configuration wizard for Microsoft BitLocker and Monitoring starts. Use the following settings in that wizard:

1. On **CM01**, in the configuration wizard, click **Add New Features**.
2. On the **Select Features** screen, scroll to the bottom, select **System Center Configuration Manager Integration**, and click **Next**.

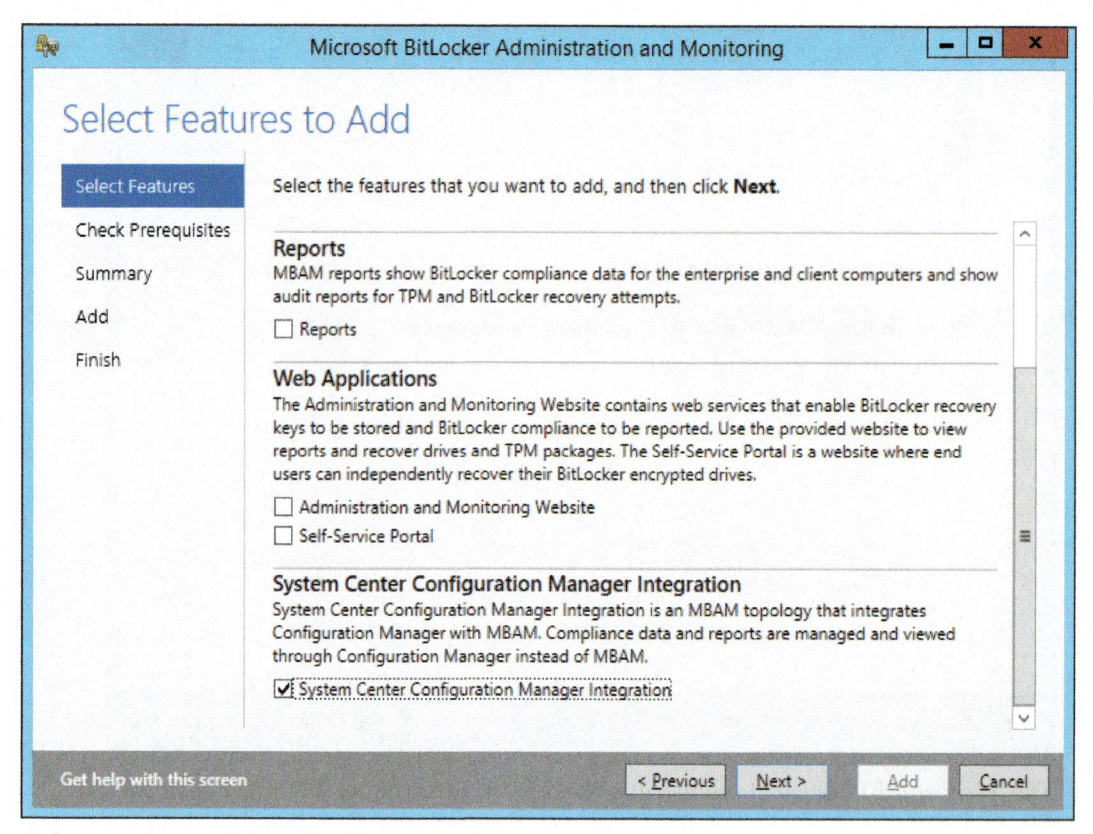

Chapter 13   Enforcing BitLocker with MBAM 2.5

*Selecting System Center Configuration Manager Integration.*

3. On the **Check Prerequisites** screen, everything should be okay, so click **Next**.
4. On the **Configure Integration** screen, for the **SQL Server Reporting Services Server** field, enter **CM01.CORP.VIAMONSTRA.COM** and click **Next**.
5. On the **Summary** screen, click **Add**.
6. On the **Finish** screen, click **Close**.

## Chapter 13  Enforcing BitLocker with MBAM 2.5

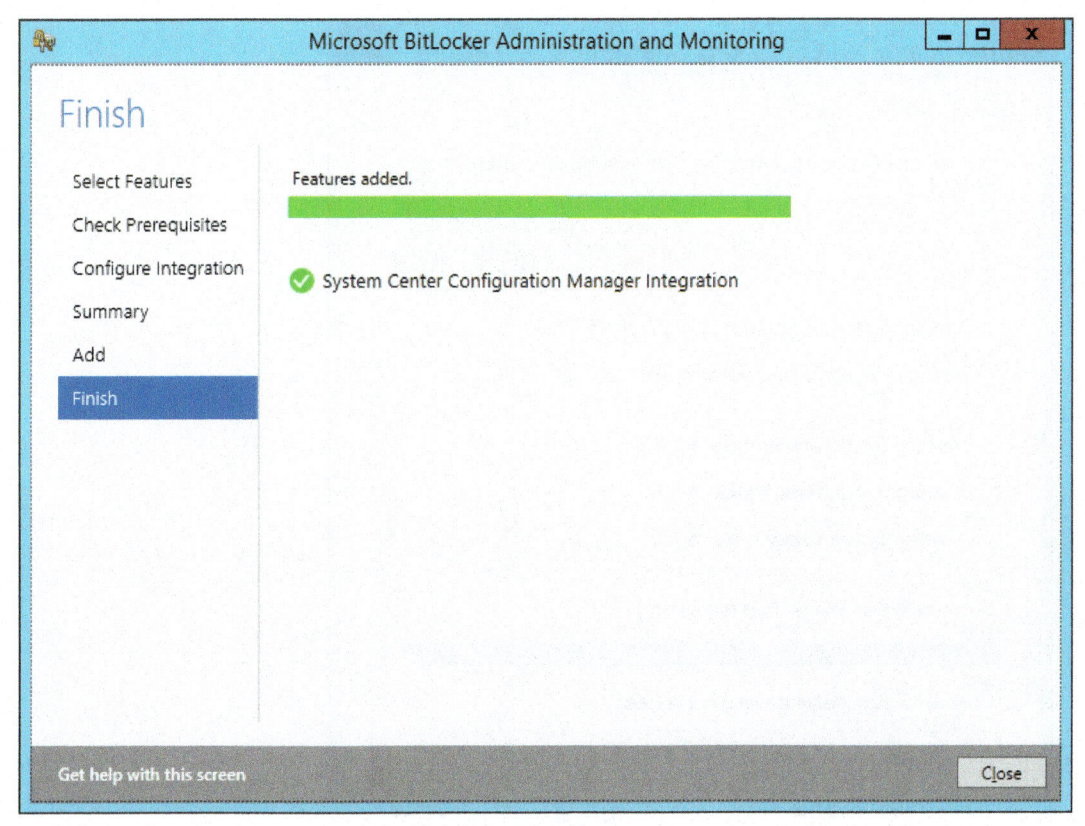

*MBAM Server has been integrated with ConfigMgr.*

## Edit the Collection Query
To allow MBAM to work with Generation 2 Hyper-V virtual machines, edit the query on the MBAM Supported Computers collection. To edit the collection, do as follows:

1. On **CM01**, in the **ConfigMgr console**, select **Assets and Compliance / Device Collections**, right-click the **MBAM Support Computers** collection, choose **Properties**, and choose **Membership Rules**.

2. Select the **BitLocker Compliant Computers** rule, click **Edit** and then click **Edit Query Statement**. Click the **Criteria** tab, double-click the line having "Virtual Machine" in it, remove **Virtual Machine** from the list of values in the query **Criteria**, and click **OK** four times to close all windows.

Note: If you want to test in VMware, you can remove the VMware Virtual Platform value as well.

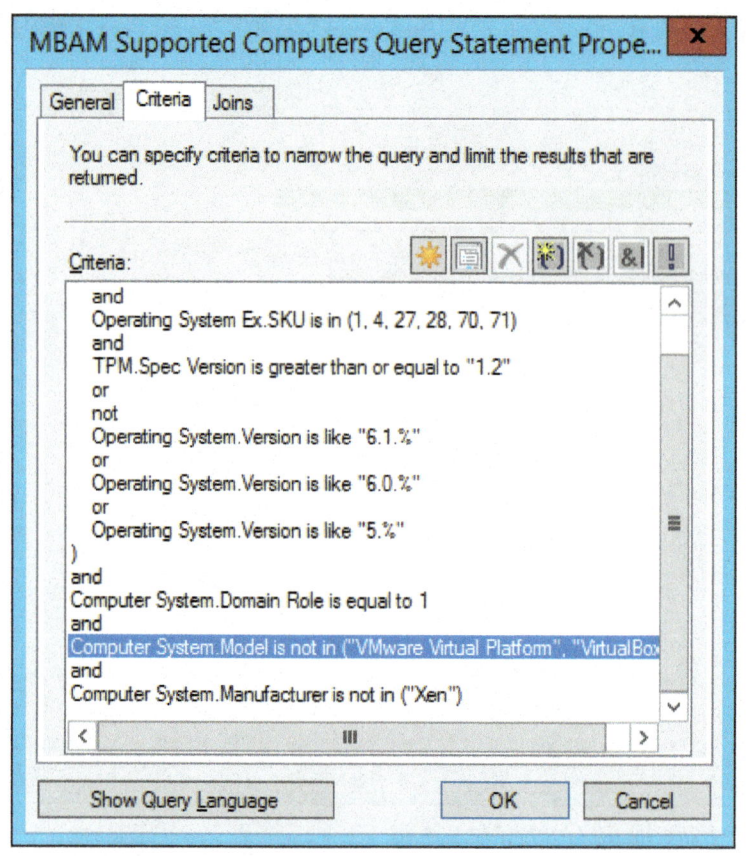

*Virtual Machine has been removed from this query criteria.*

## Installing the MBAM Server

Installing the MBAM server is necessary for creating the appropriate database structure and setting up services. To install and configure it follow the steps in this section.

### Prepare SQL Server

Before installing MBAM on the MBAM01 server, you add the MBAM_HD_AppPool user as a local administrator and then give that user appropriate permissions in SQL Server. To perform these actions, do as follows:

1. On **MBAM01**, log in as **VIAMONSTRA\Administrator**. Using an elevated **Command prompt** (run as Administrator), issue the following command:

   ```
   net localgroup Administrators /add
   ViaMonstra\MBAM_HD_AppPool
   ```

Chapter 13  Enforcing BitLocker with MBAM 2.5

```
Microsoft Windows [Version 6.3.9600]
(c) 2013 Microsoft Corporation. All rights reserved.

C:\windows\system32>net localgroup Administrators /add ViaMonstra\MBAM_HD_AppPool
The command completed successfully.

C:\windows\system32>
```

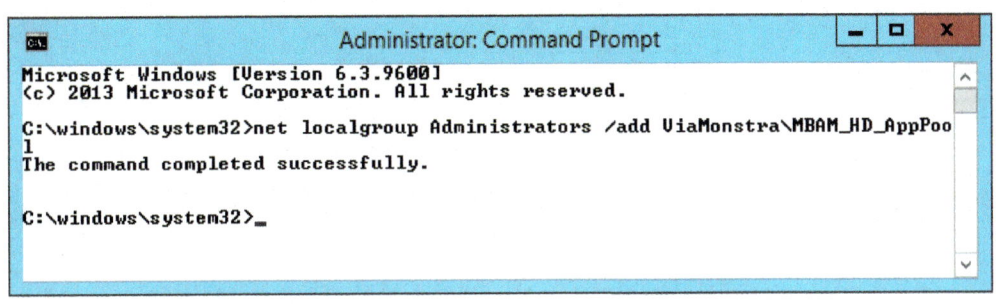

*Adding the MBAM_HD_AppPool user as a local administrator.*

2. Using the **Start screen**, start **SQL Server Management Studio**. On the **Connect to Server** window, click **Connect**.

3. In **Object Explorer**, expand **Security** and select **Logins**. Right-click **Logins** and select **New Login**.

4. On the **General** page, for **Login Name**, enter **VIAMONSTRA\MBAM_HD_AppPool**.

5. Select the **Server Roles** node, for **Server roles**, select **public** and **sysadmin**.

6. Click **OK** to apply the settings and close the New Login screen.

Chapter 13 Enforcing BitLocker with MBAM 2.5

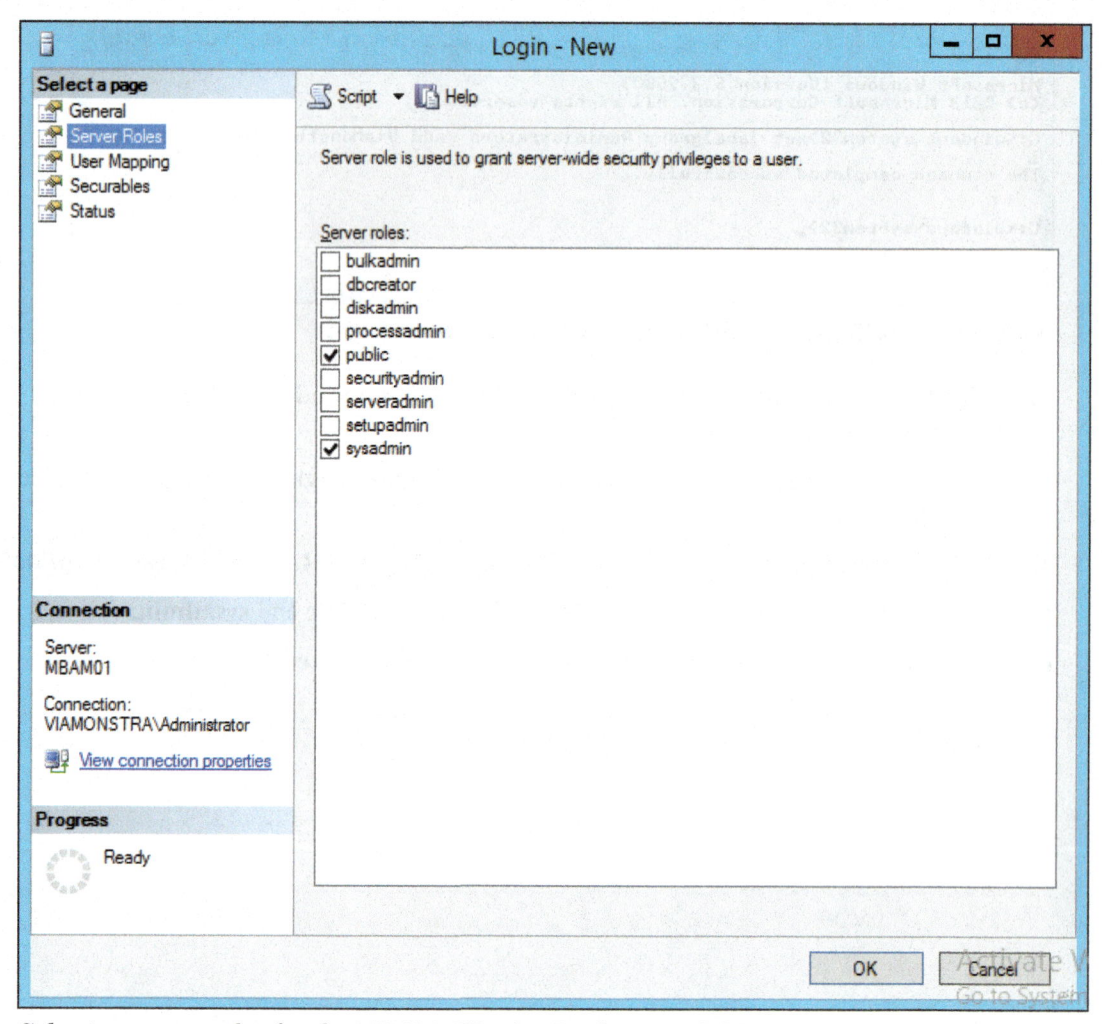

*Selecting server roles for the MBAM_HD_AppPool user in SQL Server.*

7. Close **SQL Server Management Studio** by clicking **Close**, and then sign out from the **MBAM01** server.

## Install MBAM Server

Next, you install MBAM on the MBAM01 server as follows:

1. On **MBAM01**, log on as **VIAMONSTRA\MBAM_HD_AppPool**.

2. Using **File Explorer**, copy the previously downloaded ISO for **MDOP 2014 R2** to **E:\Setup** (create the folder). Next, mount the ISO by right-clicking the file and choosing **Mount**.

316

3. Browse to the **<drive>\MBAM\MBAM 2.5\Installers\x64** folder.

4. Run **MbamServerSetup.exe** by double-clicking the file in **File Explorer**. Use the following settings for the **Microsoft BitLocker Administration and Monitoring Setup Wizard**:

   a. On the **Welcome** screen, click **Next**.

   b. On the **End-User License Agreement** screen, accept the agreement by selecting the **I accept the terms in the License Agreement** check box and clicking **Next**.

   c. On the **Microsoft Update** screen, select **Do not use Microsoft Update** and click **Next**.

   d. On the **Customer Experience Improvement Program** screen, select **Do not join the program at this time** and click **Next**.

   e. On the **Begin the Installation** screen, click **Install** and accept the UAC prompt.

   f. After the **Microsoft BitLocker Administration and Monitoring Setup Wizard** is complete, click **Finish**.

> **Note**: If you want to do this configuration using PowerShell, copy the PowerShell script E:\Setup\Scripts\Add-MbamFeatures.ps1 from the CM01 server to the MBAM01 server and then run it using Windows PowerShell ISE as Administrator. This PowerShell script can be generated by the wizard in the Summary screen by choosing the option to Export PowerShell Script.

5. In the configuration wizard that starts, click **Add New Features**.

6. On the **Select Features** screen, select all options *except* the last option, **System Center Configuration Manager Integration**, and click **Next**.

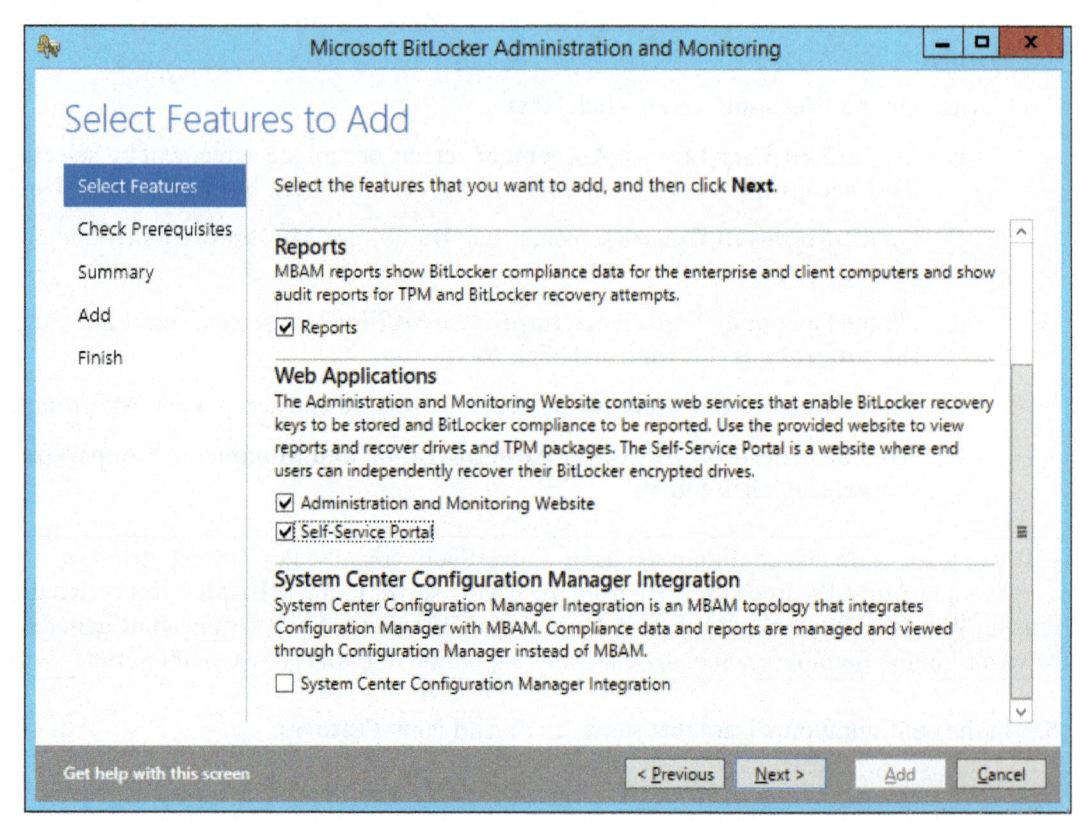

*Select everything except for ConfigMgr integration, which was already completed on the ConfigMgr server.*

7. On the **Configure Databases** screen, use the following settings for **COMPLIANCE AND AUDIT DATABASE**:

    o   SQL Server name: **MBAM01.corp.viamonstra.com**

    o   SQL Server database instance: **<default>**

    o   Database name: **MBAM Compliance Status**

    o   Read/write access domain user or group: **VIAMONSTRA\MBAM_DB_RW**

    o   Read-only access domain user or group: **VIAMONSTRA\MBAM_DB_RO**

8. Still on the **Configure Databases** screen, use the following settings for **RECOVERY DATABASE**:

    o   SQL Server name: **MBAM01.corp.viamonstra.com**

    o   SQL Server database instance: **<default>**

Chapter 13  Enforcing BitLocker with MBAM 2.5

o   Database name: **MBAM Recovery and Hardware**

o   Read/write access domain user or group: **VIAMONSTRA\MBAM_DB_RW**

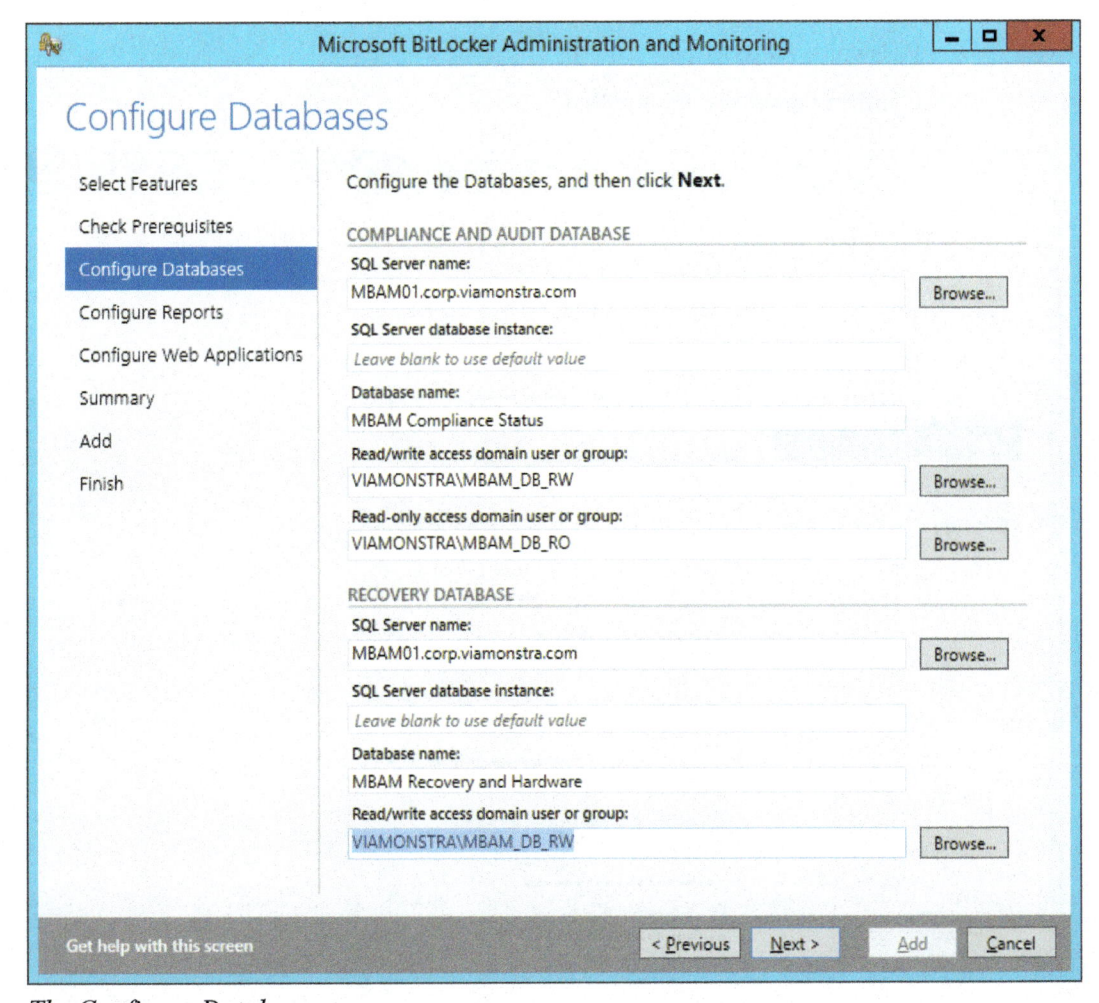

*The Configure Databases screen.*

9.  On the **Configure Reports** screen, use the following settings for **REPORTING**:

    o   SQL Server Reporting Services Instance: **<default>**

    o   Reporting role domain group: **VIAMONSTRA\MBAM_HD_Report**

10. Still on the **Configure Reports** screen, use the default settings for **COMPLIANCE AND AUDIT DATABASE CONNECTION**.

Chapter 13   Enforcing BitLocker with MBAM 2.5

11. Still on the **Configure Reports** screen, use the following settings for **Compliance and Audit Database domain account**:

    o   User name: **VIAMONSTRA\MBAM_Reports_Compl**

    o   Password: **P@ssw0rd**

    o   Confirm Password: **P@ssw0rd**

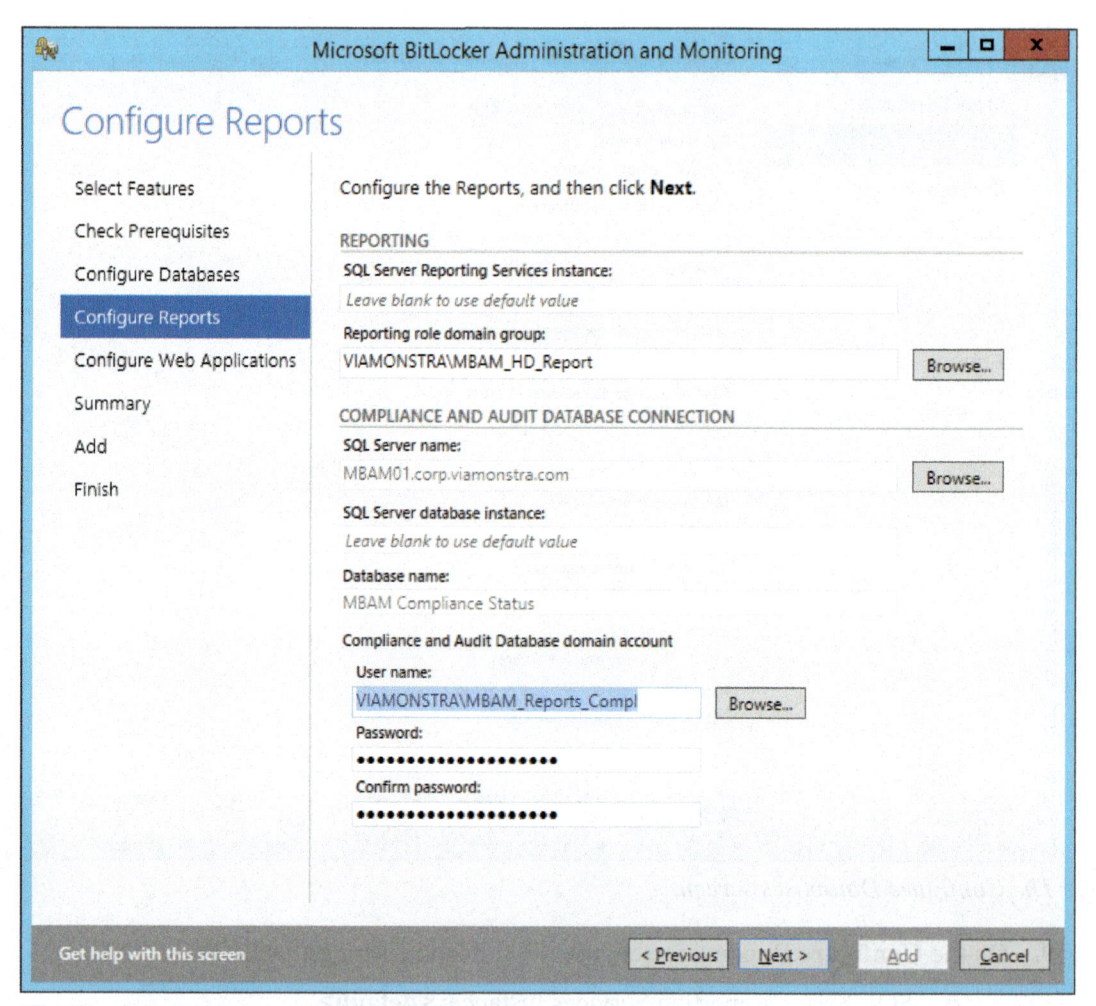

*The Configure Reports screen with its settings.*

12. On the **Configure Web Applications** screen, use the following settings for **CONFIGURATION FOR ALL WEB APPLICATIONS**:

    o   Security Certificate: **Do not use a certificate**

    o   Hostname: **MBAM01.corp.viamonstra.com**

    o   Installation Path: **C:\InetPub**

- Port: **80**
- Web service application pool domain account: **VIAMONSTRA\MBAM_HD_AppPool**
- Password: **P@ssw0rd**
- Confirm Password: **P@ssw0rd**

13. Still on the **Configure Web Applications** screen, use the default settings for **COMPLIANCE AND AUDIT DATABASE CONNECTION**.

14. Still on the **Configure Web Applications** screen, use the default settings for **RECOVERY DATABASE CONNECTION**.

15. Still on the **Configure Web Applications** screen, use the following settings for the **ADMINISTRATION AND MONITORING WEBSITE**:
    - Advanced Helpdesk role domain group: **VIAMONSTRA\MBAM_HD_Adv**
    - Helpdesk role domain group: **VIAMONSTRA\MBAM_HD**
    - Select **Use System Center Configuration Manager Integration** and use the default settings for the remaining options.

16. Still on the **Configure Web Applications** screen, use the default settings for **SELF-SERVICE PORTAL**.

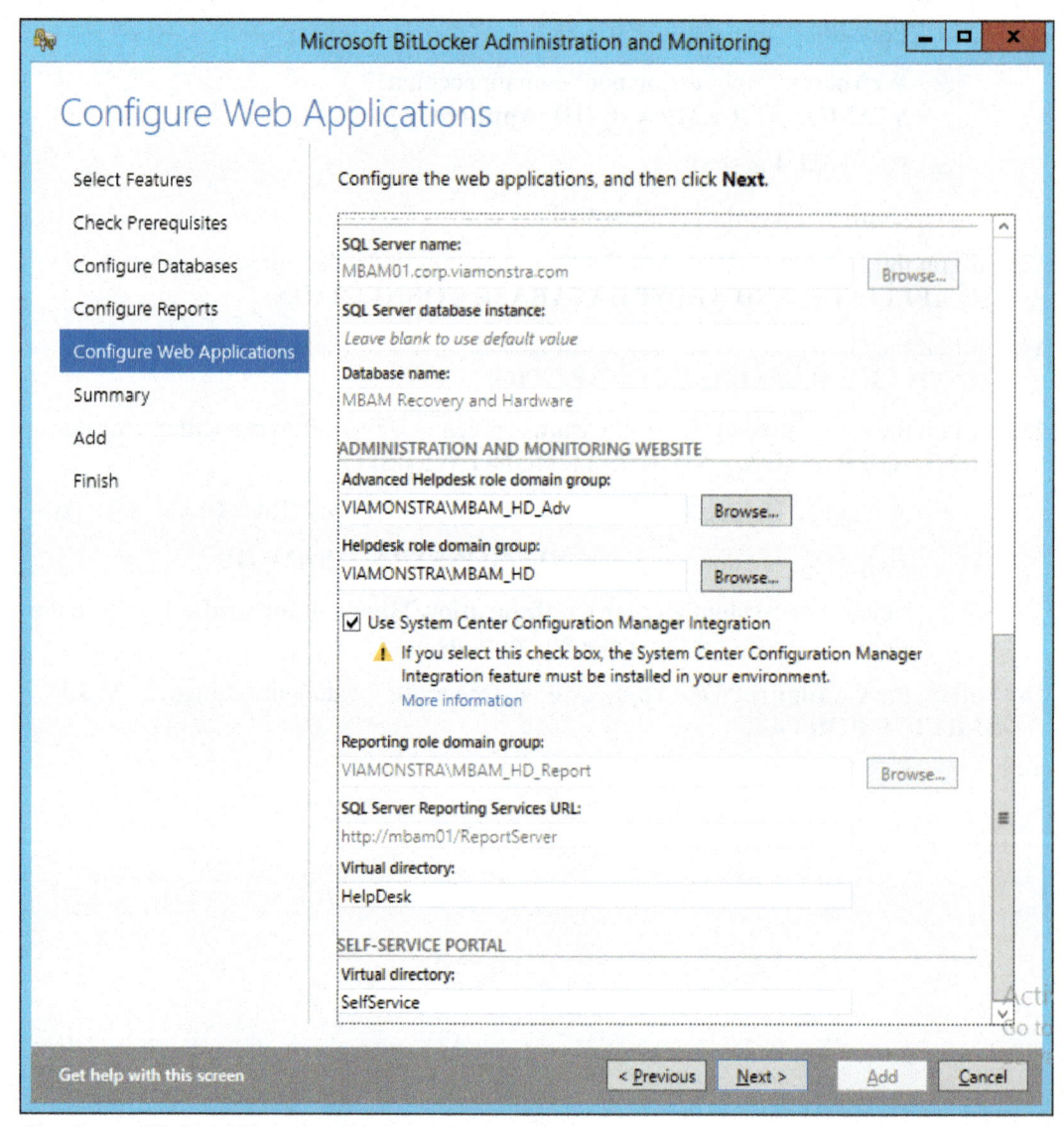

*Configure Web Applications settings.*

**17.** Click **Next**, and at the **Summary** screen, click **Add**.

Chapter 13 Enforcing BitLocker with MBAM 2.5

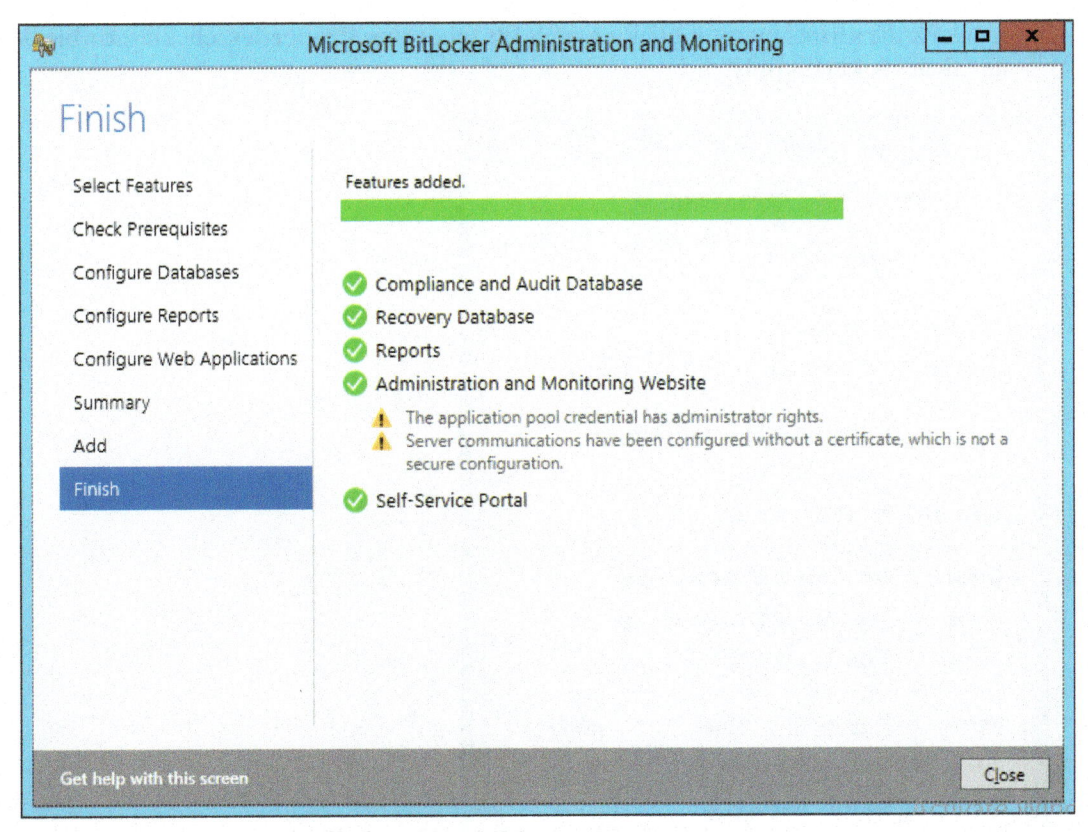

*MBAM server is now installed on MBAM01.*

> **Note**: If you have any problems with the wizard, or if it shows errors, please refer to the following URL for details on which log files and event logs you can use when troubleshooting MBAM 2.5 installation issues: https://support.microsoft.com/en-us/kb/3049652.

## Configure the Self-Service Portal

In order to avoid a blank Self-Service Portal page appearing for your end-users you need to implement the following changes. In addition, you customize the portal to use the ViaMonstra name.

1. On **MBAM01**, log on as **VIAMONSTRA\MBAM_HD_AppPool**.

2. Using **Internet Explorer**, download the following files to **E:\Setup**:

    o **jQuery-1.10.2.min.js:** http://go.microsoft.com/fwlink/?LinkID=390515

    o **jQuery.validate.min.js:** http://go.microsoft.com/fwlink/?LinkID=390516

    o **jQuery.validate.unobtrusive.min.js:**
    http://go.microsoft.com/fwlink/?LinkID=390517

323

Chapter 13   Enforcing BitLocker with MBAM 2.5

3. Unblock the scripts by right-clicking each file, choosing **Properties**, clicking **Unblock**, and then clicking **Apply**.

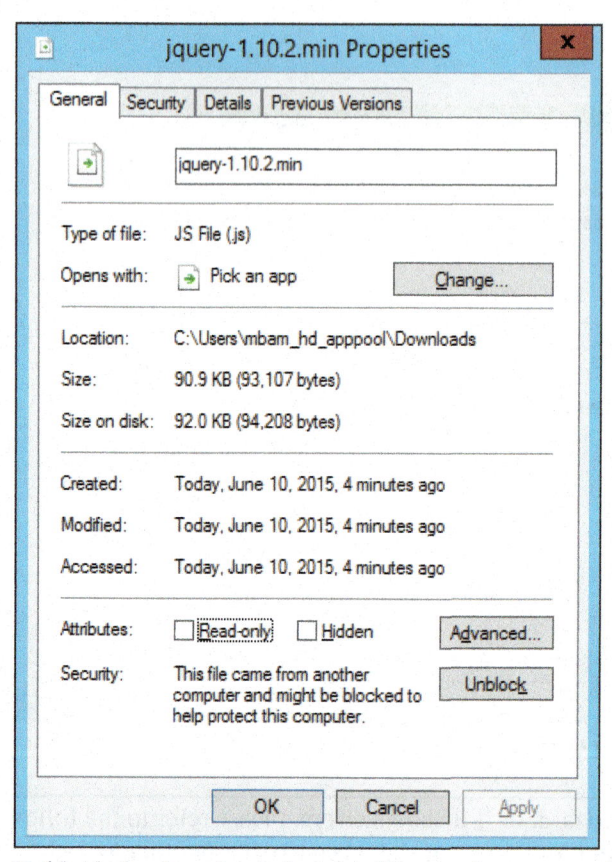

*Unblock the downloaded script files, or they cannot be used.*

4. Using **File Explorer**, copy the three downloaded files to the following folder:

   **C:\inetpub\Microsoft BitLocker Management Solution\
   Self Service Website\Scripts**

Chapter 13   Enforcing BitLocker with MBAM 2.5

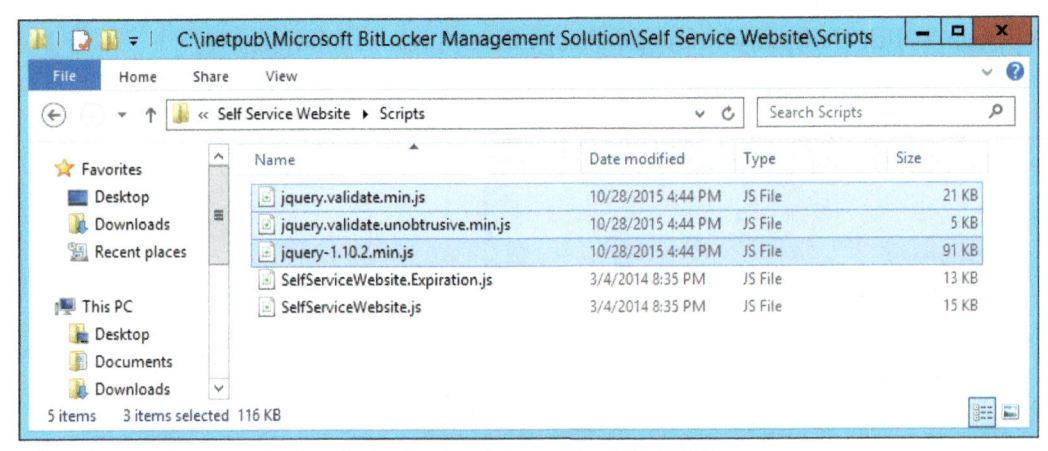

*The three scripts copied to their destination on the MBAM01 server.*

5. Open **Internet Information Services (IIS) Manager**. Under **Connections**, navigate to **Sites** and expand **Microsoft BitLocker Administration and Monitoring**. Then select **SelfService** and double-click **Application Settings** in the right pane.

6. Modify the three **jQuery** path settings to point to the new virtual path of the script files as shown in the following figure. The values are:

    o   jQueryPath: **/SelfService/Scripts/jquery-1.10.2.min.js**

    o   jQueryValidatePath: **/SelfService/Scripts/jquery.validate.min.js**

    o   jQueryValidateUnobtrusivePath: **/SelfService/Scripts/jquery.validate.unobtrusive.min.js**

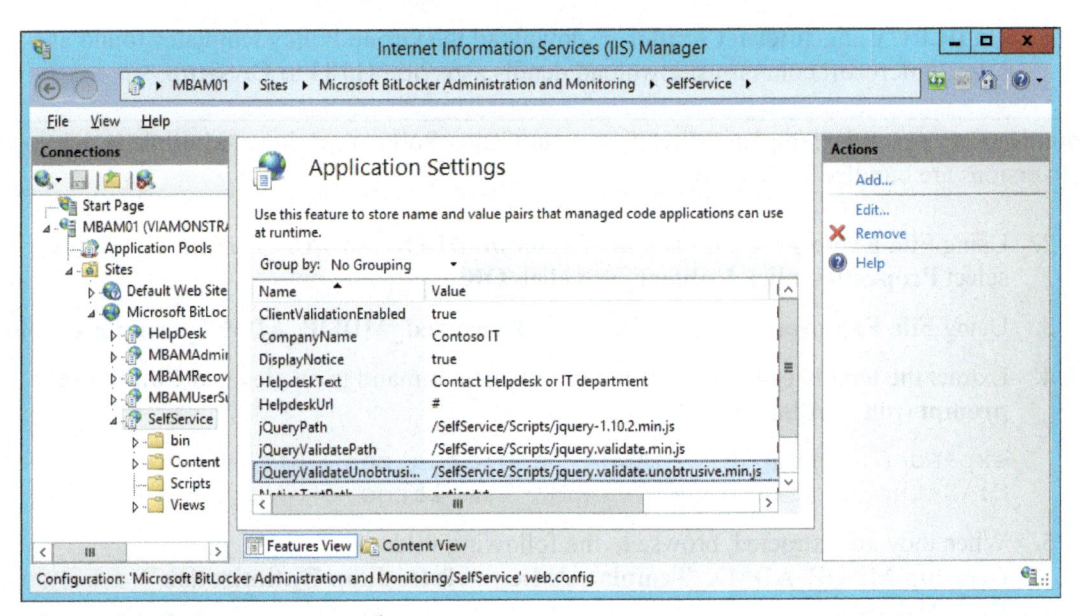

*The modified jQuery script paths.*

325

7. Double-click **CompanyName** and change the settings as follows:

   Value: **ViaMonstra**

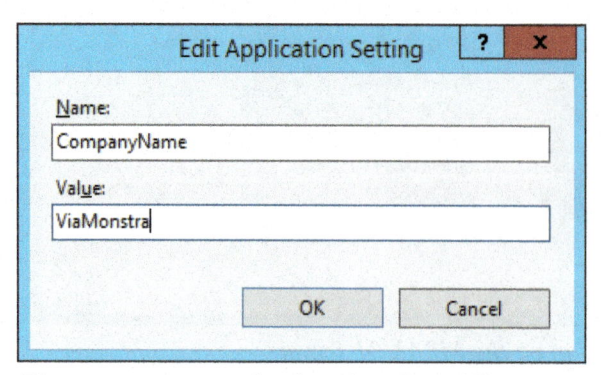

*The company name displayed in the Self Service website.*

# Configuring MBAM Group Policy

MBAM has its own set of Group Policy objects (GPOs), which can be edited and targeted to computers on which you want to control BitLocker. To configure Group Policy, follow the steps in this section.

## Copy Group Policy Templates

You need to download and then copy Group Policy templates for MBAM 2.5. To do this, do as follows:

1. On **DC01**, using **Internet Explorer**, download the Group Policy templates found at https://microsoft.com/en-us/download/details.aspx?id=41183 to **C:\Setup**.

**Note**: Do not extract the templates directly to your Group Policy repository. Multiple technologies and versions are bundled in this file.

2. Using **File Explorer**, right-click the **C:\Setup\MDOP_ADMX_Templates.cab** file, select **Properties**, click **Unblock**, and click **OK**.

3. Using **File Explorer**, create the **C:\Setup\Extracted_MDOP_ADMX_Templates** folder.

4. Extract the templates by running the following command in an elevated **Command prompt** (run as Administrator):

   ```
   expand C:\Setup\MDOP_ADMX_Templates.cab -F:*
   C:\Setup\Extracted_MDOP_ADMX_Templates
   ```

5. When they are extracted, browse to the following folder: **C:\Setup\MDOP_ADMX_Templates\Microsoft Desktop Optimization Pack\MBAM2.5**.

Chapter 13 Enforcing BitLocker with MBAM 2.5

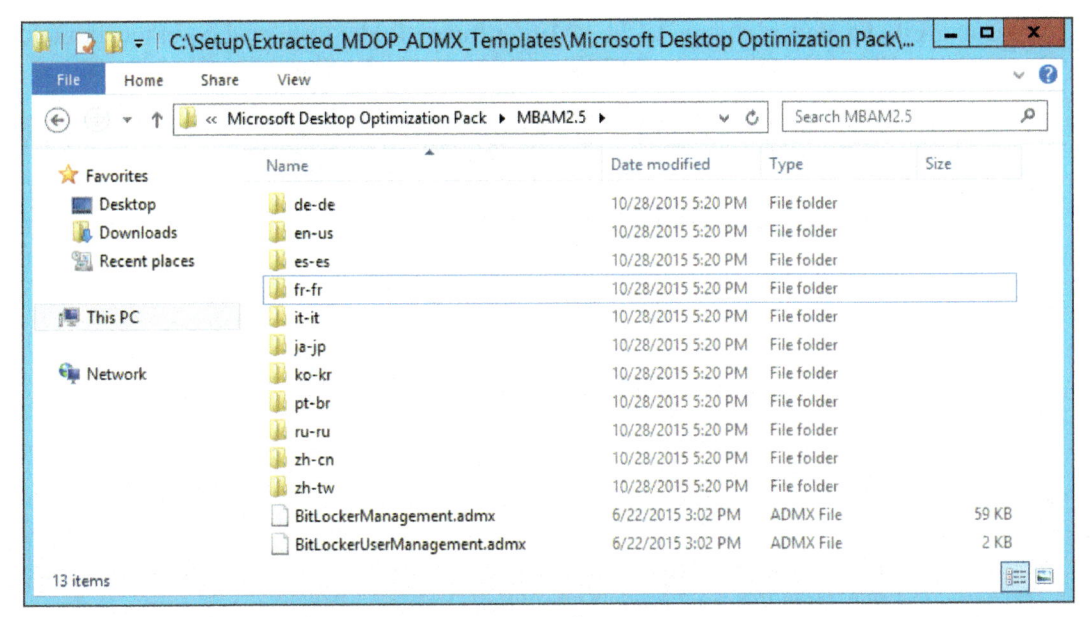

*The extracted Group Policy administrative templates.*

6. Using **File Explorer**, select the two **.admx** files and press **Ctrl + C** to copy them. In another **File Explorer** window, browse to **C:\Windows\PolicyDefinitions** and use **Ctrl + V** to paste.

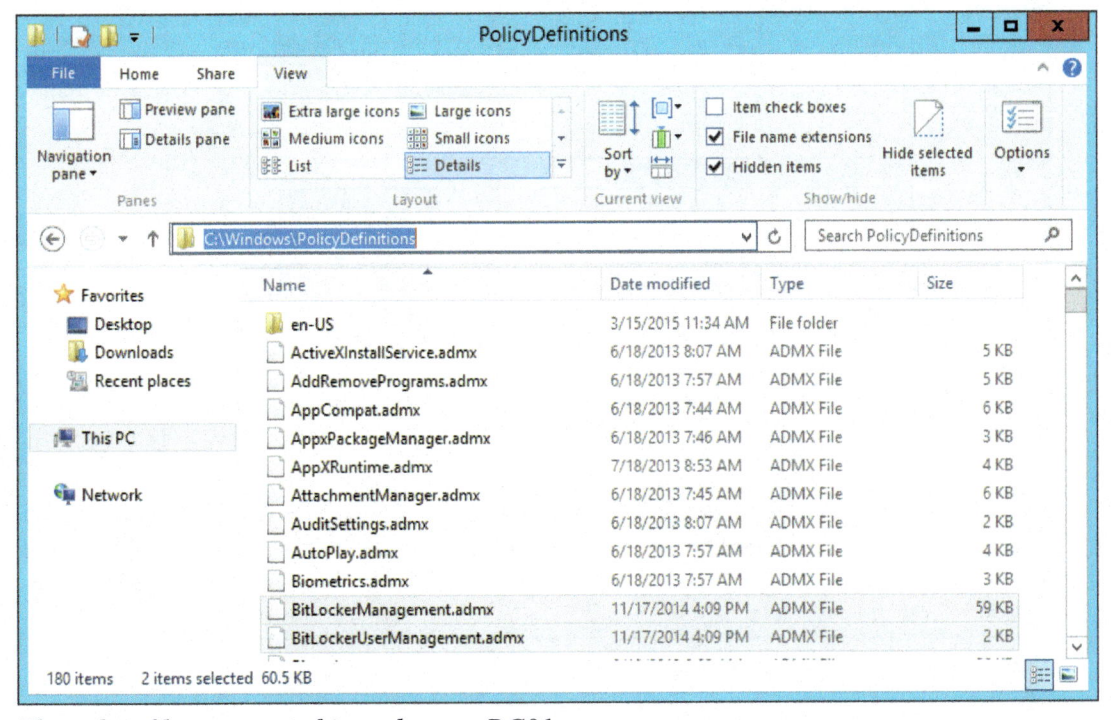

*The .admx files are copied into place on DC01.*

327

Chapter 13  Enforcing BitLocker with MBAM 2.5

7. Using **File Explorer**, change to the **<MuiCulture>** folder (e.g. **en-US**) in the extracted template files, select the two **.adml** files, and press **Ctrl + C** to copy them.

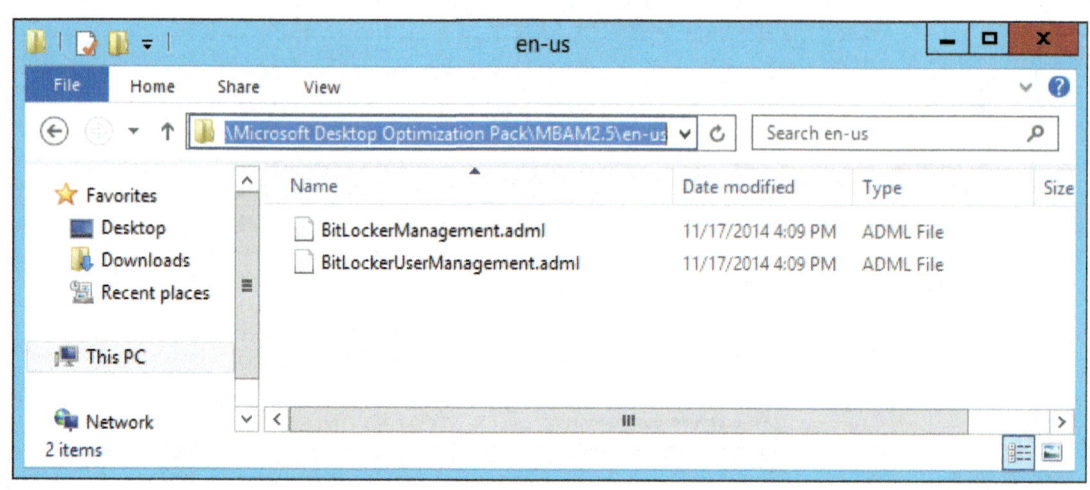

*The two adml files from the downloaded template.*

8. Paste the files into **C:\Windows\PolicyDefinitions\<MuiCulture>** where **<MuiCulture>** is the language of the OS (e.g. **en-US**) by pressing **Ctrl + V**.

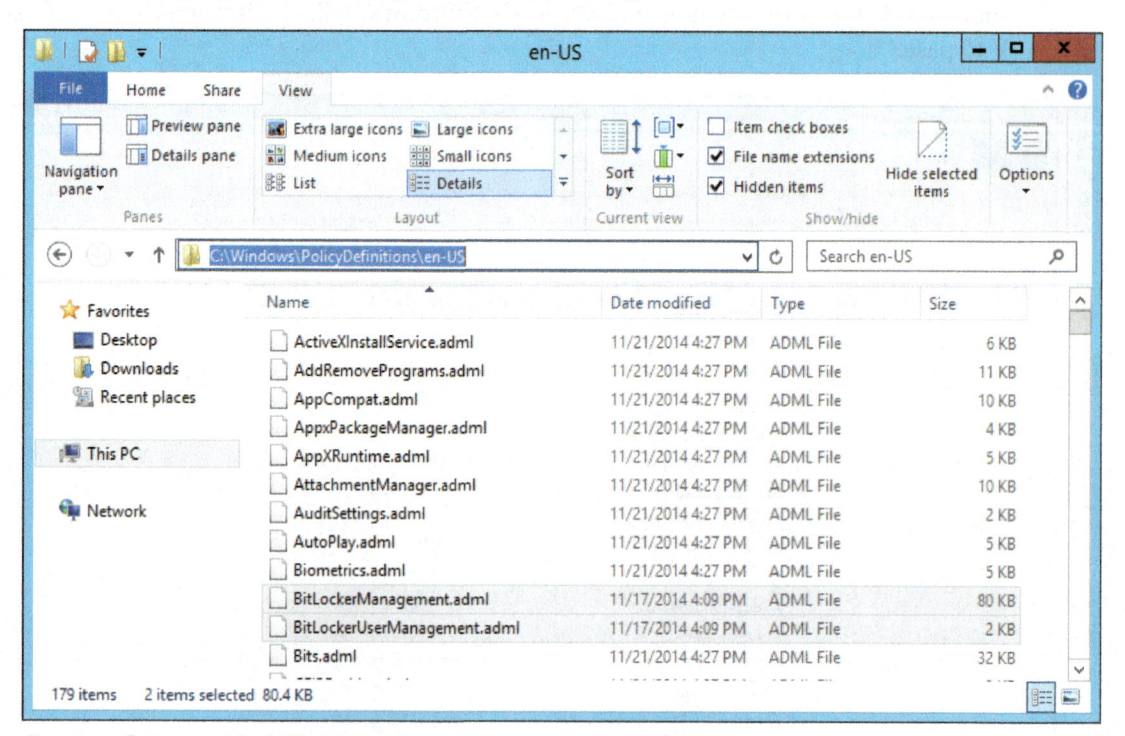

*Pasting the two .adml files into place.*

## Edit Group Policy

MBAM 2.5 comes with its own Group Policy settings, which can be customized as you see fit. In this section, you edit some of those settings. They are divided into policy groups and their respective policies. To edit Group Policy for MBAM 2.5, do as follows:

1. On **DC01**, using the **Group Policy Management Console** (GPMC.msc), expand **Group Policy Management** so that you can see the **Workstations** OU within the **ViaMonstra** OU.

2. Right-click **Workstations** and choose **Create a GPO in this domain and link it here**. This applies the Group Policy settings to this OU only. Use the following settings for the New GPO dialog box and then click **OK**:

    o   Name: **MBAM 2.5 BitLocker Policy**

    o   Source Starter GPO: **<default>**

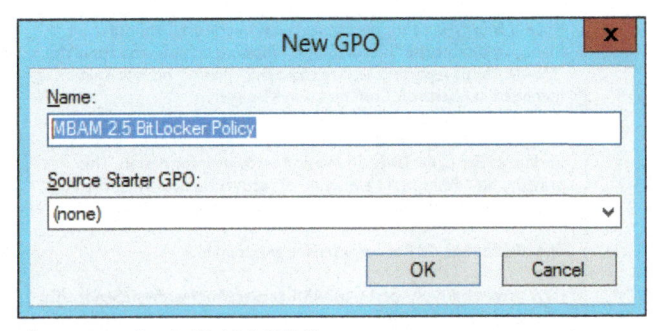

*Creating the MBAM GPO.*

3. Next, right-click the new **MBAM 2.5 BitLocker Policy** and choose **Edit**. Select **Computer Configuration / Policies / Administrative Templates / Windows Components / MDOP MBAM (BitLocker Management)**.

4. Select **Client Management** from the left pane, and double-click **Configure MBAM Services**. Set the GPO to **Enabled**, use the following settings for the options available, click **Apply** when done, and then click **OK** to close the GPO.

    o   MBAM Recovery service endpoint: **http://MBAM01.corp.viamonstra.com:80/ MBAMRecoveryAndHardwareService/CoreService.svc**

    o   Select BitLocker recovery information to store: **Recovery password and key package**

    o   Enter client checking status frequency in (minutes): **90**

    o   Configure MBAM Status reporting service: **Disabled**

Chapter 13   Enforcing BitLocker with MBAM 2.5

- o   MBAM Status reporting service endpoint: **<blank>**
- o   Enter status report frequency in (minutes): **720**

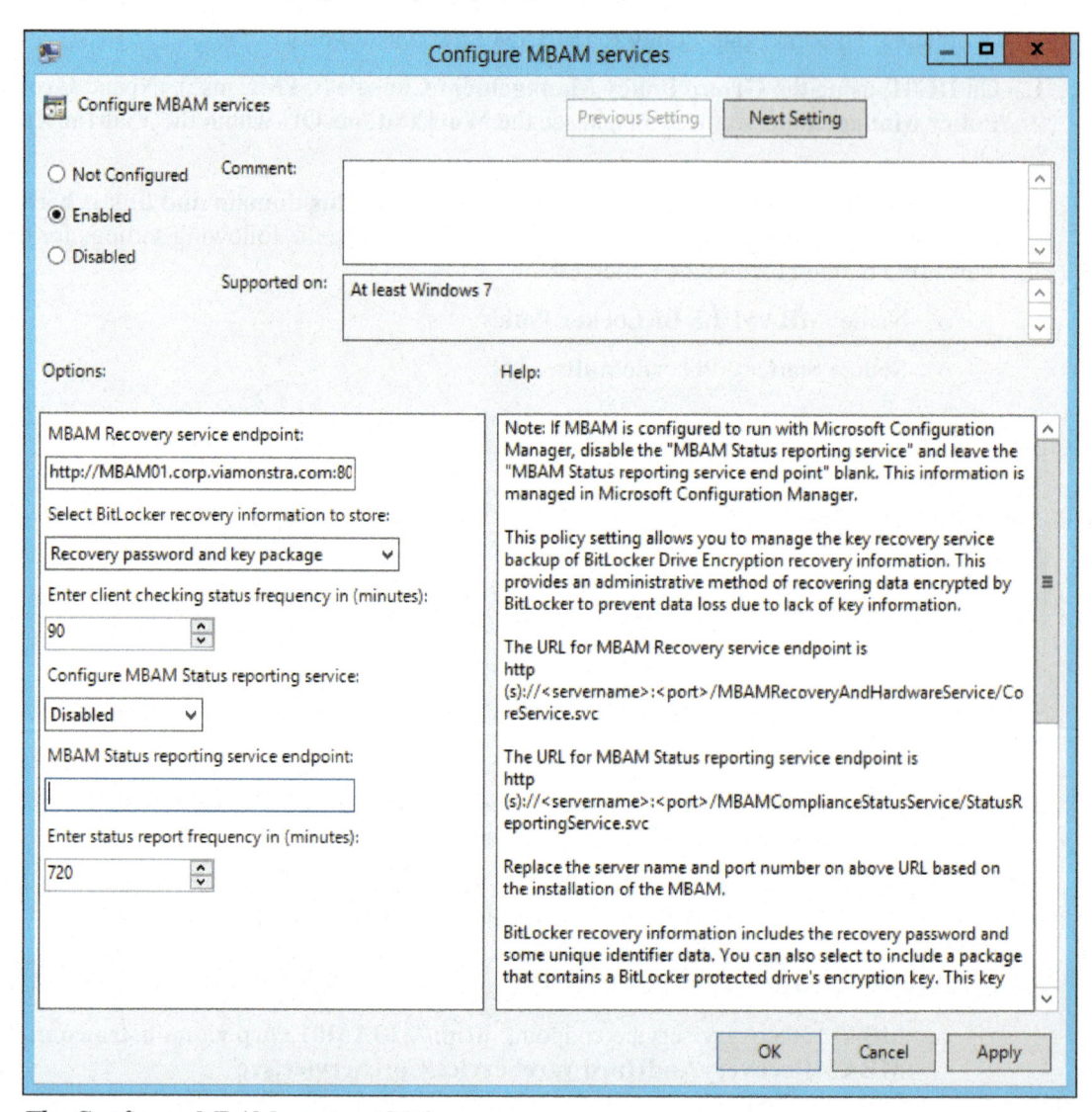

*The Configure MBAM services GPO.*

# Chapter 13  Enforcing BitLocker with MBAM 2.5

5. Select **Operating System Drive** from the left pane, and double-click **Operating system drive encryption settings**. Set the GPO to **Enabled**, use the following settings for the options available, and then click **OK** to close the GPO. The first option allows us to use BitLocker on virtual machines that support it, such as Generation 2 Hyper-V virtual machines.

     o Select **Allow BitLocker without a compatible TPM (requires a password)**.

     o Select protector for operating system drive: **TPM only**

     o Configure minimum PIN length for startup: **4**

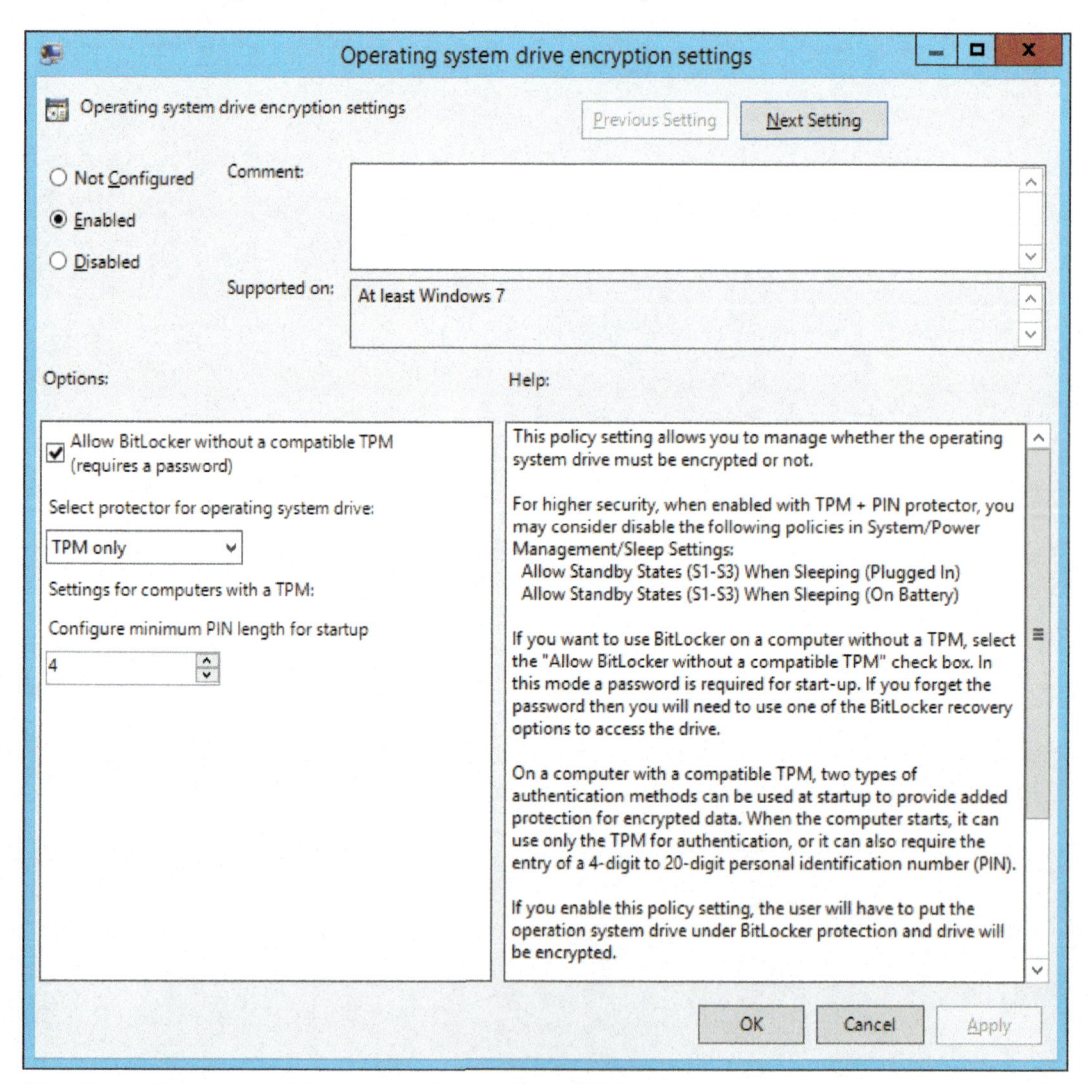

*The Operating system drive encryption settings GPO.*

# Chapter 13   Enforcing BitLocker with MBAM 2.5

6. Next, select **Configure use of passwords for operating system drives**. Set the GPO to **Enabled**, use the following settings for the options available, and then click **OK** to close the GPO.

   o Configure password complexity for operating system drives: **Allow password complexity**

   o Minimum password length for operating system drive: **8**

   o Do not select the **Require ASCII-only passwords for removable OS drives** option.

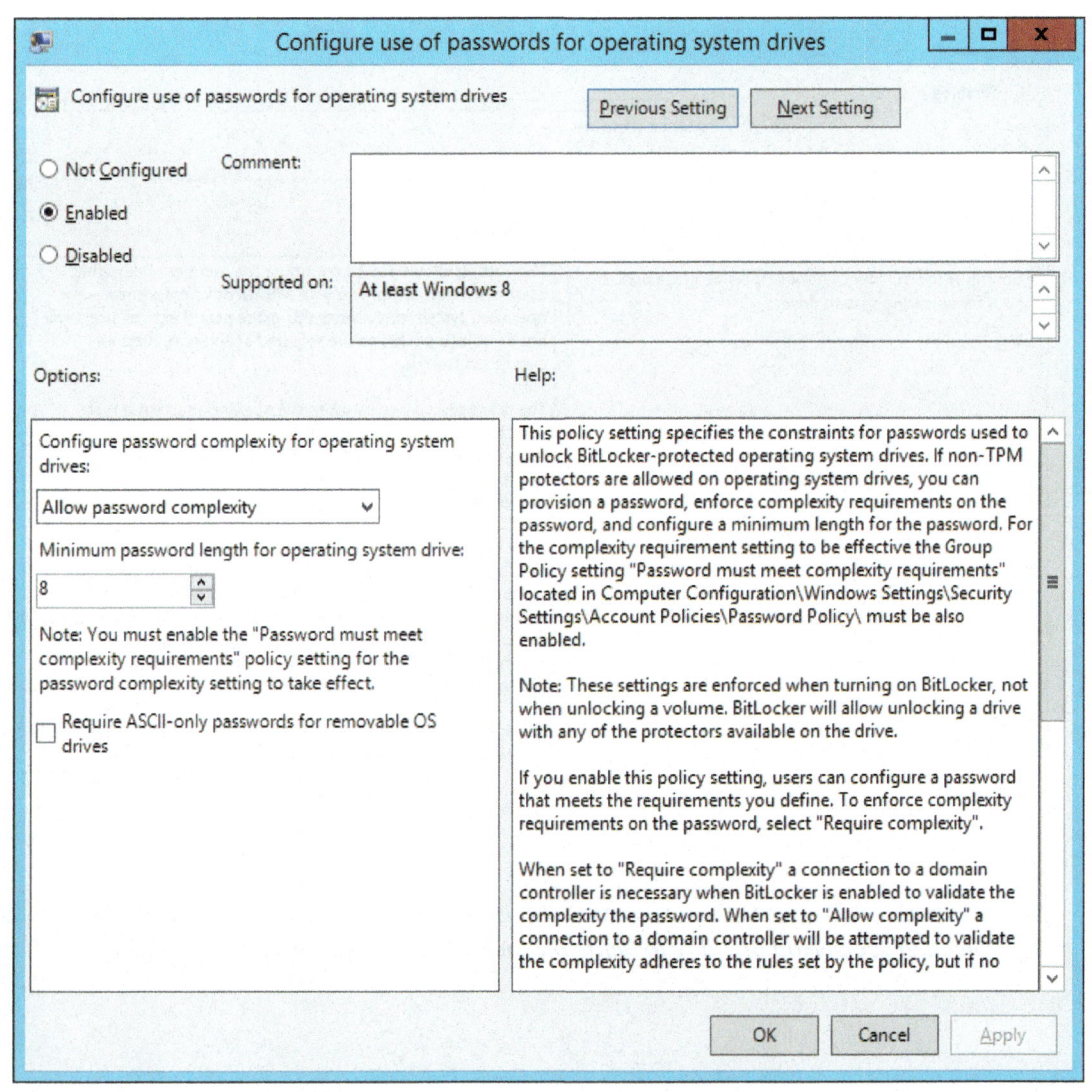

*The Configure use of passwords for operating system drives GPO.*

333

Chapter 13   Enforcing BitLocker with MBAM 2.5

7. Next, select **Encryption Policy Enforcement Settings**. Set the GPO to **Enabled** and then use the following setting, and click **OK** to close the GPO.

   Configure the number of noncompliance grace period days for operating system drives: **1**

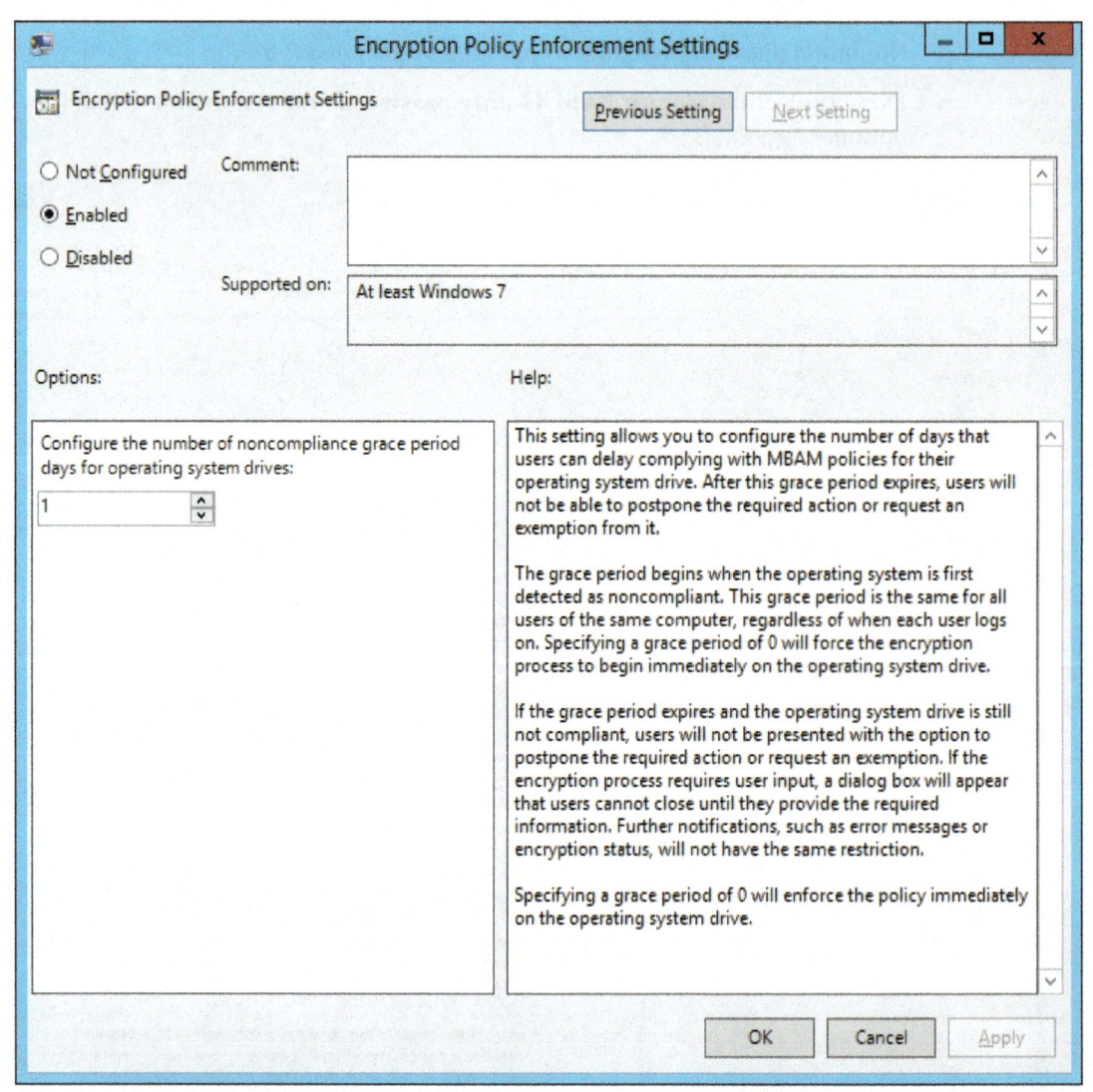

*Allowing a grace period of 1 day to delay the encryption of operating system drives.*

Chapter 13   Enforcing BitLocker with MBAM 2.5

After the changes have been added and applied close GPMC. The completed GPOs can be seen by selecting the Settings tab in the MBAM 2.5 BitLocker Policy GPO.

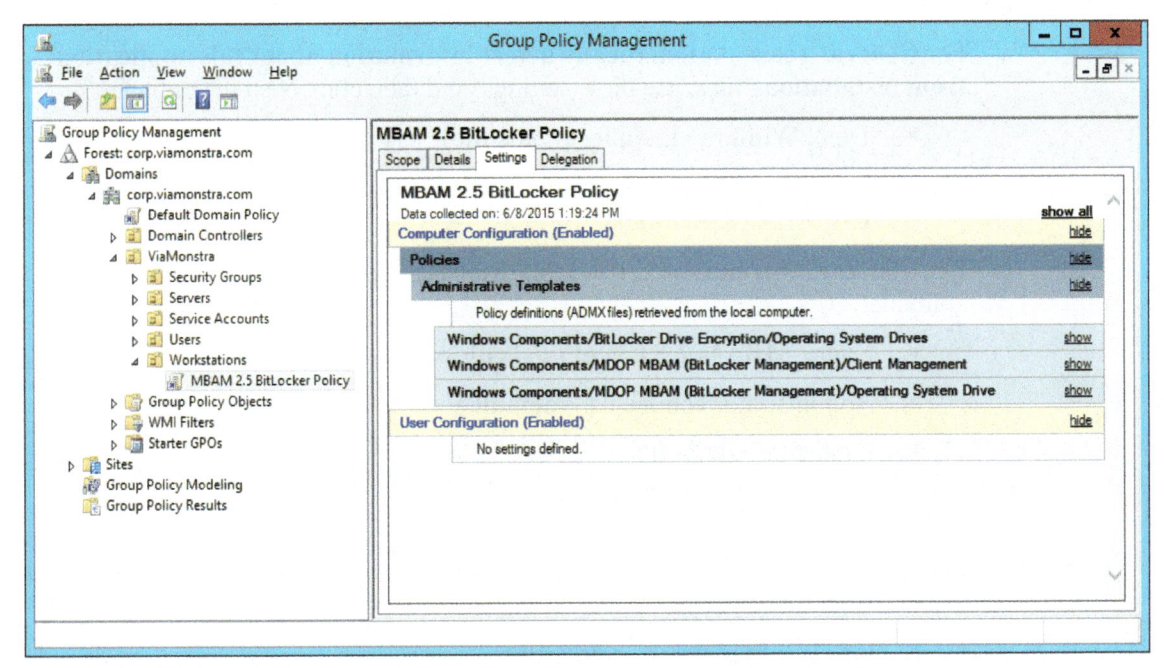

*The completed GPOs targeting the ViaMonstra Workstations OU.*

# Deploying the MBAM Client Agent

The Microsoft BitLocker Administration and Monitoring (MBAM) client software enables administrators to enforce and monitor BitLocker drive encryption on computers in the enterprise. The MBAM client itself enforces settings defined in the MBAM GPOs you configured in the preceding section and reports compliance of these GPOs to the MBAM database.

To create, distribute, and then deploy the MBAM application, follow the processes in this section.

## Create the MBAM Application

The MBAM client can be installed as an application using the supplied .msi files within the MDOP ISO. To create the MBAM 2.5 x64 client application in ConfigMgr, follow this process:

1. On **CM01**, using **File Explorer**, navigate to the **E:\Sources\Software\Microsoft\** folder and create the **MBAM 2.5 x64** subfolder.

2. Copy the **MBAM Client x64** installation file (**MBAMClient.msi**) to the following folder: **E:\Sources\Software\Microsoft\MBAM 2.5 x64**.

3. Using the **ConfigMgr console**, in the **Software Library** workspace, right-click **Applications** and select **Create Application**. Use the following settings for the **Create Application Wizard**:

   a. For **General**, select **Automatically detect information about this application from installations files**, use these settings, and then click Next to continue:
      - Type: **Windows installer (*.msi file)**
      - Location: **\\CM01\Sources\Software\Microsoft\MBAM 2.5 x64\MBAMClient.msi**

   b. For **General Information**, use the following settings and then click **Next** to continue:
      - Name: **MBAM 2.5 Client (x64 edition)**
      - Administrator comments: **<default>**
      - Publisher: **<default>**
      - Software version: **<default>**
      - Optional reference: **<default>**
      - Administrative categories: **<default>**
      - Installation program: **<default>**
      - Run installation and uninstall program as a 32-bit process on 64-bit clients: **<default>**
      - Install behavior: **Install for system if resource is a device otherwise install for user.**

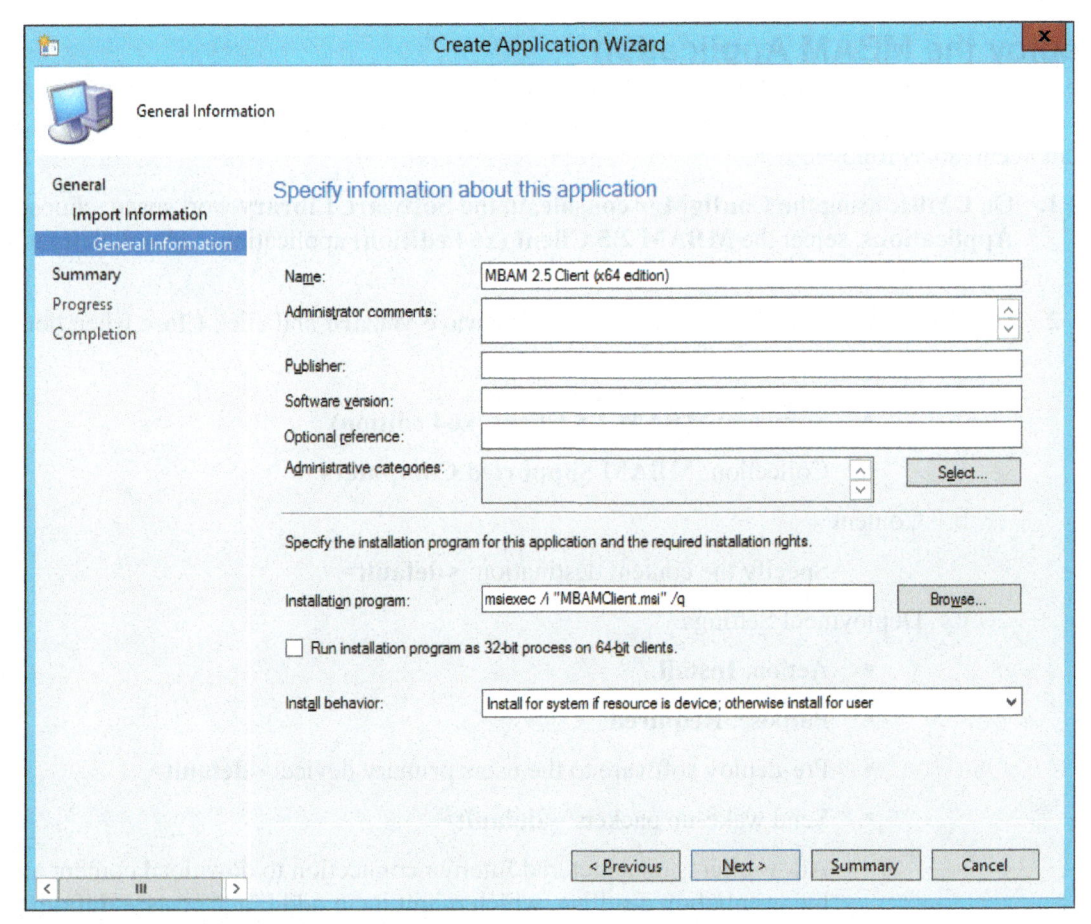

*Creating the MBAM 2.5 client application.*

4. Continue through the wizard until complete.

## Distribute the MBAM Application

In order for client computers to install the MBAM client agent, the content needs to be present on at least one distribution point. To distribute the content for the MBAM 2.5 client agent, follow this procedure:

1. On **CM01**, using the **ConfigMgr console**, expand the **Software Library** workspace, select **Application Management / Applications**, and then locate and select the **MBAM 2.5 Client (x64 edition)** application you created previously.

2. Right-click the application and choose **Distribute content**. Use the following setting for the **Distribute Content Wizard**:

    Content Destination: **CM01.CORP.VIAMONSTRA.COM**

3. Continue through the wizard until complete.

## Deploy the MBAM Application

Next, you want to deploy the MBAM application so that your MBAM-compatible computers get the agent installed and start enforcing the configured MBAM group policy. To deploy the MBAM client agent, do as follows:

1. On **CM01**, using the **ConfigMgr console**, in the **Software Library** workspace, choose **Applications**, select the **MBAM 2.5 Client (x64 edition)** application, right-click it, and choose **Deploy**.

2. Use the following settings for the **Deploy Software Wizard** and click **Close** when done:

    a. General

    - Software: **MBAM 2.5 Client (x64 edition)**
    - Collection: **MBAM Supported Computers**

    b. Content

    Specify the content destination: **<default>**

    c. Deployment Settings

    - Action: **Install**
    - Purpose: **Required**
    - Pre-deploy software to the users primary device: **<default>**
    - Send wake-up packets: **<default>**
    - Allow clients on a metered Internet connection to download content after the installation deadline, which might incur additional costs: **<default>**

    d. Scheduling

    **<default>**

    e. User Experience

    **<default>**

    f. Alerts

    **<default>**

    g. Distribution Points

    **<default>**

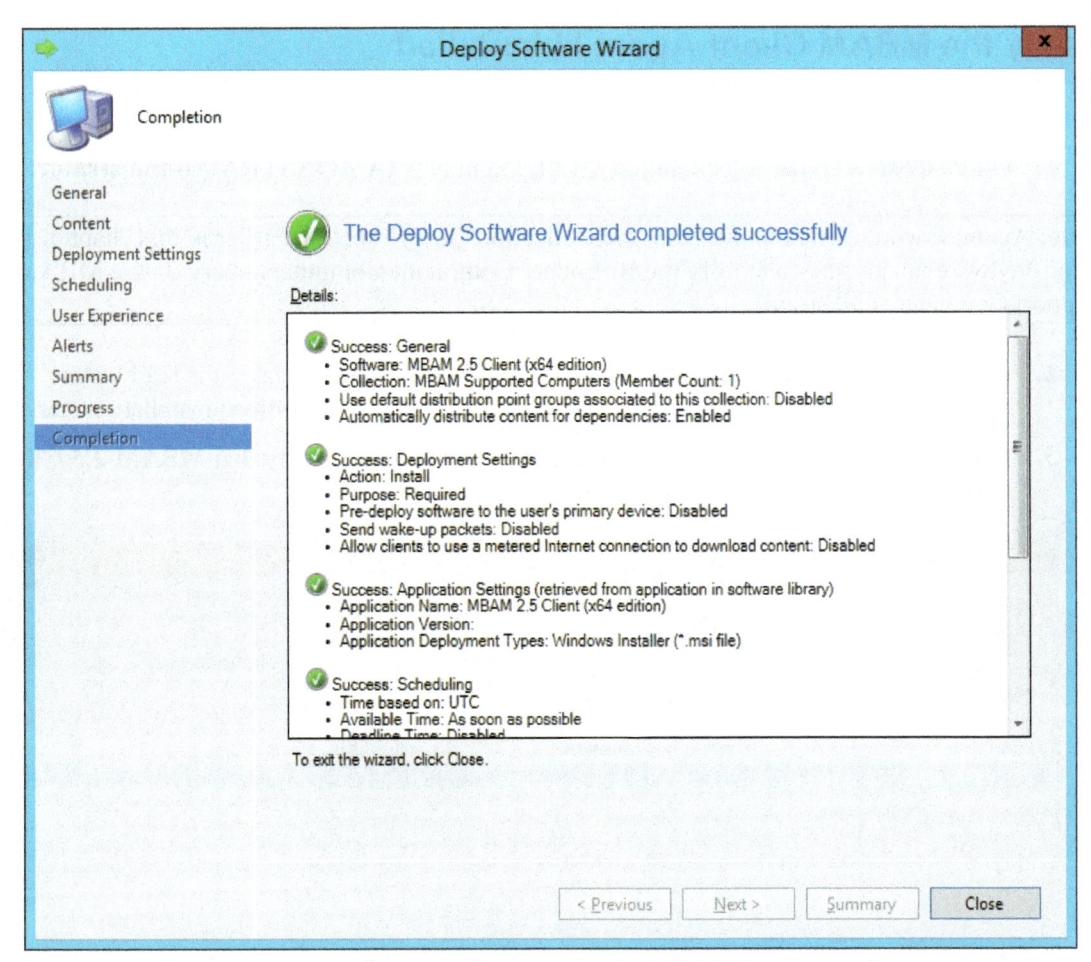

*The MBAM 2.5 Client (x64 edition) is deployed to the MBAM Supported Computers collection.*

## Verifying MBAM Client Agent Functionality

In this section, you see how to verify that the MBAM client agent is installed, check that the GPO settings are set, verify MBAM is retrieving policy, and enable BitLocker on a virtual machine without a Trusted Platform Module (TPM chip).

Saving the recovery key on a network share is not necessary on properly equipped hardware (hardware with a TPM) and is only done to prove the proof of concept. In addition, you learn how to verify that the MBAM client agent is correctly storing the recovery key ID in the MBAM database.

## Verify the MBAM Client Agent Is Installed

On a Hyper-V generation 2 virtual computer that has appeared in the MBAM Supported Computers collection, do as follows (I used the PC0001 machine in this example):

1. On **PC0001**, a Hyper-V generation 2 VM, log in as **VIAMONSTRA\Administrator**.

> **Note:** Again, as you learned in the "Edit the Collection Query" section earlier in this chapter, if using VMware, make sure to modify the BitLocker Compliant Computers query on the MBAM Support Computers collection.

2. If necessary, install the ConfigMgr agent on **PC0001**. When the agent is ready, start **Software Center** and wait until the **MBAM 2.5 Client (x64 edition)** installation starts.

3. In **Software Center**, select the **Installation Status** tab and verify that **MBAM 2.5 Client (x64 edition)** has installed.

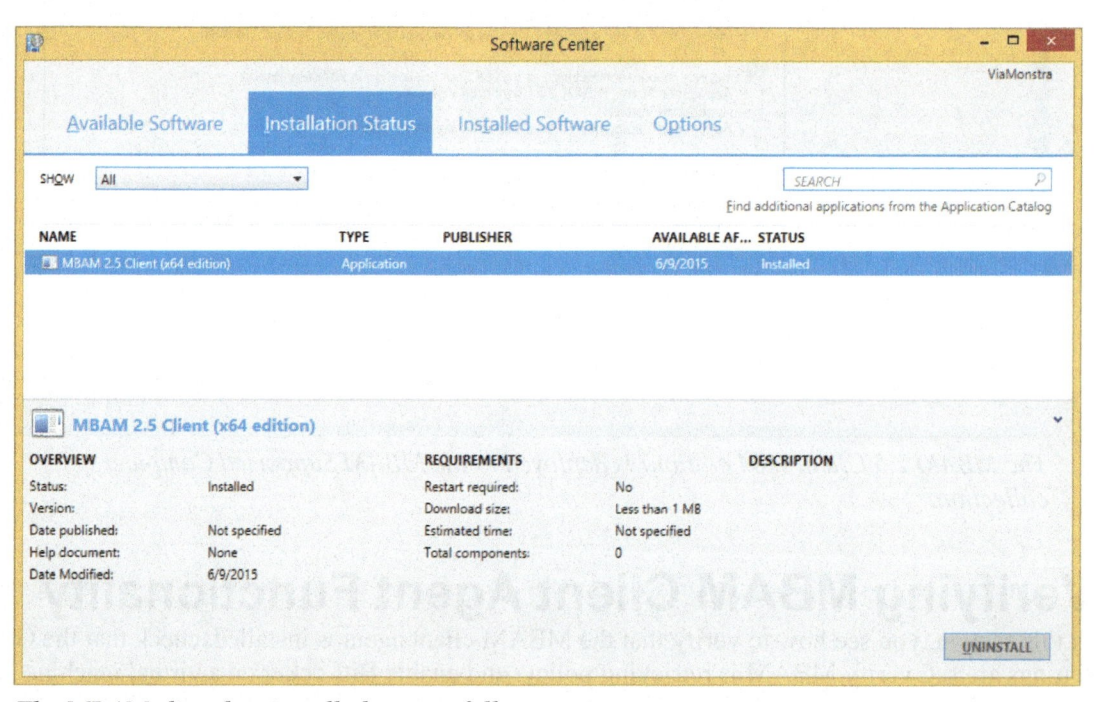

*The MBAM client has installed successfully.*

## Verify MBAM 2.5 BitLocker Policy

To verify that the computer has received the MBAM 2.5 BitLocker Policy GPO, do as follows:

1. On **PC0001**, using an elevated **Command prompt** (run as Administrator), enter the following:

   ```
   gpresult /v
   ```

Chapter 13 Enforcing BitLocker with MBAM 2.5

2. Scroll up and down through the results to verify the presence of the **MBAM 2.5 BitLocker Policy** GPOs as shown in the figure.

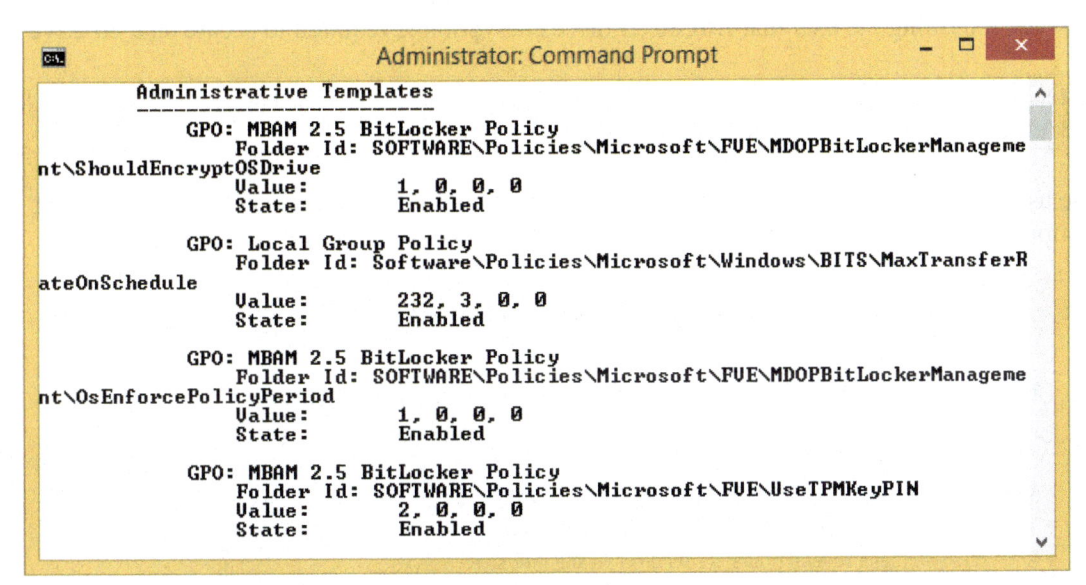

```
                Administrative Templates
                ------------------------
        GPO: MBAM 2.5 BitLocker Policy
            Folder Id: SOFTWARE\Policies\Microsoft\FVE\MDOPBitLockerManageme
nt\ShouldEncryptOSDrive
            Value:         1, 0, 0, 0
            State:         Enabled

        GPO: Local Group Policy
            Folder Id: Software\Policies\Microsoft\Windows\BITS\MaxTransferR
ateOnSchedule
            Value:         232, 3, 0, 0
            State:         Enabled

        GPO: MBAM 2.5 BitLocker Policy
            Folder Id: SOFTWARE\Policies\Microsoft\FVE\MDOPBitLockerManageme
nt\OsEnforcePolicyPeriod
            Value:         1, 0, 0, 0
            State:         Enabled

        GPO: MBAM 2.5 BitLocker Policy
            Folder Id: SOFTWARE\Policies\Microsoft\FVE\UseTPMKeyPIN
            Value:         2, 0, 0, 0
            State:         Enabled
```

*Verifying the MBAM GPO is applied using gpresult.*

3. To verify that the registry keys are set, using an elevated **Command prompt** (run as Administrator), open **regedit**. Browse to the following registry keys. These keys are set by the MBAM 2.5 BitLocker Policy GPO and govern how the MBAM client agent functions.

    o **[HKEY_LOCAL_MACHINE\SOFTWARE\Policies\Microsoft\FVE]**

    o **[HKEY_LOCAL_MACHINE\SOFTWARE\Policies\Microsoft\FVE\MDOP BitLockerManagement]**

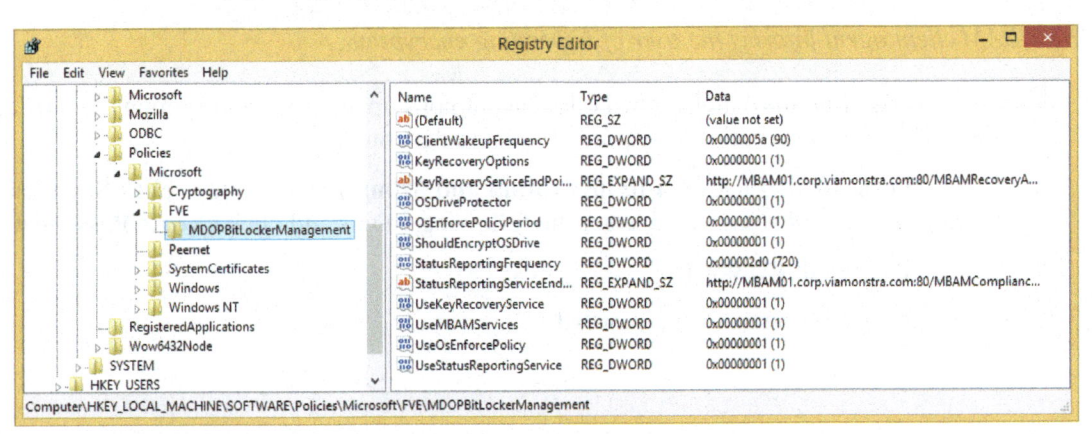

*The registry keys contain settings defined in the MBAM GPOs.*

341

## The MBAM Client Agent

After a computer with the MBAM client agent has received its policy, the agent pops up a message informing the user that BitLocker drive encryption is required to secure data on drive C:.

> **Note**: To speed up the MBAM client agent receiving policy, see the next section, "Speeding Up MBAM Policy Retrieval and Status Reporting in a Lab."

The user can postpone drive encryption by one day as configured in the GPO in the preceding section, or they can click Start to start the encryption process.

*The MBAM client agent informs the user of impending encryption.*

1. On **PC0001**, wait until the MBAM client agent pops up a message informing the user that BitLocker drive encryption is required to secure data on drive C:.

2. In the **Microsoft BitLocker Administration and Monitoring** window. click **Start**, and when prompted for a password, enter the following values and click **Create Password**:
   - Password: **P@ssw0rd**
   - Confirm password: **P@ssw0rd**

## Chapter 13  Enforcing BitLocker with MBAM 2.5

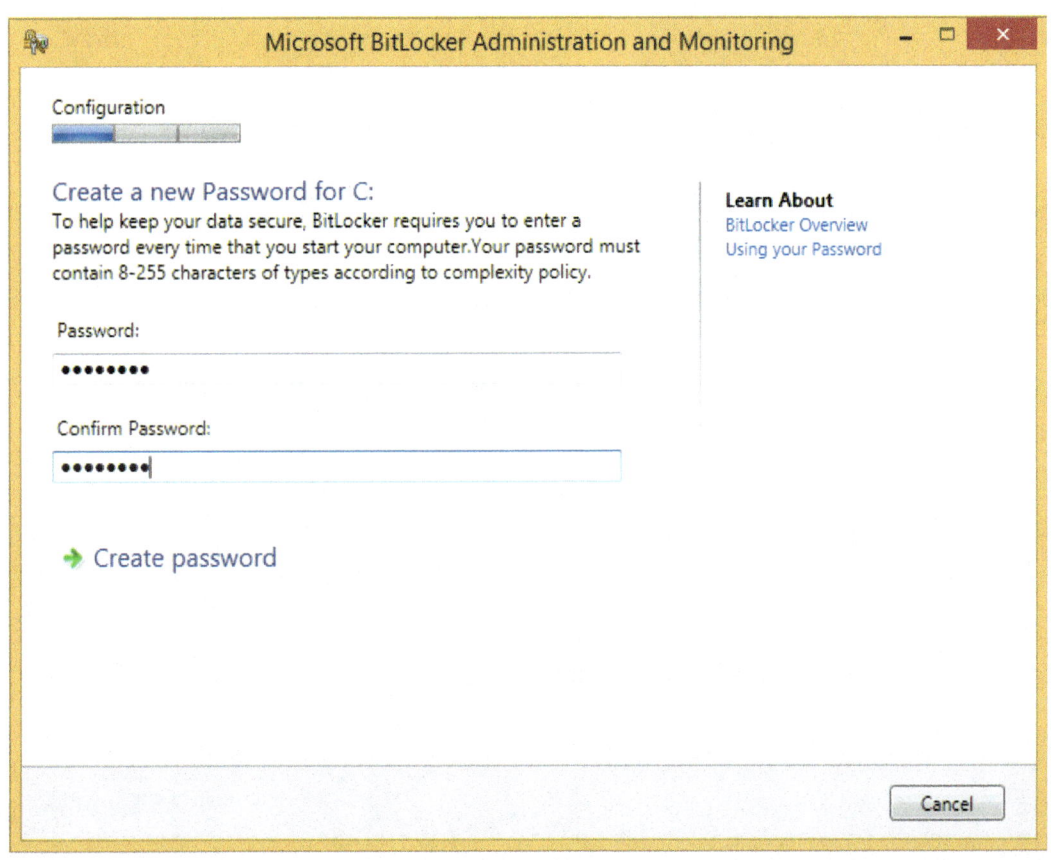

*Entering the password for drive C:, which wouldn't be required if the computer had a TPM.*

After a few moments the message in the following figure appears. This is normal for non-TPM-based virtual machines and can be safely ignored.

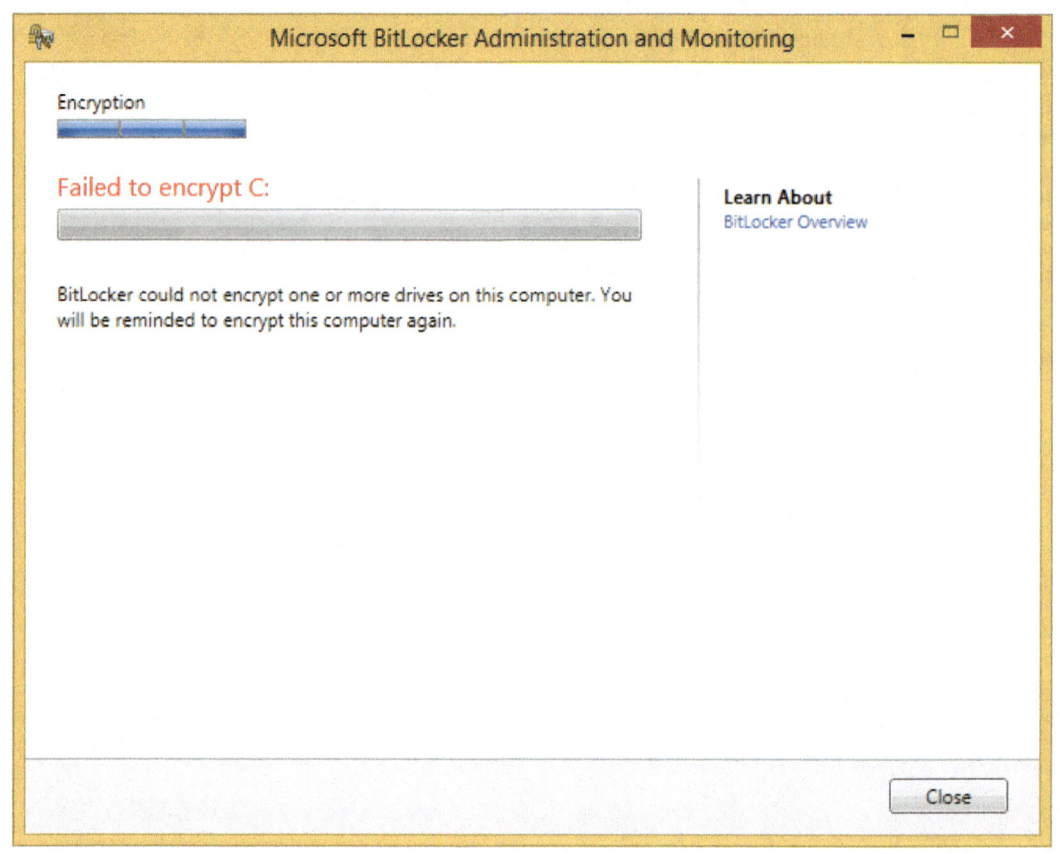

*The MBAM agent informs the user of encryption failure.*

## Speed Up MBAM Policy Retrieval and Status Reporting in a Lab (Only)

To speed up MBAM policy retrieval and status reporting, you can merge the registry settings in the following guide on a computer with the MBAM client agent installed in a lab. The registry settings are present in the NoStartupDelay.reg file that is part of this book's sample files. This is a useful way of speeding up the testing and verification of MBAM policy changes.

> **Real World Note**: Do not use these settings in production, as they make the MBAM client agent poll for policy every minute (instead of every 90 minutes). It also reports status to the MBAM database once a minute (instead of every 720 minutes). In addition, this can cause the MBAM agent to pop up once every minute until you have encrypted the operating system drive. Lastly, the registry settings do not take effect until the computer is restarted or the MBAM client agent service is restarted.

1. On **PC0001**, using the provided registry file, **NoStartupDelay.reg**, (available on E:\Setup\MBAM on CM01), double-click the file and answer **Yes** when prompted to make changes to the computer.

2. After applying the preceding registry settings, restart the MBAM client agent service running the following command in an elevated **Command prompt** (run as Administrator):

   ```
   net stop mbamagent & net start mbamagent
   ```

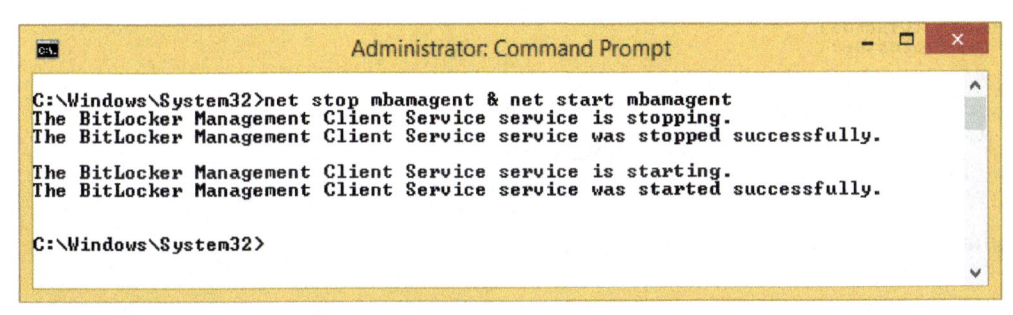

*Stopping and then restarting the MBAM client agent.*

## Verify That the MBAM Client Agent Is Storing Recovery Information in the MBAM Database

On a computer that both has the MBAM client agent installed and the operating system driver protected by BitLocker, you can verify that the MBAM client agent is sending the information correctly via the following process:

1. On a BitLocker encrypted virtual machine that has the MBAM client agent installed, open an elevated **Command prompt** (run as Administrator).

> **Note:** If you want to know how to enable BitLocker in a virtual machine, like PC0001, check out the "Enable BitLocker on Virtual Machines" section later in this chapter.

2. As you will want to test the storage and retrieval of BitLocker recovery keys using"

345

Chapter 13   Enforcing BitLocker with MBAM 2.5

3. Verify the recovery password by running the following command:

   ```
   Manage-bde -protectors -get C:
   ```

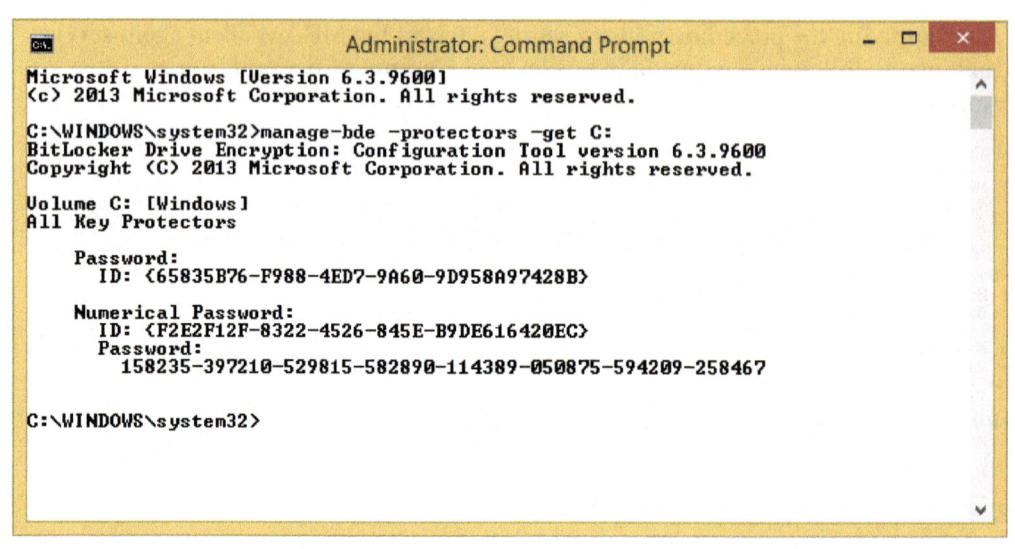

   ```
   Microsoft Windows [Version 6.3.9600]
   (c) 2013 Microsoft Corporation. All rights reserved.

   C:\WINDOWS\system32>manage-bde -protectors -get C:
   BitLocker Drive Encryption: Configuration Tool version 6.3.9600
   Copyright (C) 2013 Microsoft Corporation. All rights reserved.

   Volume C: [Windows]
   All Key Protectors

       Password:
         ID: {65835B76-F988-4ED7-9A60-9D958A97428B}

       Numerical Password:
         ID: {F2E2F12F-8322-4526-845E-B9DE616420EC}
         Password:
            158235-397210-529815-582890-114389-050875-594209-258467

   C:\WINDOWS\system32>
   ```

*Verifying the recovery password locally.*

Next, you can verify that the BitLocker recovery key ID is stored in the MBAM database. To verify, follow this process:

1. Log on to **MBAM01** using **ViaMonstra\MBAM_HD_AppPool** credentials, start **Microsoft SQL Server Management Studio**, and click **Connect** when prompted.

2. In **Object Explorer**, expand **Databases**, and expand the **MBAM Recovery and Hardware** database.

## Chapter 13  Enforcing BitLocker with MBAM 2.5

3. Expand the **Tables** node, then right-click the **RecoveryAndHardwareCore.Keys** table, and choose **Select Top 1000 Rows** from the menu.

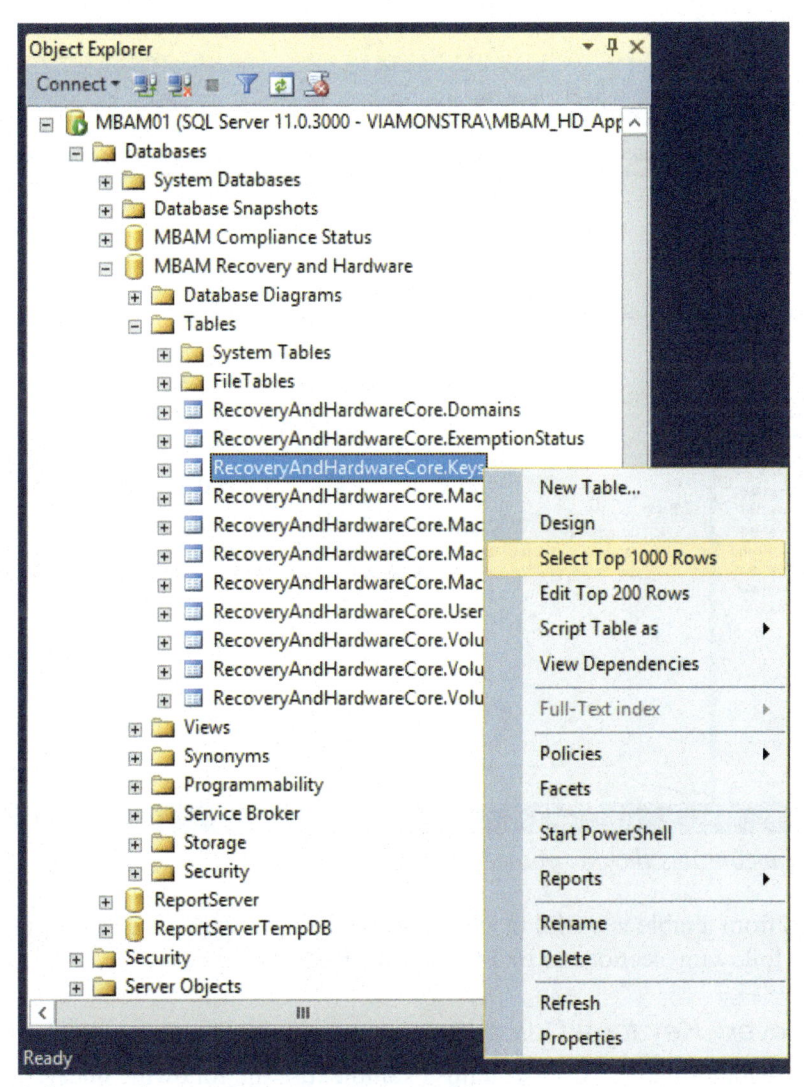

*Selecting the top 1000 rows from a table.*

Chapter 13   Enforcing BitLocker with MBAM 2.5

4. From the values listed, verify that at least one entry in the column labeled **RecoveryKey** matches the corresponding **Numerical Password: Password** field obtained on the client machine.

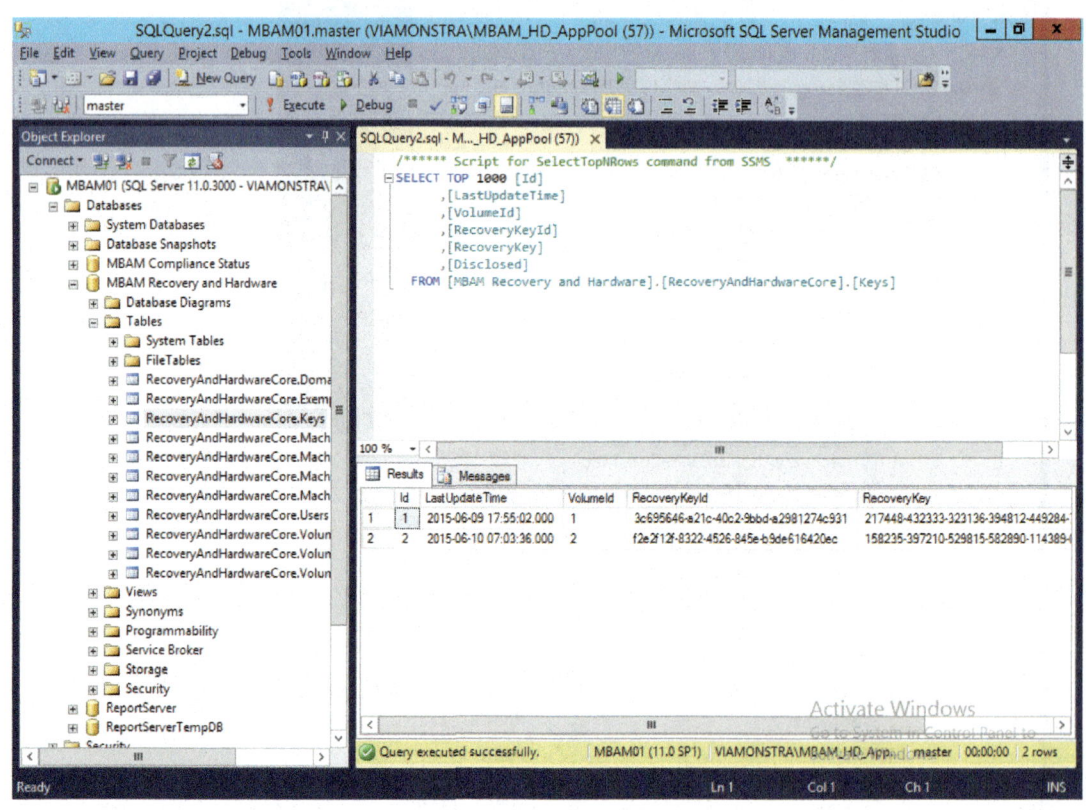

*The RecoveryKey column contains the info you need to verify.*

Selecting the top 1000 rows from a table is useful in a lab environment, but you may want to use queries such as those in the following sections to find the information more quickly.

### *Find the BitLocker Recovery Key for a Computer*

To find a system based on computer name, PC0001 in this example, use the following query:

```
use [MBAM Recovery and Hardware];

select a.Id, a.Name, b.VolumeId, c.RecoveryKeyId, c.RecoveryKey,
c.LastUpdateTime from RecoveryAndHardwareCore.machines a inner
join RecoveryAndHardwareCore.Machines_Volumes b ON a.Id =
b.MachineId inner join RecoveryAndHardwareCore.Keys c ON
b.VolumeId = c.VolumeId where a.name LIKE 'PC0001%'
```

## Chapter 13  Enforcing BitLocker with MBAM 2.5

### *Find the BitLocker Recovery Key Based on Date*

To find recovery details based on date added, use the following query:

```
use [MBAM Recovery and Hardware];

select a.Id, a.Name, b.VolumeId, c.RecoveryKeyId, c.RecoveryKey,
c.LastUpdateTime from RecoveryAndHardwareCore.machines a inner
join RecoveryAndHardwareCore.Machines_Volumes b ON a.Id =
b.MachineId inner join RecoveryAndHardwareCore.Keys c ON
b.VolumeId = c.VolumeId where c.LastUpdateTime >= '2015-06-10'
```

### *Find All BitLocker Recovery Keys for a Computer*

To find all recovery keys in MBAM by computer name, PC0001 in this example, use the following query:

```
use [MBAM Recovery and Hardware];

select a.Id, a.Name, b.VolumeId, c.RecoveryKeyId, c.RecoveryKey,
c.LastUpdateTime, c.Disclosed from
RecoveryAndHardwareCore.machines a inner join
RecoveryAndHardwareCore.Machines_Volumes b ON a.Id = b.MachineId
inner join RecoveryAndHardwareCore.Keys c ON b.VolumeId =
c.VolumeId where a.name = 'PC0001'
```

**Note:** Using Microsoft SQL Server Management Studio is useful for an administrator who knows what they are looking for; however, for end users, point them to the MBAM Self-Service Portal for retrieving recovery keys.

## Use the Self-Service Portal

The Self-Service Portal allows users to retrieve the BitLocker recovery key ID if they get locked out of their computers by BitLocker (which can occur if, for example, a motherboard is replaced). To use the Self-Service Portal, follow these steps:

1. On a computer that has access to the network, open **Internet Explorer** and browse to the following URL: **http://mbam01.corp.viamonstra.com/SelfService**.

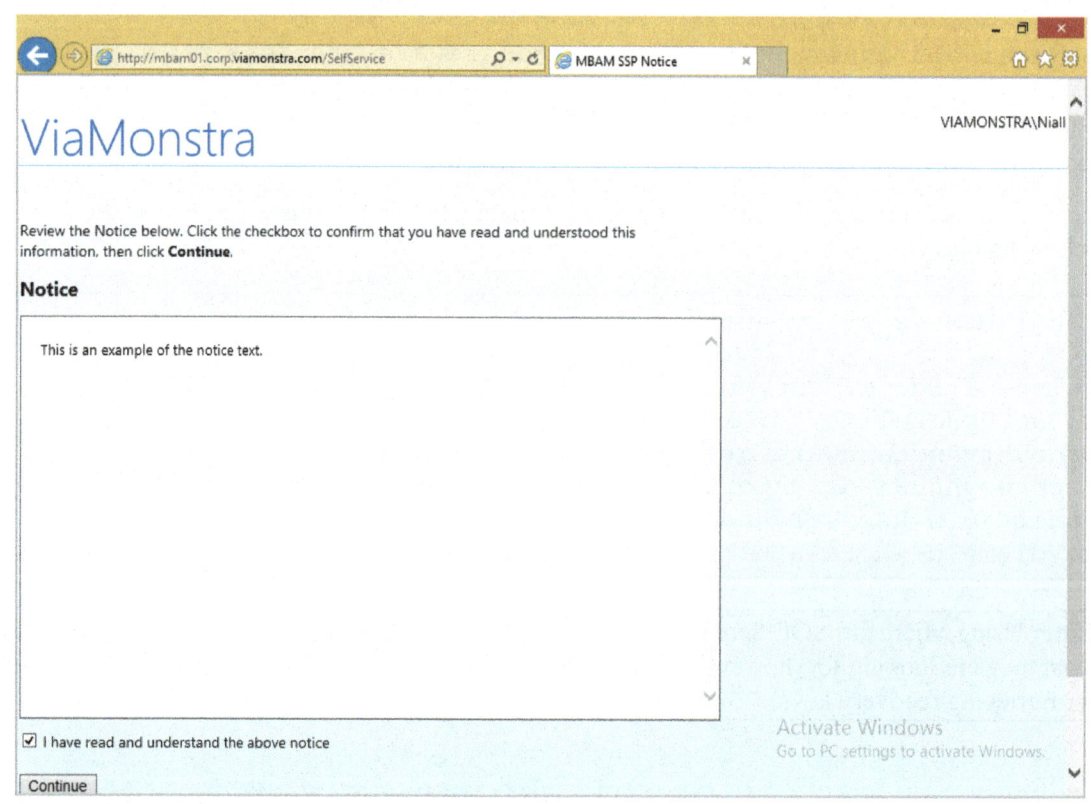

*The MBAM 2.5 Self-Service Portal.*

2. Accept the agreement by selecting the **I have read and understand the notice above** check box and then clicking **Continue**.

3. In the **Recovery Key ID** field, enter the first eight characters of the numerical password ID as shown on the **BitLocker recovery** screen. Select a reason from the **Reason** drop-down list and click **Get Key**.

> **Note:** If you need a reminder on how to get the Recovery Key ID, check the "Verify That the MBAM Client Agent Is Storing Recovery Information in the MBAM Database" section earlier in this chapter.

Chapter 13   Enforcing BitLocker with MBAM 2.5

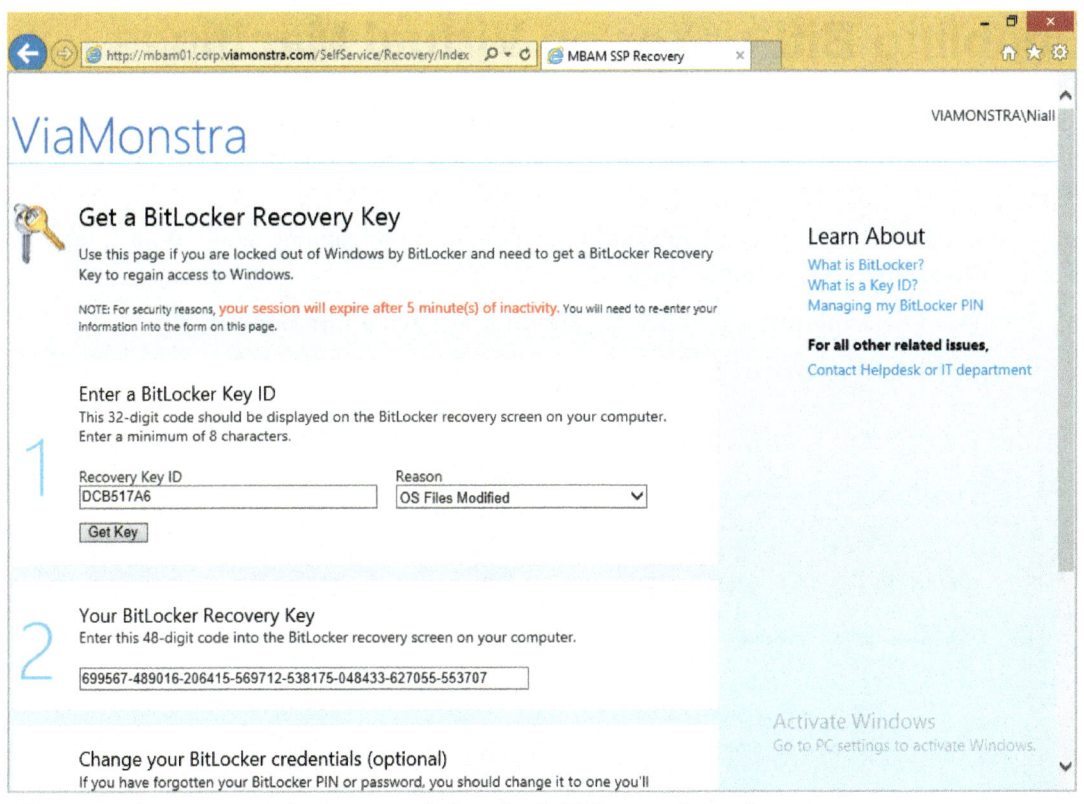

*The BitLocker recovery key is revealed in the Self-Service Portal.*

**Real World Note**: If the BitLocker recovery key has been revealed in the Self-Service Portal, it is changed by the MBAM client agent as soon as the computer boots back into the full operating system. The new BitLocker recovery key is also uploaded to the MBAM database.

# Enabling BitLocker on Virtual Machines

As you will want to test the storage and retrieval of BitLocker recovery keys using MBAM, you need one or more virtual machines to be encrypted with BitLocker. There are some manual steps involved as the machines don't have a TPM chip. To enable BitLocker on a Hyper-V Generation 2 virtual machine, do as follows:

1. On **PC0001**, a **Hyper-V Generation 2** virtual machine running Windows 8.1, log in as **VIAMONSTRA\Administrator**.
2. Open **File Explorer**, right-click **C:**, and choose **Turn on BitLocker**.

    The **BitLocker Drive Encryption** window appears.

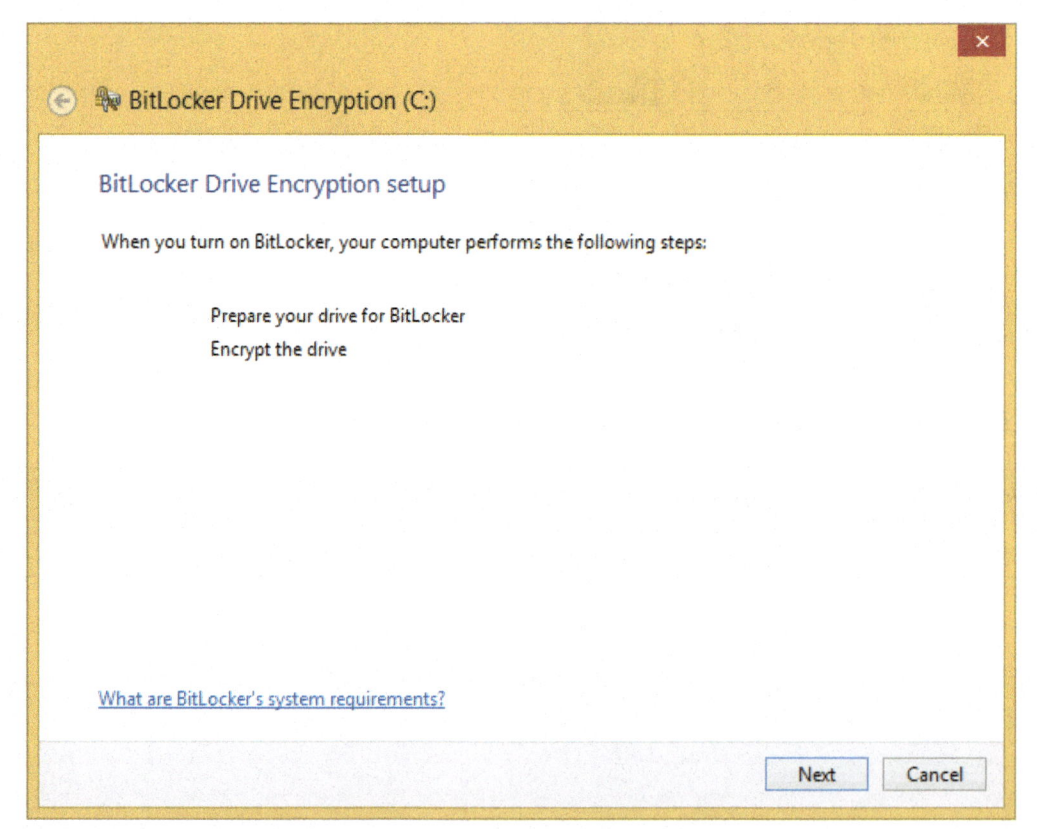

*BitLocker drive encryption being enabled via manual methods.*

3. Click **Next** to start the BitLocker drive preparations and encrypt the drive.

4. Select **Enter a password** from the options available, enter the following values, and then click **Create Password**:
   - Password: **P@ssw0rd**
   - Confirm password: **P@ssw0rd**

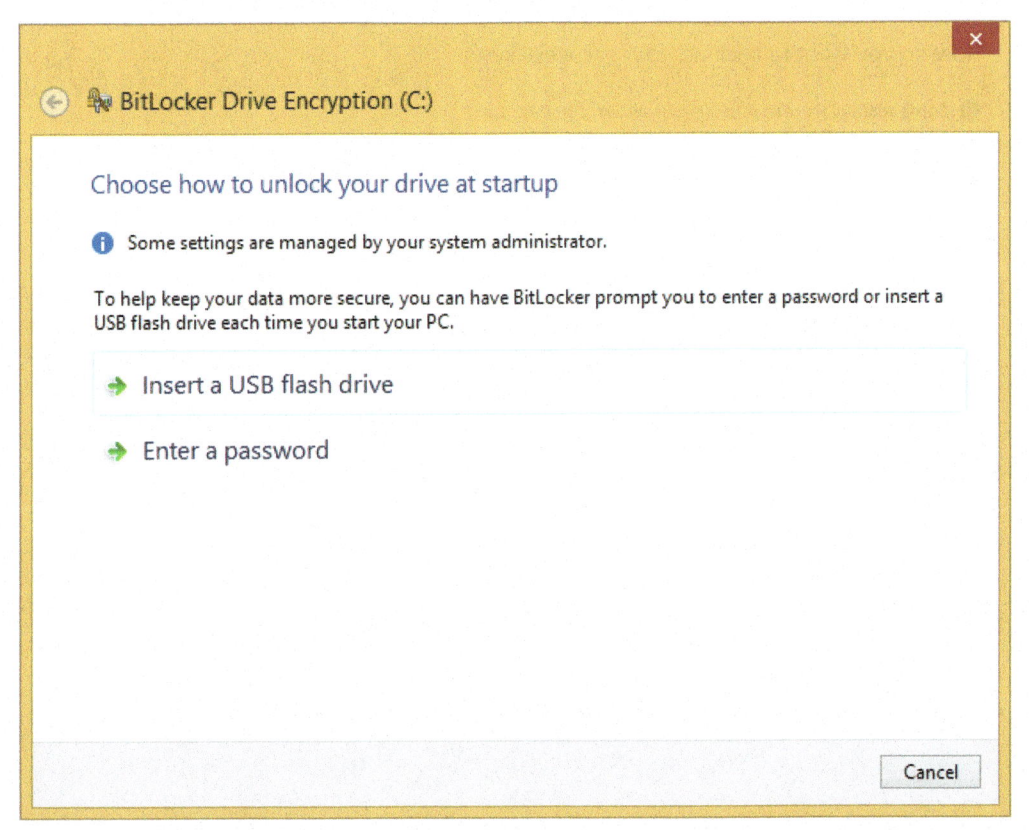

*Click Enter a password to continue, and then enter a password and confirm it.*

Chapter 13 Enforcing BitLocker with MBAM 2.5

5. When you are prompted for where to save the key, click **Save to a file**.

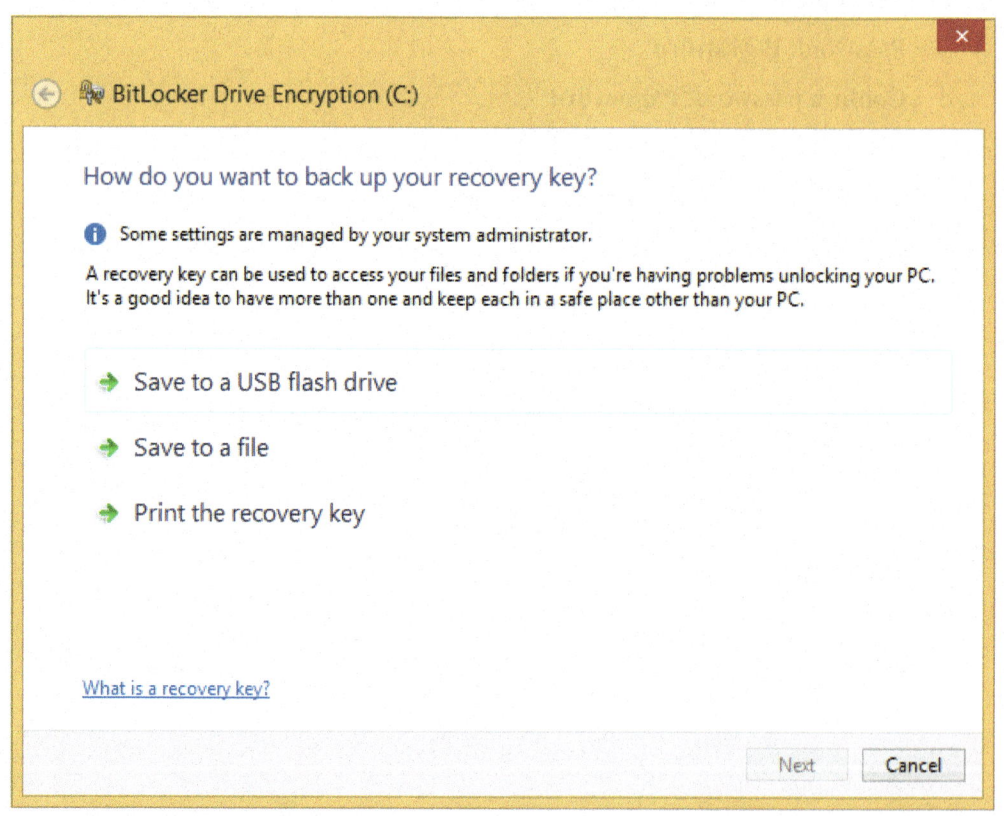

*Saving a copy of your recovery key is vital in case things go wrong.*

Chapter 13   Enforcing BitLocker with MBAM 2.5

6. On the **Save BitLocker recovery key as** screen, choose a network location, such as a share on the CM01 server to which you have write access.

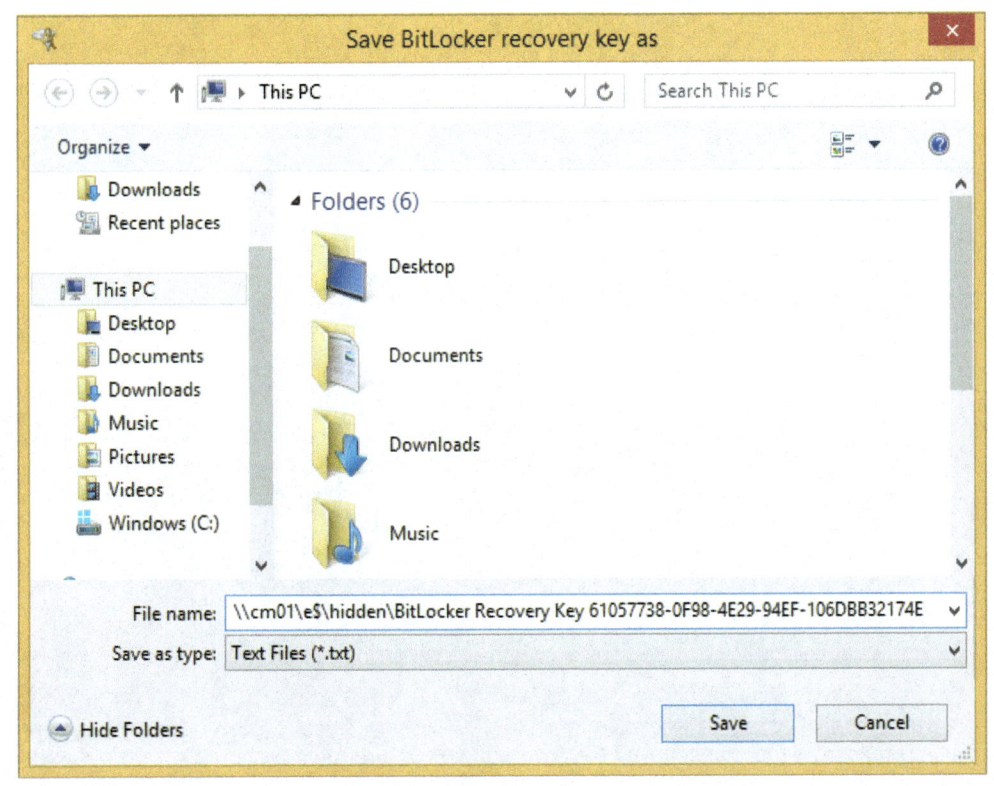

*Saving the recovery key to a share on CM01.*

7. After saving the recovery key to the network location, click **Next** and then click **Continue** to start the BitLocker checks. When prompted to restart the computer, click **Restart Now**.

8. After the restart, the computer prompts for the BitLocker password to unlock the drive; enter **P@ssw0rd** and press **Enter** to continue.

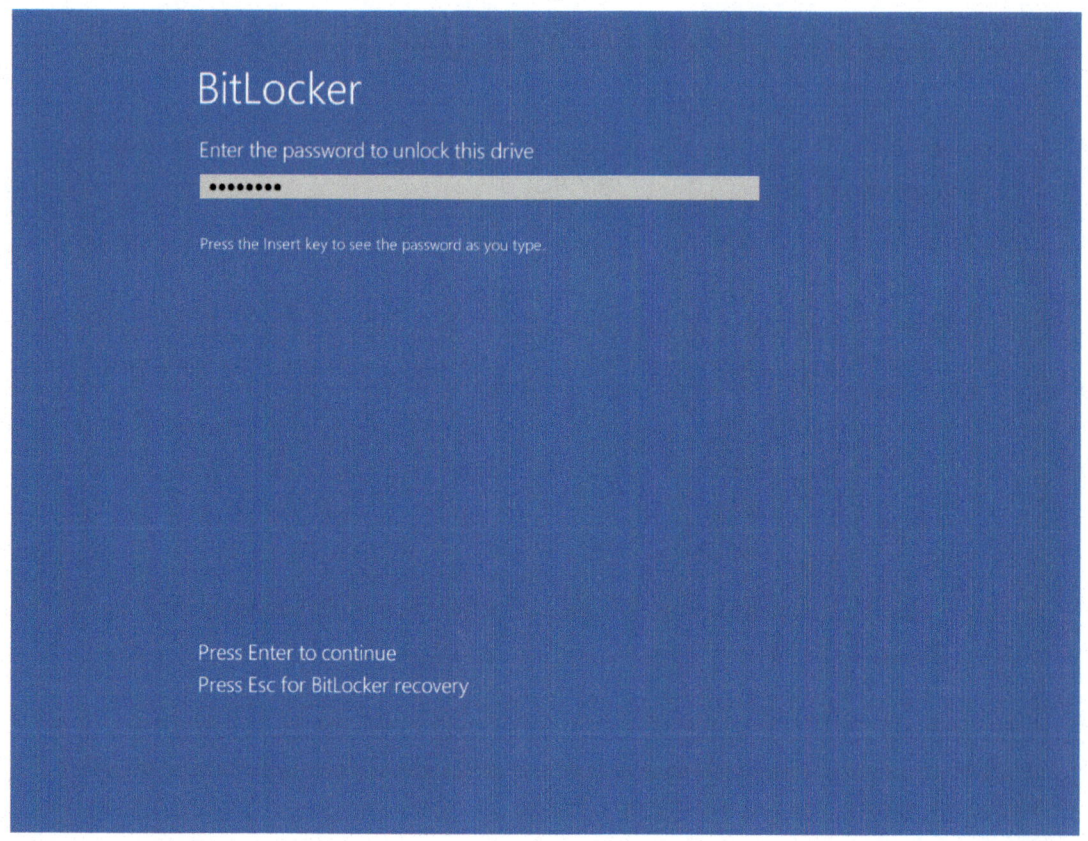

*BitLocker is prompting for a password to unlock the drive. This is normal when no TPM is available.*

## Verify BitLocker Encryption Status

On a virtual machine that has had BitLocker enabled and has the MBAM client agent installed, verify the status of the BitLocker encryption as follows:

1. On a virtual machine, log in to **Windows** using administrative credentials.

2. Open an elevated **Command prompt** (run as Administrator), and enter the following command to review the status of the encryption:

   ```
   Manage-bde -status
   ```

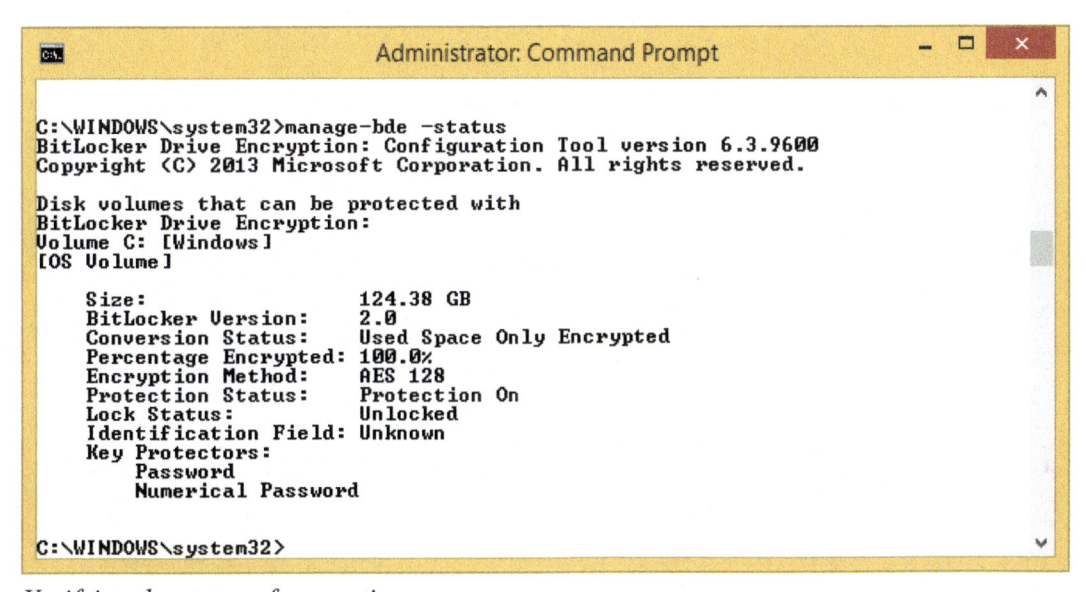

```
C:\WINDOWS\system32>manage-bde -status
BitLocker Drive Encryption: Configuration Tool version 6.3.9600
Copyright (C) 2013 Microsoft Corporation. All rights reserved.

Disk volumes that can be protected with
BitLocker Drive Encryption:
Volume C: [Windows]
[OS Volume]

    Size:                 124.38 GB
    BitLocker Version:    2.0
    Conversion Status:    Used Space Only Encrypted
    Percentage Encrypted: 100.0%
    Encryption Method:    AES 128
    Protection Status:    Protection On
    Lock Status:          Unlocked
    Identification Field: Unknown
    Key Protectors:
        Password
        Numerical Password

C:\WINDOWS\system32>
```

*Verifying the status of encryption.*

The Percentage Encrypted field should read 100.0%. If it does not, then wait a few minutes and check the status again.

# Chapter 14
# The CM12 UEFI BitLocker HTA

The CM12 UEFI BitLocker HTA is the Swiss Army knife of HTAs. The primary goal of the HTA is to supplement technicians who need to back up, reinstall, or perform new computer scenarios on BitLockered (encrypted) UEFI (or legacy) hardware.

When you think about all those new tablet devices out there today, they are more than likely UEFI only, and that presents challenges when BitLockered. This tool not only handles those modern devices but can deliver Hyper-V generation 2 virtual machines with BitLocker enabled out of the box.

All these features, however, require a decent backend, and the backend the HTA depends on runs web services and uses Microsoft BitLocker and Monitoring (MBAM) services. To get your organization into the 21st century for OSD, follow the guidance in this chapter.

## Step-by-Step Guide Requirements
If you want to follow the step-by-step guides in this chapter, you need a lab environment configured as outlined in Chapter 2 and Appendix A. In this chapter, you use the following virtual machines:

DC01    MBAM01    CM01    PC0001

*The VMs used in this chapter.*

You also need to have installed and configured MBAM 2.5 as described in Chapter 13.

## Adding a Web Service
Maik Koster's excellent Deployment Webservice (7.3) is used in this guide, and you install it on the CM01 server. The Webservice is included in the book sample files.

## Add a Web Service Service Account

In these steps, you create a new Active Directory user account in the ViaMonstra\Users OU called CM_WS. This user is used by the DeploymentWebService application pool later in this chapter.

1. On **DC01**, log in as **VIAMONSTRA\Administrator** using a password of **P@ssw0rd**.

2. Using **Active Directory User and Computers**, in the **ViaMonstra / Service Accounts** OU, create a user with the following settings:

    a. Name: **CM_WS**

    b. Password: **P@ssw0rd**

    c. Clear the **User must change password at next logon** check box.

    d. Select the **User cannot change password** check box.

    e. Select the **Password never expires** check box.

    f. Description: **Deployment WebService Account**

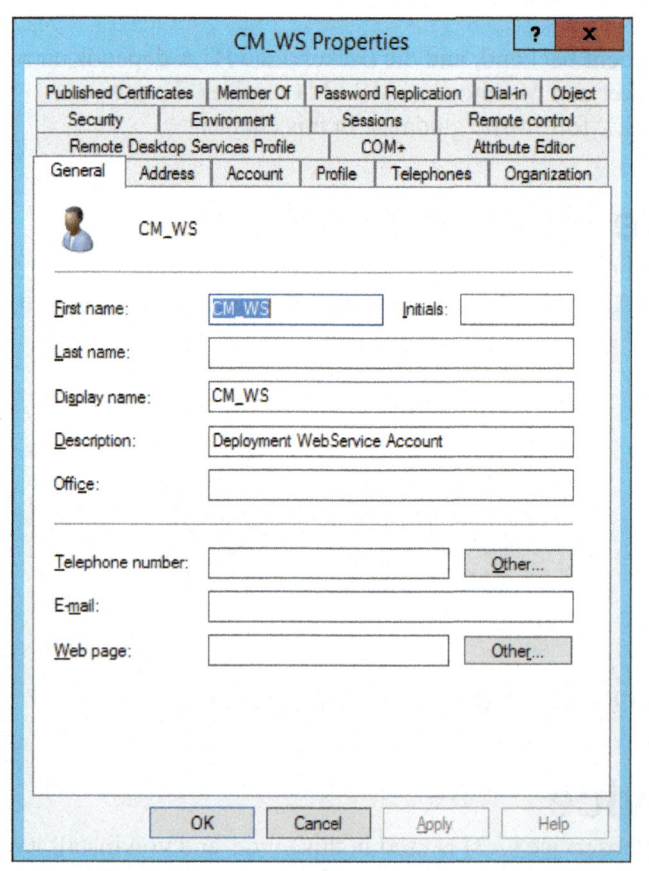

*The CM_WS Service account properties in Active Directory.*

Chapter 14   The CM12 UEFI BitLocker HTA

## Prepare Maik Koster's Deployment Webservice Version 7.3

In this guide I assume you have extracted the book sample files to E:\Setup on CM01.

1. On **CM01**, using **File Explorer**, create the **E:\ViaMonstraWebServices\DeploymentWebService** folder structure and assign the **ViaMonstra\CM_WS** account **Modify** permissions to it (NTFS Permissions).

2. Using **File Explorer**, copy the contents in **E:\Setup\MaikKoster.Deployment.Webservice_v7_3** to **E:\ViaMonstraWebServices\DeploymentWebService** as shown in the figure.

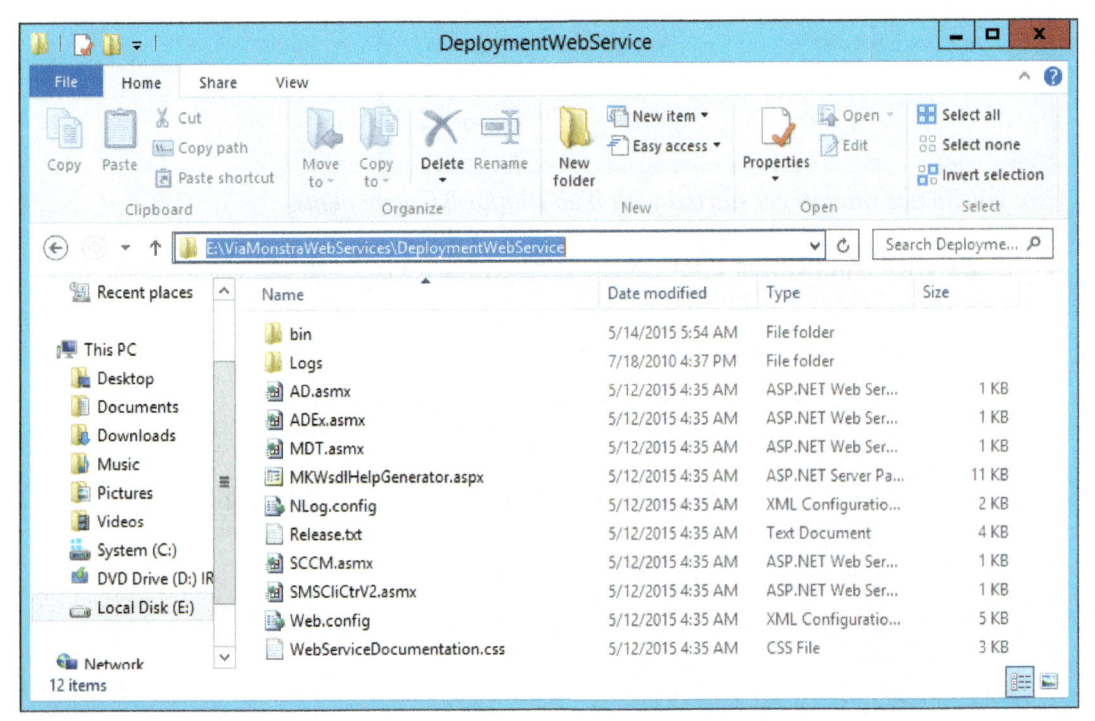

*The extracted files are copied to the DeploymentWebService folder.*

361

## Add an Application Pool

To add Deployment Webservice as a new application pool in IIS, follow this process:

1. On **CM01**, start **Internet Information Services Manager**. If you get prompted for **Web Platform Components**, select the **Do not show this message** check box and click **No**.

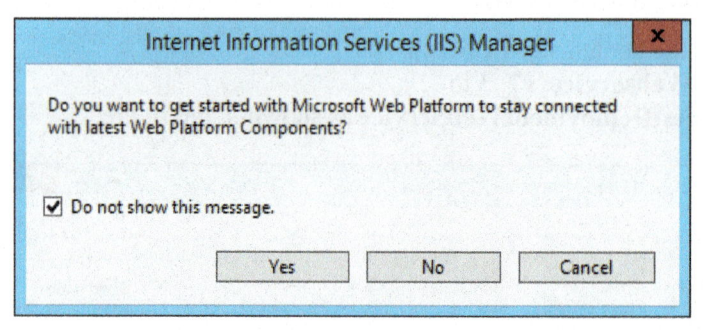

*No, you do not want to get started with Web Platform Components.*

2. Right-click **Application Pools**, select **Add Application Pool**, and use the following settings with the new application pool:

    a. Name: **DeploymentWebService**

    b. .NET CLR version: **.NET CLR Version v4.0.30319**

    c. Managed pipeline mode: **Integrated**

    d. Select the **Start application pool immediately** check box and click **OK**.

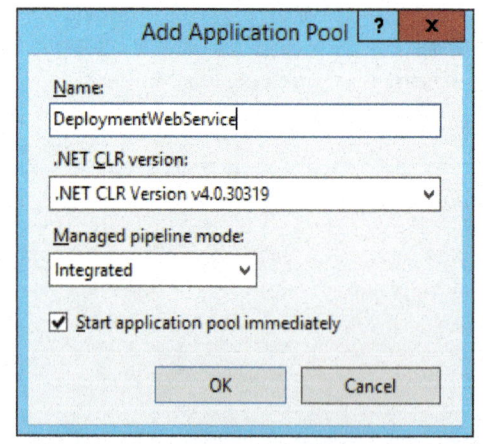

*Adding the DeploymentWebService application pool.*

3. Select the **Application Pools** node, right-click the new **DeploymentWebService** application pool, and select **Advanced Settings**.

4. Click the **Identity** line and then click the **browse** button (…).

# Chapter 14   The CM12 UEFI BitLocker HTA

5. Select **Custom Account** and click **Set**. Use the following settings for the **Set Credentials** dialog box:

    a. Username: **VIAMONSTRA\CM_WS**

    b. Password: **P@ssw0rd**

    c. Click **OK** twice.

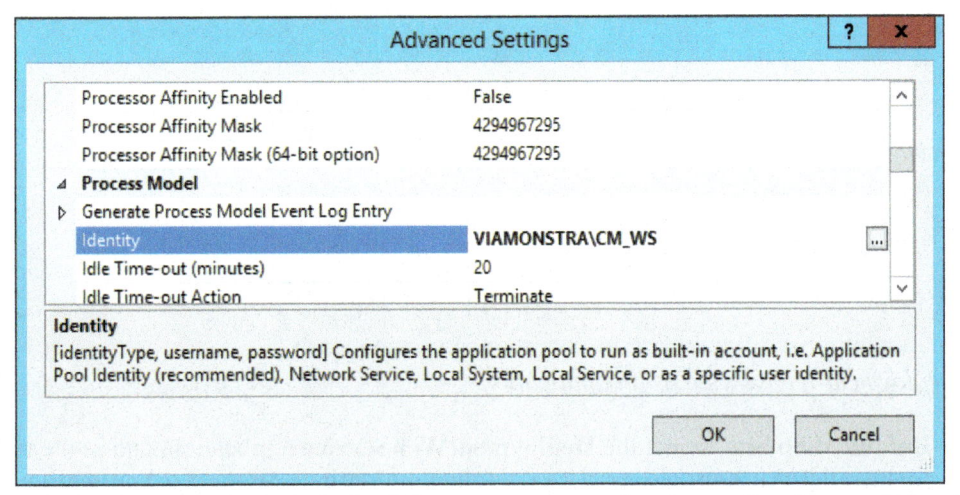

*Adding the VIAMONSTRA\CM_WS service account for the application pool identity.*

## Install Deployment Webservice
Everything is in place to install Deployment Webservice. Follow these steps to install the web service:

1. On **CM01**, using **Internet Information Services Manager**, expand **Sites**, right-click **Default Web Site**, and choose **Add Application**. Use the following settings for the application:

    a. Alias: **DeploymentWebService**

    b. Application pool: **DeploymentWebService**

    c. Physical path: **E:\ViaMonstraWebServices\DeploymentWebService**

    d. Click **OK**.

363

Chapter 14   The CM12 UEFI BitLocker HTA

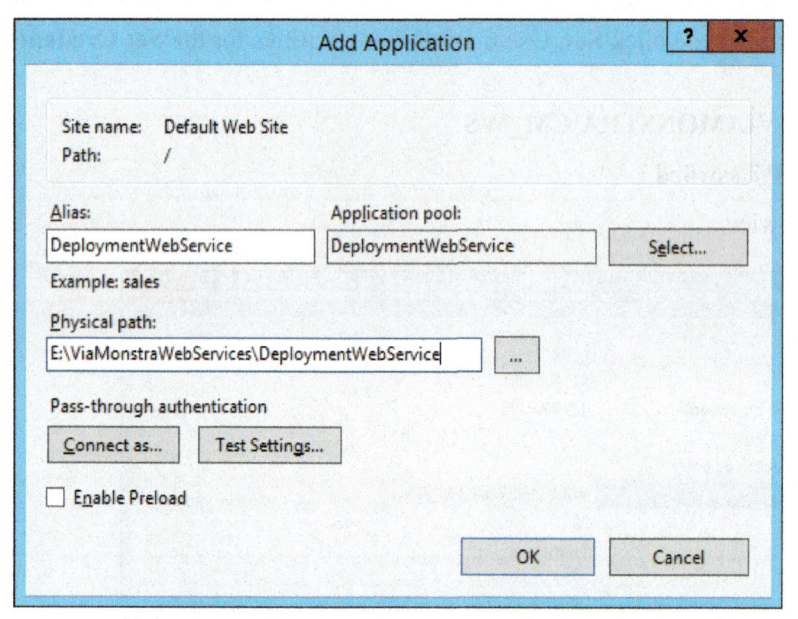

*Adding Deployment Webservice as an application.*

2. In the **Default Web Site**, select the **DeploymentWebService** application, and in the right pane, double-click **Authentication**. Use the following settings for the **Authentication** dialog box:

    a. Anonymous Authentication: **Disabled**

    b. ASP.NET Impersonation: **Disabled**

    c. Forms Authentication: **Disabled**

    d. Windows Authentication: **Enabled**

Chapter 14   The CM12 UEFI BitLocker HTA

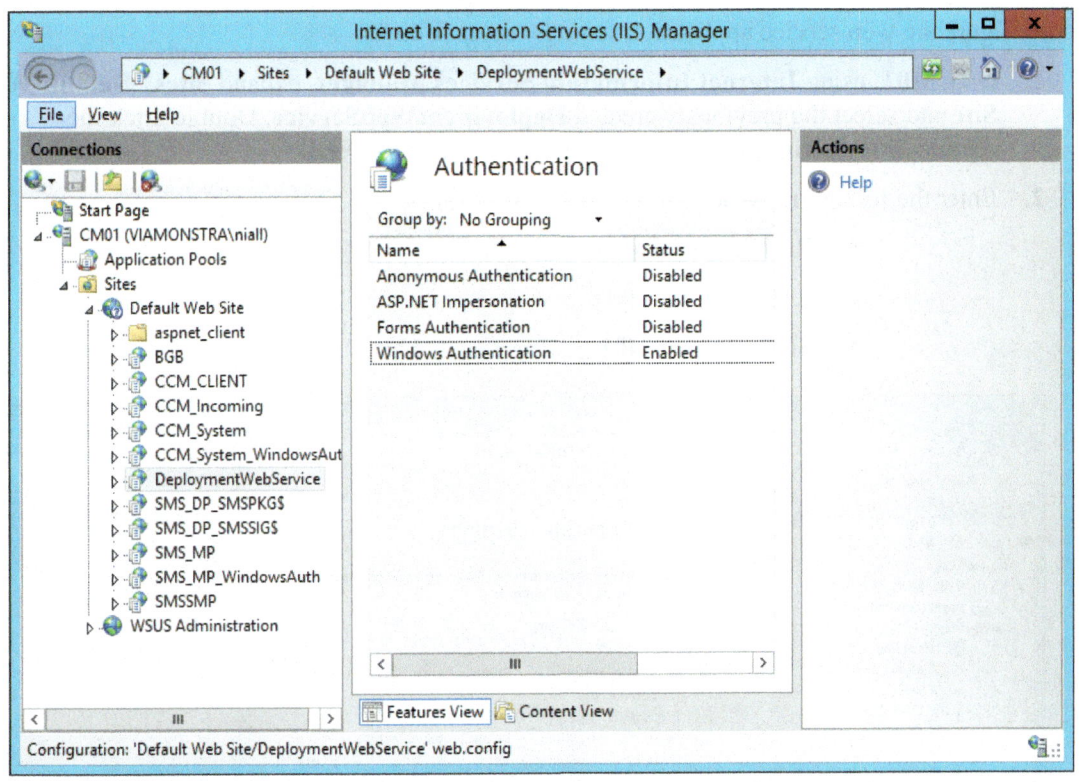

*Configuring the Deployment Webservice authentication settings.*

## Configure Application Settings

Next, you need to configure the web service application settings, failure to do so means the web service cannot do anything as it won't be able to communicate with your ConfigMgr site server.

By default, the web service uses the configured application pool user for authentication. It requires only a couple of application settings to be set:

- **RootServer**: The ConfigMgr primary site server
- **RootSiteCode**: The ConfigMgr site code
- **SLPServer**: One ConfigMgr server with the Server Locator Point (SLP) role

**Real World Note:** In ConfigMgr 2012, the Server Locator Point (SLP) role is no longer available, and its functionality is moved to the Management Point (MP) role.

To configure the web service application settings, do as follows:

1. On **CM01**, using **Internet Information Services Manager**, expand **Sites / Default Web Site** and select the previously created **DeploymentWebService**. Double-click the **Application Settings** icon in the right pane under **ASP.NET**.

2. Enter the following values for the specified settings:
    - RootServer: **CM01**
    - RootSiteCode: **PS1**
    - SLPServer: **CM01**

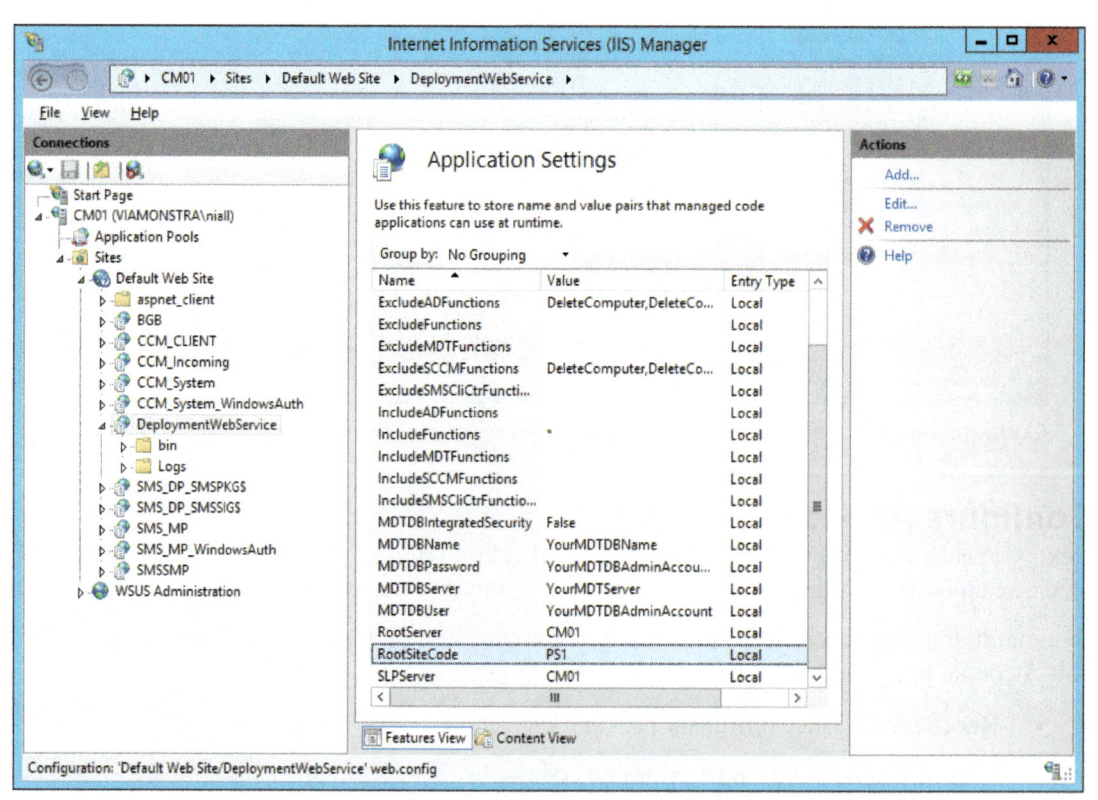

*Configuring application settings for Deployment Webservice.*

## Add the Web Service User to ConfigMgr

In order for the web service user account to search for computers (and other actions on the site server), it needs to be granted a role. To do this, follow these steps:

1. On **CM01**, using the **ConfigMgr console**, in the **Administration** workspace, select **Security / Administrative Users**. Right-click and choose **Add User or Group**.

2. For **User or group name**, click **Browse** and use **VIAMONSTRA\CM_WS**.

3. For **Assigned Security roles**, click **Add** and choose **Operating System Deployment Manager**. Click **OK** to close the **Add User or Group** wizard.

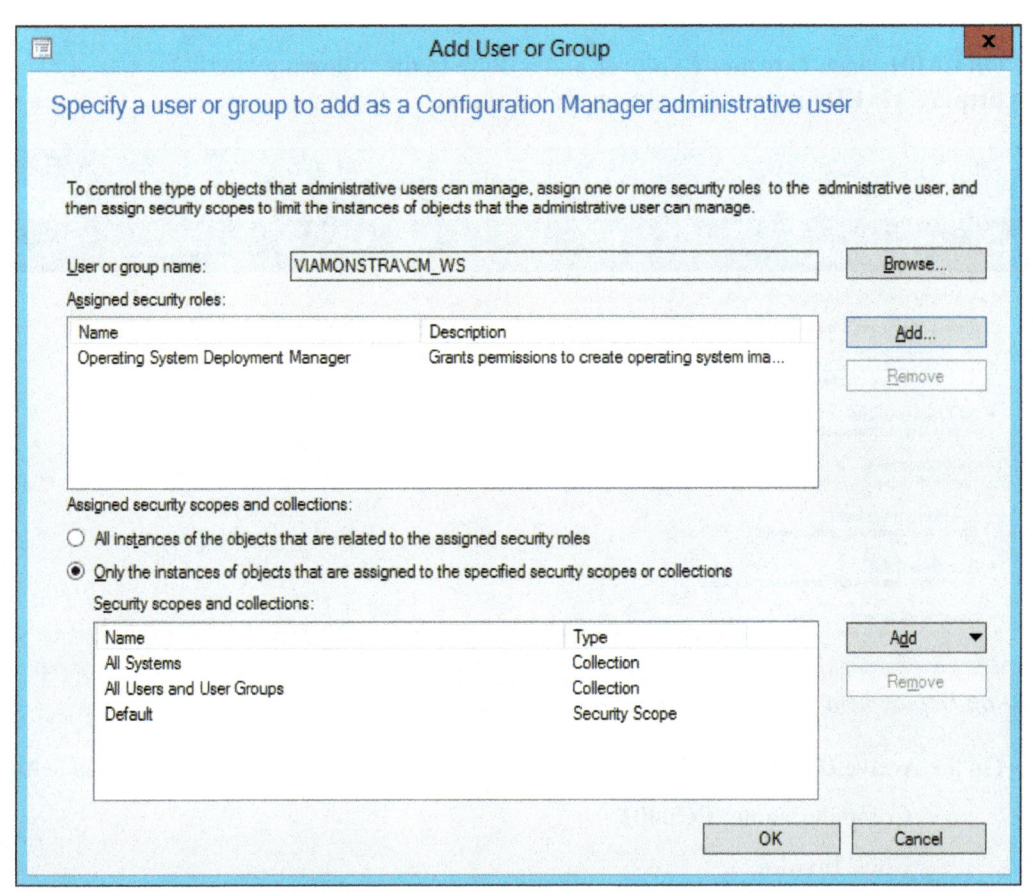

*Adding the Deployment Webservice user to ConfigMgr.*

## Test the Web Service

Now that you've installed Deployment Webservice, it's time to test it. To quickly test it, follow this process:

1. On **CM01**, open **Internet Explorer** and browse to the following URL: **http://CM01/DeploymentWebService/ad.asmx**.

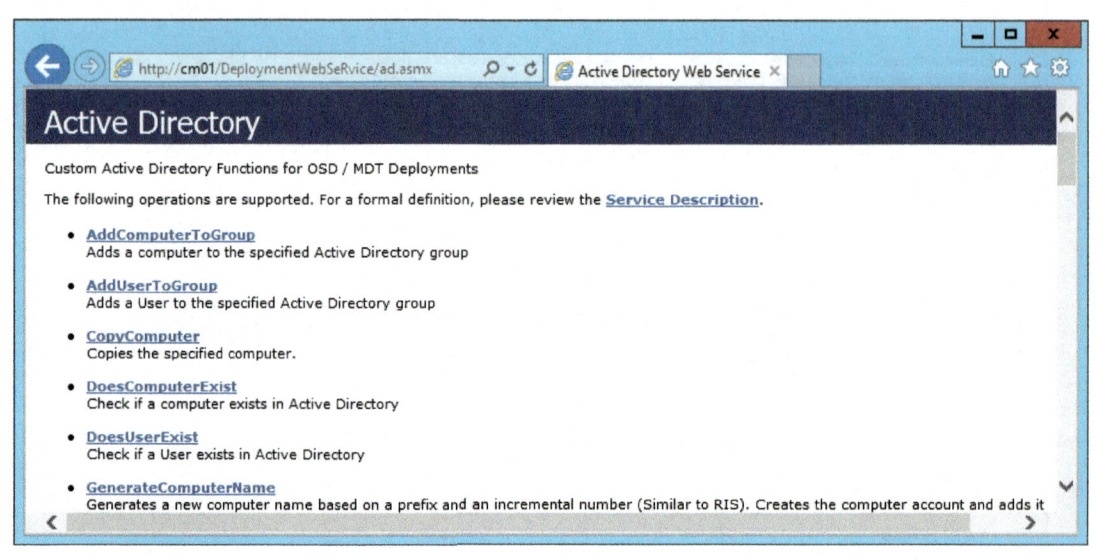

*Testing Deployment Webservice using Internet Explorer.*

2. On the **Active Directory** page, select **DoesComputerExist** and use the following settings:

    a. ComputerName: **PC0001**

    b. Click **Invoke**.

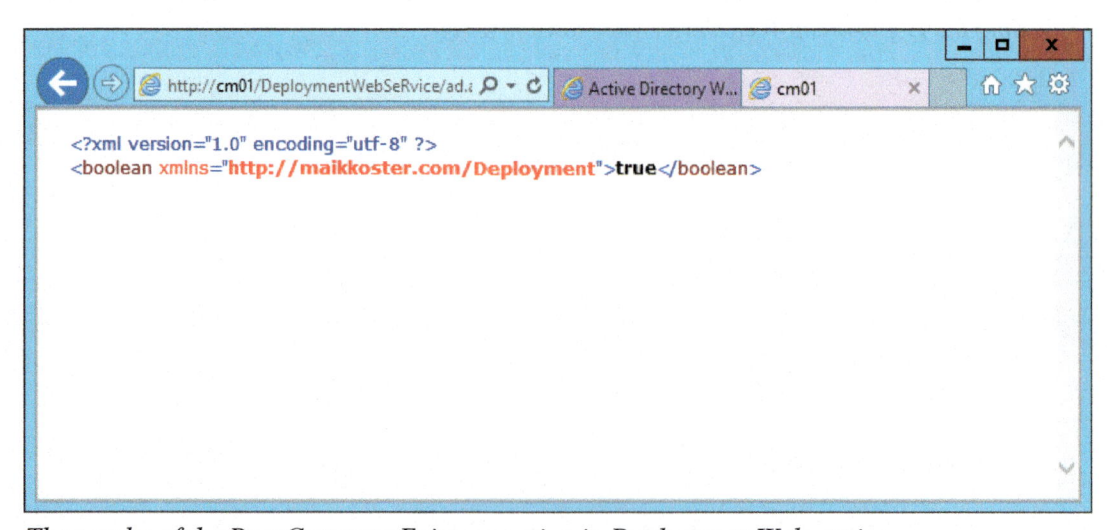

*The results of the DoesComputerExist operation in Deployment Webservice.*

# Adding Language Packs

Microsoft provides language packs to extend the language capabilities of its operating systems. All installations of Windows 8.1 contain at least one language pack and the language-neutral binaries that make up the core operating system. Additional language packs can be downloaded and installed as necessary either via Windows Update or directly from the MSDN or the Volume Licensing Service Center (https://microsoft.com/Licensing/servicecenter/default.aspx).

The CM12 UEFI BitLocker HTA offers you the ability to install one or multiple language packs by selecting the appropriate drop-down menu in either reinstall or new computer scenarios.

## Download the ISO

To download the ISO containing 36 language packs for Windows 8.1, do as follows:

1. On **CM01**, using **Internet Explorer**, browse to **http://msdn.com** or your **Volume License Service Center** and log in using adequate credentials. Search for **Windows 8.1 Language Pack with Update (x64) - DVD (Multiple Languages)**.

2. Click **Download** to the right of the ISO to start the download. Save the file to somewhere useful.

## Create Language Pack Folders

To create language pack folders for all the languages you intend to support, do as follows:

1. On **CM01**, using **File Explorer**, create the **E:\Sources\Software\Microsoft\Windows 8.1 Language Packs with update (x64)** folder structure.

2. In the **Windows 8.1 Language Packs with update (x64)** folder, create a folder for each language you intend to support (e.g. Danish, Swedish, Finnish, Norwegian, and German).

3. In addition to these folders, create a separate folder called **Multi**. This special folder will contain all the language packs you intend to support.

Chapter 14   The CM12 UEFI BitLocker HTA

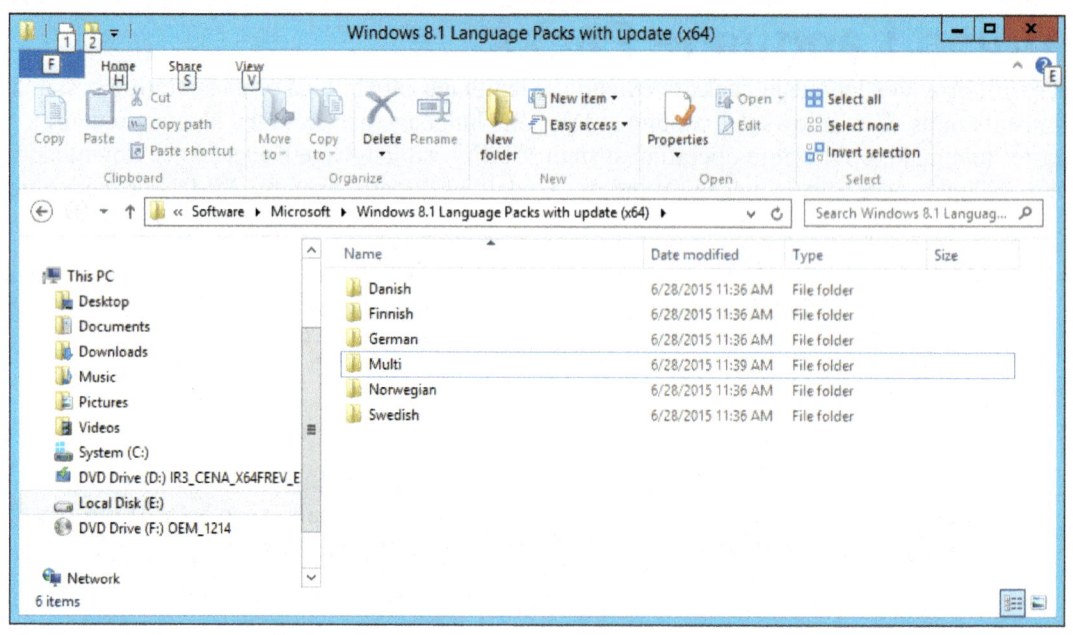

*Creating folders named after the languages you intend to support in which you later place the language pack files.*

## Extract the Language Packs

To extract the language packs from the downloaded ISO, do as follows:

1. On **CM01**, using **File Explorer**, mount the **Windows 8.1 Language Pack with Update (x64)** ISO (mu_windows_8.1_language_pack_with_update_x64_dvd_6066963.iso) by right-clicking the file and select **Mount**.

2. In the mounted drive that appears, select a language pack that you intend to offer, such as Danish (**da-dk**), from the 36 available language packs and copy it by pressing **Ctrl + C**.

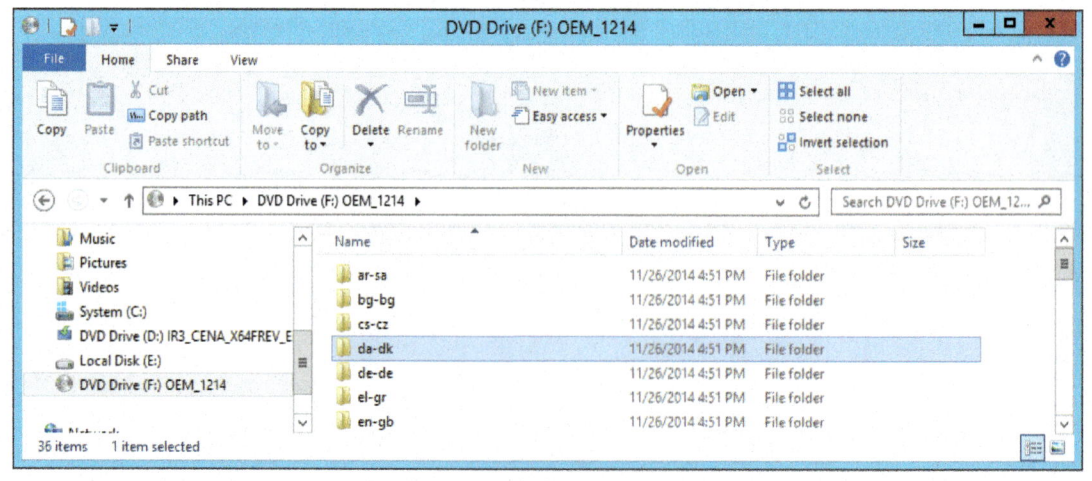

*Copying one language pack from the mounted ISO.*

370

# Chapter 14  The CM12 UEFI BitLocker HTA

3. Using **File Explorer**, paste the selected language pack into its corresponding language pack folder name by pressing **Ctrl + V**.

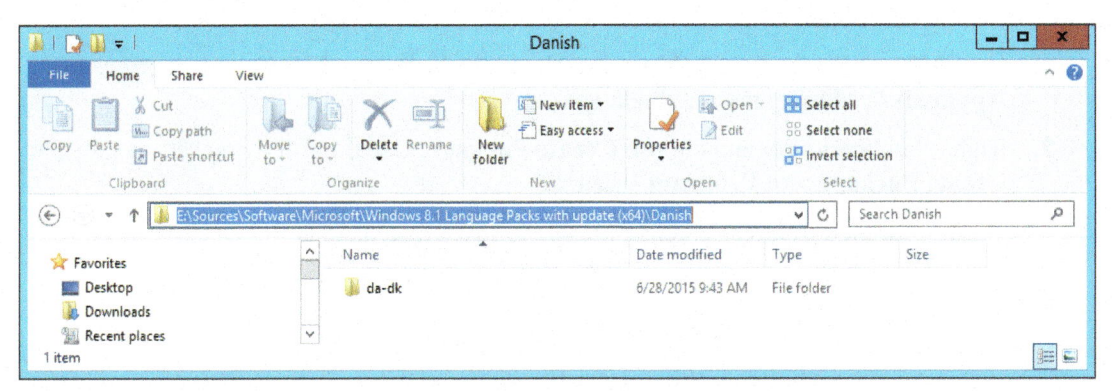

*Pasting the da-dk language pack into the Danish language pack folder.*

4. Repeat the process for each language pack you intend to support so that the correct language pack files are populated in a folder matching the language pack name.

The Multi folder is a little bit special and should contain an additional copy of each language pack you want to make available in case the user selects the option to install multiple language packs. Populate the Multi folder by doing as follows:

1. On **CM01**, using **File Explorer**, copy the language pack files you intend to support from the mounted ISO and into the **Multi** folder located in **Microsoft\Windows 8.1 Language Packs with update (x64)\Multi**.

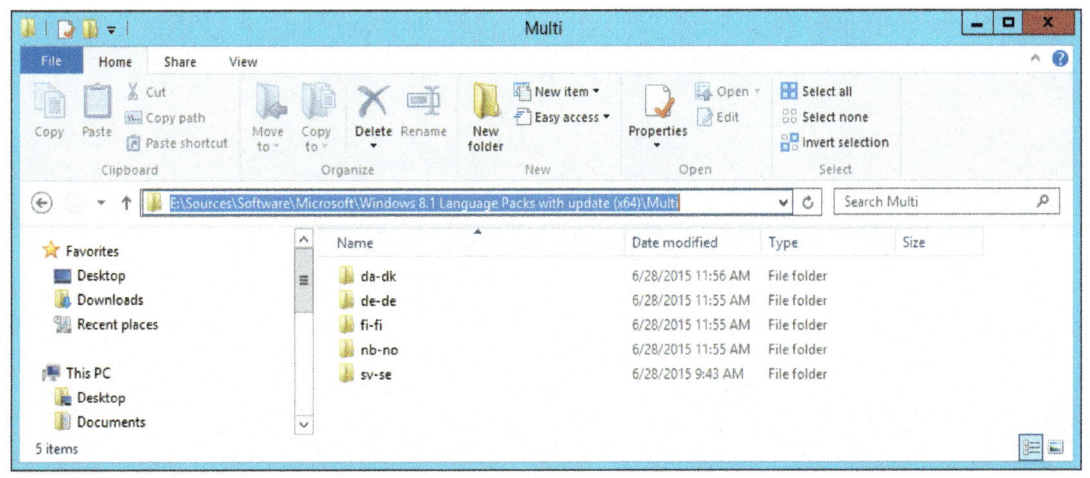

*The Multi language pack folder is populated with additional copies of the language packs.*

371

## Create Language Pack Packages

The task sequence needs one language pack package for each language pack you intend to make available in the task sequence. To create each language pack package, do as follows:

1. On **CM01**, using the **ConfigMgr console**, in the **Software Library** workspace, select **Application Management / Packages**.

2. Right-click **Packages** and choose **Create Package**. Use the following settings for the **Create Package and Program Wizard**:

    a. On the **Package** screen, enter the following settings and then click **Next**:
    
    - Name: **Windows 8.1 x64 Danish Language Pack**
    - Description: **<default>**
    - Manufacturer: **<default>**
    - Language: **<default>**
    - Version: **<default>**
    - Data Source: **\\CM01\Sources\Software\Microsoft\Windows 8.1 Language Packs with update (x64)\Danish**
    
    b. On the **Program Type** screen, select **Do not create a program** and click **Next**.
    
    c. Then continue through the rest of the wizard until completion.

3. Repeat the process for each language you intend to support, including the **Windows 8.1 x64 Multi Language Pack**.

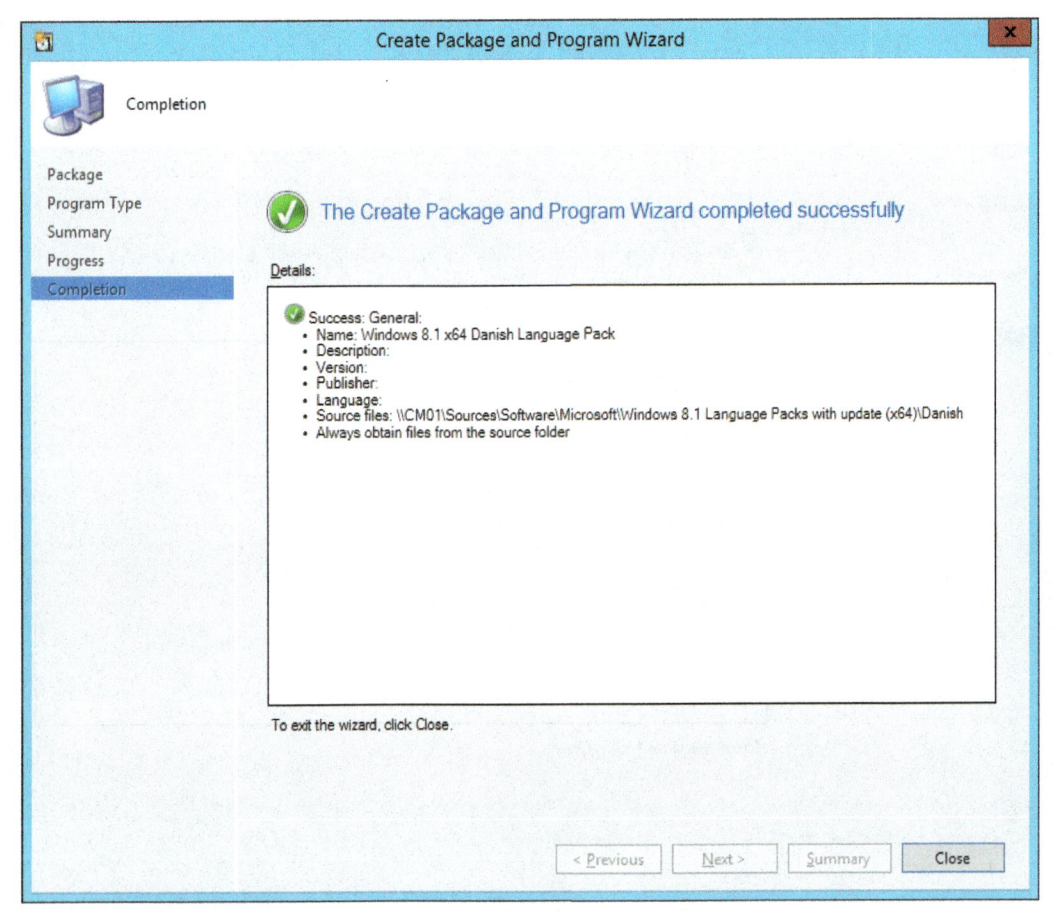

*The Danish language pack package is created.*

## Distribute the Language Packs
Now that the language packs are created, you need to distribute them. To distribute the language packs, follow this process:

1. On **CM01**, using the **ConfigMgr console**, in the **Software Library** workspace, select **Application Management / Packages**. Select all of the previously created language packs by pressing and holding down the **Ctrl** key and then selecting each language pack until they are all selected.

2. Right-click and choose **Distribute Content**, and continue through that wizard until completion.

Chapter 14   The CM12 UEFI BitLocker HTA

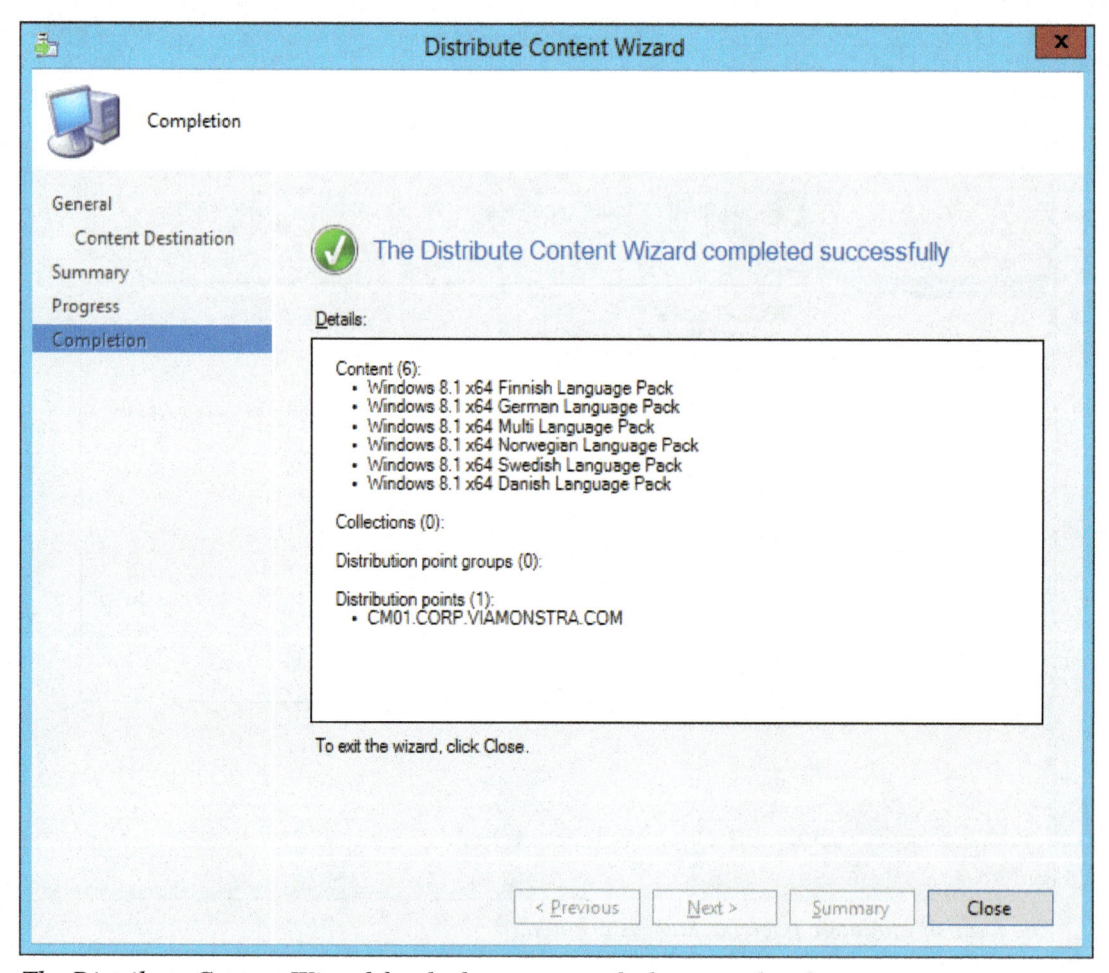

*The Distribute Content Wizard for the language packs has completed.*

## Importing the Task Sequence

This task sequence is so extensive that it's easier to just import it rather than build it from scratch. This saves a lot of time, but it does involve editing in order to make it usable.

### Import the Task Sequence

In this guide I assume you have extracted the book sample files to E:\Setup on CM01.

1. On **CM01**, using **File Explorer**, copy **the E:\Setup\The CM12 UEFI BitLocker HTA** folder to **E:\Sources\Software\ViaMonstra**.

2. In the **ConfigMgr console**, in the **Software Library** workspace, select **Operating Systems / Task Sequences**. Right-click **Task Sequences** and choose **Import Task Sequence**.

Chapter 14   The CM12 UEFI BitLocker HTA

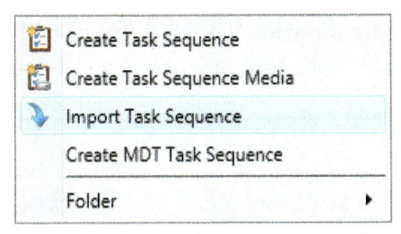

*Importing a task sequence in the ConfigMgr console.*

3. Use the following settings for the **Import Task Sequence Wizard**:

   a. On the **General** screen, for **File**, enter the following and click **Next**:
      **\\CM01\Sources\Software\ViaMonstra\The CM12 UEFI BitLocker HTA\The CM12 UEFI BitLocker HTA.zip**.

   b. On the **File Content** screen, select **Ignore Dependency** in the **Action** drop-down menu and click **Next**.

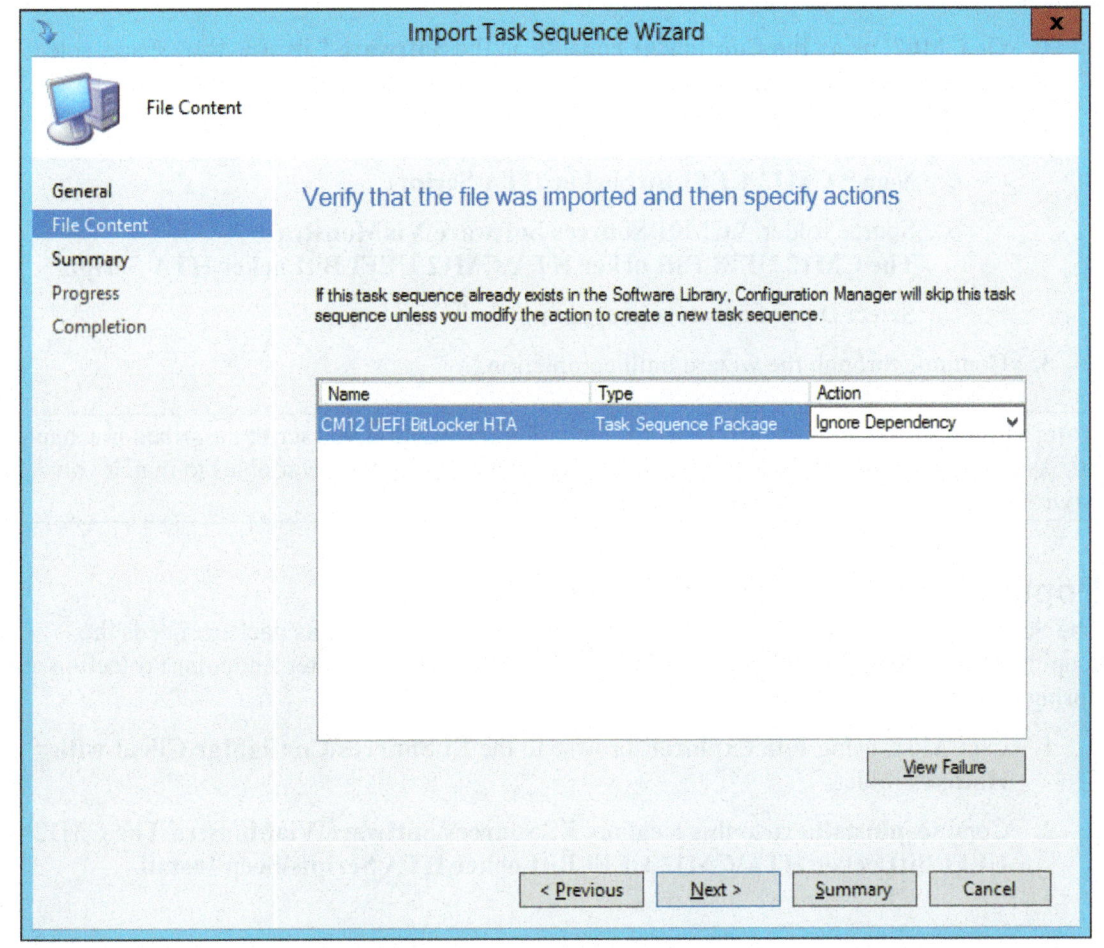

*Choosing to ignore a dependency during a task sequence import.*

375

> **Note:** For any packages not found in your ConfigMgr environment during a Task Sequence Import, on the File Content screen, you can select the option to Ignore Dependency. To get details on which package it is complaining about, click View Failure.

    c. On the **Summary** screen, click **Next**.

    d. On the **Completion** screen, click **Close**.

## Creating Required Packages

The CM12 UEFI BitLocker HTA needs a few packages, or things won't work. To create the required packages, follow the steps in this section.

### Create a CM12 UEFI BitLocker HTA Scripts Package

The CM12 UEFI BitLocker HTA Scripts package contains scripts needed during the task sequence. To create the package, do as follows:

1. On **CM01**, using the **ConfigMgr console**, in the **Software Library** workspace, select **Application Management / Packages**. Right-click and choose **Create Package**.

2. Use the following settings for the **Create Package and Program Wizard**:
   - Name: **CM12 UEFI BitLocker HTA Scripts**
   - Source folder: **\\CM01\Sources\Software\ViaMonstra\The CM12 UEFI BitLocker HTA\CM12 UEFI BitLocker HTA Scripts**
   - Select **Do not create a program**.

3. Continue through the wizard until completion.

> **Note:** This package contains many scripts, including the maillog.vbs script described in Chapter 10. As a result, you should edit that script to change the mail-related variables to match your environment; otherwise, it will not function correctly.

### Populate the Scep Install Folder

The Scep Install folder within the CM12 UEFI BitLocker HTA Scripts package needs the scepinstall.exe file populated in it to correctly install the System Center Endpoint Protection agent during OSD. To resolve this, do as follows:

1. On **CM01**, using **File Explorer**, browse to the **E:\Sources\ConfigMgr Client with Hotfixes** folder.

2. Copy **scepinstall.exe** to this location: **E:\Sources\Software\ViaMonstra\The CM12 UEFI BitLocker HTA\CM12 UEFI BitLocker HTA Scripts\Scep Install**.

Chapter 14 The CM12 UEFI BitLocker HTA

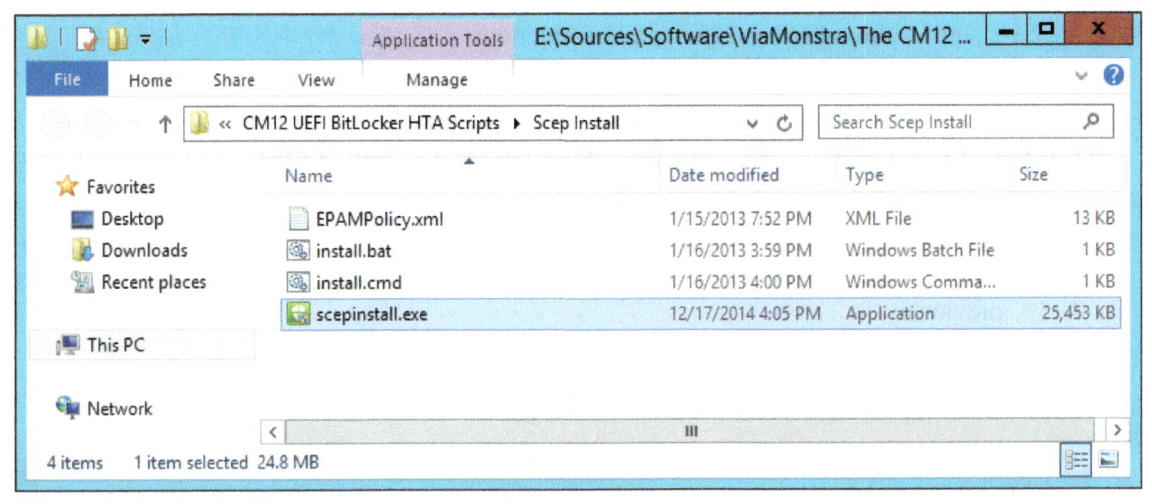

*The scepinstall.exe filed copied.*

## Create an UEFI BitLocker HTA Package

The UEFI BitLocker HTA package contains the files and scripts necessary to display the HTA (HTML application). To create the package, do as follows:

1. On **CM01**, using the **ConfigMgr console**, in the **Software Library** workspace, select **Application Management / Packages**. Right-click and choose **Create Package**.

2. Use the following settings for the **Create Package and Program Wizard**:

    o   Name: **UEFI BitLocker HTA**

    o   Source folder: **\\CM01\Sources\Software\ViaMonstra\ The CM12 UEFI BitLocker HTA\UEFI HTA**

    o   Select **Do not create a program**.

3. Continue through the wizard until completion.

## Create an Unattend.xml Package

The Unattend.xml package is needed to define regional and language settings for the operating system being deployed (Windows 8.1 Enterprise x64). Without this package, languages and regional settings fail to apply. To create the Unattend.xml package, do as follows:

1. On **CM01**, using the **ConfigMgr console**, in the **Software Library** workspace, select **Application Management / Packages**. Right-click and choose **Create Package**.

2. Use the following settings for the **Create Package and Program Wizard**:

    o   Name: **Windows 8.1 x64 Unattend.xml**

    o   Source folder: **\\CM01\Sources\Software\ViaMonstra\The CM12 UEFI BitLocker HTA\CM12 UEFI BitLocker HTA Scripts\Unattend**

    o   Select **Do not create a program**.

377

Chapter 14   The CM12 UEFI BitLocker HTA

3. Continue through the wizard until completion.

## Distribute the New Packages

Distribute the packages created in the preceding steps to the CM01.CORP.VIAMONSTRA.COM distribution point by following this process:

1. On **CM01**, using the **ConfigMgr console**, in the **Software Library** workspace, select **Application Management / Packages**. Press **Ctrl** and select each of the packages created previously.
2. Right-click the selected packages and select **Distribute Content**.
3. Continue through that wizard until completion.

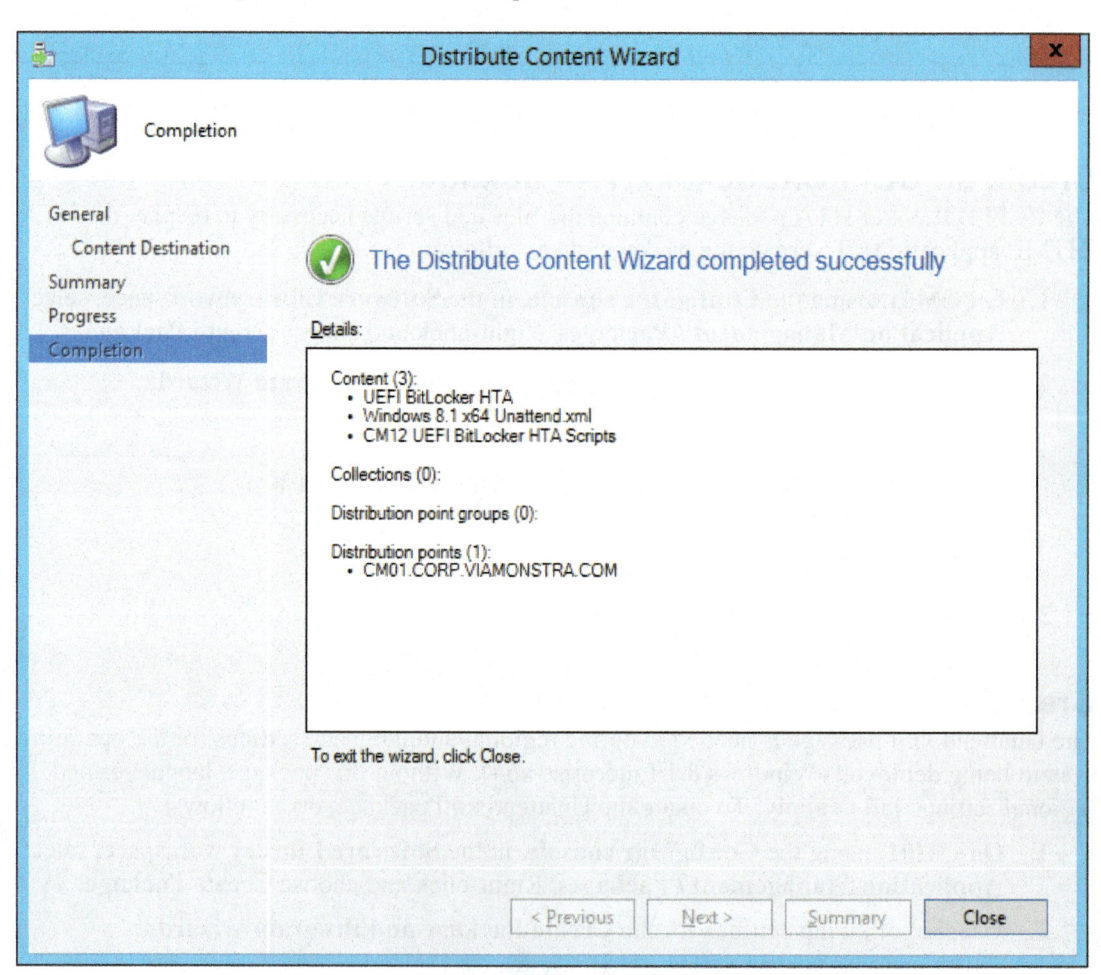

*The newly created packages are distributed to CM01.CORP.VIAMONSTRA.COM.*

# Adding a SQL Server User

The task sequence uses a SQL Server user that is defined in the Set MBAMUser task sequence step to connect to the MBAM 2.5 database while in Windows PE. To set this up correctly, do as follows:

1. Log on to **MBAM01**, using **ViaMonstra\MBAM_HD_AppPool** credentials, start **Microsoft SQL Server Management Studio**. Then click **Connect** when prompted.

2. In **Object Explorer**, browse to **MBAM01**, choose **Properties**, and then select **Security**.

3. Under **Server Authentication**, select **SQL Server and Windows Authentication Mode**.

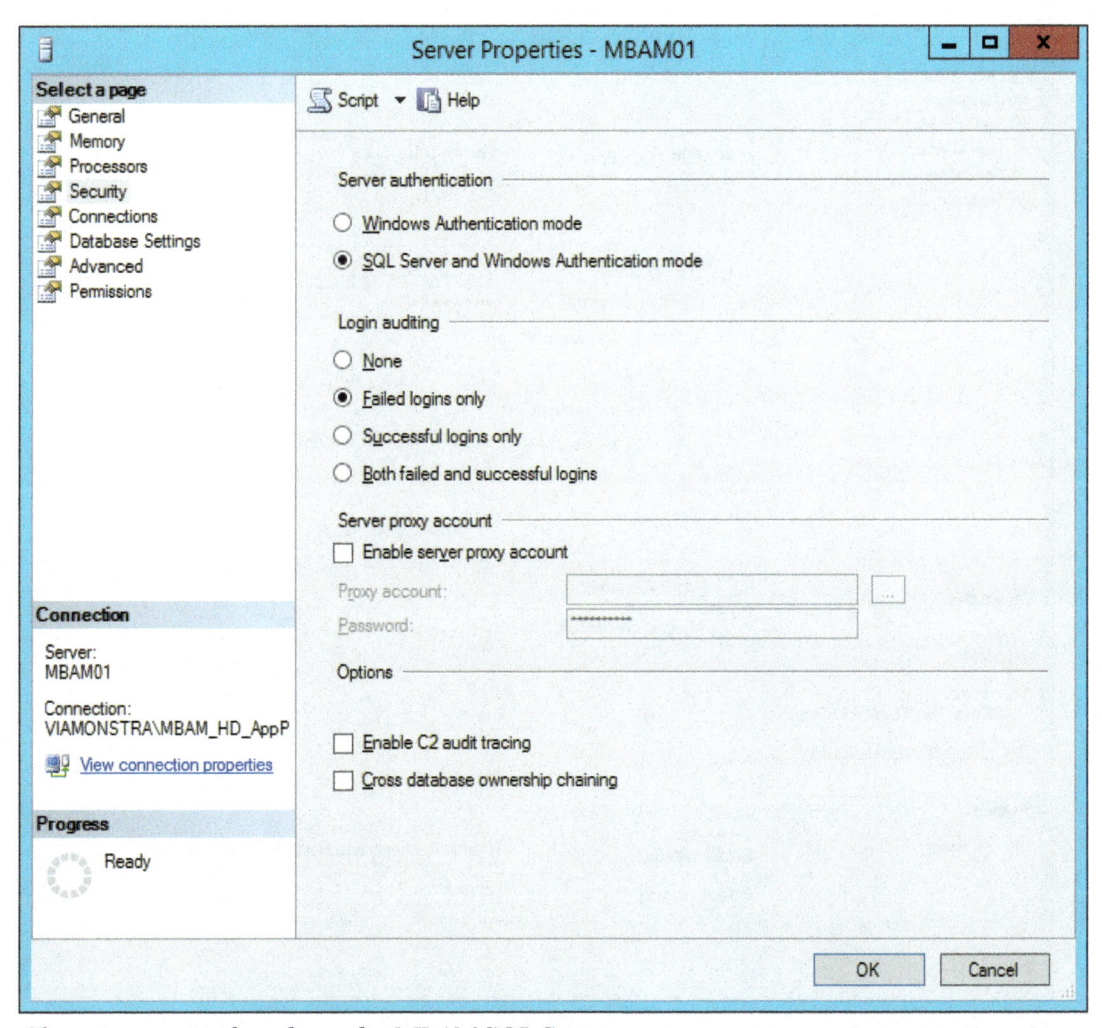

*Changing to mixed mode on the MBAM SQL Server.*

4. Click **OK** and review the notice. In **Object Explorer**, expand **Security**, expand **Logins**, right-click it, and then choose **New Login**.

Chapter 14   The CM12 UEFI BitLocker HTA

5. In the **New Login** window, enter the following values:
    a. Login Name: **MBAM_OSD**
    a. Select **SQL Server Authentication** and enter the following values:
        - Password: **P@ssw0rd**
        - Confirm password: **P@ssw0rd**
6. Clear the **Enforce password policy** check box.
7. For **Default Database**, select **MBAM Recovery and Hardware.**

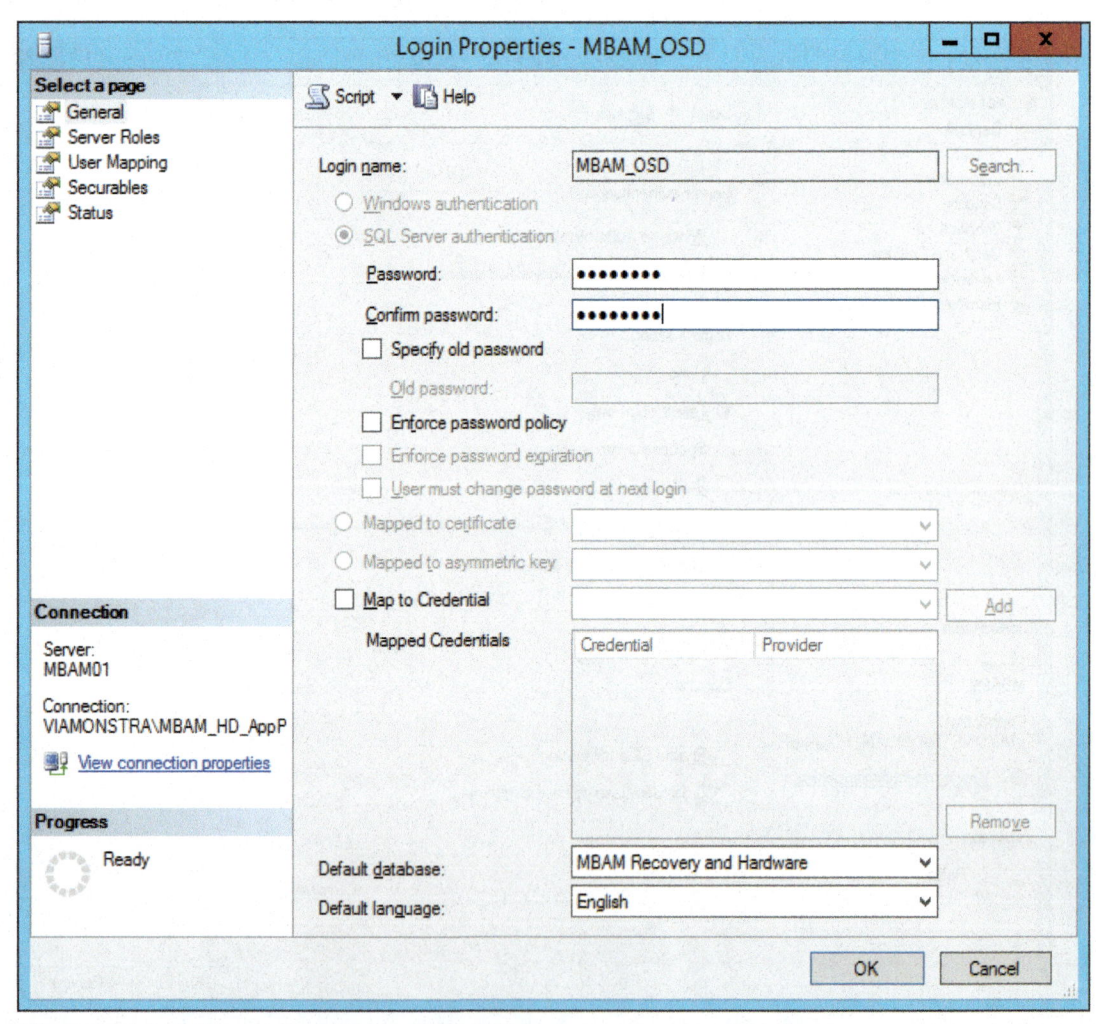

*The MBAM_OSD user is added to SQL Server.*

8. Change the **User Mapping** to **MBAM Recovery and Hardware** as shown in the figure. Make sure that **db_datareader** is set.

380

9. Click **OK**.

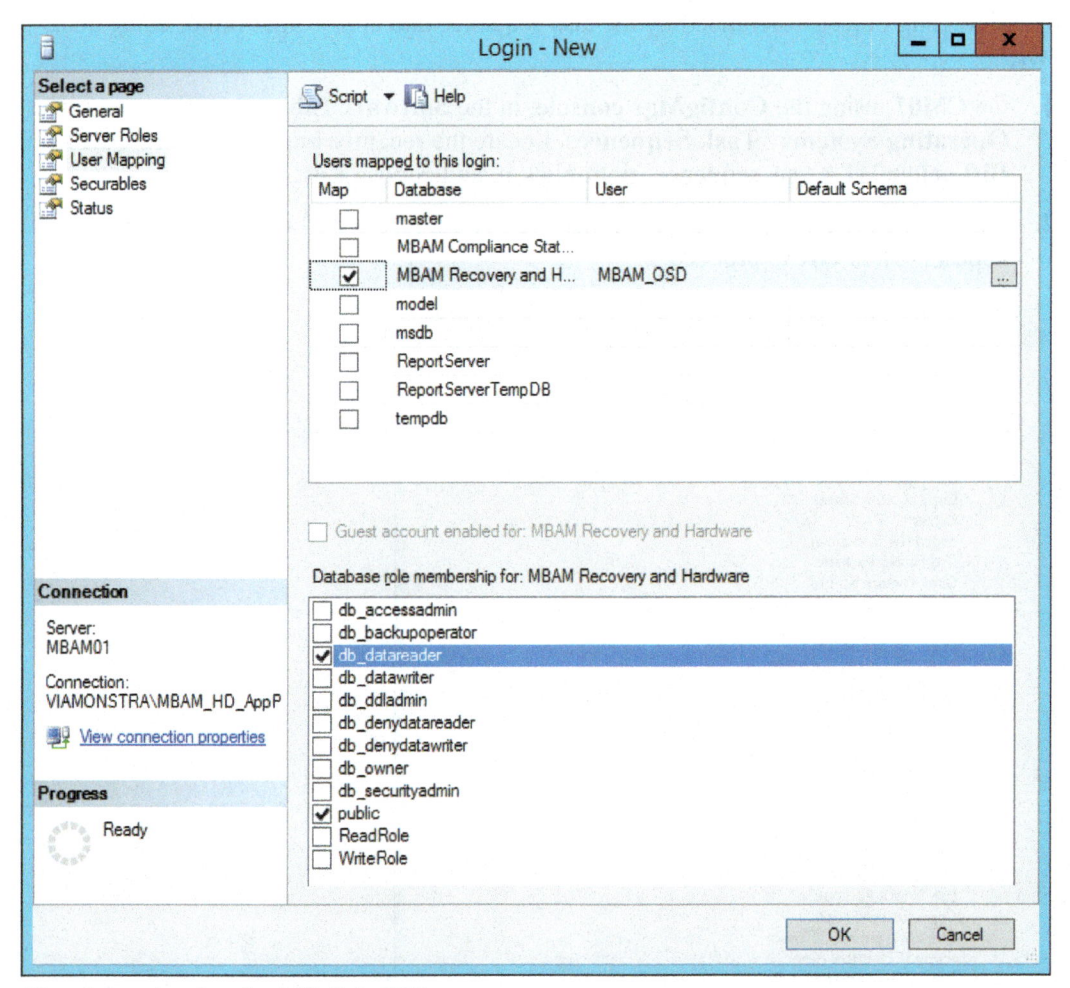

*User Mapping for the MBAM_OSD user.*

# Editing the Task Sequence

Now that the CM12 UEFI BitLocker HTA task sequence has been imported, it's time to edit it to fix all the package references that need to be resolved and define what values the variables will require.

The first time you edit an imported task sequence, you are prompted to resolve the missing references. To edit the task sequence, follow the guidance in this section. Note that this is time consuming, but it is a one-off process.

## Fix Package References

To fix the missing objects referenced by the task sequence and apply other minor edits, do as follows:

1. On **CM01**, using the **ConfigMgr console**, in the **Software Library** workspace, select **Operating Systems / Task Sequences**. Locate the recently imported **CM12 UEFI BitLocker HTA** task sequence, right-click it, and choose **Edit**.

2. After some moments, a long list of missing objects referenced in the task sequence appears. Click **OK** to proceed.

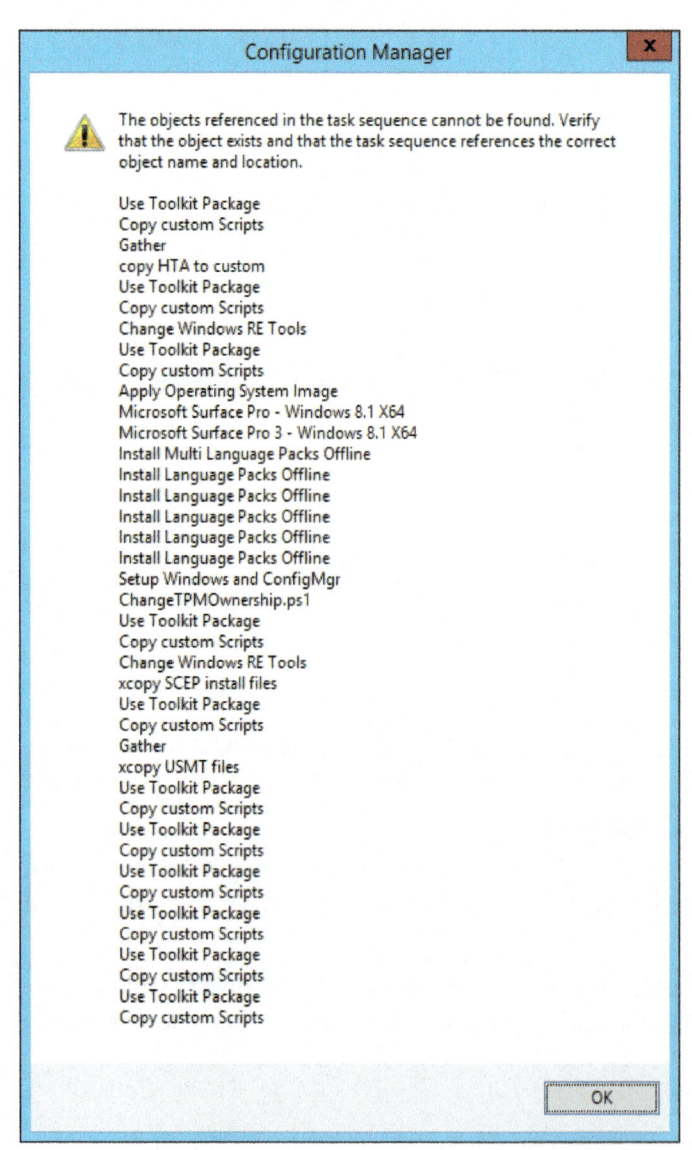

*A long list of missing objects is shown. Don't panic!*

Chapter 14   The CM12 UEFI BitLocker HTA

3. Starting at the top of the task sequence, scroll down and select the first **Use Toolkit Package** step as shown in the figure.

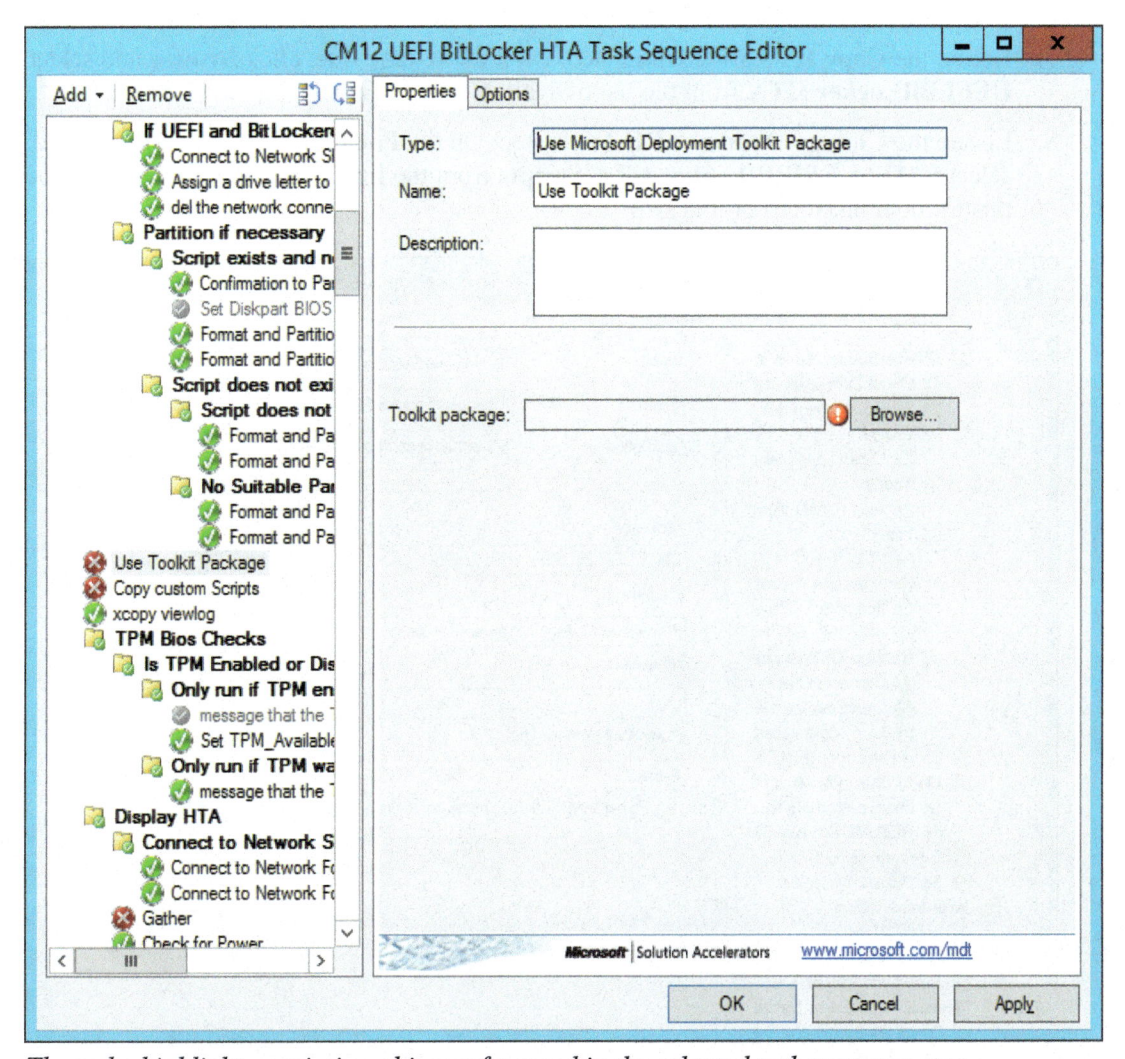

*The red x highlights a missing object referenced in the selected task sequence step.*

4. Click the **Browse** button beside **Toolkit package** and select the **MDT 2013 Toolkit** from the list of available packages. Repeat this process for every **Use Toolkit Package** step in the task sequence. (It is repeated several times throughout the task sequence.)

5. Locate the first **Copy Custom Scripts** step. On the **Package** line, click the **Browse** button and select the **CM12 UEFI BitLocker HTA Scripts** package from the list of available packages. Repeat this process for each and every **Copy Custom Scripts** step referenced in the task sequence.

6. Locate the first **Gather** step. On the **Settings Package** line, click **Browse** and select the **MDT 2013 Settings** package from the list of available packages. Repeat this process for every **Gather** step in the task sequence.

7. Locate the **Copy HTA to Custom** step. On the **Package** line, click **Browse** and select **UEFI BitLocker HTA** from the list of available packages.

8. Locate the **Change Windows RE Tools** step. On the **Package** line, click **Browse** and select **CM12 UEFI BitLocker HTA Scripts** from the list of available packages. Repeat this for both instances of this step.

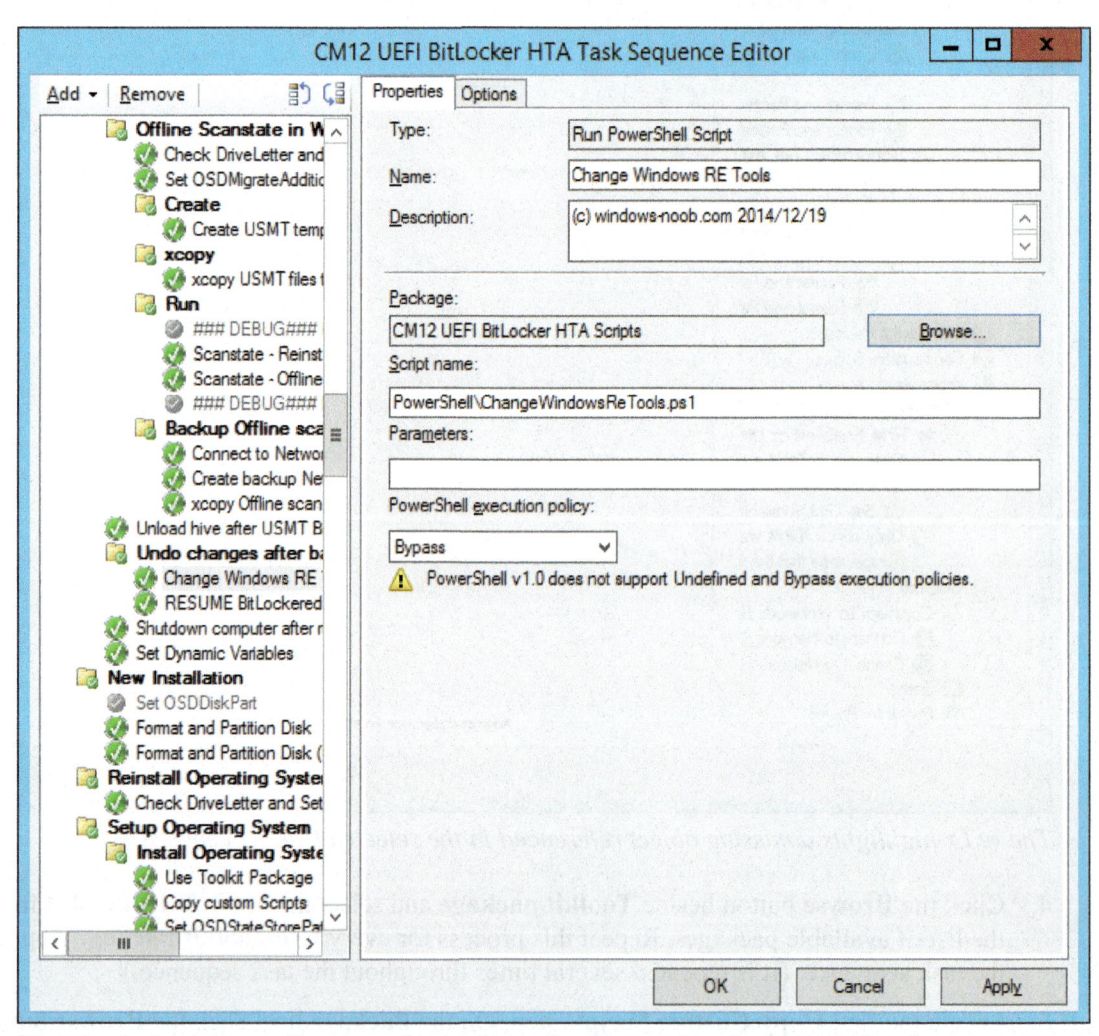

*Fixing missing objects (for example, packages) referenced in the imported task sequence.*

9. On the **Apply Operating System Image** step, use the following settings:

   a. For the **Apply operating system image from a captured package** option, use the following values:

      - Image Package: **Windows 8.1 Enterprise - 150301 x64 en-US**
      - Image: **<default>**

   b. For the **Use an Unattended or sysprep package** section, use the following values:

      - Package: **Windows 8.1 x64 Unattend.xml**
      - Filename: **<default>**

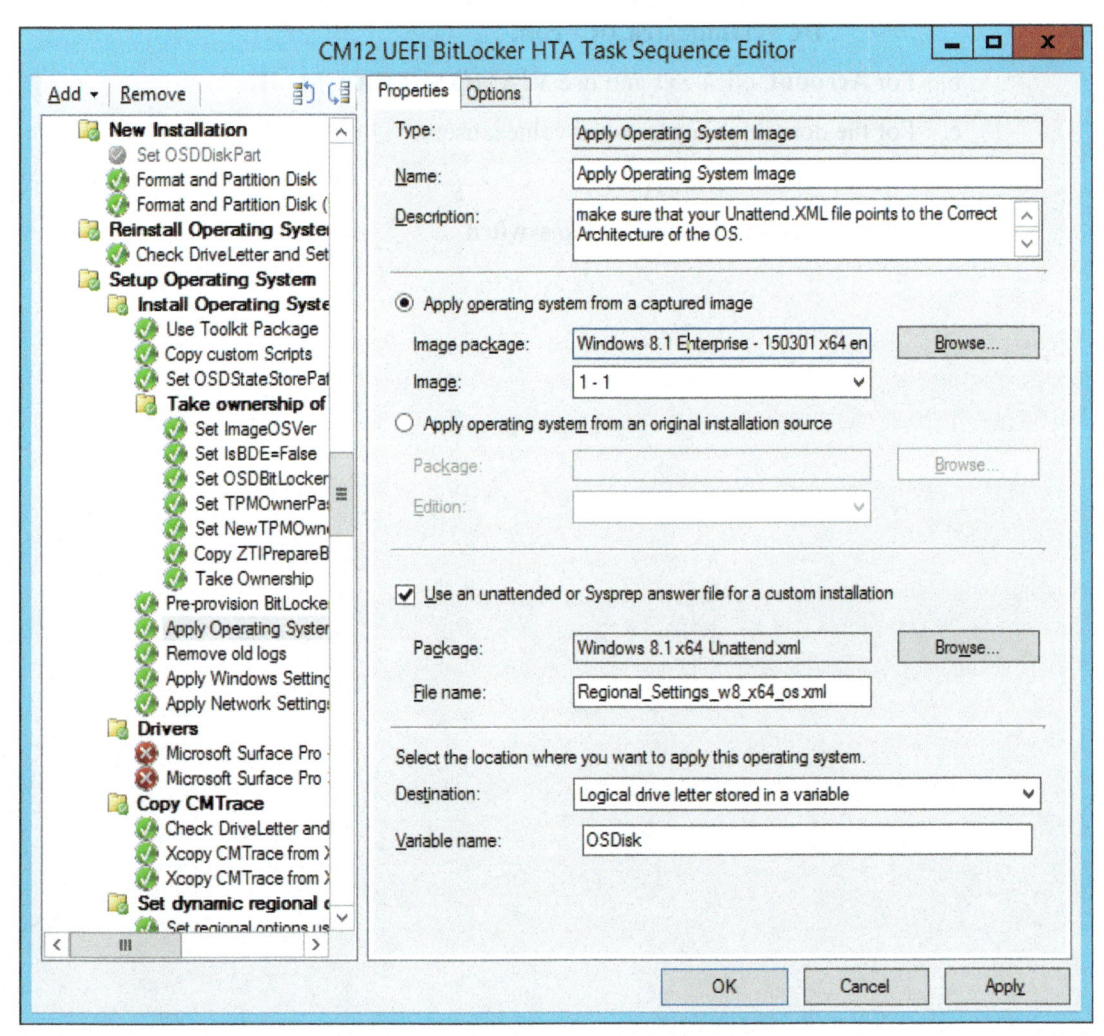

*The Apply Operating System Image step after editing is complete.*

10. Locate the **Apply Windows Settings** step, select it, and use the following settings:

   For the **Enter licensing and registration information for installing Windows** section, use the following values:
   - User name: **ViaMonstra**
   - Organization name: **ViaMonstra**

11. Locate the **Apply Network Settings** step, select it, and use the following settings:

   a. For the **Join a Domain** line, use the following values:
      - Domain: **corp.viamonstra.com**
      - OU: **LDAP://OU=Workstations,OU=ViaMonstra,DC=corp, DC=viamonstra,DC=com**
   
   b. For **Account**, click **Set** and use **VIAMONSTRA\CM_JD**.
   
   c. For the domain join password values, use:
      - Password: **P@ssw0rd**
      - Confirm Password: **P@ssw0rd**

Chapter 14   The CM12 UEFI BitLocker HTA

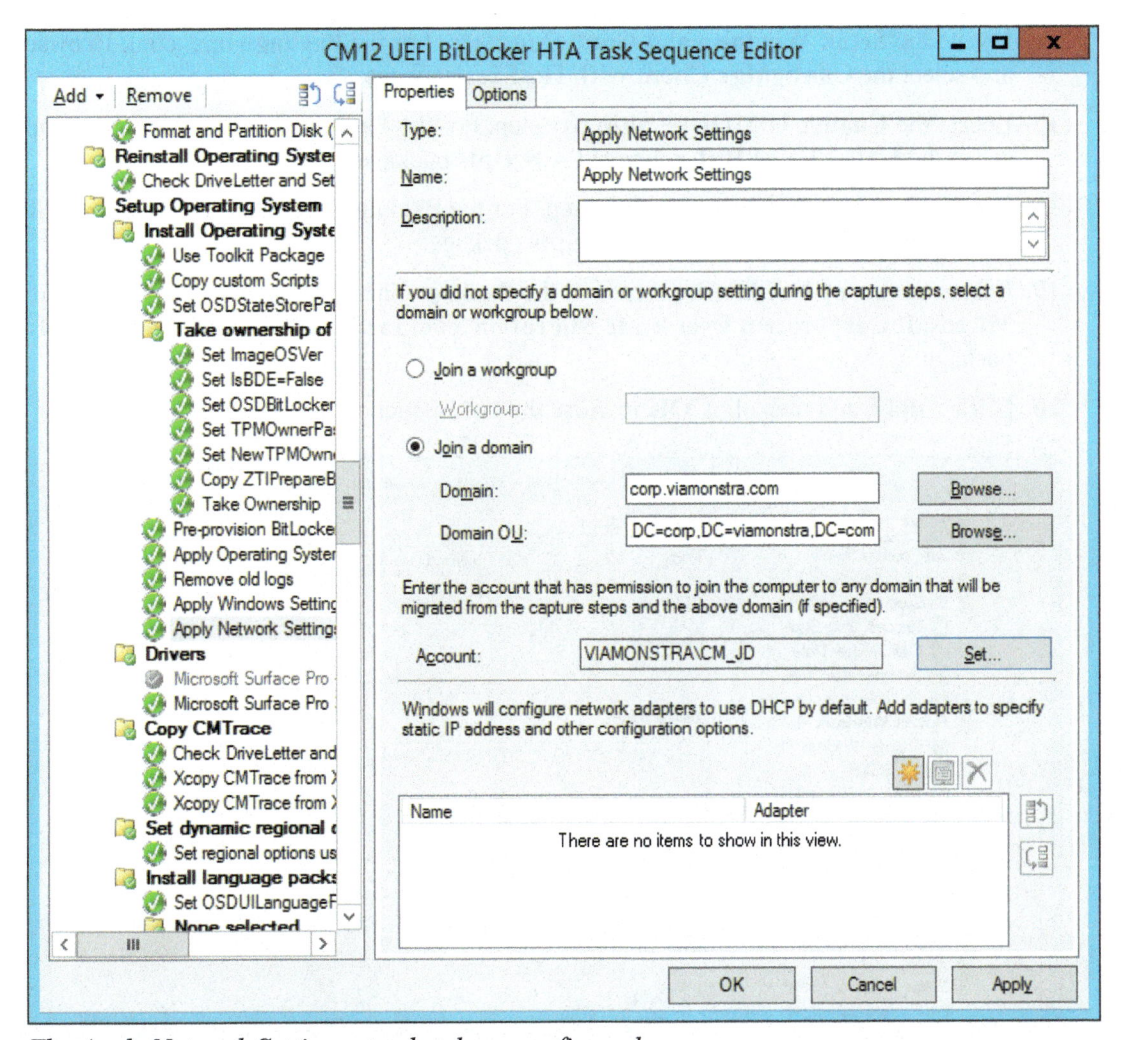

*The Apply Network Settings step has been configured.*

12. On the **Microsoft Surface Pro - Windows 8.1 X64** step, click the **Options** tab and select the **Disable This Step** check box.

13. On the **Microsoft Surface Pro 3 - Windows 8.1 X64** step, click **Browse** on the **Driver Package** line and select the **Windows 8.1 x64 - Microsoft Surface Pro 3** driver package.

14. Locate the **Install Multi Language Packs Offline** step, and for the **Language pack package** line, click **Browse** and select the **Windows 8.1 x64 Multi Language Pack** package.

15. For each language listed, locate the appropriate **Install Language Packs Offline** step and for the **Language pack package** line, click **Browse** and select the corresponding language package from the list of available language pack packages.

Chapter 14   The CM12 UEFI BitLocker HTA

16. Locate the **Setup Windows and ConfigMgr** step. For the **Package** line, click **Browse** and select the **ConfigMgr Client with Hotfixes** package.

17. Locate the **ChangeTPMOwnership.ps1** step. For the **Package** line, click **Browse** and select the **CM12 UEFI BitLocker HTA Scripts** package.

18. Locate the **xcopy SCEP install files** step. For the **Package** line, click **Browse** and select the **CM12 UEFI BitLocker HTA Scripts** package.

19. Locate the **xcopy USMT files** step. For the **Package** line, click **Browse** and select the **Microsoft Corporation User State Migration Tool for Windows 8 6.3.9600.16384** package.

20. Click **Apply**, and then click **OK** to close the task sequence.

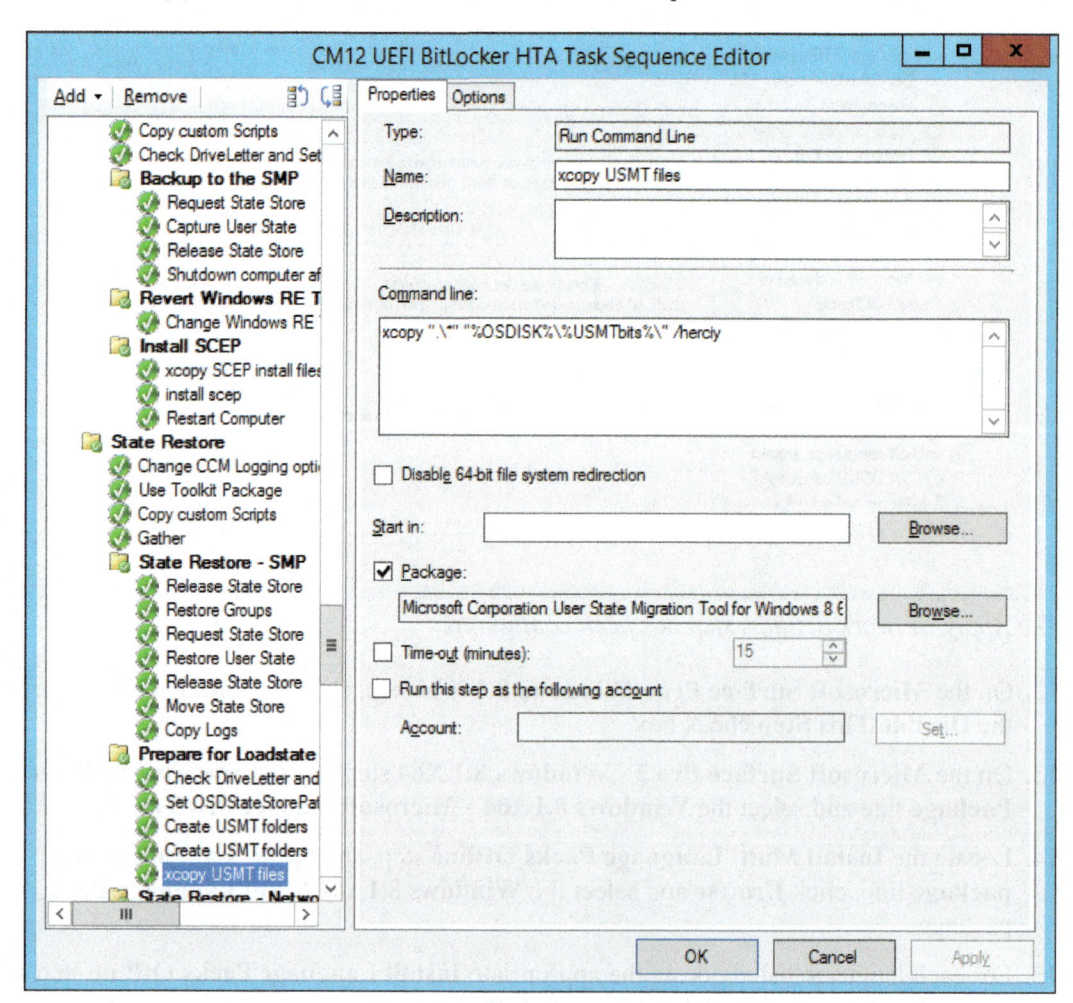

*Time to breathe a sigh of relief after fixing the missing objects referenced in the task sequence.*

388

## Edit Variables in the Task Sequence

The task sequence uses variables to define many settings used in the HTA.

> **Note**: Some of the folders specified in these variables are created and shared automatically using the Create-ConfigMgrFolders.ps1 PowerShell script located in E:\Setup\Scripts.

To set the variables correctly, follow these steps:

1. On **CM01**, using the **ConfigMgr console**, in the **Software Library** workspace, select **Operating Systems / Task Sequences**. Locate the recently imported **CM12 UEFI BitLocker HTA** task sequence, right-click it, and choose **Edit**.
2. Locate the **Set Domain** set task sequence variable step and change the **Value** to **corp.viamonstra.com**.
3. Locate the **Set Domain User** set task sequence variable step and change the **Value** to **CM_NAA**.
4. Locate the **Set MBAMServer** set task sequence variable step and change the **Value** to **mbam01.corp.viamonstra.com**.
5. Locate the **Set MBAMUser** set task sequence variable step and change the **Value** to **MBAM_OSD**.
6. Locate the **Set MBAMPassword** set task sequence variable step and change the **Value** to **P@ssw0rd**.
7. Locate the **Set BackupServer** set task sequence variable step and change the **Value** to **cm01.corp.viamonstra.com**.
8. Locate the **Set BackupShare** set task sequence variable step and change the **Value** to **Backups$**.
9. Locate the **Set USMTStoreShare** set task sequence variable step and change the **Value** to **USMTStores$**.
10. Locate the **Set USMTLacPassword** set task sequence variable step and change the **Value** to **P@ssw0rd**
11. Locate the **Set TargetDomain** set task sequence variable step in the **Add Local Administrator** group and change the **Value** to **corp.viamonstra.com**.
12. Click **OK** to save the changes and close the task sequence.

## Add a Step to Copy the USMT Binaries

When it comes to USMT binaries, they can be added in two different ways. First, you can (optionally) copy the USMT binaries from the Windows ADK installation folder to the root of the MDT package and then update that package to the distribution points. Or, second, add a step in the task sequence that copies the files. To do the second alternative, copying the binaries via a step in the task sequence, do as follows:

1. On **CM01**, using the **ConfigMgr console**, in the **Software Library** workspace, select **Operating Systems / Task Sequences**. Locate the recently imported **CM12 UEFI BitLocker HTA** task sequence, right-click it, and choose **Edit**.

2. Scroll down to the **xcopy** group, which is a sub group of the **Offline Scanstate in WinPE** group.

3. Click **Add / General / Run Command Line**. In the new **Run Command Line** step, use the following settings and click **Apply** and then **OK**:

    a. Name: **xcopy USMT binaries**

    a. Description: **<default>**

    b. Command line:
    **cmd.exe /c xcopy ".\*.*" "%OSDISK%\%USMTbits%\" /herciy**

    c. Package: **Microsoft Corporation User State Migration Tool for Windows 8 6.3.9600.16384**

Chapter 14   The CM12 UEFI BitLocker HTA

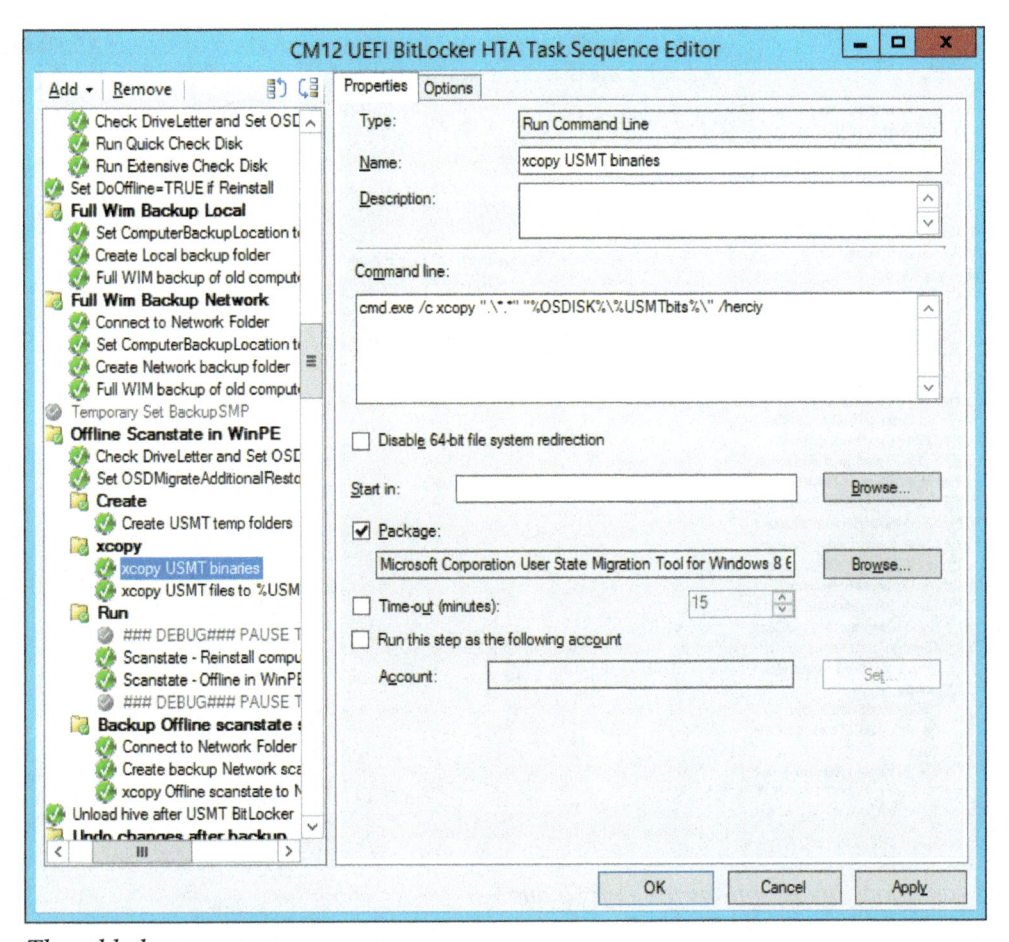

*The added xcopy step.*

## Fix a Bug
On the **Create USMT temp folders** step, the options will not run correctly if the specified folders already exist. To fix this, do as follows:

1. On **CM01**, using the **ConfigMgr console**, in the **Software Library** workspace, select **Operating Systems / Task Sequences**. Locate the **CM12 UEFI BitLocker HTA** task sequence, right-click it, and choose **Edit**.

2. Locate the **Create USMT temp folders** step, in the **Options** tab, remove all conditions currently added by clicking **Remove All** and replace them with the following:

    If **None** of the conditions is true:

    - Folder **%OSDISK%\%USMTStateStore%** exists
    - Folder **%OSDISK%\%USMTbits%\x86** exists
    - Folder **%OSDISK%\%USMTbits%\amd64** exists

391

Chapter 14   The CM12 UEFI BitLocker HTA

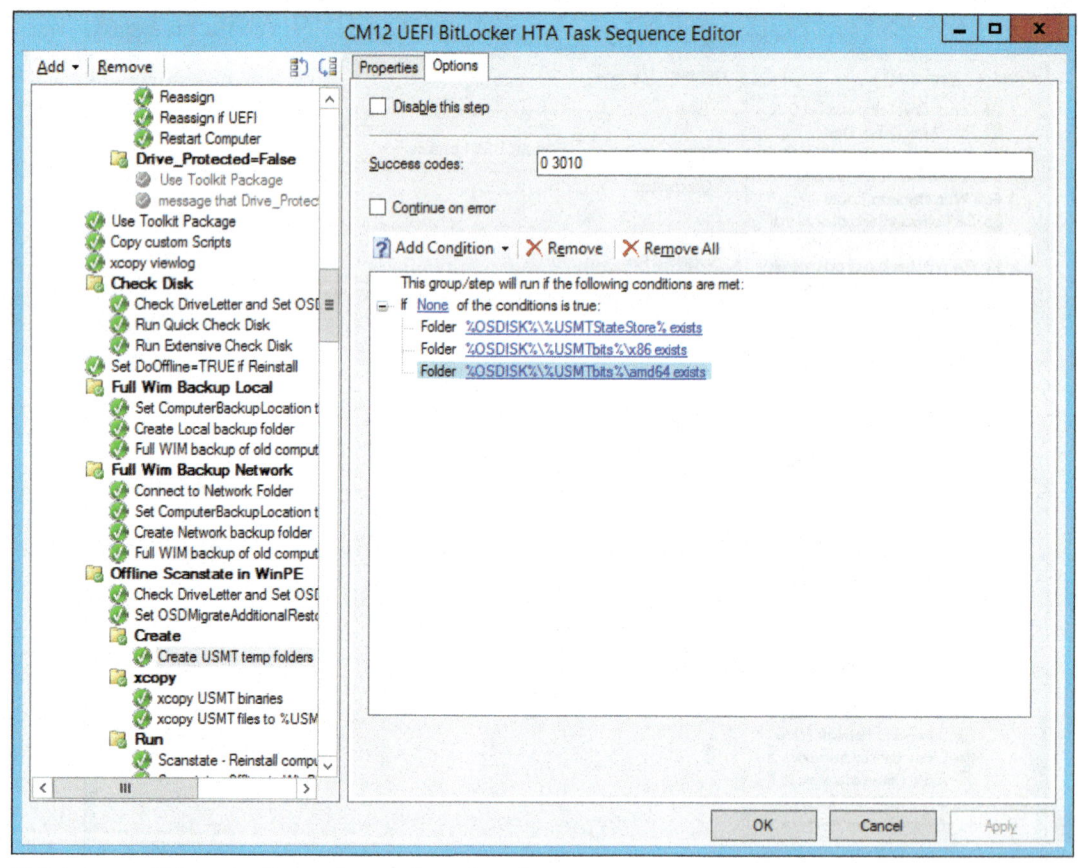

*Editing conditions in the options tab to fix a bug.*

## Set the Password to Connect to Network Shares

There are several steps that need to be edited to set the password required by the specified user to connect to the specified share. To set the password in these steps, do as follows:

1. On **CM01**, using the **ConfigMgr console**, in the **Software Library** workspace, select **Operating Systems / Task Sequences**. Locate the recently imported **CM12 UEFI BitLocker HTA** task sequence, right-click it, and choose **Edit**.

2. Locate the **If UEFI and BitLockered** group, select the **Connect to Network Share** step, and click **Set** on the **Account** line.

3. In the **%Domain%\%DomainUser% Windows User Account** screen, use the following settings:
    o   Password: **P@ssw0rd**
    o   Confirm password: **P@ssw0rd**

**Note**: As these values are variables, you cannot use the Password Verify functionality, so type the passwords carefully.

392

4. Locate the **Connect to Network Shares** group, select the **Connect to Network Folder for USMT state stores** step, and click **Set** on the **Account** line.

5. In the **%Domain%\%DomainUser% Windows User Account** screen, use the following settings:
   - Password: **P@ssw0rd**
   - Confirm password: **P@ssw0rd**

6. Locate the **Connect to Network Folder for storing Full backups** step and click **Set** on the **Account** line.

7. In the **%Domain%\%DomainUser% Windows User Account** screen, use the following settings:
   - Password: **P@ssw0rd**
   - Confirm password: **P@ssw0rd**

8. Locate the **Full Wim Backup Network** group, select the **Connect to Network Folder** step, and click **Set** on the **Account** line.

9. In the **%Domain%\%DomainUser% Windows User Account** screen, use the following settings:
   - Password: **P@ssw0rd**
   - Confirm password: **P@ssw0rd**

10. Locate the **Backup Offline scanstate store to the Network** group, select the **Connect to Network Folder** step, and click **Set** on the **Account** line.

11. In the **%Domain%\%DomainUser% Windows User Account** screen, use the following settings:
    - Password: **P@ssw0rd**
    - Confirm password: **P@ssw0rd**

12. Locate the **State Restore - Network** group, select the **Connect to Network Folder** step, and click **Set** on the **Account** line.

13. In the **%Domain%\%DomainUser% Windows User Account** screen, use the following settings:
    - Password: **P@ssw0rd**
    - Confirm password: **P@ssw0rd**

14. Click **OK**.

## Add the MBAM Client

The task sequence is set to install the MBAM client as part of the task sequence; however, it's not aware of the MBAM Client application yet. To make it aware, follow these steps:

1. On **CM01**, using the **ConfigMgr console**, in the **Software Library** workspace, select **Operating Systems / Task Sequences**. Locate the recently imported **CM12 UEFI BitLocker HTA** task sequence, right-click it, and choose **Edit**.

2. Locate the **Install MBAM Client** step and click the **yellow asterisk** button to add an application. Select **MBAM 2.5 Client (x64 edition)** from the list of available applications.

3. Click **OK**.

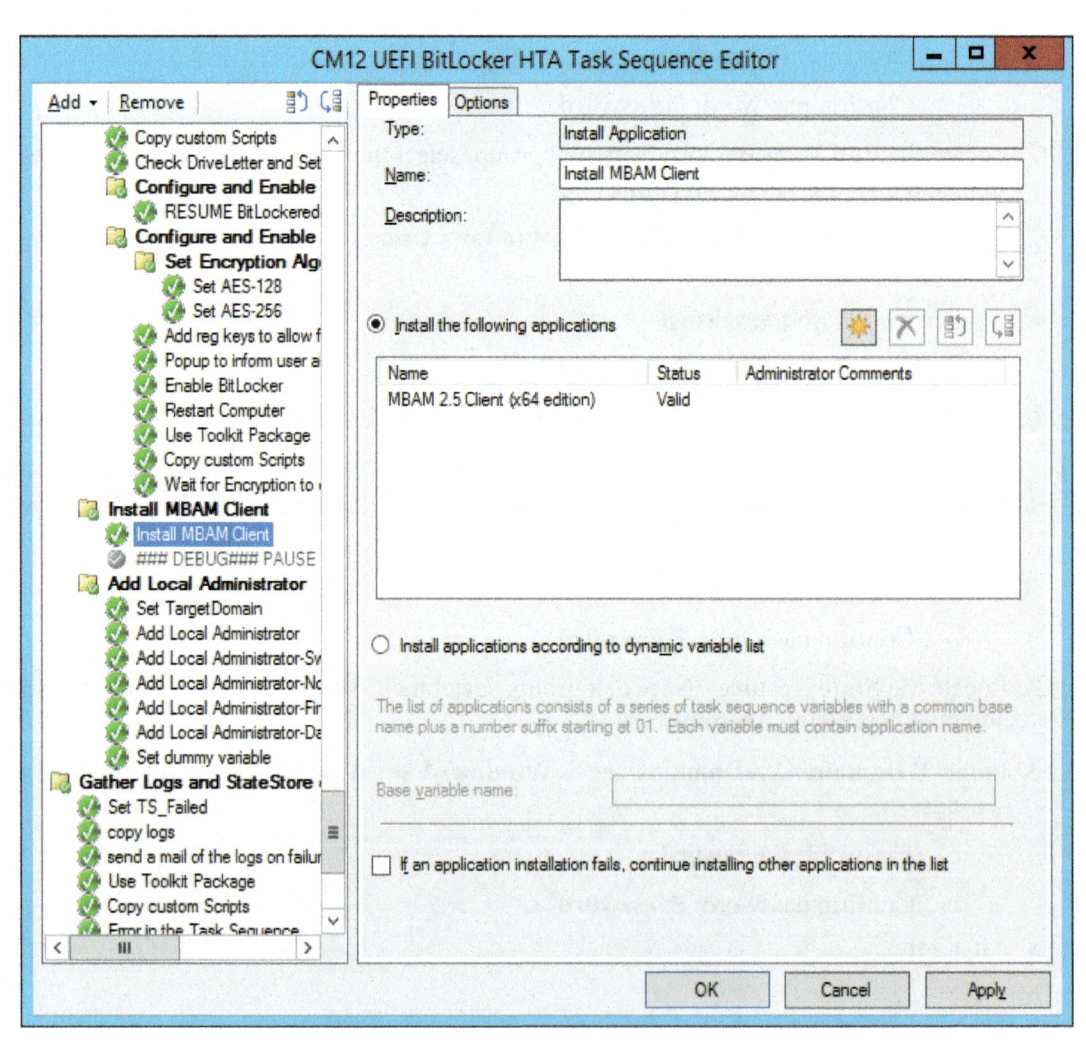

*Installing the MBAM 2.5 Client (x64 edition).*

# Editing the CustomSettings.ini File

The CustomSettings.ini file contains values that need to be adjusted in order to use the web services installed previously. To edit the CustomSettings.ini file, do as follows:

1. On **CM01**, using the **File Explorer**, browse to **E:\Sources\Software\ViaMonstra\The CM12 UEFI BitLocker HTA\CM12 UEFI BitLocker HTA Scripts** and open the **CustomSettings.ini** file using **Notepad**.

2. Replace all instances of **http://sccm/NewWebService** with **http://CM01/DeploymentWebService**.

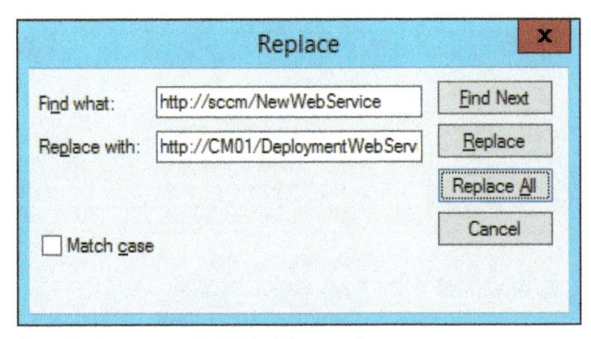

*Replacing one URL with another.*

3. Click **Save**. Next, copy the file to the root of **MDT 2013 Toolkit** package using a command prompt like so:

   ```
   copy "E:\Sources\Software\ViaMonstra\The CM12 UEFI BitLocker
   HTA\CM12 UEFI BitLocker HTA Scripts\CustomSettings.ini"
   "E:\Sources\OSD\MDT\MDT 2013"
   ```

4. Update the **MDT Toolkit Package** to the distribution points by right-clicking the package in the **ConfigMgr console** and choosing **Update Distribution Points**. Continue with the wizard until the end.

## Copying a Script to a Share

In order to allow for OSD on UEFI BitLockered machines, you use a script that can either be placed directly in your boot WIM image or copied to a share. (OSD fails otherwise during new computer or refresh scenarios as the task sequence is not able to stage any content to the hard disk.) To copy the script to the share, do as follows:

On **CM01**, using the **File Explorer**, browse to **E:\Sources\Software\ViaMonstra\The CM12 UEFI BitLocker HTA\CM12 UEFI BitLocker HTA Scripts** and copy the **ReassignOSDiskandAssignWindowsReTools.vbs** file to **E:\Backups** (the share specified in the **Set BackupShare** step of the task sequence).

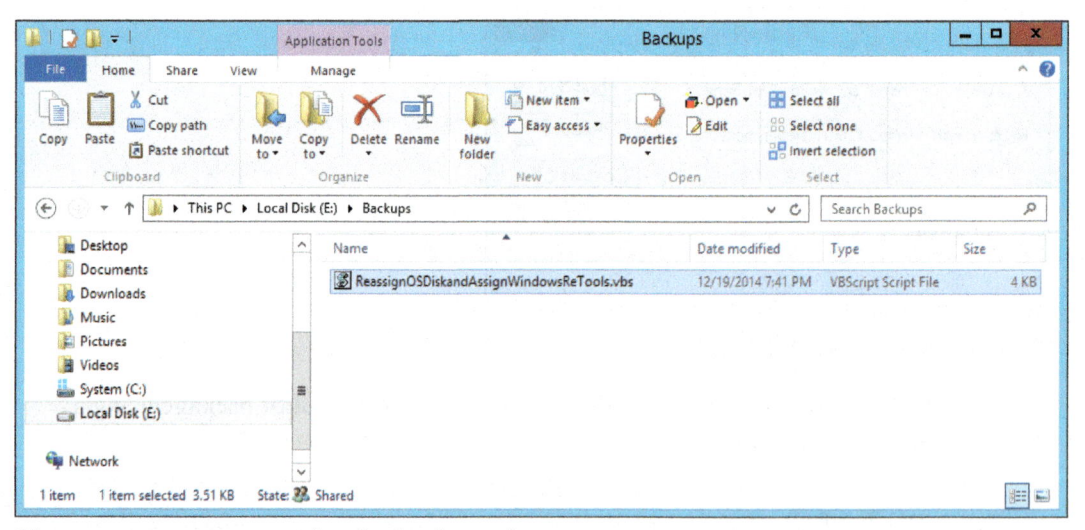

*The reassign script copied to the backups share.*

**Note**: If you decide to insert the script into the boot WIM image instead of placing it on a share, then you have to modify the If UEFI and BitLockered group in the task sequence, remove the network connection, and then change the drive letter to X:\ and the path to the script to correspond to the new path.

## Boot Image Changes

The boot image used in the task sequence needs additional powers (optional components) added to it, and then it needs to be attached to the imported task sequence. Follow the guides in this section to accomplish that.

## Add MDAC and HTA Support to the Boot Image

Allowing connections from Windows PE to your SQL Server and permitting the HTA to display in Windows PE require that some optional components be added to the boot image. To add these optional components, follow these steps:

1. On **CM01**, using the **ConfigMgr console**, in the **Software Library** workspace, select **Operating Systems / Boot Images**. Locate the **Boot image (x64)** boot image, right-click it, and choose **Properties**.

2. Select the **Optional Components** tab, and add the following components:
   - **HTML (WinPE-HTA)**
   - **Database (WinPE-MDAC)**

3. Click **OK** twice when done and click **Yes** to update the distribution points.

4. Then continue through the wizard.

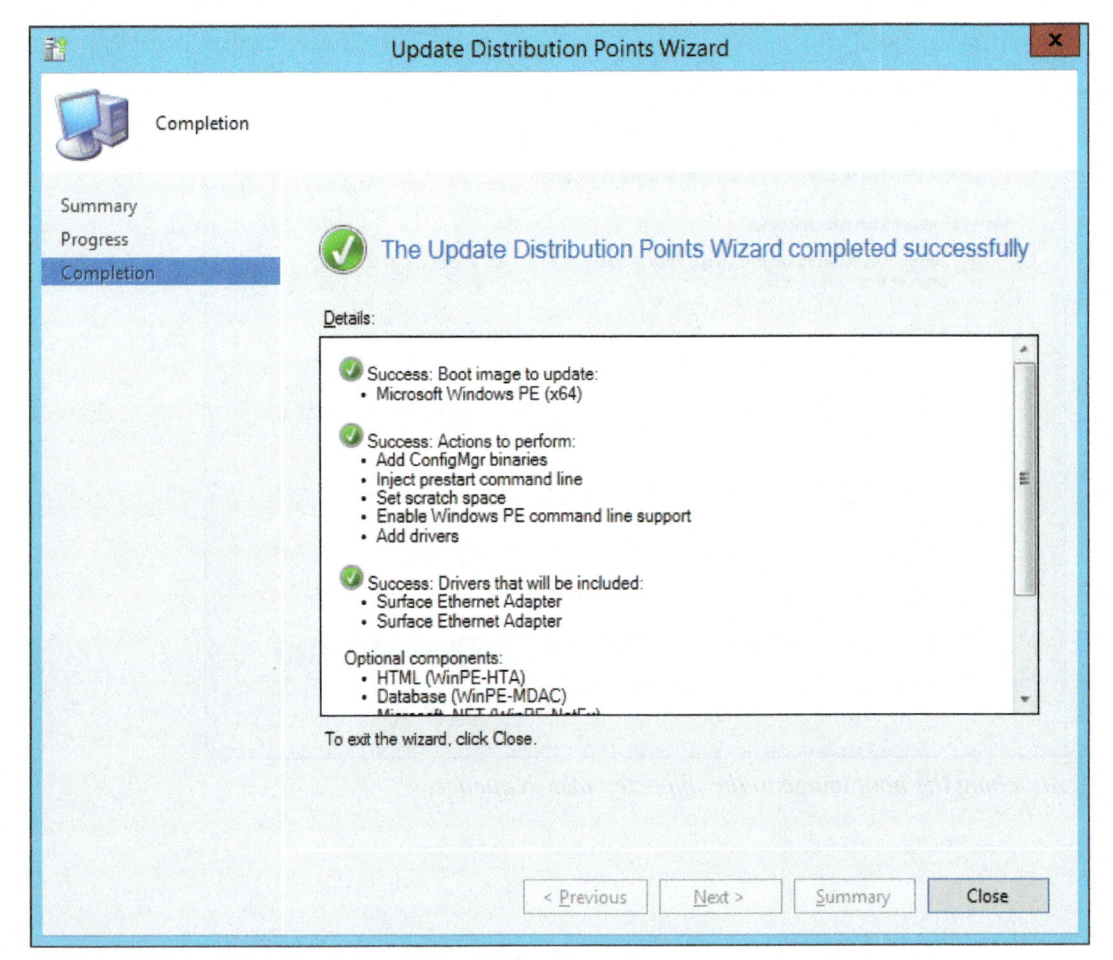

*Adding HTA and database support to the boot image.*

## Attach the Boot Image to the Task Sequence

When the task sequence was imported, it lost its boot image. To add the boot image back, follow these steps:

1. On **CM01**, using the **ConfigMgr console**, in the **Software Library** workspace, select **Operating Systems / Task Sequences**. Locate the **CM12 UEFI BitLocker HTA** task sequence, right-click it, and choose **Properties**.

2. Select the **Advanced** tab. On the **Use a boot image** line, click **Browse** and select the following boot image: **Boot image (x64)**. Click **OK** when done.

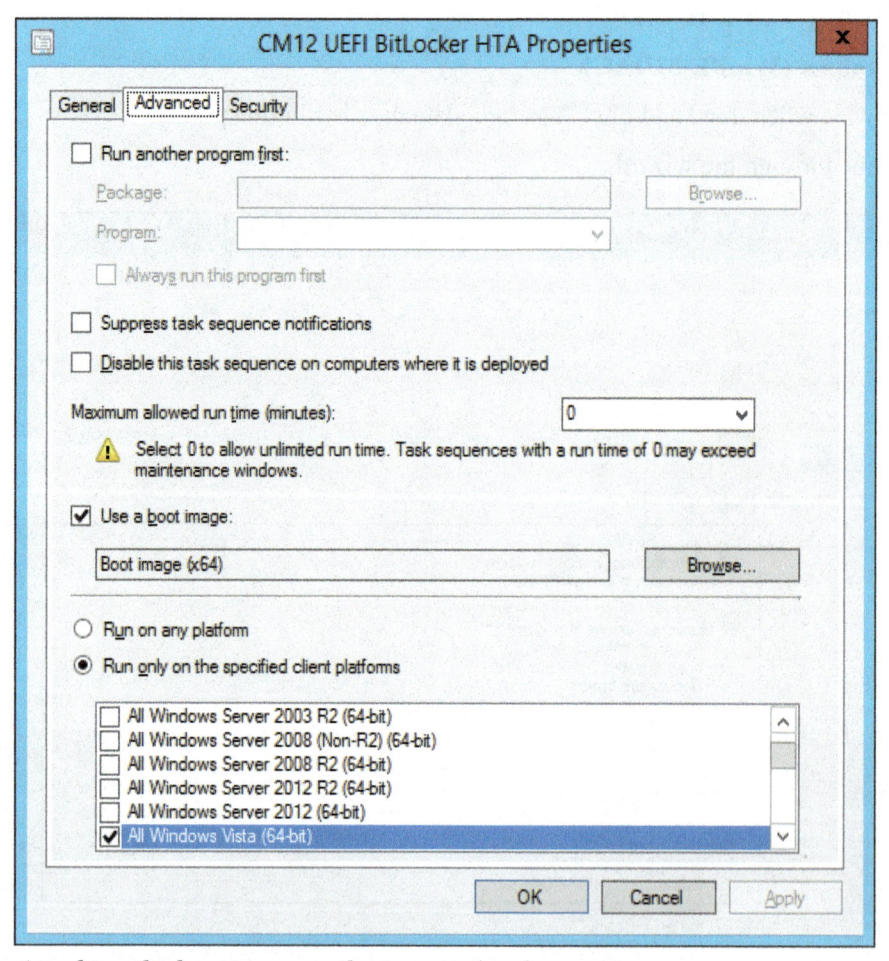

*Attaching the boot image to the imported task sequence.*

## Deploying the Task Sequence

In order for your users to be able to use this task sequence, it needs to be deployed.

1. On **CM01**, using the **ConfigMgr console**, in the **Software Library** workspace, select **Operating Systems / Task Sequences**, select the **CM12 UEFI BitLocker HTA** task sequence, and then select **Deploy**.

2. Use the following settings for the **Deploy Software Wizard**:

    a. General

       Collection: **OSD Deploy**

    b. Deployment Settings

       - Purpose: **Available**
       - Make available to the following: **Only media and PXE**

    c. Scheduling

       &lt;default&gt;

    d. User Experience

       &lt;default&gt;

    e. Alerts

       &lt;default&gt;

    f. Distribution Points

       &lt;default&gt;

## Using the Features

The CM12 UEFI BitLocker HTA offers many features which are explained here. However in a nutshell think of it as an all in one toolbox for doing BitLocker enabled OSD deployments on UEFI and legacy hardware via PXE boot.

The HTA itself is navigable via different tabs, and each tab offers different abilities explained below.

### About

The About tab is the default view when the HTA loads and gives some information about the tool. In addition, the About tab gives visual information about the computer name and user name.

The HTA checks whether the current computer name is already in Active Directory, and if so, displays it in blue.

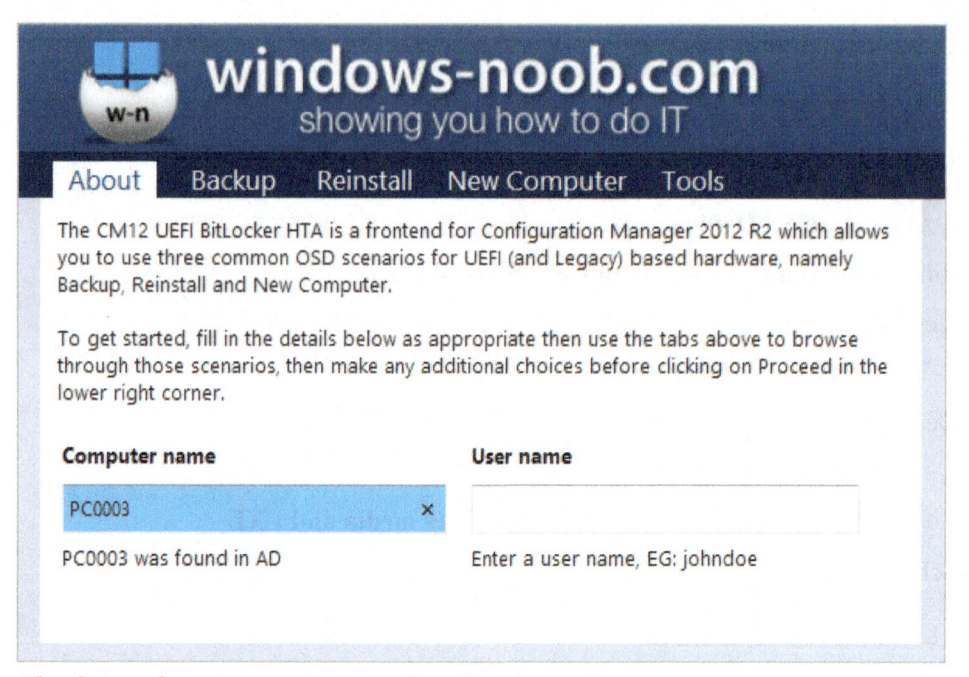

*The detected computer name was found in Active Directory.*

If the computer name is not found in Active Directory, it is displayed in red.

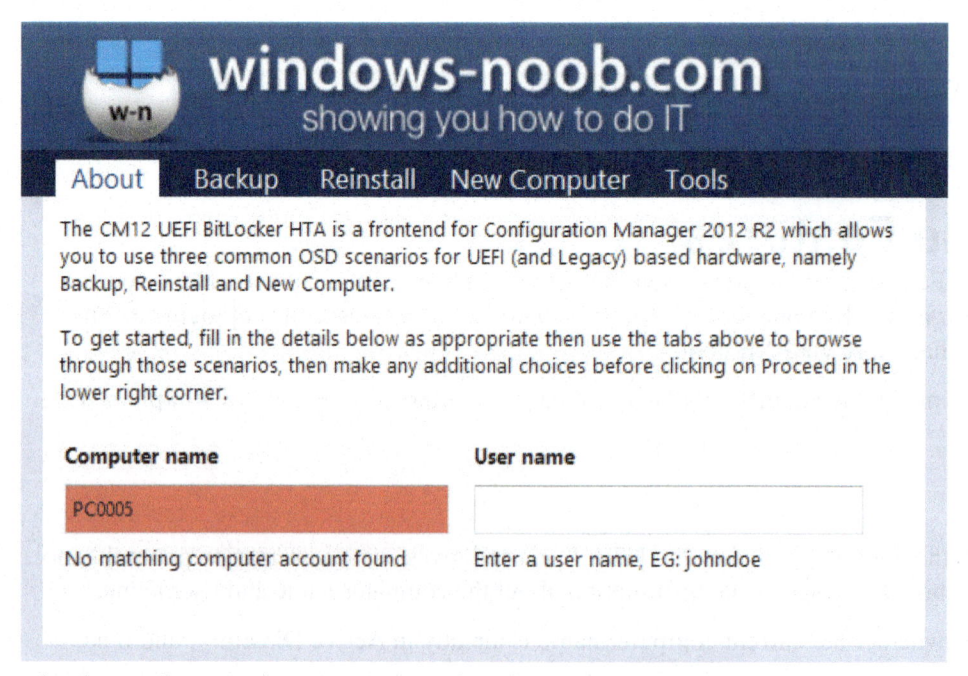

*The detected computer name was not found in Active Directory.*

If you enter a user name in the User name field, that user is granted Local Administration abilities on the computer being imaged. (Of course, you can disable this capability by disabling the group in the task sequence.) In addition, the user name entered is assigned as the Primary User of the computer.

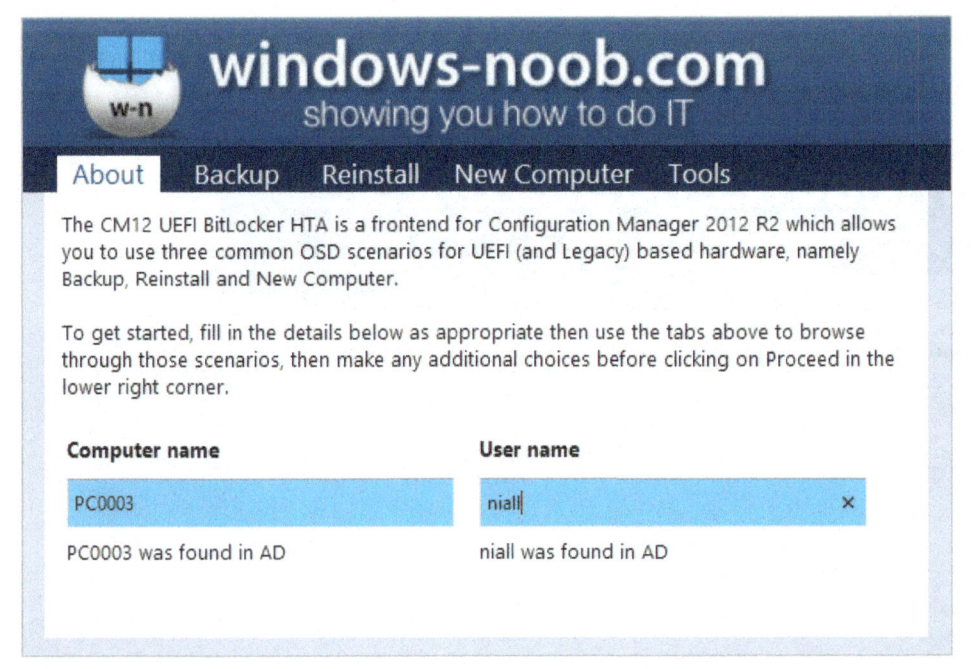

*The user name entered was found in AD and will become the Primary User of the computer.*

## Backup

The Backup tab is used for backing up the computer in a variety of ways depending on your needs. In addition, there are disk-checking options (quick or extensive) in case the operator believes the hard disk may have bad sectors (which can cause problems with backup).

There are two Full WIM backup options. One is local, and that means it backs up the computer to a WIM file stored locally on the computer. The other option is Network, and the full WIM backup file is stored on the network in the share specified in the Set Backupshare step of the task sequence.

### Chapter 14   The CM12 UEFI BitLocker HTA

In addition to Full WIM backup, the last option (xcopy to network) allows you to use scanstate to back up the users' data while offline in WinPE, which is stored on a network share as specified in the Set USMTStoreShare step in the task sequence. This state is placed in a folder named after the detected computer name and can be used when doing a new computer scenario via the drop-down menu for restoring data.

All of the backup options work whether the computer is BitLockered (encrypted) or not, as the disk is unlocked prior to backup via a call to the MBAM SQL server.

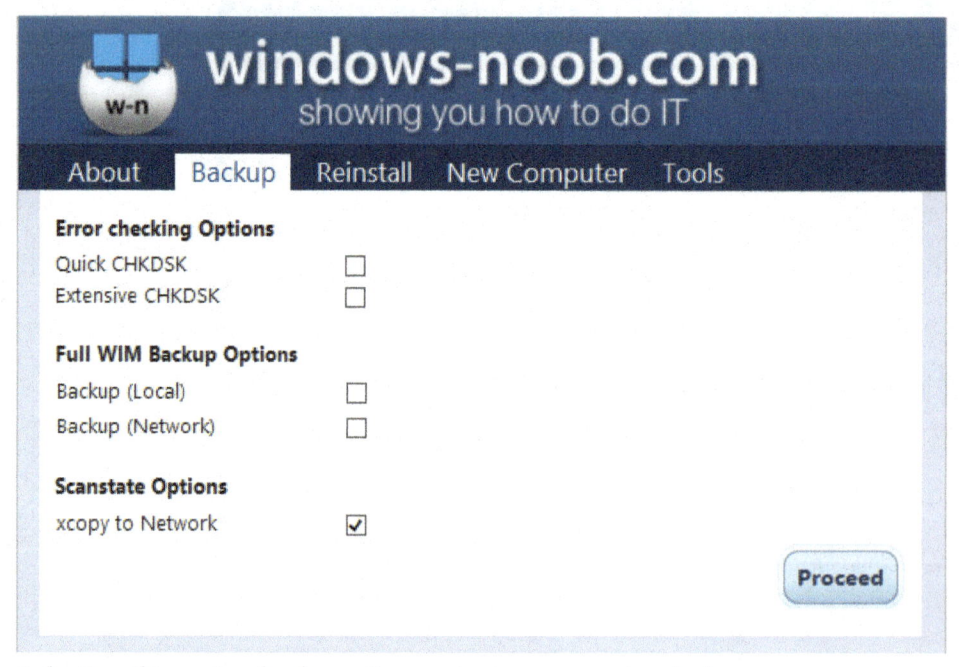

*Selecting this option backs up the user's state to a network share.*

## Reinstall

The Reinstall tab offers the capability to reinstall the operating system, which could even mean upgrading the operating system from Windows 7 to Windows 8.1. The reinstallation automatically migrates the user's files and data using hardlinking (files and data are kept locally on the system and indexed during the operating system reinstallation).

In addition to reinstalling the operating system, the user can select to install the System Center Endpoint Protection antivirus client and choose from a variety of regional and language options.

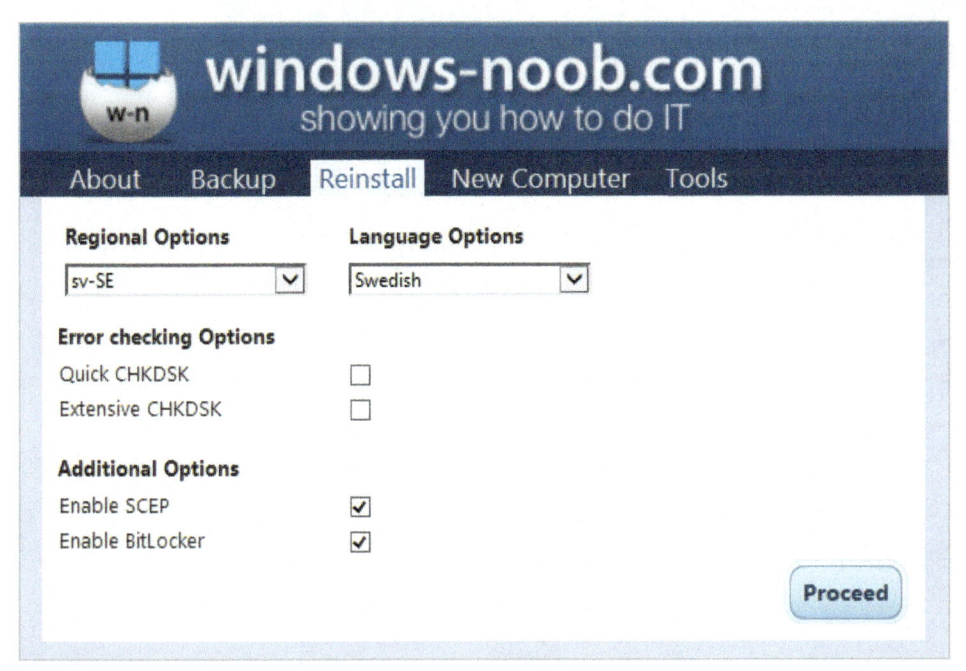

*Reinstall options allow for language and regional choices.*

## New Computer

The New Computer tab allows the operator to clean install a computer with an operating system (Windows 8.1). In addition, the drop-down menus for regional and language options are the same as for the Reinstall tab, allowing you to select different regional settings and even mixing and matching them. Selecting Multi in the drop-down menu installs all regional and/or language packs made available to the task sequence.

Chapter 14   The CM12 UEFI BitLocker HTA

If you want to set the BitLocker encryption algorithm, then select the AES level as appropriate. There also is a State Restore Options drop-down menu that allows you to select from previously captured user states stored in various formats; for example, the computer names listed were from previous offline backups to the network share via the Backup tab. The SMP option requires a previous computer association set up either in the ConfigMgr console or via the Tools tab.

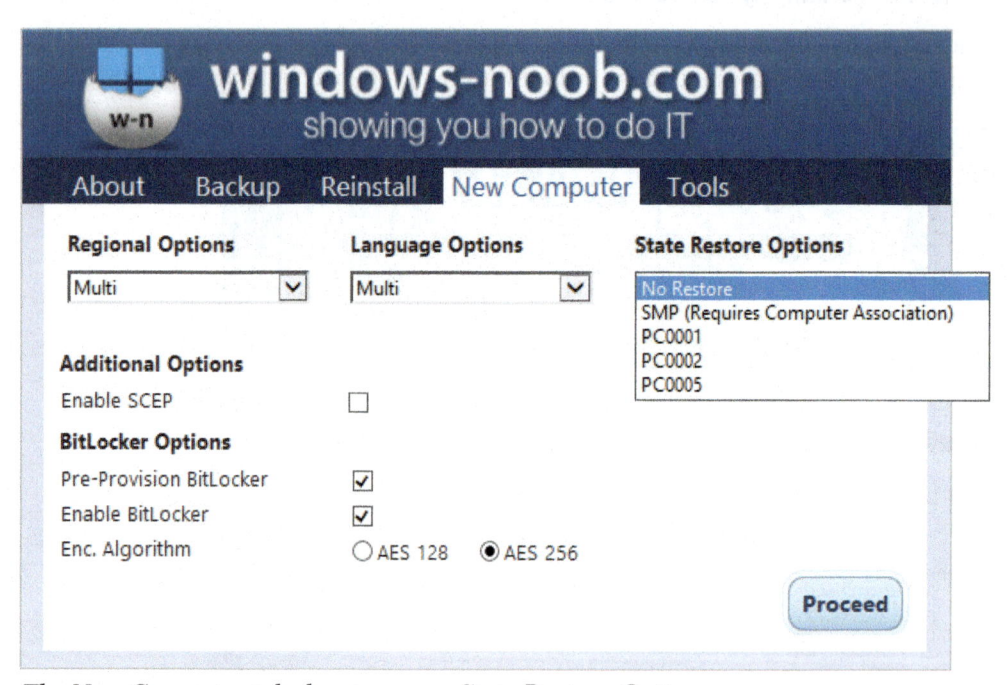

*The New Computer tab showing some State Restore Options.*

## Tools

The Tools tab offers quite a few options, including getting relevant deployment information as shown in the following figure.

**Deployment Information**

| | |
|---|---|
| Computername | PC0004 |
| Computername in SCCM | PC0004 |
| Make | Microsoft Corporation |
| Model | Virtual Machine |
| Memory | 2045 |
| Is On Battery | False |
| Is UEFI | True |
| Is Encrypted | True |
| Is VM | True |
| Virtual Platform | Hyper-V |
| Asset Tag | 0670-3010-7577-5550-4895-7976-49 |
| Serial Number | 0670-3010-7577-5550-4895-7976-49 |
| IP Address | 192.168.1.101 |
| MAC Address | 00:15:5D:00:AC:4F |
| UUID | 614EFCCB-D82C-44C9-81D2-340D86D4589D |
| Client Identity | GUID:58442226-fd5b-45ff-ac3f-f109d31c086e |
| Assigned Site Code | PS1 |
| This computer is known: | true |
| The ResourceID is: | 16777282 |

Click outside this window to close it.

*Detailed deployment information of the computer in question.*

There also are buttons to pop up a command prompt for troubleshooting or a CMTrace session with the smsts.log file loaded, and a Restart button that simply restarts the computer.

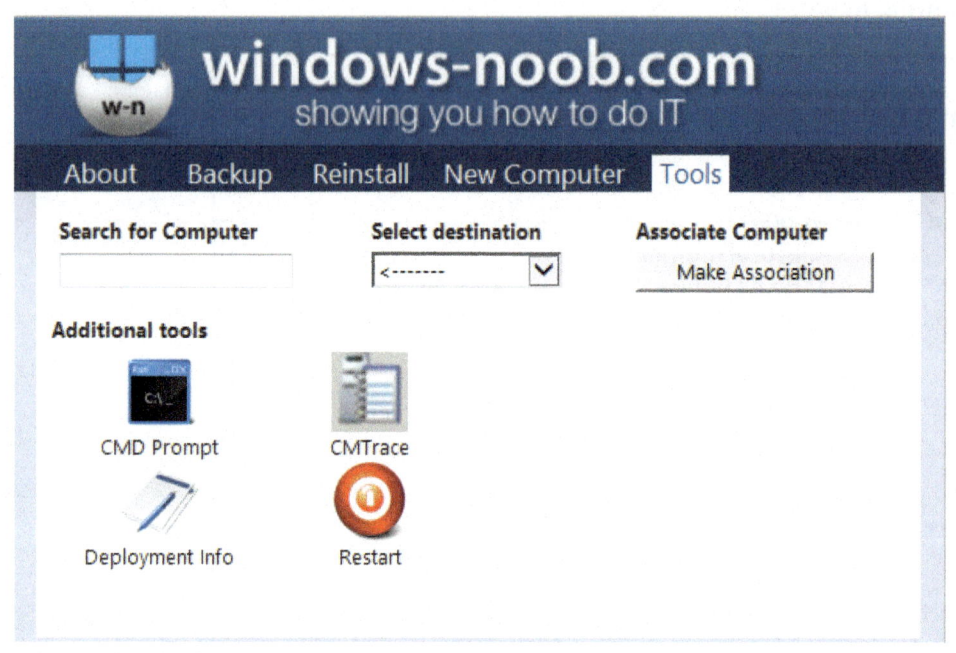

*The Tools tab showing the options available.*

At the top left of the Tools tab is a search window in which you can type all or part of a computer name. When done, the tool searches the ConfigMgr database for names matching what you typed. If any results are found, you are informed via a popup and you can then click the Select Destination drop-down menu to review/select the target computer for a computer association.

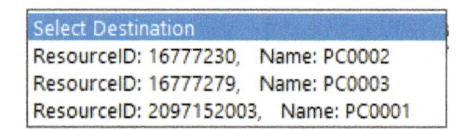

*Selecting a destination computer for a computer association.*

If you want to make a computer association for the state migration point (SMP), select the resource you want and click Make Association. When the association is complete, you are informed of the success (or failure) via a popup and can review the association in the ConfigMgr console in the Assets and Compliance / User State Migration node.

Chapter 14   The CM12 UEFI BitLocker HTA

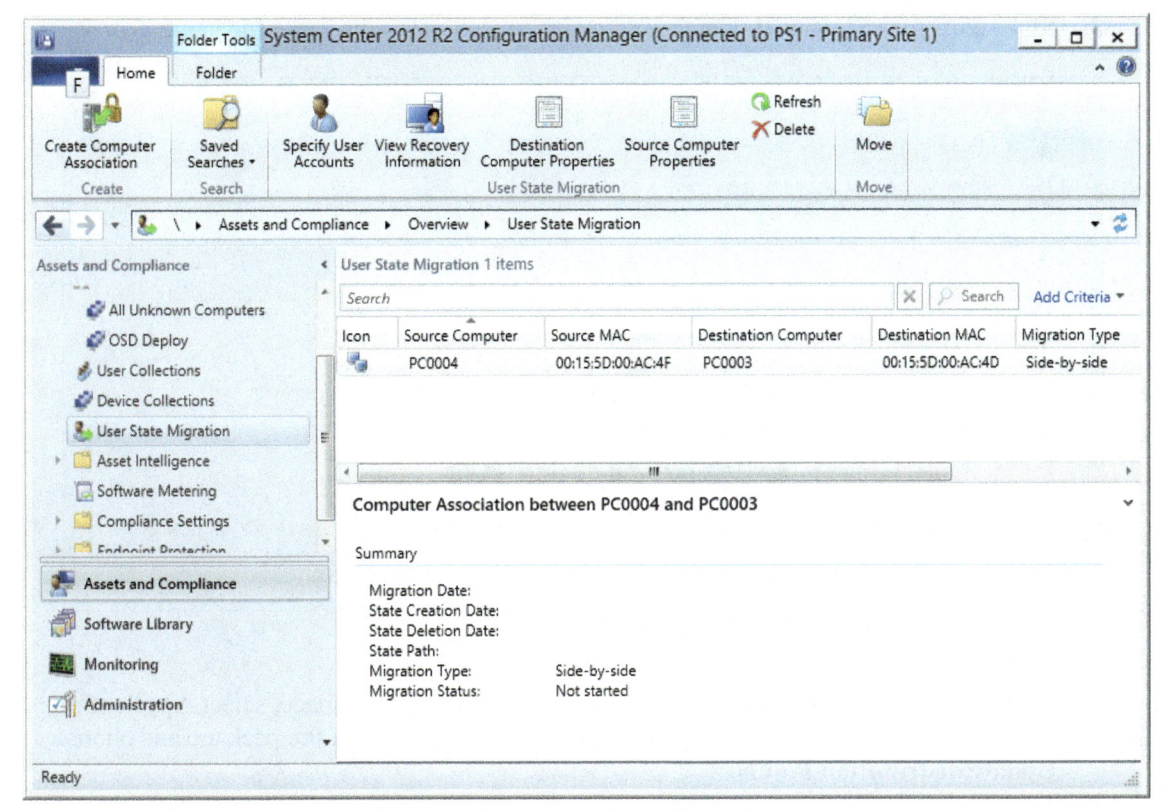

*An association created via the CM12 UEFI BitLocker HTA tool.*

# Customizing the HTA

Now that you've seen what it can do, you'll want to enable it in your organization, but you probably want to customize it to suit your branding (colors and logo, for example).

### Change the Logo
To change the logo, do as follows:

1. On **CM01**, open **File Explorer** and browse to **E:\Sources\Software\ViaMonstra\The CM12 UEFI BitLocker HTA\UEFI HTA\theme\UEFI\images**.

2. Locate the **wnb logo3.png** file, and open it with **MSPaint** or your favorite photo-editing application.

407

3. Make edits to the logo and when done save the result using the same file name.

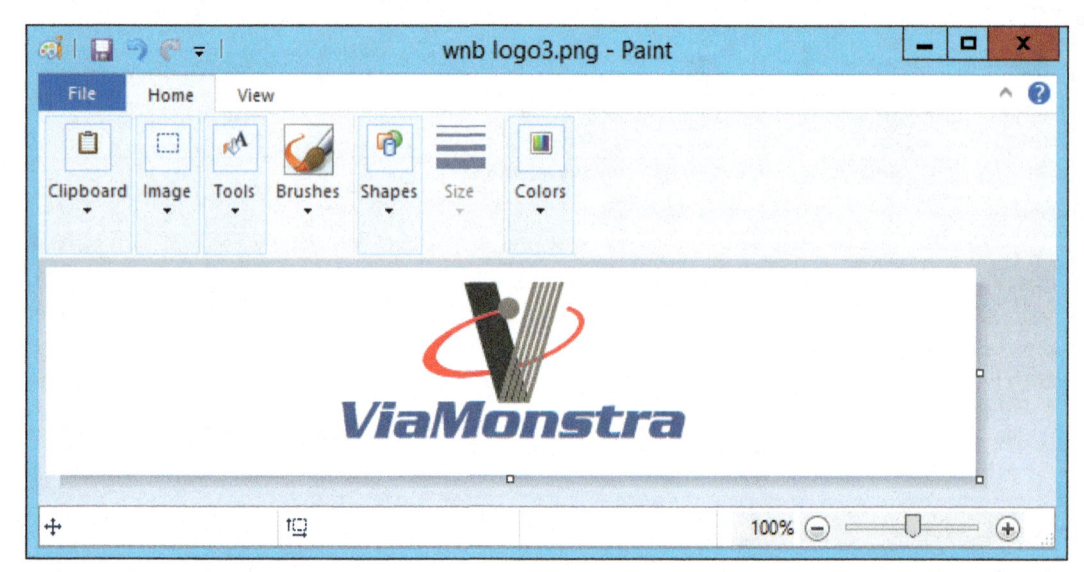

*Editing the logo used in the HTA.*

4. Using the **ConfigMgr console**, in the **Software Library** workspace, select **Application Management / Packages / UEFI BitLocker HTA**. Right-click the package and choose **Update distribution Points**.

## Change the CSS
To change the tab colors, do as follows:

1. On **CM01**, open **File Explorer** and browse to **E:\Sources\Software\ViaMonstra\The CM12 UEFI BitLocker HTA\UEFI HTA\theme\UEFI\**.

2. Locate the **UEFI.CSS** file, and open it with **Notepad** or **Notepad++**.

3. Scroll down to the **Tabs** section at the end of the file and change the colors or font sizes to your liking. Save the file when done.

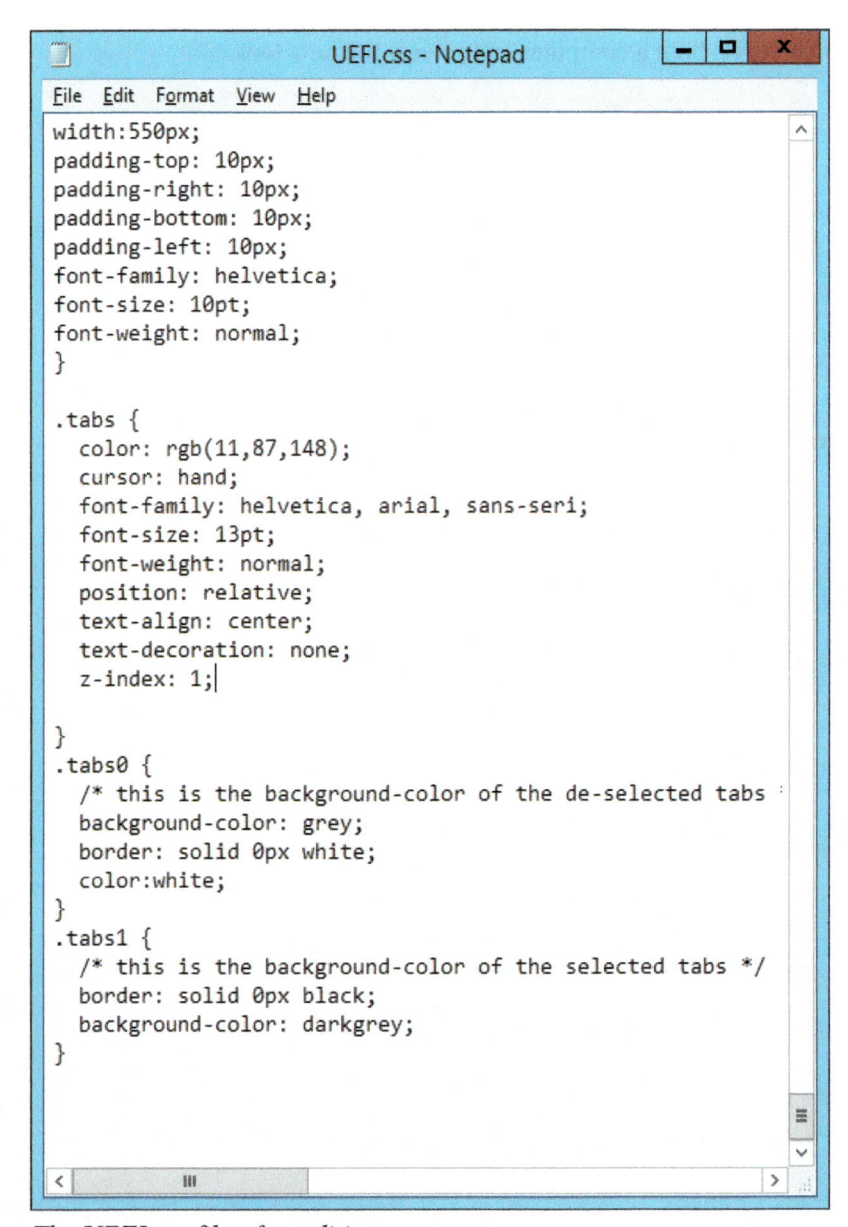

```css
width:550px;
padding-top: 10px;
padding-right: 10px;
padding-bottom: 10px;
padding-left: 10px;
font-family: helvetica;
font-size: 10pt;
font-weight: normal;
}

.tabs {
  color: rgb(11,87,148);
  cursor: hand;
  font-family: helvetica, arial, sans-seri;
  font-size: 13pt;
  font-weight: normal;
  position: relative;
  text-align: center;
  text-decoration: none;
  z-index: 1;
}
.tabs0 {
  /* this is the background-color of the de-selected tabs */
  background-color: grey;
  border: solid 0px white;
  color:white;
}
.tabs1 {
  /* this is the background-color of the selected tabs */
  border: solid 0px black;
  background-color: darkgrey;
}
```

*The UEFI.css file after editing.*

4. Using the **ConfigMgr console**, in the **Software Library** workspace, select **Application Management / Packages / UEFI BitLocker HTA**. Right-click the package and choose **Update distribution Points**.

5. After editing is complete, PXE boot a computer and review the new look.

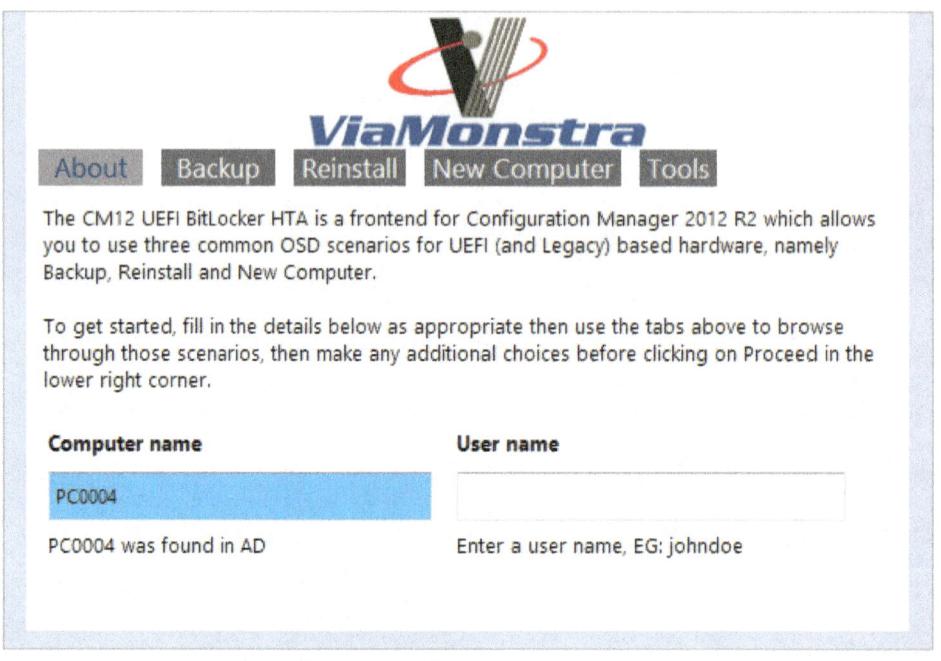

*The new logo and color scheme is added.*

# Appendix A

# Using the Hydration Kit to Build the PoC Environment

Hydration is the concept of using a deployment solution, like MDT 2013, to do a fully automated build of an entire lab, or proof-of-concept environment. This appendix is here to help you quickly spin up a lab environment that matches up with all the guides you use in this book.

I recommend using Hyper-V in Windows Server 2012 R2 as your virtual platform, but I have tested the hydration kit on the following virtual platforms:

- Hyper-V in Windows 8.1 and Windows Server 2012 R2
- VMware Workstation 11.0
- VMware ESXi 5.5

As you learned in Chapter 2, to set up a virtual environment with all the servers and clients, you need a host with at least 16 GB of RAM, even though 32 GB RAM is recommended. Either way, make sure you are using SSD drives for your storage. A single 480 GB SSD is enough to run all the scenarios in this book.

**Real World Note:** Don't go cheap on the disk drive. If using a normal laptop or desktop when doing the step-by-step guides in this book, please, please, please use a SSD drive for your virtual machines. Using normal spindle-based disks is just too slow for a decent lab and test environment. Also, please note that most laptops support at least 16 GB RAM these days, even if many vendors do not update their specifications with this information.

## The Base Servers

Using the hydration kit, you build the following list of servers.

### New York Site Servers (192.168.1.0/24)

- **DC01.** Domain Controller, DNS, and DHCP
- **CM01.** Member Server
- **MBAM01.** Member Server

## The Base Clients
In addition to the servers, you also use a few clients throughout the book guides.

### New York Site Clients (192.168.1.0/24)
- **PC0001.** Windows 8.1 Enterprise x64
- **PC0002-PC0013.** New clients that are deployed in the various guides in this book

## Internet Access
As you learned in Chapter 2, some of the guides in this book require you to have Internet access on the virtual machines. I commonly use a virtual router (running in a VM) to provide Internet access to our lab and test VMs. You can use the Vyatta and VyOS (Vyatta community fork) routers, or a Windows Server 2012 R2 virtual machine with routing configured, as well.

> **Real World Note:** For detailed guidance on setting up a virtual router for your lab environment, see this article: http://tinyurl.com/usingvirtualrouter.

## Setting Up the Hydration Environment
To enable you to quickly set up the servers and clients used for the step-by-step guides in this book, I provide you with a hydration kit (part of the book sample files) that builds all the servers and clients. The sample files are available for download at http://deploymentfundamentals.com.

### How Does the Hydration Kit Work?
The hydration kit that you download is just a folder structure and some scripts. The scripts help you create the MDT 2013 Lite Touch offline media, and the folder structure is there for you to add your own software and licenses when applicable. You can use trial versions for the lab software, as well. The overview steps are the following:

1. Download the needed software.
2. Install MDT 2013 Lite Touch and Windows ADK 8.1.
3. Create a MDT 2013 deployment share.
4. Populate the folder structure with your media and any license information.
5. Generate the MDT 2013 media item (big ISO).
6. Create a few virtual machines, boot them on the media item, and select what servers they should become. About two hours later you have the lab environment ready to go.

Appendix A   Using the Hydration Kit to Build the PoC Environment

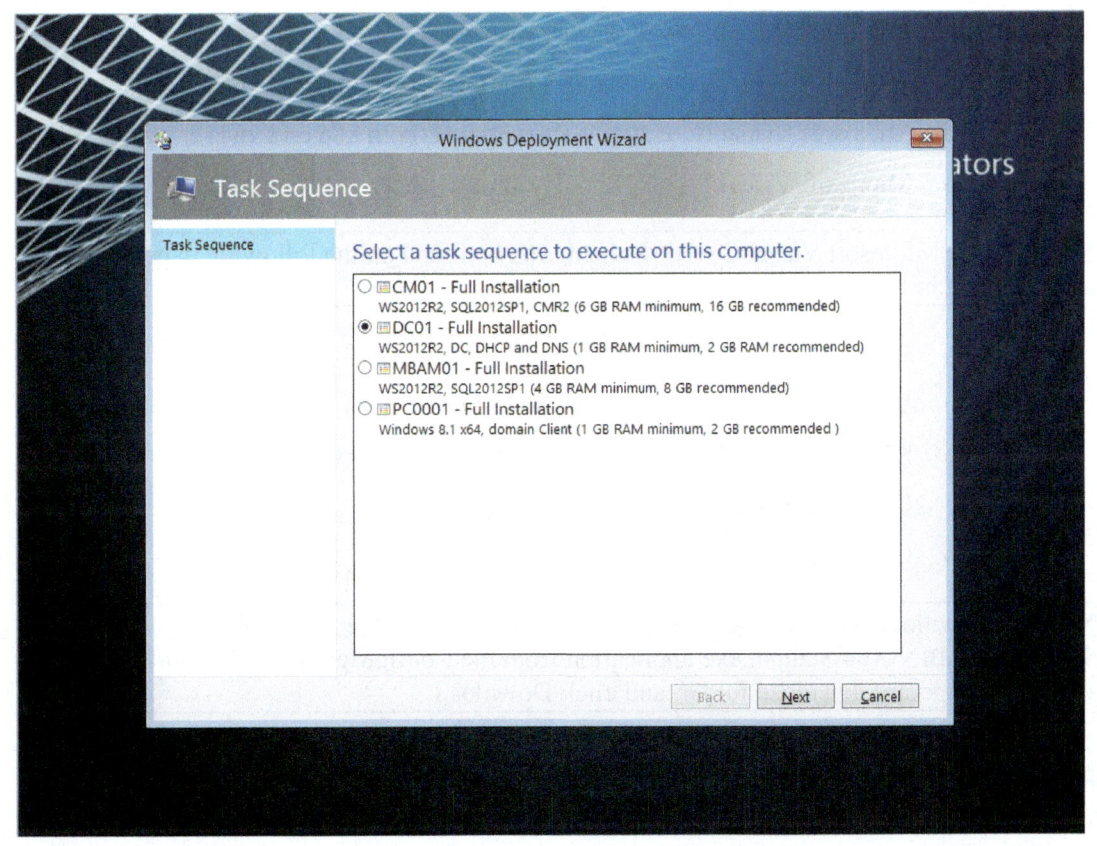

*The end result: You boot a VM from the ISO and simply select which server to build.*

## Preparing the Downloads Folder

These steps should be performed on the Windows machine that you use to manage Hyper-V or VMware. If you are using Hyper-V or VMware Workstation, this machine also can be the host machine.

### Download the Software

1. On the Windows machine that you use to manage Hyper-V or VMware, create the **C:\Downloads** folder.

2. Download the following mandatory software to the **C:\Downloads** folder:

    o   The book sample files (http://deploymentfundamentals.com)

    o   Windows ADK 8.1 (To download the full ADK, you run adksetup.exe once and select to download the files.)

    o   BGInfo

    o   MDT 2013 (http://tinyurl.com/mdt2013download)

413

Appendix A   Using the Hydration Kit to Build the PoC Environment

- Microsoft Visual C++ 2005 SP1 runtimes (both x86 and x64)
- Microsoft Visual C++ 2008 SP1 runtimes (both x86 and x64)
- Microsoft Visual C++ 2010 SP1 runtimes (both x86 and x64)
- Microsoft Visual C++ 2012 SP1 runtimes (both x86 and x64)

**Note:** All the Microsoft Visual C++ downloads can be found on the following page: http://support.microsoft.com/kb/2019667.

- Windows Server 2012 R2 (trial or full version)
- Windows 8.1 Enterprise x64 (trial or full version)
- SQL Server 2012 Standard with SP1 x64 (trial or full version)
- ConfigMgr 2012 R2
- ConfigMgr 2012 R2 PreReqs

**Note:** To download the ConfigMgr 2012 R2 prerequisites, run the SMSSETUP\BIN\X64\Setupdl.exe application from the ConfigMgr 2012 R2 installation files, specify a temporary download folder, and click Download.

## Preparing the Hydration Environment

The Windows machine that you use to manage Hyper-V or VMware needs to have PowerShell installed.

**Note:** MDT 2013 requires local administrator rights/permissions. You need to have at least 60 GB of free disk space on C:\ for the hydration kit and about 200 GB of free space for the volume hosting your virtual machines. Also make sure to run all commands from an elevated PowerShell prompt.

### Create the Hydration Deployment Share

1. On the Windows machine that you use to manage Hyper-V or VMware, install **ADK** (**adksetup.exe**) selecting only the following components:

    - **Deployment Tools**
    - **Windows Preinstallation Environment (Windows PE)**

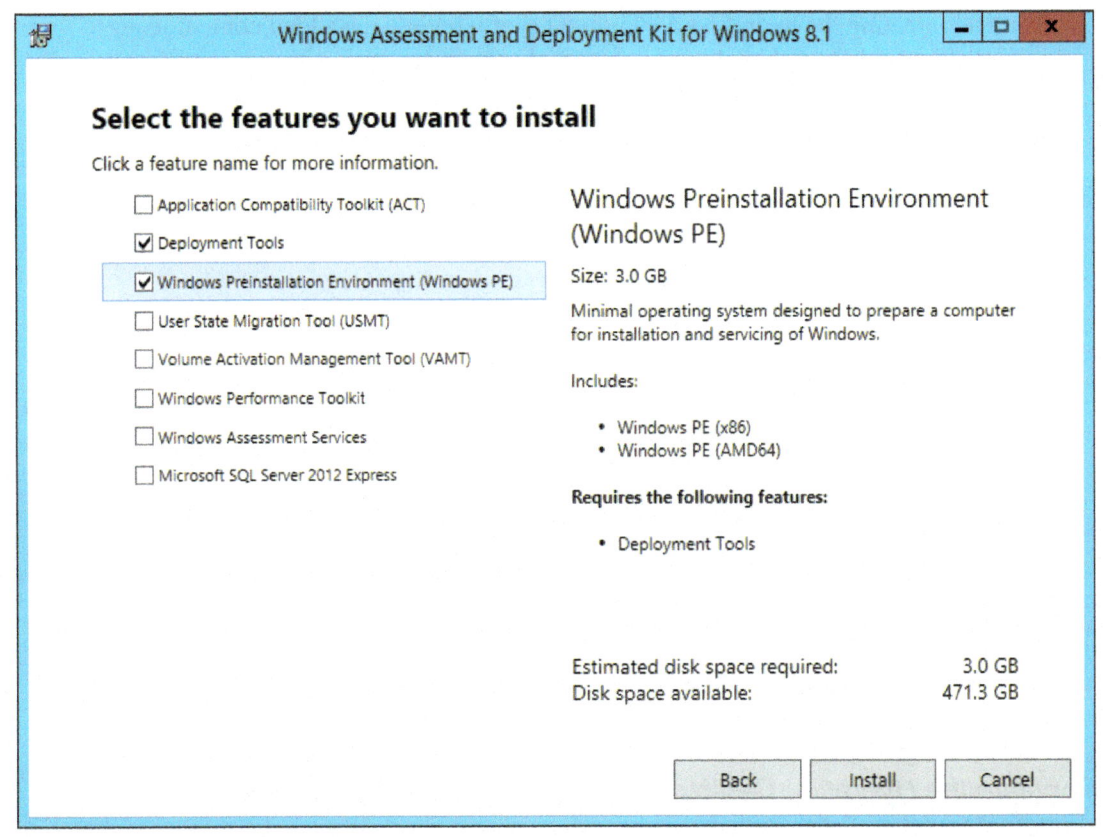

Appendix A   Using the Hydration Kit to Build the PoC Environment

*The Windows ADK 8.1 setup.*

2. Install **MDT 2013** (**MicrosoftDeploymentToolkit2013_x64.msi**) with the default settings.

3. Extract the book sample files and copy the **HydrationNoob** folder to **C:\**.

   You should now have the following folder containing a few subfolders and a PowerShell script:

   **C:\HydrationNoob\Source**

4. In an elevated **PowerShell prompt** (run as Administrator), create the hydration deployment share by running the following command:

   ```
   C:\HydrationNoob\Source\CreateHydrationDeploymentShare.ps1
   ```

415

Appendix A  Using the Hydration Kit to Build the PoC Environment

5. After creating the hydration deployment share, review the added content using **Deployment Workbench** (available on the **Start screen**).

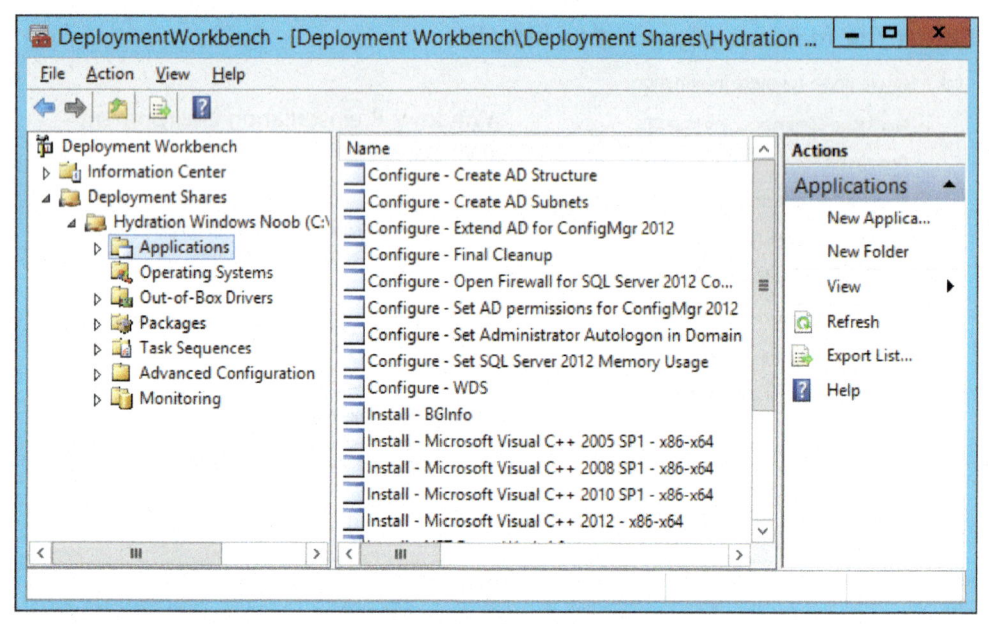

*Deployment Workbench with the readymade applications listed.*

## Populate the Hydration Deployment Share with the Setup Files

In these steps, you copy the installation files to the correct target folder in the hydration structure:

1. Copy the **Windows ADK 8.1** installation files to the following folder:

    **C:\HydrationNoob\DS\Applications\Install - Windows ADK 8.1\Source**

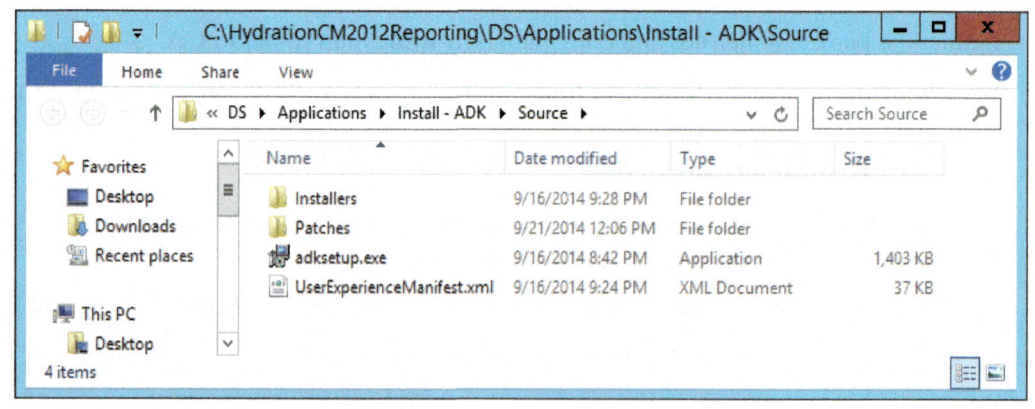

*The Windows ADK 8.1 files copied.*

2. Copy the **BGInfo** file (**bginfo.exe**) to the following folder:

    **C:\HydrationNoob\DS\Applications\Install - BGInfo\Source**

Appendix A   Using the Hydration Kit to Build the PoC Environment

3. Copy the **Microsoft Visual C++ 2005 SP1 x86** and **Microsoft Visual C++ 2005 SP1 x64** installation files (**vcredist_x86.exe and vcredist_x64.exe**) to the following folder:

    **C:\HydrationNoob\DS\Applications\
    Install - Microsoft Visual C++ 2005 SP1 - x86-x64\Source**

4. Copy the **Microsoft Visual C++ 2008 SP1 x86** and **Microsoft Visual C++ 2008 SP1 x64** installation files (**vcredist_x86.exe and vcredist_x64.exe**) to the following folder:

    **C:\HydrationNoob\DS\Applications\
    Install - Microsoft Visual C++ 2008 SP1 - x86-x64\Source**

5. Copy the **Microsoft Visual C++ 2010 SP1 x86** and **Microsoft Visual C++ 2010 SP1 x64** installation files (**vcredist_x86.exe and vcredist_x64.exe**) to the following folder:

    **C:\HydrationNoob\DS\Applications\
    Install - Microsoft Visual C++ 2010 SP1 - x86-x64\Source**

6. Copy the **Microsoft Visual C++ 2012 x86** and **Microsoft Visual C++ 2012 x64** installation files (**vcredist_x86.exe and vcredist_x64.exe**) to the following folder:

    **C:\HydrationNoob\DS\Applications\
    Install - Microsoft Visual C++ 2012 - x86-x64\Source**

7. Copy the **Windows Server 2012 R2** installation files (the content of the ISO, not the actual ISO) to the following folder:

    **C:\HydrationNoob\DS\Operating Systems\WS2012R2**

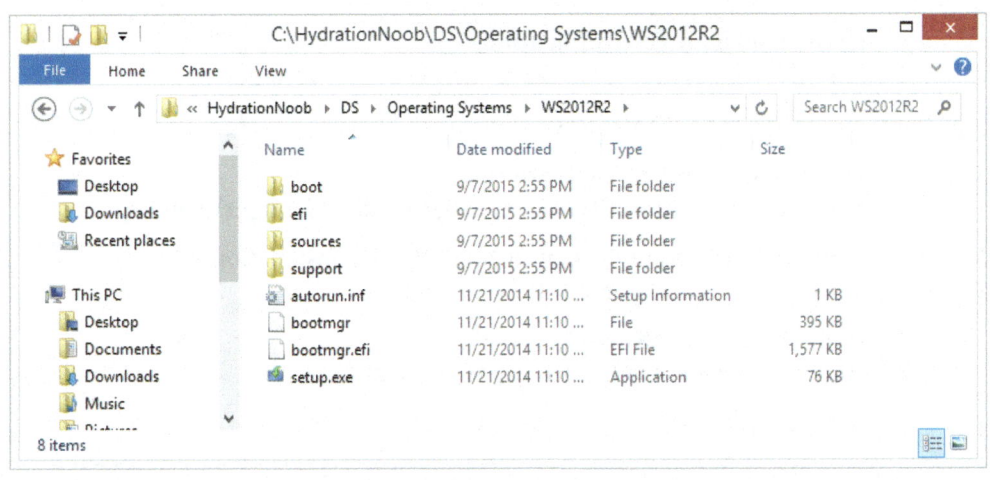

*The Windows Server 2012 R2 (November 2014 ISO) files copied.*

8. Copy the **Windows 8.1 Enterprise x64** installation files (again, the content of the ISO, not the actual ISO) to the following folder:

    **C:\HydrationNoob\DS\Operating Systems\W81X64**

Appendix A   Using the Hydration Kit to Build the PoC Environment

9. Copy the **SQL Server 2012 Standard with SP1 x64** installation files to the following folder:

    **C:\HydrationNoob\DS\Applications\Install - SQL Server 2012 SP1\Source**

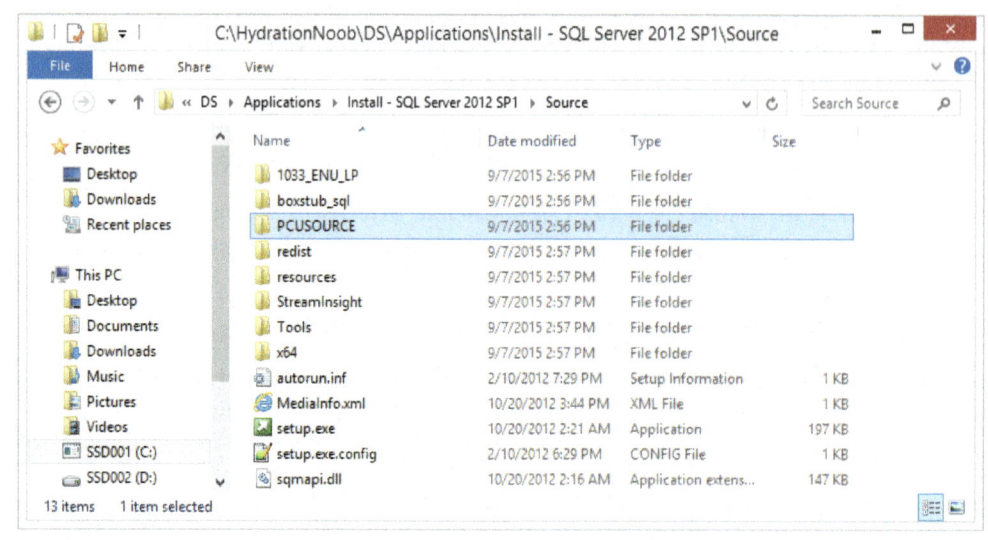

*The SQL Server 2012 Standard with SP1 x64 setup files copied.*

10. Copy the **ConfigMgr 2012 R2** installation files (extract the download) to the following folder:

    **C:\HydrationNoob\DS\Applications\
    Install - System Center 2012 R2 Configuration Manager\Source**

11. Copy the **ConfigMgr 2012 R2 PreReqs** files to the following folder:

    **C:\HydrationNoob\DS\Applications\
    Install - System Center 2012 R2 Configuration Manager\PreReqs**

12. Copy the **extadsch.exe** file from the ConfigMgr 2012 R2 installation files (SMSSETUP\BIN\X64 folder) to the following folder:

    **C:\HydrationNoob\DS\Applications\
    Configure - Extend AD for ConfigMgr 2012\Source**

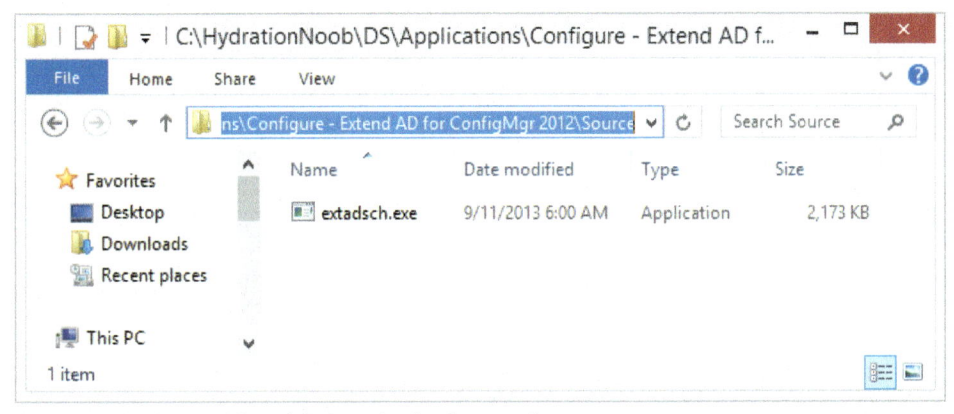

Appendix A   Using the Hydration Kit to Build the PoC Environment

*The extadsch.exe file added to the hydration kit.*

## Create the Hydration ISO (MDT 2013 Update Offline Media Item)

1. Using **Deployment Workbench** (available on the **Start screen**), expand **Deployment Shares**, and expand **Hydration Windows Noob**.

2. Review the various nodes. The **Applications**, **Operating Systems**, and **Task Sequences** nodes should all have some content in them.

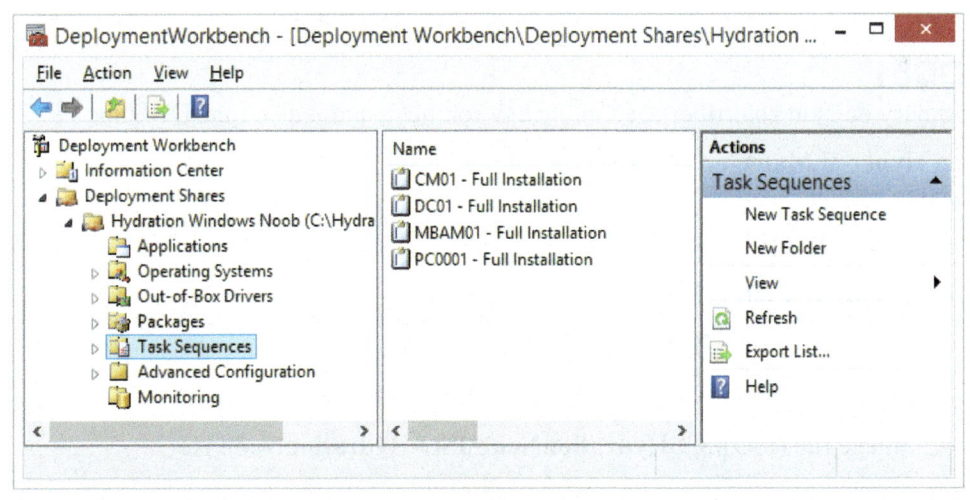

*The hydration deployment share, listing all task sequences.*

3. Expand the **Advanced Configuration** node, and then select the **Media** node.
4. In the right pane, right-click the **MEDIA001** item, and select **Update Media Content**.

**Note:** The most common reason for failures in the hydration kit are related to antivirus software preventing the ISO from being generated correctly. If you see any errors in the update media content process, disable (or uninstall) your antivirus software, and then try the update again. Anyway, the media update will take a while to run, a perfect time for a coffee break. ☺

After the media update, you have a big ISO (HydrationNoob.iso) in the C:\HydrationNoob\ISO folder. The ISO will be between 15 and 17 GB in size depending on which Windows media you have been using. (You have probably noticed that Microsoft offers ISO files with updates already installed, and these ISO files are larger.)

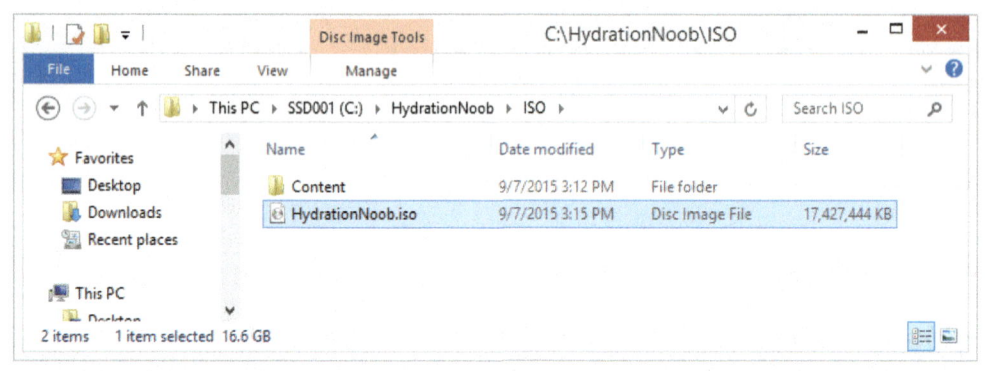

*The hydration ISO media item.*

## Deploying the New York Site VMs

In these steps, you deploy and configure the virtual machines for the New York site.

### Deploy DC01

This is the primary domain controller used in the environment, and it also runs DNS and DHCP.

1. Using **Hyper-V Manager** or **VMware Sphere**, create a virtual machine with the following settings:

    a. Name: **DC01**

    b. Memory: **1 GB** (minimum, 2 GB recommended)

    c. Hard drive: **100 GB** (dynamic disk)

    d. Network: The virtual network for the New York site

    e. Image file (ISO): **C:\HydrationNoob\ISO\HydrationNoob.iso**

    f. vCPUs: **2**

Appendix A   Using the Hydration Kit to Build the PoC Environment

2. Start the **DC01** virtual machine. After booting from **HydrationNoob.iso**, and after WinPE has loaded, select the **DC01** task sequence.

> **Real World Note:** Using a dynamic disk is really useful for a lab and test environment because the host PC uses only the actually consumed space on the virtual hard drive and not the size that you type in like a fixed disk would.

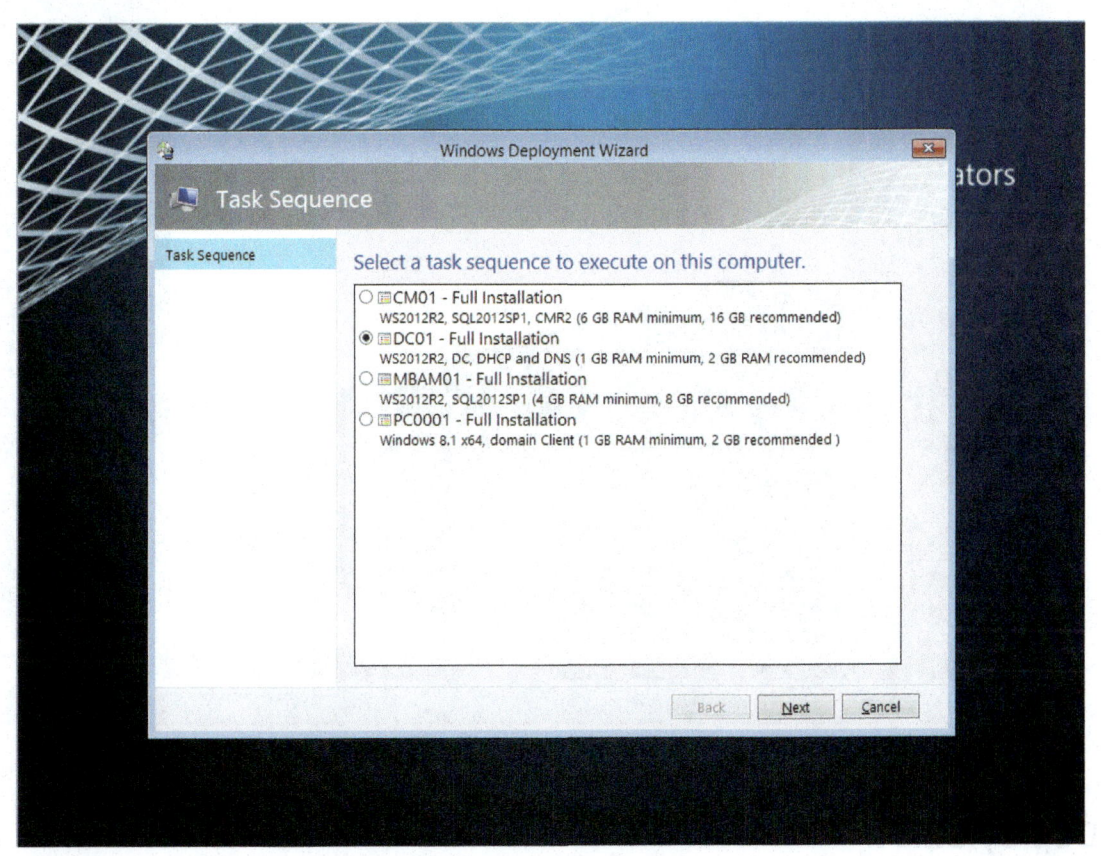

*The Task Sequence list showing the hydration task sequences.*

421

# Appendix A  Using the Hydration Kit to Build the PoC Environment

3. Wait until the setup is complete and you see the **Hydration completed** message in the final summary. Then leave the **DC01** virtual machine running.

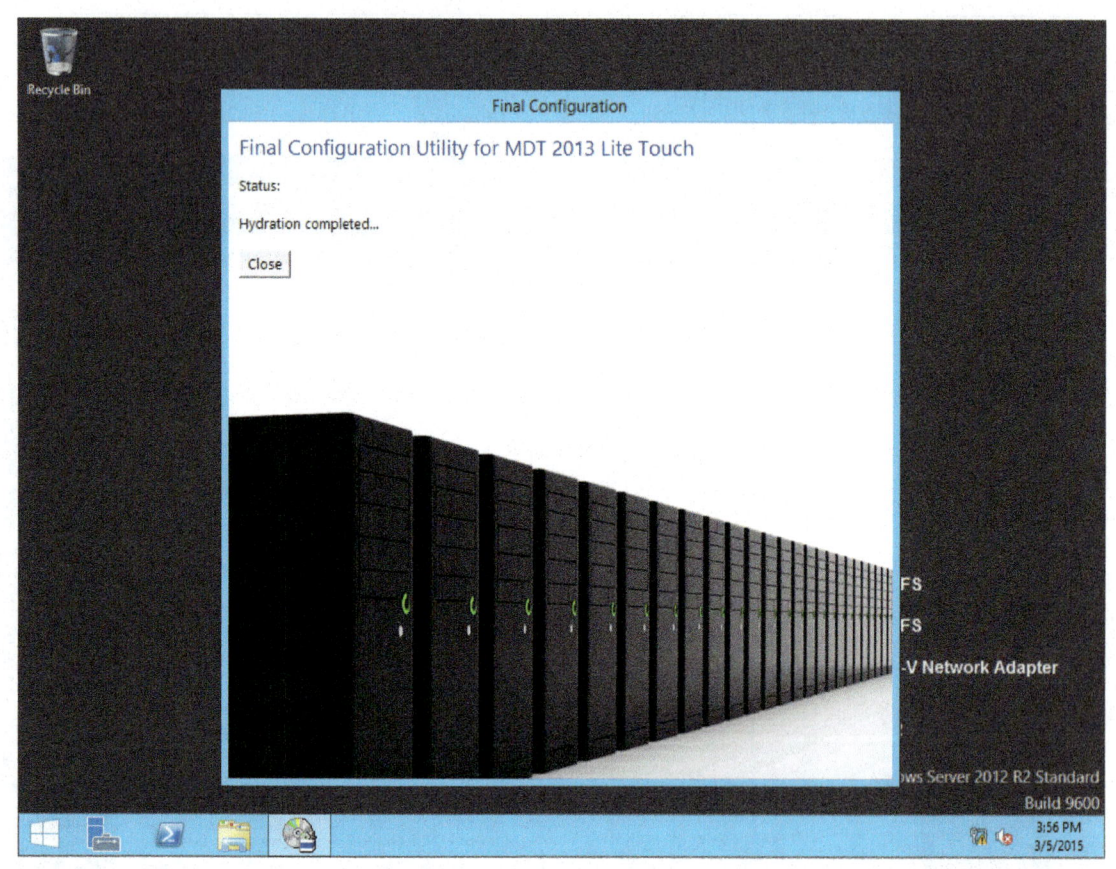

*The deployment of DC01 completed, showing the custom final summary screen.*

## Deploy CM01

CM01 is the server used for Configuration Manager 2012 R2.

1. Using **Hyper-V Manager** or **VMware Sphere**, create a virtual machine with the following settings:
    a. Name: **CM01**
    b. Memory: **6 GB** (minimum, 16 GB recommended)
    c. Hard drive: **300 GB** (dynamic disk)
    d. Network: The virtual network for the New York site
    e. Image file (ISO): **C:\HydrationNoob\ISO\HydrationNoob.iso**
    f. vCPUs: **2** (minimum, 4 recommended)

2. Make sure the **DC01** virtual machine is running, and then start the **CM01** virtual machine. After booting from **HydrationNoob.iso**, and after WinPE has loaded, select the **CM01** task sequence. Wait until the setup is complete and you see the **Hydration completed** message in the final summary.

## Deploy MBAM01
MBAM01 is the server used for MBAM 2.5.

1. Using **Hyper-V Manager** or **VMware Sphere**, create a virtual machine with the following settings:
   a. Name: **MBAM01**
   b. Memory: **4 GB** (minimum, 8 GB recommended)
   c. Hard drive: **300 GB** (dynamic disk)
   d. Network: The virtual network for the New York site
   e. Image file (ISO): **C:\HydrationNoob\ISO\HydrationNoob.iso**
   f. vCPUs: **2** (minimum, 4 recommended)
2. Make sure the **DC01** virtual machine is running, and then start the **MBAM01** virtual machine. After booting from **HydrationNoob.iso**, and after WinPE has loaded, select the **MBAM01** task sequence. Wait until the setup is complete and you see the **Hydration completed** message in the final summary.

## Deploy PC0001
This is a client running Windows 8.1 Enterprise x64 in the domain.

1. Using **Hyper-V Manager** or **VMware Sphere**, create a virtual machine with the following settings:
   a. Name: **PC0001**
   b. Memory: **1 GB** (minimum, 2 GB recommended)
   c. Hard drive: **60 GB** (dynamic disk)
   d. Network: The virtual network for the New York site
   e. Image file (ISO): **C:\HydrationNoob\ISO\HydrationNoob.iso**
   f. vCPUs: **1** (minimum, 2 recommended)
2. Start the **PC0001** virtual machine. After booting from **HydrationNoob.iso**, and after WinPE has loaded, select the **PC0001** task sequence. Wait until the setup is complete and you see the **Hydration completed** message in the final summary.

# Appendix A  Using the Hydration Kit to Build the PoC Environment

# Index

**7**
7-Zip, 13, 71
**A**
Active Directory Forest Discovery, 21
Active Directory Group Discovery, 25
Active Directory permissions, 41
Active Directory System Discovery, 22
Active Directory User Discovery, 24
application pools, 362
applications, 66
appsfolderlayout, 137
AssistMe, 231, 256
**B**
base clients, 412
base servers, 411
BitLocker, 297
BitLocker on virtual machines, 352
Blat, 232, 235
boot images, 52
boundary groups, 27
Brady, Niall, v
build and capture, 120
**C**
client settings, 49
CM12 UEFI BitLocker HTA, 359
ConfigMgr 2012 R2, 13
ConfigMgr 2012 R2 CU4, 15, 18
ConfigMgr 2012 R2 folder structure, 42
ConfigMgr 2012 R2 infrastructure, 15
ConfigMgr 2012 R2 MDT integration, 47
ConfigMgr 2012 R2 service accounts, 40
ConfigMgr client package, 45
Customize Start screen, 135
**D**
Deployment Webservice, 361, 363
devel mode, 209
discovery methods, 20
DISM, 82

drivers, 155, 160, 166, 280
**E**
Export a Start screen layout, 142
Extrafiles, 90
**H**
hotfixes, 157, 179
HTML application (HTA), 5
hydration, 6
hydration kit, 411
Hyper-V, 411
**I**
IE Enhanced Security Configuration, 31
importing computers, 111
Increasing log file size, 79
Installing web services, 359
Internet access, 12, 412
**J**
JavaScript, 4
**K**
Koster, Maik, 361
**L**
language packs, 369
**M**
MailLog, 231, 254
MBAM 2.5 BitLocker policy, 340
MBAM 2.5 client agents, 335, 339
MBAM 2.5 group policy, 326
MBAM 2.5 prerequisites, 305
MBAM 2.5 Self-Service Portal, 350
MBAM 2.5 service accounts, 298
MBAM 2.5 setup, 297, 307, 311, 314
MDOP 2014 R2, 297
MDT 2013, 13
MDT 2013 Zero Touch, 40
Microsoft MVP, v
Microsoft Office 365, 72
monitoring deployments, 130
Mozilla Firefox, 13, 67

# Index

## N
Network Access account, 48
network issues, identifying, 261
Notepad++, 7

## O
offline servicing, 283
OOBE package, 159
operating system images, 55
OSD collections, 61

## P
pausing a task sequence, 193
pausing using cmd, 199
pausing using PowerShell, 201
pausing using ServiceUI, 194
pen pairing support, 174
PowerShell, 4, 102
PowerShell Cmdlet Library, 153
PowerShell Integrated Scripting Environment (ISE), 7
prestart commands, 187
prompt for computer name, 62
Proof-of-Concept (PoC) environment, 11, 411
PXE, 50

## R
RBAC, 16
reference images, 101
reporting services point, 29

## S
sample files, 2
smsts.ini, 81
software, 13
software groups, 19
software update point (SUP), 32
software updates, 32, 112
software updates groups, 113
SQL Server 2012 SP1, 13
state migration point, 43
storage issues, identifying, 261
Surface Pro 3, 153, 181
synchronize updates, 37
syncing time in WinPE, 183

## U
UltraVNC, 232, 233
unknown computers, 62

## V
VBScript, 3
ViaMonstra clients, 14
ViaMonstra Inc., 1, 12
ViaMonstra servers, 13
videos, 2
ViewLog, 231, 259
VMware ESXi, 411
VMware Workstation, 411

## W
WBEMTest, 8
Web Platform Installer, 306
web services, 5
Windows 8.1, 13
Windows ADK, 13
Windows Management Instrumentation (WMI), 4
Windows PowerShell ISE, 105
Windows Server 2012 R2, 13
Windows Server Update Services (WSUS), 32
WinRAR, 232, 234
WMI Tools, 8

# Beyond the Book

If you liked the book, you will love these additional resources.

## Blog
Niall blogs on http://niallbrady.com.

## Forums
Niall frequently updates his forums with new articles and guides: http://windows-noob.com.

## Twitter
Niall also tweets on the following alias: @ncbrady.

CPSIA information can be obtained
at www.ICGtesting.com
Printed in the USA
BVOW07s2318270917
496073BV00001B/1/P

9 789187 445